ASIAN BUSINESS AND MANAGEMENT

ASIAN BUSINESS AND MANAGEMENT

Theory, Practice and Perspectives

HARUKIYO HASEGAWA
CARLOS NORONHA

First published 2009 by
PALGRAVE MACMILLAN

Palgrave Macmillan in the UK is an imprint of Macmillan Publishers Limited, registered in England, company number 785998, of Houndmills, Basingstoke, Hampshire RG21 6XS.

Palgrave Macmillan in the US is a division of St Martin's Press LLC, 175 Fifth Avenue, New York, NY 10010.

Palgrave Macmillan is the global academic imprint of the above companies and has companies and representatives throughout the world.

Palgrave® and Macmillan® are registered trademarks in the United States, the United Kingdom, Europe and other countries.

ISBN-13: 978–0–230–54506–9
ISBN-10: 0–230–54506–8

This book is printed on paper suitable for recycling and made from fully managed and sustained forest sources. Logging, pulping and manufacturing processes are expected to conform to the environmental regulations of the country of origin.

A catalogue record for this book is available from the British Library.

A catalog record for this book is available from the Library of Congress.

10 9 8 7 6 5 4 3 2
18 17 16 15 14 13 12 11

Printed in China

Contents

List of figures

List of tables

Preface

This textbook approaches Asian business and management from a new and more holistic standpoint than the narrow functionalist approach usually found in international business studies. It addresses key topical issues of modern business and considers how these issues are developing in the various systems found across the continent.

The idea for our collection of essays emerged from John Bratton and Jeff Gold's *Human Resource Management: Theory and Practice* (Palgrave Macmillan, 2003/08); we felt a book with a similar remit, going beyond standard functionalist limitations, would fill an urgent need in today's burgeoning business environment in Asia.

Accordingly, we have aimed our efforts at third and fourth year undergraduate and MBA/MA students, as well as managers and executives seeking an understanding of issues such as globalization, management, social responsibility and ethics and democracy in the Asian context. A primer on such issues will, we believe, address concerns that are becoming increasingly apparent as business and management adapt to the changing conditions of a world that is steadily becoming less resource-rich and less amenable to traditional expansionist business models. We hope the perspectives introduced in this book will stimulate fresh ideas geared towards a sustainable paradigm for tomorrow's business world.

HARUKIYO HASEGAWA
CARLOS NORONHA

Notes on the contributors

Harukiyo Hasegawa is Professor of Global Management and Human Resource Management at Dôshisha Business School in Kyoto, Japan. He was formerly Director of the Centre for Japanese Studies and currently Honorary Professor of Japanese Business at the University of Sheffield. His has authored, co-edited and contributed to numerous publications, amongst them *Steel Industry in Japan: A Comparison with Britain* (1996, Routledge); *Japanese Business and Management: Restructuring for Low Growth and Globalization* (1998, Routledge); *The Political Economy of Japanese Globalization* (2001, Routledge); *Japanese Responses to Globalization* (2006, Palgrave Macmillan); *New Horizons in Asian Management: Emerging Issues and Critical Perspectives* (2007, Palgrave Macmillan). He is the General Editor of *Asian Business & Management* (SSCI (Social Science Citation Index), Palgrave Macmillan) and Series Editor for the Palgrave Macmillan Asian Business Series.

Carlos Noronha earned his PhD from the University of Sheffield and is now Associate Professor at the Faculty of Business Administration, University of Macau, People's Republic of China. As a teacher, he has taught a variety of accounting and business subjects for 20 years. In terms of research, he has published widely in various management and accounting journals and is the author of several books, including *The Theory of Culture-Specific Total Quality Management* (2002, Palgrave Macmillan). He is also an Associate Editor of *Asian Business & Management* (SSCI, Palgrave Macmillan) and Editorial Board Member of the *Euro Asia Journal of Management*.

Philippe Byosiere is Professor at the Business School of Dôshisha University, Kyoto, Japan and a Visiting Research Professor at the University of Michigan-Ann Arbor. He received his Masters and Doctoral degrees in organizational psychology at the University of Michigan-Ann Arbor. Prior to Dôshisha, Professor Byosiere had held positions in the US (Michigan, Purdue, Rutgers and Hawai'i), Japan (Hitotsubashi, JAIST (Japan

Advanced Institute of Science and Technology)) and Europe (Louvain, Madrid). His research interests are in the areas of knowledge and innovation management, technology leadership and competitive advantage, stress in organizations and cross-cultural organizational research. He is a frequent consultant and speaker on issues of international business in Asia, Europe and North America and serves as the Honorary Consul of the Kingdom of Belgium in Kyoto.

Sow Hup Chan is currently Assistant Professor of Management at the Faculty of Business Administration, University of Macau, People's Republic of China where she teaches various courses in business communication and communication management. She received her MBA from the University of Nottingham and her PhD from Bangkok University, Thailand after completing her Joint Doctoral Program in Communication between Bangkok University and Ohio University, USA. Dr Chan's research interests include communication in organizations, interpersonal and intercultural communication, and micro-finance. She has published articles in *Management Communication Trends and Strategies; Asian Business & Management* (SSCI, Palgrave Macmillan); *Journal of Management Development; Euro Asia Journal of Management; International Journal of the Computer, the Internet and Management;* and *The Southern Communication Journal*. Dr Chan has also reviewed for journals including *International Journal of Productivity and Performance Management, Euro Asia Journal of Management*, and *Asian Business & Management*. She is continuously learning from her colleagues and students.

Mai The Cuong holds a BA and a PhD in International Economics from the National Economics University, Vietnam and an MBA focusing on Marketing from the International University of Japan and is currently a Lecturer in the Faculty of International Economics and Business at the National Economics University. He is also the Managing Director of Goodwill – a Vietnam-Singapore joint business in human resource training and consulting. He has taught International Business, International Procurement, and Marketing for undergraduate as well as graduate students. Dr Cuong has designed and facilitated marketing and sales programmes for enterprises in Vietnam. From 2004 to 2007, he was a researcher at the Vietnam Development Forum where he studied industrial policy and FDI marketing policies. His papers have been published in several books and journals in Vietnam. He networks with businesses, policymakers and researchers from Vietnam, Thailand, Malaysia and Japan. He also works as an independent consultant in evaluating official development assistance (ODA) projects.

Philippe Debroux holds a PhD from the Free University of Brussels and an MBA from INSEAD. He is currently Professor of International Management at Soka University, Japan and Visiting Professor on a regular basis at the Hanoi Economics University, Vietnam, Free University of Brussels, Belgium and Rennes National University, France. Professor Debroux's main research interests are international human resource management, corporate social responsibility and entrepreneurship. His main theme of research during the past two years has been female entrepreneurship in Asia and Europe. Recent publications include *Human Resource Management in Japan: A Time of Uncertainties* (2003, Ashgate); 'Trends in female entrepreneurship in Japan', in *Economic Dynamism and Business Strategy of Firms in Asia* (2005, China Economic Publishing House, Beijing); 'The shift toward a performance-based management system' in *The Changing Structure of Labour in Japan* (2006, Palgrave); 'Diversity management in Japan', in *International Journal of Human Resource Management* (2007, with John Benson and Masae Yuasa); and *Corporate Social Responsibility in Asia* (2008, Soka University Management Society Publications).

Raphaella D. Dwianto obtained her MA in area studies from Tokyo University and her PhD in Sociology from Tohoku University, Japan. Having undertaken her postdoctoral research at Ecole des Hautes Etudes en Science Sociales in Paris in 2006, followed by research at Tohoku University in 2007 under the fellowship of the Japan Foundation, she returned to the Department of Sociology at the University of Indonesia, where she has been a faculty member since 2001. Her work has been published as chapters in several books (in English and Japanese) including *Globalization, Minorities and Civil Society* (2008, Trans Pacific Press) and *Globalization and Asian Societies: The Horizon of Post-colonialism* (2006, Toshindo Publishing Co.), and also in various academic journals. Her research interests include empirical research on urban communities in Asia from a comparative sociological point of view and corporate social responsibility in Asian countries.

Tony Garrett earned his PhD from the University of Otago, New Zealand and is now at the Korea University Business School, Seoul, Korea. Prior to his arrival in Korea, he was a Senior Lecturer in Marketing at the University of Otago. His thesis examined national culture and group dynamics in new product development, focusing on New Zealand and Singapore. Currently, his main research interests are in innovation and service development, corporate entrepreneurship and national factors affecting the adoption of new products. He has published a number of chapters and articles, including articles in *Industrial Marketing Management*; *European Journal of Marketing*; *International Journal of Services Management*; *Services Management Journal* and the *Journal of Product Innovation Management*. He has worked on collaborative research projects with Jilin University, China, the National University of Singapore, HEC (Paris), Chulalongkorn University (Bangkok), Delft University of Technology (the Netherlands) and the University of Alabama in Huntsville, USA. Prior to his academic career he had business experience in the development of international brands in the New Zealand market.

Vipin Gupta holds a PhD from Wharton School and is the Roslyn Solomon Jaffe Chair in Strategy and Director, International Outreach at Simmons College, School of Management, Boston, USA. He is a Principal Co-investigator of the GLOBE (Global Leadership and Organizational Behavior Effectiveness) programme on the study of culture and leadership around the world. He is a recipient of the coveted 2005 Scott Myers Award for Applied Research in the Workplace from the Society for Industrial Organizational Psychologists, USA. He has edited 14 books, including 11 book compendium series on family businesses in different cultures of the world, and the seminal GLOBE book. He has authored a leading textbook on strategic management for the Indian market. He has published refereed articles in leading journals, and been invited to and/or presented at conferences and academic forums in more than 25 nations. He has been a visiting faculty at several business schools in India.

Martin Hemmert is Associate Professor of International Business at Korea University Business School in Seoul. Previously, he held research and teaching positions at the University of Cologne, Hitotsubashi University, DIJ Tokyo, the University of Duisburg-Essen and the National University of Singapore. His research interests include the management of R&D alliances, innovation systems, and organizational boundaries of firms. He has published five books and numerous articles in journals such as *Industrial and Corporate Change*; *Research Policy*; *Management International Review*; *Journal of Product Innovation Management*; *Journal of World Business*; and *Journal of Engineering and Technology Management*. Recently, he served twice as a Guest Editor of *Asian Business & Management* (SSCI, Palgrave Macmillan).

Pornkasem Kantamara earned her doctorate in General Administrative Leadership from Vanderbilt University, Tennessee, USA. Currently, she is a Lecturer at the College of Management, Mahidol University, Bangkok, Thailand where she teaches courses in general management and organizational change. She has published articles in various international journals such as *School Effectiveness and School Improvement*; *Journal of Educational Administration*; *School Leadership and Management*; *Asia Pacific Journal of Education*; and *Comparative Education Review*. Her research interests include change management, leadership, cross-cultural management, problem-based learning approach, and educational administration and reform.

Mari Kondo obtained her PhD from the Center for Southeast Asian Studies, Kyoto University, Japan and is now a Professor at the Ritsumeikan Asia Pacific University in Japan, teaching International Business, International Political Economy and Strategic Management to MBAs; and Asian HRM and Business Ethics and CSR to undergraduates. She was a faculty member of the Asian Institute of Management in the Philippines for more than 12 years, after a stint at the World Bank in Washington, DC. Her recent publications include 'Globalization and knowledge workers of the Philippines' in *Knowledge Workers in the Asia Pacific* (in Japanese, 2008), 'Twilling Bata-bata into meritocracy' in *Philippine Studies* (2008) and 'Conflict management styles: The differences among the Chinese, Japanese and Koreans' in *International Journal of Conflict Management* (co-authored, 2007), among others. Besides her continued interests in the Philippines, being in a campus of some 80 nationalities in Japan, her research interests have been sparked in diversity management and education, and CSR and peace issues.

Naoki Kuriyama is a Professor of Human Resources Management at the Department of Business Administration, Soka University, Tokyo, Japan. In his past academic career outside Japan he worked as an expert on employment for ILO, Geneva (1988–91) and was a visiting scholar at the International Institute of Labour Studies and Modern Asia Research Centre, Geneva (1999–2000). These assignments led to several publications in English including *Recent Trends of Industrial Subcontracting in Japanese Manufacturing Industry* (1990, International Institute for Labour Studies) and *Resilience of Japanese Automobile Investment in Thailand through the Asian Financial Crisis* (2000, Modern Asia Research Centre). Major Japanese publications include *A Study of Globalization and 'Labour' in the Context of Asia* (2003, Institute of Asian Studies, Soka University). His current research interest is on the relationships between internal and external stakeholders, CSR and HRM. Professor Kuriyama also coordinates a programme called 'Business Education of Sustainable Development' at the Soka University which includes extensive research visits to various European and Asian countries.

Denise J. Luethge is a Research Associate at the Institute for Technology Enterprise and Competitiveness (ITEC), Dôshisha University, Kyoto, Japan and Professor of Management at Northern Kentucky University. She holds an MBA from Michigan State University and a PhD in International Business from Indiana University-Bloomington.

Her research is in the areas of knowledge creation, organizational networks, strategic orientation in transitional economies, global strategic human resources in organizations, and pedagogical issues in business simulations and gaming. Dr Luethge has published widely in international academic journals with a primary focus on the automobile and electronics industries.

Leonard Lynn received BA and MA degrees in East Asian Studies from the University of Oregon, and MA and PhD degrees in Sociology from the University of Michigan. He is also a graduate of the US Army Language School in Chinese. Much of his earlier work concentrated on comparative US–Japanese studies of technology policy and management. He is now working with Hal Salzman and colleagues around the world on National Science Foundation (NSF)-funded studies of the globalization of technology development. Professor Lynn has published three books, as well as articles in journals such as *Science*; *IEEE Transactions on Engineering Management*; *Research Policy*; *Asian Business & Management* (SSCI, Palgrave Macmillan); and *Issues in Science and Technology*. Professor Lynn serves on the editorial boards of four academic journals and was on the American Advisory Committee of the Japan Foundation for eight years. He has received the 'Excellence in Research Award' from the International Association for the Management of Technology and is a past president of the Association for Japanese Business Studies.

Nguyen Thi Tuyet Mai holds a PhD in marketing from the National University of Singapore, an MBA from Boise State University, USA and a BA from the National Economics University, Vietnam. She is currently Vice Director of the NEU Graduate School at the National Economics University, Vietnam. She has taught international marketing, marketing management and research methodology in business for a number of PhD and MBA programmes. She has visited and worked as a visiting professor at various American and Japanese universities. Dr Mai has also developed and delivered a number of training courses and consulting projects related to marketing, management, and training need assessment for local and international organizations in Vietnam. Dr Mai's research interests include consumer behaviours in transitional economies, cross-cultural consumer behaviours, international marketing and entrepreneurship. Her research has been published in international journals including: *Journal of International Marketing*; *Journal of Business Venturing*; *Advances in Consumer Research*; and *Asia-Pacific Advances in Consumer Research*.

Agustinus Prasetyantoko obtained his PhD in Economics and Management from Ecole Normale Supérieure in agreement with the European School of Management, Paris, France. He has been a faculty member at Atma Jaya Catholic University in Jakarta, Indonesia since 1998. His publications include articles in the *Journal of Corporate Ownership and Control*; *Oeconomicus Journal*; and a chapter in *The Economic Relations Between Asia and Europe: Organization, Control and Technology* (2007, Chandos Publishing). He also participates in various international conferences as a presenter, discussant or reviewer, such as the European International Business Academy (EIBA) Annual Conference, Euro Working Group on Financial Modeling, Financial Management Association (FMA) European Conference, Annual Conference of the Multinational Finance Society, Spring Meeting of Young Economists, *Congrès Annuel de la Société Canadienne de Science Economique* and many others. His major research interests are on business cycles, corporate governance and corporate strategy.

Gordon Redding is Senior Affiliate Professor of Asian Business at INSEAD, and is based there at the Euro-Asia Centre. He is also Professor Emeritus at the University of Hong Kong, Visiting Professor at Manchester Business School and a Director of the Wharton International Forum. He is a specialist on Asian management and especially on Chinese capitalism and has spent 24 years based at the University of Hong Kong, where he established and was Director of the Business School. His research has focused on the understanding of Asian business systems comparatively, and especially on the contrasts between Chinese, Korean and Japanese forms of capitalism. As well as encompassing cultural effects this approach also includes analysis of the influence of institutions and societal processes seen historically. In addition, his work has included the implications for multinationals working in the region, and the operating problems of expatriate management. He had 11 years practical managerial experience as an executive in the UK department store industry before taking his doctorate at Manchester Business School.

Andrew Staples is currently Associate Professor in the Faculty of Business and Economics at Kansai Gaidai University in Osaka, Japan, and Managing Editor of *Asian Business & Management* (SSCI, Palgrave Macmillan). He was formerly a Lecturer in Japanese Studies at the University of Sheffield, UK where he also gained his PhD. His latest work based on his doctoral thesis, entitled *Responses to Regionalism in East Asia: Japanese Production Networks in the Automotive Sector*, is published as part of the Asian Business Series (series editor: Harukiyo Hasegawa) by Palgrave Macmillan (2008). His major research interests include the Japanese transnational corporation, particularly in East Asia, and contemporary inward foreign direct investment in Japan.

Robert Taylor has been Reader in Modern Chinese Studies and Co Director of the Centre for Chinese Studies at the University of Sheffield. During his career he has held appointments at various British and overseas universities. His research has focused on China's foreign economic relations, especially foreign direct investment and its impact on Chinese management. He has published extensively in academic journals across a broad range of Chinese Studies, encompassing education, manpower deployment, business management and foreign policy. His publications include *China's Intellectual Dilemma* (1981, University of British Columbia Press), *The Sino-Japanese Axis* (1985, Athlone) and *Greater China and Japan* (1996, Routledge). He has also contributed to programmes on radio and television.

Michael A. Witt holds a PhD and MA from Harvard University and an AB from Stanford University and is currently Professor of Asian Business and Comparative Management at INSEAD and Associate in Research at Harvard's Reischauer Institute of Japanese Studies. He specializes in exploring the different types of capitalism that have evolved around the world. The focus of his attention is on how these types differ, how they change over time, and how they predispose firms towards certain types of corporate strategies. Recent publications in this vein include a book on business in China, *The Future of Chinese Capitalism* (2007, Oxford University Press), a book on change in Japanese business, *Changing Japanese Capitalism* (2006, Cambridge University Press) and articles in journals such as the *Journal of International Business Studies*; *Asian Business & Management* (SSCI, Palgrave Macmillan); and *Wirtschaftspolitische Blätter*.

Acknowledgements

Acknowledgements are due to John Bratton and Jeff Gold for inspiration, and to Ursula Gavin of Palgrave Macmillan for her encouragement in this project and patience in its progress. Our thanks also go to Akiko Kuroda, John Billingsley and the anonymous reviewers who provided valuable feedback and guidance along the way to completion.

The authors and publishers wish to thank the following for permission to reproduce copyright material:

Cambridge University Press for Figure 8.1 from Witt, M.A. (2006) *Changing Japanese Capitalism: Societal Coordination and Institutional Adjustment*. Cambridge: Cambridge University Press.

The Economist Newspaper Ltd for 'The big picture: Chinese brands: TCL wants to become China's Samsung', © The Economist Newspaper Limited, London (8 November 2003).

Palgrave Macmillan for Figure 3.1 from Porter, M. (1998) *The Competitive Advantage of Nations*. Basingstoke: Palgrave Macmillan.

Reuters for 'How Confucianism fills the void' by Guo Shiping. © Reuters 9 May 2007.

Taylor and Francis Group for Figure 4.2 from Gereffi, G., Humphrey, J. and Sturgeon, T. (2005) 'The governance of global value chains', *Review of International Political Economy*, **12**(1): 78–104. Taylor and Francis Group.

Every effort has been made to trace all the copyright holders but if any have been inadvertently overlooked the publishers will be pleased to make the necessary arrangements at the first opportunity.

Abbreviations

AA	AirAsia (Malaysia)
AC	Ayala Corporation (Philippines)
ADB	Asian Development Bank
AFTA	ASEAN Free Trade Area
AIC	ASEAN Industrial Complementation Scheme
AICO	ASEAN Industrial Cooperation
Amcham	American Chamber of Commerce (Vietnam)
APEC	Asia-Pacific Economic Cooperation
ASEAN	Association of Southeast Asian Nations
ASEM	Asia-Europe Meeting
ASrIA	Association for Sustainable and Responsible Investment in Asia (Hong Kong)
BAPEPAM	Capital Market Supervisory Agency (Indonesia)
BBC	brand to brand complementation
BCG	Boston Consulting Group
BKKBN	Indonesia National Family Planning Agency
BKPM	Capital Investment Coordinating Agency (Indonesia)
BOI	Board of Investment (Thailand)
BOP	bottom of the pyramid
BPO	business process outsourcing
BPS	Central Bureau of Statistics (Indonesia)
BWI	Business Watch Indonesia
Calpers	California Public Employees' Retirement System
CAS	Chinese Academy of Sciences
CASE	Consumer Association of Singapore
CCP	Chinese Communist Party
CE	Common Era

CEBN	Chinese ethnic business network
CEO	chief executive officer
CEPT	Common Effective Preferential Tariff Scheme
CIA	Central Intelligence Agency
CII	Confederation of Indian Industry
CKD	completely knocked down [kit]
CLGI	Center for Local Government Innovation (Indonesia)
CLT	culturally endorsed leadership theory
CNDR	Corporate Network for Disaster Response (Philippines)
CNG	compressed natural gas
CPI	Corruption Perception Index
CQ	cultural intelligence quotient
CSR	Corporate social responsibility
DepEd	Department of Education (Philippines)
DJSI	Dow Jones Sustainability Index
DVD	digital video disc
EDSA	People Power Revolution (Philippines)
EIA	environmental impact assessment
EIU	Economist Intelligence Unit
EMS	environmental management system
EOI	export oriented industrialization
EPF	Employees Provident Fund (Malaysia)
EQ	emotional intelligence quotient
ETI	Ethical Trading Initiative
EU	European Union
Eurocham	European Chamber of Commerce (Vietnam)
FCGI	Forum for Corporate Governance in Indonesia
FDI	foreign direct investment
FTA	free trade agreement
FTSE	Financial Times Stock Exchange
GDP	gross domestic product
GE	General Electric
GEM	Global Entrepreneurship Monitor
GERD	gross expenditure on R&D
GIC	Government Investment Corporation (Singapore)
GLC	government-linked company
GLOBE	Global Leadership and Organizational Behavior Effectiveness
GNI	Gross National Income
GNP	gross national product
GPN	Green Purchasing Network (Japan)
GPN	global production network
GRI	Global Reporting Initiative
GSO	Government Statistics Office (Vietnam)
HBR	*Harvard Business Review*
HCM	Hochiminh [City]
HDI	Human Development Index
HICOM	The Heavy Industries Corporation of Malaysia *Berhad*
HPAEs	high-performing East Asian economies
HPEs	high performance economies

HQ	headquarters
HR	human resource
HRD	human resources development
HRDF	Human Resources Development Fund (Malaysia)
HRM	human resource management
HRMIS	human resource management information system
HSBC	Hong Kong and Shanghai Banking Corporation
IAI	Indonesian Institute of Accountants
IBRA	Indonesian Bank Restructuring Agency
ICFTU	International Confederation of Free Trade Unions
ICT	information and communications technology
ICW	Indonesia Corruption Watch
IDR	Indonesian rupiah
IDV	individualism
IE	International Enterprise
IGES	Institute for Global Environmental Strategies
IICD	Indonesian Institute for Corporate Directorship
IICG	Indonesian Institute for Corporate Governance
IIT	Indian Institute of Technology
ILO	International Labour Organization
IMD	Institute of International Management Development (Switzerland)
IMF	International Monetary Fund
IMPA	investment management and performance agreement
IMP3	Third Industrial Master Plan (Malaysia)
IMV	international multipurpose vehicle
INSA	Indian National Science Academy
IPO	initial public offering
IPR	Intellectual Property Right
IR	industrial relations
ISI	import substitution industrialization
ISICOM	Indonesian Society of Independent Commissioners
ISO	International Standards Organization
IT	information technology
JBA	Japanese Business Association
JETRO	Japan External Trade Organization
JIT	just-in-time
JSX	Jakarta Stock Exchange
JV	joint venture
KD	semi-knocked down [kit]
KOSIS	Korean Statistical Information Service
KRW	Korean won
LBDQ	Leader Behavior Description Questionnaire
LCA	life-cycle assessment
LCC	low-cost carrier
LCD	liquid crystal display
LEP	Look East Policy (Malaysia)
LNG	liquefied natural gas
LPG	liquefied petroleum gas
LTO	long-term orientation

MAS	masculinity
MBA	master of business administration
MBO	management by objectives
MDGs	millennium development goals
MMW4P	making markets work for the poor
MNC	multinational corporation
MNE	multinational enterprise
MNS	Malaysian Nature Society
MOFA	Ministry of Foreign Affairs (Vietnam)
MOI	Ministry of Industry (Vietnam)
MOLISA	Ministry of Labour, War Invalids and Social Affairs (Vietnam)
MPI	Ministry of Planning and Investment (Vietnam)
MPV	multipurpose vehicle
MRS	Malaysian remuneration system
MSAA	master settlement acquisition agreement
MSC	Marine Stewardship Council (WWF)
MSC	Multimedia Super Corridor (Malaysia)
MTI	Indonesia Society for Transparency
NACD	National Association of Corporate Directors (USA)
NAFTA	North America Free Trade Agreeement
NCAER	National Council for Applied Economic Research (India)
NCCG	National Committee for Corporate Governance (Indonesia)
NEP	New Economic Policy (Malaysia)
NESDB	National Economic and Social Development Board (Thailand)
NGO	non-governmental organization
NHK	Nippon Hoso Kosha
NIEs	newly industrialized economies
NSF	National Science Foundation
NSTB	National Science and Technology Board (Singapore)
NTUC	National Trades Union Congress (Singapore)
NWC	National Wage Council (Singapore)
OCHA	Office for the Coordination of Humanitarian Affairs (United Nations)
ODA	official development assistance
OECD	Organisation for Economic Co-operation and Development
OEM	original equipment manufacturing
OLI	ownership, location and internalization
OPEC	Organization of Petroleum Exporting Countries
OTOP	one *tambon* [village] one product scheme (Thailand)
PAP	People's Action Party (Singapore)
PC	personal computer
PDI	power distance index
PERNAS	Perbadanan Nasional (Malaysia)
PETRONAS	Petroliam Nasional *Berhad* (Malaysia)
PLA	People's Liberation Army
PM	performance and maintenance
PO	people's organization
PPP	purchasing power parity
QCC	quality control circle
QCDME	quality, cost, delivery and environment

Rs.	Indian rupees
R&D	research and development
RCC	Reliance Commercial Corporation
RM	Malaysian ringgit
RPN	regional production network
SAI	Social Accountability International
SAR	Special Administrative Region
SARS	severe acute respiratory syndrome
SEBI	Securities and Exchange Board of India
SEZ	Special Economic Zone
SIA	Singapore Airlines
SME	small to medium-size enterprise
SMI	small and medium scale industry
SOE	state-owned enterprise
SPRING	Singapore Productive Innovation and Growth Agency
SRI	socially responsible investment funds
SUV	sports utility vehicle
TI	Transparency International
TMAP	Toyota Motor Asia-Pacific
TMC	Toyota Motor Corporation
TNC	transnational corporation
TPS	Toyota production system
TRIMS	trade-related investment measures
UAI	uncertainty avoidance index
UK	United Kingdom
ULI	Unilever
UMRT	urban mass rapid transit
UN	United Nations
UNCTAD	United Nations Conference on Trade and Development
UNCTC	United Nations Centre on Transnational Corporations
UNDP	United Nations Development Programme
UNEP	United Nations Environmental Programme
UNOCHA	United Nations Office for the Coordination of Humanitarian Affairs
UNV	United Nations Volunteer
US/USA	United States of America
USD	United States dollar
VAT	value added tax
VBF	Vietnamese Business Forum
VCCI	Vietnamese Chamber of Commerce and Industry
VDF	Vietnam Development Forum
VGCL	Vietnamese General Confederation of Labor
VNNIC	Trung Tâm Internet Vietnam
WISE	work improvement in small enterprises
WTO	World Trade Organization
WWF	World Wide Fund for Nature (formerly World Wildlife Fund)

Glossary of foreign terms

aaram	The leisurely work ethic in India
arisan	Traditional Indonesian rotating credit associations
awa	'Compassion for people in need' in Tagalog
Badan Pusat Statistik	Central Bureau of Statistics of Indonesia
Barisan Nasional	National Front (Malaysia)
berhad	'Public limited company' in Malay
brahmin	A role (educator) in the Indian caste system
budi	The Malaysian belief system
budi bahasa	Good language manner in Malay
Bumiputera or *Bumiputra*	An official definition used in Malaysia to refer to the ethnic Malays and other indigenous ethnic groups. Literally, 'sons of the soil'
Bursa Malaysia	Formerly known as the Kuala Lumpur Stock Exchange
chaebol	Korean business groups
chalta hai	'Things being left as they are' in Indian
comrel	Short form of 'community relations' as used in the Philippines
confrontasi	The military action launched by President Soekarno of Indonesia in 1963
dalang	The single person who manipulates the puppets in traditional Indonesian puppet shadow plays
danwei	State industrial enterprise unit in China
Datuk	A title or honorific used in Malaysia
Datuk kong	Guardian spirit of sacred places in Malaysia
dewan komisaris	Board of commissioners in Bahasa Indonesian
dhabas	Traditional Indian restaurants

doi moi	The economic renovation which guided Vietnam towards an open market system in 1986
entrepôt	A centre of trade
errai-shacho	'Mini emperor' or corporate leader (Japan)
feng shui	'Geomancy' in Chinese
fukoku kyôhei	'Rich country, strong army' in Japanese
gankou keitai	'Flying geese' in Japanese
giri	'Social reciprocity' in Japanese
gotong-royong	'Mutual cooperation and help' in Malay
greng jai	'Considerate' in Thai
guanxi	'Connection or relationship' in Chinese
hajj	A pilgrimage to Mecca made as an objective of the religious life of a Muslim
halal	Meat that has been slaughtered in the manner prescribed by the *sharia*
haram	'Unlawful or prohibited' in Arabic
hormat	'Respect' in Malay
hukou	'Residence system' in China
ie	Traditional hearth of a farmhouse and so signifying the point of identity for a workgroup including a family and other non-family members as a community identified by shared work (Japanese)
ikhlas	'Sincerity' in Malay
inhwa	'Harmony' in Korean
jidoka	'Automation' (especially the self-regulated manufacturing process) in Japanese
jituan	Chinese conglomerates
kaizen	'Continuous improvement' in Japanese
kampong	'Village' in Malay
karma	'Afterlife' in Sanskrit
kebaya	A traditional blouse worn by Indonesian and Malaysian women
keiretsu	Japanese business groups
kenpo jushichijo	The Seventeen Article Constitution promulgated by Prince Shotoku in ancient Japan
keramat	A guardian spirit of sacred places in Malaysia
kibun	'Good feelings' in Korean
kohai	'Junior' in Japanese
konglomerat	'Conglomerate' in Bahasa Indonesian
Krung thep	'City of Angels' in Thai, another name for Bangkok
kshatriya	A role (ruler) in the Indian caste system
laissez-faire	An economic doctrine that opposes governmental interference in commerce beyond the minimum necessary for a free-enterprise system to operate according to its own economic laws
long kaeg	'Collective labour' in Thai
Mahurata	A branch of astrology called Electional Astrology in India, which indicates the best moment for starting any undertaking in terms of gaining the greatest success or productivity

mai pen rai	'Never mind' in Thai
malu	'Shame' (for the collective) in Malay
minying	'Collective' enterprises in Chinese
monozukuri	'The spirit and ability to produce or achieve something very well' in Japanese
mulia	'Righteousness' in Malay
murah hati	'Generosity' in Malay
Nai nam mee pla, nai na mee khao	A Thai saying literally meaning 'There are fish in the water, there is rice in the paddies'
Nangyang	The South China Sea
Parsi	A member of a Zoroastrian religious sect in India
posyandu	Community health posts in Indonesia
Pribumi	'Malay-descent' in Bahasa Indonesian
priyayi	An original aristocratic court culture in Indonesia
raj	Dominion or rule, especially the British rule over India during 1757 to 1947.
Ramadhan	A Muslim religious observance that takes place during the ninth month of the Islamic calendar
ringi	Japanese collective decision-making system
sabai	'Easy going' in Thai
sahoon	'Company motto' in Korean
sanuk	'Fun' in Thai
saree	The dress traditionally worn by women in India
segan	'Shame' (for the individual) in Malay
sempai	'Senior' in Japanese
sharia	The body of Islamic religious laws
shingikai	Ad hoc consultative councils set up to inform Japanese government policy
shogun	General or military ruler in Japanese
shunto	National wage negotiations each spring between employers and unions in Japan
sia na	'Lose face' in Thai
Sistem Saraan Malaysia	Malaysian Remuneration System
sogo-shosha	Japanese trading companies
sudra	A role (farmer or craftsman) in the Indian caste system
tambon	Village in Thai
Tan Sri	A title or honorific used in Malaysia
Tao	The 'way' in Chinese
thali	Indian meal plate
timbang-rasa	'Discretion' in Malay
utang na loob	'Debt of gratitude to be repaid' in Tagalog
vaisya	A role (trader) in the Indian caste system
wa	'Harmony or consensus' in Japanese
wawasan	'Vision' in Malay
wayang kulit	Traditional Indonesian puppet shadow play
wu lun	The Five Cardinal Relationships in Confucianism
yinyang	The Chinese concept of interdependence of all things
zaibatsu	Huge Japanese conglomerates before the 1930s
zhong yong	The Doctrine of the Mean in Confucianism

Introduction

Business schools should aim to produce not just efficient, but also decent human beings whose business life is guided not just by a concern with legal compliance but with criteria of fairness, which they have worked out themselves and which their conscience makes them want to stick to. (Ronald Dore (2006). *Asian Business & Management*. SSCI, Palgrave Macmillan 5(1): 9)

Seven important themes run through this book; seven themes that apply to the developing format of Asian business management across the continent, and seven themes that we feel will need to be borne in mind by business decision makers now and in the future:

■ Business systems
■ Corporate social responsibility (CSR)
■ Technology
■ Production networks
■ Culture
■ Leadership
■ Living and working conditions.

We hope that our examination of these themes and the way they are played out in certain Asian countries may help to bring a fresh perspective to bear on such decisions at a time when traditional business assumptions require reassessment in the light of contemporary circumstances.

History is a chronicle of fluctuation, especially as regards centres of development and prosperity. China and India, for instance, once held over half the world's wealth until the dynamic of world economic development shifted westwards and became concentrated in Europe and America in the 19th and 20th centuries. Now the sands are shifting once more, and it is again Asia, through the momentum of globalization, that is experiencing the winds of development.

However, the growth we see today is surely more problematic than before, as now we have become aware of other factors that must be taken into account in any further development – key issues such as sustainability and the environment, which if ignored will impact upon not only business but also the whole of humanity itself; and ethics and democracy, the underpinnings of the societies upon which economies depend. We are all familiar with problems of environmental pollution, energy resources, climate change, wealth disparity and poverty, democracy and human rights, but these are parts of a whole within which we as individuals and companies are also a part. It is necessary to be aware of causation processes and interrelationships between such problems and ourselves, whatever social role we play.

The company is a fundamental institution in civil society, and executives should understand that their organization is part of a web of causal interrelationships covering the social and natural environments. Too often, though, current perspectives in international business studies allow companies to stand aloof from the environment in which they play a part, offering theories on how to achieve business success, but little on how to understand and act on the inevitable responsibilities that go with business activity. These responsibilities may be ethical (voluntary) or statutory (obligatory), and extend to the environment, energy resources, food provision and safety, human rights, livelihood and the well-being of society and its individuals. Today's requirement of companies is for them to create management concepts that honour such responsibility and lead them to fulfil a positive role as an institution of civil society; implicit in this is democracy – not the kind of political democracy expressed through electoral systems but a liberal and diversified democracy that spreads through society on an everyday basis.

Until recently, the majority of research on Asian business management has consisted of transplanting existing theories of international business to Asia; hence, we mostly hear about globalization and market competitiveness, global strategies, strategic alliance, global organization, market entry and methods, global finance, human resource management (HRM), and cross-cultural management. But these are, essentially, narrow functionalistic perspectives focused on how to increase profitability. To understand the future development and resolve the challenges of Asia requires a different approach – one that embraces the interactions between business and its wider environment. Whether a global corporate, joint venture, local business or some other organizational structure, this means developing an inclusive attitude to civil society and a considerate attitude towards the natural environment and its constraints upon economic growth.

A strategy consisting primarily of profit-seeking cannot serve the ends of an equitable or sustainable global society or business. Asia's new economic strength is revealing shortcomings in the functionalist paradigm at the expense of regional environments and social democracy. At this time, therefore, business management theorists in Asia today can, instead of employing traditional profit-led perspectives, develop a distinctive 'introspective development' perspective, redirecting economic paradigms and business priorities towards a sustainability ethic.

APPROACH AND STRUCTURE

The framework used in this textbook is systems theory, adapted for a systems-focused approach. The structural elements of a business system, such as meaning, order and coordination, play a causal role through social dynamics – a conceptual overview which, while a framework for understanding reality, is also effective for understanding issues such as corporate social responsibility (CSR), sustainable development, technological development, production networks, cultures, leadership, working conditions and living standards in relation to business management. These are the kind of ideas we deal with in this book, and an advantage of systems theory is that it can explain potential interactions, circularity and organic development between the whole and individual components. This distinguishes it from the functionalist approaches, and in our view makes a systems-based perspective a better lens through which to view Asian business management.

Parts 1 and 2 therefore address our objectives from different angles. Part 1 offers a thematic discussion, outlining our seven themes as found across Asia in general: business systems, CSR and sustainable development, technological development, production networks, culture, leadership approaches, and working and living conditions. These chapters will give the reader an idea of how the development of Asian business and its local forms are related to active factors like regional history, social structure, culture, value systems, technology and democracy. Part 2 looks at how each of these themes is represented in a particular Asian country – Japan, China, India, Korea, Singapore, Vietnam, Thailand, Malaysia, Indonesia and the Philippines – and explains why these countries were chosen.

CONTRIBUTORS

This is not a textbook compiled by a single author; it would be extremely difficult for one person to write about all of Asia. We therefore invited contributions from leading scholars with expertise on a specific topic or country. Although we hope the whole textbook holds a general sense of unity under a value umbrella of ethical thoughts in business systems, each chapter stands on its own, reflecting the author's viewpoint, interest and individuality. Such differentials, we feel, enrich this book and enhance our sense of Asia's complexity and diversity. Throughout, we maintain an academic stance rooted in social science – not applying a narrow functionalist argument, but a perspective seeking to analyse and understand business management in relation to people, social systems and social relations.

FEATURES

The text has several features intended to assist students to understand the points raised.

- *Chapter outline*: Providing the general topic area, structure and development of information and knowledge in each chapter.
- *Chapter objectives*: A guide for the student to assimilate the key topics and issues raised in the chapter.
- *Blue highlighting*: Important terms or short phrases/sentences are highlighted in blue.
- *Summary points*: Reminders of key elements in the section.
- *Reflective questions*: These encourage students and readers to think over the topics critically and to develop their ideas about them. These questions can be used for group or class discussions, to further digest and develop the knowledge acquired.

- *Cross-chapter reflective questions*: These questions are provided in the chapters in Part 2. They are intended to stimulate the students to compare and contrast important issues across the various Asian countries under study.
- *Chapter summary*: A useful and compact digest of the information presented, by which readers can understand the relative importance of the contents and the author's perspective.
- *Key concepts*: An aid to grasping the definition of terms appearing in the chapter, to assist with clear understanding of the material.
- *Review questions*: Questions relevant to the points raised provide a reference for students to assess and enhance their understanding of the material.
- *Learning assignments*: These activities encourage students to engage in their own research and thereby deepen their understanding of the relevant issues.
- *Mini-cases*: These stories offer real-life scenarios illustrating the issues and theories of the chapter, and are useful for class discussion of linkages between reality and theory.
- *Related web-links*: Providing supplementary avenues of information for those wishing to explore the issues further.
- *References*: A list of sources/works cited in the chapter, essential for backing up discussion and developing personal perspectives.

RECOMMENDED USE OF THE TEXT

Our expected class format would be an initial lecture, followed by presentations of personal research from students or a case study followed by discussion. Mini-cases, reflective questions and activities can be used for class discussion in order to link theory and practice, enhancing students' understanding. The aim is always to encourage a holistic grasp of Asian business management issues and foster the development of initiatives and leadership, thus contributing to Asia's overall economic and social development.

HARUKIYO HASEGAWA
CARLOS NORONHA

Part 1

Asian Management: Business Systems and Perspectives

The interdisciplinary and holistic approach to our understanding of business and management practices in Asia requires the introduction of a series of key topics in the first part of this textbook. The seven chapters in this part thus each cover a key topic.

Chapter 1   In 'The Business Systems of Asia', Gordon Redding outlines the concepts and gives an overview of business systems in Asia, emphasizing the fact that, though a single continent, Asia can be regarded as an immensely varied concept in itself, comprising a huge variety of cultures, customs and relations.

Chapter 2   Philippe Debroux devotes an entire chapter to discuss 'CSR and Sustainable Development in Asia'. The business concept of CSR (corporate social responsibility) is highly prominent in contemporary business worldwide, but the idea of social responsibility in business is not a new one and has been practised in the developed West for many years.

Chapter 3   A country can use technological developments to enhance its economic position in the global economy, as Leonard Lynn explains in 'Technology Development in Asia'. Although the West has been known for its technological advancement, abundant opportunities for technological development, whether in human resources or techniques, are apparent in many Asian countries, such as China, Japan and India.

Chapter 4   Andy Staples' 'Production Networks in East Asia' explains international and regional production networks from the perspective of foreign direct investment theory, and applies the concept to East Asian production networks.

Chapter 5   In 'Culture and Business in Asia', Carlos Noronha addresses the issue of culture, for in any attempt to understand business from an open and multi-disciplinary approach, the social and cultural aspects of business organizations are not to be ignored. Culture forms the building blocks of meaning in organizations.

Chapter 6   'Asian Leadership', by Philippe Byosiere and Denise J. Luethge, compares and contrasts conventional understandings of leadership from a Western perspective and the indigenous traits of Asian-style leadership.

Chapter 7   Finally, in 'The Role of Business in Asian Living and Working Conditions', Naoki Kuriyama suggests a new approach to living and working conditions in Asia, emphasizing the reciprocity between working (enterprise) and living (community) conditions in the creation of work–life balance.

Chapter outline

- Variety in the region and general features
- What is a business system?
- The business system of Japan
- The business system of China
- The business system of South Korea
- The business system of the regional ethnic Chinese
- The business system of Southeast Asia
- The business system of IndoChina

Chapter objectives

After reading this chapter you should be able to:

1. Understand the basic components of the region's variety of business systems
2. Understand how a business system works
3. Grasp the main features of the business systems of the major economies
4. Have an initial understanding of the smaller economies of the region

Chapter 1

The business systems of Asia

Gordon Redding

INTRODUCTION

The first thing to understand about business systems in Pacific Asia is their variety. This is not ordinary variety, but immense variety; more, for instance, than across Europe. They range from the largest country in the world, China, to some of the smallest (for example Singapore), and from some of the richest (for example Japan) to some of the poorest (for example Cambodia). The area contains a wide range of political systems, ethnic types, religions, and historical experiences. So, in order to discuss them, it is necessary to moderate the variety by placing some of them in clusters, each cluster containing some similarities within its membership. This simplifying entails missing out on some of the richness in the detail, but that may be found in the specialized chapters that follow.

The main subdivisions are as follows:

- Japan
- China
- South Korea
- The regional ethnic Chinese
- Southeast Asia
- Indochina

The distinct nature of the Indian subcontinent, and its base in quite different traditions of civilization from those of Pacific Asia, means that it is better for it to be treated in its own right, and this will be done in a chapter devoted to that theme. Otherwise the constant making of exceptions from the patterns further east will interrupt the flow of what is already a complex story.

VARIETY IN THE REGIONAL AND GENERAL FEATURES

A number of regional features of geography and history need to be considered first as they have an impact in several countries. Over millennia the populating of the region tended to be in waves, with people coming in from the north-west and eventually pushing south and eastwards. The result is a layering of different ethnic types, seen very simply as:

■ essentially Malay (that is, in ethnic terms) to the eastern and southern edges of the region in countries such as Malaysia, the Philippines and Indonesia
■ Sinic (or Chinese) in China itself and penetrating Indochina
■ a distinct Japanese ethnic stock, and
■ a very mixed set of ethnic groups in the Indochina peninsula, most notably the Thai and Vietnamese.

The region extends from the equator to the cold regions of northern China and encompasses all types of natural environment. In terms of human geography and history it contains the active heritages of several great religious and civilizational traditions. Dominant among these is that of China, whose influence lies deep in the formative processes that made Japan, Korea, and Vietnam. Within this is the Confucian tradition that brings much order to societies, but contains also the balancing influences of Taoism and Buddhism, each also visible in the make-up of both Japanese and Korean society. Elsewhere, and especially in Malaysia and Indonesia, Islam penetrates deep. Thailand is an example of a predominantly Buddhist society and the Philippines has retained the dominance of Catholicism, established during four hundred years of Spanish rule.

External influences have historically overlain these traditions in many countries. The British in what was Malaya, Singapore and Hong Kong, the French in Indochina, the Dutch in Indonesia, the US Americans in the Philippines (after the Spanish) and the Japanese in the 20th century in Taiwan, Korea, and Manchuria, have all left behind institutions and connections that have marked those countries. Less by way of invasion and colonization, but equally significant has been the influence of India established through trading connections, especially in Southeast Asia. A final wave of influence, similar to that of India, has been the impact of the regional ethnic Chinese who left China in the past 150 years and settled as business people in the countries around the rim of the South China Sea. In more recent decades the influences of multinational corporations on the region have been very strong, not only on management practices, but also on government policies, the importing of technology, and the creation of alliances to link with the markets of the rest of the world. The only country that has remained free from direct foreign influence has been Thailand, protected as it always has been by the strength of its monarchy.

In the period from the end of World War II, the region went through three distinct phases of evolution as various societal experiments took place to meet the challenges of modernization. The first of these, lasting roughly from 1945 to 1975 was a period of turbulence as countries tried to establish their new identities and independent political structures after the retreat of the colonial powers. The wider world, it must be remembered, was still in tension as the communist ideal and the liberal market democratic ideal faced each other across the cold war divide. Wars broke out: the Korean War; the American War in Vietnam; a long guerrilla war in Malaya; a bitter civil war in Indonesia; struggles for independence; and a period of *confrontasi* in Southeast Asia. Other more localized outbreaks of hostility were widespread. In the same period China went through the damaging chaos of the Maoist experiments: the Great Leap Forward; and the Cultural Revolution.

A second period of relative calm then followed, between 1975 and 1997, as the region settled down to the more peaceful pursuits of doing business, and in particular of exporting to developed country markets. This saw a rise in foreign direct investment into the region and also the moving of many factories out of Japan into regional countries with lower labour costs. After Mao's death China went through a major reappraisal of its economic philosophy, and came to terms with the stark facts of the collapse of communism elsewhere, striking out with its own formula of a 'socialist market economy'. This was the period of the Japanese miracle, and saw also the impressive growth of the South Korean economy.

This long period of stable growth and accumulating success contained within it the seeds of its own destruction as it began to run out of phase with the systems of the advanced world. Not at that time clearly visible in China, but suddenly obvious elsewhere, the problem of what had earlier been termed ersatz capitalism had lain hidden. This means that inefficient use of capital was covered up by the availability of easy money, either from governments, or from over-optimistic foreigners enchanted by the lure of emerging markets. And the system could not keep up the pretence forever as it became increasingly sensitive to a downturn in the economic cycle. That downturn hit the region in 1997, and the Asian Crisis signalled the end of the easy money and the beginning of reforms.

China had been largely insulated from these effects (although its own form of financial weakness would be later revealed in non-performing loans) and so too, to a degree were Malaysia, Hong Kong, Taiwan and Singapore. But everywhere else became an industrial bloodbath, and many companies disappeared. Japan suffered from the huge bubble created in its economy by the inflation of asset values, especially in property, and is still in recovery from that. Korea was hit badly by the logics that flow from borrowing short and investing long. The economies of most ASEAN countries saw heavy losses, currency devaluation, and the closing of many firms.

As a result of the crisis the region entered a third phase, a period of reform. Since 1997 this has moved at a different pace in different countries, and recovery has therefore been slow in some cases, notably Japan and Indonesia. Even so the direction of movement has been consistent and has displayed the following broad features:

1. Improvements to accountability and disclosure in the financing of industry.
2. The reduction of favouritism and corruption caused when officials control access to licences and capital.
3. The opening of markets to foreign competition.
4. The adoption of international standards in accounting, trading, and intellectual property rights, often via bodies such as WTO.
5. A general rise in professionalism, in both management and administration.
6. The adoption of democratic processes in politics.

Part of this same raft of 'reforms' was the notion of corporate social responsibility (CSR), an idea that forced firms to be accountable publicly for the ethics of their behaviour. It is not possible to argue that one society is more ethical than another, and the various forms of enterprise in Asia display the same variety from bad to good as do firms in the Western world, from where this specification came. But at least one might argue that the open accountability and disclosure that accompany the ethical wave are likely to assist in making firms more legitimate in their societal settings. At the same time, it should be stated that the West has as much to learn from the East as vice versa in this field, and the rise of consciousness about the issue should lead to a two-way flow of advice and borrowings, in which the 'bad' universally may become less so.

An important point here is that such trends do not necessarily mean that these countries are converging on a Western formula for organizing their societies and economies. They will still find ways of interpreting the core principles in ways that fit local cultures. In other words, they will converge to some degree but then remain distinct, and 'true to themselves'. Because of that we need to account for the continuing variety of the region's business systems.

SUMMARY POINT

The region is one of great variety, not just in people, culture, and geography but also in terms of history and stage of development. As a result it contains extreme contrasts.

REFLECTIVE QUESTION

Compare Pacific Asia with Europe or Latin America and consider which contains the most variety and what is the basis of that variety.

WHAT IS A BUSINESS SYSTEM?

A business system is a complex adaptive system in which the business component of a society is analysed against the context of that society, thus 'the American business system' compared with the 'Japanese business system'. Complex adaptive systems theory is relatively new when applied this way, and the reason it is used is that it allows for the complexity of reality to be considered, whereas some disciplines attempt to reduce that complexity to a simple framework and in the process perhaps miss out things that matter. The core idea is that an economy is a process affected by the logics of economic behaviour, but also by culture, history, and specific societal events and experiences. It is also affected by external influences such as world markets, technology, and changes of values. All these forces, economic, technical, and social interact in complex ways, and the system evolves to take on a distinct flavour, society by society.

The analysis proposed for use here can be seen in Figure 1.1. The culture is seen as the base layer of *meaning*. Here we analyse how each society constructs its own way of making sense of its surrounding context, and it does so in three main fields. First is that of *rationale*, or the basic reasons adopted by people to explain the way they have chosen to make the economy work: why do they act and in what ways do they prefer to conduct exchange, employment, financing, control, and so on? Next comes *identity*, or the core ideas in the society about the place of the person in the social structure: is it an individualist or a collectivist system, and in what ways are such ideals interpreted? Next is *authority*, or the way in which power is typically exercised in the society and its organizations. These three aspects of culture have long-lasting and subtle effects.

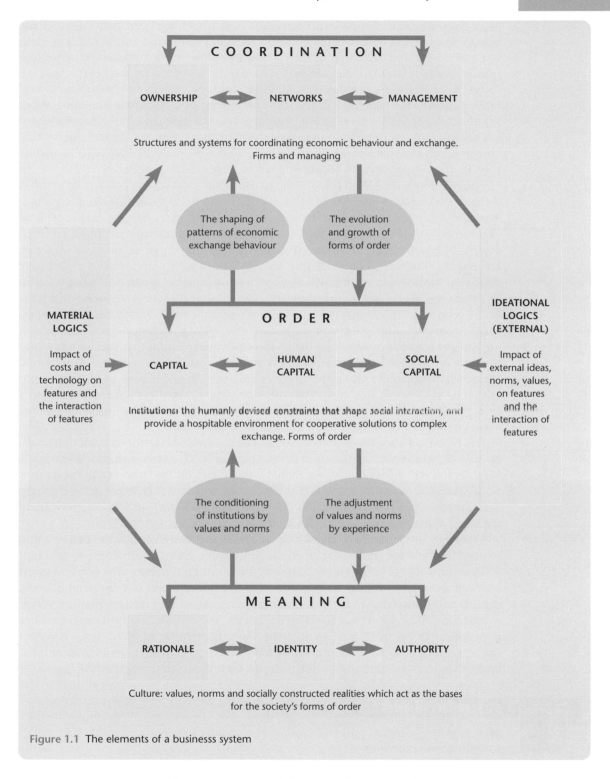

Figure 1.1 The elements of a businesss system

The middle layer of the model is that of the society's institutions. This is the realm of *order*, and the job of institutions is to standardize and regulate conduct so that it becomes predictable. People can then learn how to act, and can better predict the behaviour of others. The society's economic system can expand and intensify if there is a widespread understanding of the rules of the game and if compliance with those rules is ensured. The main areas in which such order is needed are the fields where the society's main assets are found and allocated into the system for use. These are its finance *capital*, its *human capital,* and its forms of trust or *social capital*. Capital is about where money is sourced, and how it is allocated for use. Human capital is about where talents and skills are found or encouraged, and how the labour market structures work. Trust is about the relative uses of personal trust (as with personal networks) as against trust in 'the system' (as with reliance on law or bureaucratic process).

The business system itself is at the top of the picture and emerges over time in inter-action with the other two sets of influences. It is the field of *coordination*, the pulling together of the resources needed to make economic processes efficient and capable of expansion. This is achieved in three ways: firms come into existence under forms of *ownership,* and these do not follow a universal rule. The Japanese are biased towards *keiretsu*, the Koreans towards *chaebol*, the Chinese tend to favour *smaller personally dominated* firms. These are different ways of holding together sets of assets and controlling their use. Secondly there are different ways of arranging the *relations between firms* in the economy, with a preference in some cases for alliances, cartels, and oligopolies, and in other cases for purer competition. Lastly, within each firm there are societal preferences for ways of *managing* the cooperation needed to bring together efficiently the human, technical and financial assets. In some societies firms are run with strong top-down discipline. In other societies they are run with much more participation and fair process. Although these responses differ between firms, there is nonetheless much evidence that a societal pattern makes itself felt and produces recognizable differences between national economies. Each society becomes distinct.

The history of a society will also have an effect. Taiwan bears the imprint of its half-century of Japanese occupation, and the Philippines its US American and Spanish herit-ages. So too will government policies have an impact on the end result. You cannot understand China without studying the waves of policy change it has gone through. Nor can you understand South Korea (also referred to as Korea) without acknowledging the series of five year plans begun under the Park government in the 1960s.

I shall use this framework to describe the business systems of Asia, but before doing so need to advise the reader that much simplification is inevitable in doing so, and that it is not intended to substitute for detailed studies of each society. The pictures given are outlines only. It will not be possible to go into every aspect of the model in every case, as this is intended to be an introductory chapter, not a final statement. It serves to make two main points: each society does things its own way; and although societies may appear to be drifting closer in some ways, they never meet to make a perfect convergence. The fact that they do not finally converge is what presents international business with its interest and its dilemmas, in both theory and practice.

SUMMARY POINTS

- A business system is a way of looking at a country's economy so as to compare with other countries.

- It also allows us to deal with emerging and evolving socio-economic systems and to understand their complex dynamics.

REFLECTIVE QUESTION

What do you think should be included in the description of a country's way of doing business, if someone asks you to explain one?

THE BUSINESS SYSTEM OF JAPAN

The Japanese business system developed as one of the world's most powerful, and especially in industries requiring:

- high levels of technical skill in manufacturing
- the building of globally significant brands
- complex organizational coordination at high levels of efficiency, and
- an ability to engage workers in product improvement and quality assurance.

Typical fields of dominance in global competition are automobiles, machine tools, consumer electronics, and communications equipment. How did this dominance come into being? Why is performance in certain other fields such as the service sector less dramatically competitive globally? Why is it taking so long to recover the high rates of growth typical of the 1980s? And what is it about the Japanese business system that allows it to deliver wealth per capita at one of the highest levels in the world, and organizations of immense scale and dramatic efficiency?

History and Politics

Japan went through a key societal revolution in the early years of the 17th century when the Shogun Tokugawa imposed his design on a newly unified nation, in the interests of achieving peace and stability. Key in this were two elements: first, the decentralization of much decision making into local hands along with an encouragement of participation and the seeking of consensus; and second, the development of a highly effective administrative bureaucracy responsible for strict rules of order, and for keeping the Centre informed about what happened locally. Tokugawa's influence on Japan was massive and lasted for two and a half centuries, only coming to an end when the outside world forced an entry and showed Japan that other countries had left it behind in industry, science, technology, and weaponry. The stability had come at the cost of conservatism. The subsequent overthrow of the old regime in 1868 led to the modernization of the state, and the deliberate searching for external models to adopt and adapt.

The subsequent industrialization of Japan happened twice. Between the 1880s and the 1930s Japan built huge conglomerate organizations – the *zaibatsu* – and relied upon their owning families to control and direct them. Government worked in close collaboration with such firms. World War II destroyed them all and in 1946 Japan began again, but this time under conditions of democracy imposed by the conquering US. Public ownership took over from private, and professional management took over from that of personal and family networks. Recovery was fast, especially as the markets of the advanced economies were open. New industrial conglomerates grew and began to make a global impact. By the end of the 1980s 'Japanese management' had become the world's most respected form, and its economy the most formidable. Deep competencies in the managing of technical and organizational complexity, in cooperation within the overall system, and in control of global activities, had made the Japanese company the envy of the world.

But keeping a business system in perfect balance is never easy and Japan was no exception. Through the 1980s a large bubble in asset prices had blown up, inflated by years of success and weak financial rationality, and added to by administrative corruption favouring the construction industry. The bubble collapsed in a downturn, and Japan entered a period of relative stagnation that lasted through the 1990s and into the new millennium, its capital market never recovering to the crazy peaks of the unreal asset prices that brought it down. The lost decade is extending to two decades and the reforms attempted by various governments have not taken hold to the extent needed to return Japan to its dominant position. Certain industries have remained unscathed as they were capable of radical adaptation, and they are the ones listed above. Others are victims of the rigidities of a highly inflexible structure, in which ministries, industries, labour unions, banks, and systems of distribution are all intertwined in bonds of reciprocity, and unable to orchestrate serious change. The absence of flexibility in both labour and capital markets is a handicap in such circumstances, when at earlier periods it was a strength.

It would be wrong to exaggerate the weakness of Japan, as much of its strength was retained, but its slowness in growth in recent years has been marked, and so too its apparent inability to adapt. How did this combination of power and inhibition evolve?

Culture

At the centre of Japan's economic culture is the idea that the firm exists to keep people employed, and that return on capital for the advantage of shareholders is not a primary rationale for economic action. Affecting this is the cultural tradition traceable to the Tokugawa period in which identity for the individual was centred on the *ie*, the traditional place of work and of belonging. The assertion of individual views remains constrained by the instincts for conformity to group norms. Authority came to be exercised under the conditions that subordinate dependence provided reliable workers but only if leadership took responsibility for their care. The underlying moral framework made sense of this mutual vertical bonding. It led also to a tendency for the firm to be seen as a vertical entity, separate from other entities, and in rivalry with them. A further related cultural legacy was the tradition of decentralized decision making that fostered extensive consensus seeking, and that released high levels of group creativity and commitment in the workforce.

Institutions

The institutions of finance in Japan – principally the banks, the insurance companies, and the stock markets – are providers of patient capital to industry. They have typically existed in close alliance with the major business groups and acted as clearing houses for the flows of capital needed in a relatively stable system pursuing long-term goals for growth. They have not been designed to achieve the highest rates of allocative efficiency in the short term. The system has resisted the incursion of outside influences to pursue this, doubtless judging that the short-termism that would result challenges a crucial principle of the overall design, as it actually does.

A similar rigidity occurs in the labour market. The core of the employment system is a set of permanently employed workers – perhaps 40 per cent of the total workforce –

and firms invest substantially in their training over years. This solid and reliable group is supplemented by two other groups – those employed on temporary contracts and those employed part time – and these two groups provide the necessary flexibility to the system. Compared with other societies, the technical skills derive more from the firm than from the education system and the latter is usually seen as being conservative and centralized, even though standards are high.

Social capital – or forms of trust – is at a higher level in Japan than in any other Asian society, and it engenders an unusually high level of cooperativeness between firms, firms and government agencies, subcontractors and supply chain members, unions and management, and members of the elaborate business networks and 'industry clubs' that tie the economy together. The origins of this capacity to cooperate and to trust lie most probably in the centuries-old tradition of high-quality professional administration typical of Japan. It will also have some connection with the high quality of information, in terms of both quantity and reliability that the economy is accustomed to.

The Business System

The coordination of economic exchange and control is done in Japan through the medium of two main types of firm. The heights of the economy are commanded by the very large business groups, known generally as either *keiretsu* or *sogo-shosha* depending on whether they are in manufacturing or trading. The rest of the economy is dominated by small and medium enterprises, often privately owned, and often connected to the large firms through networks of sourcing or distribution. The networking between firms is elaborate and extensive, and industry associations flourish. Within firms 'Japanese management' continues to create high levels of employment stability, and to operate with strong mutual dependence between management and workers. The relative stability and long-term nature of employment relations match the equivalent long-term nature of 'patient' capital. In these conditions firms are able to make long-term plans, to invest heavily in technology and training, and to build their strategies around product quality based on deep labour skills and incremental product improvements as opposed to constant product–market change. The ability of Japanese firms to handle complex coordination is a distinct strength in global markets and remains a primary reason for the nation's competitiveness. Few societies can handle the mixture of quality, brand building, and adaptiveness to market, at global scale, that the Japanese firms have mastered.

SUMMARY POINTS

- Japan has a distinct and very advanced industrial economy, based on its unique history, and its special combination of features.

- Its ability to handle very complex industry derives from its high levels of trust, its stable sources of patient capital, the professionalism of its management and the high skills of its workforce.

THE BUSINESS SYSTEM OF CHINA

The story of China is very different from that of Japan, and although there are some common features of heritage, notably language form and religion, their divergent trajectories over the past thousand years mean that the differences between the two societies are now profound. In brief terms Japan built itself into one of the world's greatest industrial powers following its opening up in 1868, whereas China suffered relative decline for most of the 19th and 20th centuries, and only recovered following the reforms begun by Deng Xiaoping in 1980. China's recovery has been quite simply miraculous and high respect is due for the political and economic skills exhibited in the recent transformation of its economy into 'the workshop of the world'.

History and Politics

China was a great civilization long before any other now surviving in the world. It achieved prosperity well ahead of other regions, flowering especially in the Tang and the Sung periods over a thousand years ago. Although it subsequently achieved much in science and inventions, and in statecraft, these were pre-modern achievements, and the industrial revolution passed it by in later centuries, leaving it stranded and isolated by its own wishes. Its system of government has always been highly centralized and has continually displayed the same three components, adapting them to changing surroundings:

- reliance on a powerful emperor-like figure providing direction
- use of an administrative apparatus to extend the will of the central figure into the entire society, and
- reliance on the family unit as the primary focus of belonging, duty, and welfare; this unit also providing the pride that underpins compliance to the rules of proper conduct, and the vehicle for the carrying of achieved status.

This basic architecture has not changed except in two ways. During the Mao experiments the family was temporarily destroyed and the emperor role vastly expanded. And in recent years that emperor role has diffused across a group of technocrats, as the family role expanded again to its traditional significance.

The 20th century for China was a period of high turbulence, with a revolutionary end to the Ching dynasty, civil war, invasion by Japan, World War II, the Mao years, and the post-Mao experiments. The Mao period, although giving China back its pride in a reasserted independence, led also to mass destruction of assets and lives. Emerging from the turbulence that followed, a series of controlled experiments posed a radical challenge to earlier orthodoxies, but their instigator, Deng Xiaoping, is likely to be judged by history as the true revolutionary saviour of China in its search for a modern condition. He created the special economic zones, tried various formulae for the revival of agriculture and industry, and permitted the return of the private entrepreneur.

The period since 1980 has seen dramatic shifts in the fortunes of three sectors. The state-owned enterprises (SOEs), originally accounting for 75 per cent of the economy, have been reduced to about 15 per cent and left with mainly the strategic industries that the state needs to control. The firms that remain in this category are now under the control of a state commission and are required to meet international standards of efficiency. The sector earlier known as 'the collectives', that once accounted for 36 per cent of the economy, has been partially eroded by the emerging private sector, but remains robust in many cases, having acquired great stimulus in recent years from new opportunities, local support and alliances bringing in new talent, technology, and capital. The state retains a significant interest in many of these organizations. Known now as the local corporates, this sector accounts for about 20 per cent of the economy. The private sector, of mainly small and medium enterprises (SMEs), now accounts for about 65 per cent of the economy, and has grown spectacularly from a condition of being illegal in 1980.

A modern society is one in which power has been dispersed throughout the society to a point where people can be engaged in decisions affecting their lives without the political structure being destabilized. In contrast to this it is still common to think of China as a totalitarian state. And yet, a most remarkable political process – a form of quiet revolution – has in recent years seen economic decision-making power pass from the Centre to the provinces and cities in a way that leaves them largely autonomous. The OECD's 2005 report on China showed that revenues and expenditures are decided locally to a degree higher than in any OECD country. China's structure is now one in which the local administrations collect the taxes, and spend the major part of them. They are also set up to compete with other local administrations for investment, and to be judged by Beijing on their performance in doing so. To counterbalance this loose-ness the Party retains tight control of the key positions in the local hierarchies. The effects on the economy are to increase entrepreneurship, and to intensify competition. The central government, allocating development targets and rewarding local officials against their delivery, remains fully aware, and in control.

Culture

The culture of China was for centuries a product of the ideals of Confucius. Two and a half thousand years ago, he wrote his recommendations for the running of a stable state and a harmonious society, and because of their fundamental good sense and humane nature, they have remained the principles on which Chinese people have guided their lives ever since. The design was attacked under Mao, in his attempt at moving China into the modern world, but the attack was ill-judged, presented no viable alternative, and is now irrelevant. The Confucian ideal has returned, and so too the centrality of family in the consciousness of people.

The Confucian ideal was one in which each family took care of its own members, and was responsible for their social conduct. The role of the state was to ensure that this happened. Compliance with five principles was the basis of order, and these were essentially hierarchies of rights and duties: emperor and subject, father and child, husband and wife, siblings, friends. The emperor's role was that of father to the state, and he was subject to the mandate of heaven. Dynasties were overturned when that mandate was lost through bad administration.

Confucianism is not a religion; it is a code of conduct with much advice, but no deity and no notion of heaven. It concerns itself with this world. As a counterweight to that, other more spiritual religions came in and provided the missing component: Buddhism and Taoism, in each of which there is strong emphasis on achieving a balanced relation with nature. Chinese people tend to hold several such belief systems at the same time. The values that matter most then become respect for authority, reci-procity in relations beyond the family, and identity with family. These are interpreted in daily life through heavy socialization into appropriate role behaviour. The end result is a society in which behaviour is highly predictable, and fundamentally stable. The society is also capable of high levels of peaceful interaction.

The cultural features with most impact on economic behaviour are hierarchy and mistrust, and they operate as follows. In this society leadership positions are imbued with moral value; the boss looks after the subordinates in exchange for their loyalty. This means that power is not so much reached by performance-based merit, but by other means such as ownership or connections. Power may be abused, as it is in factories where workers are dependent. And communications tend to flow downwards only. Where the boss is an effective entrepreneur this can have positive results in certain industries, but only up to a certain scale of size or complexity. The problem of mistrust comes from dependence on personal connections in networking outside the family, so that the rules of reciprocity may be brought into play, and the absence of any means of dealing with strangers on trusting terms.

Institutions

Institutions designed to provide order in China tend still to be legacies of a state with high central control, but low participation by citizens in adding spontaneously created forms of order. Examples of the latter might be civil society institutions such as free-standing professions, independent control bodies – as for example over a stock market, or societies like chambers of commerce able to lobby government. Instead – and in line with centuries of tradition – it is widely assumed that order is the job of government and the hope is for a benevolent form of it. This results in a wide net of regulatory bodies, but a thin covering. It is one of the reasons why the growth of trust has been limited. Without a rich fabric of institutions providing reliable forms of information and conduct, in addition to government control and law, it is not possible to trust those not known (and bonded) personally. An invisible but significant outcome is the high level of competitiveness between the family-based units for scarce resources.

Capital has until recently been allocated inefficiently in China, as the state banking system had a virtual monopoly on the huge savings of the people and the rights to use them in industrial investment. Foreign banks are recent arrivals and are struggling to obtain a position against a background of changing regulations. The banking system is now under close scrutiny and its efficiency increasing, as is that in the state sector more widely. Much finance for industry is taken from retained earnings, and at the smaller scale (still significant in the larger picture) often from informal lending, with start-up capital from friends and relatives.

Human capital is available in colossal quantity as relatively unskilled but trainable labour, and it is this that gives China its competitive edge in basic manufacturing. But value-added is greater in higher technology industries, and here China struggles to catch up with the demand for higher skills, and for professional competencies in engineering, accounting, and management. Educational infrastructure is expanding at high speed in consequence, but quality of output remains – with some exceptions – below global standards. The organizing of labour markets is still weak, but new legislation has been increasing worker rights, and adding welfare provisions. The most critical determinant of labour costs, however, is location, with ChongQing in the interior offering labour at half the price of Guangzhou on the coast.

Social capital, that is trust, as earlier noted, is weak in China but with the important exception of that available inside the networks of 'clan capitalism' that so typify much industry. Clusters of cooperating firms make up the formula for handling the OEM (original equipment manufacturing) that delivers the workshop of the world. High trust, flexibility, efficient transaction costs, and market responsiveness are characteristic features of these networks, which also absorb the necessary external contributions of design, technology, brand and market knowledge, and delivery logistics. The resulting economic instrument is China's most powerful weapon in world competition at present and largely explains the power of the private sector SMEs.

The Business System

China has three business systems inside its complex economy, each a legacy of a distinct history. The state sector dates from the communist era of central planning and totalitarian control. Most of it has been sold off in recent years and its remaining industries are those seen as crucial to the national interest. Either that or, in rare cases, they have become efficient at global standards. They now operate under very close scrutiny, and account for about 15 per cent of GDP.

The second sector is known as the local corporates and it derives its nature from two events. The first was the building of extensive industry at the local level in the 1950s and onwards when the communes of the Mao era were forced to act as autonomous mini economies. This required the construction of factories to meet all local needs, although some trading took place across the society within the government plan. The second event was the decision, as reform took hold in the 1980s and speeded up in the 1990s, to permit the disposal of these assets to entrepreneurs – often in coalition with local administrators. Many such assets were acquired on very favourable terms, as people decided to 'jump into the sea' and seek wealth. Many of China's new billionaires got their start in what they term now the 'golden years' when such acquisitions were possible.

The third sector is that of private business and it has received increasing encouragement from government as the primary vehicle for the country's economic growth. China has always had entrepreneurs and a tradition of commerce, and it has also always had a tendency to grow small or medium enterprises under personal control and often connected with a family. Such enterprises would normally have a short lifespan and rarely lasted beyond three generations, as family disputes would eventually break them up, or make them inefficient by the time the power of the founder had evaporated among the successors. This is partly because of the inheritance tradition that left equal wealth to all children, a feature in strong contrast with that of Japan and northern Europe, where the assets were passed intact to the principal heir, through succeeding generations, often for centuries.

The revival of privately owned companies in China dates only from the 1980s, their having been illegal under communism. Since then the sector has received increasing legal and political support and legitimacy, and now accounts for about 65 per cent of the economy. This phenomenal growth must also be seen against the fact that the funding of such enterprises has been almost entirely by retained earnings or borrowing from friends and relatives. Only now is it feasible for such companies to switch on the extra advantage of bank support for working or investment capital. It is predictable that the arrival of foreign banks as lenders to this sector will inject new efficiencies into the processes of capital use.

Ninety-nine per cent of Chinese industrial firms are small and medium in size, and the response they make to the opportunities is most easily visible in the exporting phenomenon known as the workshop of the world. Here the role of the private company is usually to take part in the network behaviour of the OEM system described earlier. No discussion of this system is complete without reference to the role of the regional ethnic Chinese in places such as Hong Kong, Taiwan and the ASEAN countries, because their injections of capital have accounted for the majority of foreign direct investment (FDI) into China since it opened up. As well as capital, however, this same group has brought knowledge of world markets, technology, branding, and logistics, and their influence on China's growth has been high.

China's industrial future will be heavily influenced by the growth of its internal market, by the extent to which it prevents outsiders from taking large slices of the cake, and by the organizational challenges of reaching scale and scope while retaining essentially charismatic leadership in many enterprises. Innovation and adaptiveness do not flourish at global standards under conditions of centralized control.

SUMMARY POINTS

- China has emerged from a long and turbulent history to find for itself a set of successful industrial formulae.

- These are a reformed state sector, a local corporate sector, and a private sector.

- The latter has grown unusually fast and now dominates, being largely responsible for China's position as 'the workshop of the world'.

REFLECTIVE QUESTIONS

- Why does Japan have an income per capita of around US$40,000 and China around US$4,000?

- Do you think that China on its own will be able to produce the equivalent of a Lexus?

- List all the global brand names you can think of from Japan and China. What does it tell you about the nature of industry in the two societies?

THE BUSINESS SYSTEM OF SOUTH KOREA

The Korean peninsula was for centuries an autonomous state, but in a tributary relationship with its giant northern neighbour China. It absorbed from China a number of key features of its culture and societal fabric. The principal one of these was Confucianism, with all that it implied for stable hierarchies and social order built around families. It also used a form of administration similar to that of the Chinese mandarin system, including a dynastic central figure. It also closed itself from the outside world, coming to be known at the end of the 19th century as the 'hermit kingdom'. That period ended in 1905 when newly expanding Japan invaded and took over the peninsula as an extension of its modernizing economy. Much about Korea in later years can be explained by its decades under Japanese rule. It had become another tributary state, this time with foreign ownership of its industry – mainly in the north – and with its agriculture serving the needs of Japan.

The sense of independence among Korean people was not to come into full expression until the 1960s but an early sign of it was the creation in 1443 of a distinct form of writing, and that rare feature in the region – an alphabet. The Korean War in the early 1950s destroyed the country and divided it, and South Korea began after it with minimal assets except the drive and skills of its people, and the willingness of the international community to provide it with financial and technical help. The post-war period was marked by a series of five-year plans in which the government took control of the shaping of the economy, and determined upon a strategy of developing the country as a base for manufacturing exports. To achieve this, its plans were constructed to provide the ingredients needed, such as human skills, infrastructure, capital, and technology. The other key ingredients – entrepreneurship and management – were found among the business people at the time, by encouraging them with licences and loans and allowing them to prove themselves. If they produced the exports they got more support, and they were allowed to keep the ownership of the companies they had founded at the early stage.

The planning system has remained in place for decades and saw South Korea's rise from nowhere to being the world's 12th largest economy. In this the role of the entrepreneurs has been crucial, as they built the key instrument of the economy – the *chaebol* – the large conglomerate firm under tight control. There is a large sector of the economy made up of SMEs, many connected by supply chains into the *chaebol*, but the grip of the latter is firm. Many of them suffered severely in the 1997 financial crisis, as their tendency to borrow short and invest long turned against them. A number of spectacular bankruptcies followed. In the decade since there has been much realignment, rationalizing, and opening up, and many of the controlling families have retired into the background, giving way to professional managers.

Culture

As earlier noted, Korea is a deeply Confucian country and this is evident in the hierarchical nature of many of its organizations, and of its management style. There is also a strong tendency to build personalistic relations horizontally, often with school groups or place-of-origin networks. An instinct for discipline is perhaps rooted in the experience of military service by many workers and executives, and the constant sense of anxiety about a possible invasion from the unpredictable regime of North Korea. A shared ideal running through the culture, and possibly attributable to the nation's experiences of subjection, and current threat, is a fierce national pride. Firms exist, in the perceptions of many, to strengthen the nation.

Institutions

Several historical legacies have left their mark on the main institutions available for the economy. First is the respect for the professionalism of the civil service, and the power assigned to it in consequence. This has deep roots in Confucian ideals and structures of statecraft, although the more recent contribution of Christian ideals has added much to the Korean elite. Second is the derivation of much administrative routine and character from the days of the Japanese occupation, during which many society leaders were educated in Japanese. The two features flow together to facilitate what political scientists call a strong state.

In addition, a great deal of new institutional structure, such as law, financial administration and accounting, organizational techniques, and technology itself, has flowed in as Korean companies have successfully interacted with the markets of the developed world, and as those sent abroad for education have returned to apply their learning. A new injection of such ideas and techniques happened as a cost of solving the financial crisis of 1997. Along with many other societies in Asia, South Korea was given its dose of 'reform', and was moved forcibly towards the market-driven rationality of the Washington consensus.

The Business System

It could be argued that the great strength of the *chaebol* has come from the ambition and the vision of the owners who ran them, and the availability of government investment to back them, and that as these elements become diluted they will be hard to replace. Such centralization of power does bring great capacity to inspire creativity and to respond to change. As these organizations evolve into a new form, many of the earlier ways will be carried with them, and the newly rising professionals and foreigners will be able to perpetuate much of the social psychology of the past, while eliminating its negative effects. It is as yet too early to read clearly these trends but if the recent ascendance of Samsung and LG is anything to go by, the future seems to lie in that direction.

SUMMARY POINTS

■ South Korea has become a major world economy with its main form of enterprise being the *chaebol*.

■ These were originally family-dominated conglomerates built with government support from 1960 onwards.

■ They are now turning to professional management to continue new growth in world markets.

REFLECTIVE QUESTION

In how many ways is Korea halfway between China and Japan?

THE BUSINESS SYSTEM OF THE REGIONAL ETHNIC CHINESE

China had a thriving economy of small businesses for centuries. In the 19th century the society went through periods of intense strife, with overpopulation, famine, unemployment, civil war, invasion, all exacerbated by a decadent government. In the worst periods people left to find work elsewhere, and to support the families who stayed behind. They left mainly from the south, were mainly young men, and they went to the countries around the South China Sea, the *Nanyang*. They usually joined their compatriots from specific regions of China, and they found work in the new agriculture and extractive industries being established under colonial rule. Hundreds of thousands went, and after some decades a similar exodus of females took place, and the Overseas Chinese settled down and became part of the fabric of their host societies. After several generations they usually think of themselves as Malaysian, Indonesian and so on. Their number now in the region is about 30 million, with a further population in Taiwan of around 22 million.

The normal pattern was for an emigrant to work as a labourer initially, but to save and then move into self-employment on a modest scale. Over decades this trade or business might be built up and expanded over several product fields, so as to hedge risk and take opportunity. The organizational pattern was highly consistent. Ownership was tightly held, in either a partnership or a family group. One person would be the big boss and would take all key decisions and often many non-key decisions also. Personal networks of connection with key suppliers, financiers, customers, and sources of information, would be built as a form of social capital held by individuals. Employees would be treated paternalistically, but discipline maintained. These enterprises had a number of distinct virtues: they were highly efficient in terms of managerial control, and in terms of transaction costs between units in the economy. By concentrating decision power and resources into very few hands they were also able to take opportunities quickly, to adapt as need be, and to keep key employees loyal. For the colonial powers, they made excellent 'middlemen' in the developing economies, being perceived as diligent, reliable, and non-political.

Over time, surviving the turbulence of the first half of the 20th century they emerged into a key position to take advantage of the growth opportunities that followed the end of colonialism and the beginning of access to world markets for goods made in the region. They came to dominate the economies of Southeast Asia, and at the same time to build up the formidable industrial and financial bases of Taiwan, Hong Kong, and Singapore. Their bamboo network in the region tied them together as a powerful force and facilitated their taking of opportunities as they unfolded country by country, the most recent aspect of that process being their massive investments in recent years in China, they being the source of around 60 per cent of its FDI to date. In the light of this the phrase 'The China Circle' is commonly used to indicate the reciprocal nature of the ties now established with the homeland and its southern ocean.

Within the category of the regional ethnic Chinese, as noted above, are the three great 'tiger' economies of Taiwan, Hong Kong, and Singapore, and although their shared cultural heritage means that many organizational patterns are consistent across the three – especially that of personally owned and dominated SMEs – the differences between them are still obvious. These are due to quite different histories and development policies in the last half of the 20th century.

Taiwan was developed by the Kuomintang elite who fled from China having lost the struggle against communism for dominance. Its longer term future awaits a working out of the tensions left over from that, and in the meantime it acts as an autonomous state, while China awaits its return to the motherland. Its development was achieved by a state system of managing the economy, and especially by controlling the major sectors such as banking, steel, transport and so on, and then encouraging the growth of entrepreneurship. Especially significant has been the encouragement of technical education and of close ties with the hi-tech industries and research facilities of the US. This has produced one of the world's most vibrant manufacturing industries in the general field of hi-tech, making components especially for the world's brand names in computing, telecoms, electronics, electrical, and machine making.

Hong Kong, now part of China but retaining much autonomy as a Special Administrative Region until 2047, is the core city of a huge region of south China containing upwards of 150 million people. It hosts much of the ownership, management, finance, design skill, market access skill, and logistics competence needed in its hinterland, and to do so carries forward the skills acquired from its earlier existence as an outpost of the British Empire. For 50 years before the transition in 1997, it developed as one of the world's purest examples of laissez-faire economic policy. This gave it an unusual dynamism as the fierce logics of competition, combined with high-quality infrastructure, brought it to developed-country levels of wealth.

Singapore, also earlier British, became autonomous in 1959, and set about building a modern economy by attracting foreign investment, and especially pulling in industry able to respond to the opportunities of both resources and markets in the surrounding region, for which Singapore had traditionally been an entrepôt. With very strong government since, it has continued on that path, extending further into industries based in science and high technology, and supporting sectors such as banking.

As the business system of the regional ethnic Chinese overlaps extensively with that for the Chinese private sector it will not be described again here.

SUMMARY POINTS

■ The regional ethnic Chinese emigrated from China to find work in the countries to the south, and they have become prosperous because of their business skills.

■ They now play a very important part in many Southeast Asian economies and their links with China grow in significance.

THE BUSINESS SYSTEM OF SOUTHEAST ASIA

The countries covered here are Indonesia, Malaysia, and the Philippines (Thailand will be included in the final section on IndoChina). The three countries share two features: they were all colonized and bear the traces of that history in their present institutions; and they have all struggled with development during the past fifty years, and been outpaced by their Confucian neighbours. Their current GDP per capita is Indonesia US$730, Malaysia US$3,850, and the Philippines US$990. In Indonesia and the Philippines this is partly a reflection of huge populations, with 215 million in Indonesia and 77 million in the Philippines. In a famous early critique, by Kunio Yoshihara, they were described as having a form of ersatz capitalism (that is, an imperfect form, just about able to stay intact). His main concerns were with the quality of the administrations in terms of policy and planning, and the difficulty those societies had in blending in new technology to their systems of production and business. Two other features need to be noted also. Indonesia and the Philippines especially have displayed unusually high levels of corruption, worsening the administrative weakness. So too were they very badly hit by the Asian financial crisis of 1997. As emerging markets they had been the recipients of vast amounts of loose and adventurous money flowing in from Western investors. The money rushed out again at the first signs of trouble and they were left to carry the blame and to see their finances laid waste by excessive valuations and debt. The years of 'reform' that have followed have seen them move clearly in the direction of greater openness, more rational resource allocation, greater professionalism, and more market-based competitive discipline, all sharpened by the arrival of more foreign competition in their own markets.

Much has been achieved in the post-crisis decade to bring order to the financial systems, and to bring corruption under control, but the building of an economy able to attract outside investment, and able to compete in world markets – especially now against China – takes time, and their ratings do not inspire confidence yet. In terms of the quality of the business environment for doing business, they are rated 123rd (Indonesia) and 133rd (Philippines) in the world. By contrast on the same scale Malaysia is rated 34th.

The Philippines was for centuries a Spanish colony, and the main legacy of that period for the economy is a land-holding 'aristocracy' of a semi-feudal character, that has retained a strong grip on political power, and frustrated many attempts at land reform and the redistribution of wealth. It has been joined by a parallel elite of ethnic Chinese business owners, capable of skilled management, and capable also of co-opting the political support needed in an essentially patrimonial state. These two groups dominate the business scene, and the only other significant players are the foreign companies seeking stable sources of labour skill for manufacturing. The fluency in English of many local people has often attracted many firms from the West. Significant also have been the strong ties with the US stemming from the period of American protection in the first half of the 20th century, with its legacies of democracy, law and education.

In Indonesia the legacy was of Dutch colonial control, in place from the early 17th century until the end of World War II, and still visible in many systems such as law and administration. After independence the state was for several decades in the hands of two powerful leaders with military backing – Soekarno and Suharto – and it was not until the fall of the latter, under charges of corruption, that new forms of government could be introduced. Eventually full democracy was reached for the first time and the country has remained stable since. In the economy the ethnic Chinese have played a major part for a long time, and have displayed great political skill in maintaining or reconstructing their positions as the various patronage networks have been reshaped. As in the Philippines ethnic Chinese population numbers are small (about four per cent in Indonesia and about one per cent in the Philippines), but economic strength is great, amounting to more than half of the ownership of the major local conglomerates in both countries.

In Malaysia, the case is different. It is a much smaller country in population terms, with around 22 million people, although its GDP stands at about 60 per cent of Indonesia's. This stems from its success in developing further the industries taken over after the colonial period, and in attracting large amounts of foreign investment. The latter has come in because of the government's willingness to create effective infrastructure and to invest in education. The end result is a powerful set of manufacturing industries bringing in new technology, and management, and making use of not just the relatively low-cost local labour, but also lower cost labour imported from Indonesia. Malaysia is an Islamic country, but unlike Indonesia which is very consciously secular in the political sphere, Malaysia takes religion – or at least ethnicity – into policy-making. In business this is clear in the attempts to protect Malay business against the intense pressures of competition from ethnic Chinese business.

THE BUSINESS SYSTEM OF INDOCHINA

For our purposes, although this region contains Myanmar (formerly Burma), Cambodia, and Laos, our attention will be given to the larger economies of Thailand and Vietnam, countries of respectively 63 million and 78 million people. Their different histories have resulted in Thailand being now about four times the weight of Vietnam in economic terms, although the latter is growing now very fast.

Thailand is distinguished among most Asian countries for its long history of independence from colonial domination. It is a constitutional monarchy, and the role of the king has long been crucial in holding the country together in the face of shifting political alliances and manoeuvres. One of the king's ancestors, King Rama IV, was instrumental in the late 19th century, in opening up the country to modern ideas and technology. This process ran parallel to the opening of Japan in the Meiji era, the more hesitant opening of China in the late Ching dynasty, and the slow dismantling of the barriers around Korea in the same period. Many of Thailand's institutions, such as law, education and administration, are traceable to that period, and they have had time since to become Thai in their workings.

In recent years industry has poured in from abroad attracted by a favourable business environment, and manufacturing industry is well established, especially in zones along the east coast and around Bangkok. Again, as in several other regional countries, the ethnic Chinese Thai have established a powerful dominance in local business, and operate on the 'bamboo network' across the region and into China. The first outside company to be registered in China after the communist era was the CP group, a family-owned firm that began in Bangkok selling animal feedstock and seeds.

The other large economy in the IndoChina peninsula is Vietnam and its story is again different. For about a thousand years it was a tributary state of China, until it gained independence in 938. This millennium left an indelible mark in the form of Confucian ideals and centralized government using a mandarin-type system. But for the subsequent thousand years Vietnam was a country under its own government until the interests of France destroyed its autonomy and led to colonial control from 1887. This built upon a long history of French interest, dating back to 1651 when a Jesuit priest adapted the language into a romanized alphabet still in use as standard today. French colonial policy was even more exploitative than the average around the region and – in the views of some – left the country worse off than when they started. There was however a residual legacy of strong administration and law, and an education system that could be later extended to more of the population. A series of uprisings in favour of independence marked the 20th century, including the expulsion of the French after Dien Bien Phu in 1954. Such movements culminated in what US Americans call the Vietnam War (and locals the American War), after which the Vietnamese regained their country. For the next ten years it was in the grip of hardliners and dogmatists, but after 1986, an opening up began that has not stopped and in fact gains continuing momentum.

Under the opening up known as *doi moi*, the state sector has declined and the private sector has grown fast. It is like watching a rerun of the China miracle but in slower motion (at least so far). The dismantling of a strong state, with a tradition of central planning and interference in the economy, cannot be achieved overnight, but the direction of movement is clear. At present it is ranked the 138th country in the world for business freedom, much of this handicap stemming from weak property rights and from corruption. The one-party state is no longer regarded as heavily interfering. Three forms of organization are emerging. The state sector companies, as in China, are succumbing to the forces of the market and being forced to reform their management. The private sector is booming and expanding entrepreneurially using SMEs. These are flexible enough, as in China, to cope with the uncertainties of their surroundings. The third form is that of foreign investors, attracted especially by the large reserves of low-cost and easily trained labour.

CONCLUSION

The variety of business systems on display here reflects the underlying contrasts in religions, in political preferences, in histories and the injections of ideas they often brought with them, and in ethnicity and culture. But at the same time many continuities are visible across the variety: the Confucian family ideal runs through many countries; the strong state is found widely; paternalism in authority systems is widespread; personal systems of trust are widely relied upon; and a powerful work ethic is widespread. But the separating out of these distinct business systems, resulting in virtually every society having its own formula, is due to the rich set of ingredients that goes into each recipe. The variety comes from the combination, and that is why there are so few replications, and why each of these societies needs to be seen in its own right, and with its own reasons for being as it is.

CHAPTER SUMMARY

- Asia is a region of immense variety and contrasts in terms of people, geography, culture, religion, history and so on.
- A business system is a way of looking at a country's economy, a way of understanding how the economy is affected by the unique social and cultural environment thus shaping the type of business system in question.
- Japan's business system and management style are highly influenced by its cultural heritage, strong social trust and the ability to deal with complex coordination.
- China's business system model has evolved after many years of turbulence and changes. Today China's private sector is developing at an astonishing speed and has taken the role of 'the workshop of the world'.
- South Korea's originally family-oriented conglomerates have in the past developed into very successful business groups or *chaebol*, which are famous worldwide.
- It is also possible to trace the development of the business systems of the ethnic Chinese who have, due to historical reasons, settled all over Southeast Asia.
- In fact it can be seen that many Asian business systems are commonly influenced by similar cultural elements such as Confucianism. Nevertheless each Asian business system has its own salient characteristics and features.

KEY CONCEPTS

Asian variety: Since Asia is a region of immense varieties, it is impossible to generalize Asia. In order to simplify our discussion, we can categorize the varieties into clusters based on geographical or cultural differences.

Business system: A complex adaptive system in which the business component of a society is analysed against the context of that society.

Culture: The base layer of 'meaning', that is how a society constructs its own way of making sense of its surrounding context.

Institutions: The middle layer of 'order', that is, the instruments through which a society standardizes and regulates conduct so that it becomes predictable.

Varieties of capitalism: Different forms of capitalism such as 'ersatz capitalism'

referring to the inefficient use of capital covered up by the availability of easy money, and 'clan capitalism' which is largely based on social trust.

REVIEW QUESTIONS

1.   What are the main business systems of the region?
2.   What are the principal components of a business system?
3.   Give examples of how culture (that is, meaning) affects institutions (that is, forms of order) in different societies.
4.   What are the most representative forms of enterprise in Japan, China and South Korea?
5.   What explains the slower growth of Indonesia and the Philippines, compared with Korea, China, and Singapore?

LEARNING ACTIVITIES

1.   Draw a picture like Figure 1.1 and fill in the boxes with one example in each box to show what is meant, describing one society in the region.
2.   Draw lines between the boxes to show the complexity of the connections.
3.   Add to the diagrams the key facts of the society's history, showing their effects.
4.   Consider what kind of firm is likely to be successful in that environment and explain why you think so.

MINI CASE

THE BIG PICTURE: CHINESE BRANDS

TCL wants to become China's Samsung[1]

Perhaps it was predestined. When France's Thomson announced on November 3 that it was in effect shedding its TV manufacturing business to a partner called TCL, few people had heard of the other firm. Was it a surprise? Not to TCL's chairman Li Dongsheng. His Western name is Thomson.

For the French company, this is a neat exit from a business in which it lost around €60 million (US$56 million) last year. Thomson gets a 33 per cent stake in the joint venture with TCL International – the mainland group's Hong Kong-listed subsidiary.

For TCL, however, the deal is bigger still. With revenues in excess of €1 billion and producing more than 18 million TV and DVD sets a year, the joint venture is being trumpeted as the industry's next global leader. So watch out Sony, Philips, Toshiba and Samsung.

Mr Li believes he is creating something new: 'the first Chinese consumer multinational with significant presence in all major markets'. And he promises confidently that the joint venture will make a profit in its first year.

This is not all hubris. The deal marries TCL's low costs with Thomson's brands, distribution and research in Europe and America. And TCL, founded only in 1981 by a group of ambitious entrepreneurs in Guangdong – the province that is China's manufacturing heartland – is aggressively commercial even though it is controlled by a city government. It survived a bruising consolidation process among Chinese TV makers to emerge as one of the two leading groups, with an 18 per cent market share.

After attempts at diversification – a common affliction among Chinese businessmen – into white goods, computers and mobile phones (with mixed results), the Thomson deal suggests a laudable focus on the core business. Comparing TCL to Haier, China's leading home-appliance maker which is also trying to build a global brand, Arthur Kroeber, managing editor of the *China Economic Quarterly*, says: 'Buying an existing brand and a sales force makes more sense. Haier is trying to build a global name from scratch, but most Chinese companies don't understand branding.'

Whether this deal will turn TCL into another Samsung is doubtful. Both Thomson in Europe and its RCA brand in America are rather tired names 'on the sort of TVs you find in drab motel rooms', says one banker. TCL will need fat margins to match Samsung or Sony at brand building and marketing. And while China's vast pool of cheap labour gives it a massive cost advantage, it is not inherently as efficient as, say, many Taiwanese contract-manufacturers, or as dedicated to process engineering as its Japanese rivals.

Even so, this deal is a warning. TCL may not turn into quite the multinational Mr Li envisions, at least not immediately. But as more mainland companies start to foster ambitions beyond their home market, it will not take long for China's first global champion to emerge.

QUESTIONS

1. What is the mixture of organizational strengths that makes the Thompson/TCL alliance viable?
2. What differences are likely to exist between this new form of China-based organization and its Korean competitors?
3. How can this new venture compete with the strong Japanese presence in the global market?
4. Will the plans succeed in your view? If so, why?

INTERESTING WEB LINKS

Organization for Economic Cooperation and Development: www.oecd.org
The World Bank: www.worldbank.org
Central Intelligence Agency: www.cia.gov/library/publications/the-world-factbook
The Asia Society: www.asiasource.org
Asian Development Bank: www.adbi.org
Asian Studies Monitor: www.coombs.anu.edu.au

Note

1 *Source: The Economist* (US) 369.8349 (8 November 2003), p. 60.

REFERENCES AND FURTHER READING

Ahn, S. and Lee, J.W. (2007). Integration and growth in East Asia. Bank of Japan Institute for Monetary and Economic Studies Discussion Paper 2007-E-14.

Backman, M. and Butler, C. (2006). *Big in Asia*. London: Palgrave Macmillan.

Chan, S., Clark, C. and Lam, D. (eds) (1998). *Beyond the Developmental State*. London: Macmillan – now Palgrave Macmillan.

Hosono, A. and Saavedra-Riveno, N. (eds) (1998). *Development Strategies in East Asia and Latin America*. London: Macmillan – now Palgrave Macmillan.

Huang, Y. (2003). FDI in China: Why surging levels of FDI in China may indicate serious economic problems. Public lecture. Washington, DC: Carnegie Endowment for International Peace.

Mathews, J.A. (2006). Dragon multinationals: New players in 21st century globalization. *Asia Pacific Journal of Management*, **23**: 5–27.

Orru, M., Biggart, N.W. and Hamilton, G.G. (1997). *The Economic Organization of East Asian Capitalism*. London: Macmillan – now Palgrave Macmillan.

Peng, M.W. and Delios, A. (2006). Conglomerates and business groups in the Asia Pacific. *Asia Pacific Journal of Management*, **23**(4).

Redding, S.G. (1993). *The Spirit of Chinese Capitalism*. New York: de Gruyter.

Redding, S.G. and Witt, M. (2007). *The Future of Chinese Capitalism*. Oxford: Oxford University Press.

Tu, W.M. (ed.) (1996). *Confucian Traditions in East Asian Modernity*. Cambridge, MA: Harvard University Press.

Wade, R. (1990). *Governing the Market*. Princeton, NJ: Princeton University Press.

Whitley, R. (1992). *Business Systems in East Asia*. London: Sage.

Yeung, H.W.C. (2006). Change and continuity in Southeast Asian Chinese business. *Asia Pacific Journal of Management*, **23**(3): 229–54.

Yeung, H.W.C. (ed.) (2007). *Handbook of Research on Asian Business*. Cheltenham: Edward Elgar.

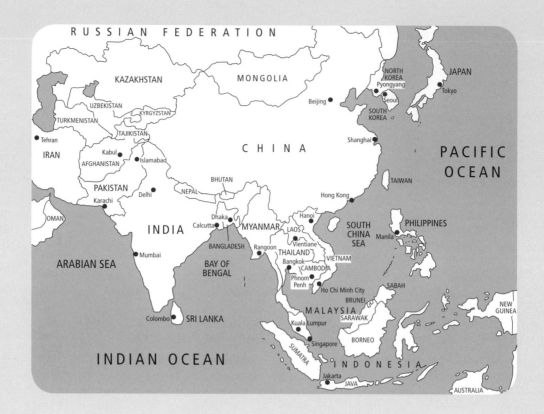

Chapter outline

- Corporate social responsibility (CSR) and sustainable development – Concept and phenomenon
- Asia positioning in the pursuit of sustainable development and CSR policies
- Adjustments required by the adoption of CSR concepts
- A pragmatic approach for implementing CSR policies
- The challenges ahead

Chapter objectives

After reading this chapter, you should be able to:

1. Understand the meaning of the CSR and sustainable development concepts in Asia

2. Identify the environmental and social problems in Asia that require a CSR solution

3. Understand the US and European positioning of CSR in their societies

4. Understand the different policies followed by the private and public actors in applying the concept of CSR and sustainable development

Chapter 2

Corporate social responsibility and sustainable development in Asia

Philippe Debroux

INTRODUCTION: CORPORATE SOCIAL RESPONSIBILITY AND SUSTAINABLE DEVELOPMENT – CONCEPT AND PHENOMENON

The Growing Importance of CSR and Sustainable Development in Asia

Asian countries face a number of social and environmental problems that are usually tackled by public authorities. But in Western countries, private business organizations play an active role to solve them. Corporate social responsibility (CSR) and the thought that corporations ought to care about the long-term sustainability of their business activities and growth pattern beyond mere compliance with the law is a concept born in the West. Nevertheless, during the past decade a growing involvement has been observed in Asian public authorities in the elaboration of policies and instruments serving to operate CSR and sustainable development strategies.

For the time being, the focus on environment-related CSR issues is dominant but a growing number of Asian companies are starting to adopt CSR practices and reporting standards embedding a broader definition of CSR including responsibility vis-à-vis workers and human rights. In a still small but growing number of them CSR activities are now internalized in the companies' organizational mechanisms. They also engage actively with their stakeholders on increasingly complex projects related to disease, biodiversity, or other issues requesting broad and diversified knowledge and experience. In doing so, they increase their social contribution and gradually acquire a valuable expertise in the field. So far, CSR-related management tools and principles have been largely elaborated in settings where Asian organizations have played a minor role. Western multinational corporations (MNCs) are still the dominant actors in Asia in terms of scope and sophistication of CSR activities. Although these organizations may have Asian members, most CSR internationally recognized norms and standards are established by organizations in which Western interests are dominant.

Both Asian governments and companies are increasingly aware of the political and economic importance of CSR and sustainable development. The concept of CSR is maturing and it is no longer considered as a merely defensive tool serving to protect companies' reputations. Besides the ethical concern, perception exists that in the future CSR and sustainable development may become the source of key business competitive advantages. This will lead to formal and informal rules that are likely to play a key role in business practices. Therefore, being late in proactively participating in the elaboration of the rules and optimizing their CSR activities may put Asian businesses at a disadvantage vis-à-vis the most advanced Western companies not only in their own markets but also worldwide.

Origin and Development of CSR and Sustainable Development

CSR has the explicit sense of voluntary, self-interest driven policies, programmes and strategies by corporations addressing issues perceived as being part of their social responsibility by the companies and/or their stakeholders. CSR was closely associated from the start with the idea of sustainable development, as identified at the United Nations Rio Earth Summit in 1992, namely, as development that 'meets the needs of the present without compromising the ability of future generations to meet their own needs'. An attempt to apprehend operationally the concept of sustainable development is found in the Three Dimensional Model presented by von Stokar (2004). Sustainable development comprises three 'bottom lines': environmental, economic and societal. All three dimensions can be measured and added to the two dimensions of time and North–South socio-economic situation. The idea is that economic development must be achieved with environmental preservation while promoting social equity in a long-term perspective taking into account the interest of the future generations.

CSR comes originally from philanthropy, with which it still shares a number of attributes. It could also be considered as an extension to social and environmental matters of the concept of corporate governance, putting emphasis on corporate economic and financial accountability factors. CSR is a product of a business environment where a combination of market and clear ownership laws is considered essential to manage a modern and economically efficient democratic society. So, the first task of CSR is to ensure that honesty, transparency and accountability are respected in business activities. But CSR goes beyond that in acknowledging that business responsibility should go not only to the market but also to all those affected by its activities, the stakeholders, that is, those who are affected, in any way, by its activities. Business may cause social and environmental problems in behaving without considering sustainability in its activity but it can also bring solutions to existing problems and prevent new ones from emerging. Respect of market principles is not incompatible, quite the contrary, with concern about the natural environment, social inequality, poverty and marginalization. CSR activities are not reserved to MNCs. On the contrary, it is recognized that solutions to sustainable development issues requires business involvement down to the lowest level of informal labour markets and local communities.

Integration of CSR in Business Policy

One important driver of CSR is the idea that there is a business case for responsibility, that is, responsible behaviour can be financially sound. However, CSR may consist in peripheral activities loosely or not at all linked with core businesses. What distinguishes today's understanding of CSR and sustainable development from the business social initiatives of the past is the attempt to manage them as part of the organization's internal activities in a business-like manner and to develop instruments for this. For instance, Toyota's participation in reforestation projects in China is outside its main activities but involves a number of the company's employees, requires managerial decisions, implies technological transfers, may lead to the development of specific techniques to achieve results, and have an impact on the level of skills and knowledge of employees and locally involved manpower. Therefore, it can be considered as CSR activity (Toyota, 2006) although a number of companies would still call it philanthropy or a 'philanthropic type' of CSR linked to market development.

Development in corporate governance, according to which not only the financial performance can be objectively measured, but the non-financial ones can also be analysed, reported and even audited and certified, led to triple bottom line reporting. This idea drew on the inspiration of the three-dimensional sustainable development concept, which links companies' financial, environmental and social performances. The response to negative publicity related to the exploitation and abusive labour practices by subcontractors of famous brands also led to the launching of codes of conduct, adopted by companies and meant to be applied to the labour practices of their subcontractors and also to their relations with the other stakeholders, such as customers and employees. These codes are important to the evolution of CSR because they address questions of business responsibility by two significant and long-term developments. The first are the new forms of business organization due to outsourcing and subcontracting practices. The second aspect is related to the increased importance of intangible assets, such as brand names and reputation, in determining the worth of a company.

The US and European Approaches of CSR and Sustainable Development

In the US approach companies must respond to the new societal norms of corporate responsibility and accountability to all stakeholders. There is no statutory requirement for CSR, but its voluntary nature is the very source of its dynamism and innovative characteristics. CSR activities are expected to enhance the motivation of the employees and evoke a positive perception of the company on the part of the stakeholders. This will induce a spontaneous and self-sustaining pattern of diffusion of the best practices from large companies down to small ones, from rich to poor countries, leading to effective market economy, liberal democracy and active civil society. The majority of US companies do not give trade unions a central role in their CSR strategy. Commitment of employees and defence of their interests is thought to be better assured through flexible human resource management (HRM) policies fitting with companies' global strategies. Private norms such as the SA8000 or initiatives such as the Global Reporting Initiative (2007) and Global Compact are favoured over those by international bodies such as the International Labour Organization (ILO). Based on flexible principles and self-regulation of their behaviour by companies they do not impose rigid constraints perceived as liable to impede business activities.

European CSR concepts are crafted on a tripartite system institutionalizing relationships between public authorities, companies and trade unions. Business input is considered as essential to solve specific issues such as unemployment, regional development and education. But the role of private initiatives is limited because CSR linked to standards privatization can weaken workers' rights in substituting for legitimate standard-setting functions of the ILO and governments. The solution promoted by the European Union is to reinforce understanding between the key stakeholders to create clear norms and standards of CSR practices complementing public regulations. CSR should remain a freely developed activity. But, the question is no longer 'why CSR' but 'how CSR'. Companies have a legal obligation to behave responsibly to society. The best example of this is the legal requirement imposed on publicly listed companies in France, the UK, Norway, and Sweden for reporting social and environmental performances.

SUMMARY POINTS

- CSR and sustainable development are concepts associating companies' and other institutions' responsibilities to economic, social and societal development in a long-term perspective.

- CSR is a voluntary activity that goes beyond mere compliance with the law but does not substitute it.

- CSR activities can be reactive and largely unrelated to business policy or proactive and integrated into the strategy of a corporation.

REFLECTIVE QUESTION

Do you think the concepts of CSR and sustainable development are conducive to fundamental changes in the manner companies are managed, the development of original corporate cultures and, eventually, to significant changes in the priority of companies' objectives?

ASIA POSITIONING IN THE PURSUIT OF SUSTAINABLE DEVELOPMENT AND CSR POLICIES

Environmental Challenges Facing Asia

As a recent report from the Asian Development Bank (ADB) indicates, a number of Asian countries have made progress in reaching a number of the United Nations' Millennium Development Goals (ADB, 2007). However, environmental and social problems are such that unless more drastic and sustained actions are taken on a large scale, they are bound to lead to major social, economic and political crises (ADB, 2007). Five hundred million out of the 850 million of the chronically food-insecure people in the world live in Asia. In developing Asia at least 500 million people are unemployed or underemployed. Another 250 million will enter the workforce over the next decade (ADB, 2007). Asian economies must grow but current growth patterns are unsustainable due to their high level of resource inefficiency and dependence on a fast growth in fossil fuel consumption. The need for oil in the next 10 years will increase by 3.4 per cent a year in China, 2.9 per cent in India and 3 per cent in other developing Asian countries (IGES, 2005). In the past 25 years, Asia has lost 50 per cent of its forests and one-third of its agricultural land has been degraded. Asia's rivers contain a much higher level of pollutants than the world average. Of the world's 15 most polluted cities, 13 are in Asia. A considerable number of Asian urban inhabitants live in slums devoid of basic facilities. About one-third of Asian people have no access to safe drinking water, and 50 per cent of them have no access to sanitation services. It is projected that 2.4 billion Asian people will suffer from water stress by 2025. At least one-third of a billion tons of solid waste across Asia remains uncollected each year (ADB, 2006).

Social Challenges Facing Asian Societies

Literacy, especially for women, has still not been achieved in many Asian countries, resulting in massive social and economic losses (Welford, 2007). The AIDS crisis is still serious despite some recent progress (ADB, 2007). It is estimated that 180 million children below 14 years old are working in Asia. Gender discrimination, exploitation of migrant labour, uncontrollable human trafficking, and child prostitution are all over the region. Unequal distribution of the fruit of growth threatens the stability of the socio-economic and political fabric, even in high growth countries such as China, India, Vietnam and Cambodia. But developed Asia from Singapore to South Korea and Japan also suffers from growing labour instability, and social and economic alienation of some part of their population. As Table 2.1 indicates, a high level of risk of social rights violations is noticeable in many countries in the region with only slow improvement if any in some of them.

Table 2.1 Comparison between Asian countries concerning the main risks of violation of social rights

Country	Forced labour	Child labour	Wages and overtime work	Discriminations	Freedom of association and collective bargaining	Other abuses
China	***	**	***	**	***	***
India	***	***	**	***	*	*
Bangladesh	*	***	***	**	***	**
Cambodia	**	**	***	**	***	*
Indonesia	**	***	***	**	**	***
Malaysia	*	***	***	***	**	**
Philippines	*	***	***	**	***	**
Sri Lanka	*	*	***	*	***	***
Thailand	**	**	***		***	**
Vietnam	*	**	***	**	***	**

Note: *** High risk   ** Medium risk   * Low risk
Source: IMPACTT Ltd (2004).

The Limited Resources of Developing Asia

With regard to Asia and the Pacific, the ADB estimated the annual investment costs required to achieve environmentally sound development based on two scenarios. Under the first one, implying no major changes in environment and development policies, the cost would be US$12.9 billion a year. Under a more ambitious scenario with the goal for developing countries in Asia to achieve the best practices of OECD countries by 2030, the cost would be US$70 billion per year. In addition, it is estimated that repairing the damage done to the land, water, air and living biotope in Asia would require US$25 billion a year (ADB, 2006). From climate change to international rivers, marine ecosystem and air pollution, the problems have almost always both an international dimension and a local one. This calls for collaboration between Asian states at sub-regional and regional levels to provide the necessary institutional framework. In the case of child labour, work hardship, human trafficking and prostitution, intervention is required at levels lower than those that are reached by public authorities because long-term solutions require the involvement and acceptance of the actions by local people at grass-roots level.

Table 2.2 Ratification of the core conventions on human rights in Asia

Countries	Freedom of association and collective bargaining		Elimination of compulsory and forced labour		Elimination of employment discrimination		Abolition of child labour	
	Convention 87	Convention 98	Convention 29	Convention 105	Convention 100	Convention 111	Convention 138	Convention 182
France	1951	1951	1937	1969	1953	1981	1990	2001
United States				1991				1999
China					1990		1999	2002
Afghanistan				1963	1969	1969		
Bangladesh	1972	1972	1972	1972	1998	1972		2001
Cambodia	1999	1999	1969	1999	1999	1999	1999	
South Korea					1997	1998	1999	2001
India		1954		2000	1958	1960		
Indonesia	1998	1957	1950	1999	1958	1999	1999	2000
Japan	1965	1953	1932		1967		2000	2001
Laos			1964				2005	2005
Malaysia		1961	1957	1958 den* 1990	1997		1997	2000
Mongolia	1969	1969	2005	2005	1969	1969	2002	2001
Myanmar	1955		1955					
Nepal		1996	2002		1976	1974	1997	2002
Pakistan	1951	1952	1957	1960	2001	1961		2001
Philippines	1953	1953		1960	1953	1960	1998	2000
Singapore		1965	1965	1960 den* 1979	2002			2001
Sri Lanka	1995	1972	1950	2003	1993	1998	2000	2001
Thailand			1969	1969	1999		2004	2001
Vietnam					1997	1997	2003	2000

Note: * Denounced by those two countries, respectively in 1990 and 1979
Source: Huchet (2007).

To make a multi-stakeholders' engagement approach successful is not possible without the right framework of norms and standards, something that requires institutional strengthening and capacity development. As indicated in Table 2.2 most Asian countries have ratified the core conventions on human rights.

But, as pointed out by the ADB, the predicament is that governments of developing countries in Asia have a problem with implementation of regulations, due to factors such as the lack of regulatory resources to enforce standards, uncertain laws with few penalties for non-compliance, corruption and inadequate infrastructure and human resources to collect evidence for non-respect of the law by companies (ADB, 2005). They suffer from a shortage of technology, governance and management skills to cope with those issues. Moreover, the high level of indebtedness of many of them makes it difficult to divert significantly higher financial resources to environmental facilities and infrastructure, and to ensure the monitoring of the laws that would solve the social issues (IGES, 2005).

A Long Tradition of Philanthropic Type of CSR

In Asia, it is pointed out that less codification of social relations was observed traditionally in business activities with more reliance on cultural mechanisms and guiding principles (Tanimoto, 2004). Asian corporations were never oblivious to their social responsibilities, though. But they were fulfilled as implicit obligations embedded in business practices and institutional frameworks. Responsibility was most often that of the owner of the corporation and it did not imply the creation of organizational mechanisms.

For instance, both in Chinese and Japanese traditional social hierarchy, the positions of the merchant and entrepreneur have been traditionally low (Dana, 2007). Their roles in society had to be legitimized by their responsible attitude to compensate for their inherently low status. This led to business cultures where companies were (and still are) expected to bear a benevolent responsibility towards those with whom they had direct relations: employees, business partners and customers, and the community surrounding the workplace, that is, the 'stakeholders' in modern CSR language. Emphasis was put on honesty, integrity and respect of ethical values by businessmen (Ho, 2006). The core values in Japanese and Chinese societies were 'faith' and 'trust', drawn from Buddhism and Confucianism (Ho, 2006). Doing something 'good' for society was regarded as a symbol of being 'successful persons', deserving respect, different from the contempt reserved for the mere 'money-seekers'. From Buddhist to Islamic influences, to minority groups such as the *Parsi* who founded the Indian Tata Group, or the Christian entrepreneurs over the whole region who have been active social reformers, all over Asia philosophical and religious doctrines have traditionally had an impact on social responsibilities. This is true as well today. It is pointed out that there is an overlap between the tenets of Islam and the concept of CSR as represented by the principles of the UN Global Compact (Zinkin, 2007). Likewise, the revival of Confucianism in China and in Hong Kong is typical of the perceived necessity of giving a moral legitimacy to the social and economic order (Ho, 2006).

Following such tradition, the Indian Tata conglomerate, the software house Infosys, and other companies indulge in community development, health, safety, and philanthropic activities. The Infosys Foundation runs orphanages, hostels, hospitals, libraries, relief shelters and homes for destitute and mentally retarded women, and invests in tribal welfare (Raja, 2004). This implies large investments that have a significant economic and social impact. Most of the activities may remain externalized as in the case of Infosys. But, in the Tata Group for example, they have acquired characteristics that are close to a systematic strategic pattern implying changes in the internal dynamics in the organization. In that sense, the Tata Group's interpretation of the concept of CSR is close to that of Western companies (Hindu BusinessLine, 2007).

Japanese (The Economist Intelligence Unit, 2005) and Korean companies (Ki-Hoon Lee, 2005) also promote partnerships with local communities in educational projects, infrastructure building and/or poverty alleviation. The nature of the CSR activities is often unrelated to their core business, although these forms of involvement tend to institutionalize CSR in company management not integrated into the core business strategy (Keizai Doyukai, 2003). However, this does not preclude stakeholder engagement as exemplified by projects of Japanese companies and some Korean ones (Ki-Hoon Lee, 2005) with NGOs and international organizations. This level of engagement is just starting in some large Chinese companies such as Lenovo and TCL. In Southeast Asia, CSR retains a paternalistic overtone, close to the former patterns found in Japan and China, that is, that of personal responsibility of top leaders, rather than organizational responsibility of a corporation.

SUMMARY POINTS

- Asian countries face a number of environmental and social problems whose resolution requires efforts from both public and private concerns.

- Solutions suppose collaboration at local, national and regional levels.

- Asian countries have a long tradition of corporate philanthropy based on philosophical and religious principles, on which the current debate on CSR and sustainable development is based.

REFLECTIVE QUESTIONS

- Is the environmental performance of our products limited by our existing technology base?

- Is there potential to realize major improvements through new technology and could technology allow us to solve environmental problems without changing the basis of the consumer-driven society in which we live and work?

ADJUSTMENTS REQUIRED BY THE ADOPTION OF CSR CONCEPTS

The Role of the State in CSR and Sustainable Policy

As the British example indicates (Lyon, 2007a), in the most progressive legal systems there is an increasing appreciation of the emerging field of sustainable development law. For the time being, there is no indication that Asian governments intend to follow European countries and impose a legal requirement for reporting social and environmental performances for publicly listed companies. But, at national level, policy documents have been developed for pursuing sustainable development in accordance with the Agenda 21 adopted at the Rio Summit in 1992. An increasing number of Asian countries are enacting laws that require environmental impact assessment (EIA) for all major projects. Some of them have applied EIA to existing and planned industrial activities as a part of industrial environmental pollution control methods. Japanese and South Korean companies are very supply-oriented in their sustainable development strategy. They believe that technological solutions are preferable to regulatory constraints. But the Japanese government is taking a proactive stance. The Ministry of Environment has developed a set of guidelines for SMEs and formulated a registration and certification programme called Eco-action 21. At the regional level, the ADB has suggested a 'greening' of the supply chain strategy, based on the establishment of environmental objectives and a programme of regular monitoring.

In China, social instability and environmental damage must be dealt with rapidly lest the whole development objective should derail. The promotion of a 'harmonious society' (Leng, 2006) is accompanied by a flurry of CSR-related activities, from laws on labour and environment, to condemnations for corruption, labour exploitation or environmental damage. CSR is thought to enhance the Chinese companies' image and improve their governance standards. The development of Chinese CSR-standards is crucial to avoid dependence on Western norms that could have negative commercial and political consequences (Ho, 2005), and to make Chinese companies competitive on the markets that emerge, based on CSR and sustainable development-related technologies.

In macroeconomic terms, the Indonesian economy has recovered after the financial crisis in the 1990s. But in creating wide social imbalance liable to create political instability as in China, Indonesia also faces major environmental challenges and is considered as one of the most corrupted countries in the world (World Bank, 2007). So, CSR laws are imposed from the top as a means of restoring a legitimate societal governance system mixed with the willingness of reinforcing economic competitiveness (Lyon, 2007b). CSR policies are likely to continue to be largely driven by the state in those two countries but it will also be the case in Singapore and in Vietnam. At first glance, the approach of CSR in those countries shares similarities with the European one of codifying rules or laws defining corporate responsibility. However, there are also differences, notably with regard to trade unions.

The Weak Involvement of Organized Labour in CSR Policy

Vietnam and China have no independent unions as in communist states. In Singapore, the tripartite system is tightly controlled by the state (Singapore Compact, 2006). In Japan, companies work with the unions on CSR activities. But the relationships between management and unions do not seem to be as close as in Europe in terms of international collaboration. A growing number of European companies have concluded so-called frame agreements with their trade unions. But, so far, no Japanese company has concluded a similar one on shared principles between international trade union organizations and MNCs, something that can be seen as the start of international collective bargaining (ICFTU, 2004). In Malaysia and Indonesia, freedom of association has long been curtailed in the export-oriented industries (Caspersz, 2006). Active labour unions have emerged in Indonesia, the Philippines and Taiwan during the past 15 years. But these countries are still characterized by anti-union behaviour in their political and business environment. In Korea, trade union movements also re-emerged as part of political liberalization and economic development but the relationships with companies remain adversarial (Lansbury et al., 2006). Admittedly, there were successful attempts in developing tripartite types of relationships in Malaysia and, more recently, in South Korea to resolve specific problems. In this latter country, a Tripartite Commission, created in 1998, produced a Tripartite Social Accord, the substance of which was almost immediately translated into law (ILO, 2008). But in view of the very different historical legacy of employment relations in Asia, and of the impact of globalization on business systems, out of Japan, it is unlikely that CSR will develop based on a tripartite system with trade unions considered as a social partner alongside management and government as in Europe. What could be expected is likely to be based more on ad hoc pragmatic attempts by management and organized labour, supported by the state in some cases, to build up profitable employment relationships, avoiding damaging labour-related disputes that companies cannot afford in a globalized world where competitive advantages can be easily lost.

A Priority Given to Environment

Asian companies disclose more detailed non-financial information related to social and environmental issues than before. In adopting the triple bottom concept, they recognize the necessity to protect their intangible assets. They are also aware of the emergence of shared workplace values appearing in the codes of conduct arena where multi-stakeholder efforts such as the Ethical Trading Initiative and SA 8000 are gathering ground (Roche, 2005). There is mounting pressure from the EU and the US to raise the CSR and environmental standards of the products imported to their markets as ethical consumption is gaining ground. But while CSR social dimensions are still often viewed as the necessary cost of doing business without fear of ostracism, environment-related CSR policies are considered easier to manage. They have less effect on companies' internal dynamics and are more potentially rewarding because they respond directly to market demand.

Western companies such as HSBC, Marks & Spencer, Tesco and Wal-Mart have either pledged to become carbon neutral or at least to substantially reduce their carbon emissions. This is bound to have a strong impact on their Asian suppliers (Crow, 2007). A few Asian countries have introduced government policies to encourage the purchase of environment-friendly products. Japan enacted the Law on Promoting Green Purchasing in 2000, requiring the national government, its affiliated organizations and local governments to purchase more environmentally sound products. South Korea followed suit in enacting a 'Green Purchase Act'. Consumers' awareness of environmental issues does seem to be growing in Asia, especially in Japan. A Green Purchasing Network (GPN) was established in 1996 in Japan. It consists of corporations, local governments and consumer organizations, and provides information on environmentally friendly products through printed materials and a web database. Local GPNs are now emerging in Japan. South Korea formed a GPN in 1999, Malaysia in 2003, and Taiwan and Thailand in 2005. Networking of national GPNs such as the international GPN is underway, which is expected to accelerate further the GPN movement in Asia (IGES, 2005).

Social labelling is almost unknown in Japan, South Korea, and Thailand but eco-labelling applies to various products, including organic food. Environmental management systems (EMS), such as life-cycle assessment (LCA), environmental reporting, environmental accounting, and the application of ISO 14001, have also grown in other Asian countries. National organizations to certify these standards have been established in Malaysia, Singapore and Thailand. Japan is well ahead in terms of ISO 14001 certificates issued, followed by China and South Korea. All three countries rank the top ten countries worldwide in the number of ISO certificates issued. Taiwan, India and Thailand have also increased their number of certified companies and the growth rate in Asia tends to be higher than elsewhere (ISO, 2007).

The Pressure from Change in Corporate Governance

In most Asian countries, stable shareholding ownership remains in place but offers companies less protection from the presence of shareholders asking for a higher return on their investments (Roche, 2005). Since the 1980s, demand for accountability and transparency spurred a shareholder activism in the US and, thereafter, in Europe, which was unknown in Asian countries until very recently. While having the objective of defending shareholders' interests, it has also been utilized to foster social and human rights-related causes. Such activism has yet to blossom in Asia but it is likely to emerge with the changes in corporate governance. The decision of the California Public Employees' Retirement System (Calpers), one of the biggest pension funds in the world, to not invest in China a few years ago and to withdraw from countries such as Thailand and Indonesia is a case in point (Association for Sustainable and Responsible Investment in Asia, 2002). The pressure exerted by Free Tibet on British Petroleum to get out of a pipeline project to Tibet in collaboration with PetroChina is another example (Dodd, 2004).

Asian companies are told that optimizing shareholders' value is the priority, but they are also expected to show more concern for other stakeholders. Protection of shareholders' rights is still an important issue in the region (Welford, 2005). Lack of transparency impedes access to information and participation in decision making for small shareholders. As a consequence, they are often deprived of their legitimate rights as investors (Welford, 2005). Asian companies must also respond to the rise of the Socially Responsible Investment Funds (SRI). It is estimated that there are about 150 SRI-related funds in Asia, draining US$20 to 30 billion. Japan has been the forefront runner of such initiatives: since the end of the 1990s, around 50 funds have been established. SRI funds still account for a negligible part of the Japanese market (2–3 per cent), though. This compares to 15 per cent in the US and 12 per cent in the UK (SiRi, 2004). In the rest of Asia, the number of SRI funds also remains small. This seems to reflect the limited interest and cautiousness so far of Asian companies to being listed on the socially responsible financial market indexes developed to measure corporate sustainability such as the Dow Jones Sustainability Index (DJSI) and the FTSE4Good. Except Japan, only a few Asian companies have this far been included in these evaluations (Van Heeswijk, 2004). It must be added that the decision of FTSE4Good to delete Toyota and Honda from its index as having failed one of its criteria (human rights in those cases) is likely to increase the cautiousness of Asian companies (Business Respect, 2007). Toyota and Honda are well known for their many initiatives linked to CSR and sustainable development and their being dropped may raise doubts about the objectivity of the evaluation criteria.

SUMMARY POINTS

- Companies in Asia must respond to the growing concern of Western and Asian consumers for environmental issues.

- The position of trade unions is weak all over Asia, preventing organized labour from playing a key role in the development of CSR activities.

- Changes in corporate governance force Asian companies to reinforce their engagement with key stakeholders.

- Companies give priority to environmental issues over social ones in their CSR policy.

REFLECTIVE QUESTIONS

- What do you think should be done in order to make the multi-stakeholders' approach workable in an Asian environment?

- In what sense and to what extent may the multi-stakeholders' framework be different in Asia from those developed in Europe and the US?

A PRAGMATIC APPROACH FOR IMPLEMENTING CSR POLICIES

Beyond the Codes of Conduct

Most CSR initiatives in Asia related to supply chain management focus on large suppliers, despite much of business in Asia falling outside the first tier of the supply chains (Welford and Frost, 2006). Moreover, the initiatives do not cover primary industries, such as mining, agriculture, forestry and fishing, where the majority of children and informal workers are occupied. Because of the cost and more importantly because of the difficulties in developing relationships with very small concerns, companies tend to narrow the number of suppliers with whom they work on CSR policy implementation. The intention is to create a critical mass of suppliers offering good wages and working conditions, and to engineer ripple effects reaching the levels below. In this respect, the sophistication of the external and internal monitoring systems that Nike (Lim and Phillips, 2007) has put in place shows that it is possible to successfully transform a competitive, arms-length market structure into an economically securer relationship with the buyer in the global value chain. The Nike approach goes beyond the mere request of applying a code of conduct. It requires the search of innovative solutions using diffusion of information, incentives and knowledge transfer in order to obtain a superior compliance of the code of conduct and, eventually, have key suppliers develop an independent ethical commitment to CSR (Lim and Phillips, 2007).

To reach levels below the first layers in the supply chains, the use or co-opting of traditional community sources of power with the help of non-governmental organizations (NGOs) may be more effective than a top-down policy. In most developing Asian countries, the development of NGOs as grass-roots organizations may offer an alternative response to the need for community level contacts. For instance, in Indonesia and the Philippines, NGOs play an important role in the rebuilding of the labour movement. But beyond purely labour-related issues they have shown the ability to develop broader local issues into international campaigns and to collaborate with multinational corporations (Ford, 2006).

For example, one of the most pressing problems in Asia is the protection of forests and the people whose livelihoods depend on them. The development of large-scale monocrop plantations in countries such as Indonesia and Malaysia has most often resulted in the rights and concerns of local people being neglected by owners and government. They are also the source of major environmental damage because of intensive irrigation and the use of pesticides detrimental to the surrounding ecosystems. The sustainable development model supposes the development of more socially acceptable large plantations coexisting with smaller locally managed plantation models. For community forestry to succeed, individual schemes must be finely tuned to reflect local circumstances. Land tenure, a voice for marginalized groups in decision making and strong institutional support are also required. It can only be done with the help of NGOs included into a multi-stakeholders structure. To cover the cost, local companies and MNCs could assist SMEs by providing hardware, such as pollution abatement technologies, specific guidance on moving up the value chain and other professional services (IGES, 2005).

A Multi-pronged Implementation of CSR and Sustainable Development Policies

Common economic instruments applied in Asia are various environmental taxes, subsidies, emission charges, user fees, custom exemptions and duties to promote clean technology. Despite their advantages, economic instruments are applied in a very uneven and limited manner (IGES, 2005). Public–private partnership has developed considerably, especially in the water and sanitation sectors. In some cases at least, positive outcomes have been reported in the form of better services and lower prices. Some failures have been registered, however. So, it is difficult at this stage to judge the extent of those partnerships' effectiveness (ICFTU, 2004).

Thailand, the Philippines and China have undertaken major reform in water management. They have strengthened their water ministry in creating an apex body set up for coordination. It sits alongside decentralization because the key success factor is the delegation of management responsibility to local communities and the strong commitment generated among local water managers by an incentive system. Other environmental issues such as haze pollution, climate change and forest management pose a set of challenges to environmental governance. Some are local in terms of the source of the harm and its impact while others are local in source but international in impact, still others are international in source and impact. That is why Asian countries are placing greater emphasis on regional participatory approaches.

A 'Regional Action Program for Environmentally Sound and Sustainable Development' was adopted at the Ministerial Conference on Environment and Development in Asia and the Pacific, in Seoul, in 2005. It provides a framework for regional cooperation on sustainable development from 2006–2010. A similar commitment to collaboration has been obtained for the sharing of information on the environment through the UNEP (2005) Regional Resource Centre for Asia and the Pacific. Specific action plans and policy integration have been formulated on biological diversity, to combat desertification and mitigate drought. At the sub-regional level, agreements have been achieved to combat acid rain, sandstorms and haze in Southeast Asia. In this latest case a legally binding policy instrument has been signed by the parties (IGES, 2005).

The creation of the Mekong River basin ecosystem-based intergovernmental body is another important regional initiative. It has set a prototype for effective ecosystem-based, natural resource management and an alternative sustainable livelihood development, in a region where few rivers and water bodies have been governed by legally binding agreements. The challenge to create a sustainable channel of commerce and prosperity in the Mekong River basin, which contains 70 million people and encompasses the 230 million people of Cambodia, China's southern province of Yunnan, Myanmar (Burma), Laos, Thailand, and Vietnam, represents the 'last frontier' in the region. Balanced, sustainable development is pitted against purely economic objectives.

In Asia, regional cooperation has traditionally relied on an informal approach with frameworks amalgamating the organizations and countries with different policy preoccupations and varying socio-economic conditions. The Roundtable on Sustainable Palm Oil is a good example of what is developing in Asia in this regard and of the limitations of the approach. It has been set up to bring the commercial sector together and involves the producers, civil society groups, governments and other stakeholders. So far only principles and criteria for sustainable palm oil production have been discussed and loosely agreed upon. It allows flexibility and pushes for consensual decision making. However, it has the disadvantage of not usually having sufficient permanent institutional support mechanisms or appropriate financing mechanisms for implementing policy measures and activities that are collectively supported by the countries concerned in the region (Crow, 2006). In that sense, the Mekong project faces an important test. It needs to be envisioned from broad perspectives recognizing the symbolic and pragmatic dimensions of the river development from being more than a transportation route or source of commodity water, to seeing it as an ecosystem worthy of preservation and protection for future generations.

SUMMARY POINTS

- There is a growing recognition that solutions to CSR and sustainable-related problems require the involvement of people and organizations down to the local level.

- Asian countries develop problem resolution mechanisms at national, sub-regional and regional levels involving private and public organizations.

CONCLUSIONS: THE CHALLENGES AHEAD

As in Western countries it seems that there is a consensus in many Asian countries on the point that CSR should be both voluntary and regulated. In that sense, the position in Asia is not very different from that of the European Union. Trade-offs between industrial development and environmental conservation will always be essential, as there are limits to the availability of win–win scenarios. The eradication of monopolies, corruption and preserve subsidies will remain difficult and politically challenging. This is all the more true where a long period of authoritarian regimes has created deeply rooted vested interests in some Asian countries.

The problem is that for the time being, the incentive not to comply often outweighs the incentive to do it in an environment of regulatory failure. As pointed out by the ADB (2006), sustainable results cannot be expected without more stringent enforcement of the existing laws and regulations to ensure that companies become minimally responsible and to avoid free riding. Conversely, however, doubts remain about the impact of 'CSR' from the top that China and Indonesia intend to develop. Any long-term solution requires an understanding of the problems of all actors at all levels and that no single strategy can encompass all types of policy. Admittedly, while things may become relatively easier for first tier suppliers to follow a consistent code of conduct, the situation gets far harder for those companies operating at lower levels. Only the use of a mix of regulatory measures, market-based measures, voluntary agreements, education and information measures can give results over time. CSR does not figure yet as a key source of competitive advantage on Asian markets. In the future, though, Asian consumers are bound to give more importance to the CSR issues in their purchasing behaviour beyond environmental concern. This likely growing assertiveness to CSR can play in favour of Western MNCs eager to penetrate Asian markets. They have developed sophisticated CSR management skills that they have already put to use in Asia. This represents a major challenge for Asian companies in their own markets. The fear of being dictated to in terms of social and economic norms is present. Recent initiatives have begun in China as well as in Indonesia, Singapore, Japan, and India to prevent Western MNCs and institutions from controlling the fields of CSR and sustainable development. The traditional fear of falling victim to non-tariff barriers that could be erected easily for alleged non-conformity to CSR rules is present (Zheng and Chen, 2006). But, countries such as China and Japan (and certainly India in the future) have a more ambitious agenda. They intend to be more assertive in the development of their own norms, participate more actively in the elaboration of international CSR standards and become 'rule makers' instead of 'rule takers' as has been the case so far.

CHAPTER SUMMARY

- The concepts of corporate social responsibility (CSR) and sustainable development have a growing impact on socio-economic modes of development in Asia. In many respects the current pattern of economic growth creates such strain in both developed and developing countries that it is unsustainable from environmental and social points of view.

- Long-term, sustainable solutions to the serious social and economic problems confronting Asian countries require the active involvement of private business beyond mere compliance with the law. There is a consensus that CSR activities must remain of a voluntary nature. However, a deeper involvement of business in the rule-making process related to environmental and social issues is expected in collaboration with the other stakeholders.

- The Asian business environment is increasingly involved in a maze of public and private initiatives whose objectives are to provide guidelines on CSR. A number of those initiatives are becoming de facto norms on corporate conduct for a growing range of issues such as labour relations, environment protection, human rights, corporate governance and consumers' protection.

- Western multinational companies have developed the most proactive, sophisticated and wide-ranging CSR policy. In the most advanced companies CSR is now incorporated into business policy. CSR is considered as a potential source of competitive advantage and not merely as a business cost necessary to preserve the company's reputation.

- So far, most Asian companies remain reluctant to develop CSR activities implying an active engagement with stakeholders who are not directly involved in the companies' activities, such as NGOs and other pressure groups. This reluctance explains why CSR activities most often focus on environmental matters and neglect the social issues.

- Nevertheless, the growing awareness of Asian public opinion to environmental and social issues, added to the pressure from Western markets, has led to a gradual change of attitude in this respect. So, CSR can be expected to play a bigger role in Asian companies' business strategies in the near future.

- At the same time Asian public authorities are becoming aware of the importance of CSR in terms of trade and autonomy vis-à-vis Western powers. This is driving them to develop their own norms and standards in order to keep local companies competitive on the world markets and become able to negotiate on equal footing with Western organizations.

KEY CONCEPTS

Business case: The concept of having a non-technical reason for a project or task. In CSR language it means that responsible behaviour can be financially sound.

Code of conduct: A set of rules outlining the responsibilities of or proper practices for an individual or organization.

Corporate social responsibility: A concept whereby organizations consider the interests of society by taking responsibility for the impact of their activities on customers, employees, shareholders, communities and the environment in all aspects of their operations.

Eco-labelling: A labelling system for consumer products (including foods) designed to avoid detrimental effects on the environment. All eco-labelling is voluntary.

Ethical Trading Initiative (ETI): An alliance of companies, non-governmental organizations (NGOs) and trade union organizations promoting ethical consumerism.

Global Compact: An initiative from the UN to encourage businesses worldwide to adopt sustainable and socially responsible policies, and to report on them.

Global Reporting Initiative: The world's de facto standard in sustainability reporting guidelines.

Philanthropy: The act of donating money, goods, time, or effort to support a charitable cause, usually over an extended period of time and with regard to a defined objective.

SA 8000: A global social accountability standard for decent working conditions, developed and overseen by Social Accountability International (SAI).

Social labelling: Labelling put on a number of products indicating that they have been produced in accordance with social and labour international norms.

Socially responsible investment: An investment strategy that combines the intentions to maximize both financial return and social good.

Sustainable development: A socio-ecological and economic process characterized by the fulfilment of human needs while maintaining the quality of the natural environment indefinitely.

Multi-stakeholders' engagement: Voluntary relationships between stakeholders in order to facilitate the achievement of objectives related to CSR and sustainable development.

Tripartite system: A system under which government, management and labour are considered as equal social partners discussing and negotiating social, business and labour relationships respectful of all the parties' interest.

Triple bottom line: Reporting of companies measuring organizational (and societal) success: economic, environmental and social.

REVIEW QUESTIONS

1. What are the main elements of the concepts of corporate social responsibility and sustainable development? In what ways are they linked to each other?
2. What differences and common points are there between the interpretation of the CSR concept in Asia, the US and Europe? What are the pros and cons of each approach?

3. How do you explain the different degree of importance given by Asian, US and European companies to the role of trade unions in CSR policy? What consequences do you think it entails in terms of protection of labour rights in Asia?
4. What do you think should be the priority of companies in terms of CSR and sustainability in Asia?
5. What roles should NGOs play in CSR? What are the pros and cons of stakeholders' engagement of companies with NGOs?
6. What roles should public authorities play in CSR at the local, national and regional levels?

LEARNING ACTIVITIES AND DISCUSSIONS

1. Gather information on concrete cases related to the subject of child labour. It could be about Pakistani soccer balls, Indian and Moroccan rugs, children working in toy factories in China, or others that you deem appropriate. Discuss the multiple facets of the issue with your colleagues. Is it a 'black and white' problem leading to the conclusion that child labour is inherently bad and should never be acceptable practice in any circumstance? If banned, what would be the likely socio-economic consequences for the country and for the children and their families? What do you think would be the most sensible policies to deal with the issue?
2. Try to find concrete examples in the developed and developing world about private–public agreements to solve social and environmental issues. Discuss the pros and cons of this type of approach. What are the key success factors and what are the elements that could cause problems?

MINI CASE

DEVELOPMENT OF THE 'BOTTOM OF THE PYRAMID' (BOP) MARKETS

Consumerism, deceptive practices or responsible behaviour fitting with the 'business case' concept?

Until recently, most companies interested in market development in developing countries concentrated their efforts on the nascent middle class with enough disposable income to afford products coming from the developed world. In doing so, they were writing off in terms of market potential the large majority of the population in those countries. But, times are changing. More and more companies show interest in the development of the so-called 'bottom of the pyramid' (BOP) markets, that is, those of people with a very low purchasing power (Prahalad, 2007).

The example of Hindustan Lever is well known. After catering for a long time to India's middle and upper classes, the company (a subsidiary of Unilever) decided to start selling to low-income people products adapted to their needs and low purchasing power. In order to do so, it had to change its business model, make smaller packaging, and distribute the products in a maze of thousands of extremely small shops spread over the rural areas. The company had to decentralize the production, marketing and distribution to take advantage of India's large pool of cheap labour, and change its price structure. The result was positive financially. Margins were lower but this was compensated for by higher unit sales. At the same time consumers had access for the first time to high-quality products that improved their standards of living. In the 1990s, during the crisis in Southeast Asia, Unilever was able to replicate the same business model and put successfully on the Southeast Asian markets smaller quantity products fitting with the market needs. In doing so, Unilever and its rival P&G are also playing a key role in the fulfilment of one of the most important objectives of the United Nations, that is, the empowerment of women in the developing world. They train tens of thousands of women to become the distributors of their products, providing additional income to the family while encouraging women's entrepreneurial spirit. In the mind of these companies, once again, this is a win–win case beneficial to both parties. Many of those women are likely to become the harbingers of change in their communities. The management knowledge they acquire will spread over to other people and enrich the potential of economic and social development (NHK, 2008).

Unilever and P&G are not isolated cases and many companies are entering the fray: from Bristol-Myers Squibb selling its AIDS drugs in Africa at a below-cost price, to Shell Solar bringing affordable solar power to poor people in Sri Lanka, India and the Philippines, with the ambition of developing the mass markets of China and Indonesia in the near future. To cope with malnutrition rampant in the developing world, Coca-Cola, Danone and Procter & Gamble are evolving similar policies. They develop innovative food products especially for poor developing countries. To avoid any misinterpretation of their activities, they take care not to repeat the mistakes committed by companies that neglected the necessary explanations about the use of the products and what could be expected or not from their consumption. To solve the difficult issue of product prices they work actively with local governments and international organizations in order to receive better treatment for the products on the markets, for instance, favourable tariffs and tax rates, speedier regulatory review of the products and subsidies from foundations.

Companies targeting the BOP markets are sometimes criticized for pushing very poor people to consume products that may not be absolutely necessary. Local substitute products often exist that are discarded although they provide similar benefits. The resources poor families spend on new products resources would be more usefully utilized for other purposes. Conversely, it is argued that those companies are of course acting from enlightened self-interest, providing early market 'pull' for new ideas. They see the developing world as an incubator for new products and sustainable technologies of the future, ranging from micronutrient-enriched food and drinks to micropower technologies such as fuel cells, microturbines and solar power. Admittedly, poverty will not be completely alleviated through their initiatives but neither should they be condemned either for exploitation of poor people. Thanks to their efforts, many children will have at least enough stamina to follow classes and become better educated. The sanitary situation has improved significantly thanks to the use of shampoo, soap and detergents. Likewise, villages in developing countries will soon have access to solar powered multimedia modems that will enable them to access the internet.

QUESTIONS

1. Do you think that BOP market development raises ethical issues? If yes, which ones and what can you propose as solutions?

2. What are the pros and cons in social and economic terms of the activities and strategies of companies attempting to develop BOP markets?
3. Which criticisms, if any, of consumerism's impact on society as a whole are found in the BOP market development? And what are the specificities you perceive in the BOP markets in this regard?

Sources: Grant, J. (2005). Check the depth of the pocket. *Financial Times*, November 16; Slavin, T. (2007). The potential in poverty. *Japan Times*, December 11; *Nippon Hoso Kosha* (NHK), India Special Issue, June 2008; Prahalad, C.K. (2007). *Fortune at the Bottom of the Pyramid: Eradicating Poverty through Profits*. Kindle Edition. Wharton School Publishing.

INTERESTING WEB LINKS

On CSR

Business for Social Responsibility: www.bsr.org
International Labor Organization: www.ilo.org
OECD: www.oecd.org
Transparency International: www.transparency.org
Global Reporting Initiative: http://www.globalreporting.org
CSR Asia: http://www.csr-asia.com

On sustainable development

Greenpeace: http://www.greenpeace.org
World Wide Fund: http://panda.org
UNESCO: http://www.webworld.unesco.org
World Health Organization: http://www.who.org

REFERENCES

Asian Development Bank (ADB) (2005). *Asian Economic Outlook 2005*. Manila: ADB.

Asian Development Bank (ADB) (2006). *Asian Environment Outlook Report*. Manila: ADB.

Asian Development Bank (ADB) (2007). *Asian Economic Outlook 2007*. Manila: ADB.

Association for Sustainable and Responsible Investment in Asia (ASrIA) (2002). *SRI and Pensions in Asia*. Hong Kong: ASrIA.

Business Respect (2007). FTSE4Good deletes Toyota, Honda, Agilent and others from index. 30 September, *Business Respect*.

Caspersz, D. (2006). The 'talk' versus the 'walk': High performance work systems, labour market flexibility and lessons from Asian workers. *Asia Pacific Business Review*, **12**(2): 149–61.

Crow, L. (2006). Business and NGOs – a force for change? *CSR Asia Weekly*, **2**(20): 1–3.

Crow, L. (2007). Global sustainability targets: Will they have an impact in Asia? *CSR Asia Weekly*, **3**(28): 17.

Dana, L. (2007). *Asian Models of Entrepreneurship*. Singapore: World Scientific.

Dodd, M. (2004). *BP in Vietnam: Social Involvement, an Evolution*. Dôshisha Business School Case. Dôshisha Business School.

Economist Intelligence Unit (2005). *The Way of the Merchant, Corporate Social Responsibility in Japan.* London: Economist Intelligence Unit.

Ford, M. (2006). Labour NGOs: An alternative form of labour organizing in Indonesia, 1991–1998. *Asia Pacific Business Review*, **12**(2): 175–91.

Global Reporting Initiative (2007). http://www.globalreporting.org/ (20 October).

Grant, J. (2005). Check the depth of the pocket. *Financial Times*, 16 November.

Hindu BusinessLine (2007). Tata Group and CSR. http://www.thehindubusiness;line.com/businessline/2007/08/26 (26 August).

Ho, B. (2005). A CSR standard for China?. *CSR Asia Weekly*, **1**(44).

Ho, B. (2006). Confucian businessmen. *CSR Asia Weekly*, **2**(43): 1–3.

Huchet, J.F. (2007). *La Responsabilité Sociale des Entreprises Étrangères en Chine.* Louvain: Institut de Recherches Economiques et Sociales (IRES).

IMPACTT Ltd (2004). *Fifth Anniversary Report*, London: IMPACTT Ltd.

Institute for Global Environmental Strategies (IGES) (2005). *Sustainable Asia 2005 and Beyond: In the Pursuit of Innovative Policies.* Kanagawa: IGES.

International Confederation of Free Trade Unions (ICFTU) (2004). *A Trade Union Guide to Globalization.* Brussels: ICFTU.

International Labour Organization (ILO) (2008), *Towards Full Employment,* Geneva: ILO.

International Standards Organization (ISO) (2007). *World-Wide Number of ISO 14001.* Geneva: ISO.

Keizai Doyukai (2003). *Corporate Social Responsibility in Japan, Selected Summary.* Tokyo: Keizai Doyukai.

Lansbury, R.D., Kwon, S.H. and Suh, C.S. (2006), Globalization and employment relations in the Korean auto industry: The case of Hyundai Motor Company in Korea. *Asia Pacific Business Review*, **12**(2): 131–47.

Lee, K.-H. (2005). Strategic CSR as stakeholder management: The business case for corporate social responsibility in Korean electronic industry. The Graduate School of Corporate Environmental Management, University of Kwang Woon.

Leng, J. (2006). The emerging discourse of CSR in China. *CSR Asia Weekly*, **2**(37): 8–9.

Lim, S.J. and Phillips, J. (2007). Embedding CSR values: The global footwear industry's evolving governance. *Journal of Business Ethics*, **56**: 43–53.

Lyon, E. (2007a). British companies in Asia: CSR is a legal requirement. *CSR Asia Weekly*, **3**(44): 1–3.

Lyon, E. (2007b). CSR law in Indonesia. *CSR Asia Weekly*, **3**(30): 1–3.

Nippon Hoso Kosha (NHK) (2008). India Special Issue, June.

Prahalad, C.K. (2007). *Fortune at the Bottom of the Pyramid: Eradicating Poverty through Profits.* Kindle Edition. Wharton School Publishing.

Raja, M. (2004). Profiting from a social conscience. *Asia Times*, http://www.atimes.com/atimes/Asian_Economy/FI30Dk01.html (30 September).

Roche, J. (2005). *Corporate Governance in Asia.* London: Routledge.

Singapore Compact (2006). *Annual Report 2006.* Singapore: Singapore Compact.

SiRi Group (2004). *Green, Social and Ethical Funds in Europe 2003.* Milan: SiRi Group.

Slavin, T. (2007). The potential in poverty. *Japan Times,* 11 December.

Tanimoto, K. (2004). *CSR Keiei.* Tokyo: Chuo Keizaisha.

Toyota Jidosha Kabushiki Gaisha (2006). *Sustainability Report 2006.* Tokyo: Toyota Jidosha Kabushiki Gaisha.

UNEP (2005). Asia-Pacific outlook http://www.rrcap.unep.org (5 November).

Van Heeswijk, J. (2004). Corporate responsibility for environmental performance. Keynote speech to the Greening of Industry Network Conference, Hong Kong, 8 November.

Von Stokar, T. and Steinemann, M. (2004). *Sustainable Development in Switzerland: Methodological Foundations.* Bern: Swiss Agency for Development and Cooperation.

Welford, R. (2005). Corporate governance in Asia. *CSR Asia Weekly,* **1**(37): 1, 8–9.

Welford, R. (2007). Gender inequality causes economic losses. *CSR Asia Weekly,* **3**(18): 1–2.

Welford, R. and Frost, S. (2006). Corporate social responsibility in Asian supply chains. *Corporate Social Responsibility and Environmental Management,* **13**: 166–76.

World Bank (2007). Environmental issues in Indonesia. www.worldbank.org/id/environment (10 October).

Zheng Y. and Chen, M. (2006). China attempts to enhance CSR in multinational companies. China Policy Institute Briefing Series Issue 11, Nottingham University.

Zinkin, J. (2007). Islam and CSR: A study of the compatibility between the tenets of Islam, the UN Global Compact and the development of social and natural capital. *Corporate Social Responsibility and Environmental Management,* **14**: 206–18.

Chapter outline

- The opportunities and challenges posed by Asian technology
- National technology systems
- Asian legacies in science and technology
- Asian responses to the Western technological challenge
- Creating national innovation systems after World War II
- The current situation

Chapter objectives

After reading this chapter you will gain an understanding of:

1. The relationship between a nation's technology development systems and various aspects of its national well-being
2. How these relationships have specifically impacted the major Asian civilizations
3. The rich technological heritage of some of the major Asian societies
4. The technological challenges facing the major Asian societies
5. The strengths and weaknesses of the Asian national technological systems

Chapter 3

Technology development in Asia

Leonard Lynn

INTRODUCTION: THE OPPORTUNITIES AND CHALLENGES POSED BY ASIAN TECHNOLOGY

In the closing decades of the 20th century and first years of the 21st century Singapore, Malaysia, Thailand and, most notably, the giant nations China and India were joining Japan, South Korea and Taiwan as major centres of technological strength. By 2003 China trailed only the US and Japan in spending on R&D (see Tables 3.1 and 3.2 for data on R&D expenditures). Overall, Asia accounted for nearly a third of the world's expenditures on R&D. India was rapidly becoming a centre of global excellence in the knowledge-intensive service sectors and in biotechnology. The Asian economies were gaining market share in high technology exports at the expense of the European Union, US, and Japan (the first modern great Asian high technology centre).

The current rise in technological strength in Asia poses both major opportunities and challenges for business people, policymakers, and citizens of other countries. Let us begin by discussing some of the opportunities.

For multinational enterprises (MNEs) there are growing new opportunities to draw on rich stocks of human resources in science and engineering in China, India, Thailand, Indonesia and other parts of Asia. Sometimes the lower costs of wages in these countries allow firms to apply more brainpower to technical problems than would otherwise be feasible. Sometimes those trained in different societies offer different perspectives or have different interests, enriching approaches to the development of technology. A pharmaceutical company, for example, may find more people with expertise and interest in infectious diseases in India than in North America or Europe. For a variety of reasons different countries may develop particular strengths in one field of science or technology. At different times in the 20th century, for example, Germany was strong in chemical technology, the US and UK in aeronautics and the development of computers, and Japan led in industrial robotics and manufacturing technology.

Table 3.1 Gross expenditures on R&D by region/country 1993, 1998, 2003 (millions of purchasing power parity US dollars)

	1993	1998	2003
Asia	95.7	143.1	229.6
US	166.1	228.1	292.4
EU-25	123.7	152.5	210.2
China	16.7	27.9	76.9
Japan	69.1	90.5	112.7
South Korea	9.9	14.8	24.3
Taiwan	NA	8.5	13.5

Note: Purchasing power parity exchange rates are calculated based on the relative costs of a fixed 'basket' of goods and services in different countries. In China official exchange rates would result in considerably lower R&D expenditures.
Source: Adapted from Table 7 in National Science Foundation (2007: 15). Original data from OECD, *Main Science and Technology Indicators* (2006/1).

Table 3.2 R&D performed in selected Asian countries by US multinationals (millions of current US dollars)

Country	1994	1998	2002
China	7	52	646
India	5	23	80
South Korea	17	29	167
Singapore	167	62	589
Taiwan	110	55	70
Thailand	3	4	22

Note: Declines in several Asian countries in 1998 over 1994 were related to Asian financial crisis.
Source: Adapted from Table 8 in National Science Foundation (2007: 19). Based on data gathered by US Department of Commerce.

Consumers around the world benefit from the enhanced ability of multinational corporations to draw on technical resources from around the world. We get new products, or products with new features. More generally, the growing technological strengths of Asia allow a far greater application of human brainpower to human problems such as disease, poverty, and environmental degradation. There are signs, for example, that major advances in alternative sources of energy may be coming from Asia's emerging economies: India has moved into a position of leadership in aspects of biotechnology and software engineering.

And yet, the rise of technological strength in India, China and some other Asian countries has also caused uneasiness among the citizens, and thus the policymakers, of Western countries (as well as Japan). Some of this unease is based on the close relationship between technological capability and military strength. Three of the large Asian countries, China, India, and Pakistan, are nuclear powers. By the end of the first decade of the 21st century the major Asian powers appeared to be beginning a space race among themselves. Overall, it seemed likely that the two-century long ability of the

West to more or less unilaterally shape the global political environment through its overwhelming military technology was coming to an end. Nor were those in certain Asian economies, and some of those in all the Asian economies, sure that they were benefiting from the emerging global technology system.

Aside from the potential military threat, some in the West see the rise of Asian technology as posing an economic challenge. In one widely circulated report, for example, a committee of the National Academies of Science in the United States said it was 'deeply concerned that the scientific and technological building blocks critical to our [US] leadership are eroding at a time when many other nations are gathering strength ... we fear the abruptness with which a lead in science and technology can be lost ... It doesn't matter whether you're a lion or a gazelle – when the sun comes up, you'd better be running' (National Academies of Science, 2007). Concerns were expressed that China and India were graduating more science and engineering students than the US and EU (see Table 3.3), and that the cost of science and engineering labour was lower in these and other Asia countries (threatening job prospects for US and European students), leading to fears that the rise of Asian technology would result in the loss of well-paid jobs, innovative capacity, and threaten continued productivity growth. Although the evolution of economies has always led to the loss of some jobs (in the early 20th century about 40 per cent of US Americans worked on farms – by the early 21st century almost all those jobs were gone), the growing concern was that the current globalization of technology and economic activities is different. In the past the twin forces of technological progress and globalization resulted in the destruction of low-paid relatively unattractive jobs in the rich countries, but also resulted in the creation of at least as many highly paid and otherwise attractive jobs. In most of the closing decades of the 20th century workers in Europe and North America may have lost mind-numbingly monotonous and dangerous jobs on automobile assembly lines and steel mills, but these job losses were more than offset by the creation of new jobs in engineering, software programming, research and development and medical technology. As the emerging economies of Asia and other parts of the world eagerly took up the less attractive jobs, attractive new jobs were created in the West. Now the situation may be different.

Two factors primarily accounted for the privileged position enjoyed by European and North American workers in the 19th and 20th centuries: they were better educated and they were backed by vastly greater levels of investment in technology. By the early 21st century these advantages were rapidly disappearing – the education gap was closing and globalization meant that capital and technology flowed freely to the Asian economies. In the memorable title of Thomas L. Friedman's best seller, today 'the world is flat.' Today it is not just blue-collar workers with a high school education or less who are worried about the loss of jobs to Asia, it is also university graduates in fields such as computer science, medical technology, and engineering. Meanwhile the reduction in international barriers to trade often puts the unskilled in emerging economies into increased competition with one another, further driving down their wages.

As far as multinational corporations are concerned, the opportunities mentioned above are partially offset by the potential threat of powerful new competitors. Just as the earlier rise of Japan, Taiwan, South Korea and Singapore presented new competitors in the automotive (Toyota, Nissan, Hyundai), home appliance (Sony, Panasonic, LG), and electronics industries (Samsung, Hyundai), firms in the newly emerging Asian economies of India, China and others are generating firms in biotechnology (Ranbaxy, SiBiono Gene Tech), personal computers (Lenovo), and software (Wipro, Infosys).

Table 3.3 Science and engineering bachelor's degrees by country (1990 or closest year and 2002 or most recent year available)

Country	1990	2002
China	268,400	533,600
India	205,000	Not available
Japan	187,900	351,300
South Korea	79,300	113,100
Indonesia	30,700	97,100
Taiwan	24,400	72,500
Thailand	24,200	31,200
US	329,100	415,600
EU (15)	284,300	506,100

Notes: 1. More recent information was not reported for India. 2. EU data are for 15 countries that were members of the EU in 1990.
Source: Table 2 in National Science Foundation (2007: 3).

To develop a better understanding of these challenges and opportunities, it is important to develop a sense of how the institutions involved in creating and using technology form a system.

REFLECTIVE QUESTIONS

■ What are the situations where it might matter in which country a technological breakthrough takes place?

■ What are the situations where it would not matter very much? Why?

■ What benefits have you received from technological developments from other countries?

■ In what ways are you worse off because of technological advances in other countries?

NATIONAL TECHNOLOGY SYSTEMS

The obvious importance of technology for a nation's economy and for its military security led to considerable discussion in the 19th century of what was needed for a country to gain a technological edge over its rivals. In the UK, the country that pioneered the industrial revolution, the concern was how to maintain leadership, and efforts were made to restrict technology exports. In Germany, Japan and China the concern was with how to catch up with and pass the leading nations.

National Innovation Systems

In the 1980s the national innovation systems framework attracted considerable attention as a way of thinking about the factors contributing to the technological strength of nations.[1] A national innovation system was defined as the network of interconnected institutions within a country that created, stored, disseminated and exploited technology. These institutions included universities, government laboratories, think tanks, corporate research laboratories, professional associations and other organizations. They sometimes were taken as also including such things as management practices and patterns of inter-firm relationship.

Japan was seen as having created a particularly effective national innovation system – one that had allowed the country to catch up with the West in a relatively short time, and that in the 1980s, seemed poised to put Japan ahead of the West in most economically important technologies. Governments in Europe and international organizations such as the Organisation for Economic Co-operation and Development (OECD) closely studied the Japanese system in an effort to find lessons that would lead to more effective systems for the creation and utilization of technology. The US and European national innovation systems were also critically examined with many calling for the incorporation of lessons from Japan. In time other Asian countries began explicitly to model some of their institutions to resemble those in Japan or the US.

Table 3.4 summarizes some of the elements attributed to the Japanese system. This model has implications that go beyond Japan, because the Japanese system of technology was seen as a model for other East Asian countries at various points, including South Korea, Taiwan, Singapore and Malaysia.

The Japanese government – most notably the Ministry of International Trade and Industry (reorganized into the Ministry of Economy, Trade and Industry in 2001), but also the Ministry of Finance, Ministry of Education, Science and Culture, and the Science and Technology Agency – was seen as playing a primary coordinating role in the Japanese system of technology. The government issued a series of visions and plans incorporating projections of technological trajectories. The technologies seen as strategic in underlying economic success in the coming decades were to be targeted. The projections were widely seen as allowing an efficient mobilization of technological resources. Firms organized into research consortia, for example, to allow them to avoid costly redundancies of efforts, and to bring complementary strengths together to leapfrog foreign competitors. The Japanese government also pressured foreign firms to share technology as a condition of entering the Japanese market. Government also worked through the financial system to assure that firms had money to invest in R&D, and in new plant and equipment (thus supporting Japan's high technology industries).

Table 3.4 A stylized model of the Japanese technology system

Role of government	Bring together industry and other leaders to reach informed consensus on future industrial and technological trends
	Support coordinated efforts to efficiently move Japan to the vanguard in these trends
	Support education system that provides good basic education in maths and science for factory workers and trains large numbers of engineers
Corporate system	Firms form *keiretsu* groups with members in finance, trade, and industrial supply chains
	Firms supported by various forms of 'patient capital'
Employment practices	Long-term employment – many scientists and engineers spend most of career at one company
	Centrally controlled career paths
	Large investment in employees

Source: Summary of the literature by the author.

A distinctive feature of Japanese capitalism was the *keiretsu*, a grouping of firms. These groups, some of which traced their origins to the pre World War II *zaibatsu*, centred on banks and other financial institutions (such as insurance companies), general trading companies, large manufacturing companies based in most key industries, and networks of smaller firms that supplied the manufacturing companies with components and services. The *keiretsu* could support each other and engage in collective long-term planning, including investment in large-scale technology projects. Because firms relied on loans from affiliated financial institutions for their capital, rather than equity and debt markets, they did not need to worry excessively about short-term results that might drive down stock or bond prices. They could plan for the long term, investing in technology.

Finally, it was often argued that Japanese employment practices contributed greatly to Japan's technological successes. Since university graduates working at major firms typically spent their careers at a single firm, the firm could invest more in the technological knowledge and skills of their employees. In a system with greater inter-firm mobility, that investment would be lost as soon as a scientist or engineer left. Indeed, Japanese firms typically undertook the advanced education of their engineers rather than relying on universities for this. The personnel offices of major Japanese firms typically exercised far more control over the positions to which employees were assigned than was true at most Western firms. They used this control to rotate engineers among key positions. Most engineers would have experience in R&D, manufacturing and customer services, giving them a most holistic view of technology and customer needs. This was thought to greatly enhance the ability of Japanese firms to commercialize technology.

National Competitive Frameworks

In a more general analysis of national competitiveness Michael Porter (1998) argues that the relative strength of nations in certain industries is based on four sets of determinants supported by government. The four determinants are demand conditions, related and supporting industries, firm structure, strategy and rivalry and factor conditions (cost of raw materials, labour, and so on.). These are often represented in what is called Porter's Diamond (see Figure 3.1). In an example of a hi-tech industry Porter makes arguments similar to those using the national innovation system framework. Again, he gives a Japanese example, that of industrial robotics. Robotics technology was initially developed in the US in the 1950s and 1960s, and US firms created the industrial robotics industry. By the late 20th century, however, the industry (and the technologies it was based on) was dominated by Japanese firms. Japanese government policies supporting development of the industry included joint research projects, tax incentives, and leasing programmes that made it easier for smaller firms to lease Japanese industrial robots. The structure of firms in Japan was also well suited to this industry. The industrial groups allowed a vertical integration that encompassed electronics and mechanical technology. The fact that there were several such groups also ensured a high level of competition. Demand conditions in Japan were also very favourable for the industry. Labour was in short supply and industrial robots were highly suitable for the industries that were growing fastest in Japan at the time, automobile production and electronics. Japan was also strong in the industries needed to support robotics, such as machine tools and electronics.

The Japanese national innovation system was widely credited with helping Japan reach the frontier in industrial technology, and move beyond it in some areas. As the Japanese economy faltered in the 1990s, however, many observers began pointing to the shortcomings of the Japanese system.

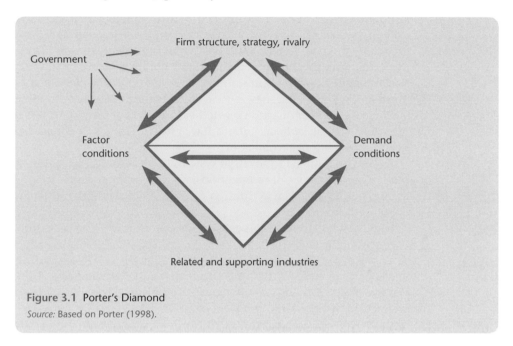

Figure 3.1 Porter's Diamond
Source: Based on Porter (1998).

While it might sometimes be possible for government coordinated groups to effectively identify technologies of the future, more often it is difficult to identify where breakthroughs may occur. Who, for example, anticipated the importance of the internet, MP3 player, and cellular (mobile) phone industries? While the Japanese forms of finance allowed firms to plan for the long term, they also allowed firms to continue performing badly over time, sometimes continuing long-term bets on technology that did not succeed. Japan's technologically powerful companies such as Fujitsu, Hitachi and Sony might have fared better in competition with fast rising firms like Samsung if they had been pressured by shareholders to move out of less promising businesses. Further, to the extent *keiretsu* firms *might* be more open to joint technology development projects with each other, they would also be *less* open to working with potential partners from other *keiretsu*.

While the Japanese employment system might allow firms to invest more in the technological expertise of their employees, it also can result in a poor allocation of science and technology human resources. Some Japanese firms, for example, appear to have 'stockpiled' electrical and electronics engineers in the 1980s, and then found they did not need them.

Finally, in Japan (and later in South Korea) the emphasis on supporting large firms entailed a de facto discrimination against small and medium sized enterprises (SMEs). Often these firms were unable to obtain the capital they needed to develop, entrepreneurship was stunted, and small-company employees were relegated to a kind of second-class citizenship.

Other Frameworks of National Technology Systems

Some observers have criticized the national innovation systems and national competitiveness frameworks for being static and simplistic – doing little more than inventory institutions and actions involved in the development of technology. One effort to add a more dynamic element is provided by the triple helix model, which conceives of evolving systems of university-led partnerships with government and industry.[2] This model allows room for the consideration of university spin-off firms, tri-lateral initiatives, and strategic alliances encompassing groups of firms, government organizations and academic research groups. Indeed this captures some of what critics see as a dynamism lacking in the Japanese system (such as the ability for technologists to start new businesses). Another question is whether in a world of increasing globalization it makes sense to focus on *national* innovation systems. Firms and intellectual property flow freely across national boundaries.

A focus on national innovation systems can lead to technonationalism, a sense that nations are in a zero sum competition with each other in which technological successes in one country are taken as threatening other countries, rather than providing a potential resource for them.[3]

Finally, scholars have struggled with the issue of how a nation's technological strength might be measured. The measures that have been used include number of patents granted, the number of scientific publications, R&D spending, the number of science and technology personnel (or the number graduating), and high technology exports. Each of these measures has its problems. Firms in some countries may be inclined to acquire large numbers of patents for strategic purposes (for example to block other firms from controlling key technologies), so the number of patents it holds may not reflect the actual creation of new technology. Some technological advances are difficult to patent, or may be more easily protected by secrecy rather than the disclosures required by patents. English language technical and scientific journals are dominant, giving an advantage to English-speaking scientists. R&D spending reflects the effort to create new technology more than the actual creation of new technology. And, in any case, different accounting practices in different countries may result in some things being counted as R&D expenses in one country that would not be in another (is the salary paid to a janitor who cleans a lab a research expense?). As we will see in the case of China a country may have a large share of high technology exports, but the value added in the country to the high technology exports may not be large. A country may train large numbers of engineers and scientists, but not be effectively using them.[4] A related issue concerns the broader ability of a country to use new technology. A country may not be particularly strong in creating technology, but may have what some scholars call absorptive capacity, the ability to identify and commercialize new technologies wherever they might come from.

SUMMARY POINTS

An understanding of national innovation systems is important for business leaders because it can:

■ Guide the strategic location of a firm's R&D and other facilities

■ Help in an assessment of international competitors

■ Help in evaluating the further economic potential of different countries.

ASIAN LEGACIES IN SCIENCE AND TECHNOLOGY

Until the European Renaissance, and, in some areas, until the Industrial Revolution of the late 18th century, the civilizations of China and India led the world in science and technology. Japan and Korea were also quite advanced in many sectors of science and technology, as were some of the civilizations of Southeast Asia. The first Chinese mechanical clock appeared early in the 8th century CE,[5] some 600 years before its European counterpart. Chinese technologists were especially advanced in studies of optics, acoustics and magnetism. Iron and steelmaking technology was far ahead of that in the West. Gunpowder first appeared in the 9th century CE, and explosive weapons were developed in China some 300 years before they appeared in Europe. Rockets enclosed in bamboo tubes were used in China at the beginning of the 12th century CE, perhaps serving as the ancestor of guns and cannons. The development and use of silk in China may have led to the development of the drive-belt and chain drive. The Chinese are also credited with inventing paper, block-printing and movable type, as well as porcelain, and may also have been the first to use biological means to control insect pests. Vaccinations were in use in China from the beginning of the 16th century CE, and possibly several centuries earlier.[6]

Ancient India also was highly advanced in science and mathematics, indeed many of the advances in Chinese astronomy, medicine and mathematics were based on knowledge transmitted to China by Buddhist monks from India. Indian scholars developed heliocentric models of the solar system before the Greeks, and India is often credited with originating a number of mathematical concepts including zero, the decimal system, the algorithm, and the square root. An Indian mathematician conceived of differential calculus in the 12th century CE.

European observers in the late 16th century considered Japan to be no more than slightly behind Europe technologically. In Korea during the early 15th century movable type was first put to extensive use, perhaps earlier than anywhere else in the world. The 'turtle ships' used by Koreans, most notably in fighting against a Japanese invasion in the late 16th century, were among the world's first iron-clad warships.

At one time a standard academic question in the West was why the advance of Chinese and Indian science and technology had halted, causing these civilizations to fall behind the West. In time, however, the question shifted to what might lie behind the acceleration of technological development in Europe. The conventional view is that there was a Scientific Revolution in Europe around 1600 CE that led to the discovery of ways to discover, which resulted in the acceleration of technical and scientific progress. This entailed the statement of hypotheses in mathematical terms and the use of controlled experiments. In a famous letter Albert Einstein said 'Development of Western Science is based on two great achievements, the invention of the formal logical system (in Euclidian geometry) by the Greek philosophers, and the discovery of the possibility to find out causal relationship by systematic observation (Renaissance). In my opinion one has not to be astonished that the Chinese sages have not made these steps. The astonishing thing is that these discoveries were made at all' (cited in Graham, 1973: 51).

During the Renaissance, Europe began importing scientific and technical knowledge from the Islamic civilizations. Some of this knowledge had been developed by the Greek and Roman civilizations, then lost to Europe and preserved by Arabs, Turks and Persians. Some had been created by the Islamic civilizations, and some transmitted by them from India, China and other civilizations. This infusion of knowledge coupled with the development of experimental science led to an accelerated development of science and technology in Europe. The Industrial Revolution, beginning in the 18th century in England, combined important technological changes including the use of new basic materials (especially iron and steel), sources of energy (coal, steam engines, electricity, petroleum), machines (such as the power loom and spinning jenny), transportation equipment (steam locomotives and ships, automobiles, aircraft), and communications equipment (telegraph, radio). The effective use of these new technologies helped enable the West to achieve economic and military dominance over much of the world, including the great civilizations of Asia.

SUMMARY POINTS

■ The great civilizations of Asia led the world technologically until recent centuries – suggesting that they can again move to a position of leadership.

■ It is not entirely clear why they lost this lead, whether because technological progress slowed in Asia, or because it accelerated so rapidly in the West.

ASIAN RESPONSES TO THE WESTERN TECHNOLOGICAL CHALLENGE

The initial responses of the Asian civilizations to the new technological challenges from the West were sometimes complacent. This is exemplified in a famous letter written by the Emperor of China to the King of England in 1793. The King had requested permission to expand trade between the two countries. The Emperor refused. He said: 'As your Ambassador can see for himself, we possess all things. I see no value on objects strange or ingenious, and have no use for your country's manufactures.' In a follow-up communication the Emperor added: 'Our Celestial Empire possesses all things in prolific abundance and lacks no product within its own borders. There was therefore no need to import the manufacturings of outside barbarians in exchange for our own produce' (Blackhouse and Bland, 1914).

Concerned about the 'subversive' activities of foreign missionaries, the Japanese government refused to allow Westerners to enter Japan – except for a small Dutch trading post in Nagasaki harbour. Korea was similarly isolated from the West. India, divided and weak, did not have the option of isolation, and after a century of gradual incursions by the British East Indian Company and various French, Dutch and Portuguese companies from the beginning of the 17th century became an English colony.

In the 19th century leaders in both China and Japan became increasingly alarmed by the Western incursions in Asia. In both countries there were moves to introduce Western technology as a means of maintaining independence from the West. Japan's greater political unity and stronger tradition of learning from other civilizations allowed these efforts to take consequential form much more quickly than was the case in China.

Concerns about a technological threat from the West reached a crisis in Japan in 1853 and 1854 with the arrival of Commodore Perry of the US Navy. When Perry's flotilla first arrived near Edo (modern Tokyo) in 1853, Perry demanded permission to deliver a letter from the US president. The clear military superiority of Perry's black ships convinced the Japanese to allow Perry to deliver the letter and to return a year later to sign a trade treaty. Perry's crew members demonstrated such achievements of Western technology as the steam engine and telegraph to the Japanese. The military implications of this technological superiority were clear to the Japanese.

The Japanese government sent young Japanese abroad to study both Western technology and the institutions involved in creating and disseminating technology. The Japanese hoped to establish a strong national technology system, but one based on Asian values. A new government drawing on the traditional authority of imperial power, but dominated by military leaders seeking a technologically strong military, was established in 1868. Thousands of foreign technical experts were brought to Japan. By the early 20th century Japan was able militarily to challenge Russia, a major European power.

Industrial technology was brought in through joint ventures and other forms of technical tie-ups involving European and US companies. In the years before World War II, Japan also successfully developed some world-class technologies of its own.

Over these decades the creation of institutions and arrangements to foster technological development was much spottier in the other Asian nations. China was torn apart by foreign powers supporting various regional war lords into the 1930s, then by civil war and the Japanese invasion in the 1930s and 1940s. Virtually all the other East, Southeast and South Asian countries were colonies until the late 1940s. Given the lack of opportunity at home, many of the brightest young Asian engineers and scientists moved to the West to build their careers.

SUMMARY POINTS

- Initially the great Asian civilizations did not feel threatened by Western technology.

- As the military and navigational advantages of Western technology become clear the Asian civilizations reacted differently: Western incursions in India prevented a coherent reaction; internal divisions in China also made mobilization difficult; the Japanese, however, responded with a high degree of success.

CREATING NATIONAL INNOVATION SYSTEMS AFTER WORLD WAR II

After World War II Japan struggled to rebuild its national technology and innovation system. Initially handicapped by widespread destruction at home, a lack of foreign exchange and a lack of access to flows of scientific and technical information, these efforts faced formidable barriers. With the end of fighting in the Chinese civil war in 1949 and India's Independence in 1947, these countries too struggled to create powerful national technology systems.

In all these countries there were strong debates about the best way to achieve technological strength. Some thought it was best to foster the development of domestic capabilities by keeping out foreign companies and refusing to pay seemingly exorbitant fees for foreign intellectual property. It was widely believed that opening the doors to foreigners would result in the Asian countries falling into a quasi colonial status. This technological protectionism slowed progress throughout the region.

Japan

After its defeat in World War II Japan found it had lost ground in its efforts to catch up with the West in technology. Sources of technology had been cut off. The country had undergone widespread destruction. Some of its best industrial plants had been bombed, others that had been built in mainland Asia were lost as Japan was forced to relinquish control of Korea and large sections of mainland China. Under the terms of its surrender Japan was not allowed to be active in certain strategic industries such as aviation and nuclear energy. Japan's devastation and the collapse of international trade also meant that Japan had few resources to acquire needed food and raw materials, let alone advanced industrial equipment and technology.[7]

To husband scarce domestic resources Japanese policymakers concentrated on the development of certain industries such as electric power generation, steelmaking and shipbuilding that were seen as key to the development of other industries. State of the art technologies were imported for these industries. Because Japan was poor in foreign exchange reserves the government implemented tight controls on expenditures for the acquisition of foreign technology. Japanese firms were constrained from bidding up the price for foreign technology and dissuaded from purchasing technology that was not seen as critical to Japan's economic development. Barriers were erected to keep large foreign firms from moving into Japan, even in cases where they might have brought technology with them. Over the years Japan became increasingly open to the import of foreign technology. Japan's technological advance was supported by a strong education system and a favourable global political and economic environment (including strong US support to build up Japanese industry during the Korean War and later during the cold war, and the liberalization of international trade). By the 1980s Japanese technology was seen by many as about to assume global leadership in a number of key sectors.

China

Once the Chinese civil war was effectively ended in 1949, the Chinese government sought to promote the advance of science and technology. Initially, China relied on its communist ally, the USSR, in its efforts to build a modern technology system. Soviet technology, know-how, and technical experts were imported on a large scale. The Soviet system also provided a model for the Chinese during this period.

The former Academia Sinica was re-established as the Chinese Academy of Sciences (CAS) and new institutions for R&D were set up. The emphasis of the new system was on the integration of research and production, with research intended to have immediate practical applications. In 1956 the government announced a twelve-year science and technology plan aimed at giving China a position of industrial leadership. Twelve areas were targeted. The basic research institutes were under the CAS, the applied and military research institutes were under the industrial ministries, and training was the responsibility of the universities. In 1960 the Soviet Union withdrew its support for China, increasing China's isolation and its attempt to move to technological autonomy.

Two decades later, under Deng Xiaoping, China initiated a series of reforms, increasingly opening the economy to foreign investment (and actively seeking it in some areas), and shifting activities to the private sector.

India

After India gained its independence in 1947, its spending on scientific research was only 0.1 per cent of gross national product (GNP). A decade later this had increased to 0.5 per cent (still far below the 2–3 per cent common in most developed nations). A system of national research laboratories was established based on the French model. Under the Council for Scientific and Industrial Research there were some two dozen institutes with scientists encouraged to develop new products for Indians. New engineering schools were established, including some of the now-famous Indian Institutes of Technology (IIT) (five were established between 1954 and 1964).

The emphasis of early Indian technology policy was on indigenous technical capability. Prime Minister Jawaharlal Nehru and Homi Bhabha (1909–1966), a nuclear physicist who is considered to be the father of nuclear physics in India) reportedly believed that 'if an item of equipment was imported from abroad, all one got was that particular instrument. But if one built it oneself, an all-important lesson in expertise was learnt as well.'[8] India's Scientific Policy Resolution of 1958 announced that one of the aims of its policy was to ensure an adequate supply within India of research scientists of the highest quality. The emphasis was on sustainable and equitable development. In a Technology Policy Statement in 1983 the Indian government reaffirmed its belief that science and technology are the basis of economic progress and declared that the country now had an impressive scientific manpower. The statement indicated such aims as to make the maximum use of indigenous resources and achieve self-reliance, making use of traditional skills and capabilities, to ensure maximum development with minimum capital outlay. It said, for example, 'We must aim at major technological breakthroughs in the shortest possible time for the development of indigenous technology appropriate to national priorities and resources.' Furthermore, India policy stated that: 'Fullest support will be given to the development of indigenous technology to achieve technological self-reliance and reduce the dependence on foreign inputs ... In view of the cost of technology development and the time necessary for successful marketing of a new or improved product, indigenously developed items are invariably at a disadvantage compared to imported products or those based on imported technologies and brands names. Support must therefore be provided through fiscal and other measures, for a limited period, in favour of products made through indigenously developed technologies, care being taken to ensure quality.'[9] Proposed technology imports were critically evaluated, and often discouraged, as was the establishment of R&D facilities by foreign firms. Many of the country's best scientists and engineers left for more attractive career opportunities in the US or Europe.

SUMMARY POINTS

- After World War II Japan quickly recovered its momentum in catching up with the West technologically. The activities of foreign firms were tightly restricted however to prevent a loss of control.

■ China and India both became free to act in a united and independent way to develop their technology systems. Both attempted to create centralized protected technology systems.

THE CURRENT SITUATION

Despite the impressive achievements of many of the major Asian countries in developing effective technology innovation systems mentioned in the introduction to this chapter, the problems still facing them should not be ignored.

Japan

In Japan the central challenge facing policymakers in the late 20th and early 21st century was how to make the country a leader, as opposed to simply being a very fast following and incremental improver of technology. Other Asian economies increasingly seemed as skilled as the Japanese at being fast followers and incremental improvers. Moreover their costs were lower. At the same time there was little evidence that Japan was closing the gap with the US in reaching the frontiers of technology development.

Wide-ranging criticisms were made of the Japanese system: its education system was said to overemphasize memorization rather than creativity, bureaucratic barriers kept its universities from contributing new technologies as effectively as their counterparts in the US, its employment and industrial systems made it difficult for entrepreneurial firms to be established and to thrive, its technological resources were overly concentrated in Tokyo and in large companies, and there was not enough diversity.

In the late 1990s and early 2000s a series of reforms were initiated to address these problems. Reforms were made in the education system, university professors were given greater freedom to work on technology development projects with companies, efforts were made to create 'Silicon Valleys' throughout the country, and changes were made in financial markets to provide more venture capital. It is not yet clear how successful these reforms will be in enhancing the creativity of Japanese technology. Still, as Tables 3.1, 3.3 and 3.5 show, Japan is a world leader in its technological capabilities.

Japan, however, has still not entirely opened itself up to potentially beneficial foreign inputs of technology. It continues to have the lowest levels of import penetration, inward foreign direct investment and foreign workers of any member of the OECD (the organization of richer countries).[10]

China

In the 1980s China began a series of innovation system reforms. The reforms were intended to be consistent with China's shift to a market-based economy. Thus in 1985 the Chinese government enacted a Resolution of the Central Committee of the Communist Party under which science and technology at public research institutes were separated from the production activities of state-owned enterprises.[11]

In 2006 the Chinese State Council released its 'National Guidelines for Medium- and Long-term Plans for Science and Technology' to cover the period until 2020. The plans identified key technologies that were to be promoted. They also announced the intention to increase China's R&D spending to 2.5 per cent of the country's GDP by 2020, around the level of the advanced economies, and to move China into the top rank of countries in terms of patents and highly cited scientific papers. China's R&D spending had already grown from just 0.60 per cent of GDP in 1996 to 1.23 per cent by 2003, and China was already the fifth leading nation in its share of publications in scientific publications, following the US, Japan, Germany and UK. Only seven years earlier it had ranked tenth in the world by this measure.

One source of China's increasing technological strength was the large number of scientists and engineers returning from the US, Europe and other technologically advanced countries. Some 81 per cent of the members of the Chinese Academy of Sciences and 54 per cent of the members of the Chinese Academy of Engineering were returned scholars during the early 2000s.

China still faces a number of challenges on its way to becoming a technology superpower. While the education system has improved greatly, the percentage of its young people receiving higher education is still relatively low, and only a relatively small number of its universities are of high quality. The Chinese system of intellectual property rights protection has been hotly criticized and may be a barrier to R&D in China. On the one hand it makes foreign firms reluctant to conduct high-level technology development activities in China. On the other it reduces the incentive for Chinese to invest in the creation of new technology. Chinese firms still must rely heavily on foreign firms for technology. This has sometimes posed problems. The Chinese DVD manufacturers, for example, were able to obtain licences for the core DVD technology only after prolonged negotiations (Sull, 2005: 5). The systems for funding R&D, compared with the US and other technologically advanced countries, are much more concentrated in public-sector research, a legacy of the pre-Deng system.

India

Reforms in the early 1990s substantially opened up the Indian economy, and since then the country has successfully built hi-tech and knowledge-intensive industries. Through the 1990s the Indian economy grew at an average rate of 8.1 per cent a year, with some of the growth attributed to the software industry – revenues of which grew from US$197 million to US$8 billion. Software exports over this period increased from US$100 million to US$6.3 billion.[12]

Government policies shifted to an encouragement of foreign R&D activities in India. Indeed, about one fourth of the *Fortune* five hundred companies have opened R&D centres in India. GE invested more than US$80 million in the John F. Welch Technology Center in Bangalore. The centre features state-of-the art-laboratories and more than 2,500 engineers and scientists. Senior officials at GE and other multinationals describe their facilities in India as equalling those in the US (National Research Council, 2007: 15). As Indian technology has globalized, official policy statements have shifted from concerns about foreign control of technology to the need for India to strengthen its protection of intellectual property rights. India's national laboratories are highly regarded, and the IITs are among the best technical universities in the world.

The Indian technology system, too, however, is faced with daunting challenges. The country's basic education system and most of its higher education system are still weak. One study found that a quarter of the teachers in public elementary schools were absent, and half of those present were not actually teaching at any given time. The percentage of India's workers with a higher education is somewhat lower than China's, and R&D

spending is much lower.[13] Critics also point out that only a small percentage of the Indian population has so far benefited from the advance of Indian high technology.

Table 3.5 Workers in selected countries with higher education: 1990 and 2000 (millions)

Country	1990	2000	(% of population)
China	11.7	20.1	.017
India	9.2	15.0	.014
Japan	9.2	12.5	.125
South Korea	2.0	4.4	
Indonesia	.2	.7	
Taiwan	.7	1.2	.04
Thailand	1.7	3.2	
US	42.7	52.8	.176
EU (15)	13.5	22.4	

Notes: 1. EU data are for 15 countries that were members of the EU in 1990. 2. 'Higher education' is education at least at level of associate degree in the US.
Source: Table 4 in National Science Foundation (2007: 8).

Other Asian Countries

Other Asian countries are also struggling to find roles in the emergent global technology system. Pakistan has felt the need to invest heavily in the development of nuclear weapons to counter the technological advance of India. The Southeast Asian states have, in a variety of ways, become integrated into the global technology value chains of multinational firms. In part this is driven by the intensification of globalization through the World Trade Organization and other international bodies that have made it increasingly difficult for countries to maintain autonomous technology policies. In part it is driven by countries seeking opportunities for economic development through cooperation with foreign multinationals. The smaller economies, however, lack the bargaining power of China, India, and Japan and doubts have been raised about the degree to which globalization is helping them to increase their indigenous technological capabilities and the degree to which they can distribute the benefits of technological globalization to their citizens. Some research suggests that Singapore, for example, has done well in this regard, while Malaysia, Thailand and other countries have been less successful.[14]

SUMMARY POINTS

■ In the last decades of the 20th century the technology systems of the major Asian countries benefited by becoming more open to the activities of foreign firms, though issues still remain with protectionism in Japan and weak intellectual property rights protection systems in China and India.

■ China has made great progress in establishing basic education for its people, but aside from a few outstanding universities has a weak system for the education of scientists and engineers.

- India has a few state-of-the-art institutions for the training of scientists and engineers, but continues to be weak in its general education system.

- Both China and India continue to have relatively low levels of private investment in R&D.

REFLECTIVE QUESTIONS

- How will the movement of the giant Asian countries of China and India to positions of leadership in more and more important new technologies impact the lives of ordinary people in Europe, North America and Japan?

- China and other emerging economies have been strongly criticized for their failures to protect intellectual property rights. One response might be to point to all the instances where the West 'borrowed' technology from China, India and other countries without any concern about Asian intellectual property rights. What do you think about this? Is it fair for Westerners to criticize emerging economies on intellectual property rights issues? Is it reasonable to make an issue of intellectual property rights in the 21st century?

- So far the benefits of technology globalization have been slow to spread to many of the poor in Asia. Do you think this is just a matter of time, or that aggressive actions should be taken?

CHAPTER SUMMARY

- The Asian economies, prominently including China and India, have recently increased their technological capabilities to world-class levels. This poses both challenges and opportunities for the world's rich countries.
- One way of understanding a nation's technological capabilities is to think in terms of national innovation or national technology systems, though this framework has some limitations that must be kept in mind.
- Before the Industrial Revolution of the 18th century, the civilizations of China and India led the world in science and technology.
- The technological rise of the West posed severe challenges for the major Asian civilizations, but (with the notable exception of Japan) most of the Asian civilizations were unable to respond until the late 20th century.
- Japan was the first modern Asian country to catch up with the West technologically, and so provided a model that was followed (in part) by other Asian countries.
- China initially tried to adopt a Soviet model of technological development, but eventually discarded this.
- India attempted unsuccessfully to foster its technological capabilities by keeping out foreign firms.
- Today Japan still sees itself as lacking sufficient technological creativity. China and India, despite their recent advances, have problems related to the protection of intellectual property, insufficient private sector spending on R&D and education.

KEY CONCEPTS

Absorptive capacity: Ability of a company or country to use technology developed elsewhere.

National innovation system: Framework for thinking about how various institutions contribute to a nation's ability to create new technology.

Porter's Diamond: Four factors determining competitive advantage of nations.

Technonationalism: Notion that technology development is a zero sum game amongst nations in which one nation's success is detrimental to the well-being of other nations.

Triple helix: Evolving interaction among universities, industries and government that provide technological capability.

Intellectual property rights: Rights the creator of intellectual property (inventions, books, music and so on) holds. May be protected by patents, copyrights, or secrecy.

REVIEW QUESTIONS

1. Why did Asia fall behind the West in science and technology?
2. Why did the Asian countries resist the import of foreign technology for so long?
3. What were the different approaches to the creation of national innovation systems taken by the various Asian countries?
4. China, India, and Japan all face significant challenges with regard to their technological capabilities. What are these challenges and how likely are they to be overcome over the next 20 years?

LEARNING ACTIVITIES

1. Use the web to find out how different Asian countries now compare in spending on R&D.
2. List the ten most important advances in science or technology created by your country, then list the ten most important advances in science or technology created by other countries. Which of these have had the greatest impact on your life?

MINI CASE

TECHNOLOGY POLICY AND BROADER SOCIAL ISSUES

The Three Gorges Dam project[15]

China's Yangtze River originates from a glacier on the Tibetan Plateau and flows nearly 4,000 miles across China before emptying into the East China Sea. Only the Nile and Amazon Rivers are longer. The Yangtze serves as China's main waterway, irrigates much of its agriculture, and its basin is home to nearly one-third of China's population. Upstream it passes Chongqing, a municipality of more than 30 million people and a major industrial city. Downstream it passes by Wuhan, one of China's most important metallurgical centres. Shanghai, Suzhou and other important cities are on the Yangtze Delta. Much of China's ancient history is tightly linked to the Yangtze.

The Yangtze has also been a source of destructive floods throughout China's history. Some of the floods have come in tsunami-like waves down the river, destroying everything in their path. On average the Yangtze has caused catastrophic floods every 50 to 55 years. In 1931 six flood waves came down the river making tens of millions of people homeless. In all, during the 20th century some 300,000 people died in Yangtze River floods. Sun Yat-sen, who was then President of China, proposed in 1919 that a hydroelectric dam be built at the Three Rivers Gorge. War with Japan, civil war and other problems kept this proposal from being acted on.

In 1992 the Chinese government announced plans for a 17-year project to dam the Yangtze River at the Three Rivers Gorge. The project would involve a quarter million workers and would inundate some 632 square kilometres (395 square miles) of land. It would be the largest hydropower station and dam in the world (the dam would be 185 metres, or more than 550 feet high). The government argued that the dam would benefit China in that it would:

1. Control the periodic devastating floods.
2. Allow ocean-going ships to go the 1,500 miles up-river to Chongqing.
3. Generate low-cost electricity. The dam could provide as much as one-ninth of China's electrical production, drastically reducing the need to burn coal. Given China's economic growth the

demand for electricity was expected to double every 15 years.
4. Reduce pollution by reducing the need to depend on coal-fired plants to generate electricity (the dam would generate electricity equivalent to about 40 million tons of coal).

The plans for the Three Gorges Project were widely criticized. Some said the dam might become an environmental disaster as toxic materials from flooded industrial sites were leached into the river. Run-off from communities around the dam might also contaminate the river. By slowing the flow of water, the dam might weaken the river's ability to flush out waste into the ocean. Some worried that the slower water flow would also result in increased silting that would actually hinder rather than facilitate river traffic. Some of the most fertile land in China would be flooded. Environmentalists also expressed concern that the dam might cause earthquakes (the massive dam would be on unstable land) and landslides, as well as disrupting ecosystems that are home to many endangered species. Concerns that the Three Gorges project might lead to earthquakes were heightened by claims that the devastating Sichuan earthquake of May 2008 may have been triggered by the filling of the Zipingpu reservoir behind a dam on a tributary to the Yangtze River (about 1,000 kilometres from the Three Gorges Dam). The Zipingpu reservoir was near the epicentre of the earthquake, but officials said the Zipingpu dam and reservoir were unrelated to the earthquake.

Other critics said that since the electricity generated by the Three Gorges Dam would all come from one site, it could not be used efficiently. There were also serious issues of social responsibility and ethics. The government estimated 1.2 million people would be displaced as cities, towns, villages and farms were flooded in the reservoir behind the dam. Others said the number of people displaced would be closer to two million. The Chinese government had programmes to help people relocate, but the aid provided seemed grossly inadequate (and much of it never reached the intended recipients). Archaeologists and historians claimed that nearly 1,300 important sites would be flooded.

QUESTIONS

1. Did the Chinese government make the 'right' decision in proceeding with the project?
2. Would the outcome have been different if the Chinese government had been more 'democratic' (with greater voice by the people most closely affected)?
3. Did the immediate needs to control flooding and boost the supply of electricity make it impossible for the Chinese government to take a more deliberative approach in deciding to build the dam?
4. What should the Chinese government have done?

INTERESTING WEB LINKS

Technology development in Japan: www.mext.go.jp/english/
Technology development in China: www.most.gov.cn/eng/
Technology development in India: http://dst.gov.in/
Technology development in South Korea: www.most.go.kr/en/
Up to date statistical information and reports can also be found from the following websites:
National Science Foundation: www.nsf.gov
OECD: www.oecd.org
World Bank: www.worldbank.org

Notes

1 Key sources on national innovation systems include Freeman (1987), Lundvall (1992), and Nelson (1993).
2 This model is developed in a number of articles by H. Etzkowitz and L. Leydesdorff. See, for example, Etzkowitz and Leydesdorff (2000).
3 For a critique of this mindset, see Lynn and Salzman (2006).
4 For a discussion of this, see Lynn and Salzman (2007).
5 Common Era: The period coinciding with the Christian era.
6 The history of Chinese science and technology is extensively documented by Joseph Needham in numerous works. See, for example, Needham (1969).
7 A good source on the evolution of technology policy in Japan until the late 20th century is Samuels (1994).
8 Greenstein, G. (1992). A gentleman of the old school: Homi Bhabha and the development of science in India. *American Scholar*, **61**(3): 417, as cited in Guha (2007).
9 Government of India, Department of Science and Technology website.
10 OECD statistics cited in *The Economist*, December 1st–7th, 2007, Special Report on Business in Japan.
11 See, for example, Simon (1988) for events in China in this period. More recent information can be found in Segal (2002), Sull (2005), and Popkin and Iyengar (2007).

12 For a readable account of the rise of one of the major Indian software companies, see Hamm (2007). Also see Popkin and Iyengar (2007).

13 To learn more about the challenges facing the Indian technology system see National Research Council (2007).

14 See, for example, Doner and Ritchie's (2003) discussion of hard drive production in Southeast Asia.

15 This case was written based on publicly available information. It is intended solely to stimulate class discussion.

REFERENCES

Blackhouse, E. and Bland, J.O.P. (1914) *Annals and Memoirs of the Court of Peking*. Boston: Houghton Mifflin, online at http://academic.brooklyn.cuny.edu/core9/phalsall/texts/qianlong.html.

Doner, R.F. and Ritchie, B. (2003). Economic crisis and technological trajectories. In Keller, W. and Samuels, R. (eds) *Crisis and Innovation in Asian Technology*. Cambridge: Cambridge University Press.

Etzkowitz, H. and Leydesdorff, L. (2000). The dynamics of innovation: From national systems and 'mode 2' to a triple helix of university–industry–government relations. *Research Policy*, **29**: 109–23.

Freeman, C. (1987). *Technology Policy and Economic Performance*. London: Pinter Publishers.

Graham, A.C. (1973). China, Europe, and the origins of modern science. In S. Nakayama and N. Sivin (eds) *Chinese Science: Explorations of an Ancient Tradition*, pp. 45–69. Cambridge, MA: MIT Press.

Guha, R. (2007). *India after Gandhi: The History of the World's Largest Democracy*. New York: HarperCollins.

Hamm, S. (2007). *Bangalore Tiger: How Indian Tech Upstart Wipro is Rewriting the Rules of Global Competition*. New York: McGraw-Hill.

Lundvall, B.A. (1992). *National Innovation Systems: Towards a Theory of Innovation and Interactive Learning*. London: Pinter Publishers.

Lynn, L. and Salzman, H. (2006). Collaborative advantage. *Issues in Science and Technology*, (Winter): 74–82.

Lynn, L. and Salzman, H. (2007). The real global technology challenge. *Change*, (July/August): 8–13.

National Academies of Science/National Academy of Engineering/Institute of Medicine (2007). *Rising Above the Gathering Storm: Energizing and Employing America for a Brighter Economic Future*. Washington, DC: National Academies Press.

National Research Council (2007). *India's Changing Innovation System*. Washington, DC: The National Academies Press.

National Science Foundation, Division of Science Resources Statistics (2007). *Asia's Rising Science and Technology Strength: Comparative Indicators for Asia, The European Union, and the United States*. NSF 07-319. Arlington, VA: National Science Foundation.

Needham, J. (1969). *The Grant Titration: Science and Society in East and West*. Toronto: University of Toronto Press.

Nelson, R.R. (ed.) (1993). *National Innovation Systems: A Comparative Analysis*. New York: Oxford University Press.

Organisation for Economic Co-operation and Development (2006). *Main Science and Technology Indicators*. Paris: OECD.

Popkin, J.M. and Iyengar, P. (2007). *IT and the East: How China and India are Altering the Future of Technology and Innovation*. Boston: Harvard Business School Press.

Porter, M. (1998). *The Competitive Advantage of Nations*. Basingstoke: Macmillan – now Palgrave Macmillan.

Samuels, R.A. (1994). *Rich Nation, Strong Army*. Ithaca, NY: Cornell University Press.

Segal, A. (2002). *Digital Dragon: High-Technology Enterprises in China*. Ithaca, NY: Cornell University Press.

Simon, D.F. (1988). *Technological Innovation in China*. Cambridge, MA: Ballinger.

Sull, D.N. with Wang, Y. (2005). *Made in China*. Boston, MA: Harvard Business School Press.

Chapter outline

- Introduction to regional production networks
- Theories and perspectives
- Regionalization, regionalism and the evolution of production networks in East Asia
- Implications, issues and debates

Chapter objectives

After reading this chapter, you will gain an understanding of:

1. The logic and structure of international production
2. The concept and rationale of production networks
3. The broader, political economy context within which production networks exist
4. The specific relevance of regionalized production to East Asia
5. The experience of Japanese production networks in East Asia
6. The relationships between corporate strategy, regionalism and economic development

Chapter 4

Production networks in East Asia

Andrew Staples

INTRODUCTION

Even a cursory glance at the relevant production, trade and investment data for the last few decades confirms for the observer that seismic 'shifts' have taken place within the geography of global economic activity (Dicken, 2003). These shifts, of which the rise of East Asia is of paramount concern here, have been led by the transnational corporation[1] (TNC) and facilitated by rapid advances in information and communications technology (ICT) and the prevailing, if contested, hegemony of neo-liberal ideology.[2] We are of course alluding to the processes of globalization yet at the same time it is increasingly clear that a regional disaggregation of these processes is necessary for us to grasp the complex realities of the contemporary internationalization of production. Indeed, while the globalization debate continues to stimulate and inform mainstream discourse, the regionalization of production, trade and investment continues apace. When considered alongside concomitant regionalism[3] the increasing importance of the region becomes clear.

Three reasons for this can be identified. First, and while we are (happily) not yet at Orwell's (1950) tripartite global structure,[4] it is nevertheless clear that global economic activity is overwhelmingly located in three regional nodes: East Asia, Europe, and North America. These nodes all exhibit greater or lesser degrees of regional economic integration, with Europe's single market, currency and parliament (political integration) at the most advanced stage while NAFTA and East Asia follow, although care should be taken to avoid overstating the limited depth and cohesion of these latter two regions. Second, our allegedly 'global' multinationals have been shown, in fact, to be overwhelmingly regional in nature in terms of both markets and organizational structure (Rugman, 2005).[5] And third, in recent years the multilateral trading system under the World Trade Organization (WTO) has stuttered to a halt as repeated attempts to conclude the Doha 'development' round of further trade liberalization have failed.[6] As a result of this multi-lateral vacuum the world has witnessed a huge expansion in bilateral and regional free trade agreements (FTAs), not least in East Asia, as Figure 4.1 shows.

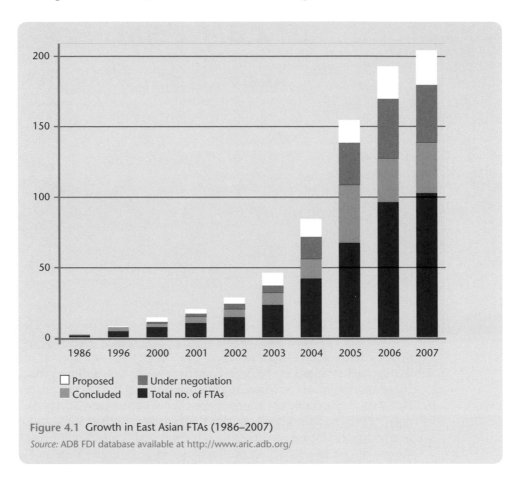

Figure 4.1 Growth in East Asian FTAs (1986–2007)

Source: ADB FDI database available at http://www.aric.adb.org/

The regional nature of much global activity, then, suggests the appropriateness of adopting a regional approach and methodology in any investigation of the contemporary internationalization of production. Yet how should this methodology be constructed and what features of regional economic activity need to be addressed? It is at this point that our attention turns to consider the regional production network (RPN) both as an organizational structure and in terms of how it relates to its regional environment. As will be examined below the continued organizational evolution of the TNC, in response to a fast paced and highly competitive economic environment, poses significant challenges for traditional firm-, and location-based explanations of international activity. In short, the complex reality of international production may only be grasped through the utilization of a conceptual framework that is able to effectively analyse the ways in which regions and networks of firms interact.

What then are RPNs and why do they, rather than individual firms, deserve our attention? Although a working definition will be provided shortly, a satisfactory answer to this question may only be gained through a review of the major theoretical approaches to internationalized production and perspectives on the regionalism/

regionalization dynamic. This will be attempted below but to allow us to continue this introductory section we may initially define a regional production network as a series of vertical and/or horizontal linkages between economic actors in a geographically defined space (the region). The precise nature and extent of these linkages will vary with industrial sector, geographic region and also the cultural embeddednesss of the firm or firms in question. With regard to the second part of the question, these networks deserve our attention as they constitute the contemporary organizational reality of production and it is rarely the case that a single firm retains within itself all aspects of the value chain.[7] This is particularly the case in the key industrial sectors of electronics and automobile production that are the focus of this chapter.

Finally our investigation into the RPN is focused on East Asia for a number of reasons, not least the remit of this book. The nature of regionalism observed, the degree of regionalization, and the varied and distinctive nature of East Asian production network 'models' means that East Asia offers a rich empirical seam to mine. At the same time the reader is urged not to limit his or her investigation of RPNs to East Asia alone as further examples may be found elsewhere, particularly between Mexico and the US and across the newly enlarged European Union. The aim of this chapter, then, is to equip the reader with the theoretical and conceptual knowledge required to understand and analyse a fundamental feature of business organization in East Asia. With this initial survey of the chapter concluded, attention now turns to consider the key themes in turn.

SUMMARY POINTS

The study of regional production networks in East Asia is important as:

■ Much of global economic activity takes place at the regional level.

■ Firms in key industrial sectors are increasingly organizing their activities on a regional basis.

■ The regionalization of economic activity in East Asia has significantly deepened in recent years.

THEORIES AND PERSPECTIVES

This section is presented in two parts. The first traces the development of theories of international production (the 'why' questions) while the second focuses more on the organizational structure of the TNC so as to attempt the 'how', 'where' and 'what' of regionalized production.

Foreign Direct Investment and International Production

Foreign direct investment (FDI) is the term used to describe the phenomenon of firms investing in foreign countries and is defined in contradistinction to portfolio investment[8] as long term in nature and exerting a degree of managerial control. When, say, Toyota builds a new production facility in Thailand it is engaging in FDI. Although defining FDI may be relatively straightforward, the question of *why* firms engage in the practice is more complicated. Why, for instance, do firms go through the expense and trouble of building overseas production capacity rather than utilizing other more arms-length forms of international interaction such as exporting and licensing? What is it that drives firms overseas and that has led to the organizational form of production that we will study below (the production network)?

Something of an evolutionary record exists with regard to attempts to satisfactorily answer these questions and contemporary approaches to FDI can be traced back to the era of classical economics and its concern with comparative advantage and international capital movements. Marxist theorizing, which continues to inform critical approaches to FDI and development, regarded such international capital flows as an inevitable consequence of the capitalist world system. Later work on international trade theory, particularly that of Heckscher and Ohlin, focuses on a nation's factor endowments and subsequent comparative advantage as an explanatory factor. However, the rapid growth of FDI in the post-war period highlighted deficiencies in these approaches and necessitated the development of new analytical models that could take into account the increasing relevance of the multinational company. In response, perhaps three broad themes have emerged which focus on the firm, trade and location, and internalization.[9]

While these approaches certainly progressed our understanding of internationalized production a considerable distance from classical economics and Marxist analysis, Dunning noted that 'no single hypothesis offers a sufficient explanation of non-trade involvement [FDI]' (Dunning, 1977: 297). That is, while the firm-based, trade and location, and internalization approaches all offered insights into the motives for FDI, no single theory existed to unify the field. To fill this lacuna Dunning sought to combine existing approaches into a paradigm that identified ownership, locational and internalization (OLI) advantages. His aptly named Eclectic Paradigm of International Production states that 'the extent, form, and pattern of international production [is] determined by the configuration of three sets of advantages as perceived by enterprises' (Dunning, 1987: 2). The eclectic paradigm hypothesized that some combination of these advantages must exist for firms to undertake FDI. Dunning's paradigm has made a significant contribution to our understanding of FDI and the MNC and is widely regarded as offering a 'unifying framework for determining the extent and pattern of foreign owned activities' (Mudambi, 2002: 263).

Dunning's paradigm has thus gained recognition as a particularly effective mode of analysis, but we must also note that this acceptance has not gone unchallenged and before we move on to consider the organizational structure of the TNC we should first take into account an alternative model that has particular relevance for East Asia. This macro-level approach originated in Japan and relates FDI to a sequential model of development based on comparative advantage, and the 'unique' features of Japanese firms. Commonly referred to as the flying geese paradigm[10] the model initially emerged in the 1930s (Akamatsu, 1962 in English) as analysis of Japan's pre-war pattern of development through interaction with advanced (Western) economies. It has since, however, become much more commonly associated with Japanese FDI and economic development in East Asian countries.

Some Japanese analysts questioned the applicability of theories developed from the study of Western firms to the experience of Japanese firms and their operations in East Asia. Kojima and Ozawa (1984) in particular took exception to two aspects of firm-based theories of FDI. First, the microeconomic focus on the individual firm (thus excluding FDI cooperation among firms or networks of firms such as Japanese *keiretsu* – see box on *keiretsu* below), and second the disregarding of macroeconomic issues including the impact of FDI on late developing economies. As a consequence they felt that the Western tradition as examined above focused disproportionately on negative aspects of FDI and overlooked the developmental potential of Japanese FDI. While some considerable criticisms of this approach exist,[11] it does nevertheless anticipate to some degree the more recent development of global production chain and network analysis and the flying geese analogy has provided a powerful, if historically contingent, visualization of East Asian development.

Table 4.1 Summary of theoretical approaches to internationalized production

Approach	Scale or focus	Features
Circuits of capital	Global system	FDI as inevitable outcome of capitalist system
Firm specific advantages	Micro	Firm has certain advantages that allow it to overcome the 'cost of foreignness'
Product life cycle	Location	The product life cycle determines location of production. Locational advantages
Internalization	Micro	Firm's internalize transactions to reduce costs and/or protect intellectual property
The eclectic paradigm	Multi	Ownership-specific advantages Location-specific factors Internalization advantages
Japanese tradition	Macro	Sequential regional 'catch-up' development based on comparative advantage Japanese firms as qualitatively distinct from Western firms

SUMMARY POINTS

Firms operate overseas for a number of reasons including:

- The possession of firm specific advantages.
- The existence of locational advantages.
- The desire to internalize operations.
- The phenomenon of Japanese firms operating in relational networks identified as *keiretsu* has given rise to an alternative model of analysis that emphasizes the broader economic context of FDI rather than the individual firm-level experience.

REFLECTIVE QUESTION

Consider a well-known TNC and identify its firm specific advantages. Next, use the company's website to learn about their overseas operations and utilize the OLI paradigm to analyse these activities.

Organizational Structure of the TNC

With this understanding of *why* firms undertake to internationalize production in hand our attention can now turn to consider the range of organizational structures[12] that firms utilize in pursuit of their global operations. Accordingly, this section reviews the evolution of our understanding of TNC organizational structure in the context of globalization before considering in greater detail perspectives designed to grasp better the complexity of regionalized production.

Dicken (2003) identifies four TNC organizational architectures and suggests that these result from organic growth and changing functional requirements as the firm faces fresh challenges from the internationalization of operations. These structures are defined as the multinational, international, global, and integrated network (see Table 4.2). Each structure is seen as the result of increasingly diverse operations across national boundaries and of the need to adopt more effective control and coordination structures. As international operations expand, the firm faces the dilemma of how best to accommodate new and urgent demands on resources while balancing the continuing demands of domestic operations. Should coordination of overseas operations be devolved and informal (the multinational model), subordinated to the domestic configuration (the international model), controlled centrally but organized regionally (the global model) or, rather, should the firm radically restructure to place the 'global' at the heart of the organization (the integrated network)? Consequently, headquarter–subsidiary relationships assume critical relevance.

Table 4.2 Organizational structure of the TNC

Model	Structure	Administrative control	Managerial attitude towards overseas operations	Emergence*
Multinational	Decentralized	Informal, loose	Independent of domestic structure	Inter-war model
International	Coordinated by HQ	Formal, tight	Extension of domestic structure	1950s/1960s US corporations
Global	Centralized hub	Formal, tight	Mode of delivery for global market	Ford (1900) Japanese firms 1970s >
Integrated network	Distributed network	Complex coordination and coordination, shared decision making	Integral component of complex network	Contemporary, emerging

Note: * Dicken stresses that observed change in organizational structure is not necessarily a sequential process and that overlaps in time and space are common.
Source: Adapted from materials in Dicken (2003).

The organizational structure of the TNC is thus determined by the increasing complexity of global competition and associated demands which have accelerated in the past few decades as we have already noted. In this environment, the 'competitive success [of the firm] thus crucially depends on a capacity to selectively source specialized capabilities outside the firm that can range from simple contract assembly to quite sophisticated design capabilities' (Ernst, 2001: 9). This leads us to consider, initially, the fragmentation of the production process, or value chain, and subsequently the geographic location or spatial scale of production. The value chain is defined here as a process whereby 'technology is combined with material and labor inputs, and then processed inputs are assembled, marketed, and distributed. A single firm may consist of only one link in this process, or it may be extensively vertically integrated' (Gereffi et al., 2005: 79). Value chain analysis, in other words, focuses on the extent to which the TNC identifies and manages core competencies internally (that is, to vertically integrate) or chooses to coordinate linkages with those external actors who are better able to perform certain aspects of the value chain (that is, outsourcing). The reality, of course, tends to lie at some point between these extremes. Indeed, Gereffi et al., (2005) identify five global value chain governance types that move from a *market* based type (where simple, codified products are purchased through arms-length transactions from the market) through to the *integrated* firm where transactions take place predominantly, if not exclusively, in-house. These governance types are seen as falling on a scale that measures the degree of explicit coordination of the value chain running from low (market type) to high (integrated firm).[13]

We should also note here that organizational form is influenced by many variables including those related to national culture and experience of development. The Japanese *keiretsu* is a clear example of where national norms and historical context have resulted in an organizational architecture distinct from that observed in many Western firms. It is also important to note here that the *keiretsu* form accommodates an intermediate position in the linear scale just identified. This is because the lead firm in the group, often the final assembler, coordinates the value chain through a networked group of companies that are in many cases affiliates (particularly nearer the top of the structure) locked into long-term relationships with their upstream customers and downstream suppliers which are further cemented through financial and historical/personal relationships.

Once we recognize that the fragmentation of production can lead to a more detached control and coordination structure, and therefore that locational advantages in production assume greater significance, we can begin to discern a rationale for a global production network (GPN) centred on a *flagship*[14] company (see in particular Ernst, 2001; Henderson et al., 2002). Within this framework, the flagship firm (the TNC) coordinates both intra- and inter-firm transactions among a global network of firms. The clear advantage of such a model is that each discrete section of the value chain may be located in that area, or region, that offers optimal performance. Crudely put, this would see labour intensive processes in developing countries with wage cost advantages and R&D facilities in locations that have excellent technical resources and high human capital. However it is important to note that due to the dynamics of localization we can also observe a growing trend of regionalizing R&D facilities.

So far this section has focused on how and where TNCs organize their activities and it is left until later in the chapter to consider what the implications of these activities may be for host economies, regional economic identity and issues concerned with governance and development. Much GPN analysis focuses on just these points and considers the 'strategic coupling' of the network (firms, subsidiaries and suppliers, customers) and regional assets (technology, organization, territory) in an attempt to understand the nature of inter-firm networks and their relationship with economic development (Coe et al., 2004). The GPN perspective therefore utilizes a spatial scale that locates regional economic activity in a broader global context by examining firm (or more correctly, industry) level relationships. In this way the finer detail provided by firm-level approaches is not lost in the broad macroeconomic brushstrokes nor is the importance of the global and regional structure eclipsed by narrow micro-level empirics. Adopting a GPN perspective thus provides us with a suitable analytical framework to examine regionalized production in East Asia.

We are now in a position to draw upon our theoretical understanding of FDI and the organizational structure of the TNC and to focus our attention on the East Asian experience of regionalized production with particular reference to activities of Japanese automakers.

Keiretsu

Networked or a collaborating family of firms, *keiretsu* (系列) in Japanese, are a characteristic feature of business organization in Japan. *Keiretsu* emerged in the early post-World War II period as either the reincarnations of former pre-war *zaibatsu* (財閥) conglomerates[15] including Mitsubishi, Mitsui and Sumitomo that had been broken up by legal reforms demanded by the occupying Allied forces; or newly emerged manufacturing firms, including Sony and Honda. Interestingly, the Chinese characters for *zaibatsu* are the same as those for present day Korean family-owned conglomerates, the *chaebol* (see below).

The prevailing (severe) economic conditions of post-war Japan and other historical factors presented a rationale for close cooperation between firms across the value chain rather than their vertical integration into one entity. These practices became institutionalized over the following years of Japan's rapid economic recovery and growth as the firms themselves expanded in size and (international) scope. In trying to understand this growth and global expansion, foreign analysts in the 1980s identified the *keiretsu* structure as a source of competitive strength for Japanese industry. They identified some 'family resemblances' across the various groups which included the practice of cross-shareholding, financing secured from a group, or main, bank rather than the stock market, long-term commercial relationships with suppliers, and personal ties, often cemented through regular meetings of company presidents and personnel exchange. In this analysis these features afforded *keiretsu* groups a number of strategic advantages over Western firms including stability in ownership, shared risk, long-termism and, in the case of the manufacturing groups, the opportunity to pursue quality and the elimination of waste through investment in human resources.

Keiretsu are conceptualized as being either horizontally (financial) or vertically (manufacturing) oriented, although examples do exist where both forms co-exist. The Mitsubishi group, which includes a bank, a general trading company, heavy industries, and automobile production, is often cited as an example of a horizontally organized *keiretsu*. In total, the Mitsubishi group is made up of over 500 companies. Toyota, on the other hand, is a classic example of a vertically organized *keiretsu* with Toyota Motor Corp. at the apex of a huge number of directly and non-directly controlled suppliers.

Finally, we should note that some debate exists over the extent, relevance and uniqueness of the *keiretsu* and further, the impact of the economic downturn in the 1990s and concomitant challenges of globalization. One of Carlos Ghosn's priorities when Renault effectively took control of Nissan in 1999 was the deconstruction of Nissan's *keiretsu* of suppliers, which were regarded as uncompetitive, costly and of decreasing relevance.

SUMMARY POINTS

- Firms adjust their organizational structures to suit the contemporary environment.

- The fragmentation of production allows for a more flexible model of value chain governance and the extent to which the TNC coordinates discrete sections of the value chain will determine its organizational structure.

- GPN analysis attempts to grasp the reality of the value chain governance in a defined spatial scale.

- Japanese firms in manufacturing industries may belong to wider relational networks described as *keiretsu*.

REFLECTIVE QUESTION

■ In what ways, if at all, are the Japanese *keiretsu* distinct from Western conglomerates?

REGIONALIZATION, REGIONALISM AND THE EVOLUTION OF PRODUCTION NETWORKS IN EAST ASIA

The preceding section surveyed the major theoretical approaches and perspectives relevant to our investigation of the production network in East Asia. It further established the rationale and logic of the production network by reviewing, in particular, the GPN approach. This section first briefly considers the broader context of the East Asian political economy, within which the phenomenon of regionalized production occurs, before examining regional integration as a political and economic process. This achieved, we then consider some examples of regionalized production in East Asia and give particular attention to Japanese production networks.

The Political Economy of East Asian Economic Development

An early attempt to distil the lessons of the East Asian experience of industrialization was made in 1993 with publication by the World Bank of the *East Asian Miracle* report. The report tackled the question of whether the 'miracle' of East Asian economic development could be attributed to, on the one hand, the 'developmental state' or, on the other, 'market friendly' strategies (Thompson, 1998).[16] This issue has not yet been satisfactorily resolved and was given further impetus by the events of the 1997/8 Asian financial crisis (Jomo, 2003). Yet in spite of these politicized debates the reality remains that the region has experienced tremendous economic gains over the past four or more decades which have lifted millions out of poverty. Japanese FDI has been a key feature in this story of development and has further served to deepen regional economic integration (regionalization) which more recently has been accompanied by *regionalist* projects (Gilson, 2004; Staples, 2006).

Regionalization and Regionalism

In contrast to the top-down experience of politically led regionalism observed in Europe, the process in East Asia is more bottom-up in that deepening intra-regional trade (both intra- and inter-firm) and investment activity has created a rationale for closer political integration. While this binary view is somewhat misleading – regionalism and regionalization are, in reality, two sides of the same coin and closely interdependent – the description is a useful and valid way of highlighting a distinctive feature of the development of a regional economic entity in East Asia. Regional economic integration is shown to have a number of consequences for inward investment as resulting market expansion and scale economies enhance a region's locational advantages in addition to offering firms the opportunity to develop ownership advantages stemming from operating in an enlarged market with improving efficiency (UNCTC, 1990; Bende-Nabende, 1999).

East Asian Production Networks

While the following section gives considerable attention to Japanese auto sector production networks in East Asia we should also be cognizant of the fact that a number of alternative models exist. It is useful to consider these from two perspectives: industrial sector and national, or at least ethnic-group, features.

As noted above, modern production techniques and a fiercely competitive market environment have led to the fragmentation of production for some products. A clear illustration of this is found in the consumer electronics sector. Global competition together with ever shortening product life cycles among other pressures has meant that reducing production costs is of paramount concern, as suggested by Vernon's (1966) theorizing. In practice this has meant that electronics firms have employed a number of strategies to reduce production costs including the redesign of production processes to allow for more (neo-) Fordist style assembly in those countries with low labour costs while retaining core technology and research and design capacity at home. In other words, the nature of the product itself creates a rationale for the construction of production networks. Borrus et al. (2000)[17] identify a range of electronics production networks in Asia that take advantage of this feature and that exhibit a diverse typology within just this one sector.

In addition to Japanese production networks further examples can be seen in the operations of the Korean *chaebol*,[18] Taiwanese and Singaporean firms (particularly in the electronics sector) and the Chinese ethnic business networks (CEBNs) (which can be far more diverse). Formal analysis of the CEBNs is challenging given their diverse, personal, and informal nature yet it is becoming clear that such groups are playing an increasingly important role in East Asian production. Peng notes that CEBNs consist of core and periphery firms where founding family members assume leading managerial positions (Peng, 2002). They are able to utilize informal information networks among Chinese business communities throughout the region including mainland China, and transcend many political and bureaucratic barriers faced by more traditional TNCs.

Given the fast paced nature of the East Asian economy, the emergence of new network models, perhaps more closely integrated with the mainland Chinese economy, and the restructuring of existing networks are inevitable. However, our attention now turns to consider an extensive and long-standing model of networked production found in the Japanese auto sector in East Asia. This example serves to illustrate the interaction between regionalism and regionalization while also highlighting the particular characteristics of production networks in the second major industrial sector.

Japanese Automaker Production Networks In East Asia

Japanese automakers have established a dominant position in East Asia both in terms of number of units produced and total sales. This is particularly true in ASEAN economies although it should be noted that this is not the case with regard to Korea where indigenous firms dominate. A combination of historical, geographical, and market factors explain this situation. Local demand was originally met through exports and local assembly of knock-down kits[19] exported from Japan. This is a common feature in the auto sector where the development of local production capacity can take years to achieve and is even more challenging in developing economies. However, increasing demands by host governments for localization throughout the 1980s forced Japanese firms to develop local production capacity. This was restrained not least by the relatively small scale of national markets and, in an industry where minimum scale economies are achieved with the production of 150,000 plus units, a rationale emerged for the development of regional networked capacity.[20] In other words, by organizing production on a regional scale, Japanese auto firms were able to compensate for locational *disadvantages*. Attempts by ASEAN governments to counter these scale economy issues centred on facilitating intra-ASEAN trade in components and a number of schemes emerged over the years.[21] Yet national priorities consistently trumped regional development and until the late 1990s most schemes had only a limited effect. By 1997, then, auto production in ASEAN was still labouring under fragmented national policies and priorities although the investment environment was certainly more conducive than in previous years as governments in the region increasingly switched from local content requirements and tight regulation of inward investment (local equity stakes, for example) to active promotion of FDI and liberalization. Figure 4.2 shows Toyota's regional production network in terms of AICO (intra-company component trade) agreements.

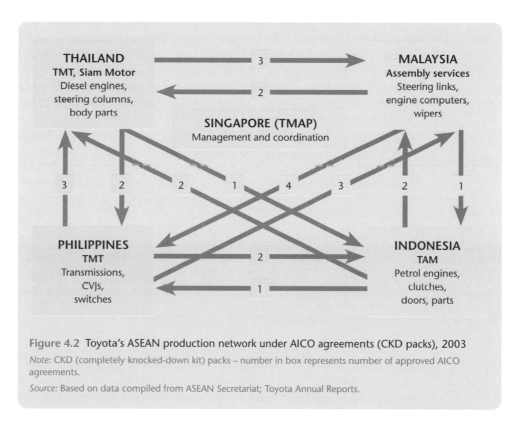

Figure 4.2 Toyota's ASEAN production network under AICO agreements (CKD packs), 2003

Note: CKD (completely knocked-down kit) packs – number in box represents number of approved AICO agreements.

Source: Based on data compiled from ASEAN Secretariat; Toyota Annual Reports.

A decisive moment came with the Asian financial crisis which had an immediate and negative impact on the region in general and more specifically on the production and sales of autos. While currencies and economies crashed Japanese automakers found themselves with excess capacity, a severe drop in demand, and increasingly expensive Japan-based supply chains. Paradoxically, the crisis is now regarded as having acted as a catalyst for the transformation of the regional economy and auto sector which has bounced back with surprising resilience. Table 4.3 documents the most significant responses to the crisis by Japanese automakers.

Table 4.3 Immediate responses to the Asian financial crisis

Issue	Response
Market orientation	From domestic to export
Excess capacity	Suspension of operations Retooling Rapid expansion of exports
Excess human resources	Increased training in country and Japan Reduction of shifts
Crisis hit affiliates	Increase equity stake
Network	Maintain

Perhaps more important, though, are the deeper responses to the crisis that continue to shape markets and structures today. Member states, for instance, agreed to accelerate AFTA implementation which limits tariffs to 0–5 per cent between member economies, with a later lead-in time for newer member states. This formalized a single, regional market and allowed Japanese automakers to both rationalize and reorganize their regional production networks. Freed of the implicit expectation that trade in components and kits should balance between member states, firms were instead able to organize networks on the basis of economic and market factors, rather than political expediency. Second, a clear push towards localization has taken place that is reflected in the establishment of not only regional management headquarters but also research and design facilities and the development of regional models or Asian cars. Toyota has also established a global production centre in Thailand that acts as a regional node for personnel training and development in a move designed to localize operational management further and to ensure consistent quality. In this way, regional production networks have expanded in terms of breadth and depth as illustrated in Table 4.4.

Table 4.4 Toyota's business activities in ASEAN 5 and China, 2005

Indonesia	Malaysia	Philippines	Singapore	Thailand	China
◎○△▲	◎○△▲	◎○△▲	★○	☆◎○△▲◆	☆◎○△▲□

KEY: ★ Headquarters, ☆ R&D centre, ◎ Production sites through FDI, ○ Sales office, △ Parts production site, ▲ Parts export hub, ◆ Vehicle export hub, □ Production site with technical collaboration
Source: Adapted from Toyota Annual Reports (various years); FOURIN Inc. (various years).

Additionally, the relationship between firm and state has experienced a significant shift. As noted above the investment environment greatly improved due to changing attitudes towards inward investment. More specifically in Thailand this led to tax exemption on imported machinery, a repeal of local content requirements, the granting of majority stakes in joint ventures and a reduction in corporate tax. The bargaining power of firms also increased in more subtle ways. Toyota, for instance, was able to secure a lower tax rate for its double-cab Hilux pickup truck, which would normally have attracted a much higher sports utility vehicle (SUV) rate, by suggesting that it would refrain from making a previously advertised huge investment in new production plant. Moreover, it was able to secure from the Thai government tax incentives which reduced the cost of the investment by 30 per cent. This issue of bargaining power and asymmetric power relations is returned to in the final section below.

A decade after the crisis tore through the region, the auto industry in Southeast Asia – and the Japanese regional production network in particular – appears to be in a strong and competitive position. Thailand, which has emerged as the regional hub for the industry, is a particular beneficiary. From the regional perspective, competitive pressures continue to exist, not least from the rapid expansion of Chinese auto production, but from the perspective of the Japanese firm, East Asia is a welcome asset.

SUMMARY POINTS

- Production networks in East Asia have been shaped by the experience of economic development.

- Regionalization of production has led more recently to regionalist projects, which have considerable implications for production networks.

- The electronics sector appears to be particularly suited to networked production.

- A number of national production network 'models' exist within the region.

IMPLICATIONS, ISSUES AND DEBATES

Two themes emerge from this investigation into regionalized production in East Asia. The first concerns the issue of economic development and industrial upgrading while the second identifies the relationship between firm and state. These two issues are not unrelated, reflecting the symbiotic nature of regionalization and regionalism as discussed above.

Development

Earlier investigations into Japanese production networks in East Asia focused on whether Japan was regionalizing its relational form of capitalism, and locking developing countries in its embrace in the process (Hatch and Yamamura, 1996; Hatch, 2001), or facilitating a sequential, Japan-led model of development premised on the implicitly developmental nature (export-oriented, based on comparative advantage) of Japanese FDI (Kojima, 2000). A full decade after the Asian financial crisis and the subsequent transformation of the East Asian political economy, further comment on these two perspectives is now warranted. First, a degree of tension will always be present where a firm wishes to exploit its firm-specific advantages for economic gain by 'exploiting' (utilizing) locational advantages and a state desires technology transfer for economic development. Earlier attempts to force auto sector (Japanese) firms to localize in East Asia failed due to lack of scale economies, the nature of the industry insofar that quality takes time to develop, and the limited capacity of host economies to absorb technology and knowledge. Yet, with the implementation of market opening and investment friendly policies, a commitment to the development of regional markets and a willingness to concede foreign ownership of the auto sector, Thailand has surged ahead of its neighbours in the development of the auto sector. This is not to suggest vindication of the flying geese model which is clearly of limited relevance in the 21st century. And at the same time this is not to negate some of the concerns espoused by the 'embraced development' theory, particularly where they relate to state–firm bargaining positions (see below). Rather, it is suggested that the focus should be on regional as opposed to national development. Coe et al. note that regional development can be conceptualized 'as a dynamic outcome of the complex interaction between territorialized relational networks and global production networks within the context of changing regional governance structures' (Coe et al., 2004: 469). Development, they go on to suggest occurs when there is a strategic fit between the needs of the global production network and regional assets. In this contemporary era of globalization and regionalism looking to this dynamic will lead us (and policymakers) to a better understanding of regional development than perhaps has been the case before.

State–Firm Relationships

As noted above, by appearing to withhold final decisions on investment and production plans Toyota was able to secure from the Thai authorities a favourable outcome in terms of tax valuation and investment incentives. What does this say about the state's power to dictate terms to TNCs? It is important to note that this is not an issue just for developing economies. The UK government in the 1980s made considerable concessions to foreign TNCs, Japanese automakers included, to secure their investments. These issues were revisited when the UK opted to remain out of the Euro. At the same time, it must also be noted that the UK received by far the largest share of Japanese FDI directed at Europe in the 1980s and 1990s and that the UK economy benefits from the presence of highly productive, largely export-oriented factories owned by Toyota, Honda and Nissan. The question thus emerges; does ownership matter? Perhaps more important than the ability to dictate terms is the capacity to attract, retain and benefit from inward investment. In other words, if the goal of the state is economic development then perhaps a better focus of attention would be the strengthening of structures designed to do this, education being chief among them.

Further Considerations

Finally, this chapter has focused on Japanese production networks in the auto sector and it should be pointed out that this is just one organizational form in one industrial sector. We have also only focused on one Japanese automaker and have not considered those in strategic partnerships with, or under the control of, foreign firms (Mazda, Nissan, and Suzuki). This can be explained with reference to the size and the extent of Toyota's presence in the region but it is also important to note that, as in the electronics sector, a range of organizational forms will always be present. In many ways the electronics sector, given the nature of its products, is far more fragmented and thus offers examples of much more complex regional networks than exist in the auto sector. Textile manufacturing, including clothes and footwear, is also a further candidate for investigation. Finally, in an attempt to develop further an understanding of regionalized production networks in East Asia, the reader is invited to consider the possible emergence of Indian networks.

CHAPTER SUMMARY

■ The complex nature of contemporary international production necessitates the development of better analytical tools, including a focus on the value chain and production network rather than the individual firm.

- Globalization has led to a fragmentation of the value chain and the emergence of global production networks which reflect increasingly elaborate geographical and organizational structures.
- East Asia as an economic entity is distinct from those found elsewhere due to its particular experience of development.
- Japanese firms have played a central role in 'networking' the region.
- Japanese automakers have regionalized production in Southeast Asia in response to national policies and are rationalizing them in response to regional polices.
- Analysing the strategic coupling of the regional production network and regional assets can offer insights into the role of the firm in economic development.

KEY CONCEPTS

Foreign direct investment: Where firms invest overseas and retain some degree of managerial control.

The eclectic paradigm: An analytical tool used to identify the reasons for the overseas activities of a firm.

Organizational structure: A firm's internal managerial architecture

Production networks: 'A set of inter-firm relationships that bind a group of firms into a larger economic unit' (Sturgeon, 2001: 2).

Value chain: 'The sequence of productive (that is, value added) activities leading to and supporting end-use' (Sturgeon, 2001: 2).

Keiretsu: A Japanese term denoting a networked or relational group of firms.

Regionalization: Some degree of economic integration in a defined regional space.

Regionalism: A political process that seeks to more closely integrate a defined regional space.

REVIEW QUESTIONS

1. In this chapter we have focused on the automotive industry. How might regional production networks differ in other industrial sectors? In other words, how far does the nature of the product determine the degree to which production can be regionalized?
2. How have the nature and experience of East Asian economic development shaped the regional organization of production?
3. In addition to Japanese firms, what other national models can be identified?

ACTIVITIES AND DISCUSSIONS

1. Select a major TNC in an important industrial sector (electronics or auto manufacture) and use the company website and other resources to build up a picture of its overseas production networks.
2. Use the WTO web page to identify regional trade agreements and consider how these impact on the production strategies of TNCs.

Toyota has moved to link a regionalized production network with global markets and in doing so has achieved a degree of localization previously unseen in emerging markets.

TOYOTA'S INNOVATIVE INTERNATIONAL MULTIPURPOSE VEHICLE (IMV) PROJECT

Although planning for the IMV project began in 1999 soon after the Asian financial crisis, its genesis is not solely attributable to this event. Sales of the Hilux pickup truck had been steadily declining in Japan, Toyota was (and remains) committed to increasing overseas production, and a strategic decision was taken to design affordable yet high quality pickup trucks and multipurpose vehicles (MPVs) for growth markets, mainly in emerging economies including East Asia. This was further compatible with the overall strategy of increasing Toyota's global market share of auto production and sales. The crisis did, however, force a critical re-evaluation of Toyota's traditional strategy of local assembly using components, particularly more complex intermediate products such as engines, from Japan. Toyota's leitmotif is *kaizen* and consistent quality and this explains why the company had been initially reluctant to relocate overseas from Japan the highly efficient production capacity which had been built up over decades. The challenges associated with replicating the Japanese model overseas are well documented (Abo, 2007) and are magnified in developing economies, such as those found in Southeast Asia. Moreover, Toyota's application of lean manufacturing is dependent on closely coordinated supplier networks. Yet the collapse of regional economies and the drop in the value of the Thai baht in particular, presented an urgent economic rationale to increase localization of component sourcing. Additionally, the previous model

of offloading older models in developing economies was coming under pressure from competitors, particularly Korean firms. The challenge, therefore, was twofold; to offer attractive models utilizing the latest technology but still suitable for developing economies, and to do so while maintaining a competitive price. Toyota's response to this is found in the IMV project, the stated aim of which is to 'realise global optimal production and supply networks' (Toyota *Annual Report*, 2003).

IMV vehicles, of which there are five models with three body styles (pickup, SUV and MPV), share a common platform, which reduces design and production costs and is becoming a common feature in auto production. This platform is also specifically designed for the sometimes challenging driving environments found in developing economies. The choice of these models reflects diverse consumer demand in developing countries. Thailand, for instance, is the world's second largest market for one ton pickups while Indonesian consumers prefer the MPV style. The IMV vehicles also act as entry level models which familiarize consumers in emerging economies with Toyota's competitive strengths, and the intention is that these consumers will be favourably disposed towards Toyota's mainstay sedans as middle classes expand and consumer tastes become more sophisticated. A similar line of reasoning can be identified at Honda with regard to power products (generators, outboard engines, agricultural tools) and motorcycles.

Production is centred on Toyota's Thai and Indonesian plants but assembly also takes place in Argentina and South Africa. Crucially, all production occurs outside of Japan and localization rates are high, reportedly 97 per cent in Thailand, which means that production does not have to rely on components sourced, expensively, from Japan. This is where the ASEAN advantages comes into play as Toyota, along with other Japanese automakers, has been developing supplier networks on a regional basis for the past two decades. It is this historical investment and development of local suppliers that allows Toyota to realize the advantages of low-cost labour while maintaining quality. Due to intense scrutiny of the supply chain and high localization rates, cost savings are reported to be around 30 per cent, allowing Toyota to compete therefore both on

cost and quality. Yet operating in emerging economies can also bring associated risks, particularly with regard to disruption of the supply chain. To mitigate this, Toyota has built in some flexibility to the demands of just-in-time production by requiring plants to maintain a two-week supply of components on site. The initial production target at the project's launch in 2002 was for 500,000 units with Thailand as the key player allocated an annual target of 280,000 units of which 140,000 were designated for export markets. The Thai plant further produces and exports diesel engines. However strong demand following commencement of the production line in 2004 saw the overall target for the project revised upwards to 700,000 units. By comparison, Toyota's total consolidated production in 2006 was approximately 8 million units.

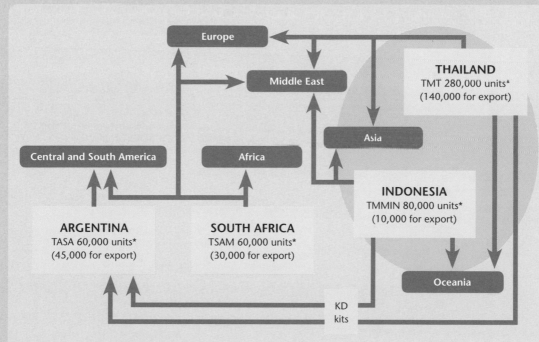

Figure 4.3 The IMV supply network

*Note *Annual production capacity*

Source: Adapted from Toyota promotional material, 2003.

IMV production is also supported by the presence of Toyota's regional HQ, Toyota Motor Asia-Pacific (TMAP), in Singapore (established in 2001) which is 100 per cent owned by TMC. In contrast to the more straightforward activities of regional management structures in North America and Europe, Toyota's organization in East Asia has emerged from the necessity of dealing with the complex nature of the regional division of labour and of a need for better coordination of supply chains and parts complementation under AFTA. Additionally, the establishment of a global production centre (an advanced, globally integrated training facility) in Thailand in 2003 supports the development of human resources in the region, further facilitating localization while maintaining quality. Finally, Toyota established its first R&D centre in an emerging economy, Thailand, in 2005 further underlining its commitment to localization of design.

The IMV project thus represents an innovative response to competitive global markets and localized demand. By drawing on an existing Southeast Asian regional production network and production and assembly facilities in other emerging economies, Toyota is successfully linking spatial scale and organizational structure. This has been facilitated by localization of production, investing in the development of regional supply chains, a commitment to local staff, and regional management. Given the surging demand for IMV models the IMV project can be regarded as a successful model of global/regional production organization.

Table 4.5 Main IMV production bases and projected unit production at launch

Country	Affiliate	Production vehicle	Start of production	Annual production	Export destination
Thailand	TMT	Pickup truck (Hilux VIGO)	2004	280,000 units (including 140,000 units for export)	Europe, Asia, Oceania,
		Sports utility vehicle	2005		The Middle East
Indonesia	TMMIN	Minivan	2004	80,000 units (including 10,000 units for export)	Asia, the Middle East
South Africa	TSAM	Pickup truck	2005	60,000 units (including 30,000 units for export)	Europe, Africa, etc.
		Sports utility vehicle	2005		
Argentina	TASA	Pickup truck	2005	60,000 units (including 45,000 units for export)	Latin America
		Sports utility vehicle	2005		

Notes: TMT: Toyota Motor Thailand Co., Ltd; TMMIN: PT. Toyota Motor Manufacturing Indonesia; TSAM: Toyota South Africa Motors (Pty) Ltd; TASA: Toyota Argentina S.A.
Source: Toyota promotional materials.

QUESTIONS

1. Is it possible to understand the IMV project with reference to the theoretical models and perspectives outlined earlier in the chapter?

2. Toyota has hedged against disruption of the supply chain by building in a degree of inventory, which is in contrast to the norm of eliminating waste found in Toyota's Japanese, North American and European facilities. What other risk factors are present with the management of a regionally constructed and globally linked production structure?

3. Given Toyota's close coordination of the value chain, in particular its relations with component suppliers, and commitment to localization, is this a model that other (Western and Japanese) automakers can emulate?

INTERESTING WEB LINKS

Toyota Motor Corporation: http://www.toyota.co.jp/en/index.html
Toyota's IMV project: http://www.toyota.co.jp/en/strategy/imv/index.html
International business resource site: http://globaledge.msu.edu/about_globaledge.asp
World Investment Report: http://www.unctad.org
World Trade Organization (Regional Trade Agreement Gateway): http://www.wto.org/english/tratop_e/region_e/region_e.htm
Global production networks research group at the University of Manchester, UK: http://www.sed.manchester.ac.uk/geography/research/gpn/

Notes

1   The transnational corporation (TNC) is used here rather than the traditional multinational enterprise (MNE) or corporation (MNC) to more accurately reflect the transnational (*across or between* nations) aspect of their operations.

2   Neo-liberal ideology is taken in this context to refer to the pursuance of free-enterprise liberalism characterized by, for instance, deregulated markets, declining state involvement in economic activity through the privatization of national assets, and a commitment to global trade liberalization.

3   Regionalization is understood here as the deepening of regional economic integration while regionalism refers to a more political process.

4   Orwell's *1984* envisaged three global super-states (Eastasia, Eurasia and Oceania) in perpetual economic competition and military conflict.

5   Rugman suggests that of the world's 500 largest TNCs, which account for 90 per cent of the world's stock in FDI and over half of world trade, only 9 can be categorized as truly global and that the vast majority (320) 'are home region based and derive an average of 80% of their sales inter-regionally' (Rugman, 2005: 224).

6   Most recently at the WTO's HQ in Geneva, July 2008 where Peter Mandelson, at that time the EU's Trade Commissioner, described the collapse of negotiations as a 'collective failure'.

7   See Key Concepts for a fuller explanation of this term.

8   Portfolio investment refers to the electronic movement of highly liquid capital for investment. Fund managers in one country may decide to invest capital in a foreign country on behalf of the investors and this process plays a vital function in capital formation. However, such funds are also seen as highly volatile and prone to herd-like behaviour and for this reason have been variously described

as 'hot' or 'mad' money. The East Asian financial crisis of 1997–98, for instance, was precipitated by massive outflows of portfolio investments from developing economies.

9   Firm-based models (see in particular Hymer, 1976) seek to identify the specific advantages (brand, technology, management) that firms hold which allow them to compensate for the presumed cost of foreignness, while trade and location analysis (see in particular Vernon, 1966) links the product life cycle with the location of production. Internalization approaches (Buckley and Casson, 1976) stem from transaction cost economics (that is, the cost involved of making an exchange) and suggest that FDI is inevitable where a firm seeks to internalize its activities as opposed to operating through licensing or subcontracting.

10 Akamatsu conceptualized economies as geese flying (*gankou keitai*) in Japanese in an inverted 'V' formation. In the original analogy Western economies, particularly the UK and the US, were the lead geese and through interaction with these economies Japan, as a following or 'catch-up' economy experienced a sequential process of economic development. This process included the progression through industrial sectors, and the shift from imports to domestic production and finally exports. In a further extension of the model exports are replaced by overseas production.

11 See in particular Hatch and Yamamura (1996) who criticize Japanese FDI as 'embracing' developing nations which leads to a form of dependency on Japanese firms, capital and technology. It should also be noted that some economies, notably Korea and more recently China, have resisted this form of investment from Japan in pursuit of their own models of economic development.

12 Organizational structure or architecture refers to the way in which a firm, or indeed group of firms, is internally organized and managed.

13 For a fuller explanation of this model, see Gereffi et al., 2005.

14 For a fuller explanation of the network flagship model see in particular Ernst, 2001.

15 A conglomerate is defined here as a corporation consisting of a number of different companies operating in a variety of fields.

16 The World Bank report points out that 'the diversity of experience, the variety of institutions, the great variation in policies among the high-performing Asian economies means that there is no East Asian model of rapid growth with equity. Rather, each of the eight economies we studied used various combinations of policies at different times to perform the functions needed for rapid growth' (World Bank, 1993: 366).

17 Borrus et al. identify five national networks (US, Japan, Taiwan, Korea, Singapore) and seven characteristics (product mix, accessibility, permanence, ability to adjust to market/technical shifts, governance, supply base preference, and exploitation of intra-Asian value-added). US firms are seen as centring on sophisticated products, are open, fluid, fast paced, decentralized, cost based and able to maximize local value-added. Singaporean firms, on the other hand, focus on particular products (PC electronics), are open, long term in nature, moderately able to react to change, centralized, utilizing local Chinese suppliers and able to maximize high domestic and low local Asian value-added.

18 The term *chaebol* refers to large Korean conglomerates including Samsung, Hyundai and LG. They are often compared with the Japanese *keiretsu* but share more similarities with the pre-war *zaibatsu* where family ownership and control was more common.

19 Localization of auto assembly and production proceeds from the import and assembly of completely knocked down (CKD) kits to semi-knocked down (KD) kits and then through limited local production to complete local production. CKD assembly commenced in Thailand in the 1960s, moved into the KD stage in the 1970s and 1980s and achieved local production in the 1990s. Complete local production is the current goal for most Japanese automakers (see also Yamashita, 1998: 61–79).

20 Toyota, for example, was producing the Corolla sedan in small numbers in five different countries.

21 The ASEAN Industrial Complementation Scheme (AIC) in 1981, Brand to Brand Complementation (BBC) in 1988, ASEAN Industrial Cooperation (AICO) in 1996 and the Common Effective Preferential

Tariff Scheme (CEPT) which was superseded by the establishment of the ASEAN Free Trade Area (AFTA) in 2003, although Malaysia delayed full implementation of this scheme in an attempt to protect its ailing national car projects.

REFERENCES

Abo, T. (2007). *Japanese Hybrid Factories: A Worldwide Comparison of Global Production Strategies.* Basingstoke: Palgrave Macmillan.

Akamatsu, K. (1962). A historical pattern of economic growth in developing countries. *The Developing Economies,* **1**(1): 3–25.

Bende-Nabende, A. (1999). *FDI, Regionalism, Government Policy and Endogenous Growth: A Comparative Study of the ASEAN-5 Economies, with Development Policy Implications for the Least Developed Countries.* Aldershot: Ashgate.

Borrus, M., Ernst, D. and Haggard, S. (2000) *International Production Networks in Asia: Rivalry or Riches.* London: Routledge.

Buckley, P.J. and Casson, M.C. (1976). *The Future of the Multinational Enterprise.* London: Homes and Meier.

Coe, N., Hess, M., Yeung, H., Dicken, P. and Henderson, J. (2004). Globalizing regional development: A global production networks perspective. *Transactions of the Institute of British Geographers,* **29**(4): 468–84.

Dicken, P. (2003). *Global Shift: Reshaping the Global Economic Map in the 21st Century.* London: Sage.

Dunning, J.H. (1977). Trade, location of economic activity and the MNE: A search for an eclectic approach. In Bertil, O. et al., (eds) *The International Allocation of Economic Activity, Proceeding of Noble Symposium.* London: Macmillan – now Palgrave Macmillan.

Dunning, J.H. (1987). The eclectic paradigm of international production: A restatement and some possible extension. *Journal of International Business Studies,* **19**: 1–31.

Ernst, D. (2001). Global production networks and industrial upgrading – A knowledge centered approach. Hawaii: East–West Center Working Papers, Economic Series (25).

Fourin, Inc. (Various). *Asian Automotive Review.* Japan: Fourin, Inc.

Gereffi, G., Humphrey, J. and Sturgeon, T. (2005). The governance of global value chains. *Review of International Political Economy,* **12**(1): 78–104.

Gilson, J. (2004). Complex regional multilateralism: 'Strategising' Japan's responses to Southeast Asia. *The Pacific Review,* **17**(1): 71–94.

Hatch, W. (2001). Regionalizing relationism: Japanese production networks in Asia. *MIT Japan Program Working Paper 01-07.* Cambridge, MA: MIT.

Hatch, W. and Yamamura, K. (1996). *Asia in Japan's Embrace.* Cambridge: Cambridge University Press.

Henderson, J., Dicken, P., Hess, M., Coe, N. and Yeung, H. (2002). Global production networks and the analysis of economic development. *Review of International Political Economy,* **9**(3): 436–64.

Hymer, S.H. (1976). *The International Operations of National Firms: A Study of Direct Foreign Investment.* Cambridge, MA and London: MIT Press.

Jomo, K. (2003). Reforming East Asia for sustainable development. *Asian Business & Management,* **2**(1): 7–38.

Kojima, K. (2000). The 'flying geese' model of Asian economic development: Origin, theoretical extensions and regional policy implications. *Journal of Asian Economics,* **11**: 375–401.

Kojima, K. and Ozawa, T. (1984). Micro- and macro-economic models of direct foreign investment: Toward a synthesis. *Hitotsubashi Journal of Economics,* **25**(1): 1–20.

Mudambi, R. (2002). The location decision of the multinational enterprise. In McCann, P. (ed.) *Industrial Location Economics.* Cheltenham: Edward Elgar.

Orwell, G. (1950). *1984*. Signet Classics. New York: Penguin, USA.

Peng, D. (2002). Invisible linkages: A regional perspective of the East Asian political economy. *International Studies Quarterly*, **46**: 423–47.

Rugman, A. (2005). *The Regional Multinationals: MNEs and 'Global' Strategic Management*. Cambridge: Cambridge University Press.

Staples, A. (2006). Japanese foreign direct investment and the transformation of the East Asian political economy: Corporate strategy in the automotive sector. In Soderman, S. (ed.) *Emerging Multiplicity: Integration and Responsiveness in Asian Business Development*. Basingstoke: Palgrave Macmillan.

Sturgeon, Y. (2001). *How do we define value chains and production networks?* MIT Industrial Performance Center.

Thompson, G. (ed.) (1998). *Economic Dynamism in the Asia-Pacific*. New York and London: Routledge.

Toyota (Various). *Annual Report*. Nagoya: Toyota.

UNCTC (1990). *Regional Economic Integration and Transnational Corporations in the 1990s: Europe, North American, and Developing Countries*. New York: United Nations.

Vernon, R. (1966). International investment and international trade in the product cycle. *Quarterly Journal of Economics*, **80**: 190–207.

World Bank (1993). *The East Asian Miracle*. Oxford: Oxford University Press.

Yamashita, S. (1998). Japanese investment strategy and technology transfer in East Asia. In Hasegawa, H. and Hook, G.D. (eds.) *Japanese Business Management: Restructuring for Low Growth and Globalization*. London and New York: Routledge.

Chapter outline

- The importance of cross-cultural understanding
- Asian cultures and management practices
- Major theories and perspectives
- Asian cultures, ethics and social responsibility
- Asian values and culture

Chapter objectives

After reading this chapter, you should be able to:

1. Understand the importance of cultural influence on management
2. Identify the major theories of values and culture
3. Identify the leading Asian cultural traits
4. Identify the major Asian management styles
5. Understand how Asian businesses use culture to create advantage
6. Understand the Asian views on ethics and social responsibility

Chapter 5

Culture and business in Asia

Carlos Noronha

INTRODUCTION

Rapid globalization has increased the volume of international trade. Take the case of China as an example. According to *The Economist* (2007), in the beginning, China's developing neighbours were worried that global foreign direct investment would all divert to China with her ascension into the World Trade Organization (WTO) in 2001. However, it turned out that it was actually an 'all-win' situation. Certainly, with her WTO membership, China became the world's third largest exporter in 2004.[1] But at the same time, foreign investment in the ten ASEAN countries had also significantly increased to a record US$37 billion in 2005. With China joining the WTO, this juggernaut export machine has actually drawn together many manufacturers in Thailand, Malaysia, Singapore, the Philippines, Indonesia, South Korea and Taiwan, creating a pan-Asia production network. As a result, trade within East Asia has grown at a much faster pace than the region's trade with the rest of the world. Even highly developed Japan has benefited from China's WTO membership as Japan imports a lot of goods from China and invests heavily in manufacturing plants in various parts of the mainland.

Like the case of China, we know that globalization is bringing more and more people from different parts of Asia and the world together. In order to succeed in this global arena, it is necessary to have a good understanding of different cultures. International business today demands multicultural interaction, multicultural understanding and multicultural communication. Conventional Western perspectives often view cultural differences in terms of an 'East–West' contrast. In fact, scholars in areas such as sociology or cultural anthropology have already pointed out that cultural differences should not be viewed as a polarized system. Rather, we should take the stance of culture being on a continuum. Just as US Americans may find it a tricky thing to negotiate business deals with the Japanese, the same may also be felt by the Chinese, the Indians or the Thais. Similarly, the Japanese may also find it difficult when dealing with the Chinese, the Indians or the Thais. Although some cultures may share certain common traits, every culture has its own uniqueness. Hence the polarized view is too simplistic.

This chapter has two broad aims. The first is to introduce to the reader the main theories of culture. The second is to present a consortium of Asian cultural systems, each with different characteristics and value orientations. Therefore, when these cultural systems interact with the respective management practices, different types of Asian management styles emerge. Understanding them is essential for conducting successful cross-cultural business.

THE IMPORTANCE OF CROSS-CULTURAL UNDERSTANDING

We will approach this issue by first looking at two real life examples.

International Enterprise (IE) Singapore[2] is a consulting firm which helps Singapore-based SMEs identify niche areas that they can enter in Japan and South Korea. These markets are often considered to be relatively 'closed' to outsiders. Winston Ho, IE Singapore's regional director commented that Singaporean companies, apart from having globally competitive products or services, must also invest considerable time and financial resources in order to succeed in these two countries. Ho pointed out that while Japan and South Korea may share some similarities, there are also key differences affecting the conduct of business. For example, due to historical and geographical reasons, Japan has strong 'dual characteristics'. On the one hand, owing to its unique culture, Japan has a natural tendency to be insular. Yet it is very much influenced by Chinese and Western technologies and practices. Therefore, Japan has been gradually opening more and more to foreign investments but in terms of the use of English as a business language, Japan is still lagging behind. Ho therefore advised Singaporean companies to invest in developing Japanese language capabilities since proficiency in Japanese may mean faster development of trust and smoother and more effective interactions. On the other hand, while South Korea is a close-knit society, it is not inward looking. The Koreans are quite receptive to foreign matters. Nevertheless, Ho advised that understanding Korean culture is the key to business success. Doing business in Korea requires a lot of patience to build up relationships. For example, the Singaporeans often like to boast of their 'Asian outlook with Western inner trait'. They are accustomed to a more rational approach. However, the Koreans place a premium on relationships because of their communal nature. Business deals are often concluded through establishing networks rather than employing fact-based marketing.

Ho also pointed out that due to their island culture, Japan has a tendency to be inward looking. The society and the corporate system are highly structured. Therefore the Singaporeans, who are accustomed to fast-paced decision making, may find it daunting in Japan where decisions are made relatively more slowly due to the multi-tier structure of Japanese corporations. Also, a lot of time has to be invested in building mutual trust. Similarly, he also advised Singaporean companies to take a long-term approach in dealing with Korean companies, since they place great emphasis on relationship building.

The above example clearly shows that culture influences business deals and how cultural awareness can possibly affect their success or failure. Imagine if Singaporean companies were to enter the Japanese and Korean markets without any cultural consciousness or sensitivity, bringing into these foreign soils their famous quick, rational and fact-based management style, what likelihood of success would one expect? While differences in culture can affect business activities, what about similarities in cultural values? Will this bring advantage and facilitate business dealings? Let us take a look at another example.

Due to increasingly tough international competition, especially challenges from the West, more and more Japanese companies are turning to South Korean, Taiwanese and other Asian companies to form partnerships. In early 2007, Nippon Oil Corporation[3] formed a partnership with South Korea's largest oil company, SK Corporation. By jointly developing energy resources, transporting crude oil and supplying each other with products, the partners enjoyed immediate benefits such as lower distribution costs and eventual opportunities to construct infrastructure together. Through this collaboration, the two companies will have a better chance to compete with major US and European oil companies. The synergistic effect in terms of information gathering, human network and political exposure will also enable the partners to take up more risk. But how do the two achieve such a synergistic effect?

Apart from hard structural factors, cultural aspects are also very important. Shinji Nishio, President of Nippon Oil, claimed in a press conference that SK Corporation is his company's 'best partner' and he ascribed this to the similarities in terms of scale, operations and culture of the two companies. Although Japan and Korea are two separate nations, due to historical reasons they share certain fundamental cultural values. Their hierarchical social structure and the influence of Buddhism and Confucianism may all have a similar effect on the way they operate their businesses. Similarities in cultural values can, to a certain extent, bring synergy. Other successful marriages can be seen in other industries. For example, Nippon Steel Industry and Posco of South Korea have tied up in order to thwart possible takeover attempts. And there are other success stories: cultural similarities are often attributed as important.

From the examples above, we can see that a strong awareness of culture, especially others' cultures, is vital to successful international business. This awareness of others' cultures can be better elaborated by introducing the emic–etic analysis originally derived from phonemics and phonetics.[4] Borrowing Berry's (1990) approach, when we view our own culture or others' cultures, we can identify three distinct phases. Although Berry's description of the concept was used to explain how cross-cultural researchers approach different cultures, we can similarly apply it to our case of cross-cultural business dealings. The first step is when one begins to analyse one's own culture from one's own point of view. This phase is known as imposed etic. At this phase, one takes everything for granted. Any culture is interpreted in 'my way'. We may call this view 'myopic'. If our cross-cultural business negotiator takes an imposed-etic approach, it means that there is very low cultural awareness. Culture shock and conflict are likely to take place and there is a slim chance of succeeding in business relationships. This is like our previous example of Singaporean companies entering the Japanese and Korean markets, bringing with them directly the Singaporean style of doing business. In the second phase, one starts to explore and appreciate the emics of a culture, that is, the specificities or principles that pertain only to that particular culture. In the third stage, one begins to compare the etics and the emics and finds commonalities between, say, two cultures. At this point, one no longer looks at others' cultures from one's own viewpoint. If our cross-cultural business negotiator takes this so-called derived etic view on others' cultures, there will be a high level of cultural awareness and sensitivity. Appropriate measures to prevent cultural conflicts and to accommodate cultural differences will be taken. Therefore, there is a much higher chance of succeeding in cross-cultural business ventures.

Some people use the contrast of ethnocentrism[5] versus polycentrism to describe a similar difference in cultural viewpoints. The ethnocentric approach is similar to the imposed etic viewpoint in that any culture is viewed in terms of one's own culture. There is little flexibility and tolerance for foreign cultures. This is often due to an assumption that one's own culture or ethnic group is superior to others. Whether this assumption is right or wrong is not the issue here but when it comes to cross-cultural business relationships, the ethnocentric approach appears to be incompatible. On the other hand, the polycentric approach is much more open. There is willingness to accept, understand and appreciate foreign cultures. Needless to say, this is the kind of attitude we need in cross-cultural business operations.

So far, we have been describing how people view cultures. However, when these viewpoints actually consolidate into cultural interactions, we are talking about how people or systems of different cultures fuse together to create new entities. We call them hybrids. Following a 'derived etic' approach, when two cultures interact, there can be three possible outcomes. The first is when there is high universality, that is to say, the two cultures have many commonalities. In hybridization theory, we call this a 'low diversity hybrid'. Thus, like in our example of Nippon Oil and SK Corporation, a successful merger takes place. However, it is possible for two cultures to result in a 'middle diversity hybrid' or a 'high diversity hybrid'. Then it will depend on how the two partners make use of the advantageous sides of both cultures to successfully create a new system. In any case, cultural sensitivity is very important. Abo (2007) and his colleagues studied Japanese manufacturers operating overseas since the mid-1980s. They agree that culture, determined by historical and social traits, is an undeniable element in shaping the qualitative nature of organizations which characterize the Japanese management system. Therefore, when an attempt is made to transfer the Japanese management system abroad, certain modifications will inevitably be made due to cultural discrepancies, resulting in what they call 'Japanese hybrid factories' all over the world. There is no need to mention that these hybrid factories have been producing products such as automobile, electrical and electronic products of the highest quality and exporting them to every corner of the globe. These hybrid factories would not have succeeded if the cultural factor had been ignored.

We have been talking a lot about culture. But what is culture exactly? In the next section, we will define the meaning of culture by introducing some major theories.

SUMMARY POINTS

Cross-cultural understanding is important in international business because it enhances:

- Companies' from diverse cultures ability to accommodate and appreciate one another smoothly.
- Companies' from similar cultures ability to boost up their synergistic effect.
- The successful creation and operation of hybrid organizations.

MAJOR THEORIES AND PERSPECTIVES

In this section, we will look into the meanings of culture and values. Then the cultural dimensions as identified in a number of representative studies will be introduced. The objective of this section is to take a bird's eye view on several major theories of culture so as to provide a foundation for the next section when we will look into various Asian cultural traits.

The Meaning of Culture

In the 1950s, American anthropologists A.L. Kroeber and C. Kluckhohn identified no less than 164 definitions of culture raised by anthropologists from 1840 onwards. After carefully analysing the various definitions of culture, they suggested that:

> culture consists of patterns, explicit and implicit, of and for behavior acquired and trans-mitted by symbols, constituting the distinctive achievement of human groups, including their embodiment in artifacts; the essential core of culture consists of traditional (that is, historically derived and selected) ideas and especially their attached values; culture systems may, on the one hand, be considered as products of action, on the other, as conditioning elements of future action. (Kroeber and Kluckhohn, 1952: 181)

This definition of culture is probably by far the most commonly cited one, and from it we can identify three main characteristics of culture. First, a culture is shared collec-tively by members of a group. Geert Hofstede simply defined culture as 'the collective programming of the mind which distinguishes the members of one human group from another' (Hofstede, 1980: 25). Thus, culture enables a group to share and see things in the same way and eventually to shape stable and consistent behaviours. Of course, no single individual will possess all the cultural characteristics of the group to which he or she belongs since there is a distinction between culture and individual personality.[6] Nevertheless, culture is a concept that rests on the collective nature of society. Second, culture is a relative concept. There is no so-called 'benchmark culture' or 'standard culture'. Every culture is distinct and relative to other cultures' ways of perceiving the world although there are ethnocentric people who do not accept culture as relative in reality. Third, culture is learned. Kroeber (1917) stated that culture is above and beyond its biological and psychological bases, having an independent existence at its own level. Culture remains relatively stable and unchanged irrespective of a large turnover in membership within each new generation. This is true as we are not born genetically with the culture we are supposed to possess. What we accumulate and cultivate to call our culture is actually transmitted to us, learned by us and shared by members of our group, just like parents pass on to their children their values, moral beliefs and so on.

Next, we will further understand culture by treating it as a system consisting of specific components. Therefore we will simply say that culture is a system that contains values, beliefs, attitudes and behaviours shared by a group of people. Of all these components, value is the most fundamental, the building block of culture. Let us trace the sequence of these components. For example, take filial piety, that is, respect for parents, a salient feature of Asian cultural values. A person with filial piety embedded inside him/herself is likely to cultivate the belief of respect for parents or the elderly. This belief can lead to an attitude of preferring experience to uncertainty. Values, beliefs and attitudes are then manifested in terms of behaviours such as ancestor worshipping, cohabitation with the elderly[7] and so on. Of course, due to modernization, many Asians may not manifest all the expected behaviours. However, filial piety remains core and is expressed in different degrees.

SUMMARY POINTS

Culture is:

- Shared among individuals belonging to a group or society.
- Formed over a relatively long period and is relatively stable.
- A relative concept.

Culture is a system containing values, beliefs, attitudes and behaviours:

- A value is what we consider important.
- A belief is what we consider true.
- An attitude is an emotion towards something.
- Behaviour is what we act out.

The Meaning of Value

Kluckhohn (1951: 395) defined value as 'a conception, explicit or implicit, distinctive of an individual or group, of the desirable which influences the selection from available modes, means and ends of actions'.

Rokeach (1973: 159–60) defined value as 'an enduring belief that a specific mode of conduct or end-state of existence is personally and socially preferable to alternative modes of conduct or end-states of existence'.

Hofstede (1980: 19) defined value as 'a broad tendency to prefer certain states of affairs over others'. From these definitions we can see that value consists of motivational and evaluative elements. It is a person's profound orientation towards something or some matters. Therefore, if we attempt to categorize these things or matters systematically and map them against the person's orientation towards them, a value system or value hierarchy arises.

Kluckhohn and Strodtbeck's (1961) variations in the value orientation concept form a widely mentioned categorization of a value system. By asking five questions, we are essentially categorizing a person's value system into five orientations.[8] They include:

1. **Human nature orientation**: What is the character of innate human nature?
2. **Man–nature orientation**: What is the relation of man to nature?
3. **Time orientation**: What is the temporal focus of human life?
4. **Activity orientation**: What is the modality of human nature?
5. **Relational orientation**: What is the modality of man's relationship to other men?

By indicating the possible variations of each orientation, a value orientation framework emerges. This framework gives a clear and broad picture of what one's value system looks like. Table 5.1 depicts the value orientation framework and the variations within.

Table 5.1 Value orientation framework

Orientations	Variations	Meanings
Man-to-himself orientation	Good	People are good and trustable
	Mixed/Neutral	People are basically good but their behaviour may be evil in some situations
	Evil	People are evil
Man-to-nature orientation	Dominant	We can change nature by technology
	Harmony	We coexist with nature
	Subjugation	We accept nature rather than try to change it
Relational orientation	Individualistic	We emphasize personal achievement
	Group	We emphasize harmony with others
	Hierarchical	We emphasize respect for authority
Time orientation	Past	We focus on the past
	Present	We focus on the short term
	Future	We focus on the long term
Personal activity orientation	Doing/Action	We work and achieve
	Controlling	We achieve a balance between the mind and the body
	Being	We enjoy life

When the framework is applied to the construct of culture, we can describe the value orientations of a culture and compare values cross-culturally. For example, Yau (1994), in a study concerning Chinese consumer values, presented a classification of Chinese cultural values based on the value orientation framework. Table 5.2 shows the cultural values identified under each orientation. We will come back to discuss more about Chinese cultural values in another section. The table serves only as a rough example of how to categorize value orientations.

Table 5.2 Classification of Chinese cultural values

Value orientations	Elements of value
Man-to-himself orientation	Harmony with nature, predestined fate
Man-to-nature orientation	Abasement, situation orientation
Relational orientation	Respect for authority, interdependence, group orientation, face
Time orientation	Continuity, past time orientation
Personal activity orientation	Doctrine of the mean, harmony with others

REFLECTIVE QUESTION

■ Think about your own culture. Can you name some possible elements of your own culture and categorize them according to the value orientation framework?

Hofstede's Cultural Dimensions

After defining the meanings of culture and value, we now come to examine a few representative studies of culture. The most well known is undoubtedly Geert Hofstede's study of work-related values. Hofstede wanted to explore how national culture can influence values in the workplace and therefore he studied data from IBM employees in 40 countries[9] during the period 1967 to 1973. His study was reported in his 1980 classic *Culture's Consequences: International Differences in Work-Related Values*. Since then, innumerable replications and validation studies have been conducted world-wide. In 2001, the second edition of his book extended the findings taken from altogether 74 countries. Due to the mammoth size of Hofstede's project and the stability and consistency of the dimensions uncovered, the Hofstede dimensions of national culture have become the most authoritative. They include Power Distance (PDI), Individualism (versus Collectivism) (IDV), Masculinity (versus Femininity) (MAS) and Uncertainty Avoidance (UAI). For each country, Hofstede calculated indices for each dimension to create country cultural profiles. Each of these dimensions is briefly explained[10] and put into the perspective of the organization here.

- **PDI**: The extent to which the less powerful members of organizations accept that power is distributed unequally. The higher the index, the greater the distance between the less powerful and the powerful. Therefore, leaders in high PDI organizations tend to manage in a more autocratic or paternalistic manner and there is less employee participation. Subordinates actually prefer autocratic management. Also, status, titles and formalities are more emphasized. On the other hand, leaders in low PDI organizations tend to be more open to employees and are likely to delegate more.
- **IDV**: The degree to which individuals are integrated into groups. The higher the IDV, the more independent and competitive people are. People pursue personal goals rather than organizational or national goals. Jobs are designed more for individuals and rewards are based on individual championship. The lower the IDV (the higher the collectivism), the more emphasis there is on collaboration and consultation. People in low IDV organizations are more integrated. Employees' interests are more protected.
- **MAS**: The distribution of roles between the genders to which a range of solutions are found. The higher the MAS, the more assertive and competitive people are. They place more emphasis on material things rather than abstract or spiritual concepts. On the other hand, the lower the MAS (the higher the femininity), the more modest and caring people's values are. Low MAS organizations place greater emphasis on the needs of the employees while those of higher MAS concentrate more on individual achievement.
- **UAI**: A society's tolerance for uncertainty and ambiguity. The higher the UAI, the less people are open to changes. They are more risk averse too. High UAI organizations rely heavily on rules, formalities and standards. Anxiety level at work is also higher. People prefer stability and they tend to remain in the same job for longer periods. Low UAI organizations encourage more unconventional thinking and risk venturing. Anxiety and stress at work also exist but they are not easily expressed outwardly. They are probably more restrained.

Now let us examine the cultural profiles of four selected Asian countries in Table 5.3. The scores run from zero, which is the lowest, to 100.

Table 5.3 Hofstede's dimensions of four countries

	PDI	IDV	MAS	UAI
China	80	20	50	60
Japan	54	46	95	92
India	77	48	56	40
Singapore	74	20	48	8

In terms of PDI, China scored the highest. This is a reflection of the hierarchical social system of China where relationships at different levels are rigidly structured. Singapore scored also relatively high due to the existence of a majority of ethnic Chinese. The caste system in India needs no introduction, hence a PDI score of 77. Japan, rather unexpectedly, scored relatively lower than the other three countries. Nevertheless, Japan is also a very hierarchical society where rules and protocols are strictly obeyed. However, at the same time, Japan is probably the most modernized country when compared with the other three. As to IDV, all four scored rather low, with China and Singapore the lowest. It has been often mentioned that Asian people are more collective than Westerners. They tend to be more 'groupistic'. It appears here that the Chinese are particularly so. For MAS, it is unnecessary to mention that Japanese society is famous for its masculinity. Even today important positions in different walks of life are mainly taken up by males. Compared with Japan, the other three countries seem to be more balanced in terms of the battle between the sexes. Finally, concerning UAI, Japan scored extremely high. This is not difficult to understand since Japanese culture values harmony and stability. On the other hand, the Singaporeans scored extremely low, probably because they are rather Westernized. However, at the same time, they are also very traditional in the sense that they are very self-restrained, not exposing their emotions casually.

SUMMARY POINTS

- Power distance: High PDI cultures emphasize social status.

- Individualism: High IDV people take care of their own business.

- Masculinity: High MAS cultures are more aggressive.

- Uncertainty avoidance: High UAI people don't like risks.

Long-term versus Short-term Orientation

As a result of Hofstede's collaboration with Hong Kong-based psychologist Michael Bond, he later added a fifth cultural dimension. In view of the rapid emergence of the 'Five Little Dragons' (Hong Kong, Japan, Singapore, South Korea and Taiwan) and other Asian countries in the world economic arena during the late 1980s to early 1990s, Hofstede and Bond (1988) believed that the real explanation for the 'East Asian Economic Miracle' can only be explored effectively by turning to the domain of culture. Since many of these countries have common cultural roots anchored on the teachings of the great ancient Chinese philosopher Confucius, it became obvious that there is a possible Confucian dynamism dimension in the cultural profile of these countries which may account for, to a certain extent, the East Asian miracle.

Truly, Confucian emphases on stability of the society, the family as the prototype of all social organizations, virtuous behaviour towards others and the virtues of acquiring education, perseverance, thrift, patience and so on are the salient features of many East Asian cultures. They generally exhibit high PDI, low IDV, middle to high MAS and high UAI. The result of Hofstede and Bond's study revealed that four of the Five Dragons namely, Hong Kong, Taiwan, Japan and South Korea, held top positions on the 'Confucian dynamism' scale. Their high Confucianism scores also coincided with their astonishing economic growth during that time. Therefore, Hofstede and Bond believed that the logical link between the cultural connection and the economic growth lies in a unique feature of East Asian entrepreneurship which possesses values rooted in Confucian thoughts and philosophy.

The notion of 'Confucian dynamism' was further developed into a formal fifth dimension known as long-term orientation (LTO) as opposed to 'short-term orientation'. LTO stresses virtuous living which values thrift and perseverance. East Asian countries high on the Confucian dynamism scale are naturally more long-term oriented. Western countries are generally more short-term oriented in that they concentrate more on satisfying immediate needs. Nevertheless, although LTO is related to Confucian dynamism, it is not entirely a Chinese or Asian concept. For example, Latin American countries also score high on LTO. But as expected, China scores the highest. A later study by Hofstede revealed an LTO score of 118 for China.

REFLECTIVE QUESTION

- Think about your own culture. Do you think that the Hofstede dimensions can accurately describe the features of your own culture?

Trompenaars' Relationship Dimensions

Although the Hofstede dimensions exhibited consistent relevance and applicability for nearly half a century, many researchers have called for a revisit of the cultural dimensions using more up-to-date data. In 1997, Fons Trompenaars and Charles Hampden-Turner published their book *Riding the Waves of Culture*. In it, they reported their study – involving over 15,000 managers in around 28 countries – on cultural differences and how they affect the process of doing and managing business. As a result, a seven-dimension cultural framework emerged.[11] These seven dimensions include:

1. Universalism versus Particularism
2. Individualism versus Collectivism
3. Neutral versus Affective
4. Specific versus Diffused
5. Achieved versus Ascribed
6. Time orientation
7. Internal versus External orientation

Let us take a look at the meaning of these dimensions.[12] Apart from Individualism versus Collectivism, which can be defined similarly to Hofstede's IDV dimension, the other six dimensions resemble to some extent Hofstede's dimensions as well as Kluckhohn and Strodtbeck's value orientation framework plus some new perspectives. The Universalism versus Particularism dimension refers to whether rules or relationships are more important. For example, in China, conducting business successfully relies a lot on 'relationships', 'connections' or what is famously known as *'guanxi'*. Therefore, China is a highly particularistic society. The Neutral versus Affective dimension determines whether people in a culture easily expose their emotion and affection. The Latin Americans are famous for their letting out of personal emotions while the Asians are usually regarded as more subtle. For example, Japan is a very neutral society. The Specific versus Diffused dimension determines whether responsibilities are specifically assigned or diffusedly accepted. For example, in diffused cultures, people may be completely immersed in business relationships, making the boundary between private life and business life blurred. Western cultures are usually more specific while Asian cultures are relatively more diffused. The Achievement versus Ascription dimension is somewhat similar to Hofstede's PDI and MAS. Achievement cultures are more masculine. They place greater emphasis on status and accomplishment. Ascription cultures are more feminine. For example, most Asian countries are usually regarded as more ascriptive. The Time Orientation dimension is similar to Kluckhohn and Strodtbeck's time orientation, looking at whether a culture is more past time-oriented or more present or future oriented. In addition, Trompenaars and Hampden-Turner also looked at whether a culture runs on Sequential Time or Synchronic Time, that is whether people do things one at a time or several things at the same time. Finally, the Internal versus External orientation tells whether a culture views nature in a mechanistic way or a more organic way. Internalistic people do not believe in fate or luck. They believe that they can control natural happenings. Externalistic people put their fate in the hands of providence. The Chinese are relatively more externalistic as compared with Westerners. This dimension resembles Kluckhohn and Strodtbeck's 'man-to-nature' orientation.

Hall's Cultural Factors

Another widely cited author is anthropologist Edward T. Hall. He is famous for his research in 'proxemics', the theory of human spaces. He believed that there is a cultural reason behind people's perception of personal space. In addition, he also studied the human orientation towards time. And perhaps most widely mentioned in the management literature is Hall's (1966) study on the context of culture. Hall distinguished between 'high context culture' and 'low context culture'.

In high context cultures, the many contextual elements provide the keys to people's understanding of how things work. By contextual, we mean things are not explicitly written. There are many covert and implicit messages. People use non-verbal communication a lot. In order to function properly in a high context culture, the bond between people must be very strong. There is strict demarcation between the 'in-group' and the 'out-group' and the commitment to this relationship is long term. Compared with Hofstede's dimensions, high context cultures appear to be more collectivistic. They also appear to be more feminine since it is the relationship that matters more than the task and the process is more important than the outcome.

In low context cultures, there are many explicit rules as to how things should be done. Messages are overt, clear and obvious. People do not communicate through body language. They speak out exactly what they mean. Due to the high degree of clarity in communication, people can easily adapt to the environment. Therefore, membership in the collective can be very fluid with new members easily learning the rules right away. This causes the bond among people to be loose and relationships become more short term. It also means that people are task-oriented and they place more emphasis on the result and achievement than on the process. Low context cultures appear to be more masculine and individualistic.

Other Theories of Culture

As well as those introduced above, a number of other cultural theories developed from areas like anthropology and psychology are often related to the management literature. It is impossible to introduce all of them here, but we can take a quick look at some of them. Serious readers should go to the References to find their sources.

Rokeach (1973) distinguished between 'instrumental values' and 'terminal values'. The former refer to personal characteristics that we think highly of: for instance, being ambitious, being clean, being independent and being self-controlled. Terminal values refer to goals in life that we think are most important: freedom, equality, wisdom and happiness are some examples.

Schwartz and Bilsky (1987) identified common values that acted as people's guiding principles in life. The Schwartz Value Inventory includes eleven value types, namely Power, Achievement, Hedonism, Stimulation, Self-direction, Universalism, Benevolence, Tradition, Conformity, Security and Super-grouping. These value types can be grouped along two continuums namely the 'Conservation–Openness' to change continuum and the 'Self-enhancement–Self-transcendence' continuum. The combinations of these elements can describe different culture types.

Stemming from the individualism–collectivism area, Triandis (1995) distinguished between idiocentrism and allocentrism. Idiocentrics are people who think that they are independent from others, are free to make decisions as they like, do not care much about how people perceive them, rely on themselves and are more task-oriented. On the other hand, allocentrics consider themselves to be interdependent, and they make decisions and search for information collectively. They also focus more on relationships rather than tasks.

Recent Developments in Cultural Theories

Two relatively newer studies of culture and business management are presented here. The first is the GLOBE project led by Robert J. House and his colleagues. The most ambitious since Hofstede's mammoth project in the 1970s, the GLOBE project represents a major contemporary cross-cultural study of culture and Global Leadership and Organizational Behavior Effectiveness (hence GLOBE). The project represents a 10-year research programme initiated in 1994, involving 160 scholars and 17,300 middle managers worldwide, examining societal cultures, organizational cultures and leadership and organizational behaviour over 62 societies. The first two phases of GLOBE have been published in an edited volume by House et al. (2004).

The main hypothesis behind the GLOBE project was that for every societal or organizational culture there will be a specific set of beliefs for leadership. Furthermore, the research team wanted to find out whether both acceptable (and effective) and unacceptable (and ineffective) leadership traits are shared among all members of a culture and among different culture groups.

The GLOBE project has identified six 'culturally endorsed leadership theory dimensions' or CLTs. These dimensions are summary indices of the characteristics, skills, and abilities culturally perceived to contribute to, or inhibit, outstanding leadership. They can be thought of as being somewhat similar to what laypersons refer to as leadership styles (House et al., 2004: 675). The six CLTs are charismatic/value-based leadership, team-oriented leadership, participative leadership, humane-oriented leadership, self-protected leadership and autonomous leadership. Due to limited space, the details of the GLOBE research and other findings are not elaborated here.

In 2003, P. Christopher Earley and Soon Ang published a book entitled *Cultural Intelligence: Individual Interactions across Cultures*. In this book, the authors pointed out that an individual's culture and cultural understanding of others' cultures will have a profound effect on the successful conduct of business; and that this understanding or awareness can be measured in terms of a 'cultural intelligence quotient' (CQ). The concept of CQ was soon popularized given its relationship with emotional intelligence (EQ). In an article published in the *Harvard Business Review* (HBR), Earley and Mosakowski (2004) admitted that CQ is related to EQ and it actually picks up from where EQ leaves off. They mentioned that people with high EQ are quickly able to know what makes a person different from another. But a person with high CQ will not only know what makes a person different from another, but also what is common to all people, what is common to groups or individual persons through analysing their behaviours. High CQ achievers are likely to excel in international business or cross-cultural dealings since they are able to delineate which features of people's behaviours are due to innate cultural reasons and which are due to, for example, universal professional knowledge.

Earley and Mosakowski (2004) pointed out that CQ can be developed. Learning other people's cultures (developing the 'head'), learning and exhibiting senses and body language compatible to other cultures (developing the 'body') and motivating oneself to overcome obstacles and setbacks (developing the 'heart') are the three approaches suggested by the authors. Through the administration of a questionnaire, one can assess one's own CQ profile by calculating a CQ score. Generally speaking, an average of 3 would indicate need for improvement, while an average of 4.5 or above means high CQ strength. Readers who are interested in the CQ questionnaire can refer to the HBR article. Today, CQ has become something frequently offered by management consultants in the form of training and workshops and the like (visit, for instance, the Cultural Intelligence Center at http://culturalq.com).

ASIAN VALUES AND CULTURES

In this section we will review the characteristics of Asian cultures. First of all, let us consider Asian values as a whole. According to the Asia Society's definition, Asia covers over 30 countries, broadly defined as the Asia-Pacific region: that is, the area from Japan to Iran, and from Central Asia to New Zealand, Australia and the Pacific Islands. This means many hundreds of ethnic communities, languages and dialects. It also means many different religions and belief systems. Asia is therefore not a homogeneous continent. Nevertheless, many Asians actually share certain common values with varying degrees such as harmony, modesty, family-orientation, respect for elders, filial piety, loyalty and teamwork. Now let us take a brief excursion through Chinese and Japanese cultures, two very important examples. Of course, they cannot represent all Asian cultures; therefore the individual chapters in the second part of the book will touch on other examples.

Chinese Cultural Values

The classical eco-cultural model stated that culture is a result of the social system, characterized by its subsistence system dependent on the ecological environment. Taiwanese cross-cultural psychologist Yang Kuo-Shu (1986) pointed out that the Chinese agricultural system regulated by the four seasons has led to a social structure emphasizing hierarchical organization, collectivistic functioning, generalized familization, structural tightness and social homogeneity. Therefore, the Chinese believe in the 'Way' (*Tao*). Man is regarded as part of nature and should not try to overcome nature. All things should be done according to the 'Way'.

Also, Chinese culture is strongly nurtured by the beliefs of Confucianism. In particular, the Five Cardinal Relationships (*Wu Lun*) are most important in connecting responsibilities and superiority of status, thus keeping the social system functioning properly. The five relationships refer to the orderly relationships between lord and servant, father and child, husband and wife, older and younger and friend and friend. *Wu Lun* emphasizes mutual responsibilities and respect between the two characters in a relationship.

Another important Confucius teaching is the Doctrine of the Mean (*Zhong Yong*). This value is manifested in a balanced life. A man's passions and impulses should not be completely oppressed. Neither should they be allowed to go astray as this will distort social harmony and deteriorate a man's morals. Therefore, the Chinese praise self-restraint and tolerance. Things are never taken too far in either social or business situations.

Japanese Cultural Values

Japan, as an island nation, is geographically isolated. This made the Japanese a very homogeneous group. The eco-cultural model explains that ancient Japan's isolation together with severe cold weather, frequent occurrence of earthquakes and the rice farming agriculture had led the Japanese to rely on tight cooperation in order to survive. Therefore, people lived in small communities and interdependence among these groups became very strong. This has cultivated a culture of social reciprocity (*giri*) or indebtedness, which places great importance on receiving and returning obligations. So, interpersonal relationships are very delicate and have to be managed carefully. Also, due to the high homogeneity in race, language and way of life, Japanese communication is very 'high context'. Empathy rather than explicit expression is the customary approach.

Japanese values also have their roots in Shintoism, Buddhism and Confucianism. Locally evolved Shintoism is a religion that reveres nature. It is believed that every element on earth has a deity within. Nature and all things given to men by nature are to be cherished. This has cultivated a culture that prizes social harmony. Also, the Confucian philosophy imported from China over a thousand years ago has been a central tenet of the Japanese way of life. Filial piety, hierarchical social relationships and virtuous behaviour towards others are still salient features of Japanese culture today. As to Buddhism, we have to mention Prince Shotoku (571–623 CE), regent for the Japanese Empress, who made Buddhism an established religion in Japan. The Seventeen Article Constitution (*Kenpo Jushichijo*) was the first writing on principles that should be observed by the Japanese government. Combining Buddhist and Confucian thought, the Constitution emphasized 'harmony' as the highest value to follow.

Like other Asian countries, Japan is constantly under Western influence, but many core values like collectivism, interdependence and harmony still predominate.

SUMMARY POINTS

- Many Asian cultures are influenced by Confucianism, especially Chinese and Japanese cultures.

- Confucianism places emphasis on proper social relationships and harmony.

ASIAN CULTURES AND MANAGEMENT PRACTICES

In this section, we will look at a few typical manifestations of underlying cultural values through management systems and practices.

First, in terms of structure, organizations influenced by Asian cultural values tend to be multi-layered. As one would expect, this is due to the Confucian emphasis on proper social relationships between different levels. For large organizations in Japan especially, the structure resembles the classic hierarchy with line and staff divisions. Michael Porter and his colleagues (2000) pointed out that the rigid hierarchical structure common to Japanese corporations can be effective in pursuing operational improvement but it may actually dampen innovative thinking. On the other hand, success and growth in large enterprises such as Sony and Orix have followed the gradual development of new organizational models.

On the other hand, many Asian countries, especially those with high PDI and low UAI, frequently demonstrate organizational structures resembling 'families' or 'tribes'. In these organizations, the boss acts in a paternal role and subordinates have no clearly defined roles and responsibilities. They have instead social roles. These organizations are characterized by centralized power and personalized relationships (Schneider and Barsoux, 1997). For example, Chinese companies are often family-based, with the founder having centralized power but at the same time acting as a caring father figure.

Since many Asian cultures tend towards the low end of the masculinity index, being more feminine and ascriptive, organizational policies and procedures tend to be more 'high context'. Compared with Western organizations, organizational processes rely more on social relationships rather than written descriptions. For example, Japanese management style stresses the importance of intensive on-the-job training and small group activities. Chinese management style emphasizes continuous learning. Therefore, experiences are accumulated through implicit social interactions rather than published company manuals. Knowledge thus becomes company-specific. This is further exemplified by the Chinese and the Japanese similar cultural distinction between the 'in-group' and the 'out-group'.

The high level of collectivism in Asian cultures also affects the organizational process. In decision making, for example, the Japanese take a collective approach. The famous '*ringi*' system, where a proposal has to be supported by all levels' endorsement before being sent to the apex of the hierarchy, is often cited as a manifestation of Japanese collectivism. However, the situation changes when the organizations are highly centralized in terms of power, like small and medium-sized family businesses of Chinese origin such as overseas Chinese or Sino-Thai companies. Here, decisions are made centrally and the number of hierarchy levels can in effect be only two.

The emphasis on relational behaviours in Asian cultures can have a great impact on human resource management practices. For example, in selection and evaluation processes, many Asian practices are labelled as nepotism by the West. This is especially serious in some Asian nations run by highly corrupted governments. The Chinese concept of *guanxi* (personal connection or network) is particularly famous. Nevertheless, *guanxi* here has a positive connotation and does not necessarily touch on corruption. Furthermore, relational behaviours also reflect the traditional concept of 'face', which is central to many Asian cultures. A harmonious situation is created when everyone respects everyone else's social status and relationships. That is, when everyone gives 'face' to everyone, harmony is preserved. Unlike Western cultures, Asian cultures avoid social and personal conflict and believe that fate is predestined. Therefore, 'face' given today can become a handsome return in the future and who knows where this might lead. Therefore, in Chinese or other Asian organizations, the personnel recruitment process involves the giving and taking of 'face' due to delicate social relationships. This is not to say that there is no competition on equal footing, but social connection is extremely important in Asian business encounters.

Schneider and Barsoux (1997) state that many cultural determinants will affect the corporate strategy adopted. For example, the relationship with nature may influence the adoption of a controlling or adapting strategy. Since most Asian cultures rest on the assumption that man should adapt to nature, not change it, an adapting strategy appears to be more in line. Nevertheless, one should bear in mind that this does not indicate a direct relationship between the kind of culture and the strategy type. As we compete in a globalized arena, a combination of different strategic approaches is often necessary.

One example is reflected in the research by Noronha (2002). He found that many quality management approaches and techniques, which in fact have a Western or Japanese cultural origin, could be implemented effectively in Chinese cultural settings. Echoing Abo's (2007) hybridization theory, management principles and practices from foreign soil when implemented will have to be transformed. This transformation is based on the fusion effect of different cultures and a culture-specific management system has to be created. Quantitative and qualitative-wise, Noronha's study indicated that the various Chinese values had an influence on the climate, processes, methods and results of the Chinese culture-specific quality system. For instance, many Chinese companies adopt Western management concepts to create a formal organizational system while reinforcing it using Confucian principles. Leadership is created through paternalistic figures giving subordinates positive personal examples. Foreign technologies are imported on a large scale but they are always modified to suit the local situation. Different from the Japanese approach, small group activities often combine voluntary participation and monetary reward.

SUMMARY POINTS

- Large Asian corporations often demonstrate multi-tier hierarchical structures while small and medium-sized companies often resemble families.

- Asian companies tend to rely more on social relationships rather than written procedures.

- Successful Asian companies are able to combine Western and local management practices.

ASIAN CULTURES, ETHICS AND SOCIAL RESPONSIBILITY

The final section will touch on ethics. Ethics is the philosophical study of values and customs of a group. It involves looking into the right and wrong, the good and the evil, and responsibility. There are three main areas, namely meta-ethics, normative ethics and applied ethics.

Meta ethics is about the origin and meaning of our ethical principles. When put into the Asian perspective, the principal origin of Asian meta-ethics comes from Buddhism and Confucianism. For example, the state of nirvana where there is no sorrow and pain, the concept of karma (afterlife) or the belief in not killing any living beings are Buddhist origins of Asian ethics. On the other hand, the Confucian emphasis on social harmony, virtuous behaviour and filial piety are also origins of Asian ethics.

Normative ethics involves ethical norms that help us distinguish between right and wrong, good and evil. Many traditional Chinese sayings have become guiding principles of how one should live an ethical life. For example, 'Reflect on our fault when we take a rest' and 'Criticize ourselves before criticizing others' are common Confucian sayings which serve as ethical guidelines for the Chinese as well as other Asians.

Applied ethics is the application of ethical theory in real-life situations. Examples are issues such as abortion and human cloning.

Putting these theories into the business setting, most Asian businesses are embraced by the Buddhist or Confucian origin of ethics which emphasizes social harmony and proper relationships among different parties. Unlike the Western practice of having written codes of ethical conduct, Asian businesses generally rely on the underlying cultural values of their organizational members as manifested in daily dealings. These values are often reflected in the emphasis on corporate social responsibility (CSR).

According to a study commissioned by the Centre for Social Markets (2003) and funded by the Department of Trade and Industry, CSR is voluntary and rooted in ethical values and is seen as an important issue by the sampled South Asian companies operating in the UK. The vast majority of the companies have engaged in certain socially responsible behaviours. Donations to charities, supporting local events, organizations and schools and environmental initiatives are examples of CSR manifestations. In general, the main spirit of CSR as perceived by these Asian businesses is to 'give something back to the community'.

Corporate social responsibility is now a hot topic in China and other Asian countries. It is important that CSR should go beyond mere donations to charities. Take China for example, the numerous reports of industrial accidents leading to loss of lives and the revelation of hazardous consumer products[13] being exported worldwide warrant a closer look at the formalization of CSR policies. With China's membership in the WTO, CSR will be a dominant issue if Chinese companies wish to maintain competitiveness. This is especially true as China received a corruption perception index ranking of 3.5 (below 5 reflects a serious level of perception of domestic corruption) according to the 2007 survey conducted by Transparency International. Although corruption does not directly indicate the maturity of CSR, it can give us a rough idea. China along with a number of Asian nations will face a long journey in building a healthier environment to foster CSR (for example other low rankings include India 3.5, Thailand 3.3, Vietnam 2.6, Indonesia 2.3). Nevertheless, some Asian countries or regions such as Singapore (9.3), Hong Kong (8.3), Japan (7.5) and Taiwan (5.7) appear to be on the right track towards sound governance and CSR.

REFLECTIVE QUESTION

- If it is said that Chinese culture emphasizes social harmony and ethical behaviour, why are we hearing news about so many unsafe products imported from China?

CHAPTER SUMMARY

- Culture refers to a society's values and norms developed through shared history and experiences over time.
- Businesses are often ethnocentric in outlook, but in the international environment, a polycentric approach is essential.
- With an open attitude to foreign cultures, their strong aspects can be transferred and successful hybrid organizations can be created.
- The value orientation framework classifies cultural values into human nature, man–nature, time, activity and relational orientations. A culture is described by the combination of them.
- Hofstede identified five cultural dimensions namely power distance, uncertainty avoidance, individualism, masculinity and long-term orientation. A culture is characterized by combining different degrees of them.
- Asian values generally derive from Confucian origin which emphasizes social harmony and proper relationships among different parties.
- Asian management practices are influenced by their cultural origins such as Confucianism and are manifested in organizational processes, structures, strategies and human resource practices.
- Many Asian nations are far behind the mature development of corporate social responsibility in spite of traditional cultural roots.

KEY CONCEPTS

Emics: Specificities of a culture.

Etics: Commonalities of two or more cultures.

Ethnocentrism: Viewing one's culture from one's own viewpoint.

Polycentrism: Willingness to accept foreign cultures.

Hybrid: The fusion of two cultures.

Culture: A system that contains values, beliefs, attitudes and behaviours shared by a group of people.

Value: A broad tendency to prefer certain states of affairs over others.

Value orientation framework: The categorization of value orientations and their possible variations.

Power distance: The extent to which the less powerful members of organizations accept that power is distributed unequally.

Individualism: The extent which individuals are integrated into groups.

Masculinity: The distribution of roles between the genders to which a range of solutions are found.

Uncertainty avoidance: A society's tolerance for uncertainty.

Confucianism: The teachings of Confucius which stress social harmony, filial piety, virtuous behaviour and proper social relationships.

Meta ethics: The origin and meaning of our ethical principles.

Normative ethics: The ethical norms that help us identify right from wrong.

Applied ethics: Ethical theory in real life situations.

Cultural intelligence: The ability of a person to function effectively in situations characterized by cultural diversity.

REVIEW QUESTIONS

1. What do ethnocentrism and polycentrism mean?
2. What are the main elements of culture?
3. How do you define value?
4. What are the five value orientations and their variations?
5. What do power distance, uncertainty avoidance, masculinity and individualism mean?
6. Is a high-context culture more masculine or feminine?
7. What are the characteristics of Confucian-influenced cultures?

LEARNING ACTIVITIES AND DISCUSSIONS

1. Select an etiquette (such as a greeting or eating habit) and contrast it under your culture with one under a foreign culture. Discuss with your colleagues the culture clash that may arise.
2. Browse the internet and find out what religions are practised in Singapore and Malaysia. Are they very different? Discuss with your colleagues their resulting impact on social and business behaviours.
3. Devise a plan to set up a business (for example a personnel recruitment agency) with two branches in Japan and the Philippines. Discuss with your colleagues the possible cultural awareness you will need to successfully run the branches.

MINI CASE

CULTURE IN PRACTICE
How Confucianism fills the void

Pop culture offerings in China these days run the gamut from Hollywood blockbusters to domestic versions of *American Idol*, but it's a book about the ancient sage Confucius that's causing the latest buzz.

Notes on Reading the Analects, by Beijing Normal University professor Yu Dan, has become the mainland's best-selling book in recent memory, defying critics who say it turns Confucian thought into self-help pulp for the modern age.

'It's good to have these teachings from old times because people are too selfish now', 60-year-old accountant Qu Juan says of the book, which has sold more than three million copies in four months. 'Everybody cares only about making money since the economic reforms', she says.

Yu shot to fame in October when she went on state TV to lecture on *The Analects*, a canon of Confucianism recording discussions between the ancient Chinese sage (551–479 BCE) and his disciples. She wrote the book based on the TV transcripts.

Cultural commentators say her mass following reflects deep anxiety about morality and beliefs in a society that has gone through disorienting transformations in recent decades.

'We were taught Marxism and Leninism in schools', says Tian Na, a 25-year-old teacher who bought the book on the internet. 'But when I became independent and went to college, I saw professors take bribes and I felt the old slogans such as "serve the people" were no longer relevant.'

Yu's book appeals across the generations, despite their vastly different experiences. Tian and her contemporaries grew up in the relatively prosperous and stable reform era of the 1980s and 1990s, unlike their elders under the tumultuous reign of Mao Zedong.

After the Communist Party took power in 1949, a series of radical political movements plunged the country into anarchy and near economic bankruptcy, culminating in the chaos of the Cultural Revolution. The turmoil of Mao's rule is blamed by many for fostering mistrust between people and causing a breakdown of traditional ethics, which were denounced as reactionary.

Confucian philosophy, emphasizing rigorous personal morality and a strict hierarchy of social relationships, was endorsed by China's imperial rulers during two millennia and still has a huge influence on East Asian countries.

The mainland's market-oriented reforms, introduced in the late 1970s, have brought dazzling growth and greatly improved living conditions, but also a yawning wealth gap and social tensions. The shattering of communist ideals and the rush to get rich – now considered almost the sole indicator of success – have left many feeling lost or resentful.

'A nation which used to value morality above everything else suddenly finds itself without a moral benchmark', says Zhu Dake, a professor and cultural critic at Tongji University in Shanghai. 'That causes inextricable anxiety.'

Yu delivers her message with a simplicity that has charmed readers but galls critics trained in the classics.

'The essence of *The Analects* is to tell us how to live the happy life that our souls crave', Yu writes in the book. 'Don't assume we should look up to it … it is simply about orienting [sic] yourself in modern life.'

Detractors argue that Yu offers little more than a mixture of distorted ancient teachings and motivational stories tailored to tell readers how to handle stress and relationships. They say she takes advantage of people's ignorance of classic literature and that her success is a symptom of, rather than a remedy for, the crazy commercialism and declining ethics of the modern mainland.

'Her moral preaching might be helpful in rebuilding more healthy social relationships, [which are] now centred on money', says Zhu, 'But she has neither the courage nor impulse to explore the ultimate meaning of life.'

Yet such criticism has failed to dampen Yu's popularity. Her fans snapped up 15,000 autographed copies of her latest book in a single day. It offers similar material but borrows from the thoughts of Zhuangzi, an ancient Taoist philosopher.

Writer Zha Jianying says Yu's books have hit the mark with a frantic readership in the ideological vacuum that has followed the collapse of communism as the 'state religion', leaving the mainland as the world's 'largest soul market'.

'So, be it Buddhism, Christianity or Yu Dan's version of Confucius, people embrace them', says Zha, the author of an acclaimed book of interviews with a dozen Chinese cultural figures.

'There are so many wounded, helpless souls who are desperate to find something to believe in and to hold onto in the wake of all these drastic changes.'

QUESTIONS

1. Do you agree that commercialism has eroded the ethics of traditional Chinese culture? Why or why not?
2. Why do you think people in China are now revisiting Confucian principles?
3. Do you think Yu Dan's massive appearance in the media is effective in promoting Confucian thoughts or is it just another example of commercialism?

Source: Guo Shiping (2007). *South China Morning Post*, 2 May.

INTERESTING WEB LINKS

Hofstede dimensions: http://www.geert-hofstede.com
Trompenaars dimensions. http://www.7d-culture.nl
Chinese culture: http://www.chinaculture.org
All things Japanese: http://web-japan.org
Asian management practices: http://apmforum..com
Global corruption ranking: http://ww.transparency.org

Notes

1 According to the *CIA World Factbook*, in 2007, China has already become the second-largest economy in the world after the US.

2 This case is taken from 'Beyond Singapore: Making inroads in Japan and South Korea' by Chan Chao Peh in *The Edge,* Singapore 28 May 2007. Copyright The Edge Publishing PTE Ltd.

3 This case is taken from 'Going global with Korean, Taiwan partners' by Yasuhiro Goto in *The Nikkei Weekly* 5 February 2007. Copyright Nihon Keizai Shimbun, Inc.

4 The terms 'phonemics' and 'phonetics' were originally coined by linguistic anthropologist Kenneth Pike (1954). The former emphasizes the intrinsic phonological differences meaningful to speakers of a particular language while the latter refers to the extrinsic aspects meaningful to linguistic analysts. These concepts in linguistics have been applied to the field of cross-cultural studies in that 'emics' refer to cultural distinctions meaningful to members of a particular society while 'etics' are extrinsic categories of a culture as viewed by scientific observers from a distance.

5 Parochialism is another concept similar to ethnocentrism.

6 According to renowned cultural anthropologist Margaret Mead (1901–1978), an individual is a product of culture that shaped the person in unique ways. Cultural traits are learned by the individual as an infant and they are reinterpreted and reinforced as he or she goes through different stages of life.

7   It is widely known that Singapore has a housing policy that encourages people to live with their parents.

8   The original Kluckhohn and Strodtbeck orientation framework consists of five dimensions. Some modern writings may add additional dimensions. For example, Lane and diStefano (2000) have added a sixth dimension called 'Man-to-space orientation' which includes three variations namely, private, public and mixed.

9   Hofstede actually collected data from over 70 countries during this period, out of which he presented findings from 40 of the largest countries in his 1980 book.

10 More detailed definitions can be found at www.geert-hofstede.com.

11 These seven cultures originate from Hampden-Turner and Trompenaars' 1993 publication *The Seven Cultures of Capitalism*, New York: Doubleday.

12 Detailed definitions of the seven dimensions can be found at www.7d-culture.nl.

13 In November 2005, an explosion at Dongfeng coal mine in Heilongjiang province, China killed 171 miners. Explosions of this kind are frequently reported. In August 2007, Mattel, the largest toy company in the US, recalled China-made toys due to toxic substance in the lead paint. Over 18 million toys worldwide were affected.

REFERENCES

Abo, T. (ed.) (2007). *Japanese Hybrid Factories: A Comparison of Global Production Strategies*. Basingstoke: Palgrave Macmillan.

Berry, J.W. (1990). Imposed etics, emics and derived etics: Their conceptual and operational states in cross-cultural psychology. In Headland, T.N., Pike, K.L. and Harris, H. (eds) *Emics and Etics*. London: Sage.

Centre for Social Markets (2003). *Giving Something Back: Social Responsibility and South Asian Business in the United Kingdom: An Exploratory Study*. UK: Centre for Social Markets.

Earley, P.C. and Ang, S. (2003). *Cultural Intelligence: Individual Interactions across Cultures*. Stanford, CA: Stanford University Press.

Earley, P.C. and Mosakowski, E. (2004). Cultural intelligence. *Harvard Business Review*, **82**(10): 139–46.

Economist, The (2007). The export juggernaut: Good for China, but good for its neighbours too, 29 March.

Hall, E.T. (1966). *The Hidden Dimension*. New York: Doubleday.

Hofstede, G. (1980). *Culture's Consequences: International Differences in Work-Related Values*. Newbury Park, CA: Sage.

Hofstede, G. and Bond, M.H. (1988). The Confucian connection: From cultural roots to economic growth. *Organizational Dynamics*, **16**(4): 4–21.

House, R.J., Hanges, P.J., Javidan, M., Dorfman, P.W. and Gupta, V. (2004). *Culture, Leadership and Organizations: The GLOBE study of 62 Societies*. Thousand Oaks, CA: Sage.

Kluckhohn, C. (1951). Values and value-orientations in the theory of actions: An exploration in definitions and classifications. In Parsons, T. and Shils, E.A. (eds) *Towards a General Theory of Action*. Cambridge, MA: Harvard University Press.

Kluckhohn, F.R. and Strodtbeck, F.L. (1961). *Variations in Value Orientations*. Evanston, IL: Row, Peterson & Co.

Kroeber, A.L. (1917). The superorganic. *American Anthropologist*. **19**(2): 161–213.

Kroeber, A.L. and Kluckhohn, C. (1952). *Culture: A Critical review of Concepts and Definitions*. Cambridge, MA: Peabody Museum.

Lane, H.W. and diStefano, J.J. (2000). *International Management Behavior: From Policy to Practice*. 4th edition. Cambridge, MA: Blackwell.

Noronha, C. (2002). *The Theory of Culture-Specific Total Quality Management: Quality Management in Chinese Regions*. Basingstoke: Palgrave – now Palgrave Macmillan.

Pike, K.L. (1954). *Language in Relation to a Unified Theory of the Structure of Human Behavior*. Glendale, CA: Summer Institute of Linguistics.

Porter, M.E., Takeuchi, H. and Sakakibara, M. (2000). *Can Japan Compete?* Basingstoke: Macmillan – now Palgrave Macmillan.

Rokeach, M. (1973). *The Nature of Human Values*. New York: The Free Press.

Schneider, S.C. and Barsoux, J.L. (1997). *Managing Across Cultures*. Hertfordshire: Prentice Hall Europe.

Schwartz, S.H. and Bilsky, W. (1987). Toward a universal psychological structure of human values. *Journal of Personality and Social Psychology*, **53**(3): 550–2.

Triandis, H.C. (1995). *Individualism and Collectivism*. Boulder, CO: Westview.

Trompenaars, F. and Hampden-Turner, C. (1997). *Riding the Waves of Culture: Understanding Diversity in Global Business*. New York: McGraw-Hill.

Yang, K.S. (1986). Chinese personality and its change. In Bond, M.H. (ed.) *The Psychology of the Chinese People*. New York: Chinese University Press.

Yau, O.H.M. (1994). *Consumer Behaviour in China: Customer Satisfaction and Cultural Values*. London: Routledge.

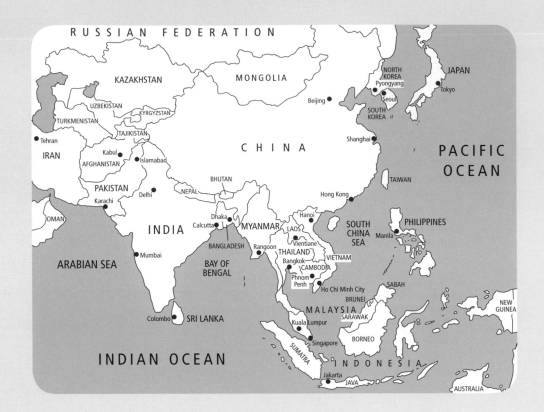

Chapter outline

- Asian business and Asian leadership
- Philosophical foundations and cultural values of Asian leadership
- Cultural differences within Asian leadership
- Leadership styles in Asia
- Traditional and contemporary Western leadership theory in an Asian context
- Asian leadership and personality, motivation, gender and CSR

Chapter objectives

By reading this chapter you will gain an understanding of:

1. The global representation of Asian business and its leadership
2. The philosophical foundations and cultural values of Asian leadership
3. The unique country differences in leadership styles between Japan, China and Korea
4. The influence of traditional Western leadership theories in an Asian organizational context
5. The differences of transactional, transformational and charismatic leadership in Asia versus the West
6. The role of personality, motivation and gender in relation to leadership in Asian business

Chapter 6

Asian leadership

Philippe Byosiere and Denise J. Luethge

INTRODUCTION

Factual and testimonial evidence of increased Asian influence in global business, particularly in the past 20 years, has been widely accepted. The continuous success of Asian leadership finds its origins in both the Asian societal and the cultural context as well as the successful adaptation of Western leadership and management models. This chapter focuses on the development of leaders and leadership theory in what is labelled 'Confucian Asia' (such as China, Japan, South Korea and Singapore). Leaders and leadership models are presented that reflect the 'indigenous' Asian character, highlighting commonalities and differences in leadership paradigms as well as in adopted Western leadership models. The chapter also provides insight into the many unique differences in leadership within Confucian Asia.

Leadership guru and business scholar D. Quinn Mills puts it unequivocally when he states that there is a direct connection between the leadership styles in a country, the developmental stage of the economy and the maturity of companies within that country (Mills, 2005). For most Asian countries, perhaps with the exception of Japan, this means seeking increased access to the global economy using a different leadership paradigm compared with that which has been used in industrialized Western countries. Although stereotypical in his expressions, Mills (2005) defines the Chinese leader as 'the head of the family,' and the Japanese leader as 'the consensus builder,' with self-knowledge and humility as the two strongest key qualities of Asian leadership. These characteristics stem from the cultures in China and Japan, and as such, it is difficult to make comparisons with Western leadership models. Thus, when examining leadership and its impact within organizations, most research and most models that stem from studies undertaken in the West have somewhat less applicability to organizations in Asia.

Prior to the discussion of an Asian leadership paradigm, we would like to point out a number of limitations of this chapter. This is not an exhaustive review of the tremendous amount of valuable leadership research in Asia and Asian companies. Before the 1970s, few Asian leadership studies found their way into Western management journals. In addition, Asia leadership studies have often been considered taboo compared with studies examining general management within the organization. However, with the 'coming of the Japanese firm' in the early to mid-1980s, a first peak of Asian leadership theory and research emerged in the 1990s, thus increasing pan-Asian leadership coverage in both Confucian and Buddhist Asia. Recently, as a direct result of the economic growth and increased market access within China, more studies on leadership in a 'Chinese' organizational context are being published today. Not all Asian leadership theories and research studies are examined in this chapter, and we encourage students of Asian leadership to extend their horizon beyond the boundaries of this chapter.

ASIAN BUSINESS AND ASIAN LEADERSHIP

It is important to recognize the fact that unlike 'Western' leadership paradigms, Asian leadership theory and research is built upon three equally important pillars: the indigenous Confucian-based leadership theory, leadership theory with a strong Western foundation and a hybrid or blending of Asian and Western leadership characteristics. These three roots of Asian leadership demonstrate both common Eastern underpinnings as well as unique country-based features resulting in specific Japanese, Chinese, and Korean leadership paradigms. This chapter recognizes the contributions of East and West leadership foundations, both indigenous and adopted in order to strike a balance between universal characteristics of leadership and the unique culturally embedded features of Asian leadership.

The study of leadership in Asia is strongly linked to the performance of the organization. The individual 'hero' status of the leader as a result of the company success is not as strong as in the West, in part due to the fact that many Western CEOs, particularly those in the US, earn extremely large salaries and bonuses, thus by US standards, making them seem 'heroic'. Even so, there are a number of extremely well-known and well-respected leaders in Asia who could be categorized as heroes, such as Akio Morita of Sony, Joo Yung Chung and Myung Bak Lee of Hyundai and Soichiro Honda of Honda. Still, Asian leadership has strong linkages to other individual and organizational processes such as personality, motivation, teams, organizational culture and organizational structure. In addition, Asian leadership's Confucian origins result in a paternalistic view of leadership, combining authoritarianism with benevolence and morality (Dorfman and Howell, 1997; Farh and Cheng, 2000; Pun et al., 2000). In other words, in order to truly understand Asian leadership, we need to examine the values and cultural characteristics impacting the actions of leaders. If the economic, financial and market success of firms can serve as an approximate measure of the effectiveness of the leadership, the past two decades have witnessed a drastic change in Asian representation in the world's largest enterprises. The composition of the Asian representation is quite different from that seen two decades ago. The rise of the Japanese manufacturing and financial firms in the 1980s has declined sharply, leaving only global automotive companies (for example Toyota and Honda, and Denso) and electronic giants (for example Panasonic, Sony, Hitachi) as major players in the global corporate world. Over the past 15 years Japan has seen a 60 per cent drop in Global

Fortune 500 company representation, dropping from 189 companies in 1990 to 67 in 2007. On the other hand, China has increased its global presence from 3 in 1994 to 24 in 2007. Slighter increases in global representation are found for Korea, Taiwan and Hong Kong over this time period. Thus, the overall trend of Asian company representation is a decrease in the number of Japanese companies along with an increase for Chinese and Korean companies.

Whereas Japanese companies have become household names in all parts of the world, the same cannot be said for many of the individuals at the helm of these companies, in sharp contrast to their Western counterparts. Why is that? The faces and names of Asian CEOs, such as Takeo Fukui (Honda), Atsutoshi Nishida (Toshiba) and Katsuaki Watanabe (Toyota), are seldom recognized in Japan. With Korea and China in different stages in their quest for globalization, it is less surprising that the names of Jong Yong Yun (Samsung), Bon Moo Koo, and Yu-Sig Kang (LG), Mong-Koo Chung and Dong-Jin Kim (Hyundai) for Korea and Wong Kwong-yu (Gome Appliances), Yan Cheung (Nine Dragons Paper Co.) and Li Ka-shing (Cheung Kong and Hutchison Whampoa) for China are not yet global household names. The anonymity that Asian CEOs enjoy, in spite of firm successes, may have less to do with the leaders than it has to do with the culture. In fact, when *Fortune* launched for the first time a ranking of the top companies for leaders in 2007, based upon surveys of human resources executives around the world, no Japanese and only one Chinese company were represented in this ranking, a remarkable result as it is in sharp contrast with the representation of Asian companies in the global ranking. It raises the question of how to put the position of leading Asian companies in perspective with regard to leadership, especially among the established Asian MNCs.

SUMMARY POINTS

- Asian leadership is highly diverse and is very different from leadership models developed in the West.

- There is also a tremendous amount of variation in leadership approaches within Asia, particularly within Confucian Asia.

- Asian CEOs are seldom heralded in the press for the successes of their firms, unlike CEOs of many European and US firms due to cultural differences.

REFLECTIVE QUESTIONS

- Why do Asian leadership models differ so dramatically from models developed in the West?

- What are the cultural dimensions that might have an impact on the reserved and 'faceless' nature of Asian CEOs?

PHILOSOPHICAL FOUNDATIONS AND CULTURAL VALUES OF ASIAN LEADERSHIP

Asian culture has had a tremendous impact on Eastern leadership and how leaders function within an organization. A number of cultural factors, very different from those which tend to be prevalent in Western firms, have a significant effect on leadership, and some of the most significant are noted here. While each of these has its own meanings, it is very difficult to separate the factors from each other, as they are intertwined among themselves. In addition, each of these factors varies from country to country within Confucian Asia, as will be discussed later.

- **Social relationships** – The development of connections, social favours and reciprocity for mutual benefit, leading to obligation on the parts of both parties (Xin and Pearce, 1996; Liu et al., 2005).
- **Harmony** – One's inner peace, equilibrium and contentment (Liu et al., 2005).
- **Face** – Pattern of social behaviours that allows people to enhance their public image and reputation.
- **Collectivism** – Society characterized by strong social networks, and the development of harmony, cooperation and the avoidance of conflict within the in-group (Rhee et al., 1996).
- **Trust** – The development of interpersonal in-group reliance, particularly between family, friends and close associates (Triandis, 1995).
- **Saving/frugality** – Traditional virtue of frugality rather than extravagance and wastefulness, especially in contrast to the willingness to spend money for hedonistic purposes (Fernandez, 2004).
- **Religion, religious symbols, and ways of living** – The importance of Confucianism within Asian cultures has a huge impact on the way business is conducted, with a focus on authority, benevolence, respect, harmony and conformity (Blunt and Jones 1997). Further, Christianity has become a growing aspect of Korean business, while the role of Soka Gakkai in the Buddhist philosophy of inner transformation and peace is important in Japanese business.

Today's contemporary Asian leadership paradigms reflect the deeply rooted philosophical aspects of Confucian thought. The Confucian conception of leadership reflects a strong humanistic, value-based, self-cultivating form of leadership striving towards social harmony (Lee, 1987; Fernandez, 2004; Alves et al., 2005). In order to present the key concepts of these leadership foundations we have integrated the conceptual work of Alves et al. (2005) and Fernandez (2004) as shown in Figure 6.1.

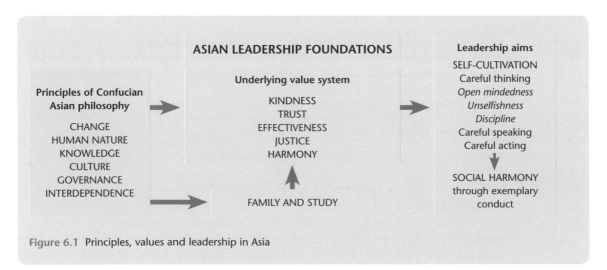

Figure 6.1 Principles, values and leadership in Asia

Alves and colleagues (2005) describe six philosophical approaches that impact leadership and management based on Confucian thought: change, human nature, knowledge, culture, governance and interdependence (*yinyang*). They note that these philosophical principles emphasize the role of social relations, collectivism, paternalism and acceptance of hierarchy (p. 13), thus resulting in Eastern leadership paradigms far different from those seen in the West. Fernandez (2004) expands upon this view of leadership by identifying the underlying leadership value system that results from these principles, characterized by kindness and justice, and leading to trust and harmony. The combination of these four elements of the value system engenders effectiveness. The continuous interaction between the six philosophical principles and the four elements of the value system, continuously reinforced through family tradition and study, forms the basis for the fundamental Asian leadership paradigm, namely, striving for a balance between self-cultivation and social harmony.

Theoretically, Asian leadership promotes trust, harmony, justice, kindness and effectiveness. However, as the stages of economic and societal development of Japan and Korea are very different from that of China, we notice a less 'indigenous and pure' form of the self-cultivation and social harmony aims of leadership. Confronted with reality, these ideal images of Asian leadership tend to face pressures of strong, often 'cut-throat' competition. Unfortunately, this competition can result in immoral leadership practices regardless of the economic stage, as seen in the increase in scandals throughout these Asian countries. The less than pure leadership resulting in corporate scandals and corruption is not only limited to China, but has occurred in Japan and Korea as well as Western countries. Confucian philosophy may be the prototype of Asian leadership, but the reality, however, may be quite different.

SUMMARY POINTS

- Western leadership tends to be much more task-oriented.

- Asian leadership is a much more holistic model focusing on trust, harmony and interrelationships among people.

REFLECTION QUESTION

- What are the underlying aspects of Asian cultures that impact Asian leadership? How do these vary by culture?

CULTURAL DIFFERENCES WITHIN ASIAN LEADERSHIP (CHINA, KOREA, JAPAN)

As noted earlier, many of the cultural factors impacting contemporary Asian leadership vary tremendously by culture within Confucian Asia. What makes understanding these differences challenging is the interrelationships among each of the factors, as these intertwining threads twist and turn in unique and confusing ways. Confucianism requires respect of superiors for subordinates, and loyalty of subordinates for superiors, leading to a highly paternalistic attitude in the workplace. Although some might see this directive type of behaviour as authoritarian, in many Asian cultures, it is more in line with familial responsibility rather than autocratic or dictatorial. In order to begin to understand how some similarities become different, we will first examine social relationships in China, Korea and Japan by looking at the networked reciprocation concepts of *guanxi*, *inhwa* and *wa*. Though some in the West might see these relationships as inhibiting fair trade or encouraging corruption, these relationships are part and parcel of the paternalistic and familial relationships that are the basis of Asian culture.

Guanxi does not have an exact translation; however, much has been written about the social connections that encompass this term. Yang (1994: 1–2) defines *guanxi* as:

> a 'relationship' between objects, forces, or persona. When it is used to refer to relationships between people, not only can it be applied to husband–wife, kinship and friendship relations, it can also have the sense of 'social connections,' … based implicitly (rather than explicitly) on mutual interest and benefit. Once *guanxi* is established between two people, each can ask a favour of the other with the expectation that the debt incurred will be repaid sometime in the future.

This type of relationship usually occurs between two individuals, and the bond that is created between the individuals is one of obligation to exchange favours rather than a bond based on personal feelings or sentiment (Alston, 1989). Should one of the partners choose not to return a favour and honour the obligation, that individual would lose the trust of the other, and along with that loss of trust would lose face. One important aspect of *guanxi* is that it usually favours the weaker of the parties, as *guanxi* often connects people who have very different ranks (Alston, 1989). Given this difference, the weaker of the two may not be able to reciprocate favours at the same level, and the higher level of the two will be accorded more respect for giving more than what is received. Alston (1989) notes that this power relationship of the weaker party to the stronger party is reflective of the Confucian ideal of family loyalty. Given the difficulty of dealing with Chinese bureaucracy and the changing nature of the legal system to enact policies that permit and assist businesses in the marketplace, *guanxi* is helpful for getting things done. *Guanxi* must be continually developed with new individuals as well as reinforced with current partners, since *guanxi* exchanges that are no longer profitable or useful can be easily discarded (Alston, 1989).

Inhwa is loosely defined as harmony in Korea. Based on the Confucian principle of family loyalty to parents and authority figures, *inhwa* focuses on the subordinate showing loyalty to the superior while the superior shows protection and concern for the subordinate. This development of personal ties means that, like the Japanese, individuals are more likely to work with those with whom they have *inhwa*. In this case, however, the group has little to do with the development of the relationship, and once *inhwa* has been established, it needs to be nurtured and strengthened (Alston, 1989; Gorrill, 2007). As part of the *inhwa* relationship, each party has the responsibility to try to support and please the other person, and neither party wants to risk upsetting the other. This building of respect, regard, patience, consideration, support and courtesy promotes good *kibun*, or good feelings (Miyataki and Whatley, 1989). Conversely, those actions that might upset or hurt someone, either through criticism and negative information or bad news would act to hurt feelings. As a result, Koreans will avoid doing anything to hurt *kibun*, even if that means misleading others or delaying decisions (Alston, 1989).

Unlike *guanxi* or *inhwa*, the Japanese *wa* refers to mutual cooperation and consensus to achieve group goals and establish group harmony. As a result, *wa* is not about the relationships between individuals, as is the case with *guanxi*, but rather it is the link between individuals and groups. *Wa* demands strong group cooperation and trust, which in most Japanese companies is built over a period of years. This strong sense of trust means that individuals will subordinate their individual needs in order to ensure harmony within the group, with the group's survival and long-term success being the ultimate goal of everyone (Alston, 1989). In addition, in order to maintain harmony throughout the organization, *wa* must be developed through the careful nurturing of a lifetime of connections that individuals have made with multiple groups within and outside of the firm. These connections must be continuously supported and maintained, thus reinforcing trust and the maintenance of harmony.

SUMMARY POINTS

- *Guanxi*, *inhwa* and *wa* are concepts that describe types of social relationships in China, Korea and Japan, respectively.

- While all are essential in organizations, each of the concepts has its own unique characteristics.

REFLECTIVE QUESTION

- How would each of these concepts impact lower and middle level managers differently from their impact on senior level managers?

LEADERSHIP STYLES IN ASIA

As noted in this chapter, much of the research in leadership has a North American focus (Den Hartog and Dickson, 2004). Unfortunately, the leadership styles that are prevalent in the US are not necessarily appropriate or effective in Asia. Given the vast differences between Asian and Western cultures, and the differences among Asian cultures themselves, it is appropriate to examine leadership styles from an individual country perspective.

Fukushige and Spicer (2007) examine preferred leadership styles in Japan, some of which are culture-specific to the country. Table 6.1 shows the categories and characteristics of the styles of leadership. Those styles marked with an asterisk indicate styles which are culture-specific preferred. Of note in this study is the description of cultural changes that will have a significant impact on leadership in the future. Three changes in particular were mentioned as being significant. First is the shift from a system of male chauvinism to one of gender equality. Although the authors admit that Japanese management has only just begun to address equality issues, demographic trends indicate a declining and ageing population. In order for firms actively to retain the best employees, they need to attract as many women as possible and leaders will have to show women that they are valued within the organization. Next is the trend from collectivism to individualism, with a shift towards a focus on individual competencies. Although the seniority system is still prevalent within Japan, changes are starting to occur. Finally, there is shift from seniority to meritocracy, in conjunction with a focus on individual competencies noted above. This is becoming more and more of a factor as individuals become more willing to switch jobs in order to secure positions with more challenges and higher levels of responsibility.

Table 6.1 Characteristics of leadership styles in Japan

Categories	Characteristics
Liberal leadership*	Fair, liberal, employs meritocracy
Trust leadership*	Proven ability, follows through on statements
Punctual leadership*	Finishes on time, works on schedule
Participative leadership	Listens, communicates, asks for suggestions
Network leadership*	Friendly, helps build subordinates' careers
Supportive leadership	Friendly, kind, supportive
Directive leadership	Gives clear orders
Protective leadership*	Protects from others in power
After-five leadership*	Tries to socialize and communicate, wants to know others better
Achievement-oriented leadership	Gives subordinates challenging opportunities, challenges them

Source: Adapted from Fukushige and Spicer (2007: 521–2).

In Korea, leadership characteristics of the most successful firms are very different from those in Japan. Shin (1998–1999) examined the characteristics that separated successful from unsuccessful firms. He found that respect for employees, initiator attitude, tenacity, network building and emphasis on competency were the key characteristics of CEOs in Korean firms. For unsuccessful firms, the corresponding traits were poor decision making, inhumane treatment of employees, lack of network building, inability to respond to environmental changes, and contempt for competency. Given these characteristics, Shin categorized the leadership styles of successful firms into three main categories. As shown in Table 6.2, the largest percentage of successful CEOs were battlefield commanders, which the author believes is uniquely Korean, and which is characterized by a leader who is people-oriented but also very much focused on what happens in the field and getting things done. The next group consists of network builders who emphasize building ties internally and externally throughout the organization. The final group is characterized by can-do spirit leaders who have a strong will to do their job coupled with a strong compassion for others.

Table 6.2 Leadership styles of successful Korean CEOs (in per cent)

Representative traits	Battlefield Commander	Network Builders	Can-do Spirit
Human respect	32.6	28.1	27.6
Initiator attitude	32.8	9.9	4.7
Tenacity and sense of calling	15.8	9.0	55.1
Network building	5.3	45.8	2.4
Emphasize competence	13.1	7.1	10.2
Total percentage of styles	58.4	24.2	17.4

Source: Adapted from Shin (1998–1999: 46).

China shows yet another very different set of leadership styles, indicative of the great variation among Asian cultures. From a study conducted with 1,446 managers (Tsui et al., 2004), Table 6.3 summarizes behavioural characteristics of good leaders into six categories: creativity and risk taking, communicating, articulating vision, showing benevolence, monitoring operations, and being authoritative. The leadership styles identified in this study each have different levels of behavioural characteristics. As shown in Table 6.3, the advanced leader, authoritative leader, progressing leader and invisible leader vary tremendously in their focus. This indicates that depending on leadership style, different Chinese leaders may choose to act in different ways. The advanced leader may be more likely to encourage subordinates to take risks or communicate with others while the authoritative leader might proffer his own solution to a particular problem rather than seek the counsel of others. In any event, these styles differ dramatically from those found in both Korea and Japan.

Table 6.3 Leadership styles in China

	Advanced	Authoritative	Progressing	Invisible
Articulating vision	High	Average	Average	Low
Monitoring operations	High	Average	Average	Low
Creativity and risk taking	High	Average	Average	Low
Communicating	High	Average	Average	Low
Showing benevolence	High	Low/average	Average	Low
Being authoritative	Low	High	Average	Average

Source: Adapted from Tsui et al. (2004: 11).

SUMMARY POINTS

- Although a number of leadership studies look at Asian leadership as one broad category, clearly there are different types of leadership styles in each Asian country.

- The type of style which is likely to be most effective will depend upon the nature of the industry, the characteristics of the leader, the type of situation and the type of followers.

REFLECTIVE QUESTION

- What aspects of a country's culture would favour one type of leadership style over another in each of the three countries noted?

TRADITIONAL AND CONTEMPORARY WESTERN LEADERSHIP THEORY IN AN ASIAN CONTEXT

Two of the most popular theories of management are based on the work of Douglas McGregor (1960) in combination with Abraham Maslow's (1943) theory of motivation. McGregor (1960) describes two basic types of factors of production and how they function within an organization. Theory X assumes that most employees are basically lazy, avoid work and have little to no ambition. These individuals are not concerned with organizational goals, and as a result, they need very strict supervision in order to perform at reasonable levels. It follows then that an authoritative, centralized structure would be the most effective means for ensuring compliance with work norms. Alternatively, McGregor (1960) also posed Theory Y. Noting that Theory X primarily addresses individuals concerned with lower order needs (biophysical and safety needs), McGregor argued that in a modern society, lower order needs were already satisfied. As such, a need that was already satisfied was unlikely to motivate individuals to perform additional work. In order to motivate employees, managers needed to focus on higher order needs, such as love, self-esteem and actualization in order to motivate employees to be more productive. In order to satisfy higher order needs and motivate individuals, McGregor suggested that firms focus on a decentralized structure that increased employee involvement in the workplace and allowed individuals more participation in decision making in their jobs.

An extension of McGregor's theory, and probably the most prominent of the theories and practices coming from Japan, is the *Theory Z* (Ouchi, 1981) approach, which combines typical practices from the US and Japan into a comprehensive system of management/leadership. This system includes the following principles of best management/leadership practice:

- Seek to establish a long-term employment culture within the organization.
- Use collective decision making as much as possible.
- Increase and reinforce the importance of individual responsibility.
- Establish a slow and long-term process for evaluation and promotion.
- Employ implicit, informal control that utilizes explicit, formal measures/tools of performance.
- Institute and use moderately specialized job descriptions and career paths.
- Develop policies and practices that support a holistic concern for and support of the individual both at work and at home (as regards family issues).

Theory Z has had a marked impact on the manner in which companies are led today. Theory Z strategies have been instrumental in building stronger working relationships between subordinates and their leaders because of the increased level of worker participation in decision making as well as leaders' higher level of concern for their subordinates.

Social scientists and philosophers have long investigated what makes a great leader (Chemers, 2000). In the early 1900s and continuing into the middle of the 20th century, much research focused on traits, such as intelligence, personality, competence and/or empathy, that were thought to be associated with good leaders. In a review of the studies examining traits and leadership, or trait theories, Stogdill (1948) concluded that although traits certainly were important, the vast number of situations leaders faced made it difficult to predict the success of one type of leader over another.

Another stream of research, known as behavioural theories, examined the styles of individuals who were thought to be good leaders in an attempt to identify those behaviours associated with successful leadership. The Leader Behavior Description Questionnaire (LBDQ) was developed to examine behavioural patterns associated with strong leadership leading to high levels of productivity (Hemphill 1950; Chemers 2000). Those behaviours that aligned most strongly to positive leadership were *initiation of structure factors*, which reflected procedural and performance variables, and *consideration* factors, which focused on empathy and support for group members and morale (Halpin and Winer, 1957). Unfortunately, these factors were more likely to explain group morale and followership than group performance, leaving the question of leadership effecting high performance unanswered. The studies based on this stream of research are particularly important as they form the underpinnings of the Performance–Maintenance (PM) Theory of leadership developed in Japan in the late 1960s and 1970s, which will be discussed later.

In part as a result of the inability of both trait theories and behavioural theories to explain the relationship between performance and leadership, researchers in the 1960s and 1970s began investigating whether or not situational factors might have an impact upon leadership behaviour and group performance. Several contingency theories posit that successful leadership is dependent upon the characteristics of the situation, the characteristics of the leader and/or the characteristics of the followers. Thus, the appropriate leadership style may change depending on the nature of the situation and participants.

Several empirical studies have been conducted testing the 'traditional' modern Western leadership theories in very specific Asian (Japan, China, Korea) organizational settings (Bass, 1990). The results of these multiple studies are inconclusive, suggesting that there may be applicability of these leadership theories on one hand, yet questioning whether direct application is completely appropriate on the other hand. The mere transfer of Western leadership styles to an Asian context requires one to examine the influence and moderation of other factors, both micro-organizational and macro-organizational in nature, such as the stage of the development of the society and the economy, the organizational structure, the organizational culture, the psychological contract between employer and employee, the national culture and the norms and value systems. We are not favouring West over East or East over West, simply acknowledging that many of the leadership theories posited in textbooks that originated in the more individualistic West, may not be applicable in the more paternalistic cultures of the East.

In part in response to the applicability issue across cultures, Jyuji Misumi adapted the LBDQ instrument to apply more appropriately to the Japanese management culture (Misumi, 1985; Misumi and Peterson, 1985) in what is known as *Performance–Maintenance Theory*. Based on this work, Misumi posited that there were two basic types of leader behaviour, task-based *performance* behaviours and group-based *maintenance* behaviours. Performance behaviours are those things that leaders do to enhance the performance of their teams, such as focusing on quality, increasing accuracy, and observing rules; while maintenance behaviours would include a focus on things such as group comfort, feelings of subordinates, and shows of appreciation (Misumi and Peterson, 1985). Four basic types of leaders are proposed: those high on performance behaviours (P), those high on maintenance behaviours (M), those high on both performance and maintenance (PM) and those low on both (pm) behaviours (Misumi and Peterson, 1985). In addition, there may be different situations where one leadership style might be more appropriate than another leadership style.

The most recent and most extensive study of leadership was conducted by House and his colleagues (House et al., 2004). Table 6.4 lists nine factors impacting leadership styles which tend to vary across cultures based on this research in 62 societies. Although there is an inherent danger in converging leadership variables into these nine broad categories and stereotyping certain cultures as higher or lower without considering the specific cultural characteristics, the study does nonetheless provide some interesting characteristics for further consideration.

Table 6.4 Cultural leadership dimensions in Confucian Asia, China, Japan and Korea

	Confucian Asia (average)	China	Japan	Korea
Performance orientation	A	4.45 (A)	*4.22 (B)*	4.55 (A)
Future orientation	B	3.75 (C)	*4.29 (B)*	3.97 (B)
Gender egalitarianism	B	3.05 (B)	3.19 (B)	*2.50 (C)*
Humane orientation	B	4.36 (B)	4.30 (B)	*3.81 (C)*
Power distance	B	5.04 (B)	5.11 (B)	*5.61 (A)*
Institutional collectivism	A	*4.77 (A)*	5.19 (A)	5.20 (A)
In-group collectivism	A	5.80 (A)	*4.63 (B)*	5.54 (A)
Uncertainty avoidance	B	*4.94 (A)*	4.07 (C)	3.55 (C)
Assertiveness	B	3.76 (B)	3.59 (B)	*4.40 (A)*

1. *Performance orientation* – the degree to which a society encourages and rewards group members for performance improvement and excellence.

2. *Future orientation* – the extent to which a society encourages and rewards future-oriented behaviours such as planning, investing in the future, and delaying gratification.

3. *Gender egalitarianism* – the extent to which a society minimizes gender role differences.

4. *Humane orientation* – the degree to which a society encourages and rewards individuals for being fair, altruistic, generous, caring, and kind to others.

5. *Power distance* – the degree to which members of a society expect power to be unequally shared with respect to power, authority, prestige, status, wealth, and material possessions.

6. *Institutional collectivism* – the degree to which individuals are encouraged by societal institutions to be integrated into groups within organizations and the society as opposed to operating as independent agents.

7. *In-group collectivism* – the extent to which members of a society take pride in membership in small groups, such as their families and circles of close friends, and the organization in which they are employed.

8. *Uncertainty avoidance* – the degree to which members of a society seek orderliness, consistency, structure, formalized procedures and laws to cover situations in their daily lives.

9. *Assertiveness* – the extent to which a society encourages people to be tough, confrontational, assertive, and competitive versus modest and tender.

Source: Adapted from House et al. (2004).

Table 6.4 shows the individual scores for each of the dimensions in the GLOBE Study. The Confucian Asia column shows the average score within that group (China, Japan, Korea, Taiwan, Singapore and Hong Kong), versus the scores on the big three countries. The numbers highlighted in blue show the outliers, indicating the tremendous variation within Asia. For example, scores for Korea are substantially lower for gender egalitarianism relative to Japan and China, indicating that gender equality has a long way to go in that country. Institutional collectivism is lowest in China while in-group collectivism is the highest, indicating that Chinese are much more collectivistic in their beliefs at the individual and family level and less so at the societal and institutional level than are their counterparts in Japan and Korea.

Three additional contemporary Western leadership paradigms have found their entrée into Asian organizational settings: transactional, transformational and charismatic leadership. Based on the work by Burns (1978), transactional leaders are those who influence followers by focusing on transactions that are based on self-interest, such as rewards or avoidance of punishment. Transformational leadership, on the other hand, is where leaders and followers interact in such a way as to raise each other to higher levels of motivation and performance, building the organization or group into a community with a common purpose. Bass and Avolio (1997) identify four inter-related components: inspirational motivation, intellectual stimulation, idealized influence and individual consideration.

Only a few studies have examined transformational and transactional leadership in Asia. In a recent study comparing transactional leadership with transformational leadership in Japan it was found that idealized influence and inspirational motivation were not endorsed as transformational leadership factors, while the Japanese were highly receptive to contingent rewards in terms of transactional leadership. As a result, this research indicated the existence of a Japanese leadership model based on leadership dimensions rooted in Japan such as liberal, trustworthy, punctual, network, protective, directive, supportive, participative, achievement-oriented, and gender-unbiased (Fukushige and Spicer, 2007).

In the Korean context, Shin and Zhou (2003) examined the relationship between transformational leadership and creativity, finding a positive relationship that was moderated by the individual value of conservation, or the desire for group harmony. In this case, the results of the study showed that transformational leadership is positively related to creativity, but that this relationship is enhanced by high levels of conservation and reduced by low levels of conservation. Since this study was conducted only in Korea, it is unknown whether or not the same results would be seen outside of Confucian Asia or even outside of Korea. When looking at research of transformational leadership in China, Shao and Webber (2006) examined the relationship between personality and transformational leadership in a replication of North American research. They concluded that transformational leadership in China differs dramatically in terms of the relationships found in studies in the West. As a result, they conclude that personality models, such as the five-factor model used in the US, are not useful for predicting transformational leadership behaviours in China (Shao and Webber, 2006).

Charismatic leadership theory was originated by Weber (1947), describing the charismatic leader as someone to whom followers attribute extraordinary characteristics or qualities (Bryman, 1993; Yukl, 1999). This leadership model involves motivating and directing followers primarily by developing in them a strong emotional commitment to a vision and set of shared values. Although from an outside point of view it would appear that in collective-based societies charismatic leadership would not be dominant, as faceless leaders are the norm rather than the exception, the reality is quite different in Japan and Asia. Apparently, the aura that bestows top leaders with authority, success and fame transforms many into exhibiting charismatic leadership behaviour. Whereas often Japanese leadership is characterized as being 'faceless', compared with the flamboyance and name recognition sometimes associated with Western CEOs, there are quite a few corporate 'mini-emperors' or '*errai-shacho*' representing Japan's charismatic leadership. The charisma may not immediately stem from the shared vision and values or from the promotion of shared identity. The charismatic behaviours of these leaders stem in many instances from the reflection of their strength (the samurai) and their extraordinary personal qualities, some of which qualities may be seen negatively in the West.

Although some leadership models have proved to be successful in the West and others have proved successful in Korea, China or Japan, attempts to duplicate one or more models in another culture may have disappointing results. The importance of cultural mores cannot be overestimated. What may work in Japan, France, or the US may not work anywhere else simply because of cultural factors. Yet Japanese management and/or leadership principles have taught managers around the world to consider new approaches in order to achieve the higher standards of organizational effectiveness necessary in today's global economy. Business leaders around the world are examining their practices in light of the success that the Japanese and others have had in the areas of strategy building, organizational development, group/team cooperation, and establishing competitive advantage.

SUMMARY POINTS

- A number of leadership theories have been tested in Asia to try to determine what leadership models are most effective and what leadership types work best.

- Evidence pointing to any one model or style is inconclusive.

REFLECTIVE QUESTIONS

- What aspects of culture in each Asian country would favour one type of leadership style over another?

- How does PM Theory fit with transformational leadership?

ASIAN LEADERSHIP AND PERSONALITY, MOTIVATION, GENDER AND CSR

Personality and Leadership in Asia

One of the most commonly used models of personality is known as the Big Five personality factor model. Originally developed in the West and tested by a number of researchers (Costa and McCrae, 1985, 1989; Goldberg, 1990; John, 1990; McCrae and Costa, 1997), this model looks at five basic dimensions of personality: openness to experience, agreeableness, neuroticism, extraversion and conscientiousness. Tested in a number of Asian countries, the model has been found to describe personality types in both Japan and Korea, with some discussion that an additional dimension of honesty should be included in the latter country (Ashton et al., 2000). In China, however, a seven-factor personality structure has been found which describes very different aspects of Chinese personalities (Wang et al., 2005). What does this mean for leadership? Given that the personalities of individuals in Japan, Korea and China tend to be different from one another, it follows that leadership styles as well as the characteristics of successful leaders also will vary from country to country. The leader that is exceptionally effective in Korea might be very different from the successful leader in Japan or China. As Asian firms increase their global reach through market expansion, consideration of personality type that is most congruent with the local leadership style might be warranted.

Motivation, Leadership and Corporate Social Responsibility in Asia

There are a number of theories that seek to describe how individuals are motivated in the workplace. Most of these theories were developed and tested in the West, and only a few have been examined in an Asian context. One of the most widely known is Maslow's Hierarchy of Needs theory. Maslow (1943) posits that there are five types of needs that individuals are motivated to fulfil in a hierarchical order. The most basic needs (physiological) are fulfilled first, followed by safety/security needs, needs for love or belongingness, need for status or self-esteem and finally, the need for self-actualization. Herzberg (1968) believes that there are two types of factors that motivate individuals. One group, called motivational factors, includes the work itself, responsibility, advancement, need for recognition, need for growth and achievement. The other group of more basic needs he calls hygiene factors, which include pay, company policies, job security and relationships with subordinates.

Herzberg's model has been studied in Korea, Japan and China (Usugami and Park, 2006). Results of that research indicate that Korean and Japanese executives recognized that both motivational and hygiene factors are important, but the Japanese were more motivated by praise for job performance and setting clear job objectives while the Koreans were more motivated by job stability. In China, on the other hand, external rewards such as money and individual bonuses are perceived as being strong motivators, along with intrinsic motivators such as promotion, career tracking and good working conditions, particularly when working for foreign firms (Jackson and Bak, 1998).

Motivating employees is one of a leader's main tasks. The factors that motivate individuals vary greatly by country. As Asian companies become more global, the likelihood of having employees from different cultures within the company increases. As companies expand operations beyond their borders, it also is likely that firms will employ foreign nationals. In order to motivate all individuals most effectively, whether at home or abroad, leaders must know how individuals from other cultures react to various motivational factors. This is especially true as firms struggle to retain the best and brightest employees within their organization, regardless of their country of origin.

Spotlight on Leadership: Female leadership in Asia

China

One of China's most influential corporate leaders is Zhang Yin, named by *Forbes* magazine as the wealthiest woman in China at US$10 billion. Founder of Nine Dragons Paper, the largest paper manufacturer in China with a market value in excess of US$5 billion, Zhang, 50, unlike most very wealthy women, did not inherit her money. Instead, she is a self-made entrepreneur. Coming from humble beginnings as the daughter of a military officer, Zhang with other members of her family now runs a vast business that recycles waste paper from Europe and the US, turns that paper into corrugated cardboard boxes, then returns the cardboard to Europe and the US filled with toys, electronics and other products in boxes labelled 'Made in China'.

Japan

In 2005, Sanyo Electric Company appointed Tomoyo Nonaka as CEO. A former newscaster with no executive experience but political connections, Nonaka served in this position until 2006 when she was replaced by the son of Sanyo's founder. Her resignation, in the midst of an accounting scandal and several product recalls, was significant, as she was the first woman to head a major electronics company in Japan (Wiseman, 2005). Fumiko Hayashi was also appointed to the top position in 2005 at Daiei, a large Japanese supermarket chain. Generally credited as being one of the most successful female executives, Hayashi had been recruited from BMW where she headed Tokyo operations for the luxury car manufacturer. In March 2007, Hayashi was demoted to vice chairwoman. Twelve months later, Hayashi left Daiei to return to the automotive industry and become a corporate vice president at Nissan (Wiseman, 2005).

Korea

In Korea, women leaders are a rare occurrence. This lack of female leadership has been called 'Korea's Unrecognized Corporate Scandal' by Renshaw and Lee (2005). This finding is consistent with the results from the GLOBE study noted earlier in this chapter. In Renshaw and Lee's research, they refer to the National Establishment Survey of 1,443 employees conducted by the Korea Labor Institute in 2002 that indicated less than 5 per cent of managers in Korea were women. This data also indicated that 64 per cent of all firms sampled had no women managers and 96 per cent had either one or no women managers. Renshaw and Lee (2005) attribute this dearth of women managers to gender discrimination inherent in Korean business culture. Despite the fact that Korean women have high levels of education and competence, they have even less presence in management than in Japan, which has a low level of 9 per cent, compared with 30 per cent in Scandinavia and 48 per cent in the US (Renshaw, 1999). Women cite factors such as the difficulty in finding a mentor, long working hours, lack of flexibility for dealing with family issues and lack of transparency in recruitment and promotion as major reasons for the glass ceiling prohibiting their movement into management (Renshaw and Lee, 2005). Further reasons, such as meetings after work, which often stress drinking and socializing, as well as an environment that either fosters or does not discourage sexual attention or innuendo, also make transition into management difficult. In essence, Korea is still a culture where 'think manager' means 'think male' (Luethge and Byosiere, 2007).

Corporate Social Responsibility (CSR) in Asia

In recent years, corporate scandals worldwide have led firms to focus upon the responsibility corporations have to society. In many cases, large corporations have been the leaders in developing policies to both ensure that their actions are in the best interests of their stakeholders (Welford, 2003, 2005) and protect their brand image and company reputation. In almost all cases, these policies come from the very top of the organization, and as a result, the leaders of the firm are highly involved in their development. Welford (2005), in a study of CSR policies and their incidence worldwide, notes that there are both internal and external measures of corporate responsibility, where internal measures focus upon things such as fair wages, equal opportunities and non-discrimination, while external aspects focus upon ethics, fair trade, corruption, bribery and the like. His results show that Asian companies focus much less on internal measures than their European and North American counterparts. However, with regard to external measures, Asian firms show similar and in some cases more involvement in the development of policies addressing these issues. Why is this? To be fair, there are a number of policies for fair wages and non-discrimination in the more developed economies of Asia, such as Japan, Korea and Singapore, but the lack of internal CSR policies in countries such as Malaysia and Thailand impact the overall numbers. In addition, the difficulties that women have with regard to discrimination in the workplace also impact internal CSR in the region. With regard to external CSR policies, Welford (2005) found that Japan, Korea and Singapore tended to be the countries in the region that were most likely to address these important areas of CSR in their corporate policies. One interesting result, which the author was unable to explain, was that Hong Kong appeared to have the least number of both internal and external CSR policies in almost all cases.

SUMMARY POINTS

- Leaders come in all shapes and sizes of personalities.

- Some types of individuals may be more successful in one country or situation than another, including leaders that are female.

- In addition, different factors motivate individuals from different Asian countries.

- Corporate social responsibility (CSR) varies in firms by culture, with many Asian firms focusing on the external aspects of CSR.

REFLECTIVE QUESTION

- How would personality and gender fit together to make a successful leader in each of the various Asian countries?

CONCLUSION

The quest into understanding Asian leadership and the development of Asian leadership models is on the rise in the field of management. Several factors are responsible for this. The global positioning of the Japanese multinationals has been increasing for almost half a century, with a focus on durable high-quality products manufactured with a process orientation based on teamwork. Korea has seen tremendous changes in product quality and global brand acceptance, particularly in the past decade. No longer the epitome of shoddy quality, many Korean brands, such as LG and Samsung, are now considered high-end products, and the companies behind those products have become very well respected. The emergence of China as a global economic power, albeit one that is still struggling for acceptance of its products, is in transition, as quality problems and a shaky reputation linger in some sectors. Given the tremendous increase in foreign direct investment, particularly in joint ventures in China in the past five years, it cannot be long before China becomes a force in the global marketplace.

There seems to be no short end to these developments and the interest in both indigenous Asian leadership as well as Western-based leadership seems to attract attention from all over the world. The collectivistic characteristics of the societies combined with the underlying Confucian philosophy and values seem to drive this interest. As China continues to develop joint Chinese–Western and Chinese–Asian companies and projects, one can only imagine what might result from the integration of East–West leadership philosophies and approaches.

Both for Westerners and Asians it is extremely difficult to 'submerge' ourselves in the deeper underlying and tacit values of leadership. It may well be the case that the connotation of leadership is so different from culture to culture that a convergence into one model or approach that is equally effective is unlikely. That there are common leadership elements is a given: however, the nature of the relationship among these elements is likely to vary tremendously from East to West and North to South.

CHAPTER SUMMARY

- The success of Asian corporations in the past 50 years has caused management scholars and practitioners to examine successful leaders and leadership in Asia.
- Unlike Western corporate leaders, Asian leaders tend to be less well known, operating quietly.
- Asian leadership is grounded in Confucian philosophy, focusing on trust, harmony and justice rather than the task-orientation of Western leadership. As a result, Asian leadership tends to have a long-term orientation as opposed to a short-term orientation seen in the West.
- Social relationships, such as those characterized by *guanxi*, *inhwa* and *wa*, are essential components of Asian business and leadership.
- Although many, if not most, leadership styles in Asia have a strong sense of empathy for workers, the styles that tend to be most effective vary greatly from country to country within Asia, and even within individual countries.
- A number of Western models have tried to characterize Asian leadership. The GLOBE study on leadership is helpful in comparing individual Asian countries with other countries on a number of leadership dimensions. Transformational leadership studies applied to individual Asian countries have shown varying results.
- Stemming from trait theories, personality has been studied widely with regard to leadership in Asia, with varying results. Since leaders are responsible for motivating employees, different motivators have been examined across cultures within Asia. Finally, the impact of female leaders is becoming more important as more and more women enter management within Asia.

KEY CONCEPTS

'Faceless' Asian executives: The relative anonymity that Asian executives enjoy that is very different from the hero worship of many executives in the West.

Confucian philosophy impacting Asian leadership: Reflects a strong humanistic, value-based, self-cultivating form of leadership striving towards social harmony.

Social relationships of *guanxi*, *inhwa* and *wa*: The development of connections, social favours and reciprocity for mutual benefit, leading to obligation on the parts of both parties.

Behavioural theories of leadership: Focus on styles of individuals who are thought to be good leaders in an attempt to identify those behaviours associated with successful leadership.

Contingency theories of leadership: Posit that successful leadership is dependent upon the characteristics of the situation, the characteristics of the leader and/or the characteristics of the followers.

Performance–Maintenance theory of leadership: There are two basic types of leader behaviour, task-based *performance* behaviours and group-based *maintenance* behaviours, where performance behaviours are those such as focusing on quality, increasing accuracy, observing rules; while maintenance behaviours focus on things such as group comfort, feelings of subordinates, and shows of appreciation.

Big Five personality factor model: This model looks at five basic dimensions of personality: openness to experience, agreeableness, neuroticism, extraversion and conscientiousness.

Corporate social responsibility: In the light of corporate scandals worldwide, firms are developing policies to ensure that they act in the best interests of all their stakeholders. These policies contain both internal (non-discrimination, fair wage, equal opportunity, human rights) and external (anti-bribery, anti-corruption, fair trade, ethics) aspects.

REVIEW QUESTIONS

1. As Asian economies further develop and parallel or even surpass the level of current Western leadership theories, which Asian leadership characteristics could be beneficial to Western business leaders?
2. The leadership typology of the GLOBE study originates primarily from Western thinking paradigms, expressing leadership characteristics in several unidimensional categories. To what extent are these typologies useful in studying Asian leadership and Asian leaders?
3. There are tremendous differences within the leadership of Chinese, Korean and Japanese companies. Which leadership characteristics are most common to all and why?
4. In recent years, we have noticed an increase in the representation of 'non-conformist' Asian leadership, such as women and young leaders. Can the current organizational and financial aspects of the Asian business climate embrace and nurture the next Bill Gates or Larry Page or Richard Branson?

LEARNING ACTIVITIES

1. Use the internet to look at the mission and vision statements for different subsidiaries of the same multinational company. What are the similarities and differences that you see? How do you think leadership will vary in different locations?
2. List the cultural characteristics that you think are most likely to work effectively for an Asian expatriate in a Western company and for a Western expatriate in an Asian company. Use the Web to gather your evidence.

MINI CASE

LEADERSHIP AT SHARP, SK TELECOM AND LI & FUNG

Sharp

Sharp, the Osaka-based company that brought the liquid crystal display (LCD) into the commercial arena, is battling fierce global competition with Samsung, Sony and LG-Philips for market domination. Sharp is highly reliant and dependent on

LCDs that account for 30 per cent of the company's bottom line, much more dependent upon that product line than its global competitors. However, the name of the game in the LCD market has boiled down to building a competitive advantage in manufacturing. This is very well understood by the recently appointed CEO, Mikio Katayama, a career-long Sharp engineer, who was the brainchild behind the Kameyama plant. Katayama decided to make a bold investment in a newly built LCD manufacturing facility, giving the world an indication of his innovative and risk-taking leadership style in conservative Japan. The multi-billion dollar Kameyama plant is widely regarded as the industry's most elite plant, where robots lift and move razorblade thin sheets of glass the size of a ping-pong table, which are then covered with liquid crystal and consequently cut into miniscule panels for cellphones, video games and other display applications. Sharp has posted record sales and profits for every year it has been in operation, and Katayama's vision focuses on being the top leader in technology. Katayama joined Sharp more than 25 years ago when he started as an engineer. He has spent his entire career at Sharp, which is not unusual in Japan, but in contrast with the typical Japanese career path, he became the CEO of Sharp at the very young age of 49. His vision and leadership style concentrate highly on perfection in manufacturing technology, production technology and innovation.

SK Telecom

Established in 1984 with a Fortune 500 ranking of 98, SK Telecom is a typical Korean company in many ways. However, its CEO since 2004, Kim Shin Bae, is anything but typical. With SK Telecom holding a 61 per cent market share in the wireless service market in South Korea,

Kim could sit back and watch, but that isn't his style. Determined to be a global communications leader, Kim believes that SK must change from the Confucian leadership tradition that is common in Asia. He thinks that a hierarchical structure with promotion based on seniority is not going to be as effective in the future as a company with open communication and knowledge sharing among employees, and that means a very flat single level manager structure. In addition to the structural change, Kim has implemented a corporate culture change to stimulate creativity and openness, such as the monthly employee talent shows in the company lobby. The change in corporate culture along with the structural change should help to stimulate communication, creativity, innovation and flexibility, all of which are needed if SK is to move ahead to become a global communications leader.

Li & Fung

Li & Fung is a family-owned business that is now operated by the third generation of Fungs. The current generation focuses on driving costs out of the value chain in the production of consumer goods – typically clothing – using highly efficient Western technology and exceptional quality control, yielding items that can be produced much more cheaply than in the West. Educated at Harvard, the current Fung leaders are truly globalizing their operation with a combination of the best of East and West. William and Victor Fung are operationalizing in the clothing production industry what William Edward Deming made popular in the automobile industry in Japan in the 1950s and 1960s – generating the manufacture of better products, more cheaply than those made outside of China. In the future, it is likely that Li & Fung, with their Western management philosophy, will favour professional managers who employ leadership styles more in line with practices in the West rather than those favoured in the East. Are these the Asian leaders of the future?

QUESTIONS

1. In order for Asian leadership to further develop globally, which characteristics of the leaders described do you consider having a major impact? Explain why.
2. Korean, Japanese and Chinese leadership styles reflect strong philosophical Confucian foundations. Which of these philosophical foundations do you recognize in these three leaders? Explain why.
3. Using contemporary Western leadership theories – transactional, transformational and charismatic leadership – discuss how these three leaders adapt different leadership styles.

Sources: Kelly, T. (2007). Go big or go home. Forbes.com, available at: http://www.forbes.com/technology/forbes/2007/0604/070.html?partner=links; *Asia Times* (2003). Korea: KTF, LG want SK Telecom market share cut. 19 December, available at: http://www.atimes.com/atimes/Korea/EL19Dg02.html; Stevens, A. (2007). Kim Shin Bae, CEO, SK Telecom. CNN.com/World Business, available at: http://edition.cnn.com/2007/BUSINESS/12/21/boardroom.bae/index.html; Mills, D.Q. (2005). Asian and American leadership styles: How are they unique? Working Knowledge: Research & Ideas, Harvard Business School, 27 June, available at: http://hbswk.hbs.edu/item/4869.html.

INTERESTING WEB LINKS

Center for Creative Leadership – Asia: http://www.ccl.org/leadership/capabilities/asia/research.aspx
Asian Leadership Institute: http://www.asianleadership.com/index.php
Asian Women in Business: http://www.awib.org/awib.html
Asian Strategy and Leadership Institute: http://www.asli.com.my/introduction.htm
Asian Business Council: http://www.asiabusinesscouncil.org/mission.html

REFERENCES

Alston, J.P. (1989). *Wa, Guanxi,* and *Inhwa*: Managerial principles in Japan, China, and Korea. *Business Horizons,* **32**(2): 26–31.

Alves, J.C., Manz, C.C. and Butterfield, D.A. (2005). Developing leadership theory in Asia: The role of Chinese philosophy. *International Journal of Leadership Studies,* **1**(1): 3–27.

Ashton, M.C., Lee, K. and Son, C. (2000). Honesty as the sixth factor of personality: Correlations with Machiavellianism, primary psychopathy, and social adroitness. *European Journal of Personality,* **14**: 359–68.

Asia Times (2003). Korea: KTF, LG want SK Telecom's market share cut. 19 December, available at: http://www.atimes.com/atimes/Korea/EL19Dg02.html.

Bass, B.M. (1990). *Bass and Stogdill's Handbook of Leadership: Theory, Research, and Managerial Applications,* 3rd edition. New York: Free Press.

Bass, B.M. and Avolio, B.J. (1997). *Full Range Leadership Development: Manual for the Multifactor Leadership Questionnaire.* Palo Alto, CA: Mindgarden.

Blunt, P. and Jones, M.L. (1997). Exploring the limits of Western leadership theory in East Asia and Africa. *Personnel Review*, **26**(1/2): 6–23.

Bryman, A. (1993). Charismatic leadership in organizations: Some neglected issues. *Leadership Quarterly*, **4**: 289–304.

Burns, J.M. (1978). *Leadership*. New York: Harper & Row.

Chemers, M.M. (2000). Leadership research and theory: A functional integration. *Group Dynamics: Theory, Research, and Practice*, **4**(1): 27–43.

Costa, P.T. and McCrae, R.R. (1985). *The NEO PI-Royal Personality Inventory Manual*. Odessa, FL: Psychological Assessment Resources.

Costa, P.T. and McCrae, R.R. (1989). *The NEO-PI/NEO-FFI Manual Supplement*. Odessa, FL: Psychological Assessment Resources.

Den Hartog, D.N. and Dickson, M.W. (2004). Leadership and culture. In Antonakis, J., Cianciolo, A.T. and Sternberg, R.J. (eds) *The Nature of Leadership*. Thousand Oaks, CA: Sage Publications.

Dorfman, P.W. and Howell, J.P. (1997). Leadership in Western and Asian countries: Commonalities and differences in effective leadership. *Leadership Quarterly*, **8**(3): 233–74.

Farh, J.L. and Cheng, B.S. (2000). A Cultural Analysis of Paternalistic Leadership in Chinese Organizations. In Li, J.T., Tsui, A.S. and Weldon, E. (eds) *Management and Organizations in the Chinese Context*. New York: St. Martin's Press.

Fernandez, J.A. (2004). The gentleman's code of Confucius: Leadership by values. *Organizational Dynamics*, **33**(1): 21–31.

Fukushige, A. and Spicer, D.P. (2007). Leadership preferences in Japan: An exploratory study. *Leadership & Organization Development Journal*, **28**(6): 508–30.

Goldberg, L.R. (1990). An alternative descriptive of personality: The big five structure. *Journal of Personality and Social Psychology*, **59**: 1216–29.

Gorrill, J.R. (2007). Doing business in South Korea: South Korean social and business culture, available at: http://www.communicaid.com/cross-cultural-training/culture-for-business-and-management/doing-business-in/South-korean-business-and-social-culture.php.

Halpin, A.W. and Winer, B.J. (1957). A factorial study of the leader behavior descriptions. In Stogdill, R.M. and Coons, A.E. (eds) *Leader Behavior: Its Description and Measurement*. Columbus, OH: Ohio State University Bureau of Business Research.

Hemphill, J.K. (1950). *Leader Behavior Description*. Columbus, OH: Ohio State University Personnel Research Board.

Herzberg, F. (1968). One more time, how do you motivate employees? *Harvard Business Review*, **46**(1): 53–62.

House, R.J., Hanges, P.J., Javidan, M., Dorfman, P.W. and Gupta, V. (2004). *Culture, Leadership and Organizations: The GLOBE Study of 62 Societies*. Thousand Oaks, CA: Sage Publications.

Jackson, T. and Bak, M. (1998). Foreign companies and Chinese workers: Employee motivation in the People's Republic of China. *Journal of Organizational Change Management*, **11**(4): 282–300.

John, O.P. (1990). The 'Big Five' factor taxonomy: Dimensions of personality in the natural language and questionnaires. In Pervin, L.A. (ed.) *Handbook of Personality: Theory and Research*. New York: Guildford Press.

Kelly, T. (2007). Go big or go home. Forbes.com, available at: http://www.forbes.com/technology/forbes/2007/0604/070.html?partner=links.

Lee, S.K. (1987). *A Chinese Conception of 'Management': An Interpretive Approach*. Doctoral dissertation, School of Education, University of Massachusetts, Amherst.

Liu, L.A., Friedman, R.A. and Chi, S. (2005). *Ren Qing* versus the 'Big Five': The role of culturally sensitive measures of individual difference in distributive negotiations. *Management and Organization Review*, **1**(2): 225–47.

Luethge, D.J. and Byosiere, P. (2007). Japanese corporations: Gender differences in re-defining tacit knowledge. *Women in Management Review*, **22**(1): 33–48.

McCrae, R.R. and Costa, P.T., Jr. (1997). Personality trait structure as a human universal. *American Psychologist*, **52**(5): 509–16.

McGregor, D. (1960). *The Human Side of Enterprise*. New York: McGraw-Hill.

Maslow, A. (1943). A theory of human motivation. *Psychological Review*, **50**: 370–96.

Mills, D.Q. (2005). Asian and American leadership styles: How are they unique? Working Knowledge: Research & Ideas, Harvard Business School, 27 June, available at: http://hbswk.hbs.edu/item/4869.html.

Misumi, J. (1985). *The Behavioral Science of Leadership: An Interdisciplinary Japanese Research Program*. Ann Arbor, MI: University of Michigan Press.

Misumi, J and Peterson, M.F. (1985). The Performance-Maintenance (PM) theory of leadership: Review of a Japanese research program. *Administrative Science Quarterly*, **20**(2): 198–223.

Miyataki, G. and Whatley, A. (1989). Human resource development in South Korea. *Asia Pacific Journal of Human Resources*, **27**: 6–13.

Ouchi, W.G.. (1981). *Theory Z: How American Businesses Can Meet the Japanese Challenge*. Reading, MA: Addison-Wesley.

Pun, K.F., Chin, K.S. and Lau, H. (2000). A review of the Chinese cultural influences on Chinese enterprise management. *International Journal of Management Reviews*, **2**(4): 325–38.

Renshaw, J.R. (1999). *Kimono in the Boardroom: The Invisible Evolution of Japanese Women Managers*. Oxford: Oxford University Press.

Renshaw, J.R. and Lee, J. (2005). Korea's unrecognized corporate scandal: The absence of women managers. Japan Policy Research Institute Working Paper No. 104, available at: http://www.jpri.org/publications/working papers/wp104.html.

Rhee, E., Uleman, J.S. and Lee, H.K. (1996). Variations in collectivism and individualism by ingroup and culture: Confirmatory factor analysis. *Journal of Personality and Social Psychology*, **71**: 1037–54.

Shao, L. and Webber, S. (2006). A cross-cultural test of the five-factor model of personality and transformational leadership. *Journal of Business Research*, **59**: 936–44.

Shin, S.J. and Zhou, J. (2003). Transformation leadership, conservation and creativity: Evidence from Korea. *Academy of Management Journal*, **46**(6): 703–14.

Shin, Y.K. (1998–1999). The traits and leadership styles of CEOs in Korean companies. *International Studies of Management and Organization*, **28**(4): 40–8.

Stevens, A. (2007). Kim Shin Bae, CEO, SK Telecom. *CNN.com/World Business*, available at: http://edition.cnn.com/2007/BUSINESS/12/21/boardroom.bae/index.html.

Stogdill, R.M. (1948). Personal factors associated with leadership: A survey of the literature. *Journal of Psychology*, **25**: 35–71.

Triandis, H.C. (1995). *Individualism and Collectivism*. Boulder, CO: Westview Press.

Tsui, A.S., Wang, H., Xin, K., Zhang, L. and Fu, P.P. (2004). Variation of leadership styles among Chinese CEOs. *Organizational Dynamics*, **33**(1): 5–20.

Usugami, J. and Park, K.Y. (2006). Similarities and differences in employee motivation viewed by Korean and Japanese executives: Empirical study on employee motivation management of Japanese-affiliated companies in Korea. *The International Journal of Human Resource Management*, **17**(2): 280–94.

Wang, D., Cui, H. and Zhou, F. (2005). Measuring the personality of Chinese: QZPS versus NEO PI-R. *Asian Journal of Social Psychology*, **8**: 97–122.

Weber, M. (1947). *The Theory of Social and Economic Organization*. Translated by T. Parsons. New York: The Free Press.

Welford, R.J. (2003). Corporate social responsibility in Europe and Asia: Critical elements and best practice. *Journal of Corporate Citizenship*, **13**(Spring): 31–47.

Welford, R.J. (2005). Corporate social responsibility in Europe, North America and Asia. *Journal of Corporate Citizenship*, **17**(Spring): 33–52.

Wiseman, P. (2005). Female CEOs signal change at Japan firms. *USA Today*, available at: http://www.usatoday.com/money/world/2005-06-07-japan-ceo-usat_x.htm.

Xin, K.R. and Pearce, J.L. (1996). *Guanxi*: Connections as substitutes for formal institutional support. *Academy of Management Journal*, **39**(6): 1641–58.

Yang, M.M. (1994). *Gifts, Favors and Banquets: The Art of Social Relationships in China.* Ithaca, NY: Cornell University Press.

Yukl, G. (1999). An evaluation of conceptual weaknesses in transformational and charismatic leadership theories. *Leadership Quarterly*, **10**(2): 285–305.

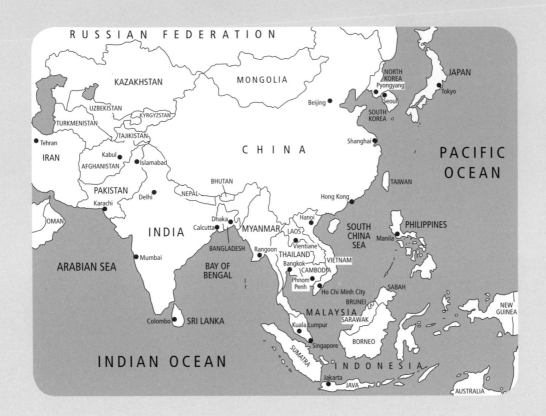

Chapter outline

- A new approach to living and working conditions
- Why should living and working conditions matter to businesses?
- Poverty and business in Asia
- Working time changes in Asia
- Corporate strategies and living and working conditions

Chapter objectives

After reading this chapter, you should have knowledge of:

1. The importance of living and working conditions for businesses
2. Management practices affecting living/working conditions
3. The situation of wealth and working hours in Asia
4. The relationship between business and poverty and working hours
5. Corporate strategies towards living and working conditions

Chapter 7

The role of business in Asian living and working conditions

Naoki Kuriyama

INTRODUCTION

Living and working conditions are becoming increasingly relevant for business and management. Globalization in the world economy, characterized by liberalization in world trade and investment, may create wealth and prosperity for some, but is accompanied by serious social and environmental problems. Capital investment is on a constant worldwide quest for lower labour and living costs, and in Asia, debate has arisen over whether this quest contributes to a decline in social factors.

Social issues, such as increasing poverty and the wealth gap, will inevitably interfere with the sustainable development of any economy and business environment, shrinking exclusive markets and the capacity for wealth creation. Most governments in Asia have come to the conclusion that a better business environment will follow from an inclusive society where all players work towards decreasing poverty and eliminating discriminatory practices.

International forums, including the UN's Copenhagen Social Summit of 1995 and the proceedings connected with establishing the UN Millennium Development Goals (MDGs), have discussed issues such as these. The International Labour Organization (ILO), as a core international forum on living and working conditions involving key tripartite constituents – governments, workers and employers – has also addressed these issues and has come up with a concept conducive to better business and, by extension, better living and working conditions – 'decent work', as proposed by the ILO, is recognized by world forums as a universally desirable target for living and working conditions.

Decent work sums up people's aspirations of people in their working lives. It involves opportunities for work that are productive and deliver a fair income, security in the workplace and social protection for families, better prospects for personal development and social integration, freedom for people to express their concerns, organize and participate in the decisions that affect their lives and equality of opportunity and treatment for all women and men. (http://www.ilo.org/global/About_the_ILO/Mainpillars/WhatisDecent Work/lang--en/index.htm)

The term sustainable enterprise was adopted and seen as a major tool for achieving 'decent work' at the ILO's 2007 conference. It was recognized that promoting sustainable enterprise would lead to improved living standards and social conditions.[1] This new approach to enterprise development in society is becoming a focus for issues such as business's relationship to living and working conditions.

This new approach is emerging in parallel to the growing emphasis on corporate social responsibility (CSR) by business stakeholders worldwide. It suggests an important change in how businesses interact with society and local communities; while such interaction has to date been largely reactive in terms of working and living conditions, a more proactive mode is appearing. In Asia, with its extraordinary ongoing economic development, business interests need to be proactive in this way to tackle the emerging social issues consequent on that development, and this chapter will outline this ongoing process.

A NEW APPROACH TO LIVING AND WORKING CONDITIONS

Corporate development is increasingly affected by the external environment, such as local communities, which have a stake in business activity on both the demand and supply side – demand, as the local community supplies market and custom, and supply, because an integral part of a business's resources, such as finance, facilities and workers, should be sourced within the community.

As the external environment determines the business-enabling environment, international business, in particular, has been geographically mobile in its quest for lucrative markets and consumers, favourable human resource conditions and good infrastructure. Nonetheless, once a plant is established, there will be resistance to further moving or restructuring; consciousness of the business and its role will grow, inevitably involving the enterprise more in external relations, in particular with the local community. Business attitudes towards involvement with local communities are becoming increasingly proactive.

The study of enterprises and the external environment has been dominated by reactive responses, as in contingency theory. More recent perspectives are generally more proactive to changing environments, embodying strategic outlooks, and they particularly affect Asian countries, where the external environment of enterprises is more diverse.

The issues of living conditions in local communities and working conditions in enterprises have previously been discussed together in the field of human resource management (HRM). Studies of HRM have also extended their perspectives to the external environment. In the early 1980s, the Harvard model (Beer et al., 1984) provided external analytical factors for HRM (Figure 7.1). HRM policies are affected by stakeholder interests and situational factors, and the resulting outcomes have long-term consequences at organizational and societal level (Bratton and Gold, 2007). Likewise, the external inputs and outputs of HRM are interconnected over time, developing the perception of 'context' in the external and internal environments of HRM (Bloisi, 2007).

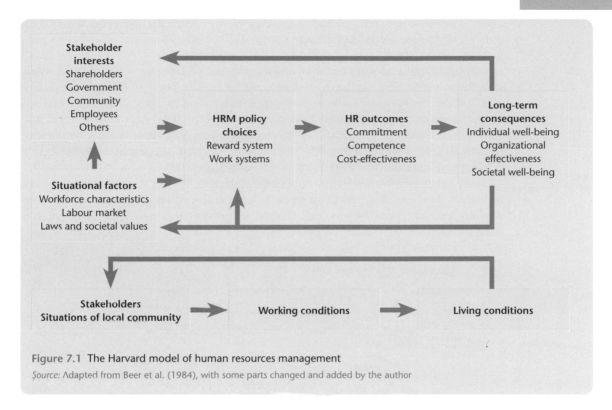

Figure 7.1 The Harvard model of human resources management

Source: Adapted from Beer et al. (1984), with some parts changed and added by the author

Although the interaction of living and working conditions is reciprocal, there is an inclination of influence from one towards the other. First is the influence of living conditions on working conditions. The internal working conditions of an enterprise are largely decided by external conditions. Wage levels in the local community, for example, are influenced by living conditions as well as factors such as industrial relations. Japan's case is typical: *shunto* (intensive national wage negotiations each spring between employers and unions) can affect the whole economy, from the industrial sector to public services. Wage negotiations at the company level during the post-war economic growth period were regulated by the general economic environment, such as increasing commodity prices and changing living conditions. This is one reason why working conditions in Japan became standardized across a large number of enterprises throughout the country.

On the other hand, working conditions also have a bearing upon living conditions. Working conditions in companies are more likely than ever to affect internal human resources, and thus external conditions in the community, via the families of employees and the communities surrounding places of business. Improved working conditions are felt throughout the local community through the improvement of workers' well-being.

Figure 7.2 demonstrates that people are internal as well as external stakeholders in enterprises. While enterprises control working conditions, the local community provides living conditions for the workers. Enterprises and local communities are therefore interconnected, and people are the catalyst between them, maintaining the relationship between working and living conditions. Living conditions are forces affecting working conditions, while recent company policy trends have indicated that changes in working conditions are becoming shaping factors on living conditions. This policy emphasizes work–life balance, a formula for optimizing the potential to integrate aspects of life as lived by the individual.

Employability is another example of the influence of working conditions on living conditions in the community. Skill development is an important working condition, as it is a determinant on income. Skills applicable to more extensive labour markets can enhance workers' bargaining power, and in turn the local community can utilize workers' skills in more extensive fields. A company may lose some capable employees, but can acquire other suitable candidates from the external labour market by increasing the employability of their workers (Rogovsky and Sims, 2001).

Thus, living and working conditions are interactive. A new strategic approach can be identified where enterprises can create a constructive spiral of interactions between working and living conditions. This chapter will review this new approach, which is most relevant for Asian business development.

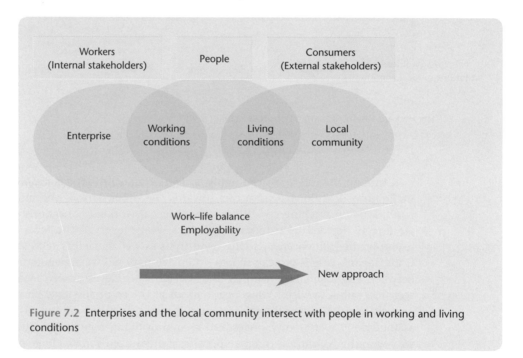

Figure 7.2 Enterprises and the local community intersect with people in working and living conditions

SUMMARY POINTS

- A business-enabling environment largely depends on living standards in the local community.

- There is growing pressure on enterprises to avoid adverse effects and create positive effects for the community.

- Living and working conditions are closely related through people in the community.

- Constructive interaction between living and working conditions is required for enterprises in the local community.

WHY SHOULD LIVING AND WORKING CONDITIONS MATTER IN BUSINESS?

The Meaning of Living Conditions and Standards of Living

The term 'living conditions' cannot be clearly defined and contains a range of meanings; it covers a broad field of life as lived, including working conditions, accessibility to available goods and services such as employment services, education, medical care and life expectancy. The meaning of 'standard of living' is defined as the level of goods and services obtainable for a given income. Standard of living can also be valued by cultural and regional aspects. Sometimes people in rural areas will place value on their existing standard of living and resist any move to cities with higher objective standards of living. Furthermore, since it is difficult to improve living conditions through public policy and legislation alone, enterprise development is regarded as an avenue for social and economic development in order to improve living conditions.

The Meaning of Labour Standards and Working Conditions

It must be noted that 'standards' are different from 'conditions'. Particularly, the terms 'labour standards' and 'working conditions' are used very differently in the contexts of labour law and workplace management. Some standards are generally set by regulation, often described as legal requirements. According to *Webster's New World Dictionary of American Language*, 'standard' is 'something established as a rule or basis of comparison in measuring or judging capacity, quantity, extent, value, quality, and so on'. Usually, labour standards mean general principles and values of labour, and codes of conduct at work regulated by national labour laws or collective agreements. Labour standards are standards concerning employment and working conditions found acceptable by employers and workers (ILO, 1998).

Moreover, labour standards are recognized as universal values based on dignity, respect, trust and fairness. International Labour Standards are globally supported by the ILO and its tripartite constituents of governments, workers and employers. International Labour Standards have been set to create a win win strategy for the entire society, including social partners.

On the other hand, working conditions are the physical, social and managerial factors affecting a worker's job environment (ILO, 1998). They reflect the current situation of workers at the workplace. For employees, working conditions include wages and working hours, health and safety, childcare, family welfare provisions, stress management, emergency loans and elimination of sexual harassment. Employees' working conditions can often determine their performance and productivity. Poor working conditions are coupled with aspects which may cause unnecessary stress and strains on employees.

The different meanings of conditions and standards have led to quite different experiences at the workplace. For example, labour standards are unable to set a fixed wage level because this is determined by various economic and social factors. However, they can set a guiding *principle* for wages, including a minimum wage system. On the other hand, working conditions are formed by financial and economic situations, internal and external circumstances and the practices and policies of companies.

'Working conditions' is a better term to use when focusing on non-legal matters. The issue of labour standards and business is another important topic. Flanagan (2006:

7) distinguishes the meanings of the two terms 'labour standards' and 'labour conditions', and includes labour rights at the core of labour standards and working conditions in labour conditions.

How Does Economic Development Improve Standards of Living?

Living and working conditions in national economies have long been discussed in the field of development research. However, discussion of relationships between business and living and working conditions is rather new, energized by the CSR debate. The major theories and views are as follows.

The Trickle-down theory set out by Simon Kuznets (1955) explains the correlation between economic development and income distribution. It indicates that although inequality between rich and poor will initially increase, it will level off at a later stage of development by 'trickle-down' benefits from the leading wealth-creating sectors to the rest of the economy. However, a number of empirical studies have indicated that there is no necessary correlation between inequality and economic growth. Furthermore, high disparity in income distribution can lead to economic stagnation.

Neo-classical economists explain that wages, the sources of living standards, should be set at market-clearing levels. They insist that regulated wage determination will bring unemployment. Ideas of '*laissez-faire*' and deregulation have been promoted in economic policies seeking to make market mechanisms work effectively. Milton Friedman, a prominent advocate of economic freedom, insisted that 'there is one and only one social responsibility of business – to use its resources and engage in activities designed to increase its profits so long as it stays within the rules of the game, which is to say, engages in open and free competition without deception or fraud' (Friedman, 1962).

However, this idea has come into question in recent times, through many empirical studies and policy directives. There is evidence that living standards can be maintained and improved by proper regulatory policies and that such policies will reduce pressure on firms to increase wages. Also, it is often pointed out that market failure occurs in the absence of public benefits in areas like law enforcement, abuse of power (monopolies), negative externality (including pollution) and asymmetric information such as insurance markets.

Consequently, certain institutional interventions are often proposed to improve living conditions without extending inequality and to deal with market failure. For businesses, living conditions matter, from the perspective of supply and demand. Living conditions in the community form the quality and quantity of the market and the quality and quantity of the workers available for recruitment from the community.

Industrial relations have played a vital role in fixing wage standards as the major point of wage negotiation. Negotiation of working conditions through collective bargaining between employers and workers has been a fundamental mechanism in major industrialized economies, enhancing industrial and social calm. Industrial relations based on freedom of association and the right to organize are a universal and fundamental right at work. Collective bargaining and dispute settlement over wage negotiations contribute to correcting the gap between working and living conditions.

It is, however, often noted that industrial relations are not the only dynamic in setting working conditions. Because of asymmetric information between workers and employers, negotiated wage levels often do not reflect real labour market situations. In addition, fixing working conditions by industrial relations is losing effect, as organized labour is declining.

As enterprise-level wage fixing spreads into the reward system, it becomes a critical factor of a company's competitiveness. It has been observed that wage fixing may be a matter of HRM rather than industrial relations (transition from IR to HRM). Nonetheless, increasing competitiveness and productivity is both a basis for creating better working conditions and a source of better living conditions (ILO, 2006). The linkages between business and living and working conditions have become more and more strengthened from the viewpoint of industrial relations and HRM as well.

Motives and Rationales of Business for Community Involvement

Living conditions are important environmental factors for the people of a community. Any business operating in a community has to be aware of the interaction between the internal and external environments. Business may have various motives for getting involved in the local community (Bronchain, 2003), such as 'awareness of impact': in a situation of 'a relatively large company in a relatively small community', the business cannot ignore the impacts of employment and produced goods and services. Other motives include compensating for limited local access to infrastructure and resources. Business is required to fill the gap between business needs and local needs.[2] Moreover, building goodwill in the community and enhancing image are important for all business interests.

Community involvement also encourages strengthening company culture and employees' social skills, making the workplace attractive, and developing and testing new products and services in the local market. In the US, employee volunteering has traditionally been the most common way of a company becoming involved in the local community. This approach is now spreading in many European countries throughout large and small companies. However, local volunteerism is an expression of a core principle of most cultures. For example, United Nations Volunteers (UNV) observed volunteerism in Thailand in that '[T]here are two major social foundations supporting volunteerism: Buddhism and mutual aid culture. There are hundred of thousands of Buddhist monks who can be considered as volunteers in different temples' (UNV Country Specific Information Thailand, UN Volunteers, 2008). Corporate volunteering in Asia should be carefully explored in practice. From a business perspective, Philip Kotler (Kotler and Lee, 2005) suggests the strengths of community volunteers for business as building corporate reputation, attracting and retaining a motivated workforce, building strong community relationships and leveraging current corporate social initiatives.

Hence, the motivation of companies to develop community involvement ranges from internal to external benefits. Increased employee motivation, development of skills and embedding company culture are examples of internal benefits. External benefits, the licence to operate and better employee recruitment motivate enterprises to involve themselves in the living conditions of their local communities.

SUMMARY POINTS

■ 'Standards' refer to levels valued by others, whereas 'conditions' mean general factors affecting the environment. These apply to the discussion of standards of living and living conditions as well as to labour standards and working conditions.

■ Theories of economic development and living and working standards range from trickle-down and neo-classical theory to institutional economics. Recent international forums have argued for the proactive involvement of companies in the living and working conditions of the workplace and local community.

■ Enterprises have various rationales for being involved in the living conditions of the local community.

POVERTY AND BUSINESS IN ASIA

One of Asia's specificities is its diversified economies. There are both emerging economies with high growth rates and impoverished territories; often, an informal sector, which operates outside labour standards and regulations, comprises a section of the population living at subsistence level. We cannot discuss living and working conditions in Asia without discussing the poverty in sectors such as this.

The high economic growth in parts of Asia has been impressive, exemplified by the remarkable rise in GDP in China and India in the past decade or so. The newly industrialized economies, such as the Republic of Korea and Singapore, have successfully improved poverty within their countries by significantly reducing the wealth gap between rich and poor.

In other social aspects of Asia's development, however, and especially in southern parts of the continent, the situation is different. Poverty remains as pervasive in Asia as in Africa; in 2006, an estimated 17.6 per cent of Asian workers lived in extreme poverty, on less than US$1 per day, and 51.9 per cent on less than US$2 a day.

If we take earnings of US$1 a day as an indicator of poverty, it appears that poverty has significantly reduced in most countries in the region when comparing data from 1990 and 2003 (see Figure 7.3). However, as Figure 7.4 shows, the picture is not so positive at the US$2-a-day level, which is also below subsistence level. Here, it is evident that most countries have not successfully reduced prevailing poverty, and around 1.9 billion people, representing 60 per cent of Asia's population (77 per cent in terms of the South Asian sub-region), were poor, earning less than US$2 a day in 2003 (ADB, 2006).

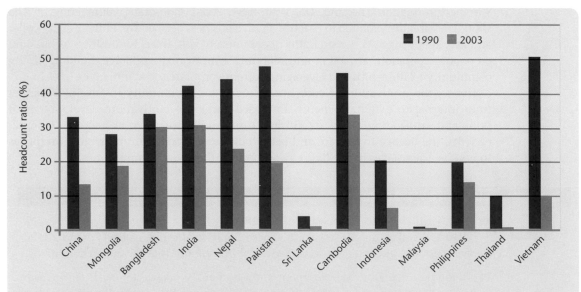

Figure 7.3 People living on US$1 a day poverty in 1990 and 2003
Source: ADB (2006).

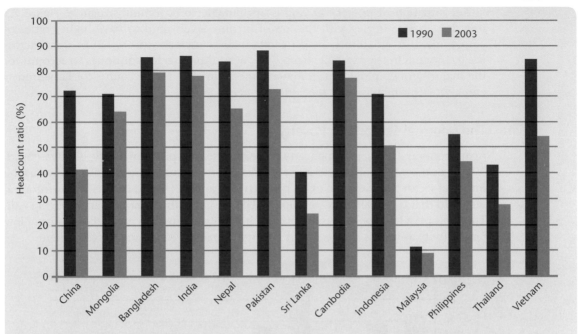

Figure 7.4 People living on US$2 a day poverty in 1990 and 2003
Source: ADB (2006).

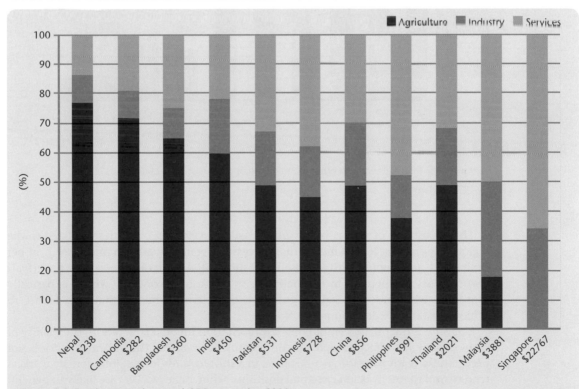

Figure 7.5 Employment share and GDP per capita, 2000
Source: ADB (2006).

The situation of poverty in Asia is attributable to economic structure. Figure 7.5 indicates that countries with the lowest income levels tend to have higher ratios of employment in agriculture. As per capita income increases (from left to right) across the economies in the available figures, the agricultural sector continues to account for the majority of employment in low-income countries. This accounts for large under-employment, which cannot meet income needs.

The Informal Sector and Poverty

Apart from rural areas, urban poverty is the most serious problem for the disadvantaged. A large number of people subsist in the urban non-agriculture sector also known as the informal sector. A correlation exists between per capita GDP and the size of the informal sector, in that the smaller the per capita GDP, the larger the informal sector (Figure 7.6). This sector is a huge pool of underutilized human resources, an inevitable source of low productivity as well as the persistent poverty characterized by underemployment.

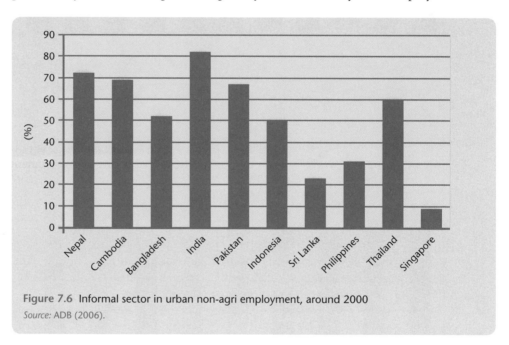

Figure 7.6 Informal sector in urban non-agri employment, around 2000
Source: ADB (2006).

The persistence of pervasive poverty in Asia's developing countries is related to the region's informal sector. It means that successful economic growth and growth of per capita GDP are coupled with an absence of substantial reduction in income poverty. It also suggests an increase in inequality in the national economy, which is basically caused by what has been called 'growth without employment', that is, a failure to achieve sustainable development.

Not only is quantity of employment important in income generation, the quality of employment also affects people's income status. Formalizing the informal sector is not necessarily a ready solution. For instance, in a shift towards formal jobs, female workers tend to find themselves in unsecured positions, while male workers are likely to benefit; in other words, a shift to formal sectors will sometimes aggravate gender inequalities (ILO, 2004).

Poverty Alleviation at the Bottom of the Pyramid Market

The idea of Making Markets Work for the Poor (MMW4P) is particularly relevant in this context. The important point of this approach is to change the structures and characteristics of markets by involving and benefiting the poor in a sustainable way. This requires creating linkages with micro- and informal-sector enterprises in the region. Value-chain systems of enterprise relations have significant potential to integrate micro, small and medium enterprises into national and global production systems (ILO, 2007a).

The term 'Bottom of the Pyramid' was coined by C.K. Prahalad (2005), who pointed out the potential for an enormous business market offering a new world of opportunity if the poor were to be seen as value-conscious consumers. Consumers at the bottom of the pyramid prefer goods and services of immediate use and are more value-conscious in costs and needs. Prahalad points out that new approaches to marketing and distribution, through the development of new products and services, can create within the poor the capacity to consume.

Business has a large stake in the lives of the poor. In reality, poor consumers pay more than rich consumers for basic services. In some developing countries, 15–90 per cent of primary education is provided in private schools, and some 63 per cent of healthcare expenditure in the poorest countries is private, almost twice that in the high-income countries of the OECD (33 per cent) (UNDP, 2004).

The informal business sector provides substandard goods and services to the poor at much cheaper prices than the formal market. If employment and income could be generated among the poorest sections of society, their living standards would improve. Then, if business could provide goods and services while increasing choice and reducing prices, interaction would be stimulated between those at the base of the pyramid and the private sector would create opportunities for direct involvement in the market economy (Rajagopalan, 2006). A well-known Unilever business model at the base of the pyramid suggests a fresh approach to consumer affordability. It challenges the traditional cost plus margin method of determining price. Business should find a cost base that supports its margin (Unilever, 2006).

Dignity at work depends on sufficient livelihood for oneself and one's family, self-respect and social responsibility (Rayman, 2001). Working conditions need a rewarding quality of life so that they create a virtuous circle for better working and living conditions.

The Millennium Development Goals (MDGs) were adopted by the UN in a global commitment to eradicating poverty, promoting human dignity and achieving peace and environmental sustainability. The key factor relating to poverty alleviation is productivity enhancement. Labour productivity has become an indicator of the MDG for poverty reduction (ILO, 2007b). To eradicate the extreme poverty of those living on less than US$1 a day is a first priority. The UN is beginning to develop a global development partnership with business, and businesses have begun to accept that they have mutual interests in attaining these goals. At the same time, there are growing international demands for companies to be more transparent and more accountable for their economic, social and environmental impacts wherever they operate. Businesses can contribute to the MDGs through community investment, more ethical supply chain management of core business activities and active engagement in public policy dialogue and advocacy activities.

For example, DHL in the Asia-Pacific region aligned its CSR initiatives with the MDGs, focusing their sustainability strategy on three major areas: disaster management, supporting future generations and creating a market for social change in line with the MDGs. Partnerships with UN organizations (UNDP and UN OCHA) have been put in place, and the DHL 'YES' award, created in 2007, is given to young social entrepreneurs in Asia who contribute to the UN's MDGs (Koh, 2007).

SUMMARY POINTS

- Although Asia is highly successful in terms of high economic growth, with the prominent examples of China and India, there is still enormous poverty. This disparity reflects negatively on sustainable development.

- There has been 'growth without employment' on a large scale in Asia.

- Poverty and the informal sector signify underemployment and underutilization of resources.

- The Millennium Development Goals require partnership between the UN and business. Business can gain advantage by creating markets for poorer sections at the bottom of the social pyramid.

WORKING TIME CHANGES IN ASIA

Working hours in Asia are changing. Global progress concerning working time is promoting shorter and flexible working hours according to economic and social development. A top priority of governments is to set statutory limits on weekly working hours. Table 7.1 shows that the progress of Asian countries in this respect is uneven, although strong policy development is seen in some countries such as Japan and the Republic of Korea.

Table 7.1 Weekly normal hours limits

	No universal statutory limit	40 hours	41–46 hours	48 hours
1984	India, Pakistan, Vietnam	Indonesia	Mongolia, Singapore	Japan, China, Laos, Malaysia, Philippines, Thailand
2005	India, Pakistan	China, Japan Indonesia, Korea, Mongolia	Singapore	Cambodia, Laos, Malaysia, Philippines, Thailand, Vietnam

Source: ILO database of working time laws (www.ilo.org/travdatabase).

Statutory standard weekly hour limits vary in Asia. Many countries have a basic regulation of 48 hours, while others have an advanced limit of 40 hours. Singapore is in between, at 44 hours a week. India and Pakistan are two of the few cases in the world where there is no generally applicable weekly limit on working hours.

Actual working hours also vary from one country to another. Comparable data are limited for OECD countries. From a historical analysis of actual working hours, it can be said that economic development is influential in reducing actual working hours up to a certain point where the impact of income on working hours becomes unclear. Actual working hours in Asia are atypical situations. Many countries have excessively long working hours. An ILO study indicated that the benefits of growth have not translated into shorter working hours, while rapid economic growth and productivity gains have contributed to rising real wages in some Asian developing countries (ILO, 2005: 23). The incidence of long working hours is rather high in newly industrialized countries among the so-called East Asian Tigers and South-Eastern Dragons. Indonesia recorded 51.2 per cent in 2004–2005, followed by South Korea with 49.5 per cent for the same period and Thailand with 46.7 per cent in 2000 (see Table 7.2).

Table 7.2 Incidence of long working hours in total employment

	1995	2000	2004–2005	Hour cut-off
Indonesia	46.9%*	49.1%	51.2%**	45+
Japan	28.8%	17.4%	17.7%	49+
South Korea		56.3%	49.5%	49+
Macau	41.0%*	41.9%	39.1%	50+
Pakistan			44.4%**	49+
Thailand	51.8%	46.7%		50+

Note: *1996 figure; **2003 figure.
Source: ILO Labour Statistics Database cited in Lee et al. (2007: 46–51).

A survey conducted by the ILO on workers with family responsibilities in seven selected countries reveals some interesting cases. Australia has a prominent gender gap with regard to weekly working hours because part-time work is widespread, and female workers can have daily starting and finishing times (flexi-time). In addition, the feeling of overwork is low. Although flexibility in working time is usually considered to be low in developing countries, Malaysian workers at surveyed companies are likely to have flexi-time practice (though it may not be institutionalized), and interestingly, the feeling of overwork among female workers is lower than in Australia. The case of the Philippines is also exceptional. Here, there is no gap between male and female working hours, and although flexi-time can be arranged, the feeling of overwork among female workers is relatively high.

Table 7.3 Working time and flexibility, 2002

Country/Gender	Length of working time (weekly hours in the main job)	Flexibility over daily schedule (can start work late or leave early if needed without losing pay, ranging from 1 absolutely yes to 0 absolutely no)	Overwork (feeling of overwork, ranging from 2 often to 1 sometimes to 0 never)
Australia Male Female	45.8 29.3	0.46 0.74	1.05 0.77
Malaysia Male Female	49.1 44.6	0.48 0.51	0.70 0.74
Philippines Male Female	45.4 45.6	0.43 0.54	1.14 1.02

Source: Adapted from ILO survey on work and family, 2002, cited in Lee et al. (2007).

In general, workers in developing countries prefer to work longer hours so as to ensure desirable living conditions. Reducing working hours is extremely difficult and only feasible if it can actually enhance productivity and competitiveness. Malaysia is a successful example. The tripartite National Labour Productivity Advisory Council has produced guidelines on introducing productivity-linked wages. This is supported by a human resources fund for investing in training for productivity improvement (Lee et al., 2007: 124). However, the introduction of flexi-time has not been fully explored in many other Asian countries, even though it has much possibility for enhancing productivity and developing decent working conditions.

OECD Experiences for Asia

Enterprises in the global market need better performance to cope with the changing external context. Flexi-time arrangements could enhance the overall performance of enterprises, though productivity is not necessarily improved in all cases (Flanagan, 2006). Studies of the OECD have admitted the following outcomes by introducing new working time arrangements. Flexi-time and reduced working hours can enhance work–life balance and have positive effects on employee attitudes and morale. Such arrangements can reduce absenteeism and staff turnover. However, some flexible arrangements, such as overtime and unusual working times, including night, weekend and shift work, might have negative effects. It is pointed out that flexi-time arrangements bring benefits only when workers' preferences and choices are taken into consideration.

Working time options would be a good alternative at this point. They allow employees to choose a work–life balance according to their needs. Work efficiency is improved through internal flexibility and adaptation of work organizations. Working time options are likely to be supported by socio-economic, demographic and cultural changes as well as public and non-public pressures in line with the promotion of work–life balance.

An OECD study (cited in Evans, 2001) lists the following factors on the positive side of working time arrangements: lower staff turnover, reduction of stress, better recruitment possibilities, greater diversity, greater overall flexibility in deploying staff, customer-oriented improvement of the public image of the company and the spread of 'ethical investment'. On the other hand, there are also negative points, such as bearing costs, direct costs, space enlargement, training costs, supervision costs, disruption caused by temporary absences, administrative costs and other adjustment costs.

Empirical studies tend to support the positive effects of work–life balance practices. A survey of 732 medium-sized manufacturing firms in the US, France, Germany and the UK found that work–life balance practices lead to higher productivity and better working conditions for employees (Bloom and Van Reenen, 2006). A recent ILO study (Lee et al., 2007) suggested that shorter working time and flexi-time arrangements would benefit enterprises by increasing productivity per hour or per unit in both industrialized and developing countries.

The reduction of working hours in the informal sector is not well documented, but the lack of good employment relations is a cause of long working hours in this sector. At the same time, the interaction of wages and working hours is a pivotal issue. It is not possible to reduce working time if workers only earn subsistence wages. Anxo (2004) pointed out that decent working time arrangements need to fulfil five interconnected criteria, namely:

- Preservation of health and safety

■ Being 'family-friendly'
■ Promotion of gender equality
■ Enhancement of productivity
■ Facilitation of worker choice and influence over working time.

Relevant legislation and collective agreements with worker representatives to secure a floor of working times with unanimous effect are necessary to realize reduced working hours in developing countries. In the Republic of Korea, for example, the use of flexible working hour systems must be preceded by an agreement between employers and workers' representatives (Lee et al., 2007: 126).

REFLECTIVE QUESTION

■ How can long working hours be reduced and hourly productivity be improved at the same time?

CORPORATE STRATEGIES AND LIVING AND WORKING CONDITIONS

Enterprises should endeavour to increase productivity and competitiveness under conditions of sustainable development. One question is how to attain this goal while improving working conditions. The extensive external changes in Asia now require a new strategy: an internal fit representing the alignment of working conditions and practices and an external fit between internal management and the external environment, to produce a new strategic approach to working and living conditions. In the globalizing economy, there is ample evidence that competitive enterprises in international trade have superior working conditions (Flanagan, 2006).

Another question is how to implement corporate strategies in society. Companies cannot do it without a business-enabling environment. Michael Porter (Porter and Kramer, 2006) once stressed the importance of integrating business and society, which is increasingly important to competitive success. The article suggests that investments in a competitive context create shared value in local community through its value chains. It introduced the case of Nestlé's commitment in a city in India, which has a significantly higher standard of living in the vicinity. This model has been applied in Thailand, and most recently in China.

Productivity and Competitiveness

Productivity is an important source of a company's competitiveness. Above all, labour productivity improvement undertaken by people is a key component of a company's competitive advantage (Pfeffer, 1998). Needless to say, corporate strategy sees its priority as creating competitive advantage in order to survive in business. The human resources of a company, among the management of various other resources, should be aligned with improvements in labour productivity. In the Asian context, the potential contribution of human resources would be enormous if synergetic interaction between business and society could become an incremental spiral though labour productivity in internal and external enterprises.

Generally speaking, labour productivity can be increased by the improvement of worker inputs, including the following factors:

1. Investment in people
2. Better workplace practices, based on better working and living conditions
3. Labour relations at the workplace.

First of all, productivity and the quality of labour input can be improved through human resources development (HRD). Skill development plays a critical role in improving the quality of human capital. One restrictive problem of training is that the return on investment in training takes time, and there is the risk of underutilization of acquired skills. Thus, the effectiveness of training depends on external conditions. In this sense, the improvement of human capital cannot be undertaken by a single company alone.

Three major actors have stakes in HRD: civil society (including the government and local community), businesses and individual workers. Human resources development needs fundamental investment in basic education, healthcare and physical infrastructure. This investment has been regarded as the task of public authorities, but businesses have also started to work with people, not only within the company, but also in the community they serve.

At the same time, companies have strengthened relations not only with local communities, but with other business entities. As Porter (1990) proposed, forming industrial clusters will strengthen competitiveness. The example of industrial clusters in South Asia is evident. Human resources development can be facilitated by collective action within an industrial cluster. The fundamental concepts in cluster theory emphasize the added advantages of trust formation, information sharing and networking. Skill development in value chains is also promoted in global supply chains. The effort of making linkage through supply chains is promoted by multinationals and international organizations. Thus, corporate strategy to improve human capital quality largely depends on externality, and business has to work with external actors in and for a synergistic effect. Diversified non-profit entities in Asia, including religious groups, could be promising partners for community development.

Secondly, in addition to human capital investment, progressive workplace practices based on good working conditions can also enhance productivity. Here is a list of key work environment and organizational factors conducive to productivity improvement (ILO, 2007a):

- Decent standards of living and economic security
- Leadership which values employees
- Safe and healthy working environment
- Mutual trust between employers and employees
- Participation in decision making
- Encouragement of initiative and creativity
- Supportive supervision at all levels
- Opportunities to use and develop skills
- Work–life balance.

The ILO report puts decent standards of living and economic security in first place, and acknowledges the interconnectedness between working conditions and living conditions. These factors signify the approach of respecting the potential of workers and their release from the subordinate role as employees to a more independent and self-regulating status. Partnership on an equal footing creates a symbiotic relationship for mutual benefit. Figure 7.7 shows a conceptual mechanism explaining why these factors contribute to productivity improvement through elevated motivation and commitment to work and organization. Intangible rewarding should be explored in Asian contexts to attract capable workers.

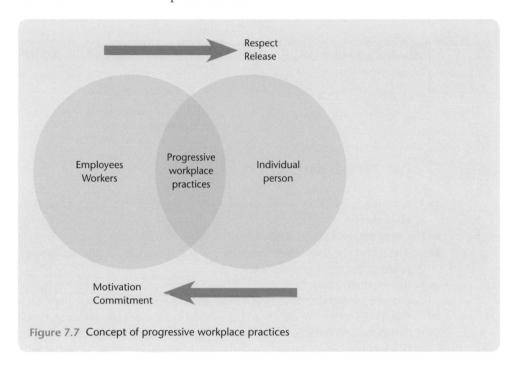

Figure 7.7 Concept of progressive workplace practices

Thirdly, labour relations can be a critical factor conducive to productivity improvement. This factor is included in progressive workplace practices, but it is worthwhile to reiterate it separately. An ILO case study has shown that some successful enterprises can increase productivity through low-cost methods involving improvements in job quality, such as cooperative work practices (Vandenberg, 2004). In fact, cooperative labour relations correlate with productivity improvement and can result in lower employee turnover, higher sales growth, customer satisfaction and total shareholder return (Kaplan and Norton, 2001). Innovation arising from active employee involvement will lead to higher competitiveness. In addition, collective bargaining and social dialogue between employers and workers contribute to an equitable distribution of benefits, resulting in productivity improvement. Here again, partnership will create symbiotic benefits. The Asian way of social dialogue might be more collaborative and harmonious than the Western way of social dialogue.

As CSR is becoming a focus in the discussion of sustainable development, businesses have started to consider the social, human and ethical impact of their corporate activities. However, it takes time to see return on this investment. Managers have to take a long-term perspective in order to reap tangible benefits. Social responsibility helps ensure that virtually every quality of a successful company will emerge over time, and thus a company's chances of long-term success will be greatly increased (Reder, 1994).

Enterprises can take the 'high road' of caring about their workers and local community, while attaining higher productivity and competitiveness. The 'race to the top' spiral will be more sustainable with good working and living conditions in society. Companies must avoid taking the 'low road' of exploiting workers and exercising market power to make profits, which would lead to a 'race to the bottom' spiral, with degraded working and living conditions. Sustainable development for business in Asia needs a high road towards a pole of excellence with strong competitiveness and decent working and living conditions.

REFLECTIVE QUESTION

- Small enterprises generally exhibit lower productivity than large enterprises. Do you think this relates to less favourable working conditions?

CHAPTER SUMMARY

- A business-enabling environment largely depends on living conditions in the local community.
- Living and working conditions closely relate to each other through people as a catalyst.
- A constructive interaction between living and working conditions is required for enterprises in the local community.
- Recent international forums have debated the proactive involvement of businesses and enterprises in the living and working conditions in the workplace and in the local community.
- Enterprises have rationales for being involved in the living conditions of the local community.
- The poor and informal sectors can be an enormous source of market opportunity and production.
- Enterprises can increase productivity and competitiveness by improving working and living conditions. We should find Asian ways for that.

KEY CONCEPTS

Competitiveness: This depends largely on the productivity of a company's employees. It is emphasized that competitiveness arises not only from economic efficiency, but also from social conditions, including living and working conditions.

Context: The external and internal environment within which an enterprise operates.

Labour productivity: The ratio of output to labour input used in production. Productivity increase is the main way to raise living standards in the long term.

Sustainable enterprise: An enterprise for sustainable development, attending to internal and external resources and conditions, such as working and living conditions.

Social enterprise: Sustainable development is the most influential factor for enterprise development. Enterprises can take various forms of business entities with social goals. Cooperative or association is one of such forms.

Labour standards: Labour standards in general are standards concerning employment and working conditions found acceptable by employers and workers.

Working conditions: Wages, working hours and occupational health and safety matters. These conditions are the physical, social and managerial factors affecting workers' job environment.

Work–life balance: People's organizational commitment is affected by their treatment by the organization. Effective human resource management endeavours to strike a balance between the two aspects of people's working and private lives.

REVIEW QUESTIONS

1. How do working conditions in a company relate to living conditions in the local community?
2. What are some possible rationales behind businesses' community involvement?
3. Can you find any examples of businesses contributing to the living conditions in your own local community?
4. Explain the meaning of 'economic growth without employment'. Give an example of this phenomenon in Asia.
5. What is the meaning of 'MMW4P'?
6. How can business improve productivity by enhancing good working and living conditions?

LEARNING ACTIVITIES AND DISCUSSIONS

1. Find any cases in which business success is correlated with improved living conditions in your country.
2. If you were appointed as the Chief Human Resources Officer of a company, what kinds of workplace practices should be introduced to increase productivity and competitiveness? Make a presentation for the rest of your classmates.
3. Devise a business plan for MMW4P after referring to the notion of 'the fortune at the bottom of the pyramid' (C.K. Prahalad, 2005).

MINI CASE

SUCCESSFUL PROGRAMMES FOR IMPROVING WORKING CONDITIONS WITH LITTLE COST BUT LARGE BENEFITS

Since the cost of improving working conditions at a company is not negligible, cost and benefit analysis is critical when introducing activities to the workplace. A study of companies in the Philippines has indicated some successful factors and practices for improving working conditions at low cost, without losing their competitiveness.

Non-monetary benefits (for example free rice, sugar and child bonus) were instituted at little cost, but had great symbolic value for employees.

Employee suggestion schemes were one of the cheapest ways of improving working conditions, allowing a sense of participation and direct communication with management. It also led to changes such as improved machine layout, simplified processes, reduced costs, enhanced quality and health and safety.

Family welfare programmes were simple to implement and cost-effective. Employee participation on a voluntary basis was beneficial in bringing about cooperation and trust. '**Family Days**', with various events for employee family members, are easy and inexpensive to organize and were popular among employees. A three-day **team-building workshop for employees' families** had a positive effect on decreasing absenteeism and raising employee motivation.

Health and safety programmes can be expensive, but all respondents thought that their costs were offset by the directly reduced expenses associated with avoiding industrial accidents. It also increased productivity among the companies studied. As a respondent put it: 'With workers' health and safety effectively addressed, downtime is lower, performance is higher and productivity increased'; while another remarked: 'Health and safety is a life-long investment that has a direct effect upon employee productivity'.

On the other hand, companies were reluctant to introduce other low-cost programmes such as **stress prevention, retirement benefits, elimination of sexual harassment and career development programmes**.

An effective technical cooperation project on working conditions is being carried out by the ILO in Asia. The project, WISE: Work Improvement in Small Enterprises, aims to improve working conditions among small enterprises in developing Asia. An early study conceptualizing the project ideas (Kogi, 1985) pointed out that identifying priority and feasibility are the key factors for effective measures undertaken by small firms in Asia. This study was based on extensive field studies in eight Asian countries, namely Bangladesh, India, Indonesia, Malaysia, the Philippines, Singapore, Sri Lanka and Thailand. It identified four fields to be prioritized: (1) workplace ergonomics such as working posture, chairs and working surface heights; (2) work organization and working time; (3) work environment and safety issues such as housekeeping, ventilation, lighting and exposure to various hazards; (4) welfare and social services including canteen and welfare facilities and provision of learning opportunities for workers. In terms of feasibility, cost and time are strongly connected. The study suggested enormous possibilities for effective measures at the workplace to improve working conditions at very low cost and effort. However, there are still difficulties for managers of small firms to put such action in place, and this is an important and challenging issue for the diffusion of improvements in working conditions.

QUESTIONS

1. What are the reasons behind each of the successful working condition improvement practices mentioned in the case?
2. Why do you think the companies were reluctant to undertake the suggested measures?
3. How do you convince managers of small firms to undertake the low-cost but effective measures to improve productivity? Describe the process of implementation and management which would be sustainable for a long-term operation.

Sources: Kogi, K. (1985). *Improving Working Conditions in Small Enterprises in Developing Asia.* Geneva: International Labour Office; Lloyd, D. and Salter, W.D. (1999). *Corporate Social Responsibility and Working Conditions in the Philippines.* Manila: ILO South-East Asia and the Pacific Multidisciplinary Advisory Team.

INTERESTING WEB LINKS

Asian Development Bank on social development: http://www.adb.org/Social Development/default.asp
ILO Regional Office for Asia and the Pacific on decent work: http://www.ilo.org/public/english/region/asro/bangkok/dw/
Asian Productivity Organization: http://www.apo-tokyo.org/index.htm

Notes

1   The International Labour Organization (ILO) has worked for the international protection of workers and fights against poverty. In other words, it has worked on improving working and living conditions as well as the application of labour standards. It was an impressive turning point that the 2007 ILO Conference discussed 'sustainable enterprise' in its plenary session, and stressed improving productivity and competitiveness for working and living conditions in a sustainable business environment.

2   Coca-Cola, for example, has committed to supply to the community the same amount of water which their plants consume for their production.

REFERENCES

Anxo, D. (2004). Working time patterns among industrialized countries: A household perspective. In Messenger, J.C. (ed.) *Working Time and Workers' Preferences in Industrialized Countries: Finding balance*. London: Routledge.

Asian Development Bank (ADB) (2006). *Labour Market in Asia: Issues and Perspectives*. Manila: ADB.

Beer, M., Spector, B., Lawrence, P.R., Mills, D.Q. and Walton, R.E. (1984). *Managing Human Assets*. New York: Free Press.

Bloisi, W. (2007). *An Introduction to Human Resource Management*. London: McGraw-Hill Education.

Bloom, N. and Van Reenen, J. (2006). Management practices, work–life balance and productivity: A review of some recent evidence. *Oxford Review of Economic Policy*, **22**(4): 457–81.

Bratton, J. and Gold, J. (2007). *Human Resource Management: Theory and Practice*, 4th edition. Basingstoke: Palgrave Macmillan.

Bronchain, P. (ed.) (2003). *Towards a Sustainable Corporate Social Responsibility*. Dublin: European Foundation for the Improving of Living and Working Conditions.

Evans, J.M. (2001). The firm's contribution to reconciliation between work and family life. Labour Market and Social Policy Occasional Papers No. 48. Paris: OECD.

Flanagan, R.J. (2006). *Globalization and Labour Conditions: Working Conditions and Worker Rights in a Global Economy*. New York: Oxford University Press.

Friedman, M. (1962). *Capitalism and Freedom*. Chicago, IL: University of Chicago Press.

ILO (1998). *ILO Thesaurus*, 5th edition. Geneva: International Labour Organization.

ILO (2004). *Economic Security for a Better World, Programme on Socio-economic Security*. International Labour Organization Social and Economic Security Programme.

ILO (2005). *Labour and Social Trends in Asia and Pacific 2005*. Bangkok: International Labour Office.

ILO (2006). *Realizing Decent Work in Asia, Report and Conclusion of the Fourteenth Asian Regional Meeting (Busan, 29 August–1 September)*. Geneva: International Labour Organization.

ILO (2007a). *The Promotion of Sustainable Enterprises, Report VI,* International Labour Conference, 96th Session, 2007. Geneva: International Labour Office.

ILO (2007b). Sustaining productivity and competitiveness on a foundation of decent work. Theme 1B at the Asian Employment Forum: Growth, Employment and Decent Work, Beijing, 13–15 August.

Kaplan, R.S. and Norton, D.P. (2001). *The Strategy-Focused Organization.* Boston, MA: Harvard Business School Press.

Kogi, K. (1985). *Improving Working Conditions in Small Enterprises in Developing Asia.* Geneva: International Labour Office.

Koh, C. (2007). A business perspective by Marcus Evans, presentation at seminar on CSR, 1 March, Kuala Lumpur.

Kotler, P. and Lee, N. (2005). *Corporate Social Responsibility: Doing the Most Good for Your Company and Your Cause.* Hoboken, NJ: John Wiley & Sons.

Kuznets, S.S. (1955). Economic growth and income inequality. *American Economic Review,* **45**(1): 1–28.

Lee, S., McCann, D. and Messenger, J.C. (2007). *Working Time around the World: Trends in Working Hours, Laws and Policies in a Global Comparative Perspective.* London: Routledge.

Lloyd, D. and Salter, W.D. (1999). *Corporate Social Responsibility and Working Conditions in the Philippines.* Manila: ILO South-East Asia and the Pacific Multidisciplinary Advisory Team.

Pfeffer, J. (1998). *The Human Equation: Building Profits by Putting People First.* Boston, MA: Harvard Business School Press.

Porter, M.E. (1990). *The Competitive Advantage of Nations.* Basingstoke: Macmillan – now Palgrave Macmillan.

Porter, M. and Kramer, M.R. (2006). Strategy and society: The link between competitive advantage and corporate social responsibility. *Harvard Business Review,* (December): 78–92.

Prahalad, C.K. (2005). *The Fortune at the Bottom of the Pyramid: Eradicating Poverty through Profits.* Upper Saddle River, NJ: Wharton School Publishing.

Rajagopalan, S. (ed.) (2006). *Bottom of the Pyramid Markets: Concept and Cases.* Hyderabad: Icfai University Press.

Rayman, P.M. (2001). *Beyond the Bottom Line: The Search for Dignity at Work.* New York: Palgrave/St. Martin's Press.

Reder, A. (1994). *In Pursuit of Principle and Profit: Business Success through Social Responsibility.* New York: G.P. Putnam.

Rogovsky, N. and Sims, E. (2001). *Corporate Success through People: Making International Labour Standards Work for You.* Geneva: International Labour Organization.

UN Volunteers (2008). UNV Country Specific Information: Thailand. Bonn: United Nations Volunteers.

UNDP (2004). *Unleashing Entrepreneurship: Making Business Work for the Poor* (Commission on the Private Sector and Development, Report to the Secretary-General of the United Nations). New York: United Nations Development Programme.

Unilever (2006). Social innovation: How value-led brands are helping to drive business strategy, speech given by Patrick Cescau, Group CEO, Unilever at the Global Forum, October.

Vandenberg, P. (2004). Productivity, decent employment and poverty: Conceptual and practical issues related to small enterprises. SEED Working Paper No. 67. Geneva: International Labour Office.

Part 2

Varieties of Asian Business Systems

In the second part of the textbook, the themes discussed in Part 1 are expanded and evaluated in the context of a number of Asian countries, which have been selected based on the following criteria.

Asia's major economic players are Japan, China and India. Each has its own distinctive history and has developed an equally distinctive society, politics and economy. While Japan has become a mature economic giant, China is undergoing an unprecedented economic development of market socialism. India, meanwhile, has been rapidly developing its IT sector, IT-enabled services and offshore operations as core industries since the 1990s. These three countries have gone through economic changes, including globalization, that have been dramatic in scale and speed and in the process have developed unique business systems which are worth examining closely. In their relation to China, Hong Kong, Macau and Taiwan have been in an idiosyncratic economic position in Asia. However, Hong Kong and Macau are now part of China and Taiwan has limited recognition as a sovereign state within the international community, so these areas are not included in this textbook. Taiwan also has high economic proximity to China; while China has recently become Taiwan's biggest export market. It is also, after Japan, Taiwan's second biggest source of imports *and the largest destination of Taiwan's foreign direct investment* (FDI).

Korea, Singapore and Vietnam are all situated in areas influenced by Confucianism and have undergone significant globalization and economic development. Korea is well known for its striking economic rise and unique business system, represented by its *chaebols*. Singapore is a small island city-state that has turned itself into an important economic hub for all of Asia, and its economic development has been characterized by its capitalist ethos, strong government intervention and Confucian democracy. Vietnam, unified since 1975, has been developing economically since the 1990s under a globalization dynamic. With the growth of overseas investment in manufacturing, Vietnam, like China, is demonstrating the emergence of a socialist market economy.

Lastly, Thailand, Malaysia, Indonesia and the Philippines are playing important roles in the Association of Southeast Asian Nations (ASEAN). Thailand, until recently an agricultural nation with abundant resources, has successfully built up an export-driven industrialization and despite a financial crisis in 1997, a 'dual track' economic policy was introduced in 2001, restoring its economy to steady growth. Malaysia is a multi-ethnic nation consisting of Malays, Chinese and Indians; since 1985, it too has been developing an export-driven industrial economy, becoming one of ASEAN's most successful nations. Indonesia, an Islamic country, has the world's fourth largest population, after China, India and the US. This huge population is a source of Indonesia's economic competitiveness, together with its rich natural resources. Indonesian politics entered a new phase following the 1997 financial crisis and the end of the Suharto government in 1998, and corporate governance has become stronger under the influence of international financial organizations. The final chapter looks at the Philippines, whose growth prospects looked promising in the 1950s following independence from the US in 1946, but failed to materialize. Uniquely in Asia, the Philippines is dominated by Roman Catholicism, which caters for over 80 per cent of the population. Fifty-three per cent of the Philippines' gross domestic product (GDP) is from the services sector, and while 33 per cent comes from manufacturing, its international competitiveness is low. A particular characteristic of its labour market is that a quarter of the Philippines' population works abroad.

Each of the focused countries above is facing issues of globalization and sustainable development. Business systems act and have effect within the dynamics of social relationships in any country. From this textbook, it is expected that students will recognize that, to maintain sustainable economic development, a business system encompassing the logics of 'introspective development' and 'democracy' in civil society will be needed, rather than an unreflective pursuit of the logic of globalization or the neo-liberal corporate governance currently in vogue in global capitalism.

Several countries or regions were not included here due to limitation of resources. ASEAN members like Laos, Myanmar and Cambodia, for example, are potentially strong players in the emergent economies, but are under-studied in terms of international business, as is Brunei Darussalam, despite its status as a rich nation. Also, the Special Administrative Regions of Hong Kong and Macau in the People's Republic of China, and Taiwan, which forms a unique model of economic development, have been left aside for future attention. Hong Kong of course is famous as an international financial centre and Macau, following the liberalization of its gaming monopoly in 2001, is now famed for its gaming and tourism industries, surpassing Las Vegas. In addition, the management practices of communist North Korea would make for interesting research. However, at this juncture we must look to the future for studies investigating these lesser known components of Asia's business and management environment.

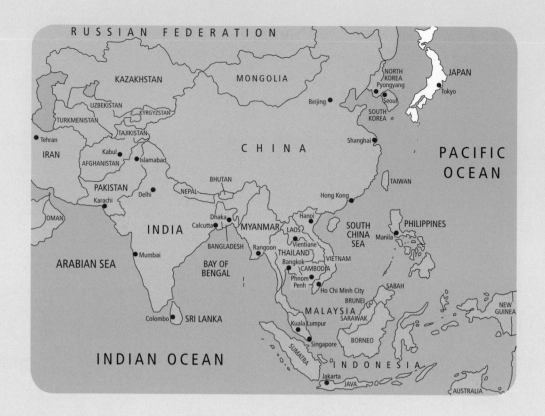

Chapter outline

- The Japanese business system
- Comparative advantage
- Continuity and change in the Japanese business system
- International activities of Japanese firms
- Corporate social responsibility (CSR) and Japanese business
- Implications for expatriates and foreign firms in Japan

Chapter objectives

After reading this chapter, you should have an understanding of:

1. The shape of the Japanese business system
2. Areas of comparative advantage and their foundations
3. Change in the business system over time
4. International activities of Japanese firms
5. CSR in Japan
6. Key implications for doing business in Japan

Chapter 8

Management in Japan

Michael A. Witt

INTRODUCTION

Japan is Asia's most developed and largest[1] economy. A densely populated country of 128 million people in an area about the size of Germany (82 million people) and somewhat smaller than California (36 million people), Japan was first among the Asian nations to industrialize.

Japan's modern economic development began in the second half of the 19th century, almost one century ahead of the Asian 'Tiger' states. It blended features of Japanese society with Western know-how. Knowledge transfer was selective and adaptive, so Japan did not become a clone of the West, but evolved its own unique ways of doing things. In this, it has been so successful that despite slow growth for most years since 1990, it still accounts for more than half of the economic output in Asia-Pacific (including China).

As a consequence, Japan's influence on Asia and the world economy has been considerable. Japan's development approach became the model for many emerging markets in Asia-Pacific, with South Korea and Taiwan at the forefront. Japanese managerial innovations have had a major impact on business worldwide, and their influence can today be found in any modern factory.

Despite its impact on the world, to many Japan remains somewhat of an enigma. The objective of this chapter is to take some of the mystery out of Japanese business.

THE JAPANESE BUSINESS SYSTEM

Culture and Key Historical Influences

Rationale

Like most firms outside the Anglo-Saxon countries, Japanese firms do not see the maximization of shareholder value as their ultimate purpose. Rather, Japanese firms exist to serve society in general and their employees in particular.

Consider these statements, taken from off-the-record interviews conducted with senior executives of leading Japanese firms (Redding and Witt, 2004):

> As an individual manager, I think the most important thing is it has to be a company that can continue to contribute to society in its own way.

> I think [most important] is the employees. … Pay the shareholder a dividend within tolerable bounds.

Implicit is a reversal of Anglo-Saxon and business school thinking that firms should maximize shareholder value, subject to the constraint of not alienating other stakeholders such as society and employees. Japanese firms instead aim to generate benefits for society and employees, subject to the constraint of keeping shareholders from revolting. While pressure from international investors has led Japanese firms to pay more attention to shareholders, the overall formula has proved resilient.

REFLECTIVE QUESTION

Different countries have different ideas about the ultimate purpose of the firm. Besides the Anglo-Saxon (shareholder value) and the Japanese views on this question, what other views do you know or can you imagine?

Even owner-managed firms exhibit a relative de-emphasis of owner interests. For instance, during Japan's lost decade of low economic growth in the 1990s and the early 2000s, many owner-managers went into debt instead of firing employees.

Understanding why Japanese business emphasizes the concerns of society and employees requires an appreciation of key historical events and their impact on Japanese business. One such key event occurred with the beginning of the Tokugawa period in Japan in 1603. After centuries of civil war, Japan was united and at peace. The new government under *shogun* (literally meaning 'general', here meaning 'military ruler') Tokugawa Ieyasu implemented a number of measures to ensure this unity and peace would last.

One step was the introduction of a Confucian social order, which is generally biased against business activities, as handling money matters is considered vulgar. The introduction of a Confucian-style four-tier social caste system reinforced this. This structure sees scholars (a role assumed by the samurai) at the top, followed by farmers and artisans. Merchants were the bottom class, as Confucius had argued that trading was a parasitic activity adding no value to society. Business under this system was closely circumscribed, with rule violations meeting severe punishment. The lasting impact on Japanese business has been to anchor in the collective mindset the necessity of firms to justify their existence to society.

Despite government hostility to business, merchants generally thrived, in some cases amassing large fortunes. This proved useful when two later key historical events compelled Japan to commence rapid industrialization. In 1853, Commodore Matthew Perry and his black ships (so called for the colour of their hulls) arrived in Japan to demand that the country open to foreign trade. Japan had imposed severe restrictions on foreign trade from 1635 onward in order to counter Portuguese and Spanish religious and colonial ambitions. Perry's arrival had several effects beyond reopening trade. One was to demonstrate how far Japanese technology had fallen behind the West. Another was to revive the fear of colonization. The United States (US) and other nations imposed so-called Unequal Treaties on Japan, and the Japanese realized that much of the world, including China, had fallen to Western imperialism.

The ineffective Tokugawa government of the time was overthrown in 1868 in the Meiji Restoration. The name of the event stems from the official pretence that it returned real power over Japan to the Emperor Meiji. In reality, the Meiji Restoration replaced one select group of rulers with another. Concluding that Japan could only remain independent if it learned to play the Western game of international politics, the new rulers initiated rapid reforms. Their objective was encapsulated in the slogan rich country, strong army (*fukoku kyôhei*): independence and security for the nation required a strong army, which needed a strong economy. Serendipitously, the merchant class had funds and business experience to propel Japan towards industrialization. Business had become useful for society.

Two further key developments occurred following Japan's World War II defeat in 1945. First, national strategy was shortened to 'rich country'. This shift is evident in the Yoshida Doctrine (after Prime Minister Shigeru Yoshida), which emphasizes economic growth while leaving international politics and defence essentially to the US. This focus on the economy further elevated the importance of business.

Second, the US occupation imposed a democratic constitution. Democracy in the Japanese interpretation became associated with equality in economic outcomes. Before the war, inequality was the norm; when, for instance, a section chief working for one of the major firms allegedly could have bought a villa from a single annual bonus. In contrast, post-war Japan evolved a system that distributed economic wealth through universal male employment, which has developed into a goal of its own over time.

In sum, the purpose of the firm is the generation of benefits for society and employees. In our discussion of the purpose, we have already encountered the key means for meeting this purpose. One is an important role for government in providing general direction for the country and in maintaining social and economic order. This implies an important role for government regulation – liberalization is seen as leading to chaos – as well as cooperative relations between government and business. Cooperation with other firms, including competitors, is appropriate for maintaining order and creating synergies, especially when Japanese firms need to catch up with foreign competitors. Further implied are measures to limit the influence of (especially foreign) investors and the acceptance of education as a means of social mobility and establishing hierarchy.

SUMMARY POINT

Japanese firms exist for the sake of society and their employees, not for the pursuit of shareholder value.

Identity

The Japanese have a relatively collectivist sense of identity that puts the interests of the group above those of the individual. Counter to what Westerners tend to expect, the available data show no clear trend towards individualism over time. For instance, the Survey on Social Consciousness by the Prime Minister's Office[2] shows people putting national over personal benefit, with the proportion of people doing so practically unchanged in recent decades. With collectivism comes conformity pressure; as the Japanese say, 'the nail that stands out gets hammered in'. Consequently, few Japanese insist on doing things their way, which contributes to low levels of entrepreneurship in Japan.

Different Asian societies emphasize different kinds of collectives (groups). The most important group for Japanese males, and in Japanese economic life generally, is the firm. This is to be interpreted in the context of lifetime or long-term employment, with many employees spending more hours with their colleagues than with their families. Even outside work, employees tend to socialize with co-workers.

Besides the company, school ties represent an important source of identity. Graduates from the same schools are expected to help one another for the rest of their lives.

Authority

Japanese society is fairly hierarchical, with authority relations structured along Confucian lines. Traditionally, Confucian hierarchies have a strong paternalistic element, with subordinates owing unconditional obedience in exchange for help and protection from their superiors. In Japan, a strong sense of community, a desire for harmony and consensual decision making combine to soften this element. It is rare for superiors to impose their views.

The Confucian influence is evident in the determinants of the hierarchy, with the most important being sex,[3] age and education. Today, both sexes enjoy equal status under the law. However, the notion of a division of labour between the sexes persists, with women in charge of household and children and men in charge of providing an income. In reality, the role of women in the workplace is considerable, though mostly in non-management positions. Career women have become more common but remain rare in middle and upper management.

Minimal age differences are sufficient to establish hierarchy. In twins, the difference in time of birth establishes a hierarchy of older/younger brother/sister. In school and work, belonging to a different intake establishes hierarchy, expressed in the terms *sempai* and *kohai* (senior and junior). *Sempai–kohai* relations tend to persist even after people have graduated or retired.

Education establishes hierarchy on the basis of the Confucian ideal that social position should be a function of educational attainment. Confucius advocated a universal education system, with attainment evaluated through state examinations. The best and brightest were to run the country as the top bureaucrats. The Japanese education system still follows this approach. The school or university one went to largely determines one's career perspectives – top-tier firms hire from top-tier schools, second-tier firms, from second-tier schools and so on.

SUMMARY POINTS

■ Japan is a relatively hierarchical society.

■ In line with Confucian thought, key determinants of the hierarchy include education, age and sex.

The Government

The role of the Japanese government in the economy is to provide stability and guidance. The Japanese generally do not share the Western, and especially Anglo-Saxon, faith that the economy is essentially stable and self-sustaining and thus best left to its own devices.[4] Market forces are perceived as potentially harmful, requiring restraint. Nor is there a strong belief that market forces alone are sufficient to guide the economy into the future, for example, by inducing the development of new technologies.

The government plays this role in a number of ways. One is to limit – not eliminate! – competition. The underlying rationale is that too much competition will weaken the viability of firms and increase the risk of bankruptcies. Because bankruptcies mean unemployment, too much competition runs counter to the purpose of the firm. The government imposes limits through formal regulations, but also through informal directives known as administrative guidance. Where regulations and guidance fail to prevent bankruptcies, the government tends to arrange for bank bailouts or mergers with healthy competitors.

A second tool is industrial policy, which aims at inducing firms to move into industries with higher value added. After the war, industrial policy was straightforward: observe more advanced countries to identify the next industry to develop, then provide incentives to a select group of companies to enter that industry, for example, through preferential access to capital and subsidies.

This model had become obsolete as Japan caught up with the West in the late 1970s. Being a developed nation means uncertainty about what industries to develop next; technologies that look promising may fail, while others may unexpectedly emerge and succeed.

The Japanese industrial policy has thus switched to promoting basic research and encouraging firms to experiment with new technologies. A common policy tool is R&D consortia. In these consortia, an average of about 20 firms conduct collaborative research on new technologies for some 6 to 10 years. This collective approach reduces the associated risk for firms, as does government funding covering part of the costs. For instance, the 10-year micromachine technology consortium of 23 firms received about US$250 million in government support (Witt, 2002).

Unlike most Asian governments, the Japanese government generally does not impose its will from above. Japanese politics involves high levels of societal coordination. This means that policymaking involves extensive consultations of government officials, business representatives and often other parties such as academics. Avenues for these consultations include deliberation councils within ministries *(shingikai)* as well as thousands of industry associations. Societal coordination takes considerable time, and if no consensus emerges, policy gets stuck (Witt, 2006). At the same time, this process helps to avoid policy mistakes and ensures that once policy is decided, implementation is typically swift and thorough.

SUMMARY POINTS

■ The role of the Japanese government in the economy is to provide stability and guidance, for instance by limiting competition and through industrial policy.

■ Policy decisions are not imposed top-down, but developed through societal coordination.

Business Environment

Financial Capital

The key characteristic of the financial system is its reliance on indirect finance, that is, bank loans. Though Tokyo is a major international financial centre, Japanese firms use banks to meet about two-thirds of their external funding needs (Witt, 2006).

Banks' lending decisions are based on a mixture of market criteria, strength of existing business relationships and government input. The relative importance of these has changed over time. In the immediate post-war era, banks essentially did as government told them. Since then, market criteria have gained importance.

Most loans are for the long term. Even in the case of debtors verging on bankruptcy, banks rarely recall their loans; instead, especially large firms may receive new loans to keep them afloat. This is partially explained by the importance of preventing bankruptcies in order to maintain employment, but also by a sense of mutual obligation from years of business relationships.

SUMMARY POINTS

■ The Japanese financial system is bank-led (indirect finance).

■ Loans tend to be for the long term.

Human Capital

The education system generally produces very good results. Basic schooling is universal, around 95 per cent of children attend high school, and more than 40 per cent enter college (Miyawaki, 2005). Attainment tends to compare favourably with that in most other advanced industrialized nations. In a 2003 OECD study of 40 nations (OECD, 2004), Japanese students were second in natural sciences, sixth in mathematics and fourteenth in reading.[5]

Despite these good results, the system has shortcomings. First, it emphasizes memorizing facts over critical and creative thinking. This is linked to Confucianism, in which standardized examinations on classical texts determined scholarly standing. Second, given the importance of education in determining one's career prospects, getting into good schools is crucial. This requires passing entrance examinations, which puts a lot of pressure on students to prepare. Many children attend private cram schools after regular school ends in the afternoon, returning home late in the evening only to spend several more hours doing homework.

The Japanese education system is relatively weak in two areas: tertiary education and vocational training. Tertiary education suffers from low motivation of students. Once students pass the entrance examinations, they are virtually guaranteed to graduate and get a job in line with the status of the school. As a consequence, most Japanese college students know more when they enter than when they graduate. The Japanese public vocational training system is weak, with most training taking place inside firms. The fact that employees typically stay for the long term allows firms to make major investments in training.

About 20 per cent of the labour force is organized in unions, predominantly at the company level. The strength of such company unions is difficult to gauge, because their interests are closely aligned with those of the company. Management tends to see unions as partners in running the company. Strikes occur mostly as a ritual component of the annual 'spring offensive' (*shunto*), during which employees may stop work briefly in support of the wage bargaining process.

While only a small proportion of workers, mostly at large firms, have the informal promise of lifetime employment, most male employees are employed for the long term. Counter to predictions of the demise of long-term employment, average tenure of male employees has risen from 10.8 years in 1980 to 13.3 years in 2000 (Inagami and Whittaker, 2005). Job tenure for women tends to be shorter. Many women quit work upon marriage, then re-enter the workforce on a part-time basis once the children have left home.

SUMMARY POINTS

- Education levels are very high in Japan.

- Labour is organized in company unions, which tend to cooperate closely with management and hardly ever strike.

- Employment tends to be for the long term.

Social Capital

Social capital is what allows people to cooperate without fear of being taken advantage of – in other words, trust. Japanese levels of trust are generally very high. At the personal level, the Japanese tend to build strong reciprocal relationships. At the systemic level, the Japanese generally believe that society helps ensure outcomes are fair. An expression of this latter point is that written employment contracts are rare. Punishment for breach of trust typically involves social sanction, such as exclusion from the group. Recourse to the legal system is possible, though relatively rare.

Strong trust enables high levels of social networking. One indicator of this is the number of industry associations, which, standardized by population size, is twice as high in Japan as in the US and some 50 per cent higher than in Germany (Witt, 2006).

SUMMARY POINT

■ Japanese levels of social capital, and thus the ability of people to cooperate, are very high.

Business System

Ownership

Most major Japanese firms are listed corporations. On average about 55 per cent of outstanding stock is owned by other firms. Of these, about 7 per cent are cross-shareholdings, in which firms own each other, and about 27 per cent constitute long-term shareholdings. Within business groups (discussed under Networking below), cross-shareholdings account for about 20 per cent of outstanding stock. Holdings by foreign investors have recently come close to 30 per cent, although foreign shareholdings move quickly with market sentiment (Witt, 2006).

As mentioned, most Japanese do not support shareholder value, but believe that the purpose of the firm is to serve its employees and society. A key implication is that corporate governance mechanisms giving shareholders control are undesirable, as shareholders may pursue their interests at the expense of employees and society. Japanese firms are insulated from shareholder pressure by having a majority of their shares owned by usually friendly firms. This makes it difficult for any shareholder to gain a controlling stake or even attempt a hostile takeover. Recently, many firms have also adopted poison pill defences against takeovers, with government encouragement. For instance, Japan's Bull-Dog Sauce Co. in 2007 invoked a poison pill defence to ward off a hostile takeover bid by a US investment fund. As a consequence of these and related measures, shareholders have little leverage, few hostile takeovers happen, and in 2001, about 10 per cent of Japan's listed companies had break-up values of at least twice their market capitalization (*Economist*, 2001).

SUMMARY POINTS

■ Most of the outstanding stock of Japanese firms is not in free float.

■ The corporate governance system gives control of the firm to employees, not shareholders.

Networking

Japan's is a network economy. Firms routinely exchange information, coordinate, and cooperate with a number of actors, such as other firms and government agencies.

One prominent type of network is the business groups.[6] These are collections of firms in different industries, about 30 to 40 on average, that maintain close ties with one another in the form of information exchange, but also in areas such as cross-shareholdings, interlocking directorates and intra-group purchasing. In the post-war period, there were six major groups, namely, Daiichi, Fuyo, Mitsubishi, Mitsui, Sanwa and Sumitomo. In 1999, they accounted for 13.2 per cent of capital, 11.2 per cent of assets and 10.8 per cent of sales in the Japanese economy (Japan Fair Trade Commission, 2001). Recent years have seen mergers across group boundaries. It is not yet clear whether this is a sign of decay or of a reconfiguration of the groups around larger, and thus potentially more competitive, firms.

Many Japanese manufacturing firms maintain dense networks with suppliers and distributors, known as *keiretsu*. These networks have received much attention in the automotive industry as an important source of competitive strength. Business relations in these networks are typically for the long term rather than by arm's-length contracting. If a supplier is temporarily uncompetitive, its customer will normally maintain the account and offer help for correcting the problem.

In intra-industry loops (Witt, 2006), firms informally exchange information ranging from technological matters to market conditions. Partners in this exchange include other firms in the same industry, the respective industry association, government and other actors connected to the industry such as researchers, banks and journalists. Through these intra-industry loops, firms keep abreast of developments in their industry and influence joint initiatives such as standards setting. The first step towards entering intra-industry loops is normally to join the respective industry association.

Figure 8.1 shows a conceptual representation of the three different network types.

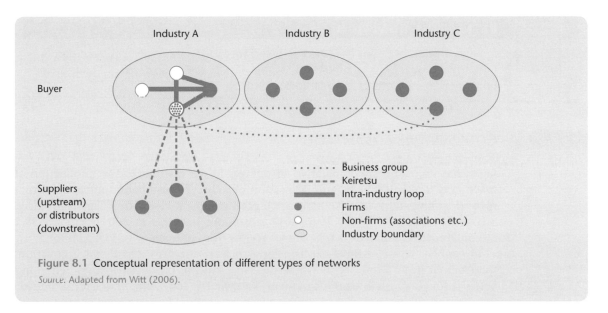

Figure 8.1 Conceptual representation of different types of networks

Source: Adapted from Witt (2006).

SUMMARY POINTS

■ Many Japanese firms maintain long-term collaborative relationships with other firms.

■ These networks include business groups, *keiretsu* and intra-industry loops.

Management

Decision making in Japanese firms is collective. Especially major decisions, such as a fundamental strategy change, rely on the so-called *ringi* system. This involves extensive consultations with the various stakeholders of the company – including, where appropriate, production workers – until an overall consensus emerges. Once this occurs, the formalized proposal is circulated to all constituents, who indicate their consent by putting their seals on the document (signatures are rarely used in Japan). This process can be extremely time-consuming. However, once everyone agrees on what to do, implementation is usually quick and thorough.

The traditional criterion for promoting people has been seniority, that is, the number of years one has worked in the company. Though some firms seem to have begun to deviate from it, the overall evidence suggest that this seniority principle is alive and well (Inagami and Whittaker, 2005). Counter to conventional wisdom, this system does account for performance variations. Of every annual intake of fresh graduates, good performers are promoted earlier than average. Those seen as less capable are side-lined over time through mechanisms such as formal promotion with no new, or less, responsibility, seconding to subsidiaries or associations and early retirement.

SUMMARY POINTS

■ Decision making inside the firm is collective.

■ Seniority and performance are key factors in career advancement.

REFLECTIVE QUESTION

Assume a tragic accident has killed all board members of a major Japanese corporation. What would be your prediction for the viability of the firm? Would your prediction differ for a private Chinese or Korean firm?

COMPARATIVE ADVANTAGE

Japan has its strongest comparative advantages in car manufacturing, production of machinery and equipment, and fabrication of radio, TV and communication equipment (Redding and Witt, 2007). Japan's biggest comparative disadvantage is in travel; according to the UN World Tourism Organization, Japanese in 2004 spent US$38.2 billion abroad, compared with Japanese receipts from tourism of US$11.3 billion.

In general, Japanese firms excel in industries relying on incremental innovation. Incremental innovation occurs where the same kind of product becomes better and better through continuous improvement (*kaizen*). The long-term character of outside finance and the weakness of corporate governance allow firms to keep employees for the long term. This enables firms to invest in training employees to produce high-quality products, as they can be sure that people will remain with the firm long enough for the investment to pay off. At the same time, long-term employment makes employees willing to acquire skills that are useful only for their present firm, as they do not have to worry about their job market value. The result is a qualification pattern that is conducive to continuous improvement and high-quality production.

Japanese firms also tend to perform well where standardization of parts and processes enable high product quality. This mode of production benefits from the integration of shop-floor workers in quality management, which has had a great impact on the development of production management worldwide. For instance, production line employees are organized in small groups (quality control circles) who take responsibility for continuous improvement of the quality of work processes, products and services. In addition, close cooperation with suppliers, often in the context of *keiretsu*, helps improve product quality and is a key enabler of just-in-time (JIT) production, in which inventories and associated costs are minimized. Cooperation among firms in the same industry, facilitated by intra-industry loops, aids standard setting.

SUMMARY POINTS

■ Japanese firms excel in industries relying on incremental innovation and standardization.

■ High product quality is enabled by extensive training and a set of quality management processes inside and outside the firm.

CONTINUITY AND CHANGE IN THE JAPANESE BUSINESS SYSTEM

The Japanese way of business has proved highly resilient to change. This is most visible in economically bad times, such as the 'lost decade' of low economic growth in the 1990s. Normally, economic pain leads to structural reforms. For example, the US business system underwent a fundamental transformation as the country encountered economic problems in the 1970s and 1980s. In the case of Japan's lost decade, however, there is little evidence of truly fundamental changes (Witt, 2006).

One cause of this rigidity is that the system is more flexible than it looks. For instance, labour costs are highly adaptable. Bonuses account for a large part of take-home pay. In bad years, companies can cut them, thus reducing labour costs significantly without firing employees. Participatory management means employees can see why the cuts are needed, which prevents disaffection. If cutting the bonus proves insufficient, firms may offer early retirement packages or transfer some employees to subsidiaries with lower pay.

However, these measures are insufficient in times of fundamental change, such as the present. The world economy is in transition from the industrial to the information technology age, and previous transitions have necessitated a thorough reform of business models. In addition, globalization has intensified cost pressures, and societal ageing paired with a shrinking population is reducing the size of the workforce.

Japan has been slow to respond for several reasons. Most Japanese are fairly content with the present system and are willing to bear the costs of maintaining it. In addition, comparative advantage of Japanese firms is dependent on the present way of doing business, as described earlier.

Most important, though, is that change requires societal coordination and, as discussed earlier under the role of government, this takes time and can get stuck. As unsolved problems accumulate, the associated economic costs should give firms an incentive to look for their own solutions by working around or ignoring the existing way of doing things. This would help firms avoid the costs of non-change and would put pressure on the coordinated decision-making process to produce results. However, in Japan, the social deviance this implies is socially unacceptable and the dense social networks in the economy increase the risk of discovery and sanction. Everyone needs to wait until societal coordination has run its course.

SUMMARY POINTS

■ Change in the business system tends to be slow and incremental.

■ Reasons for slow change include satisfaction with the way things are, the need to preserve existing comparative advantages and societal coordination.

INTERNATIONAL ACTIVITIES OF JAPANESE FIRMS

Japanese firms are active players in the world economy. One main avenue of Japanese involvement is international trade. In 2005, Japan was the world's fourth largest merchandise exporter (5.7 per cent share) and the world's fifth largest commercial services exporter (4.5 per cent). Counter to perception abroad, the Japanese economy is not highly dependent on exports, with 2005 exports accounting for about 13 per cent of GDP. This looks high in comparison with the US (7 per cent), but low compared with China (34 per cent) and Germany (35 per cent). Japan is also a major importer of merchandise (number four in the world with 4.8 per cent) and commercial services (number four in the world with 5.6 per cent).[7]

The main destination for Japanese exports is East Asia, which in 2005 received about half of Japan's exports, which within that region went mainly to Hong Kong, Singapore, South Korea and Taiwan. The US follows at about 20 per cent and the European Union (EU), at about 15 per cent. As mentioned earlier, the greatest strengths in Japanese exports are automobiles, machinery, and radio, TV and communication equipment.

The second main avenue of international activity is foreign direct investments (FDI). In 2005, Japan accounted for about 5 per cent of new FDI worldwide and held about 4 per cent of the existing worldwide stock of FDI. While Japan around 1990 was the world's leading source of FDI and a major holder of FDI stock, its present position is fairly minor, especially considering its economic size. In 2005, the US and Germany held 20 per cent and 9 per cent of the existing FDI stock. Among the Asian economies, tiny Hong Kong holds a slightly larger proportion of worldwide FDI stock than Japan.[8]

Major areas of Japanese investment are the US, Western Europe and East Asia. Of the existing stock of Japanese FDI, 35 per cent is in the US, 26 per cent in Western Europe, and 24 per cent in Asia. The ordering of new FDI is the reverse. Over the period from 2004 to 2006, East Asia received about 29 per cent of Japanese FDI, Western Europe, 22 per cent, and the US, 19 per cent. Manufacturing accounts for about two-thirds of new investments, with a focus on electric machinery and transportation equipment (including cars).

Trade and investment patterns of Japanese firms are interconnected in complex ways (Westney, 2001). One is that part of Japanese FDI has occurred in order to facilitate trade. For example, following the opening of Japan to international trade in 1868, Japanese general trading companies as well as other service firms providing trading infrastructure (banks, transport services) opened branches overseas, predominantly in Asia. Following Japan's defeat in 1945, the pattern repeated itself.

A second interconnection is that some of Japan's FDI has occurred to reduce or forestall trade frictions. For instance, Japanese car makers have made major investments in the US from the 1980s onwards. A major reason for doing so was to reduce Japanese car exports to the US, which threatened to trigger US protectionism, closing a major market for Japanese producers. Similarly, Japanese firms invested in the EU, especially in the

UK, in the 1990s, as they feared that the completion of the European Common Market might lead to a protectionist 'Fortress Europe' shutting out others.

Third, a significant part of Japanese trade involves shipments to and from subsidiaries abroad. For instance, Japanese firms investing in China often source their equipment and ship components and subassemblies from Japan. And on average about 40 per cent of the finished products of Japanese subsidiaries in China are exported back to Japan.

Counter to expectations that firms everywhere converge on the same 'best practices', Japanese multinational enterprises (MNEs) maintain distinct characteristics in their overseas investments. In particular, they tend to implement Japanese-style organizational patterns abroad and employ relatively high proportions of Japanese expatriate managers. In addition, Japanese MNEs often take many of the suppliers in their existing Japanese *keiretsu* with them to new markets.

SUMMARY POINTS

- Japan is a major exporter and importer as well as an important source of foreign direct investment (FDI).

- Counter to conventional wisdom, exports are only a relatively small part of Japanese GDP.

CORPORATE SOCIAL RESPONSIBILITY (CSR) AND JAPANESE BUSINESS

The CSR record of Japanese firms is mixed. On the one hand, service to society is, as discussed, in the DNA of Japanese business. Firms are typically concerned with the well-being of their stakeholders, including employees, society at large, customers, suppliers, and also shareholders. Larger firms in particular contribute significantly to society in areas such as the arts, education, and sports. The environment has received attention from the 1960s, with Japan now occupying a leading position among high-density population countries in terms of environmental sustainability. Corruption is relatively low, both at home and in the activities of Japanese firms abroad.

Other aspects of CSR seem less developed. Japanese firms have a tendency to attempt to cover up even major problems when they occur, such as nuclear accidents or food poisoning cases. This seems to be related to efforts to protect the firm against expected sanction from society at large. Among other areas with weaknesses, as mentioned in the literature (for example Wokutch and Shepard, 1999; Robins, 2005), are privacy policies for customers, CSR standards for suppliers, improving employability of personnel, opportunities for women and friendliness towards families, opportunities for minorities in Japan (for example ethnic Koreans) and elsewhere (for example African Americans in US plants), publication of sustainability reports, joint work with non-government organizations (NGOs), and transparent corporate governance.

Bearing in mind our earlier discussion, the causes of limited progress on some of these dimensions are clear. The implied values run counter to existing social norms and business practices. CSR is a Western product, reflecting Western thinking of what the world should look like. This overlaps only partially with Japanese views. For instance, why should Japanese firms focus on increasing employability of personnel if their focus has been on maintaining lifetime or long-term employment? And if firms do not pursue shareholder value, why would they need transparent corporate governance?

In other areas, there may be overall agreement in Japan that change is desirable, but change in Japan takes time. For instance, many Japanese would agree that women should have better career opportunities. While more firms may now hire women for the career track, the seniority system means it will take years for the new recruits to reach management positions.

SUMMARY POINTS

- Service to society has long been an important consideration for Japanese firms.

- Japanese views of how to serve society overlap only partially with the Western values underlying the CSR movement.

REFLECTIVE QUESTION

How should Japanese firms respond to pressures to follow Western CSR standards?

IMPLICATIONS FOR EXPATRIATES AND FOREIGN FIRMS IN JAPAN

Counter to its image as a market with little potential, Japan tends to be highly profitable for foreign firms. A 2002 study of 30 German and Swiss firms active in Japan found that virtually all reported that Japan was the most profitable, or one of the most profitable, markets worldwide for them (Vaubel and Höffinger, 2002). United States government statistics about company profits draw a similar picture, with Japan generating more profits for US direct investments than any other Asian market (Studwell, 2005).

Yet Japan is not an easy market. Below are the five most important considerations.

- *Compete on the right terms.* Japanese firms often compete fiercely with one another; even where they do not, they will show a strong competitive response to foreign market entrants. Japanese competition differs from that in Anglo-Saxon countries in that it is limited and hardly ever on price. Japanese firms believe that price competition is a sure way for everyone in the industry to lose as margins erode. As a consequence, the reaction to firms attempting to start a price war is typically unfavourable. Consumers may shun their products, competitors may gang up on them, and government may put pressure on them.

- *Handle employees with care.* A common mode of entry into Japan is to buy or partner with an existing Japanese firm. In these cases, the Japanese rules of the game apply, especially in human resources matters.

    One implication is that headcount reductions are difficult. Firing employees is legally difficult and will demotivate your workforce. The situation is different if the company is in trouble. In this case, the usual pattern is to reassign employees to subsidiaries; to offer early retirement; to ask for volunteers to quit; and to work with the union to identify those employees for whom the impact of redundancy would be smallest.

    Do not promote a Japanese employee over another Japanese employee with longer tenure. The person passed over will lose motivation and may quit.

- *Know when to break the rules.* Most Japanese expect foreigners not to understand the rules of the game. Foreign firms can use this to their advantage.

Breaking the rules can be effective when setting up a greenfield operation. In this case, foreign companies may follow Western lines. This allows expatriate managers to work in a familiar system, and it provides foreign firms with a way of attracting talent from the pool of Japanese who prefer a Western work environment. These include Japanese with MBAs from European or US schools expecting performance-based promotions as well as women seeking to make a career.

Breaking the rules can also be effective in situations in which a Japanese firm needs urgent help with a turnaround. Carlos Ghosn at Nissan was effective in rescuing the firm not only because of his managerial skills, but also because, as a foreigner, he could (skilfully) breach established social norms.

■ *Do not expect quick change.* Change in Japan rarely happens quickly. This is true both for the business environment and the firm. If you try to short cut the decision-making process inside the firm by imposing a solution top-down, the organization will at best ignore you, entering the collective process regardless. At worst, a divide will open up between your declared will and actual practice.

For influencing decision-making processes within the industry or at the level of the entire economy, the proper process is to go through the existing coordination structure, especially the associations. Lobbying the government for change does not produce results, and just going ahead with changes on one's own may be illegal or socially unacceptable.

■ *Realize the importance of networking.* Influencing standards, pushing change, and gathering information all occur through networks. One of your first actions should be to join your industry association. This can be expensive, but membership has a signalling effect. By paying the membership fee, you show that you are serious about your Japanese engagement and worth building a reciprocal relationship with. At the same time, you signal that you are a proper corporate citizen playing by the rules.

Getting into a network is hard. Signal commitment by continuing to try until you succeed. Consider getting introductions from a reputable and well-connected person, such as a leading professor with links to the industry.

SUMMARY POINTS

■ Compete on the right terms.

■ Handle employees with care.

■ Know when to break the rules.

■ Do not expect quick change.

■ Realize the importance of networking.

CROSS-CHAPTER REFLECTIVE QUESTION

After you have read all the remaining country chapters in this part of the book, come back to this chapter and think about the transferability of the Japanese-style management system to these foreign soils. Which aspects of Japanese management will, or will not, work where? Why?

CHAPTER SUMMARY

- Japan is Asia's largest and most developed economy. Internationally, it is second only to the US.
- Japanese firms are controlled by their employees and run for the benefit of employees and society as a whole. Cooperation within and across firms and with other organizations is pervasive. This sets Japanese business apart from firms in Anglo-Saxon and other Asian nations, but is similar to business in Europe.
- Japanese firms are world leaders in industries featuring incremental innovation as well as standardization and attendant high quality. They are at a disadvantage in industries with radical innovation and non-standard processes.
- The government plays an important role in ensuring order and guiding the economy. Liberalization is considered tantamount to chaos.
- Change in Japan is typically slow because of high levels of societal coordination. However, once change is agreed on, implementation can be quick and universal.
- Japanese firms are major players in international trade and investment.
- For foreign firms, Japan has been difficult to enter. However, once established, foreign firms have found Japan to be highly profitable.

KEY CONCEPTS

Business groups: Collections of firms in different industries that have close ties with one another while remaining formally independent.

Company unions: Groups representing the interests of labour, organized at the level of each individual firm; one of the 'three sacred treasures' of Japanese management.

Industrial policy: Government policy aimed at guiding and promoting the development of specific industries and technologies.

Intra-industry loops: Social networks connecting firms as well as non-firm organizations (for example associations) in the same industry.

Keiretsu: Strictly speaking, production and distribution networks; the term is often also applied to business groups.

Lifetime employment: Informal promise to provide continuous employment for the duration of one's career; one of the 'three sacred treasures' of Japanese management.

Quality management: A system of means for ensuring quality standards in the production of goods and services.

Ringi **system:** Collaborative decision-making process inside the firm.

Seniority principle: The practice of promoting employees based on the length of tenure with the firm; one of the 'three sacred treasures' of Japanese management.

Societal coordination: The practice of using collective consultation, deliberation, and cooperation to change rules and practices.

REVIEW QUESTIONS

1. Describe the rationale, key historical influences, identity, and authority in the Japanese business system.
2. Explain the characteristics of financial capital, human capital, and social capital in the Japanese business system.
3. Describe the aspects of ownership, networking, and management in the Japanese business system.
4. In what kinds of industries does Japan excel? Why?
5. Why is change in Japan so difficult?
6. How are Japanese firms integrated in the international economy?
7. Why is the CSR record of Japanese firms mixed as viewed from a Western perspective?
8. What advice would you give to a foreigner preparing to do business in Japan?

LEARNING ACTIVITIES AND DISCUSSIONS

1. Japanese firms are slow to change. What does this imply in the present age of globalization and rapid technological change?
2. In most Asian countries, firms rise and disappear quickly. What is the situation in Japan? Use the internet to explore the level of entrepreneurial activity as well as the age of major Japanese firms. Explain what you observe.
3. Even though foreign firms tend to make good profits in Japan, the country receives little inward FDI. By contrast, while foreign firms have had difficulties making money in China, China in a good year probably receives more inward FDI than Japan has in total since 1945. How do you explain this?

MINI CASE

TOYOTA MOTOR CORPORATION

Toyota Motors is the world's largest car manufacturer. Many also see it as the quintessential Japanese firm. The firm's origins trace back to 1933, when its founder, Kiichiro Toyoda, set up an automobile division in his father's company. Automobile production began in 1935, and in 1937, the firm was incorporated as Toyota Motor Co., Ltd.

The key to Toyota's success has been its approach to quality management, known as 'Toyota Production System' (TPS). Its original objective was to enable Toyota to remain economically viable despite low production volumes. At the time, Toyota made a few thousand vehicles per year, as compared with a daily output of 7,000 vehicles from a single Ford plant in Detroit.

To compensate for its diseconomies of scale, Toyota developed processes for eliminating waste throughout the production process.

The result is a complex, integrated quality management system that is said to hinge on three key components: *jidoka*, JIT, and *kaizen*. *Jidoka* refers to self-regulation of the manufacturing process, both at the level of the machine and the individual worker. Its most famous expression is the ability, and duty, of individual workers to stop the entire production line whenever they notice a problem that cannot be immediately solved.

JIT, or just-in-time, means that 'only the necessary items, at the necessary time, and in the necessary quantity to meet customer demand' are produced and delivered (Schvaneveldt, 2002: 257). This enables Toyota to hold little stock, which reduces the amount of capital tied up in stocks, buildings, and expensive land. JIT requires close cooperation with the supplier network (*keiretsu*). The scope of this cooperation ranges from component design to manufacturing to logistics. Toyota typically holds part of the equity of first-tier suppliers, but does not formally integrate them.

Kaizen refers to continuous improvement of processes, including the process of *kaizen* itself. The most visible manifestations are quality control circles and suggestions systems in the plants. The firm reciprocates workers' commitment to these processes through lifetime employment. Remuneration by seniority, rather than job function, enables the firm to rotate employees to different functions, thus promoting organizational learning.

What sounds simple is in reality highly complex and dependent on tacit knowledge and corporate culture. Despite decades of research into the TPS, no other firm has succeeded in reproducing it. For instance, General Motors (GM) has been unable to generate sufficient learning from its joint plant with Toyota in California, started in 1984, to compete with Toyota on quality.

Toyota has had a good record of producing efficiently what customers want. Prime examples of successful responses to market demands include the introduction of the Lexus luxury car brand in the 1980s and the development of fuel-efficient hybrid cars. The latter has allowed Toyota to cultivate an image of environmental responsibility, though critics have argued that was reflective more of clever marketing than facts.

While Toyota started to export as early as 1936, it was relatively late among Japanese car makers in producing abroad. The joint venture with GM already mentioned was its first foray. One driver of Toyota's international expansion has been the threat of trade barriers, especially in the US and Europe. Once the firm had convinced itself that TPS could be made to work outside Japan – with large contingents of Japanese managers providing training and direction – it rapidly expanded abroad. By 2002, it had produced more than 10 million cars in North America alone.

But every silver lining has a cloud. As Toyota surpassed GM to become the world's largest car maker, problems began to surface where they were least expected and most painful: vehicle quality. The firm has issued a number of embarrassing vehicle recalls, and the US *Consumer Report* no longer endorses each Toyota model automatically. In reliability measures such as the vehicle breakdown statistics collected by the German Automobile Club, Toyota has slipped from its former leading position. Ironically, it seems that one contributing factor to these problems has been Toyota's relentless push to expand production volume on its way to becoming the world's largest car maker.

QUESTIONS

1. What characteristics make Toyota a 'quintessential Japanese firm'?
2. Given what you know about the TPS, what is the likely connection between rapid expansion and quality problems?
3. Foreign firms, like GM, have tried to emulate the TPS. This has proved very difficult. Why?
4. Viewed from the perspective of Toyota, how should Japanese firms respond to calls by foreign investors to end lifetime employment, abolish the seniority principle, and focus on shareholder value?

Sources: Bird, A. (ed.) (2002). *Encyclopedia of Japanese Business and Management.* London: Routledge; Schvaneveldt, S.J. (2002). Just-in-time. In Bird, A. (ed.) *Encyclopedia of Japanese Business and Management.* London: Routledge; http://www. adac.de; http://www.bloomberg.com/apps/news?pid=20601101&sid=a._jzVOVHI8E&refer=japan; http://www.iht.com/articles/2007/10/17/business/toyota.php; http://www.toyota.co.jp.

INTERESTING WEB LINKS

Economic statistics, information on doing business in Japan and government support: http://www.jetro.go.jp
Worldwide comparisons of the ease of doing business: http://www.doingbusiness.org
Corruption in Japan and elsewhere: http://www.transparency.org
FDI statistics: http://stats.unctad.org/fdi
Trade statistics: http://www.wto.org/english/res_e/statis_e/statis_e.htm
CSR by Japanese firms: http://www.keidanren.or.jp/english/policy/csr/lists.html

Notes

1   At market exchange rates. As a general rule, purchasing power parity data should not be used in international business, as firms transact internationally at market rates.
2   Available at http:/www8.cao.go.jp/survey/index-sha.html.
3   Sex refers to biological characteristics, while gender refers to social roles. Japanese hierarchy is built around the former.
4   Recent findings suggest they may be right; see Beinhocker (2005).
5   The reading score is partially a result of the complexity of the Japanese language. Students can read a newspaper only by high school.
6   Confusingly, these are known in the West mostly by the Japanese word *'keiretsu'*, which in Japanese is typically used to refer to the supplier and distributor networks discussed in the next paragraph.
7   Trade statistics in this and the following paragraphs are available on the websites of JETRO and WTO. Investment statistics are available on the websites of JETRO and UNCTAD. Links are given at the end of the chapter.
8   Hong Kong numbers include investments from Taiwan to China channelled through Hong Kong and Chinese funds disguised as inward FDI to take advantage of government incentives.

REFERENCES

Beinhocker, E.D. (2005). *The Origin of Wealth: Evolution, Complexity, and the Radical Remaking of Economics*. London: Random House.

Bird, A. (ed.) (2002). *Encyclopedia of Japanese Business and Management*. London: Routledge.

Economist (2001). Japanese corporate raiders: Ever so polite. *Economist*. Available at http://www.electronic-economist.com/business/displaystory.cfm?story_id=E1_VDSVNG&CFID=6700295&CFTOKEN=46207aae5c3e2-2F7ADECD-B27C-BB00-014383AEB6E11ECB.

Inagami, T. and Whittaker, D.H. (2005). *The New Community Firm: Employment, Governance and Management Reform in Japan*. Cambridge: Cambridge University Press.

Japan Fair Trade Commission (2001). *Concerning the Actual State of Business Groups: Report on the Seventh Survey* (in Japanese). Tokyo: Japan Fair Trade Commission.

Miyawaki, K. (ed.) (2005). *Japan Almanac 2006*. Tokyo: Asahi Shimbun.

OECD (2004). *Learning for Tomorrow's World: First Results from PISA 2003*. Paris: OECD.

Redding, G. and Witt, M.A. (2004). The role of executive rationale in the comparison of capitalisms: Some preliminary findings. INSEAD EAC Working Paper Series. Fontainebleau, France.

Redding, G. and Witt, M.A. (2007). *The Future of Chinese Capitalism: Choices and Chances*. New York: Oxford University Press.

Robins, F. (2005). The future of corporate social responsibility. *Asian Business & Management.* **4**(2): 95–115.

Schvaneveldt, S.J. (2002). Just-in-time. In Bird, A. (ed.) *Encyclopedia of Japanese Business and Management.* London: Routledge

Studwell, J. (2005). Multinational profits: Let me down slow. *China Economic Quarterly.* **9**(4): 52–60.

Vaubel, D. and Höffinger, S. (2002). *What Really is (Still) Different in Japan: How European Firms Organize Themselves to Succeed in the World's Most Demanding Market – A Delta Study.* Tokyo: Roland Berger Strategy Consultants.

Westney, D.E. (2001). Japan. In Rugman, A.M. and Brewer, T.L. (eds.) *The Oxford Handbook of International Business.* New York: Oxford University Press.

Witt, M.A. (2002). Research cooperatives. In Bird, A. (ed.) *Encyclopedia of Japanese Business and Management.* London: Routledge.

Witt, M.A. (2006). *Changing Japanese Capitalism: Societal Coordination and Institutional Adjustment.* Cambridge: Cambridge University Press.

Wokutch, R.E. and Shepard, J.M. (1999). The maturing of the Japanese economy: Corporate social responsibility implications. *Business Ethics Quarterly.* **9**(3): 527–40.

Chapter outline

- Overview of China's market economy
- The command economy: The Soviet mentor
- Managerial traditions and a new managerial mindset
- State enterprise managerial autonomy, working conditions and labour mobility

- Property rights, corporate governance and the private sector
- Corporate Social Responsibility: The environment, human resources, corporate culture, FDI and business networks
- Working and living conditions in China

Chapter objectives

After reading this chapter, you should:

1. Have an overview of China's market economy
2. Understand the motivation for China's managerial reforms
3. Comprehend Chinese corporate governance and culture
4. Be aware of the impact of FDI on Chinese management
5. Recognize the global impetus behind corporate social responsibility in China

Chapter 9

Management in China

Robert Taylor

OVERVIEW OF CHINA'S MARKET ECONOMY

Since 1978, the date of the accession to power of China's paramount leader, Deng Xiaoping, macroeconomic reform has impacted on the structure and style of industrial management. Such change has resulted in a greater awareness of corporate social responsibility. The following summary provides the market economy perspective against which contemporary Chinese management will be viewed.

China vies with India as the most populous nation on earth and has long been seen as the world's greatest potential market. China's exponential foreign trade growth and the massive inflow of foreign direct investment (FDI) since 1978 attests to the country's emergence as a global economic player, which in turn has impacted on corporate governance, as discussed in the main body of this text. The input of foreign capital, technology and managerial expertise has contributed to unprecedented economic growth rates, averaging 9.7 per cent over the past twenty-eight years and lifted over 200 million Chinese out of abject poverty (Sheridan, 2007). China's volume of foreign trade increased from a total of US$20.6 billion in 1978 to US$1,760 billion in 2006, accounting for 70 per cent of gross domestic product and indicating China's ascent as a major trading nation. There seem no limits to China's growth and market potential. Its economy is already the fourth biggest in the world after the US, Japan and Germany and is likely to exceed that of the US in 2040 (Budworth, 2006).

Such growth reflects continuing macroeconomic and managerial reform, including industrial restructuring. The first priority of reform was the state industrial sector which, in a bid to create globally competitive multinationals, still plays a major role. To enhance state enterprise competitiveness, changes in management and corporate governance were undertaken, with simultaneous encouragement of private enterprise and foreign-invested ventures. The presence of the latter category has led observers to describe China as the world's workshop yet much FDI has been devoted to assembly or light manufacturing rather than technological innovation. Moreover, in these sectors, China faces increased competition from low wage economies like Vietnam and Indonesia, and so official policy promotes hi-tech products.

In addition, rapid economic growth has brought costs: environmental degradation and social inequality, the latter already addressed by the Chinese Communist Party (CCP) leaders in the Eleventh Five Year Plan (2006–2010). Included in the Plan is the call to create a harmonious society: social and income inequality is to be reduced through labour legislation, wages being raised and domestic consumption consequently increased. Significantly, the disposable income of the richest 10 per cent of families is calculated to be eight times greater than that of the poorest 10 per cent (Macartney, 2006). Such policy is also intended to decrease China's trade surpluses; export tax rebates are also being abolished.

Simultaneously, recent labour legislation has tightened employment law and insisted on the recognition by foreign investors of the official All China Federation of Trade Unions – Wal-Mart, the American retailer, being a case in point (Sheridan, 2007). Additionally, some sources cite wage inflation in manufacturing in Chinese cities running at 17 per cent, and while China has abundant sources of rural labour, there is a serious shortage of technical manpower and skilled management (Mortished, 2007).

The above policies and trends are a spur to further reform towards hi-tech enterprise scientific management, to which foreign expertise will contribute. This is proceeding on two fronts: state initiative in corporate governance, and technological infusion through foreign investment. One example of corporate governance reform is Netcom, the telephone company, where seven out of 13 directors are outsiders; there is thus potential for increasing managerial accountability, hitherto unusual for a state controlled enterprise. The company party secretary's task is still to ensure that state policy is upheld but shareholder interests are nevertheless protected, given CCP concerns with broader social and economic issues (Dean, 2006). In the area of technology transfer may be cited Nanjing Automobile's acquisition of part of MG Rover and the Japanese car manufacturer, Toyota's, manufacturing presence in China, designed to produce environmentally friendly vehicles for both Chinese domestic and global markets (Bolger, 2006; O'Connell, 2006).

The foregoing represents the framework within which Chinese industrial management has been conducted. It has discussed the consequences of China's impressive economic growth, the continuing pursuit of industrial restructuring and managerial reform, and attempts to reduce social inequality through increased domestic consumption. In turn, labour legislation impacts on wage costs incurred by foreign investor manufacturers. Chinese and foreign global players alike are affected by China's reformed corporate governance. The following sections examine China's post-1978 managerial reforms.

THE COMMAND ECONOMY: THE SOVIET MENTOR

The major theme of this text is contemporary Chinese management. But first of all it is necessary to examine managerial norms and values under the pre-1978 command economy, a mindset at variance with Western business practice. On their accession to power in 1949 the CCP leaders were faced with the enormous tasks of national reconstruction and economic rehabilitation; they were dedicated to transforming China into an advanced industrial country. Not only had years of warfare and civil strife taken their toll on China's infrastructure but sources of experienced managerial cadres were lacking. While technical competence was crucial, the issue of political reliability was paramount.

In the early 1950s, state sector industries were being created under the command economy, for which the mentor was the Soviet Union, whether in terms of industrial plant, managerial expertise or a higher education system geared to rapid economic development. At the same time, China began to produce its own graduates, as the universities were reorganized on Soviet lines, with specialists trained in a number of fields, especially engineering. Notably, graduates were to be assigned, without exercise of personal choice, to managerial positions in industry. The deployment of management and labour to the newly constructed state enterprises necessarily reflected the priorities of central planning devised along Soviet lines, and many Chinese technologists and engineers were also trained in Russia.

Soviet managerial structures and styles were introduced, especially in Northeast China, where much heavy industry, the main priority of the First Five Year Plan, (1953–1957) was established. Central planning and macroeconomic governance meant a vertical hierarchical chain of command between ministries in Beijing and individual industrial enterprises. The allocation of raw material inputs and capital, as well as the despatch of products, was conducted through state distribution, a system that remained until the reforms of the 1980s.

The key feature of Soviet management as transplanted in China was the single director system operated at three levels of the industrial enterprise: the factory, the workshop and the work team. In addition, functional sections at the factory level were responsible for liaising with the central planning authorities. As suggested in more detail below, three characteristics of one-man management proved to be seriously at odds with the CCP's native system of control. The single director system had been conceived in a European culture, and the individual, rather than collective leadership, had overall authority at each level. Secondly, material incentives, which could not have been utilized in the CCP's wartime rural bases, were introduced, with bonuses based on an individual's performance and awarded to party cadres, managers, technical staff and workers alike. Finally, the premium placed on technological expertise meant that specialists such as chief engineers became more important than enterprise directors and party secretaries. There were also specific technical and ideological objections which emerged in the course of implementation. Performance assessment and concomitant reward allocation demanded sophisticated accounting systems which had not been adequately developed in China. Laaksonen (1988: 197–201) refers to the creation of economies of scale involving broad amalgamation of industrial enterprises and the pressing need for coordination, the latter not always being achieved, and there were consequent deleterious effects on espirit de corps. Most importantly, the CCP had come to power on a platform of social equality, and increasing differentiation of reward threatened to create the kind of new class apparently emerging in the Soviet Union and its East European satellites.

MANAGERIAL TRADITIONS AND A NEW MANAGERIAL MINDSET

Reassertion of China's Managerial Traditions

Consequently, in 1956, on Mao Zedong's initiative, there was a decided swing to the political left when the Eighth CCP Congress inaugurated a move to wrest control from experts and hand it back to party committees in industrial enterprises. This measure, factory manager responsibility under the leadership of the party, was an integral part of a macroeconomic policy of decentralization, whereby decision-making power was devolved to provincial CCP authorities and their enterprise counterparts, even though still under the terms of the state planning mechanism. These policies followed Mao Zedong's reassertion of the mass line, part of the CCP's own tradition, whereby hierarchical vertical relationships were replaced by cooperation between managers and the workforce in decision making. This addressed both ideological and technical concerns: cadres were remoulded through participation in manual labour, while workers, together with functional staff, cooperated in solving technical problems on the shop floor. Thus innovation would supposedly be furthered by unleashing the creative energies of workers. Ultimately, however, these policies proved counterproductive: ideological incentives are so often subject to the law of diminishing returns; greater and greater exhortation is required to achieve proportionally fewer increased returns. To China's more rational economic planners material incentives and profit targets were crucial, and from 1962 to 1965 greater initiative was given to middle managers and technical experts. Enterprise production output rose but the onset of the Cultural Revolution saw a new turn in the cycle of change in management, being designed to prevent the emergence of a new technocratic elite. The mass line and collective management were revived under the leadership of revolutionary committees which included party members who had not been discredited, technicians, representatives from the People's Liberation Army (PLA) and workers who ostensibly were to cooperate in decision making, although in practice the CCP at various levels retained its dominance.

Targets were again set by central authorities, wages were based on skill levels, years of service and, more importantly, political activism. Enterprise efficiency suffered, however, and product innovation was lacking, as political meetings increased in number and managers were forced to engage in physical labour. Moreover closure of the universities and the lack of adequate training in enterprises cost China a generation of technologists. Political campaigns instigated from above against allegedly recalcitrant party members led to factionalism within enterprises, where CCP credibility was severely dented, a lesson not lost on Deng Xiaoping and his supporters when they gave back power to enterprise directors and managers in the 1980s (Laaksonen, 1988: 201–34; Child, 1994: 35–51). In fact, the reforms of the 1980s, discussed below, were intended ultimately to grant Chinese state enterprise managers the kind of autonomy enjoyed by their counterparts in the Anglo-American tradition. We now discuss the managerial reforms initiated after 1978.

Creation of a New Managerial Mindset

The Third Plenum of the Eleventh Central Committee in 1978 was a crucial watershed in that it addressed the fundamental issues of managerial reform implemented during the 1980s and beyond. In industrial reform, the intention was to make state enterprise directors and managers, who were on the lowest rungs of ministerial bureaucratic hierarchies, more accountable in the new market economy being created. Incumbent managers had been socialized in a risk-averse environment and had vested interests to defend. The pace of reform was slow; the reforms did not have a road map but a general sense of direction in which commercially oriented practices would be injected into the state sector to make it more domestically and globally competitive. It had been concluded that while spectacular economic gains had accrued from earlier five year plans, in terms of factor productivity and increasing living standards China had lagged behind other newly industrializing countries in Asia. Before the 1980s China had played a minimal role in the global economy; its foreign trade had been a supplement to make good domestic deficiencies. By the early 1980s, Chinese economic planners had realized that there were limits to autarchy, and the generation of capital for development from within China and the wherewithal for sustained growth would only come from foreign trade and investment. In turn, achievement of competitiveness demanded a change of managerial mindset, now increasingly being driven by both market competitiveness and the recruitment of returned Chinese MBA graduates trained in the West.

State enterprises were controlled by administrative fiat, not economic levers, and the acquisition of scarce supplies by directors, for instance, was secured via personal relationships within the hierarchical chain of command. Egalitarian remuneration rates applied within the managerial cadre and among the shop floor workers inhibited risk taking and entrepreneurship as well as innovation. Nor did the ideological role of enterprise party committees and their secretaries favour the individual initiative of managers. Additionally, soft skills like marketing were the province of central ministries which had the best information concerning the overall business environment.

STATE ENTERPRISE MANAGERIAL AUTONOMY, WORKING CONDITIONS AND LABOUR MOBILITY

Managerial Autonomy of the State Enterprises

Accordingly, in September 1982, the 12th Congress of the CCP unveiled a series of measures, including abolition of lifetime tenure for managerial cadres, as well as attempts to raise their educational levels and reduce their average age, in the interest of greater commercial accountability, entrepreneurship and soft skills. These reforms, however, were initially difficult to implement and in the 1980s contracts were often renewed on expiry of the cadre's term. In fact, such policy regarding term contracts was much more successful when applied to workers in general. These initiatives were an integral part of the more fundamental reforms designed to increase autonomy of individual industrial enterprises. Experimental reform, first implemented in state enterprises in Sichuan Province, was extended to those throughout the country in the early 1980s; eventually they were to become responsible for their own profits and losses. Certain rights were granted: enterprises could retain a limited amount of profit under the state plan, with an even greater percentage to be kept if derived from above quota production. This was permitted after national plans had been fulfilled. The intended uses for retained profit were technological innovation and the development of new products, in addition to spending on welfare and workers' bonuses, the latter being distributed on the basis of performance. More depreciation funds could be kept by the enterprise. Moreover market outlets were now diversified outside state commercial departments. There were problems, however, with the reforms both in terms of ineffective implementation and their extent. Bonuses lost their motivational value because they were traditionally distributed to all workers. Responding to market demand and diversity placed a premium on improved auditing and accounting. Finally, profits derived from increased productivity and market segmentation would only be meaningful if state-led pricing mechanisms were liberalized (Laaksonen, 1998: 231–38).

Thus, in 1984, the ongoing reforms were consolidated, being intended to increase the autonomy and decision-making power of state enterprises. Prices were, to an extent, allowed to float for goods produced in excess of state quotas. Prices could be set in a band within 20 per cent of their state equivalents. Certain strategic goods, however, were excepted. Moreover, that state enterprises could select their sources, from both within and outside the central planning system, effected the emergence of horizontal relationships between customers and suppliers. Significantly, enterprises were given greater freedom in recruitment; while directors and party secretaries were still appointed by their respective outside hierarchies, workers could now be engaged through formal examinations, even if under the guidance of state labour agencies. The system of the unified assignment of graduates was not to be abolished until the 1990s but for the first time directors had the right to reject those assigned. In line with moves towards performance related pay, enterprises were allowed greater leeway in wage setting (Laaksonen, 1998: 239–41).

REFLECTIVE QUESTION

■ All economies are mixed systems with the state playing a lesser or a greater role. The key to managerial reform in China is encouraging an entrepreneurial managerial mindset. In which respects do you consider that government will continue to play a role in macroeconomic and microeconomic governance?

Working Conditions and Labour Mobility

The managerial reforms discussed above were designed to induce greater competitiveness, but China's state enterprises also discharged responsibilities not generally incumbent upon Western companies. This is because the state industrial enterprise or *danwei* until the 1990s was a community as well as an employer, reflecting aspects not only of the Soviet style command economy but traditional Chinese familial type relationships and values. The *danwei* was responsible for a range of services: schools for workers' children, health provision in the form of hospitals and clinics on site, housing adjacent to the enterprise, recreational facilities and, importantly, pensions and other types of welfare. Expenses were borne by the work unit even though ultimately monies came from the state treasury. Thus, in contrast to Western companies where the employer–employee relationship was contractual, workers' allegiance to the *danwei* was social and psychological (Naughton, 1997: 169). In fact, managers would be frequently consulted by workers concerning purely personal matters.

By the 1980s two major consequences suggested that the *danwei* was ripe for reform. Firstly, given increases in longevity, the number of beneficiaries had grown and this, coupled with the fact that the sons and daughters of existing employees were engaged, often regardless of the unit's need, placed additional financial burdens on the enterprise which carried surplus labour as a result. Secondly, while in pre-reform days the *hukou* or residence system reduced physical movement and contributed to political control of the urban population, by the 1980s, the lack of earlier mobility was impeding adjustment to changing markets. Labour could not move, even if it wished, because of loss of welfare and housing. In addition, the central and local assignment of university graduates and secondary school leavers meant that after the late 1950s, with the exception of the Great Leap Forward period from 1958 to 1961 when industry was partially decentralized, there was virtually no labour market.

Labour mobility, however, was one objective of reform and the market was creating new opportunities. In the face of competition, state enterprises sought to cut costs by employing more temporary workers, such as rural migrants, but not according them welfare benefits. Moreover, with the increased incidence of the officially encouraged foreign-invested sector and the permitted revival of private enterprise from the 1980s onwards, new employment systems were emerging. Sino–foreign joint ventures and wholly owned foreign enterprises might offer provisions such as housing and be subject to the national insurance rules discussed later in relation to the state sector, but they have also introduced new Western contractual arrangements which tend to contrast with the *danwei* type social contract. In addition, private enterprises, which often are run on family lines, have not been in a position to confer *danwei* style benefits. Furthermore, with an increasingly competitive labour market, state enterprise employees have become more mobile and some are destined to move into the foreign and private sectors which offer less security of tenure. Such influences are reinforcing state sector labour reform (Solinger, 1997: 195–222).

Undoubtedly, *danwei* links have been seen as impediments to enterprise efficiency and labour mobility in response to the market. At a macroeconomic level, reformers have instituted a national social insurance system, mandated by labour legislation in 1995, as the key to labour mobility.

The benefits which the *danwei* formerly conferred were a crucial element in the management of China's state enterprises but the reform of areas like pensions and housing have altered the relationship between manager and employee, which is also being affected by the practices of the foreign-invested sector. While the latter may also offer on-site housing and pension provision via private insurers, they are also subject to Chinese labour legislation, and their human resource management practices are more contractual and in direct contrast to the former features of China's state enterprises. The separation of ownership and management, the subject of the next section, will have an even greater impact on the evolving role of the *danwei*.

SUMMARY POINTS

- From 1949 to 1978, China had a Soviet-style command economy when industrial production and distribution were subject to central planning.

- The post-1978 reforms have created greater managerial autonomy and labour mobility in order to serve a market economy, which is competitive domestically and globally.

REFLECTIVE QUESTION

- Formerly the *danwei* or enterprise unit bore responsibility for the social as well as the economic aspects of an employee's life. Do you think that such a tradition might be harnessed to create a new Western-style corporate culture?

PROPERTY RIGHTS, CORPORATE GOVERNANCE AND THE PRIVATE SECTOR

Property Rights and Corporate Governance

The inauguration of market socialism after Deng Xiaoping's Southern tour in 1992 represented a compromise between the maintenance of political monopoly by the CCP and moves towards privatization in the interests of greater domestic and global competitiveness. The earlier granting of greater managerial autonomy and the loosening of *danwei* controls had not effected the separation of ownership and management in the state sector. To achieve this there were two main prerequisites. Firstly, a managerial cadre responsible to a Board of Directors and simultaneously disciplined by the dividend demands of shareholders and secondly, a legal infrastructure including the clear delineation of property rights. The objective of creating a new system of corporate governance was set down by General Secretary Jiang Zemin in his political report at the Fifteenth CCP Congress in September 1997, even though it legitimized a number of changes already in motion. Some state enterprises had already been listed on the Shanghai Stock Exchange, founded in 1990, and that in Shenzhen, established in 1991, even though in many cases the state remained the major shareholder, with a high percentage of shares not being traded. This consolidated moves from budgetary allocation, initially towards bank lending and latterly through equity. Such measures were intended to reduce the state's liability for enterprise debt, since there were now other shareholders who could theoretically discipline management (Yakubi and Harner, 1999: 121–9). Thus joint stock companies were being created and corporations had legal person status but, while equity would play a greater role, no true privatization immediately ensued. The latter demands the creation of property rights which did not formally exist under the command economy since they were exercised through state administrative fiat. As Steinfeld (2000: 27–44) pointed out, it is not a question of property rights transfer but their creation in the first place. Moreover, legal infrastructure, still in the making in China, must provide adjudication and redress if property rights are challenged. In turn, what is needed is a corporate governance system, including shareholding, which can provide incentives for investment, monitor management and ensure the optimal use of resources (Chen, 2005: 16–29).

The ideal typology discussed above reflects the Anglo-Saxon model where shareholders monitor management on the basis of transparent auditing procedures and there exists a competitive market for mergers and acquisitions through enterprise performance (Chen, 2005: 16–29). To date, however, it cannot be said that the emerging Chinese corporate governance structure has consistently replicated this model. The Chinese attempt to create *jituan* or conglomerates as multinationals, advantaged by economies of scale, serves as an illustration. During the early 1990s, the Chinese government launched the policy of 'grasping the large and letting go the small'; successful enterprises would be retained by the state with the smaller and less competitive hived off to private interests. Larger state enterprises were subject to incorporation, characterized by clear governance and transparent accounting (Hannan, 1998: 62–104; Newfarmer and Liu, 1998: 8–13).

In this context, the Company law, implemented in 1994, enshrined the creation of a modern enterprise system. Firms would become legal entities with their own property rights and responsibility for their own profit and loss. Mergers and acquisitions, again in the interests of economies of scale, would be based on economic considerations alone. By 1997, 120 enterprise groups or *jituan* had been established in pillar industries such as automobiles, electronics, pharmaceuticals and steel. There have, however, been barriers to the emergence of a modern enterprise system. One company type envisaged by the Company law was the joint stock company, permitted to raise capital through public offerings on stock exchanges. Nevertheless, an impediment to the establishment of new corporate governance, including property rights, is that many state enterprises have been incorporated since the 1990s as wholly state-owned firms rather than shareholding companies. Thus the state is likely to remain a major institutional shareholder, even though increased public offering of shares should in time make enterprise management more accountable to external monitoring of performance (Hannan, 1998: 62–104; Newfarmer and Liu, 1998: 8–13; Shieh, 1999: 50–4; Yabuki and Harner, 1999: 130–3; Sutherland, 2003: 39–66).

In summary, it could be argued that continuing Chinese state involvement in corporate governance is more redolent of the post-war Japanese system, characterized by institutional cross-shareholding within the *keiretsu* group, even if the latter have always operated within an ostensibly free market economy.

Finally, the creation of a more effective legal infrastructure and transparent corporate governance are seen by Chinese and foreign commentators alike as the best means of eliminating corruption in business where, for instance, relations with corrupt government officials and bribery can expedite the conclusion of contracts. Another aspect of legal regulation concerns health and safety: exports of dangerous Chinese products highlight the need for more consistent law enforcement in China.

REFLECTIVE QUESTION

- It has often been said by foreign investors in China that the institution of Western-style property rights, corporate governance and a sense of social responsibility are the keys to the elimination of corruption in China. Do you think that this argument is valid, given the instances of fraud and deception in Western industrial and financial institutions?

China's Private Sector

While the institution of a modern enterprise system has been one means of disciplining China's state sector, a second involves the encouragement of the private sector, which played a minimal role during the period from 1949 to 1978, but was legitimized as an important organizational part of China's socialist market economy with legal status at the Sixteenth Congress of the CCP in 2002 and granted equal rights at the Tenth National People's Congress in 2004. There is, however, a range of entities within this sector and definition is contentious, given that in the 1980s and 1990s private enterprises were heavily reliant on local government for facilities and, in some cases, funding (Sanders and Chen, 2005: 231–45).

Private firms, varying in size, in both services and manufacturing, include former collective enterprises run by local governments but handed to private entrepreneurs to manage, as well as companies funded and run by individual owners or in partnership. Some now have limited liability while others have also diversified into high technology sectors as *jituan*, the conglomerates, or as shareholding firms. There remain, however, both exogenous and endogenous barriers to the growth of the private sector. Enterprises have often had to rely on private borrowing, the so-called social finance, rather than funds from banks which have been reluctant to lend, preferring instead the state sector. They have also been subject to double taxation, that is, on the enterprise and the individual owner in addition to miscellaneous fees exacted by local governments. Furthermore there are market barriers to specific industries, involving complex approval procedures favouring state firms. Finally, to date the private sector has often been advantaged by not paying state national insurance contributions but these charges will be increasingly difficult to evade, especially with diversification into higher wage cost, technology intensive areas (Fu, 2004: 166–77; Garnaut and Song, 2004: 1–14; Krug and Polos, 2004: 72–96; Meng, 2004: 146–65).

In fact, the issue of technological diversification impacts on the management of the private sector. To date such enterprises have been heavily concentrated in labour intensive industries like textiles in East China but, as they diversify, limitations in terms of corporate governance come into focus. Invariably ownership and management have been combined in family control which restricts growth. Technology and product differentiation demand more specialist managers not necessarily present among family insiders (Garnaut and Song, 2004: 225–35). There is now evidence, cited in Chinese economic and industrial journals, that human resource deployment is being given greater attention, with scientific recruitment of those with soft skills like marketing and accounting. Private enterprise is increasingly subject to labour legislation which in turn has a bearing on the retention of employees, maintained, for example, through assessment based training provision. Outside recruitment, scientific management and the reduction of direct family control are leading to the separation of ownership and management, with an increasing incidence of companies limited by shares, even if commercial bank loans are becoming an option as the banking system is reformed. The appointment of boards of directors and a greater dispersal of shareholding have the potential to effect closer monitoring of managerial performance in the private as well as in the state sector (Child and Pleister, 2004: 195–8; Fu, 2004: 170–4).

SUMMARY POINTS

- A competitive Chinese private sector has been encouraged to discipline the state sector.

- Private enterprises are evolving via the separation of ownership and management and diversifying technologically.

Spotlight on Geely, a private car manufacturer

Geely is an example of a Chinese private enterprise which has acquired technology through joint venture partnerships with foreign companies. It has evolved from a private firm into a multinational company and has no Chinese central or provincial government involvement. The Geely *jituan* spans a number of manufacturing and service sectors namely, construction, materials, higher education, travel and real estate. Geely was founded in 1984. It originally manufactured refrigerators but later diversified into other sectors. The enterprise accumulated capital and in 1994 it was decided to enter the motor industry but this was not possible until 2001 when government restrictions were reduced. Following technological agreements with an Italian and a Korean company and importantly, after entering a joint venture with Honda in Tianjin which enabled Geely to produce its own engine, the company penetrated a niche domestic market. Whereas the high quality and medium grade sectors have been largely monopolized by foreign global manufacturers, Geely has established a brand reputation for low priced small family saloons. By 2002, the firm had joined the group of major car manufacturers, was among the top 500 domestic enterprises and ranked 28th out of 100 in Zhejiang Province. A recent Chinese quality survey, however, suggested that doubts remain about the quality of Geely cars. Nevertheless in November 2006, Geely acquired a major shareholding in a joint venture with Manganese Bronze, maker of the London black taxi. Quality control is crucial whether for exports or an increasingly discerning Chinese domestic market.

Sources: Hutton, R. (2006). China's cut-price engine of growth. *Sunday Times*, 24 December; Wang, W. and Shi, P.C. (2005). Entry barriers and the growth of *minying* enterprises (in Chinese). *Guanli Shijie*. 4: 132–40. The above case study was included in a paper presented at the 13th Euro-Asia Research Conference held in Sapporo, Japan, in June 2007. The paper appears in Dzever, S., Jaussand, J. and Andreosso-O'Callaghan, B. (2008) (eds) *Evolving Corporate Structures and Cultures in Asia*. London and New York: ISTE/Wiley Publishing.

Changes in corporate governance and property rights have been designed to maintain domestic and global competitiveness but China's success has nevertheless had its costs in economic overheating, environmental degradation and trade deficits sustained by China's trading partners, and it is to these managerial issues that attention is turned in the following section.

CORPORATE SOCIAL RESPONSIBILITY

CSR: Environmental Protection

Corporate social responsibility (CSR) is a feature of civil society, mainly characteristic of Western advanced industrial nations, and Chinese reformers, whether intentionally or not, have created new centres of economic power, increasingly represented by associations, nominally at least, independent of government. Moreover, a number of these bodies, such as environmental lobbies and consumer groups, have emerged in reaction to such costs of economic growth as atmospheric pollution, land degradation and imperfect market practices. In fact, in China's Eleventh Five Year Plan (2006–2010) the country's leaders have sought to address the negative consequences of growth by calling for the creation of a harmonious society. Regional differentials, income inequality and environmental degradation are to be reduced, with global trade surpluses lessened by encouraging greater consumption of products at home.

These objectives are only achievable through the joint action of industry and government but focus here is on the discharge of corporate responsibility in the wider social and microeconomic contexts, using case studies of environmental protection and human resource management. Given the passage of environmental legislation since the late 1970s, the CCP leadership has shown its commitment to sustainable development, acknowledging that the country's energy efficiency and pollution reduction measures still fall far short of those in developed countries (Dollar, 2007). Such trends call for industrial restructuring towards hi-tech production, both to diversify export products and adjust to greater market segmentation and consumer discernment at home. While government seeks to direct enterprises to clean production through technical guidance and financial assistance, moves by manufacturers are constrained by the conflict between environmental protection and economic profit, especially in the high-polluting, labour-intensive sector which will still play a part in economic growth. Nevertheless, strategic targeting of new niche markets, created by greater consumer discernment regarding green issues, may facilitate cost internaliza-tion, an example being the Chinese textile and garment industries which are using less polluting, genetically variegated cotton, energy saving technology for washing wool and computer-led printing and dyeing skills (Taylor, 2007: 81–99). Such cost internalization, however, demands new expertise which large rather than small and medium-sized enterprises can afford. Capital Steel's corporate strategy has addressed the issue of environmental protection by relocation of facilities outside Beijing and moves towards production of high-grade steel based on quality, variety and service (Taylor, 2007: 81–99). The consumer also shows responsibility in the case of car owner-ship, set to increase, and vehicles are a major source of pollution in China's cities. In the wake of government initiatives in 2000, like the fuel tax designed to encourage such energy saving technology as electric batteries and the creation of a market for small vehicles with low petrol consumption, manufacturers have conducted research into the use of liquefied petroleum gas (LPG) and compressed natural gas (CNG) and experimented with improving battery performance to further the commercial viability of electrically-powered cars (Hildebrandt, 2003: 16–21; Turner, 2003: 22–5; Taylor, 2007: 81–99).

In summary, sustainable development may only be achieved by a socially responsible strategic management responding to segmented market-led industrial restructuring.

CSR: Human Resource Management, Recruitment and Training

Corporate social responsibility, however, is directed not only to the wider community but relates to satisfying the personal and professional needs of the workforce within the enterprise. Human resource management is nevertheless derived from Anglo-American practice and alien to the state-directed unified assignment of managers and workers as well as to the Marxist–Leninist assumptions characteristic of the command economy. Since the 1990s, state enterprises have enjoyed greater freedom in labour deployment, and the introduction of hi-tech industries, often through the medium of Sino-foreign joint ventures, demands that employees, particularly when given greater initiative, be subject to more scientific and sophisticated means of control, a charac-teristic of a more complex modern economy, given the increases in white-collar staff. Human resource management, which considers labour as capital rather than cost, may be defined as directing a motivated workforce dedicated to a company's success. Thus a corporate mission unites individual and company interests (Child, 1994: 157–8). As Chinese companies embrace Western managerial styles, human resource management is being regarded as a complete process encompassing recruitment, remuneration, evaluation, training, retention of employees and social welfare. By the 1990s, managerial positions in state enterprises were being increasingly advertised, with technical specialists especially being employed through the market, in some cases directly from science and technology departments in universities, and even through headhunting.

Scientific recruitment, in the form of systematic testing and interviewing tech-niques, is being introduced. Given that remuneration is one motivator, pay and promo-tion are increasingly based on educational level, responsibility, performance and innovation rather than age and seniority. As important in motivation as remuneration, however, are job satisfaction and career advancement, to which training through apprenticeship for the shop floor workforce and courses both internally and externally, especially in the fields of soft skills like accounting and marketing, for managers, contributes. Nevertheless the provision of targeted training requires a credible evaluation process, more common in foreign multinationals in China, which in turn are influencing state enterprises (Warner, 1986: 326–42; Child, 1994: 172–80; Tang and Ward, 2003: 81–2; Taylor, 2005: 5–21).

Training, however, may prove a mixed blessing. On the one hand its incentives may facilitate the retention of managers and technical experts; on the other, unless the skills acquired are company specific, employees in search of higher pay may carry their knowledge to company competitors. But, as a hedge against defection, companies may insert clauses in labour contracts requiring employees to repay training costs if they leave before the end of a stated period (Melvin, 2001: 30–5, 43).

CSR: Corporate Culture, FDI and Business Networks

Essentially, the above aspects of human resource management are designed to effect identification between individual employees and company interests. Similarly, the provision of social welfare by enterprises is an inducement to employee commitment and an area where foreign-invested companies have taken the lead. The *danwei* is being replaced by nationally legislated welfare; the private insurance benefits and assistance with mortgages increasingly provided by foreign-invested ventures may well be emulated by the state sector, as service providers from overseas enter China under the terms of the World Trade Organization (WTO) (Melvin, 2001: 30–5, 43). Finally, loyalty in Western settings has been instilled through the establishment of a corporate culture; again, foreign companies are the pioneers but it is possible that the familial type solidarity of the *danwei* may be harnessed to respond to a competitive market, forming a hybrid of Chinese tradition and Western practice.

In conclusion, corporate social responsibility in China is emerging in relation to both the wider domestic community and within the enterprise. Reference has been made to the influence of FDI on Chinese managerial practices. But China's conglomerates, the *jituan*, both state and private, are increasingly engaged in globalized operations as multinationals through outward investment, and this is likely to have an even greater impact on managerial areas like corporate social responsibility. Initially, during the 1990s, China's outward FDI was motivated by the industrial need for minerals and oil, witness current Chinese relations with countries as diverse as the states of Central Asia, Africa and South America. Increasingly, however, two concerns have dictated company policy: the imperative to circumvent trade barriers, for example in the European Union (EU), and the search to obtain high technology from overseas companies via merger and acquisition in order to expand into new markets through regional and global networks in the EU and the US as well as in Asia. Instances of the latter that may be cited include the purchase by Lenovo of a controlling stake in IBM's personal computer business in 2004, Shanghai Automobile Industrial's acquisition of an almost 50 per cent stake in South Korea's Ssangy-ang Motor Company and Haier, the whiteware manufacturer's construction of a production base in the US (Smith and Rushe, 2004). Consequently, Chinese companies' corporate social responsibility and their commitment to ethical standards, will necessarily evolve as they become major players in global management.

WORKING AND LIVING CONDITIONS IN CHINA

Western traders have long seen China as a vast market eldorado, a view enhanced since the initiation of China's open door policy in 1978 and the country's admission to membership of the WTO in 2001. Consequently, more and more company representatives have come to negotiate and work in foreign-invested enterprises. While the Chinese have encouraged such foreign investment through legislation, the motives of the Chinese government and potential foreign investors have differed. While the former have sought capital, technology and managerial expertise to further exports, foreign partners have aimed at both foreign sales and Chinese domestic markets. The entry into WTO has brought new opportunities in more Chinese economic sectors.

China is often described as the world's workshop and a source of cheap labour. In fact, however, Chinese labour legislation is now placing upward pressure on wage costs. Moreover the CCP encourages technology dissemination and innovation, while foreign investors seek to protect intellectual property. There is thus a clash of interests.

The Western media portray China largely in terms of the economically advanced Eastern seaboard which differs markedly from the poorer agricultural hinterland; China is becoming a nationwide market, although it is not there yet.

Regional inequality also impacts on the lifestyle of foreign expatriates, with China often regarded as a hardship posting. Increasingly, however, China's growing urban middle class is enjoying living standards similar to those of Western countries. Rising income in Eastern China has brought enjoyment of quality consumer durables, dietary changes and better amenities more attuned to Western taste. Living and working in China may cease to be a hardship posting.

SUMMARY POINTS

■ Reform of property rights and corporate governance is designed, through transparent auditing and shareholding, to monitor Chinese management more effectively in both the state and private sectors.

■ Emerging corporate social responsibility in China relates to such issues as environmental protection in the wider community and the effective management of human resources within the enterprise.

■ Chinese companies are part of global business networks, given inward and outward direct investment.

CROSS-CHAPTER REFLECTIVE QUESTION

■ After reading this chapter and Chapter 8 on Japan, have you recognized that there are actually certain similarities as well as differences between the Chinese and the Japanese management systems? Can you list them one by one and provide a brief explanation for each of them?

CHAPTER SUMMARY

- China is a country with a population of over a billion but only since the 1980s has it played a major role in world trade.
- From 1949 to 1978 China had a command economy characterized by an uncompetitive state industrial sector, governed by central planning.
- The reforms of the 1980s were designed to create a new managerial culture by granting more autonomy in decision making to state enterprises.
- In the 1990s, new systems of corporate governance were introduced. The separation of ownership and management in state enterprises was initiated, with the private and foreign-invested sectors cited as examples for emulation, as China moved from a command to a market economy.
- Western managerial traditions have brought awareness of corporate social responsibility to Chinese enterprises in areas like environmental protection.
- The creation of new Chinese corporate cultures is motivational, enhancing the competitiveness of Chinese companies as Asian regional and global players.

KEY CONCEPTS

Soviet-style command economy: A system where the state planned production and distribution.

Danwei: Both an employer and an agency looking after employee welfare.

Hukou: What determines one's residence in China. It acts also as a means of political control.

Jituan: Conglomerates formed from state enterprises.

REVIEW QUESTIONS

1. Why were the existing sources of managers seen as inadequate for the command economy?
2. What do you consider were the main defects of China's command economy?
3. Why did the reforms of the 1980s fail to separate ownership and management in state enterprises?
4. How is the delineation of property rights crucial for the creation of a new system of corporate governance in China?
5. What are the political impediments to the discharge of corporate social responsibility in China and how may they be overcome?

LEARNING ACTIVITIES AND DISCUSSIONS

1. It has been assumed that the Chinese should adopt Western managerial practices. In this context, and in the light of your own experience, examine the strengths and weaknesses of Western management and its suitability for emulation by the Chinese.

2. Examine, through examples drawn from media reports and the internet, the extent to which Chinese companies are discharging corporate social responsibility.

3. Collect examples, drawn from the media and the internet, of Chinese conglomerates engaging in Asian regional and global networks.

4. In all countries government plays a role in the economy. Consider the changing role of the Chinese state in the economy and its impact on management in the light of the transition from a command to a market economy.

5. Using case studies, assess the impact of Chinese managerial practices on the ventures of Chinese multinationals in host countries.

6. Branding is seen as key to the diversification and competitiveness of Chinese products worldwide. Compare Chinese brands with equivalent Western products.

7. As an aid to enhancing your up-to-date knowledge of the issues discussed in this chapter, it is recommended that you consult the journal, *Management and Organization Review*, published by Blackwell, in addition to sources cited in the references.

MINI CASE

CAPITAL STEEL

Corporate social responsibility

China's steel industry is being compelled to adjust both to market demand and pressure to engage in clean production. An example of a company undertaking such corporate social responsibility is Capital Steel.

In China, steel has been designated as a pillar industry, since it produces material necessary for the development of infrastructure and the diversification of consumer durables. Capital Steel, a major state enterprise, even in the wake of reform, continued to pursue quantitative goals and the expansion of scale but after 1995 increased funding for environmental protection. By the year 2000, on-site atmospheric pollution was said to have greatly declined. Subsequently, there has been greater emphasis on the ecological issue of resources, recycling of waste water and, significantly for corporate responsibility, the disposal of urban refuse. These measures have been enshrined in Capital Steel's corporate strategy, related to both the environment and the market. Ecological targets have included reduction in energy and water consumption per ton of steel, aiming at a projected decline in discharged dust, smoke and sulphur.

Pollution in Beijing, where Capital Steel's production is concentrated, has been exacerbated by the location of industry there. Thus, in addition to technological reform in the interests of clean production, some capital plant is to be relocated outside Beijing. In fact, integral to Capital Steel's strategy, is social concern for the environment, which will necessarily impact on the local economy. In addition, economic demand is being addressed. In the domestic market especially, steel supply exceeds demand, and there is now emphasis on quality, variety and service rather than quantity. As well as this move towards high-grade steel, since 1995 diversification has begun so that eventually non-steel products are projected to constitute over 50 per cent of income from sales. As in the case of other aspects of state enterprise reform, the above objectives are only achievable through a change of managerial mindset effected through a new corporate culture encompassing social responsibility and production targets.

The focus in the above discussion concerning China's steel sector has been on the impact of production processes on the environment. But with respect to the car industry, social responsibility rests with the manufacturer and the consumer, in addition to the government. In the year 2000, for example, China had over 16 million car users consuming about 85 per cent of the country's total oil production. Chinese domestically produced vehicles have in the past been more heavily polluting than foreign imports and still represent a major source of pollution in China's large cities. Car ownership is also growing with the emergence of an affluent middle class. A United Nations' forecast suggests a tenfold increase from an average of 10 to a hundred cars per 1,000 residents over the period from 1995 to 2020.

As a developing country, China has been slow to formulate and enforce regulations relating to car-derived pollution. Nevertheless, measures are currently in train at both national and local levels. In June 2000 there were moves to encourage the use of unleaded petrol through a fuel tax and in September of that year the Car Pollution Prevention Law was being implemented, with local bureaus responsible for enforcement. In June 2001 measures to recycle car scrap metal were put in motion, even though implementation has been inadequate.

Attempts to curb car use derived pollution, however, are being hampered by the structure of the motor industry and technological deficiencies. Currently, the industry lacks concentration and economies of scale; this is a legacy both of central planning and ironically also the decentralization under-taken as part of the post-1978 reforms. Car production is widely distributed; Beijing, Shanghai and Tianjin, for instance, all have manufacturers, led by central and local industrial bureaus. The production process is slow, innovation weak and costs high. Management is also steeped in the seller's market values of the command economy. Chinese sources have therefore called for a change of managerial mindset and greater coordination among the country's manufacturers, especially in terms of the establishment of national research and development centres linked to innovation for green production. Environmental concerns may be allied to economic profit. The fuel tax is a central government initiative to encourage energy saving technology, for example, electric batteries, and a market for low fuel consuming small vehicles. Already manufacturers of models like Santana and Red Flag have conducted research into the use of LPG and CNG.

Additionally, ongoing experiments are improving the performance of batteries to further the commercial viability of electricity-powered cars. In fact, the industry's research has been complemented by funding from the Ministry of Science and Technology which has promised to invest US$106 million to expedite the development of electric vehicles. Furthermore, there has been input from a global NGO, the International Institute for Energy Conservation which from 2000 to 2002 worked with the Chinese motor industry, the Ministry of Finance and other central agencies responsible for motor production to create efficiency safeguards for the Chinese car industry.

QUESTIONS

1. Is corporate social responsibility compatible with China's developing economy?
2. China's Capital Steel is an example of the discharge of corporate social responsibility. By reference to media reports, find other instances of corporate social responsibility in China.

3. What attempts are being made to reduce car use derived pollution in China and what are the barriers to the implementation of such policy?

Sources: Luo, B.S. (2003). Sustainable development of the steel industry [in Chinese]. *Guanli Shijie.* **2**(1–3): 22; Nogales, A. and Smith, G. (2004). China's evolving transportation sector. *China Business Review.* **2**: 24–9; Ou, X.M., Zhang, X.L. and Hu, X.J. (2003). Enabling green automobile development in China [in Chinese]. *Huanjing Baohu.* **1**: 56–8. This mini-case first appeared in a chapter entitled 'Corporate Social Responsibility in China: The enterprise and the environment', in Sharpe, D. and Hasegawa, H. (2007) (eds) *New Horizons in Asian Management.* Basingstoke: Palgrave Macmillan.

INTERESTING WEB LINKS

The Asian Development Bank: http://www.adb.org
China Daily: http://www.chinadaily.net/
Far Eastern Economic Review: http://www.feer.com/
The World Bank: http://www.worldbank.org
Xinhua: http://www.xinhua.org

REFERENCES

Bolger, J. (2006). Woman who lost her heart to IBM plans new assault. *The Times,* 29 August.

Budworth, D. (2006). London is your gateway to China's boom. *Sunday Times,* 22 October.

Chen, J. (2005). *Corporate Governance in China.* London: Routledge Curzon.

Child, J. (1994). *Management in China in the Age of Reform.* Cambridge: Cambridge University Press.

Child, J. and Pleister, H. (2004). Governance and management. In Garnaut, R. and Song, L.G. (eds) *China's Third Economic Transformation: The Rise of the Private Economy.* London and New York: Routledge Curzon.

Dean, J. (2006). China turns to Western style governance. *Sunday Times,* 8 October.

Dollar, D. (2007). China faces its environmental challenges. *APEC Economies Newsletter,* 5.

Dzever, S., Jaussand, J. and Andreosso-O'Callaghan, B. (2008) (eds). *Evolving Corporate Structures and Cultures in Asia.* London and New York: ISTE/Wiley Publishing.

Fu, J. (2004). Private enterprises and the law. In Garnaut, R. and Song, L.G. (eds) *China's Third Economic Transformation: The Rise of the Private Economy.* London and New York: Routledge Curzon.

Garnaut, G. and Song, L.G. (2004). *China's Third Economic Transformation: The Rise of the Private Economy.* London and New York: Routledge Curzon.

Hannan, K. (1998). *Industrial Change in China.* London: Routledge.

Hildebrandt, T. (2003). Making green in Bejing. *China Business Review,* **6**: 16–21.

Hutton, R. (2006). China's cut-price engine of growth. *Sunday Times,* 24 December.

Krug, B. and Polos, L. (2004). Emerging markets, entrepreneurship and uncertainty: The emergence of the private sector in China. In Krug, B. (ed.) *China's Rational Entrepreneurs: The Rise of the New Private Business Sector.* London: Routledge Curzon.

Laaksonen, O. (1998). *Management in China During and After Mao.* Berlin: de Gruyter.

Luo, B.S. (2003). Sustainable development of the steel industry [in Chinese]. *Guanli Shijie.* **2**(1–3): 22.

Macartney, J. (2006). Wealth gap worries communist elite. *The Times,* 12 October.

Melvin, S. (2001). Retaining Chinese employees. *China Business Review,* **6**: 30–5, 43.

Meng, X. (2004). Private sector development and labour market reform. In Garnaut, R. and Song, L.G. (eds) *China's Third Economic Transformation: The Rise of the Private Economy.* London and New York: Routledge Curzon.

Mortished, C. (2007). China boom under threat by loss of cheap labour. *The Times,* 23 June.

Naughton, B. (1997). Danwei: The economic foundations of a unique institution. In Lü, X.B. and Perry, E.J. (eds) *Danwei: The Changing Chinese Workplace in Historical and Comparative Perspective.* New York: M.E. Sharpe.

Newfarmer, R. and Liu, D.M. (1998). China's race with globalization. *China Business Review.* **4**: 8–13.

Nogales, A. and Smith, G. (2004). China's evolving transportation sector. *China Business Review.* **2**: 24–9.

O'Connell, D. (2006). Toyota to sell China cheapies. *Sunday Times,* 2 April.

Ou, X.M., Zhang, X.L. and Hu, X.J. (2003). Enabling green automobile development in China [in Chinese]. *Huanjing Baohu.* **1**: 56–8.

Sanders, R. and Chen, Y. (2005). On privatization and property rights: Should China go down the road of outright privatization? *Journal of Chinese Economic and Business Studies.* **3**: 231–45.

Sharpe, D. and Hasegawa, H. (2007) (eds) *New Horizons in Asian Management.* Basingstoke: Palgrave Macmillan.

Sheridan, M. (2007). Chinese laws may push up labour costs. *Sunday Times,* 15 October.

Shieh, S. (1999). Is bigger better? *China Business Review.* **3**: 50–4.

Smith, D. and Rushe, D. (2004). Devoured by the dragon. *Sunday Times.* 12 December.

Solinger, D.J. (1997). The impact of the floating population on the danwei: Shifts in the patterns of labour mobility control and entitlement provision. In Lü, X.B. and Perry, E.J. (eds) *Danwei: The Changing Chinese Workplace in Historical and Comparative Perspective.* New York: M.E. Sharpe.

Steinfeld, E. (2000). *Forging Reform in China: The Fate of State Owned Industry.* Cambridge: Cambridge University Press.

Sutherland, D. (2003). *China's Large Enterprises and the Challenge of Late Industrialization.* London: Routledge.

Tang, J. and Ward, A. (2003). *The Changing Face of Chinese Management.* London: Routledge.

Taylor, R. (2005). China's human resource management strategies: The role of enterprise and government. *Asian Business and Management.* **4**: 5–21.

Taylor, R. (2007). Corporate social responsibility in China: The enterprise and the environment. In Sharpe, D. and Hasegawa, H. (eds.) *New Horizons in Asian Management.* London: Palgrave Macmillan.

Turner, J.L. (2003). Cultivating environmental–NGO business partnerships. *China Business Review.* **6**: 22–5.

Wang, W. and Shi, P.C. (2005). Entry barriers and the growth of *minying* enterprises [in Chinese]. *Guanli Shijie.* **4**: 132–40.

Warner, M. (1986). The long march of Chinese management education, 1979–1984. *China Quarterly.* **106**: 326–42.

Yabuki, S. and Harner, S.M. (1999). *China's New Political Economy.* Oxford: Westview.

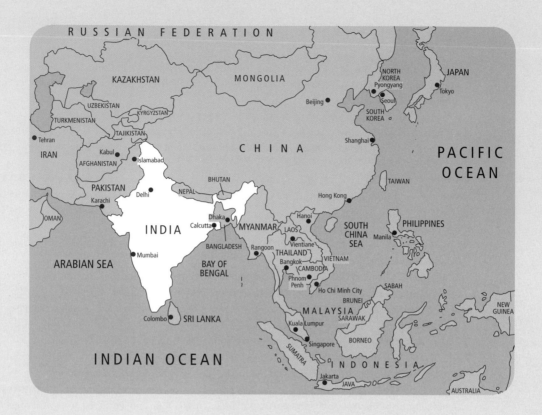

Chapter outline

- A sustainable model of management in India
- India's developmental policy and business systems
- Managing corporate and business strategies in India
- Culture, management and leadership in India
- India's management compared
- Human resource management in India
- Gender in management and leadership in India
- Corporate social responsibility, governance and ethics in India
- Working and living in India

Chapter objectives

After reading this chapter, you should have an understanding of:

1. The core drivers of India's technological and economic surge
2. The diversity of business systems in India
3. The specific features of Indian management and their cultural foundations
4. The Indian approach to managing human resources
5. How Indian firms fulfil social responsibility

Chapter 10

Management in India

Vipin Gupta[1]

INTRODUCTION: A SUSTAINABLE MODEL OF MANAGEMENT IN INDIA

Management in India has entered a fascinating period of change and success. Indian industry has been growing at a rate of 10 per cent annually since the mid-1990s, up from a historical rate of 3.5 per cent since independence. Per capita income has tripled between 1995 and 2008, and the stock market value more than quadrupled, before dropping by 50 per cent due to a global financial meltdown. While the growth in the 1990s was driven by information technology (IT), IT-enabled services, and off-shoring, several other sectors are now growing at double-digit rates including aviation, entertainment, real estate development, financial services, and hospitality (Government of India, 2007).

India is on a rapid growth path, just like China. However, China followed a traditional growth strategy, by becoming a low-wage manufacturing centre for exports. India's development is led by value-added designs and services, which show a higher growth potential at the international level. Considering the world's top 50 companies in terms of market capitalization, India boasts the highest intangible component as a percentage of total enterprise value – 75 per cent – the same as that of the US. In 2007, the global average among 32 nations was 65 per cent, with China at 58 per cent (Dhobal and Pande, 2007).

Although much progress remains to be made, the emerging story of sustainable management in India is one of striving for an inclusive approach. Managers are rapidly qualifying suppliers and workers from smaller towns and from under-represented and underprivileged backgrounds through training, gender sensitization programmes, and interior-reaching networks and collaborations, and then retaining and advancing them through more complex, diverse and broader engagements with international business-to-business clients. They are focused on reaching the customers from second tier towns

219

and increasing the capacity of the rural people to participate in the markets, through innovative use of IT-intensive solutions and supplying lower priced value-intensive products on a huge scale. In parallel, the growing Indian middle class is showing a willingness to spend more, purchase luxury products, and respond to creative financial and marketing efforts such as loyalty programmes, sales, and finance options.

INDIA'S DEVELOPMENTAL POLICY AND BUSINESS SYSTEMS

India is an ancient land. Her development policy and business systems have evolved from several diverse and well-established cultures and institutions spanning several decades, centuries and millennia. Below we examine the formative policy influences on the different types of business systems that exist in India today. These influences are examined over the following periods: British colonialism, early independence, post-1980 enabling industrial policy, post-1995 public policy reforms, and recent trends.

British Colonial Policy and Bureaucratic Business System

India was perhaps the wealthiest nation of the ancient world, as reflected in her nick-name at the time – the 'Golden Sparrow'. India became a British colony in the 18th century after the 1765 Treaty of Allahabad. The British introduced a bureaucratic business system, characterized by a leisurely work ethic (*aaram*); things being left as they are (*chalta hai*); elaborate procedures and numerous approvals (red tape); expectation of private rewards for official work (corruption); public resources used for private indulgence and family favours (nepotism); an expectation of favours for bosses (yesmanship); and superficial employment (employees who have little actual work).

To facilitate colonial administration, postal, telecom and railroad technologies were introduced into India in the 1850s as 'engines of social improvement' (Bear, 1994). The interior of India was substantially altered. English machine-made goods, made from Indian raw materials, squeezed out skilled Indian village artisans, and transformed them into unskilled workers doing jobs in the colonial British factories.

Post-independence Mixed Economy Policy and Extension Business System

At the time of independence in 1947, India's agricultural sector was growing at a mere 0.3 per cent, and its manufacturing sector was miniscule (INSA, 2001). India's first Prime Minister, Jawahar Lal Nehru, advocated adoption of the Soviet-type Five-Year Plan system, along with a Non-alignment Policy (Nehru, [1936]1972).

The Mixed Economy policy entrusted heavy industry projects, such as steel and hydro-power, to the public sector, and introduced a Licence Raj to regulate the investments of larger private sector companies. The public sector firms built extension networks with small-scale enterprises for sourcing various intermediate inputs. Similarly, the private sector subcontracted to the smaller enterprises in order to bypass licensing restrictions.

The Soviet bloc chipped in by helping construct a steel plant in 1955, licensed aircraft, tank and other military technology, and expanded assistance to oil, machinery, power generation equipment and tractors. A network of 40 national R&D labs was created, along with technology and engineering colleges. The nation became 90 per cent self-sufficient in capital goods by the late 1970s, although substantial consumer goods supply constraints emerged, along with economic stagnation, inflation, unemployment of the educated and growing urban poverty.

Furthermore, with the aid of the US, institutions of higher education in management and the fields of technology (engineering) and medicine were created, and high yielding breeds, new pesticides and new agricultural implements were adopted. By the late 1970s, agricultural growth had risen to 3 per cent, for the first time since independence outpacing population growth, and facilitating a dramatic fall in rural poverty from 60 per cent in the late 1960s to 40 per cent in late 1980s (Mulford, 2004).

Post-1980 Enabling Industrial Policy and Professional Business System

In 1984, India's new Prime Minister Rajiv Gandhi laid out a vision of taking India into the 21st century. The government policy called for an integrated development of software for the domestic and export markets by promoting the use of computers for decision making. Public sector computerization generated large complex assignments, and built capacity in the private sector. The imports of knock-down computer kits from Taiwan and Korea were liberalized in order to create opportunities for software development firms. To manage their costs, Indian firms performed low-end software work in the US, and shifted higher end work offshore to India (Mulhearn, 2000).

Post-1995 Public Reforms Policy and Entrepreneurial Business System

In the mid-1990s, the Indian government started massive public sector reforms. Unviable public sector firms were closed, while the potentially viable ones were disinvested. The Ministry of Information Technology (IT), set up in 1999, sponsored hundreds of R&D projects at scores of enterprises, labs and institutes, including the use of Indian languages for computers and a stronger extension of IT to rural India. The charge of growth was entrusted to the private sector firms, and the markets were opened to the foreign multinational firms.

By 2000, the majority of Fortune 500 companies outsourced their IT services to India (Raipuria, 2002). Soon, India had evolved from the world's software programmer to the world's back office to the world's laboratory, where the knowledge workforce made the cost of risk-taking affordable for companies around the world. Over 100 multinational firms, including General Motors, Intel, Microsoft and IBM, set up R&D operations in India. Many global investment banks set up research units and hired Indian mathematicians to design models for risk analysis, consumer behaviour and industrial processes. Several Indian companies in IT-enabled services, pharmaceuticals and engineering became the preferred suppliers to the world. In 2006, besides exporting US$30 billion of software and software services, India exported US$20 billion of business services, including accounting, auditing and environment services (trading in carbon credits), growing 80 per cent annually (India Brand Equity Foundation, 2007).

Recent Trends

In 2005, the government launched a new programme, *Bharat Nirman* (Making India) to unleash rural India's potential as a growth engine. The concept of gender budgeting was introduced, and special funds were allocated for women's development. With reforms in the cooperative movement, microfinance was promoted with the support of non-government organizations and self-help groups. Initiatives were promoted to scout out and harness indigenous knowledge at the grass roots.

Over recent years, the strategy of large private sector firms relying on imported technologies, services and capital goods is losing some of its early momentum in India. Many technology collaborations with foreign firms have fallen apart. Some large private sector firms, such as Reliance, have started emphasizing internal R&D, rather than continuing to depend on imported know-how. They have begun pioneering new frontiers of technology at the global level that they then leverage to offer niche services to foreign firms. The government also appears to be shifting its role from being the nation's primary financier of knowledge and technology, to a secondary supporter of innovations by well-managed private sector enterprises, and then to a tertiary governance and organization of the distributed knowledge in diverse communities. The government is also striving to bring about a second Green Revolution in the nation, as agriculture absorbs two-thirds of the workforce in India. Many companies are forming direct contract farming agreements with farmers to grow specific high-quality crops, and are providing these farmers with relevant technical know-how and extension services.

For many foreign companies, new India is becoming a design house, a tooling centre, a components base and a manufacturing hub. For instance, Germany's Heubach group produces pigments in India, 90 per cent of which are exported to help paint the cars of Mercedes, General Motors and other major auto firms in the US, Europe and Japan (India Brand Equity Foundation, 2007).

In 2008, agriculture accounted for 20 per cent, manufacturing 25 per cent and services 55 per cent of India's domestic income. With policy reforms allowing foreign and domestic private investments, infrastructure growth was growing by 8 per cent (Government of India, 2007).

The new India has also become sensitive to the heterogeneity of her people with respect to ethnicity, languages, religion, education, economic wealth, gender and castes. This sensitivity is challenging people to find ways that will allow the nation to harness this heterogeneity as a positive creative force of development. Some interest groups are also using the heterogeneity as a way to promote their own agenda. However, although such promotion is detrimental to growth on first sight, it also activates the hidden forces of democracy and thereby helps to strengthen the core ethos of unity in diversity.

The new economic development model of India is thus becoming intrinsically integrated with a grand model of corporate social responsibility. Such integration is resulting in serious challenges arising from competing on a global scale, while responding to the local sensitivities of the community and the grass roots. Tata Group, for instance, was forced to abandon its plans to situate the factory for its world's least-cost car, the Nano at $2000, in West Bengal, as it faced the backlash from forcible taking over of fertile agriculture land by the government fiat from farmers.

SUMMARY POINTS

- Management in India is about the development of intellectual properties to leverage and enhance the value of intangible assets.

- There is a great interest in learning why India has been successful in becoming a world leader in the development and execution of a management model based on intellectual properties.

■ Management in India has been about rediscovering and redeploying the culturally embedded local operational and servicing endowments that were lost during the colonial times, and recalibrating and re-aligning them through the assembly of networks in the global markets.

■ On one hand, the system has forged innovative links with local subcontractors and geographies; on the other hand, it has established creative links with global multi-nationals and investors.

■ It is interesting to explore why the managers in India have been unusually successful – compared to all other nations in Asia – in arbitraging intellectual servicing cost differentials between the local interior and the global exterior.

MANAGING CORPORATE AND BUSINESS STRATEGIES IN INDIA

Since the mid-1990s, Indian managers have been forced to drastically restructure their business methods, following the dismantling of licences and controls, reduction of import tariffs and quotas, virtual elimination of public sector reservations and a much more liberalized regime for foreign direct and portfolio investments. They have sold under-utilized assets, using capital in creative ways, and are intensely focused on the top and bottom line. Many companies and business groups that were on the top of the pecking order in the 1980s have been relegated. Next we discuss the strategies used by Indian managers to meet these challenges.

Corporate Strategies

Traditionally, Indian businesses – under the joint family umbrella – engaged in multiple activities. Among the top 50 business houses, such as the Tata Group, there was an average of 18 businesses in the 1990s. Some family business groups which restructured early after the national economic liberalization in 1991 have been well placed to exploit globalization opportunities. However, many have faced tough challenges. In 1991, 22 of the top 50 firms were controlled by families that increased their power during the Licence Raj. But by 2000, only 4 out of the top 50 were run by the older business families. Of the top 50, 35 were professionally managed, of which 14 were first generation businesses (Goswami, 2000).

To meet competitive challenges, many diversified family businesses are going through family splits. Managers often use family splits to recognize the synergies among different business operations and make each business group more focused and cohesive. When the split is done simply to serve the family sentiments, the independent family businesses lack critical mass and must expend time and resources on divesting unviable business lines.

Business Strategies

Indian managers are shifting away from a mindset focused on opportunistic resource accumulation and trading that traditionally prevailed as the basis for the unrelated diversification strategy. In general, they have started building a cost leadership, thereafter enhancing service leadership, and finally evolving into a recognized technology leader in the global marketplace (Das, 1999).

Service leadership: The traditional trading business families were not cost leaders – indeed they sought to keep their business within their communities, if not families, so they would not be undercut. Even today, an employee in a typical family-run *saree* (the dress traditionally worn by women in India) store unfolds a hundred sarees within minutes, trying to sell just one. Similarly, waiters in most family-run *dhabas* (the traditional Indian restaurants) deliver a customer's *thali* (a set meal) in two minutes. Many managers are now rediscovering the secrets of service leadership. Service leadership generates value by delivering superior service through trained knowledge workers.

Technology leadership: Since mid-1990s, Indian companies have shown the highest return on equity in Asia. In 2006, return on equity in India was about 21 per cent, compared with 9 per cent in China. India has followed a business-to-business model globally. However, domestically, the focus has been on a business-to-consumer model. Increasing salaries have resulted in increasing consumer expenditure. It has allowed many entrepreneurs to make large investments and benefit from economies of scale. By 2006, India boasted the highest number of billionaires in Asia – 36, valued at US$191 billion; it also had more than one million millionaires.

Now, supported by a huge supply of funds, favourable policy changes and globally competitive business practices, a number of Indian firms – both large and small – are acquiring companies abroad to tap new overseas markets, gain customer portfolios, and acquire niche technologies. For instance, small clinical research firms are acquiring overseas firms in clinical research, bio-equivalence and data management. India's overseas acquisitions exceed those of China and Russia combined, but mergers and acquisitions within India are less than 10 per cent of global acquisitions (Gadiesh, 2007). All this made India's outward Foreign Direct Investment (FDI) greater than her inward FDI in 2007, making her companies global contenders. For instance, Mahindra & Mahindra has cultivated a dominating market share in the hobby farmer market for its low horsepower tractors in the US; these tractors were inspired by the small farms of India, and did not compete directly with the high horsepower tractors used on larger farms in the US. Indian firms are successfully diversifying their customer and investment portfolios from the US to Europe as well as in Asia.

SUMMARY POINTS

■ Management in India has been about devoting close attention to the fundamentals – technological capabilities, investments and servicing, as well as trading and exchange – for achieving rapid growth for investors, clients and employees.

■ The impetus comes from the failed expectations of easy solutions, such as relying on the technology of foreign partners, and recognizing that managers must author the destiny of Indian companies themselves.

■ Great interest exists in exploring why managers in India have been unusually successful – compared to all other nations in Asia – in multiplying the equity investments and in creating new billionaires.

CULTURE, MANAGEMENT AND LEADERSHIP IN INDIA

The GLOBE (Global Leadership and Organizational Behavior Effectiveness) Research Project suggests using a nine dimension framework to study culture (House et al., 2004). We use these dimensions below to study the culture of India, as it relates to management and leadership.

Performance orientation: Indian society as a whole recognizes and celebrates accomplishments. Formal performance appraisal systems exist in most medium- and large-size organizations. At the same time, Indian society tries not to devalue failures; thus poor performance ratings are avoided. The leaders are accordingly expected to follow a nurturing style while maintaining a focus on performance (Chhokar, 2007). As such, weight is also sometimes given to an individual's identity and situational factors; for instance, seniority and suitability play a role in promotions, in addition to performance.

Future orientation: Indian society has historically put a priority on acting now for improving the 'hereafter'. Saving money and resources is encouraged in families as well as organizations. Reusing and recycling resources and products is a common practice; even in services, firms strive to develop refined and mature processes to conserve human effort. A related doctrine of *mahurata* states that if the time is not auspicious, then the actions may not be as fruitful. Given this complexity of balancing *act now* with *act at the right time*, outstanding leaders in India are expected to be visionary and inspirational.

Gender egalitarianism: Indian society has traditionally been male-dominated. Men primarily make the decisions in families, organizations and society, and there are very few women leaders at the top of such arenas. At the same time, several women role models are celebrated in Indian folklore. These role models have been invoked by the social reformers focused on the re-empowerment of women within a merit-based framework. As Gandhi ([1947]2003) observed, 'Women, and for that matter any group, should disclaim patronage. They should seek justice, never favours.' To meet the challenges of skilled-worker shortages, there is now an increasing emphasis on training, mentorship, and enabling social attitudes, family systems and organizational structures for women in management.

Humane orientation: From very early times, India's culture has been characterized by a great sense of fairness in social and civic relations (Chhokar, 2007). Commenting on the culture of India in the 1st millennium BCE, Basham (1967: 8) noted: 'The most striking feature of ancient India's civilization is its humanity.' Managers in India tend to be highly sensitive to the rights of the workers, who are often seen as members of one's extended family. The worker and consumer rights are also well protected by law. There is a strong tradition of benevolent rulers in India.

Power distance: Indian society and businesses have traditionally been quite stratified. Historically, in the so-called caste system, *Brahmins* as educators were spiritual leaders, *Kshatriyas* as rulers were administrative leaders, *Vaisyas* as traders were business leaders, and *Sudras* as farmers and craftsmen were masters of their trade. During the colonial times, the British introduced a hierarchical system of governance for society and organizations. Social reformers have sought to give voice to the underprivileged. In addition, deference to elders is an integral aspect of culture, and so employees tend to be respectful of the leaders. The power distance corresponds with the autocratic-paternalistic style of leadership and micro management; but if the leaders are not nurturing, the employees may use their power of resistance or show dissent.

Institutional collectivism: The community is a fundamental principle in Indian society. It is about nurturing each other's voice despite differences, unity in diversity, communal harmony and democratic pluralism. Effective managers are those who are adept at finding a third solution as a way to reconcile seemingly opposite interests. Simultaneously, defending one's self-esteem and uniqueness in the face of oppressive, hegemonic and homogenizing forces is also a critical aspect of India's culture. Leaders are expected to be introspective, keep important secrets, protect followers and help save face.

In-group collectivism: The family is one of the basic units of Indian society. Support from the family, particularly parents-in-law, is an important factor for women working in outside managerial and leadership positions. Key positions in family business management are often held by members of the extended family as well as close family friends and confidants. Professional managers in these businesses gain top leadership positions usually after having worked for several years (Gupta et al., 2008).

Uncertainty avoidance: Attempts to reduce and regulate uncertainty are common in Indian society. Life in India is guided by elaborate social customs and religious rituals, especially for major life events such as birth, marriage and death. Experiential knowledge and oral knowledge passed down the generations are held in high regard, although in recent years, professional academic qualifications have become a passport to fast-track careers. The leaders in India are expected to be administratively competent, that is, to enact policies fairly and proficiently.

Assertiveness: One finds that humility, gentility, and charm go along with firmness in Indian society. Indian media encourages and seeks multiple sides of an argument. Culturally, meanings, reality and interpretations are seen as multi-dimensional in India, just like the multiple forms of God. The leaders in India are expected to be decisive, diplomatic and team integrators (Chhokar, 2007).

The foregoing cultural characteristics play an important role in the models of leadership in India. The popular image of Indian leaders is one of an action oriented force of development and change. In general, Indian society prefers proactive, morally principled and ideological styles of leadership, compared to reactive, pragmatic and instrumental styles.

SUMMARY POINTS

- Management in India is about the humane mobilization of group loyalties, while carefully negotiating the reduction of dysfunctional hierarchical and male-dominated power stratifications.

- Outstanding leaders are those who dissipate dysfunctional tendencies, and focus group energies using an egalitarian approach for constructive future and goal-oriented endeavours.

- Many are interested in finding out if the culture of India played a positive, negative or neutral role in Indian business leadership, and in the success of Indian managers.

INDIA'S MANAGEMENT COMPARED

Table 10.1 uses the GLOBE study to provide a comparative snapshot of the culture of India, with that of Confucian East Asian societies, Protestant Anglo and Northern

European societies and Catholic Southern and Eastern European and Latin American societies. The scores on the nine dimensions of societal culture are on a scale of 1 = low to 7 = high.

Table 10.1 Comparative snapshot of the culture (societal practices) in India and the world

	India	Confucian Region	Protestant Region	Catholic Region
Performance orientation	4.25	4.58	4.23	3.84
Future orientation	4.19	4.18	4.28	3.53
Gender egalitarianism	2.90	3.18	3.42	3.54
Humane orientation	4.57	3.99	3.97	3.86
Power distance	5.47	5.15	4.82	5.27
Institutional collectivism	4.38	4.80	4.46	3.99
In-group collectivism	5.92	5.42	4.09	5.29
Uncertainty avoidance	4.15	4.42	4.91	3.79
Assertiveness	3.73	4.09	4.12	4.16

Source: Computed using data provided in House et al. (2004).

Compared to the Protestant and Catholic societies, India in particular, and the Confucian Asian region also to some extent, stand out because of their low gender egalitarianism and assertiveness, but high power distance, in-group collectivism and humane orientation. India and the Confucian Asian region also share a moderate degree of future orientation and uncertainty avoidance. However, Confucian Asia stands out for its institutional collectivism, which is moderate in the case of India.

In the case of India, the cultural features reflect the presence of several internally cohesive groups, stratification of power within and amongst these groups, subjugation of the rights and power of women, soft assertion of one's rights and a cultural sensitivity about inclusiveness. Caste is one major dimension of groupism, but there are other equally, and sometimes even more, important lines of cohesiveness including language, ethnicity, religion, education and economic power. These groupings generate several differences, but underlying these divisions, a sense exists of human equality, as encapsulated in the deep ethos of unity in diversity.

In the case of the Confucian region, however, the cultural features reflect the comparative ethnic and/or ideological homogeneity of the groups within Confucian Asia, and a sense of social order. These groups acknowledge the authority of the families and members that are ahead economically or politically. Few special systems regarding women exist – they are either assigned subordinate positions, or encouraged to be gender-neutral and take up the same roles as men.

These cultural differences have important implications that one should be aware of regarding management in India versus Confucian-influenced Asia.

HUMAN RESOURCE MANAGEMENT IN INDIA

Pre-British and British colonial roots have influenced human resource management in India. This influence has resulted in attempts to correct some of the past injustices after independence in 1947, and the adoption of some of the world's best practices after liberalization in the 1990s.

Pre-Independence

The early model of human resource management in India was created in the British colonial factories (Ramaswamy, 1997). In busy times, the workers, including women and children, 'had to work 22 hours a day for seven consecutive days' (Report of the Indian Factory Labour Commission, 1908). 'Those working these excessive hours frequently died' (British Parliamentary Papers, 1888).

The indigenous welfare movement gained pace with the setting up of the Dorabji Tata Graduate School of Social Work (later renamed as the Tata Institute of Social Sciences) by the Tata business family. The Tata School offered training in casework, group work and community organization techniques to deal with individuals, group and community problems in the workforce.

Post-Independence

Under the 1947 Industrial Disputes Act, the Indian government established an elaborate management–labour dispute mechanism. In the public sector, industry-level bargaining on a nationwide scale is common in core industries such as coal, steel, banks, insurance and ports. In the private sector, industry-level bargaining on a regional scale flourishes in industries such as textiles, plantations and engineering, where professional managers from the industry association, the Confederation of Indian Industry (CII) negotiate region-cum-industry agreements for the member firms. Basic wage rates, benefits and working conditions decided at the company level are adjusted for local conditions at the plant level. Guided by the concept of the Welfare State in the Constitution of India, the collective agreements cover every aspect of business that influences the workforce, including compensation, work norms, staffing arrangements, transfer and promotion procedures, job and income security, techniques and technologies (Venkata Ratnam, 1998). While about 90 per cent of the workforce in the public sector has been unionized, the private sector has sought to minimize the union effects by subcontracting to small and medium firms.

Since the 1980s, private firms in India have pioneered many approaches for flexible restructuring to cope with the restrictive labour legislation and the emerging global competition. There has been a shift from regional and national-level unions to enterprise-level unions, often not linked with the National Federations, to negotiate willingly on the basis of the business conditions of companies. The restructuring of the larger private sector firms has opened up subcontracting for the small units in the informal sector.

Recent Developments

Since the late 1990s, more dramatic changes have occurred in human resource (HR) management. To manage growth, firms have scouted for talent in the smaller cities. They have rapidly escalated the metrics to support HR's contribution to their organizations and help measure effectiveness. Many firms deal with attrition rates as high as 70 per cent. The firms with lower attrition rates are focused on increasingly complex, integrated and challenging projects to generate higher unit values and to keep the more valuable employees from leaving. Many local firms have formed collaborations with universities to start specialized programmes. Similarly, some US firms have used their corporate universities, such as Motorola University and Cisco networking academies, to collaborate with vendors in India to provide training in soft and technical skills (Srivastava, 2007).

In this backdrop, a 2007 global survey of 17 nations by the Swedish research and consulting firm Kairos Future reports that Indian youth (16–29 year olds) are the happiest in the world. The AC Nielson Consumer Confidence Survey also finds that since 2001, Indian consumers are the most optimistic in the world, with faith in their personal finances (90 per cent optimistic) and job prospects (94 per cent optimistic). At the same time, Indian men and women also wish to balance family and social life, and are not solely focused on work.

Diversity initiatives have also gained prominence to bring new talent. The proportion of women employees in new economy businesses is twice the average urban rate of 15 per cent; and the percentage of women in managerial positions has doubled from 6 per cent in the late 1990s. However, many firms experience 50 per cent attrition in the women employees by the age of 30, because of marriage and/or childbirth. Firms such as IBM India, who have managed their gender-centring programmes well, report single-digit overall attrition rates, an even lower attrition rate for female employees, and an ability to scale up local operations rapidly and successfully.

GENDER IN MANAGEMENT AND LEADERSHIP IN INDIA

There are three schools of thought on women managers in India (Mehra, 2002). The first school labels women in management to be part of the 'boys club' – these women adopt a masculine style of management, take on tough assignments, are assertive and dominating, and sacrifice their family lives. This school holds that women can be effective managers only by behaving like male managers. The second school assumes that both men and women can be equally effective managers, but holds that women have special needs – such as maternity leave, flexible work arrangements and relocation to their partner's place. The third school posits that women bring special talents and skills to management, including their more interactive, intuitive and cooperative style of leadership, and the organizations that are sensitive to gender in management are likely to benefit from this diversity.

Over the years, there have been three generations of attempts to address the issue of under-represented women in management and leadership in India. The first generation of issues was defined by the lack of managerial opportunities for women, because of an assumption that they were only capable of holding easy jobs. The second generation issue was the oppression of women using subtle barriers, even in the face of equal opportunity policies. These barriers included a paucity of mentors and role models and masculine policies such as working late nights and rigid hours. The introduction of flexible work hours and other gender-sensitive policies allowed women to enter non-traditional jobs and sectors. Yet, the percentage of women in management positions has remained very low.

In the third generation of change, in response to the shortage of managerial and leadership talent, many multinational enterprises, leading domestic firms and family businesses are beginning to re-evaluate their policies. Anecdotal reports suggest that women managers in India are opposed to the idea of women-specific policies – such policies are seen to demean the accomplishments of the women who have made it to management and leadership positions based on merit. In fact, women-focused policies have resulted in a growing new perception amongst Indian men that the gender sensitization policies are overhyped. It has made many Indian men uncomfortable about working with women bosses, feeling that they will be asked to do extra work while the women will have it easy.

Therefore, in firms such as ICICI, India's largest financial institution where women dominate the leadership ranks, emphasis has been on designing policies that address the need for varying work–life balance over the careers of the employees – women as well as men, managers as well as non-managers. Interestingly, men have become increasingly active users of the flexible work arrangements, and of the options to work from home for one or more days a week.

Women in India have rejected the introduction of a gender-based quota system in management or leadership positions. However, the Government of India has reserved one-third of the seats in rural governing bodies for women leaders. Of the 2.8 million elected officials in India, one million are women – more than all elected women representatives worldwide!

SUMMARY POINTS

■ Management in India is also about engaging employees as partners in development and growth of the firm, the local communities and the nation.

■ It is important that human resource management policies be formed taking into account the life needs of diverse groups, but those policies ought to be applied universally to provide equal opportunities for every group.

■ An important question to explore is whether the talent shortage is offering opportunity and motivation for Indian managers to take the lead in improving the fundamentals of human resource management.

REFLECTIVE QUESTION

■ Is the enormity of social challenge a drag on the success of Indian managers, or an opportunity for new business models?

CORPORATE SOCIAL RESPONSIBILITY, GOVERNANCE AND ETHICS IN INDIA

Historically, managers of Indian businesses sought to ensure multi-generational continuity of firms' values and resources by satisfying a variety of different interests of community and showed ecocentric values (Sundar, 1999). After independence, the government began enforcing social altruism values. Some public sector companies invested up to 5 per cent of their profits on corporate social responsibility (CSR) activities. The conventions of the International Labour Organization heavily influenced public policy. The high corporate and personal income taxes of up to 55 per cent and 98.75 per cent respectively, however, encouraged widespread tax evasion.

In the post-1980 era, the new professionally owned firms saw the government as a partner (Sidel, 2000). The Confederation of Indian Industry, India's largest industry and business association, developed a voluntary code of corporate governance conduct in 1996 for listed companies, ahead of the East Asian crisis. The initiative has propelled the capital market regulatory authority of India – SEBI – to introduce a statutory code to elevate corporate governance to international standards. The financial institutions have adopted an aggressive market-oriented stand, lifting their unconditional support of management. They have begun converting their outstanding debt to equity, and selling their shares in underperforming companies to professional entrepreneurs and managerial groups.

The policy framework has sought to resolve the shareholder vs stakeholder debate by promoting the rights of shareholders, while ensuring that the interests of other stakeholders are not adversely impacted. Secured credits such as banks, financial institutions and insurance companies offering long-term debt have the right to appoint their representatives as 'nominee directors' on the board of the client companies. They have exercised this right with almost all major listed companies that have a sizeable debt. Well-defined laws protect the interests of employees, insofar as the labour market is very restrictive, where adjustments, retrenchments and downsizing are difficult to implement. Increasing popularity of equity stock options, particularly for the managerial and leadership level, has aligned employee and shareholder interests.

As the firms have faced competition for capital, human resources, customers and public goods, the pressure groups have become vocal, asking for support in poverty alleviation, addressing unemployment, fighting inequity and carrying out affirmative action. Similarly, foreign clients have demanded new CSR activities, including advancing women to managerial and leadership teams, and grass-roots action for eliminating adverse impacts on the environment, human rights and child rights. The Indian CSR initiatives have evolved to cover employees, customers and stakeholders, as well as sustainable local and national development through corporate citizenship.

India has gained the dubious distinction of having the world's largest slum population. In Mumbai, half the population now lives in slums because of the migration from rural areas and real estate values that are reputed to be the highest in the world. Therefore, many public, private and non-profit firms have launched initiatives for making urban life accessible within the villages. For instance, the State Bank of India introduced the concept of no-frills accounts to give poor and rural people access to banking, affordable credit and financial literacy. Through a range of IT-enabled initiatives, corporate India is blurring the line between corporate philanthropy and business (Soota, 2007).

In 2007, India ranked in the 60th percentile on the transparency index of Transparency International. Public institutions continue to be compromised by corruption. In 2005, the Right to Information Act was passed to allow civic institutions to hold public institutions accountable and create an empowered citizenry. Indian judiciary has also supported Public Interest Litigation as a way to spur public bodies to positive social action. The economic growth has resulted in improved social indicators such as reduced poverty, morbidity and mortality rates, and higher literacy levels, with rapid improvements in the Human Development Index. However, with growing income inequalities, India's score on the Human Development Index in 2005 was 0.62, ranked at a dismal 28th percentile internationally.

Given the vast scale of the challenge, Indian managers recognize that for sustainable development, they need to take a greater responsibility for linking economic growth with social development. In addition to improving the overall quality of life and increasing social stability, it will also make India an international destination of choice for socially responsible investment and differentiate Indian firms for long-term, high-quality investors.

SUMMARY POINTS

■ Management in India is also about trusteeship of various and diverse constituencies, including employees, community, investors, lenders and vendors, particularly around rural and urban boundaries.

■ Socially and culturally sensitive strategies are essential to sustainable management in India.

REFLECTIVE QUESTION

■ Can managers make an unprecedented impact on the world's population hitherto excluded from the developmental processes and rewards?

WORKING AND LIVING IN INDIA

A growing number of expatriates are being hired by Indian firms and by multinational firms in India. The most popular category of expatriates is people of Indian origin who have studied and lived in other nations, and who may want to relocate to India for emotional or family reasons. In addition, many firms in the knowledge process outsourcing sector employ expatriates for six to 12 months, and charge them with the development of global contacts. For the expatriates, working in India has become increasingly lucrative. Since 2000 Indian workers have enjoyed the world's highest percentage of annual salary increases (nominal: 12 per cent–14 per cent; inflation adjusted: 7 per cent–9 per cent), according to surveys conducted by Hewitt Associates. During the late 1990s, senior/top management enjoyed the highest salary increases, but since 2000, entry-level professional/supervisor/technical positions have received the highest increases. While the top 10 cities in India account for 45 per cent of the shoppers' base, the most rapid growth has now shifted to urban uptowns, emerging uptowns, and other towns. The expatriates find healthcare to be very economical in India, but the cost of housing is extremely high.

Most expatriates find the diversity of Indian religious and social life, and its influence on management and leadership, to be a refreshing eye-opener. Yet a major psychological challenge is to reconcile the vast differences in income and opportunity. At the base, India has a 700 million strong bottom of the pyramid, comprised of poor people living in urban slums and rural areas. At the top, a quiet but dramatic rise is noticeable in India's rich, comprising more than a million millionaires and a few billionaires. In 2006, the upscale, premium and luxury market in India was US$15.6 billion (Technopak, 2007). The middle class is distinguished by the rise of the twenty-something Indian urban consumer. From 1996 to 2006, middle-class families with an annual household income of US$5,000 and above tripled to 100 million (lower middle class being another 200 million strong) (NCAER, 2007).

CROSS-CHAPTER REFLECTIVE QUESTION

■ If you compare Chapters 8 (Japan), 9 (China) and 10 (India), it appears that Chinese and Japanese management systems are to a certain extent commonly influenced by Confucianism. However, Indian culture is not based on Confucianism. So, how does this difference in terms of underlying cultural assumption affect management styles and methods?

CHAPTER SUMMARY

- India is fast emerging as a major economic power. India has transformed herself from a lower income to lower middle income nation. The role of government has shifted from that of tight control to partnership with the private sector for inclusive and sustainable development.
- The backbone of the growth of India's economy has been information technology, but new areas such as biotechnology are fast emerging as new growth drivers.
- The Indian management style is built on craft traditions and community values. However, it also received an imprinting of British bureaucratic and human rights exploitation and welfare-oriented socialist policy.
- Women are playing an increasingly important role as entry-level workers and as managers in Indian companies, although the number of women in leadership remains quite limited.
- Expectations for corporations to be socially responsible have become very high. Although philanthropy, donations and welfare-oriented employee policies remain important, the emphasis has now shifted to business models that are inclusive and enable sustainable engagement of under represented, underprivileged, and under served segments.

KEY CONCEPTS

Business-to-business model: Direct relationship between two businesses or business partners.

Business-to-consumer model: A relationship where businesses interact with the end-consumers.

Cost leadership: Developing an ability to compete on the basis of low cost structure.

Extension services: Services offered by an academic or public institution to the larger public.

First generation family business: Family businesses that are owned and run by the founders.

Green Revolution: A significant increase in agriculture productivity arising from the introduction of scientific methods and systematic management models.

Licence Raj: The bureaucratic system of controlling the economy through licence permits for investment capacity and production outputs.

Mixed Economy: A system of economic governance where the public and private sector collaborate and play an equally important role.

REVIEW QUESTIONS

1. Why did the Indian economy transform and grow so fast after the mid-1990s?
2. What are the distinguishing features of Indian culture? What are the implications of this culture for the management and leadership of Indian firms?
3. What is the role of gender in Indian firms? How has this role been transforming? What other forms of diversity are important in Indian management? What factors are influencing the salience of these forms in the strategies of Indian firms?
4. How are Indian companies acquiring and advancing their workers and managers?

LEARNING ACTIVITIES AND DISCUSSIONS

1. Search for Indian businesses in your community and evaluate them broadly (in terms of price, quality, ethnic uniqueness, product diversity, inclusiveness and service). What distinguishes them from similar businesses from other countries in your community? Think about whether and how the features of these Indian businesses can be related to the peculiarities of Indian management.
2. Imagine you are working for an Indian company. Discuss with your classmates how you would be able to deal with the Indian management style, and what would probably be the biggest cultural challenges for you to accommodate in such an environment.
3. Indian firms have increasingly globalized their activities in recent years and acquired subsidiaries overseas. To what extent can they learn new practices from their subsidiaries in Southeast Asia to enhance Indian management? What can be expected to be some crucial areas where the Indian style of management will be worthy of research and consideration by the local firms in Southeast Asia?

MINI CASE

RELIANCE GROUP
Emergence of an elephant from an ant

The origins of the Reliance Group – India's largest business house – date from 1958, when Dhirubhai Ambani founded Reliance Commercial Corporation (RCC) with a borrowed capital of Rs.15,000 to export spice commodities to Yemen. In 1966, he left the spice business and launched Reliance Textile Industries with a borrowed capital of Rs.280,000. He started this business after the government announced an export promotion programme to allow the import of nylon fibre against the export of rayon fabrics. Reliance enjoyed rapid growth under a follow-up government programme in 1971, which allowed the import of polyester fibre against the export of rayon fabrics – in fact, 60 per cent of all firms' exports under this programme were from Reliance.

After the government decided not to renew these programmes beyond 1978, Reliance decided to shift its focus to the domestic market. Reliance went public in 1977 and roped in 58,000 middle-class investors from the smaller cities in one of the largest public issues of the time. That was revolutionary in a market dominated by state financial institutions, and when the stock market was deemed something only for the rich.

Reliance bypassed wholesalers and focused on non-metro urban markets where the power of bigger wholesalers was weaker. Within two years, Reliance gained a national reach. Reliance rejected the model where a few experts run a company as if it is a secret operation.

In 1981, Reliance decided to integrate backward by starting its own polyester fibre plant. It produced at a capacity almost twice the current demand. Dhirubhai brought in his elder son, Mukesh, who had just finished his MBA from Stanford, to start the polyester fibre plant from scratch. At this time, the government had decided to reserve polyester fibre for the small scale sector. Reliance designed a subcontracting programme wherein it would sell its polyester yarn to small mills for spinning, and then buy the spun cloth back for finishing and sell it under its Vimal brand name. Since no other large mill offered polyester cloth, Reliance enjoyed rapid growth once again.

To sustain its growth, Reliance remained diligently focused on talent management. Reliance hired managers from the public sector to introduce the best practices for setting up standard operating procedures and processes. Different groups of people were given charge of different competencies. Some were entrusted with obtaining government licences, such as for importing something quickly to reduce the cycle time. Others were responsible for timely project execution. And still others focused on the operations – how to run the company efficiently.

To outsiders, it seemed that Reliance's success was mostly based on the web of relationships it created with influential politicians, government officials and the media. These relationships helped it lobby with the government and gain favourable policies, licences, approvals and foreign exchange for its expansion and diversification initiatives. However, for the same reason, Reliance was constantly criticized by its rivals, including one who owned a major national newspaper, for manipulating government policies through bribes and unfair influence.

Reliance was committed to use its competencies and cash flows to invest in the businesses of the future, and to make a difference in the lives of millions of Indians. Therefore, it moved further upstream backward integration into polyester resins, and produced a range of petrochemical end products such as detergent intermediaries whose capabilities were related to the manufacturing of these resins. Consequently, by 1990, Reliance's stock market value had soared to nearly Rs.10 billion.

Reliance consolidated its capabilities to move further upstream into petrochemical intermediaries in 1991, by building the world's largest ethylene cracker plant. The stock value reached nearly Rs.100 billion by 1995, when Reliance became the first Indian company to report a net profit of Rs.10 billion. As after liberalization, the government reduced tariffs first to 150 per cent, then to 30 per cent and finally 10 per cent, thus creating a booming opportunity for Reliance.

When the government decided to offer licences for cellular phones in 1997, Reliance decided to take the plunge into the growing information technology sector.

Reliance moved further upstream in its core business into oil refining in 1999 with a state-of-the art integrated complex which accounts for 25 per cent of India's refining capacity. For the next three years, Dhirubhai was rated 'India's most admired CEO' in the Business Barons – Tylor Nelson Sofres-Mode Survey. In July 2002, Dhrirubhai passed away, leaving his legacy behind. As India's largest company, and India's only Fortune 500 company, Reliance had given its original investors a compounded annual return of 43 per cent over its 25 years as a public company. Indian corporate history had been rewritten, and the way Indian business thought and operated had been changed forever.

In June 2005, Dhirubhai's wife decided to split the group to sort out the rivalry between Mukesh and his younger brother Anil. Mukesh was given Reliance Industries (oil, gas and petrochemicals) worth 70 per cent of the family's equity in the group worth US$23 billion of market capitalization, and Anil received 20 per cent in the form of Reliance Communications (telecom), Reliance Energy (power utility) and Reliance Capital (financial arm). Their two sisters received 5 per cent each.

Under Anil, Reliance Communications grew into the country's second biggest in subscriber numbers, and Reliance Capital became the biggest private sector mutual fund within a year. Reliance Energy announced a major expansion plan to transform India's power landscape. Anil also acquired an entertainment company Adlabs Films to enter the entertainment business. By mid-2006, his Group was worth nearly half of Mukesh's Group.

Mukesh's Group grew more modestly by 50 per cent in one year, as he focused on projects that proved more socially controversial. One of the unfulfilled dreams of Dhirubhai was for Reliance to enter agribusiness and make a difference in the lives of the 60 per cent of the Indian population engaged in agriculture. Mukesh believed that fragmented landholdings of the farmers could be integrated with technology, and farmers could become world-class with proper inputs. For that to happen, distribution had to be fixed by putting world-class technology at Indian costs, to connect the small farmers directly to the US market so that they could get market price for their fresh produce. Mukesh planned to invest Rs.250 billion in retailing, structured into 34 independent companies for each of the verticals that might in future be listed as a public company, and to form global alliances. The vision was to create one million new jobs for college graduates by 2010, and increase farm incomes by 6 to 10 times. However, the small traditional food retailers in the unorganized sector were soon out in the streets to protest the entry of Reliance in groceries. Mukesh's other major plan was to invest in Special Economic Zones (SEZs) that would offer integrated airport, seaport, transportation, power and housing capabilities at sensible costs. The vision was to bring in global employers to different sectors to tap the talent that India had to offer.

In 2008, Forbes ranked Mukesh as the fifth richest person in the world and the richest in Asia, with an estimated wealth of US$43 billion – double that of a year earlier. Anil's wealth grew even faster and tripled over the year to reach US$42 billion. Reliance group was worth about US$200 billion, having grown 8.5 times since the split in 2005. By the end of 2008, the value of Reliance Group fell by about 50 per cent as a result of the global financial meltdown. Yet, overall, it appeared that sibling rivalry had played an important role in driving respective businesses to excellence.

QUESTIONS

1. Which internal and external factors have helped Reliance Group to grow into its current position?
2. In which aspects has the management at Reliance Group been typical for Indian management? In which aspects has it been atypical?
3. Do you think Reliance Group has to transform itself fundamentally to remain successful in the future? Why or why not?

Sources: Majumdar, S. and Shetty, S. (2002). The Dhirubhai legend: The bond with the market still endures. *The Financial Express*, June 27; Srinivasan, R. (2002). Driven by the power to dream big. *Business Line*, July 8; Karmali, N. (2002). A lifetime achievement. *Business India*, July 8–21; The Rediff interview with Mukesh Ambani, chairman, Reliance Industries Ltd, 'Always invest in businesses of the future and in talent', January 17, 2007; Ambanis first to hit $100 billion mark, but together, newindexpress.com, Oct 30, 2007.

INTERESTING WEB LINKS

On the story of India: india.gov.in
On the success story of Brand India: www.ibef.org
On tourism in India: www.incredibleindia.org
On news from India: samachar.com

Note

1   I thank Jessica Rudis, Simmons College '08, for her careful editing of this chapter.

REFERENCES

Basham, A.L. (1967). *The Wonder that was India*, 3rd edition, London: Sidgwick and Jackson Limited

Bear, L.G. (1994). Miscegenations of modernity: Constructing European respectability and race in the Indian railway colony, 1857–1931. *Women's History Review*, **3**(4): 531–48.

British Parliamentary Papers (1888) LXXVII, No. 321.

Chhokar, J.S. (2007). India: Diversity and complexity in action. In Chhokar, J.S., Brodbeck, F.C. and House, R.J. (eds) *Culture and Leadership Across the World: The GLOBE Book of In-Depth Studies of 25 Societies*. Mahwah, NJ: Lawrence Erlbaum.

Das, G. (1999). The problem. *Seminar, Special issue on family business: A symposium on the role of the family in Indian business*, 482.

Dhobal, S. and Pande, B. (2007). India emerges Top 3 economy in the world. *The Economic Times*, December 10.

Gadiesh, O. (2007). Looking at acquisitive India: An M&A scorecard. *The Economic Times*, December 10.

Gandhi, M.K. ([1947]2003). Gandhi on women in politics: A voice from the past. *The Hindu*, September 28. http://www.hindu.com/mag/2003/09/28/stories/2003092800280400.htm.

Goswami, O. (2000). *The Tide Rises Gradually: Corporate Governance in India*. Paris: OECD Development Centre.

Government of India (2007). *The Economic Survey 2006–2007*. Government of India.

Gupta, V., Levenburg, N., Moore, L., Motwani, J. and Schwarz, T. (2008). *Culturally-Sensitive Models of Family Business in Southern Asia: A Compendium Using the GLOBE Paradigm*. Hyderabad: ICFAI University Press.

House, R.J., Hanges, P.J., Javidan, M., Dorfman, P.W. and Gupta, V. (2004) (eds). *Culture, Leadership, and Organizations: The GLOBE Study of 62 Cultures*. Thousand Oaks, CA: Sage Publications.

India Brand Equity Foundation (2007). www.ibef.org.

INSA (Indian National Science Academy) (2001). *Pursuit and Promotion of Science: The Indian Experience*. New Delhi: INSA.

Karmali, N. (2002). A lifetime achievement. *Business India*, July 8–21.

Majumdar, S. and Shetty, S. (2002). The Dhirubhai legend: The bond with the market still endures. *The Financial Express*, June 27.

Mehra, P. (2002). Women managers: To the top and beyond. *Hindu Businessline*, April 7, http://www.thehindubusinessline.com/

Mulford, D.C. (2004). US–India partnership: Creating economic opportunities in agriculture. Talk delivered at the Confederation of Indian Industry, Chandigarh, India, April 16.

Mulhearn, J. (2000). Birth, evolution, and globalization of the Indian information technology industry: Protected insular state enterprises to private global software exporters, http://www.contrib.andrew.cmu.edu/~mulhearn/india.html. Accessed January 13, 2005.

NCAER (National Council for Applied Economic Research) (2007). *The Great Indian Middle Class*. Delhi: NCAER.

Nehru, J.L. ([1936]1972). Introduction to M.R. Masani: Soviet sidelights. Reprinted in *Selected Works of Jawaharlal Nehru* (New Delhi, 1972), **7**: 128–9.

newindexpress.com (2007) Ambanis first to hit $100 billion mark, but together, 30 October.

Raipuria, K. (2002). What size the 'new' economy? A conduit approach. *Economic and Political Weekly*, **37**: 1062–7.

Ramaswamy, E.A. (1997). Why ask unions to do management's job? In Ramaswamy, E.A. (ed.) *A Question of Balance: Labor, Management, and Society*. Delhi: Oxford University Press.

Report of the Indian Factory Labour Commission (1908). Vol I. Simla: Government Press.

Sidel, M. (2000). New economy philanthropy in the high technology communities of Bangalore and Hyderabad, India: Partnership with the state and the ambiguous search for social innovation. Paper presented at the Rockefeller Foundation Conference 'Philanthropy and the City: A Historical Overview', September 25–26.

Soota, A. (2007). Business with a heart: The Mind Tree and India stories, 6th Annual Business and Community Foundation CSR Lecture, New Delhi, April 5.

Srinivasan, R. (2002). Driven by the power to dream big. *Business Line*, July 8.

Srivastava, S. (2007). Indians to get a big raise. *Asia Times*, February 9.

Sundar, P. (1999). *Beyond Business: From Merchant Charity to Corporate Citizenship, Indian Business Philanthropy through the Ages*. New Delhi: Tata McGraw-Hill.

Technopak (2007). *India's Luxury Trends 2006,* KSA Technopak, February.

The Rediff interview with Mukesh Ambani, chairman, Reliance Industries Ltd, 'Always invest in businesses of the future and in talent', January 17, 2007.

Venkata Ratnam, C.S. (1998). Industrial relations in India. In Chandram, A., Mund, H., Sharan, T. and Thakur, C.P. (eds) *Labor, Employment and Human Development in South Asia*. Delhi: B R Publishing Corporation.

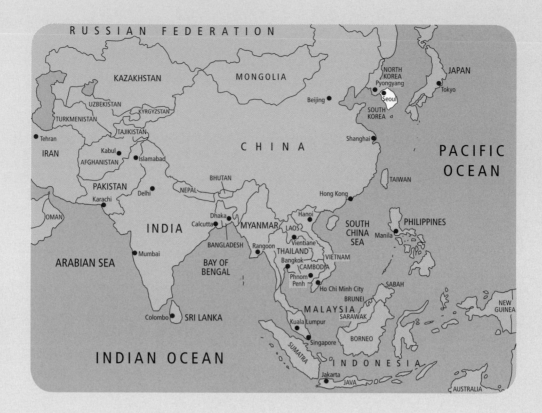

Chapter outline

- Overview of the Korean economy
- Economic development, corporate growth and business–government relations
- Korean culture and management
- Leadership and decision making
- Human resource management
- Corporate social responsibility and corporate citizenship
- Working and living conditions in Korea

Chapter objectives

After reading this chapter, you should be able to:

1. Identify the major reasons for Korea's dynamic economic development
2. Understand the specific features of Korean management and their cultural background
3. Identify the major potential strengths and weaknesses of Korean management
4. Understand how Korean firms exert social responsibility

Chapter 11

Management in Korea

Martin Hemmert

OVERVIEW OF THE KOREAN ECONOMY

South Korea (subsequently referred to as Korea) is a geographically small country with an area of approximately 99,000 km^2 which covers the southern half of the Korean peninsula. However, in contrast to its limited geographic size, it is a major economic power. The Korean GDP amounted to almost US$1,000 billion in 2007 and was thereby the fourth largest in Asia behind Japan, China and India. The country's population is slightly less than 50 million people, and the estimated per capita income level in 2007 was approximately US$20,000 at current exchange rates and US$25,000 on a purchasing power parity adjusted base, illustrating the fact that Korea has reached the group of very high income countries, with the remaining income gap to the richest countries narrowing in recent years (CIA, 2007; OECD, 2007). Moreover, income level per capita has increased by approximately 250 times between 1962 and 2007, reflecting the country's stunning economic development throughout the past 50 years (Bank of Korea, 2007).

Notwithstanding its large size, however, the Korean economy shows a relatively strong pattern of specialization. The weight of the manufacturing and construction sectors amounted to 40 per cent of the total economy in 2006 (with 3 per cent falling to agriculture and 57 per cent to services) and is thereby one of the highest in the world among developed countries (OECD, 2007). Moreover, within manufacturing, Korean firms are strongly specialized in a few industries, such as automobiles, electronics, microelectronics, telecommunications, steel and shipbuilding, which account for most of the country's exports. Aside from this pronounced sectoral specialization, however, Korea's economy is also very specialized in a vertical sense. Korean firms often focus only on specific steps within the industrial value chain. Whereas they concentrate largely on the final assembly of products such as cellular phones or digital displays, most of the parts and components are purchased from outside and often imported.

Taken together, the Korean economy is characterized by a strong horizontal and vertical specialization in activities where it possesses strong competitive advantages.

Korea's business sector also has some other distinctive characteristics. Most of the country's large companies are members of business groups (*chaebol*) which dominate the export oriented industries. However, most Koreans do not work in these large firms. On the contrary, small and medium-sized enterprises (SMEs) with less than 300 employees accounted for almost 85 per cent of the country's total business sector employment in 2005 (KOSIS, 2007). Compared with large firms, wages and salaries are much lower in these SMEs. In other words, a pronounced division between SMEs and large firms can be observed in Korea. Large firms possess a strong international competitiveness and are concentrated in the export oriented industries, whereas SMEs are mostly focused on domestic business activities.

ECONOMIC DEVELOPMENT, CORPORATE GROWTH AND BUSINESS– GOVERNMENT RELATIONS

Whereas Korea has evolved as an independent kingdom throughout its long history, it was – much like other East Asian countries – technologically backward when Western colonization reached out to the region in the late 19th century. After a failing struggle to maintain independence, it came eventually under Japanese influence and was formally annexed by Japan in 1910. During the period of Japanese rule which lasted until 1945, the country's infrastructure was somewhat modernized, and an industrial manufacturing sector was created. However, all developmental priorities were set according to the preferences of the Japanese rulers, not those of the Korean people themselves.

After achieving independence from Japan, the country split into a Southern half which developed under American influence and a Northern half under Soviet and, later, Chinese influence. Following a military attack by the North, the country was devastated by the Korean War which lasted from 1950 to 1953. This war cost not only the lives of several million people, but also destroyed large parts of the infrastructure and manufacturing facilities. In short, the Korean government after the war found itself in charge of a country that was extremely impoverished in terms of technological, material and financial resources. Moreover, Korea had also been deprived of any autonomous development and leadership for the previous 50 years. As a result, aside from a gradual postwar reconstruction that was backed by development aid, no rapid improvement of the economic situation could be achieved in the first years after the war.

Rapid Economic Development and High Growth Since the 1960s

The situation changed, however, during the government of President Chung-hee Park, who seized power through a military coup in 1961. Under authoritarian rule, resources were concentrated on activities in specific sectors that were designed to achieve rapid industrialization. In the beginning, priority was given to the development of basic industries such as cement and petroleum, and light, labour intensive industries, such as textiles and footwear (Chung et al., 1997). Since the late 1960s, however, the focus of Korea's industrial policy shifted to heavy industries such as steel and shipbuilding, and later on in the 1970s to advanced assembly industries such as automobiles and electronics. Korea's industrial policy during this period included not only concentration on specific sectors and industries, but also preferential treatment of certain companies and business groups in these industries which were evaluated as most capable by the government to contribute to the country's economic and industrial development. These firms were provided with priority access to scarce resources through the granting of import licences which secured availability to foreign exchange and almost unconditional bank loans.

The Emergence of Korean Business Groups

Korea's industrial policy during this period was widely regarded as extremely successful. Double digit annual growth rates were continuously achieved, resulting in a rapid upgrade of the country's status from a developing to an emerging economy. The economic and technological development in the 1960s and 1970s clearly occurred under the leadership of the government which steered and controlled the private business activities through a wide range of direct and indirect measures (Chang, 2003). However, as a consequence, the corporate sector grew rapidly. In particular, numerous diversified business groups (*chaebol*) emerged in Korea. A common feature of these groups was that they expanded into a large number of products and industries which were often technologically unrelated. This lateral corporate growth was partially the result of the preferential treatment of specific companies by the government which allowed them to pursue aggressive expansion strategies. However, at least during the early stages of development, it was also a consequence of the lack of industrial development and weakness of markets for resources and intermediate products which induced companies to expand into other industries to become and stay competitive (Kim et al., 2004). To illustrate, LG chairman Cha-kyung Koo recalled the early development of his business group like this (Aguilar and Cho, 1985):

> My father and I started a cosmetic cream factory in the late 1940s. At the time, no company could supply us with plastic caps of adequate quality for cream jars, so we had to start a plastics business. Plastic caps alone were not sufficient to run the plastic molding plant, so we added combs, toothbrushes, and soap boxes. This plastics business also led us to manufacture electric fan blades and telephone cases, which in turn led us to manufacture electrical and electronic products and telecommunication equipment. The plastics business also took us into oil refining, which needed a tanker shipping company. The oil refining company alone was paying an insurance premium amounting to more than half of the revenue of the then largest insurance company in Korea. Thus, an insurance company was started. This natural step-by-step evolution through related businesses resulted in the Lucky-Goldstar group as we see it today.

Later on, from the 1980s, the government gradually retreated from the direct control of the corporate sector and its support of specific firms. By this time, some *chaebol* had grown into giant industrial groups which not only accounted for a large part of the Korean economy, but also competed globally in a wide range of industries. At the same time, many Korean firms also made steep technological advances (Kim, 1997). Whereas they were strongly dependent on foreign technology in the early stages, from the 1980s they increasingly acquired indigenous technological capabilities through research and development (R&D) activities. As a result, Korean firms moved into technologically advanced fields, such as semiconductors, cellular phones and digital displays. In certain fields, they emerged subsequently as global industry leaders, such as Samsung Electronics in the memory chip industry since the early 1990s. Recently, supported by heavy investment in wireless communication networks, Korean companies are also rapidly advancing into internet-related products and services, though many of them still appear to target primarily the domestic rather than the international market.

The Financial Crisis of 1997 and Structural Reforms

Notwithstanding the gradual reduction of government interference in the business sector and the country's democratization which occurred in the late 1980s, Korea was still considered largely a closed market by foreign investors in many industries until the 1990s. Many formal restrictions as well as informal practices, accompanied by a widespread hostility in the government and the business community towards foreign influences, made it difficult for multinational enterprises (MNEs) to penetrate the Korean market through imports or foreign direct investment.

However, the business climate drastically changed as a result of the Asian financial crisis of 1997, which had a huge impact on Korea and forced the government to seek the IMF's financial assistance in order stay solvent internationally. Subsequently, many restrictions for international investors were removed, and a large number of financially troubled Korean firms were acquired by foreigners. At the same time, the *chaebol*'s structure and business model, which had previously been praised as a major reason for the country's economic success, came under strong attack. About half of the 30 largest business groups underwent bankruptcy or bank-sponsored restructuring programmes in the years immediately after the crisis (Kim et al., 2004), with Daewoo, which together with Samsung, Hyundai, LG and SK was one of the five leading *chaebol* in Korea but ceased to exist as a group after 1999, being the most prominent victim. Moreover, the surviving *chaebol* were also being criticized for their lack of transparency and poor corporate governance which allowed the groups' owners to exert almost unlimited power regarding strategic business decisions through a network of majority ownership in group companies. The management of the *chaebol* were urged to improve transparency through the set-up of holding companies and to dispose of technologically unrelated activities.

Many *chaebol* made significant efforts as regards the latter point, with the Hyundai group, which split up into two groups – one being focused on the automobile business and some related activities and the other one accommodating most of the other group companies – being the most well-known case. Notwithstanding these developments, however, most Korean business groups still have to be regarded as extremely diversified when compared with conglomerate firms from other advanced economies, and the extremely strong influence of their owners prevails in most cases (Hemmert, 2007). In fact, some *chaebol* have recently even started to diversify again since the aftermath of the economic crisis has been overcome. Furthermore, whereas the government's influence on business has weakened in the course of the country's economic and political development, it still appears to be stronger than in most other OECD countries, as some politicians and administrators continue to interfere with the private sector through occasional discretionary actions and rulings.

Taken together, notwithstanding the rapid transformation of Korea's economic and political system throughout the past 50 years, some previously important features of the Korean economy still partially prevail. In particular, large business groups continue to play an important role in Korea. Cultural features, which will be reviewed subsequently, contribute to explaining this structural inertia.

SUMMARY POINTS

■ Since the 1960s the Korean economy has developed rapidly under authoritarian government rule.

■ Conglomerate business groups (*chaebol*) play a leading role in the Korean economy.

■ After democratization in the late 1980s and the Asian financial crisis of 1997, Korea opened up to foreign companies and investors.

KOREAN CULTURE AND MANAGEMENT

In order to understand the peculiarities of the Korean management style, a brief review of some features of the Korean culture is helpful. The country's cultural tradition is strongly linked to a specific interpretation of Confucianism which particularly emphasizes the following values (Chang and Chang, 1994; Chung et al., 1997; Grainger and Ananthram, 2007):

■ Loyalty to senior individuals within a hierarchy
■ Filial piety and respect for parents
■ Emphasis on education and diligence
■ Trust between friends and colleagues.

As can be seen from this list, there is a particular emphasis on hierarchical relationships, family values and group harmony in this cultural tradition. This heritage of Korean Confucianism which has shaped the country's culture over many centuries is still strongly prevalent in the contemporary management of Korean firms. However, Korean management also received some important foreign influences in more recent history. Japanese managerial practices had a lasting influence on the Korean management style in the first half of the 20th century and American-style management in the second. Specifically, it appears that Korean management inherited the introduction of well structured corporate ranks and managerial procedures from the Japanese and a strong focus on competition and performance orientation from US influences.

As a result, contemporary Korean management can be qualified as a hybrid which incorporates traditional Korean (Confucian), Japanese and American practices. It embraces the following features (Chung et al., 1997; El Kahal, 2001; Chen, 2004; Grainger and Ananthram, 2007):

■ Centralized management
■ Top-down decision making
■ Authoritarian and paternalistic leadership
■ Long-term oriented, but flexible employment practices
■ Compensation and reward based on both seniority and merit.

REFLECTIVE QUESTION

■ Think about the management style of firms in your home country. Is it also affected by foreign influence, and can be therefore qualified as 'hybrid'?

LEADERSHIP AND DECISION MAKING

In a Korean business group or firm, the CEO is typically the owner. Thus, there is mostly no separation between ownership and management. The CEO and company owner assumes the role of the father in a Confucian family. He makes all major decisions and expects his subordinates (the 'family members') to respect and implement them swiftly. As a consequence, most of the power in Korean firms is centralized at the top level. Moreover, for top managers, there is no need for extensive consultation and consensus seeking within the organization in the wake of major decisions.

In large *chaebol*, the owner typically relies on a staff organization which is personally attached to him, named 'planning and coordination office', 'central planning office' or 'office of the chairman', to gather the information needed for important decisions (El Kahal, 2001). This staff organization is typically not integrated into any of the *chaebol* group firms, thereby avoiding any dependence of the owner on the resources of a specific group firm and enabling him to develop his views and decisions independently.

The directions given by senior managers in Korean firms are often rather general and unspecific in nature. This gives subordinates a relatively large amount of freedom regarding implementation details, but also requires them to understand the managerial directions properly and to have the capability to implement them satisfactorily and quickly (Chung et al., 1997).

In formal meetings, there is typically no open communication and discussion of managerial decisions. In particular, opposing views are not aired, as challenging the superior's views in front of others would damage his 'face' and authority and would therefore be regarded as unacceptable behaviour, regardless of the validity of the argument. Instead, subordinates often interact with their superiors informally on the basis of personal one-to-one communication to discuss managerial directions and facilitate mutual understanding.

In general, vertical human ties tend to be close in Korean firms and are often extended beyond narrowly defined working relationships. Managers expect their subordinates to be respectful and to do their best to follow their directions. At the same time, they assume personal responsibility for the well-being of their subordinates and give them advice on work-related as well as on private matters. In sum, whereas harmonious human relationships are regarded as important in Korean firms, such harmony is particularly emphasized in vertical rather than horizontal relationships (Chen, 2004).

The Korean management and leadership style bears a number of specific opportunities and risks. As there is little need for discussion and consensus seeking, managerial policies tend to be implemented with high speed in Korean firms. At the same time, the fate of Korean companies depends to a great extent on the quality of managerial decisions made by top managers. If a top manager is highly competent and his managerial directions are enlightened, Korean companies have the potential to emerge as extremely strong and dynamic competitors – domestically and internationally. However, if the prescribed managerial policies are bad, they can lead the respective companies into serious difficulties, as there is no effective organizational mechanism in place to control or correct them. Furthermore, a lack of professionalism has been identified as a major problem in some large *chaebol* and Korean companies. As ownership and management are not separated in most cases, it sometimes turns out that the competent management of large businesses is beyond the intellectual or professional capacity of their owners (Chang, 2003). In fact, recently many *chaebol* are relying more and more on professional managers to overcome this problem (see for illustration the Samsung Electronics mini case at the end of this chapter).

Furthermore, as a result of the Korean organizational culture and the country's recent economic history, the firms' managerial policies often tend to be bold and entrepreneurial. As outlined in the previous section, Korean businesses often lacked any significant resources or competitive advantages when they started their operations in the first decades after liberation and the Korean War. Often, innovative and risk-taking approaches were the only way to overcome this situation and to make a business viable and sustainable. This risk-taking attitude has persisted in the managerial strategies of many Korean firms during the past decades. It could be observed not only domestically, but also internationally. For example, Korean firms often entered emerging markets such as India or Central Asian countries at an early stage to grab business opportunities and achieve first mover advantages. Likewise, *chaebol* often advanced aggressively into new industries and product lines, leading to very high diversification levels, as discussed earlier in this chapter. Moreover, the Korean firms' aggressive expansion strategies were often extensively debt financed, resulting in highly leveraged balance sheets with debt/equity ratios of 5:1 or higher (Chung et al., 1997).

Similar to the organizational culture of Korean firms, their entrepreneurial, risk-taking strategies bring certain opportunities and risks. On the one hand, their aggressive approach was often rewarded with high growth and profitability when new markets were successfully penetrated through product or geographical diversification. On the other hand, however, it also makes them vulnerable to the consequences of managerial errors or unfavourable changes in the business environment. Therefore, it was not a coincidence that so many *chaebol*, notwithstanding their previous growth and profitability, went bankrupt after the Asian financial crisis.

SUMMARY POINTS

- Ownership and management are often not separated in Korean firms and business groups.

- Managerial power and leadership are highly centralized.

- Vertical, rather than horizontal, human relationships are emphasized.

- Korean firms often apply aggressive growth and diversification strategies.

REFLECTIVE QUESTION

- Why do you think Korean firms are particularly successful when entering markets of developing and emerging economies?

HUMAN RESOURCE MANAGEMENT

Korean firms pay strong attention to the field of human resource management, as their home country is not blessed with any significant natural advantages or other resources except human skills and knowledge. Moreover, their human resource management strongly emphasizes education, which is a core value in the country's Confucian culture.

Recruiting

There are two groups of employees in Korean firms for which sharply different conditions and rules apply: regular and non-regular employees. For regular employees, a highly formalized recruiting process is applied, whereas non-regular employees are hired on a more casual basis. Accordingly, a relatively high amount of job security is provided to regular employees, whereas non-regular employees are often laid off at the convenience of the company, such as during business downturns.

Regular employees are hired twice a year (in spring and fall) by most companies, and traditionally the recruiting process has been centred on new university graduates. In many large companies, only graduates from prestigious universities used to be hired as core employees, that is, employees with good career opportunities. However, in recent years, a university diploma has in many companies become a requirement in order to be considered as a normal regular employee, or sometimes even as a non-regular employee. The rising expectations of Korean firms regarding the qualifications of job applicants reflect the increasing competitive pressures they are exposed to, but are also a result of an education boom in Korea which shows the strong emphasis on education in the country's society. In recent years, Korea has had the highest proportion of high school graduates, as well as one of the highest of university graduates among the younger population within OECD countries (OECD, 2005).

New employees are hired through an extensive review of application materials and multiple interviews. Moreover, large companies also conduct additional written tests and use assessment centres to screen the actual skills and capabilities of applicants (Chung et al., 1997). Aside from the formal education level and the reputation of the educational institution they graduate from, the applicants' personality and their range of practical skills and foreign language capabilities are also strongly considered in the recruiting process. As an overall tendency, strictly performance oriented criteria, as opposed to personal networks and social ties, have become more and more important in the selection process for Korean companies' new employees.

Training and Skill Formation

There are extensive internal training programmes in Korean firms. Many large firms have set up their own training facilities. Moreover, the companies' internal training programmes are not exclusively targeted at providing basic training for new recruits only, but also organize various skill enhancement programmes for veteran employees. The great emphasis many Korean companies place on training their employees can be seen from the fact that they set aside around 5 per cent of their employees' regular working hours for participation in training programmes (Chen, 2004). As well as skill development, the internal training is also aimed at enhancing the employees' group cohesiveness, *esprit de corps* and emotional attachment to their company. In the same vein, Korean companies use company mottos (*sahoon*) to communicate that they do not just provide a working place for their employees, but also promote broader values such as 'trust', 'credibility', 'excellence' or 'responsibility' (Chung et al., 1997).

Thus, Korean companies not only enhance the professional skills of their employees, but also promote collectivistic values, such as harmony and group cohesiveness. In this context, it is noteworthy, however, that Korean workers' and managers' work values and attitudes are strongly individualistic, though group oriented. Whereas they are used to and willing to work in groups, they are striving for individual achievements, such as receiving positive evaluations, within this group context. In other words, Koreans are group oriented workers, but do not abandon their individual ambitions by becoming group members. In this sense, groups of Koreans can be described as 'salad bowls' in which each member keeps his or her individual profile, as compared with 'melting pot' groups in Japan which absorb each member's aspirations and create a coherent group consciousness (Chang and Chang, 1994). As a consequence, conflicts can quite easily evolve between working group members in Korea, and companies feel a strong necessity to promote common values and group cohesiveness.

Compensation, Promotion and Retirement

Koreans tend to be very diligent and ambitious, and the prospect of promotion can motivate them strongly, as with promotions come recognition, prestige and status gains, which are highly valuable rewards in a Confucian cultural context. However, wage increases and, in particular, job security are also strong motivators (Chen, 2004). To illustrate, as a result of the rising competitive pressures in the business sector which give many employees the feeling that their jobs may not be safe in the long run, recently many highly qualified individuals in Korea have been applying for jobs in the public sector, which provides only moderate career opportunities and salary levels, but high job security.

Compensation and promotion systems traditionally used to be strongly seniority oriented. However, throughout the past few decades, performance orientation has become more highly regarded. Some companies, such as Samsung Electronics, have become famous for strongly linking their managers' compensation to business results in their fields of responsibility (refer to the mini case at the end of this chapter). In general, whereas most Korean companies still retain a certain seniority component in their promotion policies, it appears that performance on the individual and group levels has become the predominant evaluation criterion for workers and managers. This change was further triggered by the impact of the Asian financial crisis, when many Korean firms were forced to lay off large numbers of their employees and had to abandon stable, long-term employment relations (Park and Yu, 2002). At the same time, the loyalty of many employees to their companies is not very high, although some Koreans still spend their whole working life within the same company. Even traditionally, however, loyalties were often felt more strongly on the individual level (particularly with superiors) than on the organizational level, implying that when a senior manager changed his employer, he often brought some of his subordinates to the new company. In recent years, partly as a reaction to the introduction of flexible employment practices by many companies and decreasing job security, many Koreans are open to considering a change of employer when a better position or compensation is offered, and they actively search the external job market if they are dissatisfied with their current work or compensation level.

Companies have specific retirement ages which are commonly between 55 and 60 years of age. However, the retirement age often varies between managerial ranks, with executives and senior managers given the opportunity to stay for longer in their company than lower level managers and workers.

Industrial Relations

One further important aspect of human resource management for Korean firms lies in their relationship with labour unions. During the period of authoritarian government from the 1960s to the 1980s, the labour movement was suppressed and labour unions were severely restricted regarding their permitted range of activities. Only in 1987, was government regulation regarding industrial relations largely removed (Chung et al., 1997). Since then, labour unions have evolved as powerful negotiation partners for companies and have enforced high rates of wage increases, significant reductions of working hours and various other improvements in working conditions. While this development has certainly contributed to an improvement in living standards for many Koreans, it also drove up the labour cost for Korean companies and induced them to move significant parts of their operations to countries with lower wages, particularly China. Furthermore, many firms have increased the proportion of non-regular employees, as their compensation is much lower and they can be laid off more easily. As a result, the share of non-regular employees has increased steeply and now amounts to more than 40 per cent of the total workforce in Korea (OECD, 2007).

Furthermore, many labour unions tend to be hostile with companies and readily call for strikes if their demands are not fulfilled. In many cases, there appears to be a deep-rooted mistrust between the firms' management and labour representatives. These problems are so widespread that industrial relations are often cited as a major hurdle for investment in Korea by representatives of multinational firms. In other words, the development of peaceful and productive relationships with labour unions constitutes an important challenge for many Korean companies.

REFLECTIVE QUESTION

■ Given the Confucian cultural tradition that stresses harmony, why are there so many conflicts between companies and labour unions in Korea?

CORPORATE SOCIAL RESPONSIBILITY AND CORPORATE CITIZENSHIP

During the period of authoritarian rule, the Korean government gave preferential treatment to many firms and business groups in order to enhance the country's economic development, as mentioned before. Part of this implicit contract between government and business was that the *chaebol*, through their rapid growth, provided employment opportunities for many Korean people. In this sense, Korean firms certainly showed a high degree of corporate social responsibility towards the public during that stage of economic development. Since the government retreated from the direct regulation of the business sector, however, firms have increasingly come under criticism for only maximizing their profits and not showing responsibility towards the general public, particularly after the Asian financial crisis which resulted in layoffs on an unprecedented scale. This public reaction shows that in Korea large companies are expected to take some responsibility not only for the benefit of their shareholders and employees, but also for the Korean economy and the country as a whole. Many Koreans have ambiguous feelings about the *chaebol*. On the one hand, people are proud of the large firms and their achievements, as they display the country's economic achievements and success. On the other hand, *chaebol* are accused of selfish and irresponsible behaviour, particularly after corporate scandals which periodically come to the surface.

Many *chaebol* owners have often shown a certain willingness to share their wealth with the Korean public, however. Repeatedly, they have given large donations for the development of educational infrastructure or other activities of high public interest. One particularly spectacular case was the endeavour of Ju-yung Chung, former chairman of the Hyundai group, to set up a tourist resort in North Korea's Kumgangsan region in the early 1990s, a time when there was still almost no communication between the two Koreas at the governmental level (see also the box below, 'Spotlight on CSR'). Arguably, chairman Chung thereby made a major contribution to inter-Korean conciliation. The fact that after many years of operation, Hyundai's tourist business in North Korea still does not appear to be very profitable also suggests that the whole initiative was indeed not primarily profit seeking, but rather intended to contribute to an improvement of the political situation on the Korean peninsula.

Spotlight on CSR: The Hyundai Group

Since the 1970s, the Hyundai group, a family owned *chaebol*, emerged as one of Korea's largest business groups. Its founder and chairman, Ju-yung Chung, later developed political aspirations and made an unsuccessful bid for the country's presidency in 1992. Moreover, he also endeavoured to achieve inter-Korean reconciliation and agreed with the North Korean government to set up a tourist resort in the Kumkangsan region. In 1999, Hyundai Asan was created as a group subsidiary to develop the Kumkangsan business. Hyundai Asan also played a leading role in the development of the Kaesong industrial park, a special economic zone set up in North Korea in 2004. However, Mong-hun Chung, chairman of Hyundai Asan and a son of Ju-yung Chung, committed suicide in August 2003, after being accused of corruption and embezzlement charges related to secret money transfers to North Korea.

In the wake of the Asian financial crisis, Hyundai split into two business groups: the Hyundai Kia Automotive Group, which focuses on the automobile business, and the Hyundai Group, which absorbed most other group companies, including Hyundai Asan. The Hyundai Kia Automotive Group thrived in recent years under the leadership of chairman Mong-koo Chung, another son of Ju-yung Chung. However, the group's chairman was arrested in April 2006 on charges of embezzling US$100 million of company money to a slush fund which was used for paying lobbyists as well as for personal matters. Shortly before his arrest, Chung apologized to the Korean public and pledged to donate KRW1,000 billion (more than US$1 billion) of this personal wealth to society in various ways, such as building cultural facilities.

During the two months until chairman Chung was released from prison, Hyundai Kia's management was largely paralysed because major business decisions could not be made. After a three year prison sentence had initially been given to Chung in February 2007, an appeal court suspended the prison term for five years in September 2007 on the conditions that Chung keeps a clean record during this period and fulfills his earlier promise of donating KRW1,000 billion. The presiding judge declared that the chairman was too important to the Korean economy to go to jail.

Sources: CNN World Business News, February 5, 2007, 3 years to Hyundai chief on fraud; CNN World Business News, September 6, 2007, Hyundai chairman to avoid prison; *Asia Times Online*, August 7, 2003, The sad tale of Hyundai scion's demise; Hyundai Asan homepage http://www.hyundai-asan.com; *The New York Times*, December, 13, 1992, Thousands in Seoul rally for a candidate.

WORKING AND LIVING CONDITIONS IN KOREA

As mentioned earlier in this chapter, the Korean people made an intense national effort in the decades after the Korean War to reconstruct and develop their economy. During this period, annual working hours were among the longest in the world, and economic development was given clear priority over cultural or environmental concerns. As a result, the country has been perceived as subjecting its population to harsh working and living conditions.

The situation has changed considerably since the 1980s, however. Working hours, while still longer than in other OECD countries, have been reduced, and the five-day working week has gradually been introduced since 2004. Moreover, infrastructure related to public transportation, culture and leisure has been rapidly built up, particularly in the metropolitan area around Seoul which accommodates almost half the country's population. Whereas environmental problems remain a concern, energy efficiency has been increased and air pollution has been significantly reduced in recent years, and efforts for a further improvement of the situation are ongoing (OECD, 2007). Taken together, working and living conditions in Korea have been greatly improved throughout the past few decades.

From an international perspective, Korea has also become a much easier place in which to live and work. English is more widely spoken now, particularly by the younger generations of Koreans. The country's well-developed infrastructure combined with its natural beauty makes it a pleasant place in which to live. Koreans also commonly display friendly behaviour towards foreigners, particularly those from Western countries. In fact, surprise about the high level of development and the pleasant overall living environment is a frequent response of foreigners newly arrived in Korea, suggesting that its image in many other countries is outdated. The ratio of foreigners among the total population stood at about 2 per cent in 2007 and is therefore still lower than in many other countries (OECD, 2007), but has been rapidly increasing since the 1990s, reflecting Korea's greater openness to the world.

CROSS-CHAPTER REFLECTIVE QUESTION

- Going back to Chapters 8 (Japan) and 9 (China), how do you compare the Korean *chaebol*, the Japanese *keiretsu* and the Chinese *danwai* or the modern state-owned enterprises?

CHAPTER SUMMARY

- Korea is a geographically small country, but a major economic power. The country emerged within 50 years from extreme poverty to high affluence through an intense collaborative effort by business and government.
- The Korean economy has a large manufacturing sector and is strongly specialized in specific industries, such as automobiles, electronics, microelectronics, telecommunications, steel and shipbuilding. Highly diversified business groups (*chaebol*) play a leading role in it.
- The Korean management style is built on Confucian traditions, but also received Japanese and US influences. It features a strong centralization of power, top-down manage-

ment, authoritarian and paternalistic leadership, long-term oriented, but flexible employment practices and a strong performance orientation.

■ In Korean companies, the owners and CEOs have extremely strong managerial power. Korean firms tend to display entrepreneurial, aggressive strategies which lead them into new business fields and geographical regions.

■ Korean workers and managers are diligent and highly motivated. They work in groups, but their motivation is strongly individualistic. Korean companies select their regular employees carefully, train them extensively and expose them to strong performance pressures.

■ Large firms are being criticized by the Korean public for displaying selfish profit-seeking behaviour, but they occasionally make large donations to society.

KEY CONCEPTS

Economic dynamism: Korea has transformed itself from a low-income developing country to a major economic power in less than 50 years.

Korean business groups (*chaebol*): Large, diversified groups of companies which are tightly controlled by their owners.

Confucianism and hierarchical Korean management: Korean cultural traditions support a paternalistic, top-down management style.

Entrepreneurial business strategies: Korean firms pursue aggressive growth strategies into new product lines and geographic regions.

Korean human resource management: Employees of Korean firms are carefully selected, extensively trained and exposed to strong performance pressure.

REVIEW QUESTIONS

1. What are the specific features of the Korean economy?
2. Why did the Korean economy develop so fast after the 1960s?
3. What are *chaebol*? Why are they important in Korea?
4. What is typical for Korean management? What are the implications of this management style for the competitive strategies of Korean firms?
5. How do Korean companies hire, train and evaluate their workers and managers?

LEARNING ACTIVITIES AND DISCUSSIONS

1. Search the internet for information about the four largest *chaebol* (Samsung, Hyundai-Kia Automotive, LG and SK). Compare their structures with each other and with leading conglomerate firms from Japan.
2. Imagine you are working for a Korean company. Discuss with your classmates how you would be able to deal with the Korean management style, and what would probably be the biggest cultural challenges for you to accommodate in such an environment.

3. Analyse Korea from the viewpoint of a foreign MNE. For which industries and products do you think the country is an attractive location to do international business, and why?
4. Korean management is strongly influenced by Confucian traditions. However, Confucianism has also had a broader regional impact on other East Asian countries, such as China or Japan. What are main differences between Korean, Japanese and Chinese management, and how can these differences be related to different interpretations and traditions of Confucianism in these countries?
5. Korean firms have increasingly globalized their activities in recent years and created many subsidiaries abroad. To what extent can they probably establish Korean-style management in their subsidiaries in North America, Western Europe, Eastern Europe, India and China? What can be expected to be some of the crucial areas where the management of Korean companies' subsidiaries needs to be adjusted to the local environment in these regions and countries?

MINI CASE

SAMSUNG ELECTRONICS

The emergence of a Korean flagship company

Samsung Electronics was founded in 1969 as an affiliate of the Samsung group, one of Korea's leading *chaebol*. Since the 1980s, it emerged as Samsung's leading group company and later as the country's largest industrial enterprise in general.

The company's beginnings were humble, as it was established initially as Samsung-Sanyo Electric, a joint venture with Japan's Sanyo Electric intended to produce household and consumer electronics in Korea based on the Japanese partner's technology. In the 1970s, the company grew rapidly, and it produced relatively simple electronic products, such as TVs, refrigerators and microwave ovens. However, technological independence was gradually achieved during this period.

The next stage of the company's development in the 1980s was signified by a first wave of internationalization. Overseas production and sales affiliates were established in different parts of the world, and a large part of the revenue now came from overseas markets. However, the company's business was still mainly focused on mature, low-tech products.

In 1987, Byung-chul Lee, Samsung's founder and chairman, died and his son, Kun-hee Lee, became the new chairman of the Samsung Group. Later on, in 1998, he also assumed the position of chairman at Samsung Electronics. He led the company into a new direction by allocating more resources to high technology products, particularly semiconductors. This strategy was apparently successful, as Samsung Electronics entered the highly competitive semiconductor industry from a latecomer position, but achieved global leadership in the memory chip market by 1992. It became the world's leading memory chip producer and still retains this position. Its success has been largely attributed to its aggressive investment in R&D and production facilities and its ability to dominate rivals through shorter development and ramp-up cycles, which are crucial in this industry where every few years one generation of products is replaced by a new one. In particular, Samsung's initial success was a result of its counter-cyclical behaviour during the global memory chip market recession of 1990–1, when it aggressively built new capacity at a time when its main rivals cut or delayed their investments.

Whereas Chairman Lee's leadership has definitely played an important role in the company's strategic direction throughout the past 20 years, his approach is clearly different from those of many other *chaebol* owners, as he transferred much of the responsibility for ongoing business decisions to professional managers and focuses himself on the formulation of long-term, overarching strategies. In April 2008, following a corporate scandal, he resigned from the chairman's position.

Since the late 1990s, the following managerial policies have been particularly pursued at Samsung Electronics:

■ *Technological leadership and innovativeness*: The company has continued to invest aggressively in R&D. It is now one of the leading R&D spenders in the world and accounts for more than a quarter of Korea's total business R&D. It has also become a leading global patent producer. Moreover, employees of all ranks are encouraged to develop new ideas and problem-solving approaches.

■ *Efficiency drive through internal competition*: Internal business divisions, while still assisting each other when appropriate, have been encouraged into an intense company internal competition which is also enhanced by compensation of managers based on their relative performance within the company.

■ *Enhanced global marketing and brand management*: Whereas the company's marketing and branding efforts were formerly dispersed throughout the world, strong attention has been given to the creation of a strong, coherent Samsung brand. As a result, the company's brand value is now evaluated as one of the highest among Asian companies.

■ *Further globalization*: Samsung Electronics' global sales, production and R&D networks have been considerably extended and deepened, giving it a strong presence in all parts of the world.

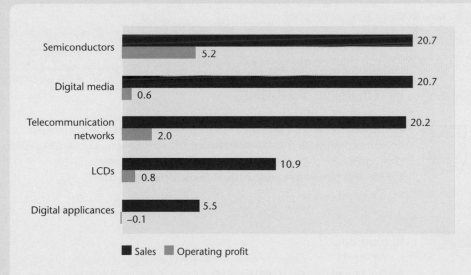

Figure 11.1 Samsung Electronics' sales and operating profits by division (unit: KRW1,000 billion, 2006)

As shown in Figure 11.1, the company has five large business divisions, and as a whole is very profitable. However, the data also hint at some continuing challenges Samsung Electronics is facing. Most of the profits are generated by the semiconductor division which itself relies strongly on the highly profitable memory chip business. A stronger performance from the other divisions would reduce the company's dependency on the earnings of a single division. Moreover, a stronger diversification into logic chips would make the semiconductor division less vulnerable to the business cycles in the field of memory chips.

At a more fundamental level, the company is likely to face two other key challenges. First, how to balance the innovativeness and creativity needed to be a global technology leader with traditional Korean top-down management. Second, how to become a truly global company without giving up accumulated strengths which appear to be strongly embedded in the country's home base.

QUESTIONS

1. Which internal and external factors have helped Samsung Electronics to grow into its current position?
2. In which aspects has the management of Samsung Electronics throughout the past decades been typical for Korean management? In which aspects has it been atypical?
3. Do you think Samsung Electronics has to transform itself fundamentally to remain successful in the future? Why or why not?

Sources: Samsung Electronics, Annual Report 2006; Samsung Electronics homepage http://www.samsung.com; Jang-Sup Shin and Sung-Won Jang: Creating First-Mover Advantages: The Case of Samsung Electronics, SCAPE Working Paper No. 2005/13, Department of Economics, National University of Singapore; H. Cho, H. Chun and S. Lim: *Dijital chungbokcha Samsung Chuncha* [Digital Conquerer Samsung Electronics], Seoul: Maeil Kyungjae Sinmunsa, 2005; Interbrand: Best Global Brands 2006 http://www.interbrand.com/best_brands_2006.asp; *The Times*, April 23, 2008, Samsung chairman Lee Kun Hee resigns after corruption probe.

INTERESTING WEB LINKS

Macro-economic data on Korea: http://ecos.bok.or.kr/EIndex_en.jsp
Korean economic and business statistics: http://www.nso.go.kr/eng2006/
On *chaebol*: http://www.sjsu.edu/faculty/watkins/chaebol.htm
On life and culture in Korea: http://www.lifeinkorea.com/

REFERENCES

Aguilar, F.J. and Cho, D.S. (1985). *Gold Star Co. Ltd.* Case No. 9-385-264. Boston, MA: Harvard Business School.
Asia Times Online, (2003). The sad tale of Hyundai scion's demise, August 7.
Bank of Korea (2007). *Bank of Korea Statistics System.* http://ecos.bok.or.kr/EIndex_en.jsp.

Chang, C.S. and Chang, N.J. (1994). *The Korean Management System: Cultural, Political, Economic Foundations.* Westport, CN: Quorum.

Chang, S.J. (2003). *Financial Crisis and Transformation of Korean Business Groups: The Rise and Fall of Chaebol.* Cambridge: Cambridge University Press.

Chen, M. (2004). *Asian Management Systems: Chinese, Japanese and Korean Styles of Business.* 2nd edn. London: Thomson.

Cho, H., Chun, H. and Lim, S. (2005). *Dijital chungbokcha Samsung Chuncha* [Digital Conquerer Samsung Electronics], Seoul: Maeil Kyungjae Sinmunsa.

Chung, K.H., Lee, H.C. and Jung, K.H. (1997). *Korean Management: Global Strategy and Cultural Transformation.* Berlin: Walter de Gruyter.

CIA (Central Intelligence Agency) (2007). *World Factbook 2007.* https://www.cia.gov/library/publications/the-world-factbook/.

CNN World Business News (2007). 3 years to Hyundai chief on fraud, February 5.

CNN World Business News (2007). Hyundai chairman to avoid prison, September 6.

El Kahal, S. (2001). *Business in Asia Pacific: Text and Cases.* Oxford: Oxford University Press.

Grainger, R. and Ananthram, S. (2007). Managing industrial development through learning, the family and competition in South Korea. In Chatterjee, S.R. and Nankervis, A.R. (eds) *Asian Management in Transition: Emerging Themes.* Basingstoke: Palgrave Macmillan.

Hemmert, M. (2007). The competitive potential of Asian business groups: A comparative analysis of Kigyo Shudan and Chaebol. In Yau, O.H.M. and Chow, R.P.M. (eds) *Harmony Versus Conflict in Asia Business: Managing in a Turbulent Era.* Basingstoke: Palgrave Macmillan.

Hyundai Asan homepage http://www.hyundai-asan.com.

Interbrand: Best Global Brands 2006 http://www.interbrand.com/best_brands_2006.asp.

Kim, H., Hoskisson, R.E., Tihanyi, L. and Hong, J. (2004). The evolution of diversified business groups in emerging markets: The lessons from Chaebols in Korea. *Asia Pacific Journal of Management,* **21**(1/2): 25–48.

Kim, L. (1997). *Imitation to Innovation: The Dynamics of Korea's Technological Learning.* Boston, MA: Harvard Business School Press.

KOSIS (Korean Statistical Information Service) (2007). *Saeobje kijo tongke* [Basic industry statistics], http://www.kosis.kr/.

New York Times (1992). Thousands in Seoul rally for a candidate, December 13.

OECD (Organization for Economic Co-operation and Development) (2005). *OECD Economic Surveys: Korea 2005.* Paris: OECD.

OECD (Organization for Economic Co-operation and Development) (2007). *OECD Economic Surveys: Korea 2007.* Paris: OECD.

Park, W.S. and Yu, G.C. (2002). HRM in Korea: Transformation and new patterns. In Rhee, Z. and Chang, E. (eds) *Korean Business and Management: The Reality and Vision.* Elizabeth, NJ: Hollym.

Samsung Electronics, Annual Report 2006.

Samsung Electronics homepage http://www.samsung.com.

Shin, J.S. and Jang, S.W. Creating First-Mover Advantages: The Case of Samsung Electronics, SCAPE Working Paper No. 2005/13, Department of Economics, National University of Singapore.

The Times, (2008). Samsung chairman Lee Kun Hee resigns after corruption probe, April 23.

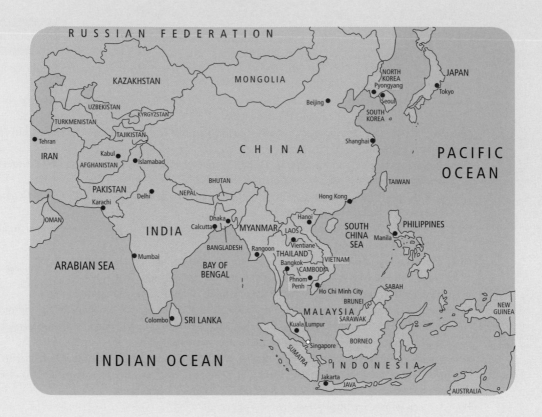

Chapter outline

- An overview of the Singapore economy
- Singapore's development and business system
- Culture and leadership in Singapore
- Human resource management in Singapore
- Singapore and corporate social responsibility
- Living and working in Singapore

Chapter objectives

After reading this chapter, you should be able to:

1. Identify the major reasons for Singapore's dynamic economic development
2. Understand the specific features of Singaporean management and their cultural background
3. Understand the Singaporean approach to managing human resources
4. Understand how Singaporean firms exert social responsibility

Chapter 12

Management in Singapore

Tony Garrett

AN OVERVIEW OF THE SINGAPORE ECONOMY

The Republic of Singapore (subsequently referred to as Singapore) is a small island city state with an area of about 650 km² located at the tip of the Malay Peninsula. Although Singapore is a small country it has become one of the major hubs for the Southeast Asian region. It has a dynamic economy, one of Asia's four Tiger economies, with strong service and manufacturing sectors. It has a well-developed infrastructure, with its port, airport and roads among the best in the world. Singapore's GDP is US\$135 billion with a GDP growth rate of 7.4 per cent. It has one of the region's highest GDP per capita of approximately US\$35,000 (Statistics Singapore, 2008) and US\$48,900 on purchasing power parity adjusted base, placing it near the top of the world. Singapore has been duly described by an HSBC economist as a 'developed country that grows at developing country rates' (*Economist*, 2007a).

Singapore's economy has been strongly reliant on international trade and on the sale of services. Its merchandise trade is three times its GDP. A large volume of re-exports is represented in this figure reinforcing Singapore's role as a trans-shipment hub. Its major industries include petroleum refining, electronics, oil drilling equipment, rubber products, processed food and beverages, ship repair, financial services and pharmaceutical manufacturing. It is, however, moving to reduce its reliance on the manufacturing and exports by developing its services sector, as well as its chemical, petrochemical and biotechnology industries. Although manufacturing still accounts for 25 per cent of GDP, it has found new niches in marine engineering and biomedical firms, with annual growth of 40 per cent, and it dominates the region in private banking (*Economist*, 2007a).

Singapore's small population, 4.5 million, and dependence on external markets and suppliers pushed Singapore towards economic openness, free trade, and free markets. Governmental policies that encourage and foster economic development underpin this and are key factors in Singapore's historically strong economic performance. The Singapore government, a key player in the economic life of Singapore, continues to pursue an outward-looking, export-oriented economic policy that encourages two-way flows of trade and investment. It has introduced policies to enhance Singapore's position as a hub for financial, education and transport services. The 'knowledge economy' has been a key focus of the government's education and training policies for Singaporeans. It is supportive of regional and international multilateral trading initiatives particularly through the World Trade Organization (WTO), the Association of Southeast Asian Nations (ASEAN), the Asia-Pacific Economic Cooperation (APEC), and the Asia-Europe Meeting (ASEM), and bilaterally through free trade agreements (FTAs) with a range of key trading partners.

Singapore positions itself as the region's hub and regional proponent of economic development and reform. Singapore has faced and faces several challenges however. Globalization and the increasing competition from fast-growing lower cost regional producers like China and India, highlight the need for Singapore to move from a labour-intensive manufacturing-based economy to one which is focused on being a value-added services hub. Past challenges, which Singapore has been successful in overcoming, include the 1997 Asian financial crisis, the global economic slowdown in 2001, the growth in regional security concerns, and Severe Acute Respiratory Syndrome (SARS) in 2003. Singapore was faced for the first time with negative growth in 2001 followed by a sluggish economy in 2002 and 2003. The Singapore government has continued to focus on upgrading and restructuring its economy to help it through potential crisis. In 2007, for example, it announced a 2 per cent cut in corporate tax and a provision of partial corporate tax exemption. To further its objective of expanding Singapore's services and biomedical research sectors, the government announced a $500 million supplement to existing funding for R&D in 2007. It also introduced measures to promote the growth of its legal, financial, logistics, maritime and aviation services sectors.

History of Singapore

Singapore's strong tradition in trading and as a shipping hub is historic. Although accounts exist of Singapore from the 3rd century, it is commonly accepted that modern Singapore was founded in 1819, by Thomas Stamford Raffles, of the British East India Company, as a regional base for the British Empire to ward off the power of other colonial powers in the region, particularly the Dutch. Raffles found Singapore to be an ideal location to establish a port, fulfilling basic requirements such as having a deep water harbour, water supplies and timber for the repair of ships. After negotiation with the Sultan of Johor, the nominal leader of the island, a treaty was signed to establish the colony of Singapore.

During its time as a colony of Britain, Singapore developed as a key trading area, built upon the opening market of China and the raw products coming from Malaya. During this time, the colony attracted a number of immigrants with the population in the early 1900s being approximately 62 per cent Chinese, 16 per cent Indian, 13.5 per cent Malay and 8.5 per cent European. Prosperity existed until World War II when the Japanese occupied the colony from 1942 until 1945. The colony took some time to recover to pre-war levels of prosperity after the war, but notably the credibility of the British as its rulers took a blow since they were unable to defend the state from occupation. Subsequently, Singapore was granted self-government from the British in 1959 and after a brief period in the Federation of Malaysia, 1963–1965, it became an independent republic.

Singapore was seen by many to be incapable of surviving as an independent national state, so the national policy initiatives made national survival its core basis for national policy (Koh and Wong, 2005). The following sections examine the role of government and the phases of economic development.

SINGAPORE'S DEVELOPMENT AND BUSINESS SYSTEM

Singapore is a modern society epitomized by a combination of a modern capitalist system and high government intervention. Its business system has stemmed from this unique combination that has assisted its development into one of the leading economies in the region. The principal influences are examined below.

Singapore Government's Role in the Economy

The authoritarian/semi-authoritarian approach by the government to the economy is well noted. Singapore has been ruled by a single political party, People's Action Party (PAP), since independence. The party holds 82 out of the 84 electable seats in parliament, gaining between 60 and 84 per cent of the popular vote. In spite of PAP's power, Singapore is regarded as one of the least corrupt countries in the world, ranking fourth overall, and number one in Asia (Transparency International, 2008). The PAP has been central to the state's political, social and economic development. The ideology of the party was in its early years to ensure that Singapore could survive using a social democrat model. The major ideologies of the PAP subsequently have been pragmatism, meritocracy, multiculturalism and Asian values. Although it has rejected the idea of a Western style of liberal democracy, many of the ideals of Western liberalism do permeate the policies that the government pursues. The philosophy underlying governmental policy has been to 'maximize political cooperation and minimize contention' (Bhasin, 2007).

The Confucian democracy that exists is central to understanding the government's policy. Opposition or disruption to the role of the government is regarded negatively. The view held by the government is that the strong rule is necessary to promote political stability, which in turn leads to rapid economic development.

The government has fostered economic development through the maintenance of peace and harmony among the multi-ethnic population, and by focusing on the needs of the global marketplace (Haley and Low, 1998; Bhasin, 2007). It has done this through careful management of the following core values that have been identified and continually modified for a good society (Haley and Low, 1998; Bhasin, 2007):

1. Community over self
2. Upholding the family as the basic building block of society
3. Resolving major issues though consensus instead of contention
4. Stressing racial and religious tolerance and harmony
5. Honest government
6. Compassion for the less fortunate.

The government maintains that these values are at the centre of the Confucian/Asian approach and should be the guide to structure a society that will serve and be successful in a changing global environment. The tenets of the stated values are for a hierarchical structure and a compliant society, reminiscent of early Chinese society. The community, the centre of collectivism and Confucianism, rather than the individual, is the important element in the overall Singapore environment.

The manifestation of the values is evident in many elements of Singapore society through campaigns by the government to modify social behaviour – no littering, family planning (procreate more), be courteous and so on. Legislation was implemented and strictly enforced, unfortunately labelling the country as a 'fines' country (Bhasin, 2007).

Governmental policy has been instrumental in the development of the skills required for changes in the needs of the economic environment. Initially the focus was on meeting skills shortages for the MNCs which have come to dominate society. Specialization is required at an early age, with a student's educational path being stratified by their ability and aptitude, creating what could be called a hierarchical society.

Nowhere is this more apparent than in those who were selected for government posts. The government was renowned for recruiting the best and brightest, through the education system and scholarships, to get the best people for leadership in politics, the military and business. Government traditionally therefore had a monopoly of the top talent (Haley and Low, 1998; Chew and Chew, 2003; Chew and Sharma, 2005; Bhasin, 2007).

The end result is that the government takes a somewhat technocratic approach to achieve the country's shorter term goals through the channelling of academic talent to meet their own aims. There has been some comment and criticism of this approach indicating that it creates a dearth of talent for entrepreneurial or innovative activity in the business sector (Chew and Chew, 2003).

Singapore Inc.

The Singapore government has been an active participant in Singapore's economy since its independence. The use of the government-linked companies (GLCs) has been the main mechanism for government intervention in the business environment.

These GLCs were established in the 1960s and 1970s to help facilitate the building of infrastructure and to support economic development. Companies were also established in the 1980s and 1990s to further expand the privatization of government departments and statutory boards. There was a clear rationale stated by the government of the time to 'compensate for the lack of private sector funds or expertise' (Ramirez and Tan, 2003). Many of these GLCs have subsequently become monopolies and national icons.

The investment in the GLCs has extended to many key sectors of Singapore's economy such as finance, trading, transportation, shipbuilding and services. Examples of GLCs include companies such as Singapore Airlines, SingTel (Singapore Telecom) and Natsteel, among others. It is estimated that GLCs account for 60 per cent of the domestic economy (Ramirez and Tan, 2003; Bhasin, 2007).

There has been increasing argument as to whether the GLCs can contribute to the country's entrepreneurial environment especially in a time of many changes in the regional business environment (Bhasin, 2007). Their links with government, particularly the ability to access funds, tenders and opportunities, have closed large areas of the economy to the private sector and have stifled the growth of entrepreneurship (Ramirez and Tan, 2003). One paper indicated that the GLCs were rewarded through this special relationship with government by premiums of 20 per cent in financial markets (Ramirez and Tan, 2003). Reports have borne this out. The index of economic freedom states that Singapore receives approximately 22.75 per cent of its total revenues from state-owned enterprises and government ownership of property (Bhasin, 2007).

Temasek Holdings is the commercial mechanism of the Singapore government. Established in 1974, it has a portfolio of some US$100 billion. With involvement in telecommunications and media, financial services, property, transportation and logistics, energy and resources, infrastructure, engineering and technology and pharmaceutical and biosciences, the company regularly announces shareholder returns of 18 per cent annually. It accounts for approximately 30 per cent of the economy.

The role of the government in Temasek Holdings is large. The company is 100 per cent owned by the Singapore Ministry of Finance, with the Chief Executive generally having strong political links. The government also has strong links to the management team of the organization.

The second important investment arm of the Singapore government is the Government Investment Corporation (GIC). This organization invests Singapore's foreign reserves, which are some of the largest in the world, totalling some $US130 billion. The fund managed by GIC is shrouded in secrecy. The government's stated rationale behind this is to ward off speculative hits on the Singapore dollar as foreign reserves are frequently used to stabilize the national currency (Bhasin, 2007).

Due to the dynamic nature of the environment there are increasing calls for the government to decrease its participation in private enterprise together with giving more transparency in its current involvement. These calls have come across the board. The response by government is to defend its involvement, stating that foreign pressures should not be heeded if the Singapore public is happy with it, and that government involvement in fact fosters growth.

Phases of Economic Development

Singapore has undergone three key phases of economic development spanning the period from 1959 (self-government) until the present day (Soon and Tan, 1993; Haley and Low, 1998; Koh and Wong, 2005; Wong et al., 2006). Policies implemented in the first phase were geared towards the provision of jobs for the unemployed while the latter phases emphasize upgrading the economy.

Phase One: Labour Intensive Economy (1960s–1970s)

The key impetus in the first phase of development was focused on industrializing the nation, providing employment and diversifying away from a dependence on *entrepôt* trade. Singapore had a high unemployment rate in the 1960s, which was compounded by the decision of the British government to withdraw its troops from Singapore in 1968. This is known as a factor driven growth strategy (Porter, 1990; Koh and Wong, 2005).

During the period 1966 to 1973 a labour-intensive export-oriented manufacturing strategy was implemented. Attractive incentives that included tax relief, a stable labour situation and availability of skilled workers prompted a surge in investments by foreign multinationals (Soon and Tan, 1993).

By 1973, the level of foreign investments had grown to such a level that a labour surplus situation was replaced by a labour shortage situation. Workers had to be imported from neighbouring countries. This brought about (1973–8) the shifting of the economic strategy from one of attracting labour-intensive industry to one that sought high-technology industries. A portfolio of incentives, covering wage rates, manpower development, tax regimes and ease of entry of qualified foreign professionals succeeded in attracting further investments. By 1979, foreign firms were playing a major role in the economy of Singapore. The slowdown in industrialized economies around this time alerted the government to the need to diversify the economy (Soon and Tan, 1993; Koh and Wong, 2005).

Phase Two: Capital Intensive Economy (1980s–1990s)

During the period 1979–84 an economic restructuring was implemented, whereby both the economic activities and markets were diversified and expanded. Wages were also adjusted upwards to discourage the inflow of labour-intensive and low-technology investments that posed obstacles to upgrading and restructuring. Promotions to attract firms in 11 selected industries with high-technology components were undertaken. These included: automotive components, machine tools and machinery, medical and surgical apparatus and instruments, specialty chemicals and pharmaceuticals, computers, computer peripherals equipment and software development, electronic instrumentation, optical instruments and equipment, advanced electronic components, precision engineering products, and hydraulic and pneumatic control systems. Large inflows of foreign direct investment into the desired industries resulted. MNCs became firmly established as a key element within society.

During this period the country's first severe recession occurred in 1985. Wage rates and other costs of doing business were reduced and the country quickly recovered from the recession the next year. At the same time, the government continued its unrelenting efforts to promote high-value-added technology-based manufacturing industries. Incentives are given to firms to conduct their research and development (R&D) activities in Singapore (Soon and Tan, 1993; Koh and Wong, 2005).

Phase Three: Knowledge Intensive Economy (2000s)

The third economic phase saw the government strongly committed to the development of science and technology. The budget committed was S$2 billion for the 1991–5 period, S$4 billion for the 1996–2000 period, with a further S$7 billion allocated for the period 2001–5 (National Science and Technology Board, 2000a), with increased budget allocations having occurred over the subsequent periods. The public funds earmarked for R&D-related activities are administered by the National Science and Technology Board (NSTB), a statutory body tasked to stimulate R&D and build up capabilities in certain fields of science and technology. The nine technology fields targeted are: information technology; microelectronics; electronic systems; manufacturing technology; materials technology; energy, water, environment and resources; food and agro-technology; biotechnology; and medical sciences. This signalled policymakers' focus on moving from an economy that uses technology to one that creates it.

Public spending in R&D focuses on meeting four main challenges to be overcome in order to spur the undertaking of economically relevant R&D. These challenges are: meeting the demand for manpower; making it advantageous for industry to undertake R&D; strengthening the country's technological capability; and fostering technological innovation and commercialization (National Science and Technology Board, 2000a).

A number of schemes are currently in place to deal with the above challenges. In the area of meeting manpower needs, NSTB offers scholarships for bright undergraduates to pursue postgraduate research study. Furthermore, the government has maintained an 'open door' policy of admitting foreign technical professionals with the relevant expertise to boost the manpower base (National Science and Technology Board, 2000a).

A series of support activities and incentives are in place to create a conducive environment for industry to undertake R&D. Financial support, in the form of grants, is available for co-funding R&D activities. Physical infrastructure includes the development of a technology corridor – a 15 kilometre region containing a synergistic mix of higher education establishments, research institutes and private sector laboratories. The proximity of these institutions, especially the Science Park, provides a vibrant environment for researchers who can interact on a frequent basis.

The task of strengthening the technological capability of the country falls on the research institutes and universities. Research institutes are set up to develop generic technologies for strategic industry clusters. These institutes collaborate with industry partners to develop pre-competitive technologies. In the process, manpower training and technology transfer are affected. The universities are not only expected to fulfil their role in training researchers but are also expected to provide leadership in research on areas of strategic importance.

Mechanisms to help foster technological innovation and commercialization are manifold. Information on technologies is made available through the National Technology Databank and National Patent Information Centre. Innovators wishing to protect their invention can apply for financial assistance through the Patent Application Fund. Financial assistance for technical entrepreneurs is available in the form of the Technology Development Fund, which helps a start-up through its initial years when it is difficult to secure funding from the traditional sources. Finally, incubators help ease small companies into their new business.

There is subsequently no lack of funding or initiatives on the part of the government to upgrade the technical skills and competencies of the country. The bulk of the proposed budget is allocated to manpower training and development. This is identified as one factor that attracts foreign multinationals to base part of their research operations in Singapore. These foreign multinationals play an important role in the economy and are expected to be the primary drivers of R&D activities in Singapore.

Despite the major impetus and large funding given to R&D by the government, private sector spending in R&D outstrips government spending. The private sector accounted for 62 per cent of the country's gross expenditure on R&D (GERD) during 2000. The manufacturing sector and the service sector account for 99.7 per cent of private sector spending on R&D. Foreign MNCs account for 71 per cent and 81 per cent of the R&D spending in the manufacturing and services sector respectively. The electronics industry is the most important industry within the manufacturing sector, accounting for 53 per cent of private sector investments in R&D. Out of this amount, foreign MNCs accounted for 77 per cent of the commitments in the electronics industry (National Science and Technology Board, 2000b).

The private sector funds most of its R&D activities internally. Only 2.3 per cent of the funds used come from the government. This figure is consistent with the government policy of allocating their R&D budget to ensuring the availability of trained manpower that the private sector, and especially foreign multinationals, require for their R&D activities. Thus, the government may perceive its role as that of providing the environment and opportunity for R&D rather than that of funding the incremental costs of specific R&D activities. This strategy seems to be working when evaluated in light of the commitments and R&D activities taking place in the private sector.

It is noted that a substantial amount of R&D work is carried out in a cross-cultural setting where the innovating firms are non-Singaporean (and even non-Asian) while the researchers are predominantly Asian. This sets up a situation where an understanding of the values and culture of the local staff becomes essential for a firm to maximize the research productivity of such workers.

The second core factor in driving a knowledge-based economy is the development of the local entrepreneur. As noted earlier, elements of Singapore society may in fact hinder entrepreneurial behaviour. The Global Entrepreneurship Monitor (GEM) 2006 rated the total entrepreneurial activity in Singapore at 4.9 per cent – a ranking of 16 among the 22 OECD nations that were surveyed (GEM, 2006). A number of agencies have been set up in Singapore to assist in the development of entrepreneurial activity including: Singapore Productive Innovation and Growth (SPRING); Enterprise One Singapore; International Enterprise Singapore and so on (Bhasin, 2007). Incentives for entrepreneurial activity were also given, such as tax exemptions for start-ups, tax incentives, government financing, matching funds from the Economic Development Board Startup Enterprise Scheme and so on. Many of these are initiatives that have only occurred in the last phase of economic development, and the jury is still out to see if they are successful. The GEM survey would suggest, however, that entrepreneurial intensity has slipped between the 2001 and 2006 reports (National Science and Technology Board, 2000b ; Bhasin, 2007).

Commentators have remarked on the lack of entrepreneurial activity concluding that 'although Singapore displays many of the characteristics typical of a knowledge-based economy, Singapore's new economy seemingly lacks a stimulating climate conducive to imagination, innovation and adventure that will attract globally mobile talent' (Tan, 2003 in Wong et al., 2006).

SUMMARY POINTS

- The Singapore economy has developed since self-rule through a clear and focused economic policy.

- MNCs, through the government opening up the economy and GLCs play important roles within the economy.

- Confucian principles underlie government policy within the country.

- Since the economic downturn and SARS in the 2000s, the government is moving to create a knowledge-based society in which technology is not just used but created.

REFLECTIVE QUESTION

- In your opinion, will the reliance on the government detract from the development of entrepreneurial behaviour among its citizens?

CULTURE AND LEADERSHIP IN SINGAPORE

Singapore has been grouped with other Confucian Asian economies – China, South Korea, Hong Kong and Taiwan – in terms of its national cultural tendencies. These nations share similar attributes when rated on a number of dimensions that have been used to measure cultural values and beliefs, for example the Global Leadership and Organizational Behavior Effectiveness (GLOBE) programme's dimensions, and Hofstede's cultural dimensions. The GLOBE dimensions are used to discuss the culture of the nation (Hofstede, 1984; House et al., 2004):

Assertiveness: Singapore society tends to operate at two levels. Society as a whole is encouraged to be modest and tender with one another, however, on the other level there is assertiveness in the business environment. Leaders in Singapore are expected therefore to be caring to the group, but very goal orientated.

Future orientation: Singapore is highly future orientated. The Singapore government is an exemplar of this through implementing policy initiatives, which at inception were difficult but in the longer term have led to economic success for the country. Organizational leaders and other members of society are also expected to share similar values. Students, for example, will work hard and diligently from an early age for a secure future.

Gender differentiation: Singapore has traditionally been male dominant. This is changing, however, with women now making it to the top echelons of society and the business world. Although representation in government, similar to many other countries, is low, women are now making large inroads into business and other areas of society.

Uncertainty avoidance: Singapore has been found to be very concerned about avoiding uncertainty. Singaporeans wish to avoid uncertainty generally. Singapore personnel for example would prefer to work for larger organizations, rather than risk 'face' and finances on starting their own (Low, 2006a). High levels of codified procedures are found in Singapore organizations and upper management is expected to take responsibility for the workgroup (Garrett et al., 2006).

This dimension shares elements with the Hofstede dimension of uncertainty avoidance from his famous study conducted in the early 1970s (Hofstede, 1984). In this study Singapore was rated as one of the least uncertainty avoidance countries in the world. The reversal in the interim time period has been hotly debated. In one study looking at the lack of entrepreneurial activity in Singapore, the following conclusions were made (Low, 2006a; Bhasin, 2007):

- Young people are cautious due to society under the PAP being very compliant and lacking in diversity of ideas.
- The education system has a strong focus on learning facts and figures rather than being creative.
- Singaporeans in modern society are somewhat more pampered and less street-smart, relying on textbooks and being left-brain (logically) orientated.
- There is a strong reliance on government to do things for them.
- Failure is an embarrassment.

Power distance: Singapore has a high level of power distance. Although not necessarily born into a class-based society this is evolving as individuals see the way to break through this by education. Leadership tends to be autocratic and seniority-based. Performance, however is now becoming an important criteria to succeed (Chia et al., 2007).

Institutional emphasis on collectivism versus individualism: The values of Singaporean society lead to an institutional emphasis on collectivism, the basis of Confucian values as advocated by the government. The overall community therefore is important. This value is not shared, however, by some employees, so the workplace leaders and managers are therefore needed to maintain in-group cohesion within the workplace, rather than relying on the individual themselves. This is in keeping with the notion of the paternal state (Low, 2006b).

In-group collectivism: The family is one of the basic units in Singapore society. Although the Singapore family is getting smaller, the family and family occasions are very important. Seniority plays an important role within the family, and traditionally in the workplace.

Performance orientation: Singapore is very oriented towards performance at all levels of society. In the work environment Singapore workers have been found to be very oriented to individual success and career advancement (Garrett et al., 2006). This seems at odds with the Confucian principles of the society, however Singapore society has been geared towards economic and social success through its economic development. Performance has also been a key element in appraisal systems within organizations, with the National Wage Council (NWC) urging that pay scales should not be based on seniority alone, but rather on competitive forces and performance (Leggett, 2007). Singaporeans will work diligently and hard at all levels to achieve their personal ultimate aims, along with those of the organization and the country. Although Singapore belongs to the same group as other Confucian Asian economies, its leadership style differs significantly from the others. Employees in Singapore prefer their leaders to be charismatic and value-based which includes being visionary, having high integrity, being inspirational and having strong performance orientation (Li et al., 2002). They do not like their leaders to be non-participative, autocratic or concerned about saving their own face. These values correspond strongly with the national cultural tendency of the country. Singapore's government is a good example of the leadership qualities that Singaporeans look for. It is perceived within Singapore as having a high charisma and good values – a high future orientation.

SUMMARY POINTS

- Singapore is a Confucian oriented society sharing many cultural values with other Asian countries.

- Singapore has higher levels of power distance, uncertainty avoidance and performance orientation than other Confucian countries.

REFLECTIVE QUESTION

- What elements of a Confucian oriented society will be ideal for the modern business world? How do these elements differ from those in the West? If you could blend the two cultures together, what elements would you take from each?

HUMAN RESOURCE MANAGEMENT IN SINGAPORE

Human resource management (HRM) has always been important within the Singapore context. As a country of limited natural resources, human capital has been a key cornerstone of Singapore's development both at the governmental and organizational levels, although HRM is set to become even more important with the emphasis on a knowledge-based economy. This major strategic focus necessitates the recruitment, motivation and retention of highly skilled human capital. This refocus has large ramifications for local businesses in Singapore, which although having benefitted from the government efforts to provide a well-educated workforce have traditionally focused on technical and capital resources at the expense of their human capital (Horwitz et al., 2006; Low, 2006a). This is changing, with indicators showing that companies are becoming much better at retaining their workforce. For example in 2004, recruitment and resignation rates had shifted from 6.9 per cent in 2000 to 4.4 per cent (Horwitz et al., 2006; Ministry of Manpower, 2008). Singapore, however, does not produce enough knowledge workers for its economy and is therefore heavily reliant on imported and often expatriate skills (Ministry of Manpower, 2008).

The dual nature of the Singapore economy has traditionally meant differing HRM practices between Singapore owned and operated businesses and MNCs. MNCs have frequently been benchmarked by Singapore companies to understand what the best practice is to implement for competiveness and, in the case of larger local companies, to move them to becoming Asian MNCs themselves (Huang et al., 2002). Singapore companies are therefore in a state of transition.

The differences between Singapore companies and MNCs have been found in many guises (Huang et al. 2002):

- First the orientation of the businesses towards their employees has been different. MNCs have traditionally viewed their human capital as being somewhat more crucial to their strategic performance than their local counterparts (Huang et al., 2002; Chew and Horwitz, 2004). In addition, Singapore companies have previously valued their employees on a historical cost or expenditure basis rather than on a human capital asset basis. However the movement to a knowledge-based economy is changing this view among enterprises (Huang et al., 2002).
- Job recruitment approaches are similar in both contexts. The use of online adverts, general advertising and headhunters are very common approaches beyond graduate recruitment for knowledge-based staff (Horwitz et al., 2006). Technical, industry, job knowledge and work experience have traditionally been the main criteria for the selection of employees within the Singapore enterprise. Singapore's educational focus has for a long time been on quality, particularly in engineering and science-based technical skills. Singapore emphasizes quality education in all disciplines as it works towards its objective of becoming an educational hub for the region. Good qualifications are therefore seen as being important recruitment criteria. Although qualifications are important for MNCs, additional criteria include teamwork, honesty, creativity, intelligence and leadership (Horwitz et al., 2006). There have been many studies that suggest that working for the government, GLCs or MNCs is highly attractive for Singaporean graduates (Haley and Low, 1998; Chew and Chew, 2003; Chew and Sharma, 2005; Bhasin, 2007).
- There tend to be extensive training programmes in larger firms operating in Singapore with high expectations on the part of their employees that training is avail-

able (Taormina, 1998). MNCs and Singapore-based companies, however, differ on the training and development focus. In line with the recruitment procedure for their employees, technical and IT skills are emphasized. MNCs will additionally focus on social-cultural training. In both cases training may lead to additional rewards from the company in terms of salary increments.

■ In a time of staff shortages, it is not surprising that career management has become a vital issue. Singapore companies, due to their performance orientation discussed earlier, have a strong tendency to use work performance, employee behaviour and achievements to appraise their employees, reflecting a results or bottom line oriented approach. Although these elements have been found to be important in MNCs, other measures such as employee abilities and training needs are also included, which have been argued to foster more staff loyalty (Horwitz et al., 2006).

Singapore knowledge-based employees tend to be somewhat individualistic in orientation. Key human resource (HR) strategies to motivate employees, for example, include having the freedom to plan and work independently, having challenging projects to work on, having access to leading-edge technology and products, good top management support and fulfilling work (Horwitz et al., 2006). They are less motivated by HR practices such as flexible work practices, working with a large group of knowledge workers, generous funding for conferences or studies, cash rewards for innovations and seeking recruits who fit the culture. Preferred retention strategies are similar. There is a high level of motivation for challenging work, financial rewards such as competitive pay packets, performance incentives and bonuses, along with management support and opportunities to develop in a specialized field and gain access to leading edge technologies and products (Horwitz et al., 2006). Less effective retention strategies are having flexible work practices, critical mass of knowledge workers, transparent pay and benefit decisions, and a fun and informal workplace. These motivations appear to be at odds with the Confucian culture of the Singapore society, although not at odds with the Singaporean desire to succeed. Although Singapore, at the level of the government, is a collective society, individualism is evident in the workplace (Horwitz et al., 2006).

Singapore has had a stable record in industrial relations. As with other elements of the economy, the government, through the PAP, has played a key role in all elements of collective bargaining and dispute settlement. To encourage the industrialization of Singapore and the end of colonialism, the PAP enacted the Industrial Relations Ordinance in 1960, with the purpose of regulating collective bargaining and dispute settlement. Unionists were brought together under the National Trades Union Congress (NTUC) that effectively saw the end of politicized labour and a decline in disruptive labour disputes in the period 1960–1967. During the 1970s the government enacted a number of laws which highly regulated industrial relations within Singapore. The government wanted to work with the NTUC in a collective role to assist in the economic development, although by being a partner with government the NTUC had to restrain its union activities. The end result is that industrial relations have become highly regulated with large government involvement.

One further advisory body, a tripartite forum with representatives from employees, trade unions and government, which has a strong influence on industrial relations, is the National Wage Council (NWC). Set up in 1972 this body recommends annual wage increases for the entire economy; ensures that wage recommendations promote social and economic development; and assists in incentive schemes to help national productivity. Its guidelines are not mandatory, although they are followed by the large public sector and have a strong influence and are widely followed in the private sector. At times of national crisis therefore, such as the Asian Financial Crisis, its recommendations to cut labour costs, which were largely implemented, assisted Singapore in getting through successfully. Similarly, in the development of the knowledge-based society, the NWC is influential in recommending a competitive base wage system which urges a move away from seniority-based wages with a 70 per cent basic wage, a 20 per cent annual variable component, and a 10 per cent monthly variable component for task employees, and 40 per cent and 50 per cent variable components for middle and top managements respectively (Leggett, 2007). The aim is to make the compensation system more flexible in times of dynamic business environments.

SUMMARY POINTS

- Human capital is very important for Singapore as a country with limited natural resources and an emphasis on developing a knowledge-based society.

- Singapore seeks to implement best practice HRM policies including through benchmarking with MNCs.

- Singapore has a stable industrial relations record.

REFLECTIVE QUESTIONS

- What are your key motivations to work diligently?

- What do you expect from your manager?

SINGAPORE AND CORPORATE SOCIAL RESPONSIBILITY

Social responsibility has been a key element underpinning the development of Singaporean society, although it is only recently that increasing attention has been paid to corporate social responsibility (CSR) (Tan, 2008). In 2005, a comparative study indicated that Singapore had one of the lowest levels of CSR penetration compared to seven other (poorer) Asian countries (Chapple and Moon, 2005). This was a paradox which was not lost on the government agenda. In 2004, a tripartite approach involving government, private sector and labour movement was set up to drive CSR. This culminated in the formation of the Singapore Compact for Corporate Social Responsibility in 2005. This body's stated objectives are (Compact Singapore, 2008):

- To broaden the base for dialogue and collaboration between policymakers, businesses, trade unions, the government, social partners, civil society, academics and other stakeholders on CSR.
- To create awareness among the stakeholders of the value and importance of social responsibility in helping the socially disadvantaged.
- To develop effective strategies and approaches to promote CSR in Singapore.
- To conduct research and surveys and highlight best practices and successful examples on CSR.
- To establish a CSR training unit and offer learning, benchmarking, and capacity building opportunities on CSR.
- To facilitate the implementation and follow-up of CSR through sectoral networks or other appropriate groupings.

There is no current legislative framework on CSR in Singapore; rather the government has been reliant on persuading organizations to work in accordance with Singapore's political and cultural values (Tan, 2008). This is in line with the fundamental socially responsible nature of these values. Although Compact Singapore's agenda has predominately been oriented towards organizations within the domestic environment, the rise of the Singaporean MNC and GLCs' regional and international investments means that increasingly CSR and the Singaporean values that the organizations are being persuaded to use to apply outside the confines of Singapore. This is particularly apparent with some of the recent backlashes against Singapore in the region (*The Economist*, 2007b).

Ethical business considerations are therefore becoming more and more important in Singapore. Consumer watchdog groups, such as the Consumer Association of Singapore (CASE), along with government are increasingly making businesses accountable for the actions that they take. Given the government's agenda and overall the public's desire to make Singapore a hub for good business practice, the importance of CSR and business ethics will only be more heavily promoted.

LIVING AND WORKING IN SINGAPORE

Singapore has built its country upon the hard work and diligence of its citizens and the foreigners bought in to help. It has maintained its political and economic stability and is considered a safe country in which to live. The results of its economic success are evident. The streets are among the cleanest in the world and it has a cosmopolitan lifestyle. The society is a blend of many cultures with the population being made up of approximately 70 per cent Chinese, 15 per cent Malay and 7 per cent Indian, together with many other significant ethnic groups. With skilled human capital being in short supply, Singapore organizations will continually seek skilled workers from outside their borders.

Singapore is an easy place to live and provides a high standard of living. It is ranked as the 9th most expensive place in Asia (ECA International, 2007) so can be a relatively inexpensive city for expatriates to live. With education as one key of its success, it has a well-developed education infrastructure with numerous international schools. It also has one of the best quality healthcare systems in the region. Purchasing a vehicle is expensive as the government controls the number of vehicles on the road through a vehicle quota system and issuing a Certificate of Entitlement, the price of which is managed through an open bidding system. The public transport infrastructure is, however, well developed, doing away with the need for a car. With English being the official language of the city and a large expatriate population, assimilation is relatively easy. The laws of Singapore are fairly authoritarian and are strictly enforced and people are quite compliant to them. The laws are however very transparent.

Although it is regarded as a city state, Singapore is not overly developed. With some 58 surrounding islands and the city covering one-third of the main island, there has been an attempt to create open leisure spaces for the population. Although clean, on occasions it can encounter air pollution problems often generated by the clearing of land from neighbouring Indonesia.

Singapore has continually been ranked as one of the world's freest economies (*The Economist*, 2008). To set up and undertake business is very simple, with low corporate tax rates, a well-educated skill base, well-developed infrastructure and English being the business language. As the other economies in the region continue to develop and become competitive, Singapore is seeking ways in which to make the country even more competitive and maintain or increase its success. Business policies therefore will be continually reviewed, with businesses which find themselves to be less competitive exiting, to be replaced by new and even more exciting ones.

CROSS-CHAPTER REFLECTIVE QUESTION

- In this chapter we have read that the most salient feature of the Singapore economy is probably the government's intervention through GLCs. How do you compare these GLCs with China's state-owned enterprises (Chapter 9)?

CHAPTER SUMMARY

- Singapore has emerged as a major economic hub in Southeast Asia. It has moved from a manufacturing-based economy to a knowledge-based economy in which it creates its own technology. Governmental policies have encouraged foreign direct investment and supported GLCs to develop key infrastructure.
- Singapore's economy has grown through R&D, with a focus on information technology, microelectronics, electronic systems, manufacturing technology, materials technology, energy, water, environment and resources, food and agro-technology, biotechnology and medical sciences.
- Singapore is a Confucian-based culture. Similar to other Confucian cultures it does have high power distance, uncertainty avoidance and performance orientation. Confucian principles also underlie government orientation for the society.
- Human resources (HR) are key to the knowledge-based society. There is a strong focus on identifying best practice to make the knowledge-based economy a success.
- A principle underlying Singapore society is social responsibility, although corporations have only more recently recognized this.

KEY CONCEPTS

Value-added services hub: Singapore is set to become a central player within the region to provide added value for services, whether these be education or R&D activities.

Knowledge-based economy: Movement away from a reliance on manufacturing technologies brought into the country, towards the development of unique technologies which will give the country a distinct competitive advantage.

Singapore Inc. and GLCs: Singapore Inc. is the colloquial name given to state intervention in the economy through the use of government-linked companies (GLCs). These are large companies which often have a monopolistic position within the market or have become national icons.

Factor driven growth strategy: A strategy followed by the Singapore government in the 1960s and 1970s which focused on building-up the economic fundamentals that allowed future growth. These included the policies that allowed foreign direct investment that built upon the manufacturing and skill base for the economy.

Confucian approach: This is a cultural approach of government that reflects the view of the national culture. The government has formulated the nation in line with these Confucian values.

REVIEW QUESTIONS

1. How has the Singapore economy transformed and grown so fast since the 1960s?
2. How has the Singapore government been instrumental in the success of Singapore?
3. What are GLCs? Why are they important in Singapore?
4. What are the distinguishing features of Singaporean society? What are the implications for the management and leadership of Singaporean firms?
5. What are the key fundamentals of Confucian culture that should make the implementation of CSR easier?

LEARNING ACTIVITIES AND DISCUSSIONS

1. Search the internet for information on two GLCs: Singapore Airlines and SingTel. Compare their structure and management with other large multinational companies. Think about whether, and how, these GLCs can be related to the peculiarities of the Singapore environment. Do they differ from other MNCs in the world?
2. Think about working in Singapore for a Singapore-based firm. Would you be able to work with the management style and what would you consider the biggest cultural challenges that you would have to accommodate to in such an environment?
3. Singapore is a base for many multinational companies in the region. What cultural elements do you think are important for a MNC to consider when doing business there? Do you think that Singaporean companies could learn from the MNC?

MINI CASE

SINGAPORE AIRLINES
A world-leading operator

'The Best Way to Fly', Singapore Airlines' (SIA) positioning statement is certainly one that this Singapore company has lived up to. Singapore's national carrier has a long list of awards to back its claim, among them being Asia's leading airline. It is one of the world's most admired companies, ranked 17th by *Fortune* magazine. It has a strong brand name, excellence in spotting and initiating trends, innovation, profitability and service. An airline company that leads the way in the very competitive airline market is a credit to the vision and management style of the company. SIA is an example of the successful GLCs who are significant players in the Singapore economy.

Singapore Airlines was born in 1947, when Malayan Airlines scheduled three services a week from Singapore's Kallang Airport to Kuala Lumpur, Ipoh and Penang. It became Singapore Airlines in 1972 with Malaysian Air Systems upon the split of Malaysia-Singapore Airlines. The ubiquitous 'Singapore Girl' with her distinctive 'kebaya' uniform appeared in 1968, and has been central to the image and branding of the airline. Since its incorporation, SIA has been very successful in managing its rapid growth. It has consistently been first in the market with new innovative offerings, culminating in 2007, with the world's first delivery and flight of the Airbus A380 on the 'Kangaroo Route' between Australia and Europe. There is a management commitment to leading the airline industry through quality service innovation.

As a GLC with a 54 per cent ownership by Temasek Holdings, the Singapore government investment and holding company, SIA and the Singapore government have made it clear that there is a separation between government and management. Independent audits and research have verified that it gets no government funding, subsidies or any other form of preferential treatment. In spite of this, the Minister Mentor, Lee Kuan Yew has made public his advice on how the company should go forward and has on occasions intervened in industrial disputes. A point he has also made is that SIA stands alone, with no preferential treatment from Singapore's Changi Airport which aims to become an international air hub. It is held up, however, as a flagship of the corporate excellence that is expected and has prevailed in Singapore.

Singapore Airlines has no intention of letting itself become uncompetitive. It has a strong commitment to training its staff, with one of the most competitive and rigorous training regimes. Singapore Airlines is also a significant investor in other airlines with significant stakes in Virgin Atlantic Airways, Tiger Airways and China Eastern Airlines. It has a wholly owned subsidiary, SilkAir, along with 24 other subsidiary companies, 32 associated companies and two joint venture operations. It is more than an airline company now, although some suggest that it should be more focused on its core business. Singapore Airlines, however, has demonstrated that it will be a major force in the aviation industry in the years ahead.

QUESTIONS

1. What do you think of SIA as a company?
2. What do you think makes SIA competitive in an era of low-cost airlines?
3. Why do you think it is important to prove that there is not a strong link between the government and SIA's management? Would such a link impede SIA's intentions in its globalizing business?
4. What do you believe SIA's intention is in investing in other airline companies? How will this make it grow?

Sources: SIA homepage http://www.singaporeair.com; 'Lee Kuan Yew: Government cannot let pilots have their way', *The Straits Times*, 3 December, 2003; money.cnn.com/magazines/fortune/globalmostadmired/2007/top50/index.html; 'Minister says Singapore Airlines should sell off two subsidiaries', *Airline Industry Information*, 30 December 2005; 'Changi Airport prepares for battle', *The Straits Times*, 8 April 2004.

INTERESTING WEB LINKS

Information on Singapore generally: www.sg/
Official Singapore tourism site: www.visitsingapore.com
Gateway to Singapore Government: www.ecitizen.gov.sg
Singapore business and statistics: www.singstat.gov.sg

REFERENCES

Airline Industry Information (2005). 'Minister says Singapore Airlines should sell off two subsidiaries' 30 December.

Bhasin, B.B. (2007). Fostering entrepreneurship: Developing a risk-taking culture in Singapore. *New England Journal of Entrepreneurship*, **10**(2): 39–50.

Chapple, W. and Moon, J. (2005). Corporate social responsibility (CSR) in Asia: A seven country study of CSR web site reporting. *Business and Society*, **44**(4): 415–41.

Chew, I.K.H. and Horwitz, F.M. (2004). Human resource management strategies in practice: Case-study findings in multinational firms. *Asia Pacific Journal of Human Resources*, **42**(1): 32–56.

Chew, I.K.H. and Sharma, B. (2005). The effects of culture and HRM practices on firm performance: Empirical evidence from Singapore. *International Journal of Manpower*, **26**(6): 560–81.

Chew, S.B. and Chew, R. (2003). Promoting innovation in Singapore: Changing the mindset. *International Journal of Entrepreneurship and Innovation Management*, **3**(3): 249–66.

Chia, H.B., Egri, C.P., Ralston, D.A., Fu, P.P., Kuo, M.C., Lee, C.H., Li, Y. and Moon, Y.L. (2007). Four tigers and the dragon: Values differences, similarities, and consensus. *Asia Pacific Journal of Management*, **24**: 305–20.

Compact Singapore (2008). Available at: www.csrsingapore.org.

ECA International (2007). Worldwide cost of living ranking 2007. Available at: www.eca-international.com.

Economist, The (2007a). Country briefings: Singapore. Available at: www.economist.com/countries/singapore.

Economist, The (2007b). Let's all bash Singapore. *The Economist*, 8 February.

Economist, The (2008). Economic freedom. *The Economist*, 24 January.

Garrett, T.C., Buisson, D.H. and Yap, C.M. (2006). National culture and new product development integration mechanisms: A cross-cultural study between New Zealand and Singapore. *Industrial Marketing Management*, **35**(3): 293–307.

GEM (Global Entrepreneurship Monitor) (2006). *Singapore Report 2005*. Singapore: National University of Singapore Entrepreneurship Center.

Haley, U. and Low, L. (1998). Crafted-culture: Governmental sculpting of modern Singapore and effects on business environments. *Journal of Organizational Change*, **11**(6): 530–53.

Hofstede, G. (1984). *Culture's Consequences*. Newbury Park, CA: Sage.

Horwitz, F.M., Heng, C.T., Quazi, H.A., Nonkwelo, C., Roditi, D. and Eck, P.V. (2006). Human resource strategies for managing knowledge workers: An Afro-Asian comparative analysis. *International Journal of Human Resource Management*, **17**(5): 775–811.

House, R.J., Hanges, P.J., Javidan, M., Dorfman, P.W. and Gupta, V. (2004). *Culture, Leadership, and Organizations*. Thousand Oaks, CA: Sage Publications.

Huang, G.Z.D., Roy, M.H., Ahmed, Z.U., Heng, J.S.T. and Lim, J.H.M. (2002). Benchmarking the human capital strategies of MNCs in Singapore. *Benchmarking*, **9**(4): 357–73.

Koh, T.H. and Wong, P.K. (2005). Competing at the frontier: The changing role of technology policy in Singapore's economic strategy. *Technological Forecasting and Social Change*, **72**: 255–85.

Leggett, C. (2007). From industrial relations to manpower planning: The transformations of Singapore's industrial relations. *International Journal of Human Resource Management*, **18**(4): 642–64.

Li, J., Fu, P.P., Chow, I., and Peng, T.K. (2002). Societal development and change of leadership style in oriental Chinese societies. *Journal of Developing Societies*, **18**(1): 46–63.

Low, C.P.K. (2006a). Cultural obstacles in growing entrepreneurship: A study in Singapore. *Journal of Management Development*, **25**(2): 169–82.

Low, C.P.K. (2006b). Father leadership: The Singapore case study. *Management Decision*, **44**(1): 89–104.

Ministry of Manpower (2008). Employment situation in fourth quarter 2007. Available at: www.mom.gov.sg.

money.cnn.com/magazines/fortune/globalmostadmired/2007/top50/index.html.

National Science and Technology Board (2000a). *National Science and Technology Plan 2005*. Singapore.

National Science and Technology Board (2000b). *Year 2000 National Survey of R&D in Singapore*. Singapore.

Porter, M. (1990). *The Competitive Advantage of Nations*. Basingstoke: Palgrave – now Palgrave Macmillan.

Ramirez, C. and Tan, H.L. (2003). Singapore Inc. vs. the private sector: Are Government-Linked Companies different? *IMF Staff Paper*, **51**(3): 510–28.

SIA homepage http://www.singaporeair.com.

Soon, T. and Tan, C.S. (1993). *The Lessons from East Asia: Singapore – Public Policy and Economic Development*. Washington, DC: The World Bank.

Statistics Singapore (2008). Per capita GDP at current market prices. Available at http://www.singstat.gov.sg/stats/themes/economy/hist/gdp.html.

Tan, E. (2008). Molding the corporate social responsibility agenda in Singapore. Available at: http://knowledge.smu.edu.sg/index.cfm?fa=viewfeature&id=1119.

Taormina, R.J. (1998). Employee attitudes toward organizational socialization in the People's Republic of China, Hong Kong and Singapore. *Journal of Applied Behavioral Science*, **34**(4): 468–85.

The Straits Times (2003). 'Lee Kuan Yew: Government cannot let pilots have their way', 3 December.

The Straits Times (2004). 'Changi Airport prepares for battle', 8 April.

Transparency International (2008). Corruption Perceptions Index. Available at: www.transparency.org.

Wong, C., Millar, C.C.M. and Choi, C.J. (2006). Singapore in transition: From technology to culture hub. *Journal of Knowledge Management*, **10**(5): 79–91.

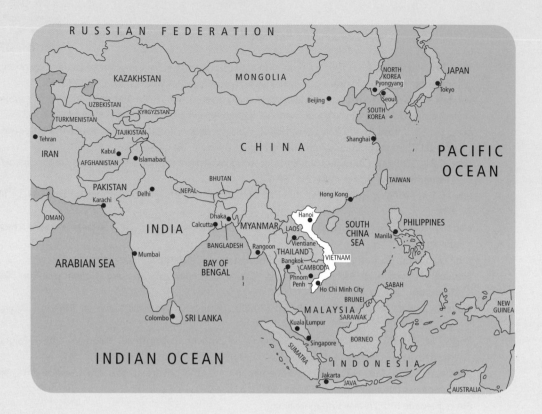

Chapter outline

- The 1986 reform policy and the new perspective of economic development
- Trends in reforms and impact of international integration
- Ownership and governance of the large state and foreign enterprises
- Vietnamese consumers: Changes in consumer values and behaviours
- Culture, ethics and CSR in Vietnam, a transitional economy
- Employment and HRM for sustainable development
- Work and living conditions in Vietnam

Chapter objectives

After reading this chapter, you should be able to understand:

1. How the government designed and implemented the integration of two different economic principles

2. The opportunities and challenges presented by international integration (ASEAN, APEC and WTO) and the need to compromise with domestic sustainable development

3. The ways in which large state-owned and private foreign enterprises are organized and controlled

4. The current issues of labour markets and the characteristics of the employment system

5. Changes in consumer values and behaviours in a transitional economy

6. Perspectives of ethics and CSR in business and society

Chapter 13

Management in Vietnam

Nguyen Thi Tuyet Mai and Mai The Cuong

THE 1986 REFORM POLICY AND THE NEW PERSPECTIVE OF ECONOMIC DEVELOPMENT

Located in Southeast Asia, Vietnam is a developing country bordered by China in the north, and Laos and Cambodia in the west. It has more than 3,200 km of coast, of which part is along the Pacific Ocean.[1] It has been considered the gateway to the ASEAN and South China for centuries.

Vietnam is one of the world's most dynamic economies today. A report by PriceWaterhouseCoopers (2007) showed that Vietnam ranked number one among 20 emerging countries in terms of attractiveness for manufacturing investment. The Asia Business Council's survey released in 2007 showed that, looking ahead, Vietnam was the third most attractive location, after China and India, for future investment in the eyes of Asian corporations for the period 2007 to 2009. Vietnam also ranked number six in the world after China, India, the US, Russia and Brazil for foreign direct investment (FDI) (UNCTAD, 2007).

Vietnamese history has been characterized by struggles against foreign aggression. After Vietnam was reunited in 1975, the centrally planned economy associated with the socialist North was extended throughout the country; however, the economic system did not perform well. In the 1980s, Vietnam experienced severe shortages of basic consumer goods, high inflation, a high budget deficit and poor living standards. Therefore, in 1986 the Vietnamese government decided to launch *doi moi* policy (that is, economic renovation), shifting the economy from a command economy to a market-oriented economy. This reform has involved state decentralization, reorganization of collective agriculture into household holdings, more autonomy for state-owned enterprises (SOEs) and more development of a private sector. Economic liberalization could be seen in many aspects of the economy, including reduction and/or elimination of both tariff and non-tariff barriers to trade, reform of the banking system with the formation of a commercial bank system, the establishment of a stock market in late 2000, and reform of the tax system.

As a result of *doi moi*, Vietnam has obtained significant achievements in economic development. The country has enjoyed impressive GDP growth rates of around 7 to 8 per cent since 1991, which is second only to China's. Inflation was controlled, reducing from triple digits in the late 1980s to single digits in the 1990s. Inflationary levels have remained low. Vietnam has been successful in poverty reduction and significant improvement of living standards for all groups of Vietnamese people.

There have been positive changes in economic structure as well. From 1990 to 2003, the proportion of agriculture, forestry and aquaculture production in the GDP reduced from 38.7 per cent to nearly 22 per cent while the contribution of industrial and construction production increased from 22.6 per cent to 39 per cent and that of services from 35.7 per cent to 39 per cent (Statistics Publishing House, 2004).

With regard to ownership, as a result of *doi moi,* non-state enterprises account for a large proportion of total enterprises in Vietnam while SOEs have been declining due to restructuring and equitizing, as illustrated in Figure 13.1. In terms of contribution to the GDP, although the contribution of SOEs remained fairly stable, non-state and foreign-owned businesses rapidly increased their contribution to the GDP of Vietnam.

Since applying *doi moi* policy, Vietnam has been very successful in attracting FDI. During the period 1989 to 2006, FDI commitment to Vietnam was US$78.3 billion with 47.6 per cent implemented. In 2006, it attracted more than US$12 billion, the largest amount ever (GSO, 2007). In terms of registered capital, the 10 biggest investors by nationality to Vietnam are Singapore, Taiwan, Republic of Korea, Japan, Hong Kong, British Virgin Islands, the US, France, Malaysia and the Netherlands (GSO, 2007).

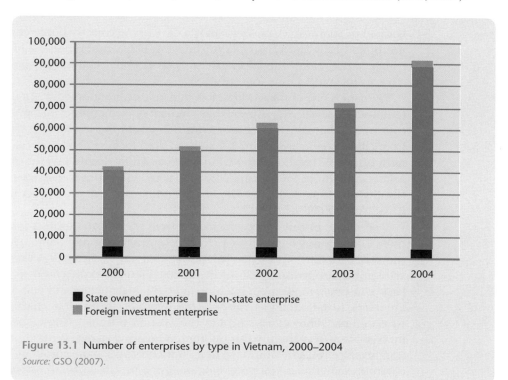

Figure 13.1 Number of enterprises by type in Vietnam, 2000–2004
Source: GSO (2007).

In recent years, Vietnam has experienced a deficit in its trade balance (see Table 13.1). Manufactured imports account for 72 per cent of total imports, largely in machinery and transport equipment, and processed materials. Its primary imports are mainly mineral fuels, lubricants and related materials.

After the adoption of the 'open door' policy, exports expanded significantly with very high growth rates in some years. Vietnam exports a variety of products from shrimp, coffee and tea to shoes and ships. Although agriculture is primarily based on small family farms, with agricultural modernization Vietnam has become the world's largest exporter of pepper and the second largest rice exporter. Manufactured exports increased from 33 per cent of total exports in 1995 to 50 per cent of total exports in 2005.

Table 13.1 Exports and imports of goods by standard international trade classification (SITC)

	Million USD				
	1995	2000	2003	2004	2005
TOTAL EXPORTS	**5,449.0**	**14,482.7**	**20,149.3**	**26,485.0**	**32,447.1**
Primary products	3,664.1	8,078.8	9,397.2	12,554.1	16,100.8
Manufactured products	1,784.8	6,397.5	10,747.8	13,927.6	16,341.0
Commodities not classified elsewhere in SITC	0.0	6.4	4.3	3.3	5.4
TOTAL IMPORTS	**8,155.4**	**15,636.5**	**25,255.8**	**31,968.8**	**36,761.1**
Primary products	1,914.5	3,527.6	5,282.7	7,317.5	9,308.2
Manufactured products	6,240.9	12,101.2	19,791.9	24,084.3	26,633.1
Commodities not classified elsewhere in SITC	0.0	7.7	181.2	567.0	819.8

Source: GSO (2007).

TRENDS IN REFORMS AND IMPACT OF INTERNATIONAL INTEGRATION

Vietnam aspires to be a primarily industrialized country by 2020, which is a popular goal in the country. By 2010, GDP will at least have doubled that of 2000.[2] In order to achieve this goal the Vietnamese government has shown commitment to continuing the reform. It is an important factor contributing to Vietnam's strong economic performance over the past years.

A key element in the economic reform is the reduction of state intervention in business. The government has been trying to reduce its direct role in supervising the economy and is providing support to the private sector to support its crucial role in the economy. Laws are going to have an increasingly important role in regulating businesses and, in fact, Vietnam has already promulgated a number of laws, including the Enterprise Law, the Labor Code and laws to protect intellectual property. After joining the WTO in early 2007, Vietnam began working on improving its legal framework to bring it into closer alignment with international standards.

The reform of the state sector has been continuing in the direction of cutting most subsidies and other privileges while giving greater autonomy to individual firms. SOEs have been restructured and the number of SOEs has been decreasing. The privatization process is the official policy of the government. Recently, thousands of SOEs have been scheduled for equitization, including those in electricity, post and telecommunications, banking and insurance sectors. Many policies have been introduced to enhance transparency and financial accountability, and to ensure effective corporate governance. Equitization of SOEs may also create opportunities for private and foreign investors to participate in this process (Meyer et al., 2006).

With regard to the implementation of regional and international integration, Vietnam has realized the consistent policy of multilateralization and diversification of its external economic relations. Since the 1990s, Vietnam has normalized relations with the US, joined ASEAN in 1995 and realized its commitments within AFTA (ASEAN Free Trade Area). This membership permits the free flow of goods within the economic area without substantial tariffs. Therefore, products manufactured in Vietnam will be able to reach a larger market.

Vietnam became a member of APEC in 1998. The Vietnam–US Bilateral Trade Agreement was signed in 2000, and since January 2007 Vietnam has been a member of the WTO. This creates many opportunities as well as challenges for Vietnam (Nguyen, 2007).

Key Opportunities

■ The greatest benefit of joining the WTO may be that Vietnam will be able to gain increased access to the global market to support its economic growth and expand export turnover.

■ As a member of the WTO, Vietnam must develop its legal framework to international standards and follow all the required management rules of the WTO. This helps improve the business environment in Vietnam, and thus contributes to greater FDI attraction and promoting all domestic economic sectors' potential for development.

■ As a member of the WTO, Vietnam holds a position equal to other members. This enhances Vietnam's ability to protect the interests of Vietnamese businesses and the country as a whole in the international market.

■ Vietnam's international integration through joining the WTO facilitates the reform process in the country in more comprehensive and effective ways.

■ By joining the WTO, Vietnam's position and image in the world can be enhanced in a way that facilitates the implementation of external affairs policies for peace and the development of the country.

Key Challenges

■ With Vietnam as a member of the WTO, Vietnamese businesses may have to cope with fierce competition in both domestic and international markets. Therefore, in order to be able to take advantage of the opportunities of WTO membership, Vietnamese businesses need to revise their business strategies and develop their competitive edge. They need to produce high-value-added products to gain more profit in the long run. This is a big challenge for Vietnamese businesses because more than 90 per cent of them are small and medium enterprises.

■ Vietnam's international integration creates challenges in dealing with many social and economic issues such as inequality in income distribution, unemployment, enterprise bankruptcies and environment protection.

■ As a part of the world economy, the Vietnamese economy may be strongly influenced by fluctuation in the international market. This challenges Vietnam in managing the economy given the incomplete legal framework and lack of experience in managing in a market-oriented economy.

SUMMARY POINTS

■ The Vietnamese government has shown commitment to continue economic reform, in which a key element refers to the reduction of state intervention in business.

■ Vietnam is working to improve its legal framework to bring it into closer alignment with international standards.

■ SOEs have been restructured, and equitization of SOEs has been gradually implemented.

■ Vietnam has been actively pursuing international integration, including joining the WTO in early 2007.

OWNERSHIP AND GOVERNANCE OF THE LARGE STATE AND FOREIGN ENTERPRISES

Vietnam is a socialist country.[3] The political system[4] in Vietnam stresses the primacy of collective goals (collectivism) in which society's goals are more important than individuals' goals. Globalization brings several types of production to Vietnam, such as Japanese integral production with *monozukuri* spirit and American/Chinese modular production as well as changes in consumer styles.[5]

Before 1986, Vietnam had a command economy in which the state owned all businesses and allocated resources to SOEs. After the collapse of the Soviet Union in 1991, Vietnam began to rigorously transform its economy into a market-oriented one with features of both a state-directed economy and a mixed economy. Privatization, which is often referred to as equitization in Vietnam, has been speeding up since 2006 under a government led by Prime Minister Nguyen Tan Dung. His industrial policy aims to make Vietnam basically an industrialized economy by 2020. While pursuing this goal, Vietnam faces policy challenges because it must follow its commitments in international and regional organizations like the WTO, APEC, and ASEAN, which do not encourage common measures to promote domestic industries. Ohno (2006) suggested that Vietnam's industrial policy in the 21st century must be different from that of other countries. Vietnam must quickly become open and a meaningful part of East Asian and global business.

Before 1986, Vietnam restricted the development of private enterprises. After *doi moi*, the private sector developed at a fast pace. Total investment increased by 20 per cent annually, of which non-state enterprises contributed the most. State investment still accounts for a large proportion of total investment (see Figure 13.2) even though the number of non-state enterprises has increased substantially.

In January 2007 Vietnam became the 150th member of the WTO and as a result laws were modified to meet international standards. Nowadays, the legal system in Vietnam has rules and laws on enterprises, property rights, anti-corruption and contracts. Contract law is regulated in the Civil Code as in other countries that apply civil law.[6]

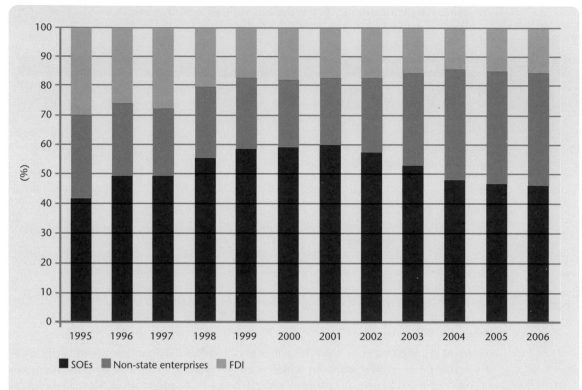

Figure 13.2 Investment by ownership in Vietnam, 1996–2006
Source: GSO (2007).

Before 2005, different laws governed the operation of different types of enterprises, which were categorized into SOEs, FDIs and non-state enterprises. The unified enterprise law, or the Law on Enterprises, came into effect on 1 July 2006 and ensures that all enterprises in Vietnam are governed under the same regulations. Under this law, SOEs must be transformed into limited liability companies or shareholding companies within four years of this law coming into effect.[7] FDIs may choose to change their legal status but this is not compulsory.

The Common Investment Law in Vietnam also came into effect on 1 July 2006 and legislates that all investors, regardless of nationality, are promoted in the same manner. There is no separation of Law on Promotion of Foreign Investment and Law on Promotion of Domestic Investment. Under the Investment Law, the Vietnamese government commits to open its market, eliminate trade-related investment measures (TRIMs) and protect the rights of investors, including exemption from nationalization.

REFLECTIVE QUESTION

■ A common debate in Vietnam is about the role of economic sectors in the economy. Imagine you are about to present your view to the cabinet. What do you go for: SOEs, FDI or non-state enterprises? Why?

The above characteristics have been reflected in the management practices in Vietnam. FDI companies, such as those from Japan, Korea and the US bring their own management styles and show strong commitment to manage existing businesses in this style. They have clear business and management processes and policies on quality, cost, delivery and environment (QCDME). Vietnamese companies, especially private ones, are learning by doing and observing. Some Vietnamese managers who work closely with foreign firms understand and exercise international standards in running their businesses. Others are struggling with learning QCDME. Nevertheless, although SOEs are being restructured, some older managers still consider their jobs to be temporary or a place to relax before they retire.

SUMMARY POINTS

- Vietnam is a socialist country where collective goals are stressed.

- Foreign and private investments are increasing but state investment still accounts for a large proportion. SOEs restructuring is a priority of the Vietnamese government.

- Since 1 July 2006 all enterprises in Vietnam have been working under the same treatment/environment, together with efforts to enhance the Vietnamese legal framework.

- Management practices are moving towards international standards of quality, cost, delivery and environment.

VIETNAMESE CONSUMERS: CHANGES IN CONSUMER VALUES AND BEHAVIOURS

Vietnam, with a population of more than 85 million, is considered a very promising market for both local and foreign investors. *Doi moi* has created a large and growing urban population with an increasing standard of living. Particularly important are the burgeoning middle-class consumers, accounting for a significant proportion of the population in major cities. They have high disposable income and consumption and entertainment habits that lead them to spend more money and time on shopping.

With regard to marketing channels, traditional Vietnamese 'wet markets' are being supplanted by modern distribution channels, including supermarkets and shopping centres such as Big C and the German Metro. Franchising contracts have also become popular for foreign consumer products and fast food such as Swatch and KFC, and for local operators such as Trung Nguyen coffee shops and Pho 24.

A variety of products and services is now available with a wide range of quality, designs and prices. Vietnamese consumers, especially those in the new middle class, who have relatively higher incomes, now enjoy the sudden increase in the availability of consumer goods like 'a drought meeting a rain storm' (Beresford and Dang, 2000).

In addition to the enhanced product availability in the market, there are various sources of information introducing new products, fashions and modern lifestyles. These sources of information include the mass media, advertising and promotion events provided primarily by foreign companies and joint ventures operating in Vietnam, and this has had a great impact on consumers' lifestyles and changes in consumer values.

Consumer Values

Doi moi in Vietnam has changed the traditional value systems that were premised on a centrally planned and subsidized economy. The modern influences brought about by *doi moi* tend to coexist with many of the values, attitudes and behaviours that are associated with the traditional Vietnamese culture (Shultz et al., 1994). Nguyen (1994: 97) noted that 'today, Vietnam is witnessing a great synthesis and integration of the various cultures present in Vietnamese society: tradition with modernity, Oriental values with Western values, preservation of national culture with international integration'. In addition, among the groups of consumers in the society, the young emerging consumers in Vietnam, similar to those in other transitional economies such as China, are often considered to be much more influenced by modernity and Western values.

Along with economic renovation, Vietnamese consumers, especially younger people seem to demonstrate increasing levels of materialism and individualism. In the past, people could have a happy life without placing importance on material values. Nowadays, however, material objects have become very important to many people. It appears that an increasing number of Vietnamese use material symbolism to signal their success and achievements which reflect their own competencies. This can help them display prestige and gain 'trust' from business partners, which is especially important for first impressions. Also, more consumers are now concerned about their own lives, hobbies and levels of satisfaction. Many young consumers, especially, are becoming more independent and competitive in their lifestyle, and these characteristics extend to their consumption behaviours.

The preference for foreign products and brands has also been noticeable among many Vietnamese consumers. Specifically, imported products (from developed countries such as Japan and the US) were generally ranked as the most preferred products. There are no obvious signs of hostility among many Vietnamese consumers for these foreign goods. For instance, many Vietnamese consumers appreciate the quality and performance of American products, and are willing to buy and consume them while overlooking the past war between the two countries.

While demonstrating a strong preference towards foreign products, a number of Vietnamese consumers believe that in the future, the attitude towards local products will change as quality improves, and more Vietnamese people will show stronger support for local products. However, in general, many Vietnamese consumers seem to demonstrate a relatively low level of consumer ethnocentrism, especially among middle-class consumers (Nguyen and Takahashi, 2007).

Consumer Buying Behaviours

The striking changes in the marketing environment in Vietnam, including the retail settings and consumer values, have contributed to the development of an environment tolerant of consumer behaviours that were not socially acceptable in the past (for example conspicuous consumption) and did not have favourable conditions to occur (for example impulse buying). Nowadays, the incidence of rampant spending on luxury products and status symbols is found in many transitional economies, including Vietnam. This conspicuous consumption may result from the sudden availability of luxury goods in these economies and the pent-up desires of consumers after years of deprivation (Belk, 1999).

SUMMARY POINTS

■ At present, traditional values seem to coexist with modern ones. Vietnamese consumers, especially younger people tend to demonstrate increasing levels of materialism and individualism, while holding relatively low levels of consumer ethnocentrism.

■ There have been changes in consumer behaviours. For example conspicuous consumption was not socially accepted in the past, but is common today.

CULTURE, ETHICS AND CSR IN VIETNAM, A TRANSITIONAL ECONOMY

Vietnamese Culture and Management Practices

Previous studies have suggested the importance of culture to management practices (for example Ralston et al., 1999; Dao and Sørensen, 2007). Traditional Vietnamese culture was deeply influenced by Confucianism, which emphasizes filial piety and obligation, altruism and the belief that man creates his own destiny. Respect for authority and social rites are very important. Influenced by Confucianism, the organizational structure of many Vietnamese companies, especially SOEs, tends to be multi-layered. Management style is more authoritative than participative.

Similar to those in many other Asian countries, Vietnamese people stress the importance of relationships and the group. It may be different from Western culture; Vietnamese business relationships often become social relationships after a while. Developing good personal relationships with local business partners is often seen as a recipe for success. In Vietnamese enterprises, especially in SOEs, policies and procedures tend to be more 'high-context'. Organizational processes rely more on social relationships rather than written descriptions. Informal networking and relationships are, on the one hand, creating favourable conditions and on the other, creating unpleasant obstacles to business and management, such as difficulties in overcoming the bureaucratic administration system or in accessing reliable information.

In Vietnamese SOEs, the collective approach is more often taken in decision making. In local small and medium-sized family businesses, the practices are different, with the organization usually being highly centralized in terms of power, and decisions are often mostly made centrally.

Vietnamese culture often avoids personal conflict. Harmony is preserved and keeping face is desirable. Support, trust and respect are important factors in relationship building between partners. The Vietnamese like to be respected and this is manifested in daily decision making and communication. Expatriate managers, working in a joint venture with local partners, who fail to adapt to this culture often have difficulty in dealing with local managers and employees.

Westerners may see the humility and modesty of the Vietnamese people as indirect and deceitful, while the Vietnamese may see the individual assertiveness of Westerners as arrogant and tactless (Ashwill, 2007). Therefore, working and getting along well with business partners is often a challenge for both sides.

The impact of Vietnamese culture on management practices is manifested differently in different types of businesses. A recent study concerning interactions between expatriates and local Vietnamese managers of MNCs in Vietnam (Dao and Sørensen, 2007) suggests that local managers in MNC subsidiaries learn more from their expatriate colleagues about management style compared with those in joint ventures (JVs). Some key elements of this management style refer to flexibility, systematic thinking, going straight to the point, taking responsibility, keeping promises and being punctual.

The development of the internet, as well as the popularity of American and Korean movies, are bringing new styles of living to the Vietnamese youth, while the development of trade and investment bring different styles of management. Vietnamese managers are generally eager to gain management skills and knowledge. The learning process, however, may not be the same for different groups of local managers. MNCs tend to look for young Vietnamese executives who have experienced international standards rather than those with experience in the former central planning system.

Ethics and Corporate Social Responsibility

Corporate Social Responsibility (CSR) is well regulated in the Labor Code of Vietnam (for labour related issues), the Law on Environmental Protection, the Anti-Corruption Law and the Intellectual Property Law. The concepts and issues of child labour, forced labour, gender inequality, social insurance, environmental protection, intellectual property, bribery and corruption are not new to the Vietnamese society. In practice, however, there exist many related concerns among consumers, such as fake products, low product quality and safety, and environmental pollution caused by the many businesses. Although child labor may still be a controversial subject, several recent studies have suggested a dramatic decline in child labour in Vietnam (see for example Edmonds and Pavcnik, 2002).

In Vietnam, numerous natural disasters such as storms and floods occur yearly. In addition, post-war consequences are still evident in many Vietnamese families. The Vietnamese Fatherland Front is an organization known as a pioneer and leader in motivating society's resources to help overcome the consequences of natural disasters as well as supporting the poor and handicapped in the country. An increasing number of companies in Vietnam actively participate in the programmes initiated by this organization. In this way companies demonstrate their social responsibility while at the same time enhancing their public image.

REFLECTIVE QUESTIONS

- Different companies use different ways to demonstrate their social responsibility. What are they?

- Imagine you are managing a company in Vietnam. The local authority asks your company to contribute to a local fund. At the same time, you receive many requests from other similar funds. What would you do?

The development of the Vietnamese stock market has also impacted the CSR issue. Since 2006, more and more companies have been listed in the Hanoi and Ho Chi Minh (HCM) city's securities trading centres. Initial Public Offerings (IPOs) not only attract investments but also promote CSR practices since public companies must be transparent in finance, operation and decision-making processes. However, to really practise CSR in management is still an issue. The following is an example from the motorcycle industry in Vietnam. To complicate matters, Vietnamese enterprises are inexperienced at keeping records of CSR management and practice (MOLISA, 2004).

Spotlight on CSR: Intellectual Property Rights in the Motorcycle Industry of Vietnam

At the end of 2005, Vietnam had 16.09 million registered motorcycles and 0.89 million registered automobiles in use. Compared with the year 1990, this is an increase of 5.8 times for motorcycles and 3.6 times for automobiles. In 2005, motorcycles served 62.7 per cent (Hanoi) and 77.9 per cent (HCM city) of travel needs, while the shares of passenger cars and taxis were only 3.5 per cent (Hanoi) and 5.9 per cent (HCM city), and the shares of buses were 8.4 per cent (Hanoi) and 5.9 per cent (HCM city).

Intellectual Property Right (IPR) infringements in motorcycles are rampant in Vietnam. It occurs in the manufacture of parts, assembly, transporting and sales. Honda and Yamaha motorcycles are the most popular targets of fakers and counterfeiters. According to official data, there were about 300 infringement cases related to motorcycles in Vietnam in the first six months of 2006. According to another source, it is estimated that about 560,000 fake Honda motorcycles were sold in the first 10 months of 2006 but only 5,986 were seized by the authorities.

The most common infringements in Vietnam's motorcycle industry are in industrial design, especially regarding external plastic covers, on which manufacturers or traders of low quality motorcycles use fake decor similar to the original. It is very difficult for law enforcement authorities to find production lines of fake products since manufacturers and traders usually assemble copies secretly instead of in registered factories. Only unfinished motorcycles, without exterior plastic covers, are in their factories to avoid prosecution. Another common way of violating companies is to produce visibly different models from the ones they register. Illegal copies can be sold with impunity since photo verification is not required at the point of sale. In addition, dishonest producers even blame enforcement authorities and complain to the public that their arrest was unlawful and caused by inconsistent policies among the authorities concerned.

Patent infringements in Vietnam mainly occur in the unauthorized use of clutch release mechanisms and frame structures. Trademark infringements are common in sales rather than in manufacturing. Violating shops display signs or logos indicating that they are authorized dealers of Honda, for example, when they are not.

The law and decrees stipulating IPR related issues in Vietnam are the Law on Intellectual Property dated 29 November 2005; Decree No. 105/2006/NĐ CP on State Management of Intellectual Property; and Decree No. 103/2006/NĐ-CP on Industrial Design. The new law on intellectual property came into effect on 1 July 2006, partly to address the problems under the old law and partly to fulfil requirements of WTO accession.

Source: MOI (2007). 'Intellectual Property Rights' Chapter 8 in *The Master Plan for the Development of the Motorcycle Industry in Vietnam,* Final draft, May, pp. 81–90.

REFLECTIVE QUESTION

■ It is said that generally Vietnamese managers are eager to gain management skills and knowledge. Why do MNCs tend mainly to look for young Vietnamese executives who have worked for MNCs and have international experience?

EMPLOYMENT AND HRM FOR SUSTAINABLE DEVELOPMENT

The most recent survey on population and family planning in 2005 showed that life expectancy had increased since 1989 resulting in an increased percentage of people over 65 years old. With 83.12 million people in 2005, giving a population rank of 13th in the world, as well as a high percentage of people in the age group 15–65, Vietnam sees around 1.5 million people joining the workforce annually.

Table 13.2 Vietnam's population structure

	1989	1999	2005
Under 15	39%	33%	27%
Over 65	5%	5.8%	6.7%
From 15 to 65	56%	61.2%	82.19%

Source: Authors' calculation based on GSO (2005), *Key Findings from 2005, April's Survey on Population and Family planning.*

The Labor Code of Vietnam governs labour related issues such as labour relations and management of labour. It was first introduced in 1994 and amended in 2002, 2006, and 2007. Vietnam also has a Law on Gender Equality, which came into effect on 1 July 2007. These two laws provide a sound framework for the management of labour in Vietnam, and help move the population towards a more civilized society as well as towards sustainable development.

Officially recognized by the constitution and laws of Vietnam, the Vietnamese General Confederation of Labor (VGCL) represents the working class in Vietnam. It was founded in 1929. This national trade union leads all trade unions in Vietnam, or in other words, all trade unions are dependent on VGCL. It has offices in all 64 provinces in Vietnam. As of 30 June 2005, Vietnam had 7,828,201 members in its 76,678 trade unions of which 62,135 were in the state sector and 14,543 in the non-state sector (VietnamNet, 2006). With such figures the power of trade unions would appear to be great; however, at industry and company levels trade unions are not eager to bargain for rewards and wages for their members. They have little control over recruitment and selection of employees, or over employee development. Collective bargaining relates more to support from management in cultural, sporting and holiday activities for employees. There are few demonstrations by workers in Vietnam, although some have occurred in FDI enterprises where official trade unions are not set up or promoted.

Vietnamese labourers are known to be hard working, talented and keen to learn. Vietnam ranked 105th out of 177 in terms of the Human Development Index (HDI) according to UNDP's 2007–2008 report. The HDI of Vietnam has increased for the past 10 years, and reflects factors such as increased life expectancy, real income and, especially, the educational attainment of the Vietnamese.

The salary of Vietnamese workers is less than those in neighbouring countries such as Thailand, Malaysia, Indonesia or the Philippines. Managers working in Vietnam must be aware of the job-hopping issue. Theoretically, in rapidly growing economies like China and Vietnam, not only managers, but also engineers and workers have opportunities to move to other companies with higher compensation. However, this is not always the case since there are other factors involved in retaining employees.

Vietnam is facing a shortage of skilled labourers, while there is an abundance of unskilled labourers. There is only 20 per cent of trained labour in the total labour force of Vietnam. In addition, work discipline is a weakness of Vietnamese workers (MOLISA, 2004). At the same time, highly skilled Vietnamese labourers are concentrated in Hanoi and HCM city. These two cities are the drivers for the economic development of Vietnam in the North and South.

Spotlight on HRM: Job-Hopping as an Impediment to Skill Development

An important issue related to human resource development is job-hopping. This prevents an accumulation of highly specific skills and reduces incentives for companies to train their workers. This phenomenon is not unique to Vietnam, with many developing countries reporting high job turnover.

In Vietnam, several Japanese moulding companies aim to establish an integrated manufacturing system within a factory from design to marketing. They train their workers to become fully fledged engineers who know how to make moulds from A to Z. However, their plans are often frustrated by middle-class engineers quitting without mastering high-level techniques. One Japanese expert criticized this trend because workers were losing the opportunity to become excellent engineers in favour of short-term gains.

In Vietnam at present, there seem to be two macro reasons for increased job-hopping. First, an increased inflow of FDI is creating labour shortages, especially in localities where FDI is concentrated. An automobile parts supplier in the North said that, as the industrial zone in which the company was located was becoming fully occupied, rising labour demand began to cause high job turnover and wage increases. The second reason is a shift in economic structure. In and around HCM city, service industries are expanding rapidly and absorbing a large amount of the workforce. An electronic parts maker in HCM city said that the average turnover of first-year employees had increased dramatically in recent years, from less than 1 per cent to 40–50 per cent at present.

However, not all firms report high job-hopping. Some said they had kept their workers successfully with very low turnovers, even less than 1 per cent per year. One reason seems to be location. An automobile parts supplier in the suburbs of Hanoi explained that it was located in an area where labour demand had not risen very much and where most of the workers were local, not migrant, with no intention of moving far. Another reason seems to be company policy towards employees. A plastic parts supplier described its worker incentive programmes, such as generous benefits, transportation allowance and delicious lunches. Workers tend to be loyal to companies which treat them well. The salary level is often not the decisive factor.

Source: VDF (2006). Supporting industries in Vietnam from the perspective of Japanese manufacturing firms. *Policy Note*, 2, (E), 13–14.

SUMMARY POINTS

- Vietnam has 1.5 million people joining the labour force each year. The Vietnamese labour force is cheaper than those of neighbouring countries. Vietnamese workers are hard-working, talented and eager to learn.

- Issues relating to the labour force include job-hopping and shortage of skilled labour.

REFLECTIVE QUESTIONS

■ Some people say Vietnamese labour and Japanese labour have many similarities. What are they?

■ Is job-hopping an exception in Vietnam?

WORK AND LIVING CONDITIONS IN VIETNAM

Vietnam has received more than 3 million foreign visitors annually since 2005. Five main reasons for attracting foreigners to Vietnam are:

■ low prices of goods and services
■ natural beauty
■ Vietnamese culture
■ adventure tourism
■ friendly people (Visa and PATA, 2007).

There were 6,761 FDI projects operating in Vietnam as of 31 October 2006 (MPI, 2007) and the number of foreigners working in Vietnam is increasing.

The cost of doing business in Vietnam is lower than that of other countries in the region. Table 13.3 provides cost comparisons in four selected Asian cities. Vietnam is improving its infrastructure system to facilitate businesses, including the renovation of roads, railways, seaports, airport networks and enhancement of the IT platform. Broadband internet is available in Vietnam with more than 17 millions users as of September 2007 (VNNIC, 2007).

The construction business is booming as Vietnam achieves its economic growth. It is easy for foreigners to rent an apartment or house in Vietnam. However, foreigners are not allowed to buy a house. Monthly rent is not high even though Vietnam is facing a land price bubble.

Table 13.3 Cost comparison in selected Asian cities

	Unit: US$			
	Hanoi	Bangkok	Shanghai	Kuala Lumpur
Worker's monthly wages (general industry)	79–119	184	109–218	202
Mid-level engineer's monthly salary	171–353	327	269–601	684
Mid-level manager's salary (section chief or department chief)	504–580	790	567–1,574	1,892
Office rent (per square meter/month)	24	11.03	37.50	9.92–17.68
Broadband internet (monthly basic charge)	76.89	82.75	73.7	162.63
Electricity tariff for business (per kwh)	0.05–0.07	0.04	0.03–0.10	0.05
Container transport (40-foot container, from nearest port to Yokohama)	1,300	1,200	700	575
Passenger car purchase price (1,500cc sedan)	26,500	12,563	10,849–13,991	13,965

Source: Mai (2005) compiled from JETRO (2004).

Traffic congestion is a big issue in Hanoi and HCM city. People face difficulties commuting to and from work and the local authorities concentrate a lot of effort on improving the infrastructure and traffic systems. Both cities want to enhance their public transport services, including introducing buses and urban mass rapid transit (UMRT). UMRT is a policy direction and is only at the start-up stage. The authorities expect that public transport services will only be able to cover 45–50 per cent of the total transport demand by 2020 (MOI, 2007).

Several business clubs and associations are in operation. Active ones include the American Chamber of Commerce in Vietnam (Amcham) with more than 400 members, the European Chamber of Commerce in Vietnam (Eurocham) with more than 600 members, the Japanese Business Association (JBA), the Vietnamese Business Forum (VBF) and the Vietnamese Chamber of Commerce and Industry (VCCI). These clubs and associations are facilitating fruitful discussions among businesses and governments.

The favourite sport in Vietnam is football (soccer). V-league, Vietnam's football tournament, is the most challenging league in ASEAN and Vietnamese people love to talk about their national team.

Resorts for vacation trips are available along Vietnam's beaches and mountainous areas. In addition, golf clubs are booming throughout the country attracting more and more foreigners and Vietnamese. There were 14 golf courses operating, with another 28 courses being planned as of July 2007 (Pike, 2007).

It is not difficult to find people who can speak English in the big cities. Besides the English language, younger Vietnamese are now studying other languages as second or third languages including Mandarin Chinese, Japanese, French, Korean, German, Russian and Spanish. At the same time, foreign food can be easily found in Hanoi and HCM city including Japanese, Chinese, Korean, French, Italian and Indian.

CROSS-CHAPTER REFLECTIVE QUESTION

■ Can you compare and contrast an emerging economy like Vietnam with a fully developed economy like Japan (Chapter 8) in terms of the governance of large organizations, consumer values, HRM sustainability and CSR?

CHAPTER SUMMARY

■ Vietnam has shifted from a command economy to a market-oriented economy since 1986, following a process known as *doi moi*. Since then, Vietnam has made some impressive achievements, including high GDP growth rate, poverty reduction and increase of HDI.

■ Vietnam has been active in regional and international integration. Joining the WTO early in 2007 created many opportunities and challenges for Vietnam in managing the country.

■ Enterprises in Vietnam, regardless of ownership, are now operating and promoting under the same scheme. CSR is well regulated by the legal system but is still an issue in practice.

■ Vietnamese culture is deeply affected by Confucianism. Personal networking and relationships are important to business and management practices in Vietnam.

■ Vietnamese labourers are known to be hard working, talented and eager to learn. However, work discipline and job-hopping are still at issue. In addition, Vietnam lacks skilled labour while having abundant unskilled labour.

■ With a large population, Vietnam is considered a promising market for investors. There have been many changes in consumer values and behaviours.

KEY CONCEPTS

Doi moi: Economic renovation or 'change for the new', which guided the Vietnamese economy towards an open market economic system.

International integration: A process in which an economy becomes an active part of the global market.

Industrialization: A process to transform an economy from an agricultural base to an industrial base.

Transitional economy: Economy going through a period of transition from a planned economy to a market economy.

Equitization: A process to transform a part of state ownership to private ownership. The state first sells shares to employees in the SOEs. It then sells shares to the public through the stock market. The state remains the dominating owner in selected enterprises.

REVIEW QUESTIONS

1. What are the key elements of *doi moi* in Vietnam? And what are its major achievements?
2. What are the opportunities and challenges for Vietnam as a member of the WTO?
3. What types of company (in terms of legal status) can be established in Vietnam?
4. What are the characteristics of the Vietnamese consumer market and its implications for investors?
5. What is important in Vietnamese business culture and the related implications for working with Vietnamese business partners?

LEARNING ACTIVITIES AND DISCUSSIONS

1. Imagine that you, as a foreign investor, want to set up a business in Vietnam. Explore information to see if you can buy a house in Vietnam, and make comparisons regarding the cost of living for foreigners in Hanoi (or other cities in Vietnam) and that in other cities in the East Asian region.
2. Vietnam has been a member of the WTO since January 2007. Discuss with your colleagues the main opportunities and challenges for foreign companies that wish to do business with Vietnam.
3. Joint ventures (JVs) are a very common form of FDI in Vietnam. In many cases, the local partners are SOEs, which may have very different management styles and lack the knowledge and experience associated with a market economy. Discuss with your colleagues potential conflicts in management styles of JVs in Vietnam and how to solve the problems.

ZAMIL STEEL POWERS AHEAD

Expansion is the key word for a company that is racing to keep up with demand in the domestic market and in markets abroad

The only Saudi Arabian investor in Vietnam, Zamil Group, is looking forward to expanding its operation, starting with a second factory and eyeing other businesses. The 24,000-square-meter factory in Noi Bai Industrial Zone, about 40 kilometres north of Hanoi, is roaring as 500 workers are kept busy. On one side are piles of raw materials. In the middle, groups of workers are involved in welding long bars of steel.

Donald I. Ghanem, a 30-year-old Lebanese and an operation superintendent, says it is very busy now as the factory is operating at maximum capacity. The final products flow out marked with 'Made in Vietnam by Zamil Steel' and are made ready for shipping.

Zamil Steel Vietnam, with an investment capital of US$30 million, is the only factory of Zamil Group in Southeast Asia. The factory produces 4,500 tons of steel products a month but it cannot keep up with the growing demand of the domestic market, which is estimated to hit 3.2 million tons this year, or a 20 per cent growth compared with last year. The company's export earnings are also surging as demand in southern Asian countries is rising due to reconstruction after the tsunami.

Zamil Steel Vietnam, a joint venture between Zamil Steel Industries with a 90 per cent stake and Japan's Mitsui with 10 per cent, has had the Noi Bai factory since 1999. Despite two expansions to 4,500 tons a month from the initial 600, output does not match demand. The investors say they need to have another factory in the south where market growth is greater than in the north.

'Zamil Steel is very well-known in the south and the market is very large. By putting another factory in the south we will be closer to our customers,' says George E. Kobrossy, Zamil Steel Vietnam's general director.

Work has started on a 45,000-square-meter area in Amata Industrial Park in Dong Nai Province, neighbouring HCM City. The second factory, with an investment of about US$10 million, is projected to start operation in the second quarter next year. The factory will cover an area of 20,000 square meters in the first phase and produce about 3,000 tons of pre-engineered steel a month.

The second factory will employ 300 workers, bringing Zamil Steel Vietnam's total employees to about 1,000. 'The second factory will give us ability to provide full coverage of the whole market in Vietnam,' Kobrossy says.

Zamil Group is one of the largest industrial groups in the Middle East. It has factories in China, Egypt, India and the United Arab Emirates. The company's presence in Vietnam dates back to 1993 when Zamil Steel Industries opened its first office to introduce pre-engineered steel buildings to the market.

After four years, Zamil's sales in Vietnam reached 10,000 tons or 60 steel buildings, making Vietnam the biggest steel importer of Zamil steel. By the end of 1996, Zamil's pre-engineered steel buildings had been introduced to most of the main cities in Vietnam. The early success led the company to set up a joint venture with Mitsui in 1997 and the first factory started production in 1999. Since then, Vietnam has become one of the fastest growing markets of Zamil Group.

Total sales in Vietnam have reached US$160 million and should reach US$200 million by the end of this year. Average sales growth over the last five years was 25 per cent. Kobrossy says that sales growth this year would rise by 50 per cent, the highest level since 2000. More than one-third of sales are exports. The main export markets are ASEAN countries and Japan.

'We expect that the second factory in Dong Nai will start running at a profit in the second year of operation, one year earlier than the first one, as the situation now is much better,' Kobrossy says, adding that Dong Nai is the best location given its easy access to human resources and good infrastructure.

'Vietnam is the second-largest production site [of Zamil Steel] after Saudi Arabia and sometimes when they are overloaded we fabricate buildings for them,' he says.

As high-rise buildings have been mushrooming in Hanoi and HCM City in recent years and the inflow of foreign investment is becoming a deluge, it is reasonable for Zamil Steel to expect growing business.

Kobrossy, who has been living in Vietnam for almost 10 years, says he sees other opportunities for Zamil Group here.

Manufacturing air conditioners and producing paint are likely to be the two sectors for Zamil Group's new businesses. The group's interests range from manufacturing air conditioners, steel, plastics, glass, paint, petrochemicals and food products, to operations and maintenance, construction and travel services.

'I'm trying to encourage Zamil air-conditioning to come and invest here because they are doing very well,' Kobrossy says. 'I think that Vietnam will be a good market for a new air-conditioning company to produce for the domestic market and for export markets.'

Aiming to become number one in the Zamil Steel family, Kobrossy expresses his belief that his company is well-positioned to grow.

'We have the Zamil Steel brand name, we have credibility, integrity and know-how, and our satisfied clients are available all over the world. So we believe we have the ability and capability to make an impact throughout the world,' he says.

QUESTIONS

1. What are opportunities and challenges that the company may have to cope with when doing business in Vietnam?
2. What are possible recommendations for Zamil Steel Vietnam in dealing with management issues such as working relationships between managers from Zamil Steel Industry and managers from Japan's Mitsui, and between foreign managers and local managers in the JV?
3. Do you think Zamil Group will be successful with the new businesses in the Vietnamese market (for example manufacturing air-conditioners, food products and operating travel services)? Use arguments related to management issues and the consumer market to support your ideas.

Source: Ngoc Mai, *Saigon Times Weekly* (internet version), 10 September 2005.

INTERESTING WEB LINKS

Asian Development Bank (ADB): http://www.adb.org/Statistics/ki.asp
The General Statistic Office of Vietnam: http://www.gso.gov.vn
Vietnamese laws: http://www.vietnamlaws.com
American Chamber of Commerce in Vietnam: http://www.amchamvietnam.com
European Chamber of Commerce in Vietnam: http://www.eurochamvn.org/
Vietnam Chamber of Commerce and Industry: http://www.vcci.com.vn/

Notes

1 Vietnamese people call their sea 'Bien Dong' which means the East Sea.
2 According to the website of the Ministry of Foreign Affairs (www.mofa.gov.vn) accessed in October 2007.
3 Socialism has been divided into two groups (i) communism and (ii) social democracy. Communists believe that the only way to achieve socialism is through violent revolution while social democrats believe that there should be no violence.
4 By political system we mean the organization and working modality of a government.
5 Integral manufacturing is implemented by Japanese manufacturers. It requires unique parts for each product and continuous technical improvement. Modular manufacturing is implemented by Chinese and American firms where parts are easily assembled into products. *Monozukuri* spirit is a Japanese term that is difficult to translate into English. Its meaning is similar to 'dedication and commitment of leaders/managers to drive a company towards success'.
6 Civil law is exercised in Germany, France and other European countries. Common law is exercised in some countries such as England, the US, Australia and New Zealand.
7 We must not equate the transformation of company types, which is mainly related to legal management of companies with the transformation of ownership.

REFERENCES

Ashwill, M. (2007). Interview with Christopher Runkel on the book *Vietnam Today: A Guide to a Nation at a Crossroads*, published in 2005 by Intercultural Press. Available at http://www.business-in-asia.com/books/vietnam_today.html.

Asia Business Council (2007). Asia's Chief Executive perspective: Results from the 2006 Annual Member Survey. Available at http://www.asiabusinesscouncil.org/research.html.

Belk, R.W. (1999). Leaping luxuries and transitional consumers. In Batra, R. (ed.) *Marketing in Transitional Economies*. Boston, MA: Kluwer Academic Publishers.

Beresford, M. and Dang, P. (2000). *Economic Transition in Vietnam*. Cheltenham: Edward Elgar Publishing, Inc.

Dao, T.L. and Sørensen, O.J. (2007). The interplay between expatriates and local managers from learning perspective. The 3rd VDIB-Workshop in Hanoi. November.

Edmonds, E. and Pavcnik, N. (2002). Does globalization increase child labor? Evidence from Vietnam. NBER Working Paper No. 8760.

GSO (Government Statistics Office) (2007). Statistical Data. Available at http://www.gso.gov.vn/default_en.aspx?tabid=491.

JETRO (Japan External Trade Organization) (2004). *The 14th Survey of Investment-related Cost Comparison in Major Cities and Regions in Asia*. Tokyo: Overseas Research Department of JETRO.

Mai, T.C. (2005). The marketing approach to FDI attraction. In Ohno, K. and Nguyen, V.T. (eds) *Improving Industrial Policy Formulation*. Hanoi: The Publishing House of Political Theory.

Meyer, K.E., Tran T.T.Y. and Nguyen H.V. (2006). Doing business in Vietnam. *Thunderbird International Business Review*. **28**(2): 263–90.

MOI (Ministry of Industry) (2007). *The Master Plan for the Development of the Motorcycle Industry,* drafted by Joint Working Group (May version).

MOLISA (Ministry of Labour, War Invalids and Social Affairs (2004). Labor and social issues emerging from the accession of Vietnam to WTO. Available at http://siteresources.worldbank.org.

MPI (Ministry of Planning and Investment) (2007). Report on FDI in the first 10 months of 2006 (in Vietnamese). Available at http://fia.mpi.gov.vn.

Nguyen, T.D. (2007). Joining WTO: Opportunities, challenges and our actions. *Vietnam Economic Times*. November 11.

Nguyen, T.H. (1994). Vietnamese traditional culture: A historical approach. *Journal of Vietnamese Studies*. 95–7.

Nguyen, T.T.M. and Takahashi, Y. (2007). Consumer behaviors in Vietnam: a transitional economy. *Journal of Commerce*. **3**(4): 107–24.

Ohno, K. (2006). Vietnam's industrial policy formulation: To become a reliable partner in integral manufacturing. *Industrialization of Developing Countries: Analyses by Japanese Economies*. 21st Century COE Program.

Pike, S. (2007). Vietnam golf boosting tourism biz. Available at http://www.hotelinteractive.com.

PriceWaterhouseCoopers (2007). Emerging markets: Balancing risk and award – The Pricewaterhouse-Coopers EM20 index. July.

Ralston, D.A., Nguyen, V.T. and Napier, N.K. (1999). A comparative study of the work values of North and South Vietnamese managers. *Journal of International Business Studies*. **30**(4): 655–72.

Shultz, C.J., Pecotich, A. and Le, K. (1994). Changes in marketing activities and consumption in the Socialist Republic of Vietnam. In Shultz, C., Belk, R. and Ger, G. (eds) *Research in Consumer Behavior*. Vol. 7. Greenwich, CT: JAI Press.

Statistics Publishing House (2004). *Vietnam Statistical Yearbook 2004*. Hanoi: Statistics Publishing House.

UNCTAD (2007). *World Investment Report 2007: Transnational Corporations, Extractive Industries and Development*. New York and Geneva: United Nations.

VDF (Vietnam Development Forum) (2006). Supporting industries in Vietnam from the perspective of Japanese manufacturing firms. *Policy Note*. 2, (E), 13–14.

VietnamNet (2006). The working class and trade unions of Vietnam in the new period. Available at http://english.vietnamnet.vn/social.

Visa and PATA (2007). Asia Travel Intentions Survey 2007. Available at http://www.visa-asia.com.

VNNIC (2007). Statistics of internet in Vietnam (in Vietnamese). Available at http://www.thongkeinternet.vn.

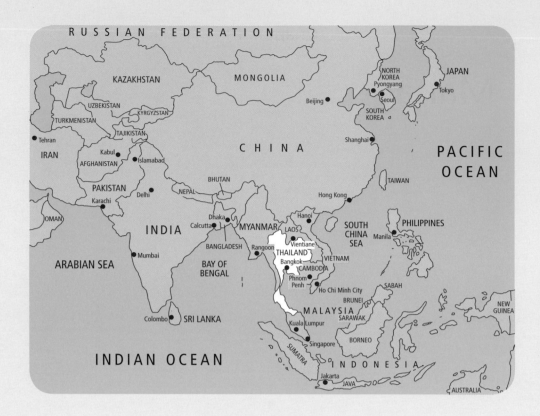

Chapter outline

- An overview of the Thai economy
- The King's Philosophy of Sufficiency Economy
- Thai culture and management
- Leadership and change
- Thailand and corporate social responsibility (CSR)
- Living and working in Thailand

Chapter objectives

After reading this chapter, you should be able to:

1. Describe the overview of the economic and business systems in Thailand

2. Describe the Philosophy of Sufficiency Economy by His Majesty King Bhumibol Adulyadej and how it influences business management in this country

3. Identify the key features of Thai culture and explain how they affect business management in Thailand

4. Understand the role of leadership and how it affects change implementation in Thai firms

5. Understand how Thai firms exert social responsibility

6. Explain key implications for expatriates working in Thailand

Chapter 14

Management in Thailand

Pornkasem Kantamara

INTRODUCTION

The Kingdom of Thailand is a developing country situated in Southeast Asia covering an area of nearly 513,115 square kilometres. It is roughly the size of France. Thailand shares land borders with Myanmar (Burma) in the north and west, the Andaman Sea in the west, Laos in the north and north-east, Cambodia and the Gulf of Thailand in the east, and Malaysia in the south. With the shape of the country resembling that of an ancient axe – the peninsula being the handle – combined with the richness of its natural resources, Thailand is also called *The Golden Axe*.

Thailand's capital and largest city is Bangkok or *Krung thep* in the Thai language, which means *City of Angels*. The national and official language is Thai, while English is widely spoken among the younger generation, particularly school or university students and businesspeople in Bangkok and in business circles. The population of Thailand was estimated at 65 million in 2007, about 10 million of whom live in Bangkok and about 25 per cent are under the age of 15. According to an estimate by the United Nations Population Information Network, the population of Thailand will be about 74 million in the year 2050. According to the National Economic and Social Development Board (NESDB), the biggest ethnic group in Thailand is Thai (75 per cent), with Chinese 14 per cent and others 11 per cent. Almost 95 per cent of Thai people are Buddhist, 4.6 per cent Muslim, Christian 0.7 per cent and others 0.1 per cent (NESDB, 2007).

AN OVERVIEW OF THE THAI ECONOMY

Thailand is an agricultural country which enjoys an abundance of natural resources: mountains, forests, rivers, minerals, sea and natural gas. The saying, '*Nai nam mee pla, nai na mee khao*', which means 'There are fish in the water, there is rice in the paddies', accurately depicts Thailand and the fertility of its land. Approximately 68 per cent of the Thai population live in rural areas and the majority are farmers with incomes reliant upon subsistence agriculture. The key agricultural products include rice, tapioca, rubber, corn, sugar cane, coconuts, soybeans, vegetables and orchards. Rice is the country's most important crop, and Thailand is the world's biggest rice exporter.

Thailand has been open to trade, commerce and diplomacy with foreign countries ever since the Ayutthaya period, the great era of international trade, particularly during the reign of King Narai the Great (1656–1688). The first European countries that traded with Thailand included the Netherlands, England, Portugal, Spain and France. Apart from Europeans, Chinese, both from the mainland and later those who became ethnic Thais, are another significant influential group contributing to the development of trade and commerce in Thailand, since they are very business-oriented and hard-working. In fact, most current successful and prosperous conglomerates in Thailand today are of Chinese descent. The United States and Japan did not start business relations with Thailand until the 19th century (1832 and 1887 respectively). However, these two countries have become important business partners of Thailand as well with the US being its number one exporter and Japan its number one supplier.

While agriculture is still the major part of the Thai economy with 49 per cent of its workforce, Thailand has become more commercialized and industrialized nowadays with an increasing number of multinational companies and industrial plants in different parts of the country. Its main industries include textile and garments, agricultural processing, beverages, tobacco, cement, electric appliances and components, computers and parts and integrated circuits. Having numerous and diverse beautiful natural attractions, tourism has also become one of the key income-generating industries of Thailand. The economy of Thailand is currently that of a middle-income industrial developing nation, heavily export-dependent, with exports of goods and services accounting for approximately 73.7 per cent of GDP in 2006 (The World Bank Group, 2008).

Foreign investment is welcomed and encouraged by the Thai government. Thailand provides an attractive environment for Foreign Direct Investment (FDI) with its central location in Asia, good infrastructure and efficient transportation, affordable wages, adaptable labour force, reasonably low-priced real estate and construction costs, and commitment to trade and investment liberalization with the countries in the Association of Southeast Asian Nations (ASEAN), the Asia-Pacific Economic Cooperation (APEC) and many other countries. A 2006 survey conducted by the Japan External Trade Organization (JETRO) showed that Thailand was the 'most optimal location for establishing a production/sales base in the coming five to 10 years'. (Board of Investment (BOI), 2008)

The 1997 Financial Crisis

Prior to the financial crisis the Thai economy performed extremely well. The growth rate in 1987 was almost 7 per cent, the highest of the Asian countries at that time. And, in 1988, 1989 and 1990, the growth rates in GDP were even more spectacular – 10.9 per cent, 13.2 per cent and 10 per cent respectively, or an 11.7 per cent average over the three years. These rates marked the Thai manufacturing-led economy as the fastest growing in the Asia-Pacific region and in the world over this period. It also placed Thailand firmly within the group of 'miracle' East Asian economies whose remarkable performance economists were so anxious to explain (World Bank, 1993; Warr, 2000).

Thailand was then referred to by the World Bank as one of the newly industrialized economies (NIEs), along with Indonesia and Malaysia (Ryan, 2000). It was also hailed as the 'Fifth Tiger'[1] (Krongkaew, 1994). The spectacular growth performance of the Thai economy during the past decade has been attributed to the regime switch from ISI (import substitution industrialization), inspired by the 'infant industry' argument, to an EOI (export oriented industrialization) strategy. The economic boom in Thailand (as well as Indonesia, Malaysia and China) was fuelled by dramatic export growth and the high level of capital inflow, including bank loans from abroad and speculative portfolio investment (Warr and Nidhiprabha, 1996). Within Thailand, the result was unprecedented business optimism, reflected in enormous property market speculation and construction in Bangkok. Risk-taking was paying off (Warr, 2000).

The Asian Financial Crisis in 1997 ended all the glory. Euphoria induced by almost a decade of high growth was a major reason for the explosion of the classic bubble economy when the rate of export growth declined to nearly zero in 1996. In addition to the drastic slowdown of exports, some other incidents also contributed to the crisis – in the case of Thailand, for example, the political events, monetary policy, increasing competition from China, and the capital market liberalization by the Bank of Thailand, as advised by the International Monetary Fund (IMF) and so on (Warr, 2000).

The crisis started in Thailand with the financial collapse of the Thai baht which was hit by massive speculative attacks. The Thai government decided to float the baht, cutting its peg to the USD, after exhaustive efforts to support it in the face of a severe financial over-extension that was in part real estate driven. At the time, Thailand had acquired a burden of foreign debt that made the country effectively bankrupt even before the collapse of its currency. This not only affected the currencies, but also the stock market and asset prices. Many businesses collapsed, and as a consequence, millions of people fell below the poverty line in 1997–8. The crisis and contagion clearly demonstrated the vulnerability of Thailand and other countries within the region and the inability to face the volatility of the world economy.

Thaksin's Dual Track Policy

The Thaksin government took office in February 2001 with the intention of stimulating domestic demand and reducing Thailand's reliance on foreign trade and investment. The government refined its economic message, embracing a dual track economic policy, known as *Thaksinomics*, aiming to simultaneously pursue the development of a strong domestic foundation for the economy as well as promoting linkages through international trade, investment and financial cooperation. These policies included:

- A three-year debt moratorium for farmers, combined with a revolving Village Fund and People's Bank project.
- Orders to Thailand's stated-owned banks to aggressively extend loans to farmers, villages and small and medium-size enterprises (SMEs) at discounted rates.
- Subsidized petrol and diesel prices.
- In the area of public health, the 30 baht universal healthcare programme was initiated, which guarantees universal healthcare coverage for just 30 baht (about US$0.75) a visit at state hospitals.
- The one tambon one product [2] (OTOP) scheme, which promoted and gave incentives for the development of rural SMEs.
- A continuous attempt to privatize state-owned enterprises, for example the electricity company.
- Increasing the Free Trade Agreement (FTA) negotiations with more countries, for example the USA, Japan, India, China, Australia, New Zealand and so on.

■ The 'mega-projects', which involve investing over US$50 billion in public works, including roads, public transit and a new international airport. (Shinawatra, 2003)

The implementation of the dual track policy led to an overall recovery of the Thai economy. By 2001, the currency rose to a reasonable, export friendly level. Thailand outpaced the rest of Southeast Asia by posting a GDP growth of 5.2 per cent, the fastest rate since the Asian Financial Crisis of 1997. The economy grew by another 6.9 per cent in 2003 outpacing the rest of the region except the People's Republic of China. In 2004, in spite of a volatile external environment and rising oil prices, Thailand still managed a GDP growth rate of 6.1 per cent. In addition, Thailand was able to repay all its debts to the IMF ahead of schedule; and the percentage of non-performing loans in the banking system had fallen.

Notwithstanding, some critics and sceptics questioned the real success of the policies. They pointed out that despite the rising export demand, domestic consumer demand had, in fact, grown only modestly. Also, consumer indebtedness had risen due to the fact that the state-owned banks made loans without proper due diligence to poor farmers and villagers who had little means to repay the loans.

Thai Economy Today: An Emerging Economy with Great Potential

After recovering from the Asian Financial Crisis of 1997–8, the Thai economy took off again. From 2002 to 2006, Thailand's growth averaged at 5.6 per cent. Today, it would be entirely wrong to think of Thailand as a second class state or inferior. Thailand's economy is emerging from the shadows of the great financial crisis and the subsequent devaluation of the country's currency. Since then, the Thai government has been trying to stimulate economic growth while adopting a prudent fiscal policy.

In the fourth quarter of 2007, the Thai economy expanded by 5.7 per cent year-on-year, which was higher than the rates recorded in the previous three quarters. This was again attributed to the acceleration in net exports and private investment, while the rate of private consumption did not grow significantly. As a result, for the whole year, the Thai economy expanded by 4.8 per cent in 2007. In fact, since the crisis, the long-term trend of social and economical development in Thailand has been strong. The poverty headcount ratio decreased in all parts of the country (see Table 14.1).

Table 14.1 Thailand poverty headcount ratio classified by region, 1996–2006 (percentage of total population)

	1996	2000	2004	2006
Thailand	14.8	21.0	11.2	9.6
Northeast	24.5	35.3	18.6	16.8
North	17.8	23.1	15.7	12.0
South	10.3	16.6	6.0	5.5
Central	6.1	9.0	4.5	3.3
Bangkok	1.2	1.7	0.8	0.5
Urban	9.9	8.6	4.6	3.6
Rural	22.9	26.5	14.2	12.0

Note: 2006 National Poverty Line is 1,386 baht/head/month.
Source: NESDB.

Figure 14.1 shows Thailand's GDP, PPP and GDP growth rates between 2003 and 2007.

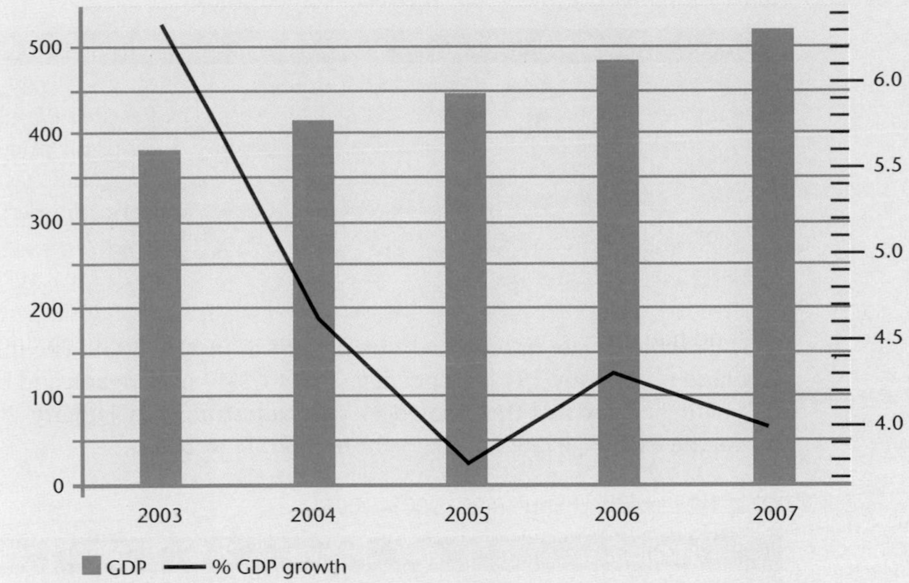

Year	GDP in billions of USD PPP	% GDP Growth
2003	379.55	6.30
2004	413.16	4.63
2005	445.37	3.80
2006	482.89	4.30
2007	519.28	

Figure 14.1 Thailand GDP, PPP and GDP growth rates 2003–2007

Source: EIU Country Data, Thailand, Economist Intelligence Unit, *The Economist*, Outlook for 2008–09

Table 14.2 shows the import/export values of Thailand between 2003 and 2007. The export-oriented manufacturing, in particular automobile production and farm output, are the main drivers of the country's economic gains.

Table 14.2 Import/export value in Thailand, 2003–2007

Import Value		Export Value	
Billion US$	**Year**	**% Billion (in US$)**	**Year**
74.3	2003	78.1	2003
93.5	2004	94.4	2004
117.7	2005	109.2	2005
126.9	2006	127.9	2006
139.2	2007p	151.1	2007p

Key: p = preliminary figures
Source: Board of Investment, 2008.

Table 14.3 shows Thailand's unemployment rate over the past five years (2003–7) which reflects the optimistic economic development.

Table 14.3 Unemployment rate in Thailand, 2003–2007

Year	Unemployment Rate	Rank	Percentage Change	Date of Information
2003	2.90%	171		2002 est.
2004	2.20%	176	–24.14%	2003 est.
2005	1.50%	11	–31.82%	2004 est.
2006	1.80%	12	20.00%	2005 est.
2007	2.10%	17	16.67%	2006 est.

Source: CIA World Factbook, 17 April 2007.

The exchange rate has reached 31 baht/US$ as of May 2008. The minimum wage in Thailand is currently 194 baht per day (about US$6) in Bangkok and between 143 and 193 baht per day in other provinces (last adjustment in January 2008). Table 14.4 shows the exchange rate for Thai baht from 2003 to 2008.

Table 14.4 Thai exchange rates, 2003–2008

Exchange rate	2003	2004	2005	2006	2007p	2008p1
Baht: US$ (reference rate)	41.5	40.3	40.3	37.93	34.56	31.46

Key: p = preliminary data; p1 = preliminary data cumulated from quarter 1 data
Source: Bank of Thailand, updated 5 May 2008.

Challenges Ahead

Despite its success in recovering from the 1997 financial crisis, below is a list of some challenges still facing Thailand:

■ *Political and policies uncertainty:* In September 2006, the army staged a *coup d'état* and overturned the government of Thaksin Shinawatra due to corruption and a lack of transparency. Thailand has returned to a democracy with its 23 December 2007 elections. The new six-party coalition government has to prove its ability to bring about stability and confidence. It is crucial for the government to demonstrate that the pace of private consumption and foreign as well as domestic investment will recover from the recent decline. Moreover, the fragmentation of the people's feelings towards government policies has also been undermining its administration.

■ *Economic and social development:* Another challenge for Thailand is to sustain the strong export growth and improve domestic demand. The slowdown of the global economy could make it difficult for Thai exports to repeat the robust performance of 2006 and 2007, while higher inflation could dampen domestic consumption. In addition, Thailand is facing a severe problem with the increasing cost of living, particularly in big cities. This is a result of the world energy prices crisis.

■ *Insurgency in the south of Thailand:* Since the Thaksin administration, the gap between the government and the extremists in the southern part of Thailand has widened. This triggered the ongoing violence in this part of the country, particularly in the four southernmost provinces, which consequently led to a stagnation of the businesses and investment in the south.

■ *Volatility from world politics and economy:* The world economy remains volatile due to various factors. For example, continuous rising energy prices, fluctuation of currencies, high international competition (particularly from China, in the case of Thailand), terrorist movements, the financial turmoil in the US and so on.

■ *Four national reforms:* The government sees the need to issue a national agenda to move Thailand towards becoming one of the high performance economies (HPEs) in the region. This includes economic reform, education reform, bureaucracy reform and corporate reform. This is an ambitious, but not impossible, vision. However, to realize it requires wise, prudent policies and serious cooperation from all parties concerned in a concerted manner.

SUMMARY POINTS

■ Thailand is a newly industrialized developing country with a middle income economy. Thailand is the world's number one rice exporter.

■ The Thai government encourages free enterprise and welcomes foreign direct investment. Since the 1997 Financial Crisis, there have been more multinational companies in the country in the form of mergers and joint ventures.

REFLECTIVE QUESTIONS

■ What do you think were the causes of the 1997 Asian Financial Crisis?

■ What is dual track policy and how can it help a country to survive a financial crisis? What are some other measures which can be adopted to comply with this policy?

THE KING'S PHILOSOPHY OF SUFFICIENCY ECONOMY

As discussed above, similar to numerous other Asia-Pacific countries, Thailand's economic policies have for decades been directed towards fostering economic growth. After the 1997 Financial Crisis, most Thai firms were forced to seek a new management approach to survive, as an alternative to the prevailing Anglo/US business model. The Philosophy of Sufficiency Economy is one of the options.

His Majesty King Bhumibol Adulyadej, who is the soul of the nation, has on many occasions graciously reminded Thai people of a step-by-step and balanced approach to development, which is now known as the Philosophy of Sufficiency Economy, particularly, after he saw how globalization affected the way of living of his subjects. The philosophy provides guidance and appropriate conduct covering numerous aspects of life. The following is an excerpt from his speech in 1974:

> Economic development must be achieved gradually. It should begin with the strengthening of our economic foundation, by ensuring that the majority of our population has enough to live on … Once reasonable progress has been achieved, we should then embark on the next steps, by pursuing more advanced levels of economic development. Here, if one focuses only on rapid economic expansion without making sure that such a plan is appropriate for our people and the condition of our country, it will inevitably result in various imbalances and eventually end up as a failure or crisis as found in other countries. (Royal Speech, 1974: 12)

After the economic crisis in 1997, His Majesty reiterated and expanded the concept to point the way for recovery that would lead to a more resilient, balanced and sustainable development, better able to meet the challenges arising from globalization and to changes that may bring future economic insecurity. The philosophy can be summed up in one paragraph, as translated from the Thai:

> Sufficiency Economy is a philosophy that guides the livelihood and behaviour of people at all levels, from the family to the community to the country, on matters concerning national development and administration. It calls for a 'middle way' to be observed, especially in pursuing economic development in keeping with the world of globalization. Sufficiency means moderation and reasonableness, including the need to build a reasonable immune system against shocks from the outside or from the inside. Intelligence, attentiveness, and extreme care should be used to ensure that all plans and every step of their implementation are based on knowledge.

> At the same time we must build up the spiritual foundation of all people in the nation, especially state officials, scholars, and business people at all levels, so they are conscious of moral integrity and honesty and they strive for the appropriate wisdom to live life with forbearance, diligence, self-awareness, intelligence, and attentiveness. In this way we can hope to maintain balance and be ready to cope with rapid physical, social, environmental, and cultural changes from the outside world. (Krongkaew, 2003)

At first glance, this philosophy may sound unrealistic, idealistic and impractical for today's world. However, it has been proved time and again by numerous Thai business owners and scholars that the philosophy was effective and necessary for the survival and sustainability of the businesses (Kantabutra, 2005; Kusumavalee, 2005; Nuttavuthisit, 2005; Thai Chamber of Commerce, 2008).

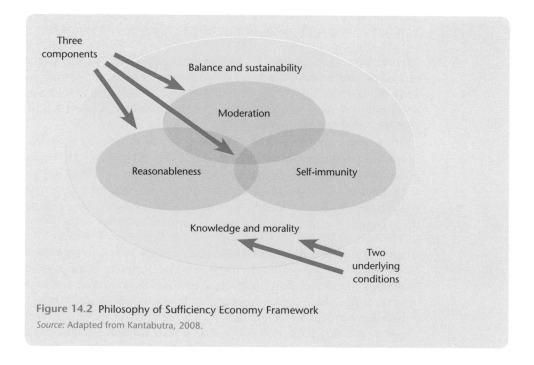

Figure 14.2 Philosophy of Sufficiency Economy Framework
Source: Adapted from Kantabutra, 2008.

The Philosophy of Sufficiency Economy, based on adherence to the middle path, is advocated to overcome the economic crisis that was brought about by unexpected change under conditions of rapid globalization, and to achieve sustainable development. The Philosophy of Sufficiency Economy framework (see Figure 14.2) comprises three main characteristics and two underlying conditions (Piboolsravut, 2004).

The three characteristics are:

1. *Moderation* has two components; sufficiency and appropriateness. The word 'sufficiency' means not lacking in anything, but having everything in appropriate amounts, that is, not too much nor too little. A balance in all our actions leads to sustainable development.
2. *Reasonableness* means both evaluating the reasons for any action, and understanding its full consequences, with the condition of having knowledge and ethics as the basis for decision making.
3. *Self-immunity system* means the readiness and ability to cope with the shocks from internal and external changes by carefully assessing the situation and considering both short-term and long-term consequences.

The two underlying conditions necessary to achieve sufficiency are:

1. *Knowledge* which consists of accumulating knowledge on various subjects from the past, present and future.
2. *Morality* means embracing the four virtues, namely kindness, unity, honesty and justice, that if practised will bring peace and prosperity to the individual and also to society (Thai Chamber of Commerce, 2008).

'Sufficiency Economy' requires breadth and thoroughness in planning, carefulness in applying knowledge, and the implementation of those plans. As for the moral and ethical condition, 'Sufficiency Economy' enforces the condition that people, particularly public officials, academics and businessmen at all levels, adhere first and foremost to the principles of honesty and integrity while conducting their lives with perseverance, harmlessness and generosity. The Sufficiency Economy Philosophy serves as a guide to the way of living and behaving for people of all levels, including business organizations, and is universally achievable (Piboolsravut, 2004; Kantabutra, 2008). Ajva Taulananda, a member of the Sufficiency Economy Movement Sub-Committee and Chairman of Private Sector Working Group, stated,

> There has been some confusion about the term Sufficiency Economy. Most people usually associate this with the poor or with farmers where as trade and industry were on another level, and therefore not applicable. This is a misunderstanding. Sufficiency Economy is a philosophy that can be applied at all levels ranging from people's daily lives and society, to business and the nation. (Thai Chamber of Commerce, 2008: 17)

The Philosophy of Sufficiency Economy is simple, and yet very effective if practised strictly. Applying Sufficiency Economy in business is a form of marketing strategy, and can be used for both niche and mass markets. Sufficiency Economy implies that there is enough and no deficiency. Having enough does not mean excessiveness to the point of extravagance, nor does it mean saving to the extent of parsimony.

To integrate the Philosophy of Sufficiency Economy and the ability to increase trade capacity, business people need to exercise caution before decision making. They need to approach with rationality and moderation, must be prepared to manage and take any risks involved. It is also natural that business needs to grow, expand and achieve a productive goal through marketing. The philosophy reminds business owners to be wise and not to act when they are not prepared to do so. They need not perform business that is beyond their own capacity or with no proper preparation (Thai Chamber of Commerce, 2008).

SUMMARY POINT

■ The Philosophy of Sufficiency Economy comprises three characteristics: moderation, reasonableness, and self-immunity system; and two underlying conditions to achieve sufficiency: knowledge and morality.

REFLECTIVE QUESTION

■ Do you agree that the Philosophy of Sufficiency Economy can assist people to cope with globalization and unexpected change from the world social and economic situation?

THAI CULTURE AND MANAGEMENT

As suggested by previous studies, culture influences management practices (for example Ralston et al., 1999; Dao and Sorensen, 2007). Thus, to learn more about Thai culture will enable us to have a better understanding of Thai people and their behaviours. In this section, Hofstede's cross-cultural framework will be applied to provide perspectives on Thai culture. This framework comprises four dimensions: *power distance; individualism vs collectivism; masculinity vs femininity; and uncertainty avoidance.*

High Power Distance: Hofstede defined power distance as 'the extent to which the less powerful members of institutions and organizations (that is, juniors) within a country expect and accept that power is distributed unequally'. (Hofstede and Hofstede, 2005: 46). Thailand was rated high in the dimension of power distance. Inequality within Thai society is visible and it is accepted that different social classes exist divided by economic status (rich vs poor); education (low vs high); profession (blue- vs white-collar); position (subordinate vs supervisor), family relation or seniority (parents vs children) and so on. This does not come as a surprise, given that Thailand has been ruled as an absolute monarchy for hundreds of years. 'Each Thai person who is trained to be a functioning member of society learns, early in life, what rank he or she holds and how he is supposed to treat others according to that rank. The "others" in his life are reckoned as his juniors, his seniors or his peers' (Holmes and Tangtongtavy, 1997: 26).

From an early age, Thai children are taught to respect, obey and not to argue with adults, such as parents, grandparents, teachers or any senior persons. As a result, in a hierarchical society like Thailand, seniority is very important. Inevitably, this high power distance, due either to the seniority or authority of a person in an organization, carries over into business and affects management. Other key characteristics of high power distance, which also apply in the Thai workplace include:

■ hierarchy
■ autocracy, centralization
■ more supervisory personnel

- a wide salary range between the top and bottom of the organization
- managers rely on supervisors and on formal rules
- subordinates expect to be told what to do
- the ideal boss is a benevolent autocrat, or 'good father'.

Collectivism: Thai people were also found to rank very high in the dimension of collectivism, which is characterized by a tight social framework in which people distinguish between in-groups and out-groups. 'Collectivism pertains to the societies in which people from birth onward are integrated into strong, cohesive in-groups, which throughout people's lifetimes continue to protect them in exchange for unquestioning loyalty.' (Hofstede and Hofstede, 2005: 76).

Traditionally, Thai people grow up within an extended family. Children are used to being surrounded by not just the parents and other children, but also grandparents, uncles, aunts, servants and cousins. They learn to think of themselves as part of a 'we' group, as opposed to a 'they' group. During the harvest season, Thai farmers in the past had a tradition called *'long kaeg'* or 'collective labour', which was the time when all the farmers in the same village gathered together to assist with the rice harvesting on the plot of one household. Then, the *long kaeg* rotated around to cover the other households. At school or at work, it is quite common to see a group of girls (and boys) walking together, dining together, or even walking to the restroom together! An organization is like a family with employees as its members.

Some key characteristics of a collective society such as Thailand are:

- the social network is the primary source of information
- saying or doing things out of the mainstream is generally discouraged or frowned upon
- harmony should be maintained and direct confrontation avoided
- friendships are predetermined
- direct appraisal of subordinates spoils harmony
- relationship prevails over task.

Femininity: According to Hofstede 'A society is called feminine when emotional gender roles overlap: both men and women are supposed to be modest, tender, and concerned with the quality of life. And, a society is called masculine when emotional gender roles are clearly distinct: men are supposed to be assertive, tough, and focused on material success, whereas women are supposed to be more modest, tender and concerned with the quality of life.' (Hofstede and Hofstede, 2005: 120). Thai people are generally not assertive and ambitious. The culture places more value on relations and quality of life rather than wealth and material possessions.

Thailand is ranked very high on femininity. Some key characteristics of a feminine society such as Thailand are:

- being responsible, decisive, ambitious, caring, and gentle for both women and men alike
- women's liberation means that men and women take equal shares both at home and at work
- people underrate their own performance: ego-effacement
- resolution of conflicts by compromise and negotiation
- rewards are based on equality
- there is a higher share of working women in professional jobs.

The degree to which Thailand is a feminine society is higher in the rural areas than in the big cities and urban areas where there is an increasing number of working women and where people's mentality has been more influenced by Western culture, which is more masculine.

Strong Uncertainty Avoidance: This dimension refers to the way people handle uncertainty, whether they tolerate or avoid it. Thailand is also found to rank high on the uncertainty avoidance dimension. This means most Thais possess the mentality of *'What is different is dangerous?'* They generally are not risk-takers and fear change, which brings uncertainty and anxiety, and see it as a threat. Job-hopping is unpopular among Thai people. Most of them prefer working for the government which offers lifetime employment, security and better benefits, despite a low salary (However, nowadays the younger generation seems to have less of this characteristic than in the past).

Some key characteristics of a collective society such as Thailand are:

- there is an uncertainty about new products and technologies
- conservative investment
- few changes of employer, longer service
- an emotional need for rules
- motivation by security and the esteem of belonging.

Significant Thai Traits and Characteristics

- ***Sanuk*** or 'fun' and ***sabai*** or 'comfortable, hang loose, or easy going' are two major characteristics of Thai people. As already stated, Thailand is located in the sub-tropical region and benefits from a richness of natural resources. The weather in Thailand is moderate to hot. Thai people hardly ever experience intense weather or natural disasters, such as hurricanes, earthquakes, volcanic eruptions, blizzards and so on, as in other parts of the world. Therefore, they tend to live their lives contentedly with low levels of stress. They are normally easy-going and do not take things seriously.

  Moreover, traditionally, Thailand is an agricultural country and their products depend very much on natural conditions. After the hard work during the planting season, Thai farmers will relax and enjoy themselves – *sabai* – while waiting for the harvesting season, when they will again work and have fun – *sanuk*. The *'long kaeg'* ritual does not only signify collectivism in Thai culture, but also a fun-loving nature. Thai people like to mix work with play; there is basically no competition in their peaceful, relaxing and fun way of living.

- ***Greng jai*** or 'considerate' is one of the most significant and intriguing Thai concepts. Thai people are expected to be considerate, to show politeness and good manners. *Greng jai*-ness may cause Thai people to do what they may not want to, or not to do what they want to. Why are people *greng jai* to other people? The answers are various: 'I don't want to bother her'; 'I don't want to hurt her feelings'; 'I don't want to offend her or make her angry (she's my boss!)'; 'I don't want to make her lose face', 'I don't want to impose' and so on. This perplexing phenomenon may be related to concepts of power distance, face saving, seniority or plain politeness.

  To illustrate a common example of being *greng jai*, after the meeting, a manager expressed his feeling with his colleagues:

I knew the decision to open up a new programme was not a good one and could even be detrimental to our own programme due to the competition for the same target group. But, we were too *greng jai* (considerate) to tell them that and offend them. So we kept beating around the bush and did not say anything. After all, they were our partner. Besides, the top management seemed to support it too. So, how could we have opposed it?

The above incident is quite common in Thailand. In a meeting, employees have a tendency to be quiet, often do not express their opinions and seem to agree. Note that these behaviours can also be associated with other cultural dimensions, such as high power distance and collectivism. A certain degree of *greng jai*-ness is appropriate and expected, if practised socially to demonstrate good manners. However, in business, if it gets to the extent that people refrain from what they should be doing, the consequences could be detrimental to the business or their job security.

- **Sia na** or 'lose face' or 'stop having respect from other people' – This could be one reason why many Thai people do not voice their opinion in a meeting; they are afraid of losing face and embarrassing themselves. Or, they may be be too *greng jai* and do not want to make their boss *sia na*, in case he/she is wrong. These two traits can be related. Face is very important for Thai people. So, again, they may do, or refrain from doing something, in order to save their own or the other's face. If someone causes a Thai person to lose his/her face, it is considered very serious, especially if that person is more senior or of higher rank. Normally, in Thailand, a student does not question a teacher's knowledge; a subordinate does not point out a supervisor's mistake.
- **Mai pen rai** or 'never mind' – As stated before, most of the time Thais do not take things seriously. *Mai pen rai* portrays this characteristic; it also goes along with *sabai*. This helps to explain the benign behaviour in Thai culture. The Thais are also peaceful people; a quarrel does not happen easily and is settled with a compromise. *Mai pen rai* could cause people to overlook a problem, underestimating the seriousness of a situation and just let it slide. As a result, things might not get done and problems not be solved. This could cause damage to a business. On the other hand, *mai pen rai* allows people to remain calm and not to panic when facing a problem, so they can solve it cautiously.
- **Thai smiles** – Thailand is often called *The Land of Smiles* because Thai people are extremely and impressively hospitable. They are known for being very friendly, generous, easy-going and fun-loving. These qualities make visitors from around the world feel at home and want to come back to Thailand again. But, a Thai smile can mean many things – *happiness; embarrassment; shame; remorse; tension; fear; or even sadness* (Holmes, and Tangtongtavy, 1997), and occasionally it can be both challenging and frustrating at the same time to interpret. The different interpretations of smiling behaviour may lead to problems, particularly if the situation in which they occur involves stress or tension. The following story told by a Japanese manager illustrates this:

When I asked, my employee reported to me with a certain smile that the project could not be completed according to the schedule, even though it has been delayed for six months already compared to other countries. I don't understand how he could have smiled about this. It's very serious and I was furious that he didn't report to me earlier.

SUMMARY POINTS

■ Thailand is a high power distance, very high collectivist, feminine, and high uncertainty avoidance society.

■ Thai people are hospitable, friendly, fun-loving, easy-going, generous, peaceful and considerate. Face saving is very important in Thai culture.

REFLECTIVE QUESTIONS

■ Which aspect of Thai culture would you find most challenging to manage in Thailand? Why?

■ What could be the cause(s) of conflict on the job? How would you deal with it?

LEADERSHIP AND CHANGE

As mentioned above, Thai culture is very hierarchical and is a high power distance culture. Leadership plays a significant role in the effectiveness of business performance. Of the most common leadership styles existing, *autocratic leadership* is still prevailing in Thai society and in organizations, where power distance is high and the overall system is hierarchical. Seniority-based management is common. An organization is a presumed family; its leader is thus a paternalistic figure who holds absolute authority to make decisions. Leaders give orders and instructions; employees are expected to follow them. Employees also have high expectations of their leaders and need to be able to depend on them in all things, professional as well as personal.

In recent years, with the increasing number of multinational companies, there has been an attempt to exert alternative leadership styles in organizations in order to involve employees more in the decision-making process, such as participatory, situational and transformational leaderships. But, the result has not been very successful, particularly in governmental agencies. Most Thai employees consider this as 'role switching' and, probably, are reluctant to take it on.

Globalization and advance technology force organizations to change the way they operate to maintain their competitiveness. A Thai manager once said, 'Making change happen in a Thai organization is not difficult. You can just order your staff to "do it". And they'll follow your order and change will happen.' But, change is a process that takes time to happen step-by-step, not something that happens overnight. People also need time to adjust to change gradually. Leading change in Thailand can be challenging. When a leader orders their employees to change, what they get is a merely superficial change, not a real one; that is, new behaviours and thinking. The staff may not resist change openly for fear of the leader's power, but they do not support it wholeheartedly either. Thus, change is not materialized. At the same time, there may be another group of staff who agree with the change, but do not show it openly for fear of being outsiders from the mainstream.

Leading change is a delicate and sentimental process. There are more ingredients required for a successful change process than just a top-down implementation and order giving. Of course, authority (that supports change) and strong leadership help, but this is not enough. We also need staff involvement, their buy-in, input and feedback, sense of ownership, supportive social network and effective strategy.

THAILAND AND CORPORATE SOCIAL RESPONSIBILITY (CSR)

Corporate social responsibility is the new social mantra in today's business world. Although many Thai firms might have been conducting some type of socially responsible activities for many years, the concept of CSR as it stands today has emerged only recently. There is no legislative framework on CSR in Thailand. As in many countries, 'the development of CSR in Thailand has been somewhat slow, piecemeal, reflective of a number of disparate positions, as well as lacking a clear theoretical framework' (Ratanajongkol et al., 2006: 67). In the past, only a few firms gave it much attention and saw the link between CSR and their business operation and its competitive advantage. Most companies only focused on increasing revenue and short-term profits and maximizing shareholder value. Or, some firms were simply too busy trying to survive and stay afloat during the economic downturn to think about CSR.

In Thailand, only 11 per cent of Thai companies donate to charities, well under the global average of 65 per cent, according to a survey by the consultancy firm Grant Thornton (BOI, 2008). Most companies do not, and are not required to, have social responsibility policies. However, recently the trend on CSR practices consideration shows an impressive increase, particularly among large, leading, well-established Thai companies or joint ventures and multinational companies (MNCs).

After the 1997 economic crisis, public scrutiny and pressure became more common for Thai companies. The press was asking tough and sophisticated questions of business leaders in areas beyond financial reporting. Human rights, human dignity, social responsibility and equitable treatment within stakeholder groups were the issues raised by activists, reporters, analysts and the public at large. As a result, all listed companies were asked by the Thailand Stock Exchange to appoint an audit committee before the end of 1999. This effort was aimed at building awareness of, and promoting implementation of, corporate governance practices in Thailand.

In Thailand, the manufacturing sector has the highest record of CSR disclosure of the industry sectors, with the dominant theme being the environment, whereas the service sector has the lowest disclosure on the same theme (Ratanajongkol et al., 2006). Triple bottom line reporting is becoming more important and more common among companies in Thailand, due to pressure from consumers, government, NGOs and society at large. CSR also ranges from a philanthropic to a policy level, such as donating money or things to charity or helping society simply as a way of image building, or continuous quality management of the product or service to becoming more user-friendly, incorporating and practising CSR as an integral and natural part of an organization's operation.

Spotlight on CSR: The Bangchak Petroleum Pl. Co. Ltd.

The Bangchak Petroleum Pl. Co. Ltd. (Bangchak) is a Thai oil company which started its operation in 1964. Bangchak imports crude oil from the Middle East and Far East regions, as well as from domestic sources, to be refined at the capacity of 120,000 barrels per day. The company mainly distributes its products through 566 standard service stations and 530 community service stations (as at the end of 2006). It also directly sells to consumers in the sectors of transport, airlines, marine, construction, industry and agriculture.

Bangchak is one of the first oil companies to seriously pay attention to CSR and actively and consistently act upon it. The company established Lemon Farm shops within its service stations, which sell natural agricultural products from rural community organizations to customers coming to fill up with petrol. In this way, Bangchak helps to provide marketing channels for farmers and health benefits to its customers at the same time. Some of Bangchak's CSR activities include: safety training for the neighbouring community; awarding scholarships for needy students; reforestation projects; youth camp; Bangchak employees volunteering to teach children in the neighbouring community after school and helping them with homework, among others things.

Bangchak partnered with a local supplier to establish the first cooperative gas station, which was expanded from supporting agricultural organizations in the community to becoming owners of Bangchak gas stations, shops, oil trucks and garment production. This helped them to learn organizational and business management skills with joint community ownership and was one more tiny effort in strengthening community economies, engendering self-sufficiency and a good quality of life.

Source: www.bangchak.co.th, 2008.

Spotlight on CSR: Red Bull

Red Bull is the brand name of an energy drink introduced in 1987, which combats mental and physical fatigue. It was originated in Thailand and, in a version adapted to Austrian tastes, is now popular throughout the world. The sale of Red Bull is prohibited in some countries, usually due to its taurine content or its alleged high level of caffeine. In Thailand, its profits are almost 400 million baht.

'Red Bull Taxi Talk', an English class for taxi drivers on the radio was initiated by Red Bull. Taxi drivers are one of the key target groups of Red Bull for many of them need to drink it to stay awake, alert or energetic. Mr Nuatthasit, the volunteer instructor for the programme, said, 'We try to make English fun and practical so the learners can use it in their daily job on the road. Hopefully, this can help them do their job more smoothly and they can develop themselves more and improve their English proficiency.'

Red Bull Spirit Project is the latest CSR project of Red Bull. The company expands its CSR role by creating networks and collaborating with other partners – private, public and NGOs alike. This year nine projects were initiated and implemented by Red Bull employees, management, some of its partners and volunteers from the public at large. These projects cover various themes such as capacity building and development for disadvantaged groups like children with special needs or children from broken families; youth leadership development; environmental conservation, particularly forests and waters; learning centres for rural children, and so on.

Source: http://www.manager.co.th, www.redbullspirit.org, 2008.

SUMMARY POINTS

- There is no legislative framework for CSR in Thailand.

- The trend of CSR is increasing in Thailand.

- CSR ranges from the philanthropy level to the policy level. In Thailand, most companies are still at the philanthropy level.

REFLECTIVE QUESTION

■ In your opinion, what organizations (in your country) are good examples of CSR practices, particularly at the policy and organizational performance level? Provide examples of what they do that makes you select them.

LIVING AND WORKING IN THAILAND

Thailand is an easy place to live in and provides a high standard of living. It is located at the heart of Asia, the largest growing economic market. Therefore, from Thailand it is convenient to trade with Southeast Asia, the sub-region, China, India and the countries of the Association of Southeast Asian Nations (ASEAN). Thailand was one of the founding members of ASEAN and has forged closer economic cooperation with ASEAN member nations.

Generally, Thailand has strong social and political stability, despite a few *coups d'état* in the past. It is a welcoming Buddhist country. The country's form of government – constitutional monarchy – allows democratic processes and reforms, and is balanced by the Thai peace-loving nature, high reverence for the Thai monarchy and devotion to the teachings of Buddhism. While the vast majority of the people of Thailand are Buddhist, all religions are welcome, and His Majesty the King is the patron of all religions. Different ethnic groups can live together peacefully in Thailand, which does not suffer from the racial tensions experienced by some other Asian countries.

The Thai economy is growing steadily. The Thai workforce is well-educated, highly skilled, hard-working, very adaptive and cost-effective. Thailand has good infrastructure for foreign investors, for example skytrain, underground trains, advanced telecommunication and IT networks.

The country's well-defined investment policies focus on liberalization and encourage free trade. Foreign investments, especially those that contribute to the development of skills, technology and innovation are actively encouraged by the government. Thailand consistently ranks among the most attractive investment locations in international surveys, and a 2006 World Bank report indicated that Thailand was the 4th easiest country in Asia in which to do business, and the 20th easiest in the world (BOI, 2008). Thailand also offers numerous support facilities and incentives for foreign investors, such as tax incentives, no local content requirement, no export requirements and so on.

Thailand's education is of an international standard. Its universities are outstanding in many fields. There are a great number of international schools and colleges that offer world-class education. Thai food is also known worldwide for its delicacy and taste; and international cuisine is easy to find. Moreover, healthcare in Thailand has developed a good reputation globally. The cost of living is generally very cheap compared to Western countries and many other Asian countries.

It is challenging and interesting working with Thais due to their unique characteristics (see above). The people have a unique charm. Many foreigners have been impressed with the natural beauty of the country and with 'Thainess', and keep coming back to this country.

Some points to consider for living and working in Thailand:

■ Do not mistake the Thais' modesty for poor performance, or silence for lack of good ideas. Underrating their own performance does not mean they do not achieve in what they do.

- Do not touch a Thai's head. The head is the locus of the soul and is treated by others with the greatest respect.
- Pointing with your foot is considered rude. And take your shoes off before entering a Thai's home.
- To work successfully in Thailand, you need to win the Thais' hearts. Take your time to get to know them. Be patient. Do not expect quick change. Focus on Thais' strengths and make the most of it. Working in Thailand can be very enjoyable, rewarding and fruitful.

CROSS-CHAPTER REFLECTIVE QUESTION

- In this chapter we have read that the rapid growth of the Thai economy was mainly triggered by the King's Philosophy of Sufficiency Economy. In fact, government or sovereign-led reforms have often been crucial in economic transformations. We can see examples like *doi moi* in Vietnam (Chapter 13), Deng Xiaoping's Open Door Policy for China (Chapter 9) and the Singapore government's involvement in the economy (Chapter 12). Can you think of some other examples in Asia or beyond?

CHAPTER SUMMARY

- Thailand has a broad-based economy with strong agricultural, service and industrial sectors. It is a middle income newly industrialized developing country with free enterprise. The government encourages FDI. Before the Asian Financial Crisis Thailand's economy was the fastest growing in the world. The country has now fully recovered from the crisis mainly through the acceleration in exports and private investment.
- The King's Philosophy of Sufficiency Economy comprises three main characteristics: moderation, reasonableness, and self-immunity system; and two underlying conditions necessary to achieve sufficiency: knowledge and morality. This philosophy can be applied to every part of society, including large and small businesses.
- Thailand is a Buddhist country and Buddhism plays a major role in every part of Thai life. Thai culture has high power distance, collectivism, femininity and high uncertainty avoidance. Some key Thai characteristics are 'sanuk', 'sabai', 'greng jai', 'sia na', and 'mai pen rai'.
- Autocratic leadership style prevails in Thailand, thus top-down and centralized management and change implementation is common in an organization.
- There is no legislative framework for CSR in Thailand; however, the trend for it is increasing, particularly among leading, well-established Thai and multinational companies.

KEY CONCEPTS

The Philosophy of Sufficiency Economy: This philosophy emphasizes taking the middle path, and comprises three main characteristics: moderation, reasonableness, and self-immunity system; and two underlying conditions: knowledge and morality.

SME: Small and medium enterprise – normally, a family or community-owned business with around 10 or 20 employees. The business can be either domestic or international.

One tambon (village) one product (OTOP): A project to promote the local industry through the manufacturing of attractive local specialty products. The movement was originally started in Japan.

Dual track policy or Thaksinomics: An economic policy which aims to simultaneously pursue the development of a domestic foundation for the economy as well as promoting linkages through international trade, investment and financial cooperation.

Triple bottom line: This is when an organization expands its traditional values and criteria for measuring its success by considering social and environmental performance in addition to financial performance.

REVIEW AND DISCUSSION QUESTIONS

1. Despite its impressive growth, Thailand is notable for the near-absence of companies that could truly be called world-class, such as Korea's Samsung and LG, China's Lenovo, India's Tata, or Singapore's Singapore Airlines. A recent study by the Boston Consulting Group (BCG) showed only two companies from Thailand meet the standards needed to belong to the 100 largest multinationals from emerging economies. In your opinion, what are the causes of this? And, how can Thailand improve and develop to be able to meet those standards?

2. Do you think the Philosophy of Sufficiency Economy is practical as a business management approach in your country, given its social, economical and cultural context?

3. Discuss some of the things you should be aware of, should you become a manager in Thailand. How do you think you could be successful in your job?

4. 'Thailand's strength derives from its diversity.' What do you think this statement means? What kinds of diversity does Thailand have and how can they help Thailand grow?

LEARNING ASSIGNMENTS AND ACTIVITIES

1. Assume that you are working for a multinational company. Your head office has sent you to replace the previous country manager in Thailand, who had some problems working with the local staff which led to a drop in performance and productivity. What would be your strategy to solve the overall problem?

2. Search for more information on the Philosophy of Sufficiency Economy on the internet. Conduct a debate on its advantages and disadvantages for doing business in today's world.

3. Having the information on Thailand, discuss the strengths and weaknesses for doing business in this country when compared with other Asian countries.

MOONRISE AT TONGSAI

Management Thai style[3]

The Tongsai Bay Cottages & Hotel is a 5-star hotel in Samui Island, Suratthani province, south of Thailand. Twenty years ago, while sailing past Tongsai Bay, a hotel chain tycoon Akorn Hunetrakul was so enchanted by its beauty that he decided to buy a piece of land in the bay area and started a hotel business with only a few small cottages. The hotel was later expanded with more one-storey cottages and a three-storey building with 75 rooms. His business concept was not to build a skyscraper which would become an eyesore on the island, not to cut down any coconut trees unless necessary, and to hire local people, especially those in the community surrounding the hotel.

When Akorn fell ill, he decided to sell all his other 10 hotels in the Imperial group and kept only Tongsai Bay Hotel. After his death, the hotel was passed on to his wife and then his son, Thanakorn and his wife Saisiri, who is currently managing director of the hotel. The new generation's management followed the Philosophy of Sufficiency Economy and emphasized even more strongly natural and environmental conservation. The new vision for the hotel was explicitly announced to everyone in the organization, 'We will neither increase the occupancy nor expand our hotel. Instead, we will maintain and improve what we already have, because we don't want to be in debt and take risk. We will remain prosperous as we are now.'

Today, Tongsai Bay has 83 rooms situated on 72 rais (about 11.5 hectares). The hotel has 250 employees who receive good wages. The hotel management was confident in the abilities of Thai people and tried to select Thai staff members before hiring foreigners. They believe Thai people should be given a chance to develop their careers in hotel management in order to compete with foreigners. This practice is in contrast to other major 5-star hotels where they usually hire foreign executives. The staff at Tongsai Bay have received very positive comments from their guests for being friendly, hospitable, caring and eager to help. Aside from the beauty of the island and the accommodation, the quality of the staff is another competitive advantage that draws customers back to Tongsai Bay Hotel. The management believes that only happy employees can deliver quality service.

In past years, Tongsai Bay Hotel has made enough profit to be able to sustain itself. The owners invest within these profits and do not overinvest through bank loans. Not only do they not believe in borrowing, they also save the profits for a rainy day. In the event of any economic crisis, they can use their savings to help the staff for a certain period of time. These savings are thus their immunity.

The second immunity is that the hotel accepts payment in Thai baht rather than US dollars. While many hotels charge their guests in US dollars, Tongsai Bay Hotel continues to charge in the local currency as they believe that earning Thai baht does not involve them in complications arising from foreign exchange fluctuations.

As mentioned earlier, natural and environmental preservation is an integral part of Tongsai Hotel business management and the hotel has initiated a 'green project' to use natural resources economically. Garbage management at Tongsai Bay Hotel is handled very seriously. Bags of different colours are used to sort out different kinds of garbage: wet, dry, poisonous, biodegradable. The hotel staff are also strictly prohibited from mistreating or killing animals or cutting down trees. Large trees are preserved and more are planted to provide food for birds and other wildlife. While other luxury hotels may have to spend a lot on landscaping and maintaining their gardens the Tongsai Bay allows nature to take care of itself. They also grow their own produce in an organic garden and the guests benefit from this chemical-free produce. To further encourage the protection of animals and the environ-ment, specialists from nature foundations are invited to educate the hotel staff. More-over, in mid 2006, Thanakorn donated 5,000 rais (over 800 hectares) to the local government to turn it into a 'community forest' to preserve water sources and feeding areas for wildlife on the island.

After 20 years, The Tongsai Bay Cottages & Hotel has changed very little, especially in its assets and investment. But what has changed is that there are more green areas with more trees that have grown bigger, more birds, insects and other wildlife, more happy faces, and the increasing reputation of The Tongsai Bay Cottages & Hotel.

QUESTIONS

1. In your opinion, is The Tongsai Bay Cottages & Hotel a successful business? What are your criteria for a successful business?
2. Do you think the management style at Tongsai Bay can be applied in other types of business or industry (aside from the hotel business)? If yes, which types and how? If no, why not?
3. From the case, which aspects of management seem to be typical for Thailand?
4. 'Doing business and nature conservation should go hand-in-hand and this will lead to a win–win result.' Do you agree with this statement? Explain and justify your point of view.

INTERESTING WEB LINKS

Official Thailand tourism site: http://thai.tourismthailand.org
General statistics on Thailand: http://portal.nso.go.th
Thailand Economy and business: http://www.boi.go.th
Sufficiency Economy site: http://www.sufficiencyeconomy.org

Notes

1   The original four Asian 'Tigers' are Hong Kong, South Korea, Taiwan and Singapore.
2   A project to promote the local industry through the manufacturing of attractive local specialty products. The movement was originally started in Japan. Each village identifies the outstanding product(s) it wants to promote. Tambon means 'village' in English. (Also see Key Concepts).
3   This case is based on publicly available information. It is intended solely to stimulate class discussion.

REFERENCES

Board of Investment (BOI) (2008). Available at http://www.boi.go.th.

Dao, T.L. and Sorensen, O.J. (2007). The interplay between expatriates and local managers from learning perspective. The 3rd VDIB-Workshop in Hanoi. November.

Hofstede, G. and Hofstede, G.J. (2005). *Cultures and Organizations: Software of the Mind*. Revised and expanded 2nd edn. New York, NY: McGraw-Hill.

Holmes, H. and Tangtongtavy, S. (1997). *Working with the Thais*. 4th edn. Bangkok: White Lotus.

Kantabutra, S. (2005). *Applying Sufficiency Economy Philosophy in Business Organizations: A case of Sa Paper Preservation House*. Unpublished manuscript, Sufficiency Economy Unit, Office of National Economic and Social Development Board, Thailand.

Kantabutra, S. (2008). *Development of the Sufficiency Economy Philosophy in the Thai Business Sector: Evidence, Future Research & Policy Implications*. Available at http://www.sufficiencyeconomy.org/en/files/26.pdf.

Krongkaew, K. (ed.) (1994). *The Making of the Fifth Tiger: Thailand's Industrialisation and its Consequences*. Armonk, NY: M.E. Sharpe.

Krongkaew, M. (2003). Available at http://kyotoreview.cseas.kyoto-u.ac.jp/issue/issue3/article_292.html.

Kusumavalee, S. (2005). *Applying Sufficiency Economy Philosophy in Business Organizations: A case of Siam Cement Group*. Unpublished manuscript, Sufficiency Economy Unit, Office of National Economic and Social Development Board, Thailand.

NESDB (2007). *The Seventh National Economic Development Plan*. Bangkok: National Economic and Social Development Board.

Nuttavuthisit, K. (2005). *Applying Sufficiency Economy Philosophy in Business Organizations: A case of Pranda Jewelry*. Unpublished manuscript, Sufficiency Economy Unit, Office of National Economic and Social Development Board, Thailand.

Onishi, J. (2006). *Working Japanese: Conflict, Cultural Difference, and the Japanese Multinational in Southeast Asia*. Philippines: CRC Foundation, Inc.

Piboolsravut, P. (2004). *Sufficiency Economy*. Available at http://www.allbusiness.com/finance/147694-1.html.

Ralston, D.A., Nguyen, V.T., and Napier, N.K. (1999). A comparative study of the work values of North and South Vietnamese managers. *Journal of International Business Studies*, **30**(4): 655–72.

Ratanajongkol, S., Davey, H. and Low, M. (2006). Corporate social reporting in Thailand: The news is all good and increasing. *Qualitative Research in Accounting and Management*, **3**(1): 67–83.

Ryan, L. (2000). The 'Asian economic miracle' unmasked: The political economy of the reality. *International Journal of Social Economics*, **27**(7/8/9/10): 802–15.

Shinawatra, T. (2003). The Opening Address at the 10th APEC Finance Ministers' Meeting, 4 September.

Thai Chamber of Commerce (2008). *Sufficiency Economy: A New Philosophy in the Global World – 100 Interviews with Business Professionals*. Bangkok: Thai Chamber of Commerce.

Warr, P.G. (2000). Is growth good for the poor? Thailand's boom and bust. *International Journal of Social Economics*, **27**(7/8/9/10): 862–77.

Warr, P.G. and Nidhiprabha, B. (1996). *Thailand's Macroeconomic Miracles: Stable Adjustment and Sustained Growth*. Washington, DC and Kuala Lumpur: World Bank and Oxford University Press.

World Bank (1993). *East Asia's Economic Miracle*. New York: Oxford University Press.

The World Bank Group. (2008). Available at http://devdata.worldbank.org.

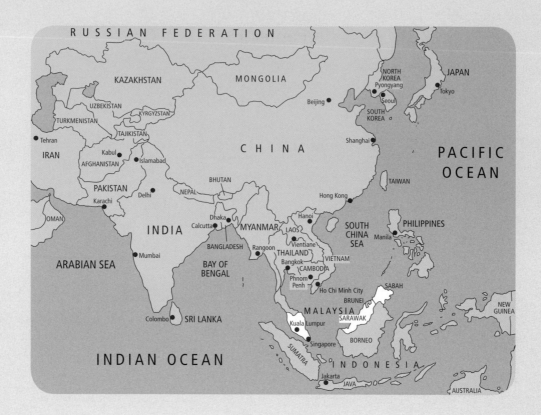

Chapter outline

- Overview of the Malaysian economy
- Economic development through the New Economic Policy (NEP)
- Malaysian culture and management
- Leadership and decision making
- Human resource management
- Corporate social responsibility and corporate citizenship
- Living and working in Malaysia

Chapter objectives

After reading this chapter, you should be able to:

1. Understand the influence of the NEP on Malaysian businesses
2. Identify the various Malaysian management styles in leadership and decision making
3. Understand the practice of human resource management in Malaysia
4. Identify what Malaysian businesses are doing to fulfil their role as corporate citizens

Chapter 15

Management in Malaysia

Sow Hup Chan

OVERVIEW OF THE MALAYSIAN ECONOMY

Malaysia is a federation of 13 states and three territories. The transformation of her economy since independence in 1957 has been spectacular. Following the successful implementation of the Industrialization Plan in 1985, Malaysia is one of the most developed ASEAN countries. Compared to her dependence on agricultural industries and primary commodities in the 1960s, Malaysia has become a diversified and modern export-driven economy.

At the time of writing, Malaysia has a stable economy with a gross domestic product (GDP) growth of 6.3 per cent[1] in 2007. Exports such as electrical and electronic products, cars and motorcycles, textiles and apparel, as well as palm oil-based, rubber-based and wood-based products played a crucial role in sustaining the rapid economic growth. Manufactured goods, especially electronics and semiconductor products, are the major contributors to the nation's GDP. Other significant contributors to the economy are commodities such as palm oil and palm oil-based products, crude petroleum, liquefied natural gas (LNG) and petroleum products. The economy is targeted to grow at 6.3 per cent[2] during the entire Third Industrial Master Plan (IMP3) 2006–20 period.

Blessed with rich natural resources, an industrious population of approximately 27.17 million,[3] and literacy rate of approximately 93.5 per cent,[4] Malaysia is the world's 19th largest exporting country according to the World Trade Organization (WTO)'s International Trade Report for 2006 and was ranked 23rd largest importer in 2006.[5] Malaysia's total trade in 2007, valued at RM1.1 trillion, was the second year trade surpassed the RM1 trillion mark.[6] Malaysia continues to enjoy a healthy surplus in external trade, has strong international reserves and high national savings. The average income of Malaysians has increased by 2.5 times within the past two decades.[7] Hard-core poverty was down to 1 per cent[8] while unemployment remained low at approximately 3.6 per cent.[9]

The inflation rate spiralled to a 27-year high at 8.5 per cent[10] from the previous 3.3 per cent[11] due to the fuel price hike. Malaysia has a labour force of 11.5 million with approximately 49.9 per cent involved in the service sector, 29 per cent in the manufacturing sector, 13.3 per cent in agriculture, 7.4 per cent in construction and 0.4 per cent in mining.[12]

Malaysia's pro-business policies provide opportunities for growth and profit. The government has invested heavily in economic infrastructure such as roads, airports and utilities, and recognized that further income growth requires a better educated workforce and a more competitive business environment. Privatization was a policy, however the programme slowed as a result of the 1997–9 economic downturn. Nevertheless, the private sector is expected to play a central role in assisting Malaysia to achieve a fully developed nation status by 2020 as declared in *Wawasan 2020* (Vision 2020).

ECONOMIC DEVELOPMENT THROUGH THE NEW ECONOMIC POLICY (NEP)

When Malaysia gained her independence, the economy was monopolized by the ethnic Chinese. Resulting from the May 1969 socio-economic strife was the New Economic Policy (NEP) formulated at the commencement of the Second Malaysia Plan (1971–5) aimed at eradicating poverty among the population irrespective of race, and at restructuring society to eliminate the identification of race with economic function. It was planned that by 1990, 30 per cent of the ownership of Malaysian companies would be in the hands of the *Bumiputeras* (literally, 'sons of the soil'), 40 per cent in the hands of the ethnic Chinese and Indians, and the remaining 30 per cent in the hands of foreign investors.

A key feature of the NEP was to elevate the status of the economically disenfranchised *Bumiputeras* through positive discrimination. Policies introduced included requiring firms to offer employment opportunities to *Bumiputera* individuals, requiring foreign and domestic non-manufacturing firms to take on *Bumiputera* partners (usually 30 per cent of share capital), requiring new listings on *Bursa Malaysia* (formerly the Kuala Lumpur Stock Exchange) to issue at least 30 per cent of its initial offering to *Bumiputera* shareholders, and making numerous funds available for the exclusive use of *Bumiputeras* to obtain finance.

With the NEP in place, government-sponsored enterprises aggressively advanced into all industries and ended up gaining a monopolistic position in some. Limits were imposed on the expansion of ethnic Chinese-owned businesses by restricting entry into various industries. Setbacks for ethnic Chinese businesses in key areas included banking. Laws requiring the participation of *Bumiputera* capital in certain types of project undertaken, and a number of other restrictions posed difficulties for local ethnic Chinese entrepreneurs in the course of doing business.

The state policies and market forces altered the control and ownership in the ethnic Chinese family businesses by imposing new licensing regulations and requiring companies to restructure their ownership and employment structures. Over time ethnic Chinese companies had to provide not just cosmetic measures and rent-seeking opportunities (see Key Concepts) for Malay[13] individuals and companies, but also meaningful participation and real decision-making powers (Jesudason, 1997). Public companies which have adjusted to the new realities, such as Genting *Berhad* and Lion Corporation *Berhad*, continue to retain family control while other public companies, such as Palmco Holdings *Berhad*, a palm-oil refining and manufacturing company, are no longer family controlled companies but companies with family interests. Nevertheless, many family businesses controlled by the second and third generation family members have been professionalized and are willing to share power and management with outsiders. Ethnic Chinese family businesses without clear-cut succession plans, however, have difficulty maintaining unity particularly when second and third generation family members are involved.[14]

There are three distinct types of business enterprises in Malaysia: state-owned companies (now referred to as government-linked companies (GLCs)); joint ventures or foreign owned companies; and local private businesses. A short description of each follows.

Government-linked Companies

The state directly intervened in productive activities and acquisition of economic assets to increase *Bumiputera* ownership of capital and economic participation. Productive enterprises and various Malay equity funds were set up (Jesudason, 1988). The government holds equity stakes, generally minority shares, in a wide range of domestic companies,[15] usually large players in key sectors, and can exert considerable influence over their operations.

Holding companies like Perbadanan Nasional (PERNAS) *Berhad* and Renong *Berhad* were created in the 1970s. State-owned companies like HICOM (The Heavy Industries Corporation of Malaysia) *Berhad* was launched to deal with steelworks, motorcycle and engine manufacture and other heavy industry, while Petroliam Nasional *Berhad* (PETRONAS) was established with the overall aim of controlling strategic resources such as oil and gas production. The number of state-owned economic enterprises grew tremendously from 109 in 1970 to 1,014 in 1985 (Jesudason, 1988) and to 1,100 by 1990 (Salazar, 2004). Generally, the state-owned enterprises (SOEs)[16] are involved in a wide range of activities, mainly in industries which require large investment outlays such as plantations, exploitation of natural resources such as oil, steel plants, public utilities, airlines, construction and heavy industrial machines and equipment. While PETRONAS has grown into a well-managed multinational, HICOM[17] for example has turned out to be a painful failure. A majority of the SOEs recorded a net loss. The SOEs' deficit reaching more than RM6.5 billion in 1984 led to privatization.

Following the Asian financial crisis, the government granted assistance to troubled corporations on the basis of three criteria: national interest, strategic interest, and equity considerations under *Bumiputera* policies. Thus, many large scale corporations which the government had privatized and which were controlled by the politically well-connected were bailed out, renationalized or bought back by the government to prevent their collapse.[18] In 2004, the government oversaw 40 listed GLCs in various sectors which accounted for around 34 per cent of the total market capitalization of *Bursa Malaysia*.

Joint Ventures and Foreign-owned Companies

Under the IMP3, tax incentives and a liberal policy on foreign equity participation and employment of expatriates were granted to encourage the establishment of promoted services activities. Industries that utilize Malaysian mineral and agricultural resources, export most or all local production, or involve the transfer of high or new technology can also benefit from attractive investment incentives. The government permits 100 per cent foreign ownership in the manufacturing sectors, has extended the full tax exemption incentive to firms with Pioneer status (see Key Concepts) from 10 to 15 years and encourages joint ventures between Malaysian and foreign companies although it limits foreign equity and employment.

Malaysia is encouraging foreign investment in Islamic banking by allowing foreign businesses to set up wholly-owned foreign currency operations, and is actively wooing foreign investment in the information technology industry, particularly in the Multimedia Super Corridor (MSC), Asia's version of Silicon Valley. Despite stiff competition for foreign direct investment (FDI) worldwide, Malaysia continues to draw FDI. There are more than 4,000 international companies from over 50 countries making Malaysia their offshore base.

Local Private Businesses

The Chinese have had a long tradition of entrepreneurship. Handing over of family businesses from father to son was the norm. Although the *Bumiputera* community was used to being either employed in civil service or focused in farming, their attitude towards entrepreneurship has improved. The assistance provided to existing and potential *Bumiputera* entrepreneurs has led to a significant increase in the establishment of *Bumiputera* enterprises, both in the corporate and non-corporate sectors. Nevertheless, ethnic Chinese private businesses still dominate.

The government continues to be supportive of entrepreneurship and has taken various steps to promote the development of entrepreneurs in general including the setting up of the Ministry of Entrepreneurship in 1995 and providing a conducive economic environment, various financing and funding schemes and tax incentives, as well as business advisory centres. Numerous sources of funding are also available to entrepreneurs and small- and medium-scale industries (SMIs).

SUMMARY POINTS

■ The NEP was an ambitious socio-economic restructuring programme

■ Numerous policies were introduced to encourage *Bumiputera* involvement in the economic community

REFLECTIVE QUESTIONS

■ In your opinion, had the NEP been successful in its stated objectives when the policy ended officially in 1990? Did the programme end in 1990? Can you think of other countries that might have similar affirmative action programmes?

MALAYSIAN CULTURE AND MANAGEMENT

The management practices in Malaysia were greatly influenced by the British. Managers and administrators practise both the Western and Asian style of management. Small businesses mostly adopt the Asian style of management. For instance, Chinese family-owned businesses run their businesses in the traditional Chinese manner – as either a clan-based or closely-knit family operation. Larger businesses, multinational companies (MNCs) and foreign-owned companies are managed more with the Western approach while incorporating some local ethnic values and practices that work elsewhere such as Quality Control Circles (QCCs) and Management by Objectives (MBO). The Look East Policy (LEP) also encouraged Malaysians to incorporate some Korean and Japanese work ethics into management.

The workplace scenario is culturally diverse. The three main ethnic groups – Malays, Chinese and Indians have remained largely separated, making it difficult to speak of a 'Malaysian culture', let alone a 'Malaysian style of management'. Each ethnic group has its own ethnic orientation at work while managing to work together relatively well. Despite differences in work orientation and ways of thinking, there are similarities in work-related values. Although the Malay belief system and ways of thinking are based on the *Budi* complex[19] and the Chinese ways of thinking are driven by Confucianism, both belief systems have a holistic view of self, are collectivist, long-term and relationship-oriented, make decisions through subjective knowing, view time as subjective and relative, and desire to be in harmony with nature (Storz, 1999).

When Hofstede (1991) defined the value systems for Malaysia, he found low levels of individualism, medium levels of masculinity and equally high levels of power distance in the three ethnic groups. He considered the Chinese and Indians in Malaysia to be more long-term oriented than the Malays, and suggested that the Chinese are more flexible than the other two groups in terms of uncertainty avoidance. In other words, they are better prepared to deal with uncertainty avoidance while their Malay counterparts choose work clarity as being of high importance (see Abdullah, 2001). Malays are slightly more oriented towards relationship building, prefer stability, and honour traditions while the Chinese prefer to incorporate business dealings into hierarchical relationships, adapt better to risks, and possess qualities such as perseverance and thrift (Lim, 1998).

The Malay culture, developed from the close-knit social unit of the *kampong* (village), provides the foundation for them to develop a sense of responsibility to help friends, relatives and neighbours in the name of *gotong-royong* (mutual cooperation) (Lim, 1998). Malay managers place more importance on relationships than their Chinese counterparts (Abdullah and Lim, 2001). Their preference for greater hierarchy than Chinese managers suggests: a stronger tendency for authoritative leadership; over-centralized decision making at the top management level by Malay chief executives; and subordinates continuing to accept centralized power and dependence on superiors for directions (Lim, 2001). A Malay manager may emphasize the values of togetherness, harmony, relationships and 'give and take' while a Chinese manager may emphasize the values of hard work and financial incentives, while an Indian manager may prefer respect for elders and harmony (Abdullah, 2001). On the other hand, the Chinese, are often portrayed as being more materialistic than the Malays – highly inspired by financial rewards and more achievement oriented (Lim, 2001) and seem to strike a balance between maintaining good interpersonal relationships and task achievement (Lim, 1998).

The common Malaysian business values that have emerged include collectivism, paternalism, respect for authority and hierarchy, and being relationship-oriented (Abdullah, 2001; Hassan and Ahmad, 2001), supported by values such as harmony, loyalty and face-saving. Paternalism, which is interconnected to a strong hierarchy, has modernized as subordinates are nowadays encouraged to communicate directly with each other.

Generally, cultural values such as tolerance, respect for elders, courtesy and compromise guide organizational behaviour. There is liberal acceptance of all religious practices and there is a tradition of tolerance in the workplace. For instance, a Malay manager may conduct a 'religious blessing' before the start of an important event such as the opening of a new bridge while a Chinese manager may precede the opening of a new business with the lion dance. A Chinese manager may also consult a *feng shui* (geomancy) expert to help make decisions to avoid adverse consequences such as the possibility of accidents or loss on the company's bottom line. It is a priority to ensure *feng shui* in business building designs, signboards, office layout, lighting, colour-scheme and even the colour of furniture and the setting to match the horoscope of the manager, the overall setting of the boardroom or meeting rooms as well as the seating position of the boss. Fortune tellers are also consulted to select auspicious days to move office, launch a new product or commemorate a significant event.

A Chinese businessperson may refuse to deal at a price which includes the figure 14. Similarly, property developers are concerned with unlucky numbers such as 4, 13, and 14 as reflected in Table 15.1. A way must be found to conclude the transaction without using unlucky numbers and a 4th floor might be replaced by a 3A floor. Home addresses in some upper middle class areas with numbers 4, 24, 94 might be replaced with 2A, 22A and 92A instead. Spirit houses and *Datuk* spirit houses may be built as illustrated by Goh (2005):

> Property developers in Penang (Malaysia) were erecting shrines and performing rituals to propitiate a Malay–Muslim guardian spirit of local sacred places known interchangeably as *keramat* or *Datuk Kong* during a period of euphoric economic growth in Malaysia in the early 1990s.

Table 15.1 Superstitions with numbers

Property around Kuala Lumpur	Missing floor
Wisma MPL	No 4th and 13th floor
Plaza See Hoy Chan	No 13th floor
Menara Aik Hua	No 13th floor
Wisma Lim Foo Yong	No 13th floor
Menara MIDF	No 13th floor
Menara ING	No 14th floor

Malaysians appreciate 'high context' communication where messages are more indirect. A lot of meaning has to be 'sensed' and analogies or metaphors might be used to communicate concern to avoid hurting the subordinate's feelings. The subordinate is expected to read between the lines and change their behaviour accordingly.

As a high power distance country, subordinates are dependent on their superiors, expect them to make decisions and not off-load any responsibilities on to them. They abide by the decisions of those who are in power, accept delegated tasks without too many questions, and will pretend to understand the instructions given in order to appear polite towards their superiors. They show deference by not challenging or even clarifying their bosses' judgments unless provoked, tend to suppress anger and will offer proposals rather than arguments since asserting viewpoints too strongly and directly shows impoliteness. Disagreements are seldom articulated in a frank manner because of the importance of group loyalty, cohesiveness, harmony and face. Generally, subordinates compromise, show high tolerance for ambiguity, avoid vertical friction and may even appear unassertive, too humble, conservative and submissive to their expatriate managers.

The cultural influence on leadership and decision making will be elaborated in the following section.

LEADERSHIP AND DECISION MAKING

The successive government policies have resulted in a pluralist approach to business and management. Leaders in GLCs tend to run their organizations in a similar way to government departments. As the workforce is generally Muslim, the leadership incorporates Islamic values rather than using money to motivate. There is less authority and freedom of action for making decisions as decisions have to be referred to the top leadership.

The major principle of family-based businesses is family exclusivity, informed by patriachical notions of tight ownership control and a delimited, face-to-face understanding of trust (Jesudason, 1997). The CEO or leader is very much in charge and often confides and assigns control to close relatives. Family connections within the clan, as well as political connections, matter. The late Tan Sri Lim Goh Tong for example ran his business closely. The business remains family controlled after passing to his son, who internationalized the operation. Many firms have remained family controlled despite becoming very large. Businesses belonging to the second and third generations of early entrepreneurs, however, are increasingly being run by professional managers – either because the younger generations have gained managerial qualifications, or by hiring professional managers. Businesses with political connections are increasingly passed from family leadership to professional management. Similarly, smaller companies and those more rooted in family practices are willingly seeking Malay partners. Naturally, the styles of leadership of the new partners influence the culture and subcultures within the organization.

Unlike early successful entrepreneurs who changed from rags to riches in one generation, having started with humble beginnings and limited education, most Malaysian business leaders are now educated. Despite their education, there is a need to adapt to local values in conducting business operations. Like other Asians, they adopt the harmonious and humanistic approach. Hence, leadership styles which promote harmonious relationships such as being humble, cordial and open are favoured.

Effective leaders inspire a shared vision and instil a sense of commitment to the organization by creating a 'family' atmosphere, since employees are more willing to innovate and try out new ideas when working with a nurturing 'parent' who does not reprimand but provides room for growth in the organization. They motivate their subordinates by developing good interpersonal working relationships with others in the organization and build a supportive organizational climate through close supervision and paternalism. As paternalistic leaders they develop trust and respect as a 'caring parent', sensitive to various cultural values and norms in the workplace. They also try to reduce social, physical and power distance, create a comfortable working atmosphere and develop a sense of belonging, through getting together around 'food' in the office, or picking up the bill when entertaining outside the work environment.

Leaders are respected when they are perceived as competent, inspiring, honest, credible, nurturing, caring and supportive. Leaders with *budi bahasa* (good manners in language) expressed through a proper choice of words and appropriate body gestures are valued by Malaysians. As employees are more receptive to the feedback and appraisal from a trusted leader, successful leaders often make a great effort to show *budi bahasa*, develop trust and understand their employees in order to maintain their dignity, support their work and personal needs, as well as provide any necessary coaching. Behaviour considered part of *budi bahasa* includes not being forthright, assertive or aggressive, not responding to a request with a direct 'no', not being too blunt or direct in expressing one's views, and not causing interpersonal conflict or 'loss of face' (Abdullah et al., 2001).

If stress and tension are felt during a meeting, the father figure usually steps in to offer 'wisdom' on the issue, succinctly, in a polite manner and drawing upon the superordinate goal of promoting harmony and peace. Compromise is often preferred. Sometimes, a respectable third party may be used to resolve a conflict or to deal with ambiguities, uncertainties and when communicating negative news.

Adaptation and accommodation of one another is valued over confrontation because frankness and open confrontation contradict the concept of face. While one may be considered tactless and unrefined for doing otherwise, the confrontational approach is also viewed as aggressive, quarrelsome, argumentative and insensitive to preserving group harmony. Such an approach may cause affected parties discomfort leading to withdrawal from a win–win solution. In negotiation, concessions are expected and given. Both parties should adopt the win–win approach because the relationship will break down once a party is made to lose face. If that happens, it would be impossible for the negotiation to proceed further.

The respect for hierarchy and status in the workplace also requires younger managers first to gain the respect, trust and support of the older subordinates before any work problems can be discussed. Many managers feel uneasy about counselling their underperforming subordinates, while some will tolerate poor performance as face-to-face discussions run counter to the issues of face and the importance placed on maintaining harmonious relationships.

Although decision making tends to be autocratic and top-down in most firms, it is common practice to look for precedents. Matters are often discussed at considerable length until common consensus is reached so that harmonious relationships are maintained. Group problem solving and decision making among subordinates, especially when dealing with new issues or projects, is preferred and the *gotong-royong* spirit needs to be taken into account. Since subordinates are not forthcoming in putting across their opinions unless invited, leaders need to be skilful in extracting information from less articulate members without causing them stress or embarrassment. It should be noted that group interest need not necessarily take precedence over personal interest as the Malays are not keen to sacrifice family or religious obligations for the company (Rashid et al., 1997: 58).

Regardless of whether a decision is made collectively or individually, the process followed is influenced by the social and cultural values of the person involved. Shephard (2001) identified several factors that may have an impact on the way decisions are made including the role of age, supernatural beliefs, *feng shui*, religious rituals, astrological signs, harmony and goodwill, consensus, acceptance of authority and face. These are summarized in Table 15.2.

Table 15.2 Malaysian values for management

Malaysian Values	Examples
Respect for age, status/authority	Elders take the lead in decision making Subordinates are invited to contribute ideas Dissenting views are expressed elsewhere
Harmony	Be sensitive to cultural nuances Allow each ethnic group to perform its own rituals (to fulfil religious obligations) since superstitions have an impact on their lives and decisions Avoid racism Seek consensus Group decision making among peers Promote a familial work environment Avoid conflict at all cost
Relationships	Respect age and social hierarchy Understand the likes and dislikes of key role players Develop 'connections' with high status associates or individuals with titles
Face	Reprimand in private Avoid negative criticism. Feedback, even if constructive, is often regarded as personal attack on an individual's character Give praise whenever the opportunity arises Communicate decisions indirectly Be vague, delay saying 'no' openly, seek clarification, invite and consider other options

Malaysians are rather accommodating in the use of time. Although employees are on time in the office, the need to build relationships over morning coffee and food prior to work is the norm in many organizations. The tendency to procrastinate and not to be precise on time when making decisions is due to the fear of loss of face or damaging relationships if the decision proves erroneous. They are unlikely to be too specific with meeting times. A negotiation might be set to begin at about 9 a.m. rather than at 9 a.m. sharp, while a ceremony which is scheduled to start at 3 p.m. might not get started until 3:30 p.m. When making business appointments, it should be noted that all states (with the exception of Kedah, Kelantan and Terengganu) observe Saturdays and Sundays as weekly rest days.[20]

Since Islamic values have increasingly been incorporated in the legislative and administrative systems in Malaysia, organizational leaders must be responsive to the local cultural and religious ethos in their operations and human resource management strategies. Some implications for management are shown in the following box.

Spotlight on Islamic values: Implications for management
The following Islamic values and practices have implications for management:

- ◼ Prohibition on drinking alcohol can limit after-work social activities
- ◼ Limited interaction with the opposite gender exists as Muslim women are not allowed to shake hands with men, look them in the eye when communicating, or be alone with them
- ◼ Praying five times daily requires management to prepare a suitable prayer room for each gender and allow time off from work for prayers

- A reduction in expected productivity during the *Ramadhan* month when Muslim employees are fasting during daylight. An understanding employer would not assign strenuous tasks to them whenever possible. One should not eat or drink in their presence either
- Friday is the day Muslims congregate to pray in the local mosque, hence, Muslim employees are expected to be away from work between 12:30 p.m. and 2:45 p.m.
- Using the left hand is considered rude. All good acts, eating, even when a fork and spoon are used, touching someone, giving or receiving something, pointing at another person or at something should be done using the right hand
- The Malays do not eat pork and only eat *halal* food. Cafeteria or canteen arrangements need to be considered
- All Muslims are expected, if possible, to perform the '*hajj*' pilgrimage to Mecca at least once in their lives. Employers need to consider time off for them to fulfil their religious obligations.

As the relationship between employer and employee is seen as one of cooperation and siblinghood, employers are obligated to look after the welfare of their workers by providing a safe working environment and offering just reward for their labour. On the other hand, employees are obligated to perform their work with due diligence.

SUMMARY POINTS

- Malaysian managers practise both the Western and Asian style of management.
- There is a tradition of tolerance in the workplace.
- Leadership and decision making tends to be autocratic and top-down.

HUMAN RESOURCE MANAGEMENT

The MNCs and large corporations tend to have a more elaborate and structured recruitment process compared with most firms which use a more simplistic approach, such as relying on recommendations from subordinates, friends or family members. The tendency to favour 'word of mouth' recommendations arises because of obligations to perform well or risk embarrassing the person who made the recommendation. Methods for recruiting new knowledge workers include channels such as 'internal contacts', networking, agency searches, websites, media advertisements and university's placement offices. Internal contacts are preferred as this shortens the learning curve and allows work to proceed more smoothly due to the expertise and reputation from a previous organization. Nepotism is still believed to be strong at the lowest level, especially when hiring is handled by the line supervisor (for example hiring production workers in manufacturing facilities), and at very high levels (for example hiring the 'know-who' people). Specifying a preference for *Bumiputera* candidates in job advertisements is acceptable. Doing otherwise is unacceptable, hence the advertisement may emphasize certain language or dialect proficiency, and appears in the vernacular newspapers. Job interviews are often conducted with an indirect approach in order to draw out the applicant's ability and confidence in performing the job. The rejection process is handled in a polite manner, either with a letter, or by informing the person who recommended the applicant. Alternatively, applicants can form their own conclusion when they do not hear from the company after a lapse of time.

Reference checking and verification of qualifications is not common practice, but is considered essential for professional positions such as financial management and senior executive positions. Even so, the new employer needs to read between the lines as references often are indirect and reluctant to provide negative information so as not to 'break someone else's rice bowl'.

Malaysians are money oriented and inclined to job hop, with little hesitation about better financial offers (Kawabe, 1991). They are unwilling to stay with their organizations for more than three years (Lim, 2001). Thus, promotion based on seniority no longer works as better access to tertiary education enables faster promotion. High performers also tend to leave for firms that reward rapid advancement. Although seniority still minimally counts to a varying degree in pay decisions, most companies practise performance-based reward systems. There is no equal pay for equal work policy in the private sector so when both sexes are employed to do the same work, men are often paid more.

Although the compensation and rewards for knowledge workers are similar to other developed countries, firms are facing aggressive competition to attract and retain talented employees. Annual turnover rates have been high and above 15 per cent (Malaysian Employers Federation, 2004, 2005). Since knowledge workers are becoming a more crucial resource for the growth of the MSC status companies, the quick turnover and shortage of professional workers leads to poaching from within the industry and unrelated industries, escalating competition in wages, compensation and rewards packages and further challenges in human resource development.

As one of the largest employers in the country, the Malaysian Public Service has taken steps to develop and retain their employees. Among the major HRD-related initiatives introduced are the Malaysian Remuneration System (MRS or *Sistem Saraan Malaysia*), training and development activities and ICT-related projects such as the Human Resource Management Information System (HRMIS). The MRS introduced in November 2002 is a comprehensive remuneration package designed to meet the public service requirement in the knowledge-based economy. It inculcates the culture of continuous learning among government employees and develops knowledge workers in the public service to meet the national objectives as expressed in *Wawasan 2020*. The system consists of four core components:

- Emphasis on competency
- Improvement of career development
- Modification to the salary structure, allowances and perquisites
- Improvement of service conditions (Mohd. Yusoff, 2003).

The government also provides study leave and sponsorship facilities for public servants to pursue both full-time and part-time studies.

Industrial Relations and Training

The industrial relations in the country are harmonious, with minimal trade disputes that result in strikes. Labour relations are generally non-confrontational and strikes are extremely rare although theoretically legal. Dismissing a redundant employee is not difficult. There is no unemployment compensation programme. However, workers are protected against loss of income due to sickness, injury, old age and death. The simple employment procedures and no national minimum wage help businesses to stay competitive.

The transformation towards a knowledge-based economy and the development of regional growth corridors is increasing the demand for skilled and knowledge workers in the country. Hiring and keeping good knowledge workers remains a challenge although there is a large pool of unemployed graduates. Graduates with a poor command of the English language (which employers stress as a major requisite in selection), take an average of one year to get a job. The education system has been blamed for creating a workforce neither skilled enough for high-end jobs nor cheap enough for low-end ones (Clifford, 1996). Nevertheless, the government is doing its part to help graduates obtain employability skills in their retraining schemes. To improve the efficiency of job-matching, the Electronic Labour Exchange is used to match employers with suitable potential employees while an internet-based training management system is used to match workers who need training or retraining with specific training providers.

The government made it an obligation for foreign companies to provide technical training for their employees. The Human Resources Development Fund (HRDF) launched in 1993 facilitates training, retraining and skills upgrading. Employers in the manufacturing and service sectors contributing to this fund are eligible to apply for grants to subsidize the costs incurred in training and retraining their workforce.

SUMMARY POINTS

- Most firms practise a performance-based reward system.

- The Malaysian Public Service has taken numerous steps to develop and retain their employees.

- Hiring and keeping good knowledge workers remains a challenge.

REFLECTIVE QUESTIONS

- Is there a Malaysian culture or Malaysian style of management? Can you identify some possible reasons to explain why that is the case?

CORPORATE SOCIAL RESPONSIBILITY AND CORPORATE CITIZENSHIP

The arrival of MNCs and foreign corporations has created employment, provided training and transfer of technology, and at the same time improved overall the competence and skills of Malaysians as well as their quality of life by allowing them to generate wealth. The government policies ensure transfer of skills by limiting the number of expatriates so that the locals are employed whenever possible. The rapid increase in public and private businesses provided further employment, improved the quality of life of the underemployed and unemployed, created wealth for the rural citizens and improved the living standard of the rural population as a whole. However, the privatizations, reforms and later the handling of the huge loss-making conglomerates lacked transparency. Although a positive act on the part of the government, the move was seen in a negative light, especially by the international community influenced by good governance and transparency. On the one hand, the bail-outs were seen as selective and directed to those who were politically well connected. On the other hand, some view the state policies as restricting business activities and focusing entrepreneurial effort on rent-seeking behaviours, and hampering the development of *Bumiputera* entrepreneurs, as contracts awarded to *Bumiputeras* were eventually subcontracted to foreigners and non-*Bumiputeras*.

Nevertheless, the government[21] will continue with previous economic policies, including privatization, which will be carried out through open bidding in future. The current government has also stressed 'know-how' rather than 'know-who' as the basis for business success and professional managers with the 'know how' are to lead organizations. The government promoted reforms to achieve greater corporate accountability and transparency. The Malaysian Code of Corporate Governance has been introduced. Various laws were amended to improve standards of governance. Despite numerous anti-graft campaigns Malaysia went down from 39th position in 2005 to 47th position amongst 180 countries in the Transparency International Corruption Perception Index (CPI) 2008.[22]

Many public corporations are increasingly recognizing they can pursue multiple bottom lines – what some people refer to as corporate social responsibility (CSR) while pursuing profits (Chan and Simpson, 2005). More firms are recognizing their ethical responsibilities and contribution to the environment such as improving product quality and safety, and improving the rights and status of workers. Many local companies have adopted the ISO 14001 Environmental Management System standards. The wider Malaysian community is benefiting from these organizations, many of whose actions are unrelated to their business and do not appear to contribute directly to their profit.

While most big corporations have been philanthropic, contributing large sums to the development of schools, sports and games, or simply making donations to welfare organizations, other large companies have gone further. Honda Malaysia has pledged a contribution of RM5 million to WWF-Malaysia for its five-year commitment to save a Malaysian national heritage – the critically endangered Sumatran rhino, so that one day the animals might flourish unthreatened in their natural habitat. The OPTIMAL Group of Companies serve society by developing an open and trusting relationship with the local community through their proactive role in environmental conservation and education in partnership with the Malaysian Nature Society (MNS), the largest and oldest NGO in Malaysia. They influence and improve the future of the community in which they operate through activities which include restoring the mangrove and surrounding coastal vegetation to its natural state, promoting long-term awareness and sustained conservation of the ecosystem, and forming a Community River Watch Group to monitor water quality and other living organisms such as fireflies and plants along the integrated river basin. Similarly, Shell's social investment programmes are often run in partnership with other private, voluntary and community-sector organizations. Contributing to society through corporate citizenship or social investments has therefore become a major focus in many companies' efforts to demonstrate their concern for an improved Malaysia and their commitment to the society where they operate.

SUMMARY POINTS

- Privatizations, reforms and handling of the huge loss-making conglomerates lack transparency.

- 'Know-how' rather than 'know-who' is stressed.

- More organizations are demonstrating their commitment to society.

LIVING AND WORKING IN MALAYSIA

The *Barisan Nasional* (National Front) still commands strong support from the people although the political tsunami that swept the country handed the opposition coalition control of five states and increased its representation in Parliament. The opposition party's brand of multiracial politics, where Malay rights will be preserved and protected but not at the expense of the other races, perhaps looks tempting to the non-Malays. The Kuala Lumpur Composite Index has fallen by more than 17 per cent since the 8 March, 2008 general election, while the stock market's value has depreciated by more than RM100 billion to RM814.9 billion. With Datuk Seri Anwar Ibrahim's political comeback after a 10-year absence, foreign investors and fund managers are worried about a possible change in government, although other factors affecting their confidence include the global economic slowdown, lower crude palm oil prices, higher cost of raw materials, lower disposable income and inflation.

Malaysia has maintained political and economic stability, and is considered a safe country in which to live and work. The living standards have improved greatly over the decades. Many Malaysians have access to services and facilities similar to those in developed countries. Malaysians are friendly by nature and possess a high level of tolerance due to the multiracial and multicultural environment. Most Malaysians speak at least two languages.

A secular state,[23] with Islam as its official religion and a political sphere dominated by the *Bumiputeras*, there are distinct religious, social and cultural beliefs, values and norms about many issues, including the role of women in society. Some practices pertaining to specific ethnic groups have now been adopted by all Malaysians. Identifying and acknowledging the differences within any group of Malaysians is very important to living and working together harmoniously.

Occasionally, Malaysians encounter air pollution problems often blamed on fires lit to clear land in neighbouring Indonesia. The worst air pollution occurred on 11 August, 2005 when a state of emergency was announced in Port Klang and Kuala Selangor after air pollution reached dangerous levels. All workplaces in the two towns had to shut except for those providing essential services. People were advised to stay indoors and wear masks if they had to venture out.[24]

Kuala Lumpur, ranked as the 33rd most expensive city in Asia,[25] is an inexpensive city for expatriates to live in. There are over 30 international schools registered with the Ministry of Education including American- and British-style international schools as well as French, German, Japanese and Taiwanese schools that have facilities ranging from pre-school to college education. Additionally, they have easy access to modern communication systems, good healthcare and medical facilities, and various entertainment or outdoor recreational activities. In sum, expatriates on a foreign salary can expect some savings while enjoying a good lifestyle during their assignment.

Work permits for varying periods depending on the employment position are required for those seeking work in Malaysia. A permit is normally obtained by the employer for the employee. Residence status for tax purposes is determined by the duration of stay in the country. Those who stay in Malaysia for less than 182 days per year are treated as non-residents. Any foreign income received in Malaysia by a non-resident is exempted from tax. Corporate tax for the year of assessment 2008 was 26 per cent, and expatriates and their employers are exempted from compulsory contributions to the Employees Provident Fund (EPF).

In recent years, all citizens of countries recognized by Malaysia were encouraged to submit applications to live in Malaysia. Under this programme, they are allowed to purchase residential property.

CROSS-CHAPTER REFLECTIVE QUESTIONS

- In this chapter we have read that *Bumiputeras* are a unique concept pertaining to Malaysia. Do you think this is as a result of a mixed race/culture society? Can you compare a mixed race/culture society with a homogeneous society like Japan (Chapter 8) in terms of economic consequences in general as well as in terms of specific managerial aspects such as HRM?

CHAPTER SUMMARY

- Malaysia has transformed its economy since independence and has emerged as a stable and fast-growing economy in the region. Malaysia's political stability and commitment to development have been critical to its economic success.
- There are three main categories of firms: government-linked companies, joint ventures and foreign-owned companies, and local private businesses.
- The pluralization of control and ownership in the Chinese family business is a major development in the country's corporate sector.
- A distinctive Malaysian management style has yet to emerge. Values such as collectivism, paternalism, respect for authority and hierarchy, and being relationship-oriented will continue to strongly influence the management process.
- Malaysian companies are finding difficulty hiring and keeping their knowledge workers.
- Many public corporations are increasingly recognizing that they can pursue multiple bottom lines.

KEY CONCEPTS

Employees Provident Fund (EPF): A social security organization that provides retirement benefits for private sector employees and non-pensionable public service employees.

Government-linked companies (GLCs): Companies that have a primary commercial objective and in which the Malaysian Government has a direct controlling stake.

Human Resources Development Fund (HRDF): A fund aimed at encouraging manufacturing and service sector participation in skill development, skill redevelopment and skill upgrade.

Look East Policy (LEP): One of Tun Dr Mahathir Mohamad's foreign policies. He called for a 'Look East' orientation among Malaysians to model themselves on the work ethics and success of the South Koreans and the Japanese.

Malay: A person who speaks the Malay language, adheres to the Malay traditions and practises Islam. The Malays and the indigenous people like the Negritoes, Dayaks, Ibans, Kadazans, Muruts and so on, have been designated as *Bumiputera* while the Chinese, Indians and people of other ethnic minority groups are referred to as non-*Bumiputeras*.

Multimedia Super Corridor (MSC): Malaysia's most exciting initiative for the global information and communication technology (ICT) industry.

New Economic Policy (NEP): An ambitious and controversial socio-economic restructuring affirmative action programme launched by the late Prime Minister Tun Abdul Razak in 1971.

Pioneer status company: A company that obtains very favourable fiscal treatment in respect of income derived from 'promoted activities' or 'promoted products'.

Rent-seeking: Generally implies extraction of uncompensated value from others without making any contribution to productivity.

Wawasan 2020: This vision calls for a self-sufficient industrial developed nation in 2020.

REVIEW QUESTIONS

1. What are the specific features of the Malaysian economy?
2. Why has the Malaysian economy developed so fast since the 1980s?
3. What are *government-linked companies*? Why are they important in Malaysia?
4. What is typical of Malaysian management? Why should management pay attention to ethnicity when applying management approaches and when designing incentive systems?
5. What is the Malaysian Public Service doing to develop and retain their employees?
6. How are some businesses demonstrating corporate citizenship?

LEARNING ACTIVITIES AND DISCUSSIONS

1. Search for a Malaysian made *halal* product currently exported to other countries. Is that product easily available in the convenience store near you? How would one distinguish a *halal* from a non-*halal* product?
2. What do you think are some of the major challenges facing Malaysia in its attempt to become a fully developed nation by 2020? Is the country ready to deal with those challenges? Why or why not?
3. What are the main differences between Malay, Chinese and Indian management styles? What are the similarities?

AIRASIA

Becoming an ASEAN brand?

Tony Fernandes took over AirAsia (AA), a full service airline, from a Malaysian conglomerate, DRB-HICOM, at a time when the airline was not performing too well. With an initial staff of 12 and two carriers, AA has been a low-cost carrier (LCC) model in Asia since December 2001.

Based on the belief that more people will fly if fares are affordable, management introduced its 'low fare no frills' concept. The average passenger profile quickly changed from a business man flying within Malaysia to people from all walks of life, including housewives, budget travellers and natives from interior Sabah or Sarawak – customers who are not seeking luxury in their short distance trips. Indeed, flying becomes possible for even the most ordinary man as reflected in the motto 'Now everyone can fly'.

In line with its 'easy to book, easy to pay and easy to fly' approach, guests can pay for their telephone bookings by credit card or by cash at any Alliance Bank branches. This ticketless airline is constantly looking for ways to improve its services. The frequency of services between various destinations was increased over time to ensure customer convenience. Recognizing the need for package deals, AA introduced the Go Holiday programme where guests can book holiday packages online in real time.

This 'no frills' airline achieved rapid growth in market share in the domestic market and was cutting into the larger full carriers like Malaysia Airlines. AA grew quickly despite challenges like the SARS outbreak and the Asian tsunami. It extended its operations to regional markets from its hub in Kuala Lumpur. Within three years, there were flights to various destinations in Thailand and Indonesia. Another maiden service to the Special Administrative Region (SAR) of Macau was launched soon afterwards and expansion has not stopped since.

A public listed company on the Malaysia Stock Exchange since November 2004, AA flies to over 60 destinations in Malaysia, Thailand, Indonesia, Singapore, Laos, Brunei Darulssalam, Macau, China, the Philippines, Cambodia, Vietnam, Myanmar and Australia. It formed two successful joint ventures, one in Thailand through Thai AirAsia, and one in Indonesia through Indonesia AirAsia, expanded its fleet from the original two to 28, and revolutionized air travel in the ASEAN countries by offering incredibly low fares through its innovative sales channels. To date, the AirAsia group has carried over 35 million passengers. It is set to begin its budget long haul flights for Europe, the Far East and across the Pacific Rim.

QUESTIONS

1. How did AA operationalize its management policies in maximizing profits while transporting people from point A to point B safely in the shortest possible time and at the most affordable price?
2. In your opinion, what are the circumstances leading to the sale of AA by DRB-HICOM? Why do you think this? How much do you think the CEO paid for AA?

3. Despite soaring fuel prices, AA has been able to grow. Which internal and external factors have helped AA grow to its current position? How is AA managing to expand and succeed while at the same time its competitors are struggling to keep the lights on?

4. Would AA have survived under the old management of the business conglomerate? Why or why not?

Sources: AirAsia homepage http://www.airasia.com; McCloud, T. (2007). Even dreams need wings. *Travel 3 Sixty*, **1**(1): 30–4.

INTERESTING WEB LINKS

Economic and business statistics: http://www.statistics.gov.my
Human resources: http://www.mohr.gov.my
Trade and industry : http://www.miti.gov.my
Trade development : http://www.matrade.gov.my
Multimedia Super Corridor: http://www.msc.com.my
OPTIMAL: http://www.optimal.com.my/media/media_contacts.asp
Culture of Malaysia: http://www.everyculture.com/Ja-Ma/Malaysia.html

Notes

1 http://www.statistics.gov.my/english/frameset_keystats.php.

2 http://www.hlb.com.my/wb/Research/Economic_News/Malaysia/mimp3.pdf.

3 http://www.statistics.gov.my/english/frameset_keystats.php.

4 http://www.statistics.gov.my/english/frameset_news.php?file=pressedu.

5 http://www.mida.gov.my/beta/view.php?cat=53&scat=1637.

6 http://www.matrade.gov.my/cms/content.jsp?id=com.tms.cms.article.Article_hide_Malaysia's%20Trade%20Performance%202007.

7 http://www.dfat.gov.au/publications/malaysia_an_economy_transformed/malaysia_toc_&_exec_sum.pdf.

8 http://www.suhakam.org.my/docs/document_resource/ann_report2003_chap8.pdf.

9 http://www.statistics.gov.my/english/frameset_keystats.php.

10 http://www.nst.com.my/Current_News/NST/Friday/NewsBreak/20080829190912/Article/index_html.

11 http://www.statistics.gov.my/english/frameset_keystats.php?fid=b.

12 http://www.matrade.gov.my/foreignbuyer/Msiafacts.htm.

13 As Andaya and Andaya (2001]) noted, the legal definition has permitted the inclusion of immigrants from Indonesia and the southern Philippines, and even individuals from other groups. Thus in the 1991 census tabulation for example, many Indonesians who had recently become citizens were classified as Malays, while non-citizen fellows were categorized as 'other'.

14 An example of family feuding leading to break-up of a family-run business is the Teo clan of the See Hoy Chan Group.

15 For example, PETRONAS (petroleum, oil and gas) is wholly owned by the Malaysian government. In terms of transportation and logistics, the investment holding arm of the government Khazanah Nasional (chaired by the prime minister), holds 72.74% of Malaysia Airport (listed company) and 100% of Penerbangan Malaysia (unlisted) which owns 52% of Malaysian Airline System (listed);

in terms of media and communication Khazanah Nasional holds 44.51% of TMI (listed), 41.78% of Telekom (listed), 30.04% of Time dotcom (listed), and 21.4% of Astro (listed); in terms of infrastructure and construction, Khazanah holds 100% of UEM (unlisted) which owns 58.42% of UEM World; in terms of automotive Khazanah holds 42.74% of Proton (listed); in terms of property Khazanah holds 100% of STLR (unlisted), 100% of UDA Holdings (unlisted), 75% of Iskandar Inv. *Berhad* (unlisted).

16 According to Perkins and Woo (1998), 'Government oversight of the state owned firms was so weak that the government itself did not even know how many firms there were!'

17 Manufacturer of Proton Saga, the national car. HICOM was sold to the private sector in 1996, and consolidated into the conglomerate known as DRB-HICOM.

18 Loss-making companies such as Malaysian Airlines, the Bakun Dam Project, the Indah Water Konsortium and PERNAS have been bought back by the government.

19 *Budi* 'embodies all the virtues ranked in the system of values of the society … the structure of *budi* is composed of virtuous qualities such as *murah hati* (generosity), *hormat* (respect), *ikhlas* (sincerity), *mulia* (righteousness), *timbang-rasa* (discretion), *malu* (feelings of shame at the collective level) and *segan* (feeling of shame at the individual level)' (Dahlan, 1991: 46–7).

20 Many organizations in the private sector and Government departments in Kedah, Kelantan and Terengganu observe Fridays and Saturdays as weekly rest days.

21 Prime Minister Abdullah Ahmad Badawi was elected in 2004 by a landslide vote after an anti-graft campaign.

22 http://jinjiruks.blogspot.com/2008/09/transparency-international-corruption.html.

23 The Federal Constitution clearly reflects that Malaysia is a secular state. There is much confusion on this subject. See for example http://www.bernama.com/bernama/v3/printable.php?id=281491.

24 http://news.bbc.co.uk/2/hi/asia-pacific/4140660.stm.

25 ECA International worldwide Cost of Living ranking 2007 available at http://www.eca international. com/Asp/ViewArticle2.asp?ArticleID=199.

REFERENCES

Abdullah, A. and Lim, L. (2001). Cultural dimensions of Anglos, Australians and Malaysians. *Malaysian Management Review*, **36**(2): 9–17.

Abdullah, A., Singh, S. and Gill, S.K. (2001). Communicating with Malaysians. In Abdullah, A. and Low, A.H.M. (eds) *Understanding the Malaysian Workforce: Guidelines for Managers* (revised edition). Kuala Lumpur: Malaysian Institute of Management.

Abdullah, S.H. (2001). Managing in the Malaysian context. In *Management in Malaysia*, 2nd edn. Kuala Lumpur: Malaysian Institute of Management, pp. 51–72.

AirAsia homepage http://www.airasia.com.

Andaya, B.W. and Andaya, L.Y. (2001). *A History of Malaysia*. Basingstoke: Palgrave – now Palgrave Macmillan.

Chan, S.H. and Simpson, T. (2005). Multiple coexisting bottom lines: Insights from Arvind Singhal's 'Distinguished International Scholar' address at the University of Macau. *Euro Asia Journal of Management*, **15**(2): 125–31.

Clifford, M.L. (1996). Can Malaysia take that next big step?: Without a balanced growth plan, good times may not last. http://www.businessweek.com/1996/09/b3464109.htm.

Dahlan, H.M. (1991). Local values in intercultural management. *Malaysian Management Review*, **1**: 45–50.

Goh, B.L. (2005). Malay-Muslim spirits and Malaysian capitalist modernity: A study of *keramat* propitiation among property developers in Penang. *Asia Pacific Viewpoint*, **46**(3): 307–21.

Hassan, A. and Ahmad, K. (2001). *Malaysian Management Practices: An Empirical Study*. Kuala Lumpur: Leeds Publications.

Hofstede, G.H. (1991). Management in a multicultural society. *Malaysian Management Review*, **26**(1): 3–12.

Jesudason, J. (1988). *Ethnicity and the Economy: The State, Chinese Business, and Multinationals in Malaysia*. Singapore: Oxford University Press.

Jesudason, J.V. (1997). Chinese business and ethnic equilibrium in Malaysia. *Development and Change*, **28**(1): 119–41.

Kawabe, N. (1991). Japanese management in Malaysia. In Yamashita, S. (ed.), *Transfer of Japanese Technology and Management to the ASEAN Countries*. Tokyo: University of Tokyo Press.

Lim, L. (1998). Cultural attributes of Malays and Malaysian Chinese: Implications for research and practices. *Malaysian Management Review*, **33**(2): 81–8.

Lim, L. (2001). Work cultural values of Malays and Chinese Malaysians. *International Journal of Cross Cultural Management*, **1**(2): 209–26.

McCloud, T. (2007). Even dreams need wings. *Travel 3 Sixty*, **1**(1): 30–4.

Malaysian Employers Federation (2004). *The MEF Salary and Fringe Benefits Survey for Executives 2003*. Kuala Lumpur: Malaysian Employers Federation.

Malaysian Employers Federation (2005). *The MEF Salary and Fringe Benefits Survey for Executives 2004*. Kuala Lumpur: Malaysian Employers Federation.

Mohd. Yusoff, M.S. (2003). Globalization and human resource development in the Malaysian public service. Paper presented at the 19th General Assembly EROPA Conference, New Delhi, India, 5–10 October. http://unpan1.un.org/intradoc/groups/public/documents/EROPA/UNPAN014373.pdf.

Perkins, D.M. and Woo, W.T. (1998). *Malaysia in Turmoil: Growth Prospects and Future Competitiveness*. http://www.econ.ucdavis.edu/faculty/woo/davosmal.html.

Rashid, M.Z.A., Anantharaman, R.N. and Raveendran, J. (1997). Corporate cultures and work values in dominant ethnic organizations in Malaysia. *Journal of Transnational Management Development*, **2**(4): 51–65.

Salazar, C. (2004). The legacies of Mahathir's privatization policy. Asean focus group Asian analysis, ANU, Canberra, March. http://www.aseanfocus.com/asiananalysis/article.cfm?articleID=721.

Shephard, P. (2001). Making decisions. In Abdullah, A. and Low, A.H.M. (eds) *Understanding the Malaysian Workforce: Guidelines for Managers* (revised edition). Kuala Lumpur: Malaysian Institute of Management.

Storz, M.L. (1999). Malay and Chinese business values underlying the Malaysian business culture. *International Journal of Intercultural Relations*, **23**: 117–31.

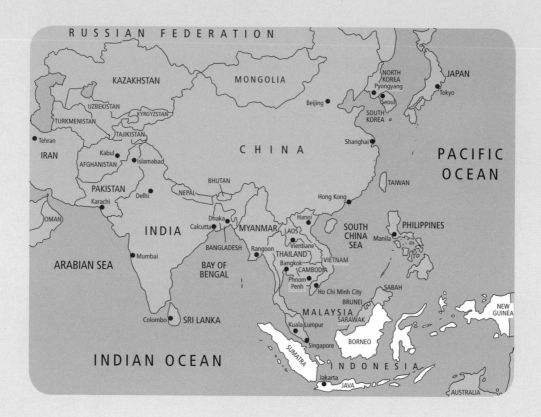

Chapter outline

- An overview of the Indonesian economy
- Economic development, financial liberalization and crisis
- Indonesian culture and management
- Leadership and decision making
- Corporate governance in the new business environment
- Working and living conditions in Indonesia

Chapter objectives

After reading this chapter, you should be able to:

1. Identify the major events and reasons for Indonesia's dynamic economic development

2. Understand the specific features of Indonesian management and their cultural background

3. Identify the major potential strengths and weaknesses of Indonesian business

4. Understand the evolution of corporate governance and corporate social responsibility (CSR) practices in Indonesia

Chapter 16

Management in Indonesia

Agustinus Prasetyantoko and Raphaella D. Dwianto

AN OVERVIEW OF THE INDONESIAN ECONOMY

In 2007, Indonesia's estimated gross domestic product (GDP) was US$408 billion with nominal per capita GDP of US$1,812.[1] The service industry plays a major role in the country's economy, followed by manufacturing and agriculture. Indonesia's main export markets are Japan (22.3 per cent of all Indonesian exports in 2005), the US (13.9 per cent), China (9.1 per cent) and Singapore (8.9 per cent). The major suppliers of imports to Indonesia are Japan (18.0 per cent), China (16.1 per cent) and Singapore (12.8 per cent).[2]

With more than 17,000 islands, Indonesia is recognized as the world's largest archipelagic state and has a long history of trade going back centuries. In the 13th century, Sriwijaya Kingdom, which was situated on Sumatra Island was one of the most important trade centres in the world, linking Chinese, Indian and Arabic traders. Historically, the Island, with a background of Arabic and Chinese cultural influences was, until recently, crucially important. Although officially Indonesia is not an Islamic state, it is the most populous Muslim-majority nation. On the other hand, even though Indonesian people who are of Chinese descent are in the minority in terms of number in the population, their role in the economy is indispensable. Big business and finance in the Indonesian private sector have been dominated by family-owned business groups, almost all of which are owned by those of Chinese descent (Mackie, 1990).[3]

With a population of over 234 million people in 2007,[4] Indonesia is referred to as the world's 4th most populous country, after China, India and the United States. The country is also richly endowed with extensive natural resources, including crude oil, natural gas, tin, copper and gold. Due to its important exports of crude oil, Indonesia is Southeast Asia's only member of OPEC.[5] The oil price rises in the 1970s provided an export revenue windfall that contributed to sustained high economic growth rates.

These two features, a large population and an abundance of natural resources, have become the main competitive advantage of Indonesia's economy. In general, Indonesia has been considered a favourable country for private sector activities since a large population means promising consumers and rich natural resources mean cheap inputs for production.

Before the 1997 financial crisis, foreign investors enjoyed investing in Indonesia, with the conviction that if they could access Indonesia, they would have a very profitable business. Simply, Indonesia meant good business. It is recognized as a market friendly economic system. The enthusiasm of foreign investors is not only supported by government policies which ease the investment procedures but also by the dynamism of firm-level strategies. Economic and financial liberalization led by the government have boosted corporate sector development. Indonesia can be praised as one of the most promising countries in Asia due to its political, economic and socio-historical background.

Until the 1997 financial crisis, Indonesia's economy was basically based on the 'growth-oriented development strategy'. Afterwards, during the post-crisis period, issues such as corporate governance, CSR, and business law were being discussed feverishly and were seriously implemented. This shows that during the post-crisis period, the 'quality of growth' was also an important element in the development strategy.

ECONOMIC DEVELOPMENT, FINANCIAL LIBERALIZATION AND CRISIS

During the early independence period (1950–1965) Dutch business activities were still dominant.[6] During that time, the revolutionary movements of the Indonesian people were fierce and aggressive. Inevitably there were several serious conflicts between the indigenous people and the business sector which was controlled by Dutch companies.

It is estimated that at that time business activities contributed to about 25 per cent of Indonesia's GDP and most of the business activities were controlled by Dutch, US and British companies. During this period, there were political movements by nationalist activists to take over many foreign companies as part of a transformation from the colonial economy into a national economy. Officially, the Indonesian government nationalized all Dutch companies and changed them into state-owned enterprises (SOEs) in early 1959. Political leaders and military officers were appointed as company managers.

After the emergence of a new government in 1966, which also marked the beginning of the Soeharto era known as the 'new order' government, the business climate changed significantly. The new government tried to open the economy to foreign investors. It was a landmark in Indonesian business activities. The new order government's top priority was to recover the economy which was suffering from hyperinflation and macroeconomic instability. Under the 'old order' government of the Soekarno era, inflation reached over 600 per cent and had practically collapsed.

One of the most important actors in saving the economy from instability and collapse was the private sector. The 'new order' government tried to attract foreign private enterprises to play a bigger role in the economy. The new business activities commenced with the Foreign Capital Investment Law of 1967, which opened the country to fresh foreign direct investments (FDI). This law contained various attractive incentives, including generous tax concessions (for example tax holidays and duty-free imports of capital goods) and guarantees, including the free transfer of dividends and profits and a guarantee against arbitrary nationalization of foreign enterprises. To administer the new inflows of foreign investment, a Technical Team for Foreign Investment (which later became the Capital Investment Coordinating Agency, (BKPM)) was established, which was also put in charge of foreign investment promotion (Sadli, 2003).

In the domestic market, the government protected selected industries from foreign competitors since they were still infant industries. This kind of intervention in industrial policies allowed several business groups to boost their activities extensively by taking advantage of these privileges. These policies were subsequently cited as an important factor in the rapid development of Indonesia under Soeharto's new order.

The rapid economic growth was accompanied by the emergence of big business groups which happened to be mainly controlled by Indonesians of Chinese descent. For instance, the Salim group, owned by a first-generation overseas Chinese from Fujian province, was the largest business group in Indonesia with 38.5 per cent in terms of business size among the 10 largest groups and 18.5 per cent among the 100 largest groups (Sato, 1993).

Basically, the two salient features of the industrialization policies during Soeharto's government were liberalization, permitting foreign investors to develop investment in Indonesia, and protection or intervention policies followed by the emergence of dominant business groups. These processes resulted in high-performing growth not only at the industrial level but also in terms of the national economy. Since the 'new order' government, economic growth was relatively high and stable with an annual average growth of 7 per cent. In 1993, the World Bank referred to Indonesia as one of the high-performing East Asian economies (HPAEs)[7] with 'miraculous' growth, due to its fundamentally sound development policies and an unusually rapid accumulation of physical and human capital.[8]

Unfortunately, Indonesia's high-performing economy was wiped out by the 1997 Asian financial crisis. In 1998, the Indonesian annual GDP dropped severely to minus 13 per cent. Subsequently, unemployment increased significantly from 6 million people in the pre-crisis period to 20 million in the aftermath of the crisis. Meanwhile, the number of people living under the poverty line is estimated to have risen to 80 million, or about 40 per cent of the population. Following a free-floating exchange rate system decided on by Bank Indonesia (the Indonesian Central Bank) in August 1997, the Indonesian rupiah (IDR) depreciated sharply from 4,900 IDR to the US dollar in December 1997 to 15,000 IDR to the dollar in June 1998.

What are the real sources of growth? Financial liberalization is a major force to boost business development and economic growth. However, the Indonesian financial system only started in 1966 when the commercial banks were born. It can be said that before 1966 a financial system hardly existed in Indonesia, a fact commonly attributed to economic disruptions like the consecutive runs of fiscal deficit and hyperinflation under the old order government's administration (Hamada, 2003).

According to Hamada (2003), the Indonesian financial system developed in five phases from 1966 until recently. The first period (1966–1972) was its formative period, the second (1973–1982) its policy-based finance period under soaring oil prices, the third (1983–1991) its financial-reform period, the fourth (1992–1997) its period of expansion and the fifth (1998–2002) its period of financial restructuring.

In the first wave of financial system development, the Parliament of the Republic of Indonesia engaged with the legalization of the banking system in Indonesia. Law 14/1967 on the Principles of Banking was enacted by the Parliament to redefine the role of banks and improve access to credit. The law characterized the banking system as an instrument of national development to improve economic growth, equitable distribution of wealth and national stability (Hofman et al., 2004). One year later, the Parliament issued Law no.13/1968 to authorize Bank Indonesia as the national central bank.

Liberalization policies in Indonesia were substantially implemented in the 1980s due to the sharp decline in oil revenues in late 1982 and again in 1986. During the financial reform period, many policies were issued to liberalize and deregulate the financial market. In October 1988, the government of Indonesia launched the second major policy package for banking deregulation. These reforms were mainly aimed at enhancing the efficiency of the financial sector by encouraging competition and increasing the availability of long-term finance through the development of a capital market. This deregulation was quickly followed by several dynamic policies in December 1988 and March 1989 with the main objective of accelerating capital market development.[9] The reforms contributed to an explosion of financial activities. Domestic credit jumped and the number of banks increased from 111 in 1988 to 240 in 1994.

The policy package in October 1988 basically eased the capital requirement for establishing a bank, which required only 10 billion IDR. Since the requirement was relatively easy, the number of banks in Indonesia increased tremendously.[10] This drastic increase was also due to the policy which permitted banks to open branches in rural areas. Therefore, banks were able to accumulate more money from the people.

This fast development of the banking sector turned Indonesia into one of the Asian countries with the highest number of banks.[11] This drastic increase was accompanied by unhealthy business competition resulting in low respect for the banking system. The credit market was characterized by related bank credit in which firms could easily access short-term borrowing without enough collateral. Business groups or *konglomerat* were allowed to establish commercial banks to serve the needs of other corporations within the same group.

At the same time, Bank Indonesia lacked sufficient regulations and supervision. However, it successfully promoted economic growth by providing low-cost funds and a high supply of credit to the corporate sector. Unfortunately, since the regulations and institutional system were relatively weak, rapid growth changed quickly into a deep crisis. Banks became a major source of credit since at that time the capital market was underdeveloped. Nevertheless, the capital market in Indonesia rapidly evolved in the early 2000s, especially with the merger of two capital markets, namely the Jakarta Stock Exchange and the Surabaya Stock Exchange into the new Indonesia Stock Exchange by the end of 2007.

SUMMARY POINTS

The business sector in pre-crisis Indonesia had several characteristics, namely:

■ Extensive control by family groups.

■ Finance provided by banks in their own groups was dominant.

■ Expansive growth in investment and capital accumulation.

■ Lack of supervision due to weak governance system.

REFLECTIVE QUESTION

■ Why do you think Indonesian firms are particularly vulnerable when facing external shocks such as currency depreciation?

INDONESIAN CULTURE AND MANAGEMENT

The influence of national culture on management is a key issue in organization science (Hofstede, 1983). Now we will take a look at Indonesian culture. Although it is well known that Indonesia is a country with various traditional local cultures, in sum it is said that the contrast of life, business and art in Indonesia can be compared to Indonesian *wayang kulit* (Kemp, 2001). It is a kind of traditional shadow puppet play where one not only notices the actions portrayed on the oil lamp-illuminated screen, but also the artistry of the *dalang*, the one and only person behind the screen who moves all the puppets and manipulates the images on the screen. It is the *dalang* who determines what we see. As a consequence, it is not easy to really differentiate black from white among characters in the traditional puppet play. Similar things can be said about Indonesia – it is one of the most complex cultures to understand and to penetrate. Despite its modernity, easily seen in its big cities, Indonesia's business, political and community cultures continue to be flavoured by tradition.

The tendency to concentrate authority, such as in the case of the *dalang* in *wayang kulit*, can also be traced back in Indonesian history. For two-and-a-half centuries Indonesia was a colony of the Dutch and was ruled by one of the biggest, most enduring and least socially responsible colonial trading companies. Colonialism in Indonesia left a legacy of a complex melange of patronage, monopolies and the commensurate concentration of wealth and power, which still remains in the Indonesian consciousness.

Another thing that emerged under the reign of the Dutch East India Company and continues to exist is the division between the elite (ruling elite) and the masses. During that time, the colonial government formed a seamless blend with the Javanese culture, which is an original aristocratic court culture known as *priyayi* culture, derived from the large sultanates of Java. The class of *priyayi* people is seen as an exclusive rather than inclusive social class.

The consciousness of patronage, monopolies, concentration of wealth and power, as well as the division between the elite and the masses has survived the colonialism of the Dutch. When Soeharto, a Javanese commoner, took his place as the second president of Indonesia in 1966, this subsequently resulted in the concentration of capital in his hands, and those of his family and selected clients and cronies. During his regime, large businesses in Indonesia were marked by the presence of *konglomerat* – that is, well-connected groups of businesses linked to Indonesian political elites – and large state-owned enterprises (SOEs), which are bureaucratic corporations protected by the power of government and patronage (Wibisono, 1991). In other words, the management style in Indonesia is highly personal, encompassing only family members or those known to the family. Similar styles of management practices can be seen also among businesses owned by Indonesians of Chinese descent.

Looking at the above-mentioned historical and cultural background of management practices in Indonesia, it is easy to understand why in his country scoring, Hofstede gave Indonesia a score of 78 in the Power Distance Index (PDI). This is above the average of all other Asian countries which, according to him, tend to have high PDI scores. Since the level of power distance in organizations is related to the degree of centralization of authority and the degree of autocratic leadership (Hofstede, 1983: 81), in the case of Indonesia with its historical background, it can be clearly seen that there is an unequal distribution of power, with the one with power and authority having the position of 'patron' or 'father'.

The next dimension to be highlighted in the case of Indonesia is the dimension of Individualism versus Collectivism. According to Hofstede, the score for Indonesia is 14, which is low compared to an average of around 20 for other Asian countries. In Hofstede's argument, the individualistic and the collectivistic societies are integrated wholes, but the former is loosely integrated, while the latter is tightly integrated (Hofstede, 1983: 79). With a low score of 14, it indicates that in Indonesia, ties between individuals are strong in in-groups. This also means that each person is expected to look after the interests of his or her group, and in return, the person will get protection. And since a person is also expected to have the same opinions and beliefs as his or her in-group, it results in a high degree of trust among people of the same in-group, which in the case of business groups, tend to be extended family members. With personal relations regarded as being of more importance, it is then natural to have a higher score for uncertainty tolerance in Hofstede's Uncertainty Avoidance dimension.

The influence of traditional culture on management in Indonesia was, to a certain degree, punctuated with the stepping-down of Soeharto in 1998. Regarding business ethics and governance, it is clear that after more than three decades of Soeharto's patriarchal system, overnight change is not possible. Even though Indonesia is emerging from decades of dictatorship, it can be said that the country is still struggling to stand on its own feet. During this process, two cultural tendencies in managing business in Indonesia are worthy of notice. One is the growing influence of Islam, and the other is the changing management systems among large ethnic Chinese-owned businesses.

As the world's most populous Islamic country, sharia law also enters into business dealings. The law demands that property should not be acquired by acts of bribery, looting or deception, which are considered *haram* or prohibited. Sharia specifies that the fruits of productivity should benefit the community and that Muslims as individuals cannot own publicly used utilities such as roads, schools or hospitals, or production facilities where the cost of the good far exceeds the cost of production – some have argued that this includes gold mines and oil production or refinement. Meanwhile large ethnic Chinese-owned businesses, which comprise an important part of the Indonesian economy, are changing their insular management style which is highly personal, to modern, accountable management practices. However, the patriarchal structure still exists (Adnan and Goodfellow, 1997).

Yet from a broader perspective, following the 1997 financial crisis and the end of Soeharto's regime in 1998, the Indonesian government and society are gradually changing business practices into becoming increasingly proactive for social justice and transparency. New laws and government reforms since 1997 are changing the business environment. For example, the new corporate financial reporting and shareholder accountability laws will increase transparency in business practices. New bankruptcy and capital market laws will clarify the firms' obligations to creditors and shareholders. Other new laws will also cover anti-competitive behaviours. Beyond doubt the implementation of these laws will take time. Nevertheless, they will eventually result in changing the 'old ways of doing business'.

LEADERSHIP AND DECISION MAKING

Indonesian management in general tends to be traditional, patriarchal and hierarchically oriented. Leadership and decision making are no exceptions. To begin with, we can refer to the research conducted by Sato (2004) covering the top 100 non-financial public firms. It confirmed that ownership was still highly concentrated; and ownership and management were still entwined. However, the findings also showed that concentrated ownership and non-separation of ownership and management do not necessarily equal poor company performance. Firms associated with established business groups such as Sinar Mas, Astra and Salim, which happen to be under the control of people of Chinese descent, performed better compared to firms not affiliated with groups, or firms that are associated with more recent groups from the 1980s such as Bimantara and Humpuss which are controlled by Soeharto's sons.

With this trend in management, according to the 2003 White Paper on Corporate Governance in Asia, powers of boards of directors in Indonesia cover the following:

1. Appointment and compensation of senior management
2. Review and adoption of budgets and financial statements
3. Review and adoption of strategic plans
4. Major transactions outside the ordinary course of business (shareholders' approval needed)
5. Changes to capital structure (shareholders' approval needed)
6. Organization and running of shareholders' meetings
7. Process of disclosure and communications
8. Company's risk policy
9. Transactions with related parties (independent shareholders' approval needed).

And to be one of the directors in an Indonesian firm, one has to pass the 'fit and proper test', that is, one should have no criminal convictions or prior bankruptcies. Yet there is no minimum or maximum age for directors and no professional experience requirements. To be an independent director, a person who has a kinship relationship (whether it is by blood or by marriage) with any member in a management position or with any major shareholder, is eligible, unless they have some investment in the firm. However, employees of affiliated companies and representatives of companies having significant dealings with the company are excluded.

To get a better picture of leadership and decision making in Indonesia, we will refer to the cases of Sinar Mas Group and Astra Group as reported by Habir and Larasati (1999). Sinar Mas Group, founded by Eka Tjipta Widjaja (of Chinese descent), who started the business in the 1950s as CV Sinar Mas, is a diversified international business group employing 180,000 people of different nationalities. The group is now one of the largest Indonesian business groups and has four core businesses, namely pulp and paper; agribusiness, food and consumer products; financial services; and real estate and property development. The group bases its core corporate values on the key success factors set out by the founder–owner–chairman, Eka Tjipta Widjaja, namely hard work, thrift, honesty, loyalty, perseverance and zeal. It can be said that leadership in Sinar Mas Group is very much influenced by the family culture of the Widjaja Family. As in many other Indonesian business groups, the family members and Indonesians of Chinese descent dominate top management.

Astra Group has been recognized as the most well managed and professionally run Indonesian business group. According to Sato (1996), the main features of the group include the following:

1. It is the largest car maker in Indonesia with over 50 per cent market share. Its joint ventures with Japanese car manufacturers have provided the business foundations for the manufacture of cars and machinery.
2. It was initially a family business founded by William Soeryadjaya, and was owned by the family until 1992. Following the bankruptcy of another family business, the family sold its shares, and the firm is now held by multiple owners including Indonesian government financial institutions, domestic private capitalists and foreign firms.
3. It is a pioneer of Indonesian modern management, the first Indonesian business group to have its holding company listed on the domestic stock market, and has a high reputation domestically as the most professional business group in Indonesia.

Regarding leadership, it has separated management from ownership, and has a non-discriminative employment policy. Top and middle management are a blend of Indonesians of Chinese descent and of Malay descent (known as *pribumi*). Astra Group used to also have a female CEO who is a *pribumi*. She successfully steered Astra through debt restructuring negotiations after the economic crisis hit the country in 1998 (Putranto, 1999). By also basing its modern management on the vision and philosophy of the founding family, the group survived the collapse of the family ownership, and later on survived the economic and political crisis in Indonesia in 1997.

SUMMARY POINTS

■ Due to the historical and cultural background, there is a tendency for concentrated power and authority, combined with a high degree of collectivism based on personal relations.

■ In accordance with such a tendency, leadership is also traditionally, patriarchally and hierarchically oriented.

CORPORATE GOVERNANCE IN THE NEW BUSINESS ENVIRONMENT

The issue of corporate governance is relatively new in Indonesia. Before the 1997 financial crisis, this word was almost unheard of in public discourse and especially in business practices. The background to this is, traditionally, the above-mentioned patriarchal and hierarchically oriented management, which rarely questioned corporate governance. But nowadays, the issue of corporate governance has become one of the most popular topics in academic and practitioner fields.

Among practitioners, Indonesia is usually regarded as a country with a bad reputation in corporate governance, since the judicial and political systems are not particularly conducive to good business practice. Concerning the efficiency of the judicial system, for instance, Indonesia has the lowest level, whereas it is still in the top rank of the corruption index (Claessens et al., 2000). These characteristics of the business environment could be cited as the dominant institutional business context in Indonesia.

Family-concentrated businesses are often achieved through complex cross-shareholding and pyramiding of companies. In most cases, the owners appoint and control the two-tiered board of commissioners and board of directors, as well as the top management; and they are involved in all key business decisions (Husnan, 1999; Simandjuntak, 2000).

Influenced by the Dutch legal system, Indonesia has a 'dual-tiered system' of corporate governance which means that there is a separation between managers and the supervisory board, called the board of commissioners or *dewan komisaris*. The commissioner is a representative of the shareholders, including minority share-holders. The pre-crisis corporate governance system was characterized by the absence of supervision to management decisions and there was no protection for the minority shareholders.

However, the 1997 financial crisis has progressively changed the landscape of business in Indonesia. Due to this severe crisis, almost all conglomerates were taken over by the Indonesian Bank Restructuring Agency (IBRA). This period became an important phase of industrial development in Indonesia, since most large groups were restructured because of their bad performance in finance or unpaid loans. Most of them were ridden with bad external debts and their financial positions were almost in default. The government of Indonesia responded to this condition by issuing Law No. 5 concerning Anti-Monopoly and Unfair Business Practices in 1999. Afterwards, a Commission for Supervision of Business Competition was formed in the middle of 2000.

The financial crisis has also disclosed issues around corporate governance and has exposed them as one of the most important problems in Indonesia. In general, the implementation of good corporate governance practices in Indonesia has shown positive progress since its introduction in the aftermath of the 1997 crisis. Recommended by the International Monetary Fund (IMF) and supported by the World Bank and the Asian Development Bank, a National Committee for Corporate Governance (NCCG) was established in 2000. This institution subsequently issued a Code of Best Practice in 2001.

Corporate governance initiatives were also launched by several organizations such as the IICG (Indonesian Institute for Corporate Governance), FCGI (Forum for Corporate Governance in Indonesia), and IICD (Indonesian Institute for Corporate Directorship). Table 16.1 contains a list of organizations promoting corporate governance in Indonesia.

In 2002, the IICG organized the 2nd annual Corporate Governance Awards based on its Corporate Governance Perception Index shared with all Jakarta Stock Exchange (JSX) member companies. The following are the seven corporate governance categories being used in the ranking:

1. Corporate governance commitment
2. Rights of shareholders
3. Board of commissioners
4. Functional committees (audit, remuneration and nomination)
5. Board of directors
6. Transparency and accountability
7. Shareholder relations.

Table 16.1 Organizations promoting corporate governance in Indonesia

No	Organization	Description	Website
1	Jakarta Stock Exchange (JSX)	Stock Exchange	www.jsx.co.id
2	Capital Market Supervisory Agency (*Badan Pengawas Pasar Modal* – BAPEPAM)	Stock Exchange watchdog	www.bapepam.go.id
3	Indonesian Institute for Corporate Governance (IICG)	Corporate governance development, awards and shareholder activism	www.iicorporategovernance.org
4	National Committee for Corporate Governance (NCCG)	Policy development, support structures, institutionalization and socialization driver for good corporate governance	www.nccorporategovernance-indonesia.org
5	Forum for Corporate Governance in Indonesia (FCGI)	Linking corporate governance with CSR strategy/practices	www.fcorporategovernancei.or.id
6	Indonesian Institute of Accountants (IAI)	National body to improve accounting practices	www.akuntan-iai.or.id
7	Center for Local Government Innovation (CLGI)	Supports excellence in local governance	www.clgi.or.id
8	Partnership for Governance Reform	Governance reform in decision making and resource allocation, eradicate corruption, supremacy of law	www.partnerships.or.id
9	Indonesia Corruption Watch (ICW)	Systematic freedom from corruption based on social justice – awareness, participation, enforcement, monitor/empower and so on.	www.antikorupsi.org
10	Business Watch Indonesia (BWI)	Business accountability and fairness issues researched and converted into actions and NGO network support	www.fair-biz.org
11	Transparency International (TI)/Indonesia Society for Transparency (MTI)	Leaders in corruption awareness/monitoring/avoidance and good governance to strengthen accountability	www.ti.or.id www.transparansi.or.id
12	Indonesian Institute for Corporate Directorship/Commissioners and Directors (IICD)	Strategic business partners to develop and internalize directorship skills, knowledge and ability to implement corporate governance. Affiliated with NACD (USA)	www.nccorporategovernance.org
13	Corporate Leadership Development Institute	An instrument of strategic intervention for all state-owned enterprises to develop future corporate leaders, including a healthy dose of corporate governance	www.cldi-i.com

Source: www.asria.org.

In Table 16.2, we can see several examples of corporate governance practices. It could be an important indication of how serious the concern is and the actual actions taken to deal with corporate governance in post-crisis Indonesia.

After the financial crisis, political forces in the government and parliament supported important judicial revisions enhancing good business practices in Indonesia. At the firm level, there are important changes in terms of corporate governance and CSR practices coinciding with developments in the political and judicial fields. These conditions are resulting in a more favourable environment for good business in Indonesia, although it is undeniable that the changes are not rapid.

Table 16.2 Corporate governance examples in Indonesia

No	Events	Cases
1	Lippo Bank	Investment Management and Performance Agreement (IMPA) confidentiality Dubious financial reporting Director accountability BAPEPAM regulatory enforcement
2	Kimia Farma	Dubious financial reporting Director accountability BAPEPAM regulatory enforcement
3	Texmaco	Master Settlement Acquisition Agreement (MSAA) manipulation Owner accountability BAPEPAM regulatory enforcement
4	Semen Cibinong	Asset (equity) off-balance sheet manipulation Owner accountability BAPEPAM regulatory enforcement
5	Indomobil	Credit asset (property) repurchase misappropriation Owner accountability BAPEPAM regulatory enforcement
6	Bumi Resources	Minority shareholder rights Transparency in asset acquisition Director accountability BAPEPAM regulatory enforcement

Source: www.asria.org.

SUMMARY POINTS

■ There are great changes in the business environment in the post-crisis period in Indonesia.

■ The changes not only involve political and judicial aspects, but also corporate practices, such as corporate governance and CSR.

REFLECTIVE QUESTION

■ In what ways do you think the 1997 financial crisis has helped to disclose poor corporate governance issues in Indonesia?

WORKING AND LIVING CONDITIONS IN INDONESIA

Data from the Central Bureau of Statistics or *Badan Pusat Statistik* (BPS) show that in 2005 only around 5.42 per cent of the labour force in Indonesia had a tertiary educational background; while 56.23 per cent of them are either primary school graduates or drop-outs. When it comes to gender division, the total number of female workers comprises only one-third of the total labour force in Indonesia. Although there is no significant difference in terms of the percentage of female workers by age groups, there is a slight tendency for there to be more younger female workers. These female workers seem to retire earlier than their male fellow workers. In general, we can say that the labour force in Indonesia has a mostly lower level educational background and is dominated by younger male workers.

According to BPS, in 2003, agriculture was still the industry employing the most workers in Indonesia, while the financial industry lagged behind. Needless to say, Indonesia still depends heavily on the agriculture industry, despite its massive urbanization.

Regarding the division of gender, based on data on job category in 2003, even though management posts are dominated by male workers, the numbers of professional, sales and administrative staff showed almost equal division in gender.

One thing that should be noted when it comes to employement in Indonesia is the significance of the informal sector as the employer of the labour force. The informal sector is represented by the self-employed, temporary helpers, casual employees in agriculture and non-agriculture and unpaid workers. The total of these informal workers amounts to 70 per cent of the total workforce.

When it comes to strikes, in general, they do not have much impact because they are sporadic and dispersed in different regions. Two regions that can be said to be strike centres are Tangerang in West Java and Sidoardjo in East Java. Both are centres of industry. Even though strikes are sporadic, marked by an emphasis on local issues, there are still several common issues that always emerge in every strike in the country. One common issue is rejection of the policy of labour market flexibility, in which striking workers ask the government to revise Labor Policy No. 13 of 2003. From the workers' point of view, this policy only further weakens their bargaining position, mainly on negotiations with employers, which have become individualized. The policy also lowers job security due to outsourcing.

Concerning living conditions in Indonesia, the annual average income was US$1,663 per capita as of 2006. On the other hand, the average inflation rate ranged between 5.6 per cent in 2002 to 17 per cent in 2005. Everyday life has not been easy.

The decreasing rupiah affects every part of the country, with people of middle and low income in big cities such as Jakarta being the most severely affected. A common strategy for survival when in need of extra cash is the traditional rotating credit association, known as *arisan*. In this informal association, people who know each other well gather once a month. At the gathering, every member contributes a fixed amount of money and the total will go to a member (or more than one member, in some cases) who will usually be decided by lot-drawing. The monthly gathering will go on, until each member has had his or her turn of getting the money collected at the gathering.

However, *arisan* is not only well recognized among people of middle and low income. People with higher social class also establish this kind of informal association. They treat this as more of a social gathering than an association based on economic need. The membership in such associations also tends to be limited, and is often only by the recommendation of other members. During the monthly gathering, the amount of money collected from each member is, in many cases, unthinkable for people of middle and low income.

CROSS-CHAPTER REFLECTIVE QUESTION

- It appears that both Vietnam (Chapter 13) and Indonesia had both experienced a series of economic revolutions before the national economy started to move on to a developmental track. How do you compare President Soeharto's new order economy and Vietnam's *doi moi* in terms of building economic success for the two countries?

CHAPTER SUMMARY

- Development of the business sector in Indonesia is supported by a set of government policies, such as industrial and financial liberalization and protection of infant industries.
- An unsound judicial and political system coinciding with low governance contributed significantly to the country's financial crisis.
- Indonesian businesses tend to have an unequal distribution of power and a high degree of collectivism based on personal relations.
- Indonesian management is traditionally characterized by patrimonially and hierarchically oriented leadership and decision making.
- The financial crisis disclosed central problems such as cartels, poor corporate governance and social responsibility issues.
- Issues on anti-monopoly, corporate governance and social responsibility are pivotal problems to be addressed in Indonesia's move towards an era of accountability and governance.
- Although improving, there is still a low level of higher educational attainment among Indonesian workers.

KEY CONCEPTS

Economic dynamism: Indonesia has seen aggressive economic growth since the financial liberalization in banking and the capital market in the 1980s.

Conglomerate: A large group of companies which is controlled by connected owners.

Corporate governance system: A 'dual-tiered system' of corporate governance which means that there is a separation between the managers and the supervisory board.

Paternalistic corporate culture: A corporate culture that is highly personal, encompassing only family members or those known to the family, with a high consciousness of patronage.

Indonesian human resources: A labour force that is of lower level educational background and is dominated by younger male workers.

REVIEW QUESTIONS

1. What were the determining factors affecting the rapid business sector development and the high economic growth in Indonesia during the 1997 financial crisis?
2. What are the important characteristics of the business and economic environment in pre-crisis Indonesia?
3. What are the important changes in the business environment in post-crisis Indonesia?
4. How do the cultural aspects affect business practices in Indonesia?
5. How have corporate governance and CSR evolved in this country?
6. What are the present working conditions in Indonesia?

LEARNING ACTIVITIES AND DISCUSSIONS

1. Imagine you are going to run a business in Indonesia. For example, you have to set up a small factory, open a branch or just make a deal with an existing business. What kind of strategic planning will you develop before entering the country? Identify the macro and micro factors influencing your business plan and formulate your strategy.
2. Search the internet and find a case of a foreign business (for example a multinational corporation) in Indonesia which faced turbulent conditions during the crisis. Describe how the company responded to these difficulties.
3. Discuss with your classmates what you would do to enhance your CSR programmes if you were currently running a business in Indonesia. How would you contribute to improving working conditions, including wages?
4. Having understood the evolution of corporate governance, CSR practices at the firm level, and the judicial and political system at the country level in Indonesia, how do you think business conditions in Indonesia will develop in the future? In the process of development, what dominant factors do you think will be of great influence?
5. What kind of corporate governance and CSR practices do you think will be appropriate for the present business environment in Indonesia? Do you think that multinational companies in Indonesia are better in their corporate governance and CSR practices than local companies? Why, or why not?
6. How would you explain the relationship between political factors, economic factors and firm strategies in a country undergoing rapid changes such as Indonesia?

MINI CASE

THE CASE OF UNILEVER INDONESIA'S CSR PROGRAMME

Unilever began its business in Indonesia in 1933, under the name of PT Unilever Indonesia Tbk. It is one of the major companies in Indonesia dealing with consumer products. It has more than 3,000 employees and another 20,000 workers whose livelihoods depend on small- or medium-scale businesses that have a relationship with Unilever Indonesia.[12]

Besides conducting businesses, Unilever Indonesia established a social organization in the year 2000, called Unilever (ULI) Peduli

Foundation. The ULI Peduli Foundation was set up in order to demonstrate Unilever Indonesia's commitment to sustainable social responsibility. The objective of ULI Peduli Foundation is to contribute to human and economic development in Indonesia. To accomplish this objective, ULI Peduli Foundation has organized several programmes. In 2003, the total expenditure of Unilever Indonesia on this CSR programme was around 8,616 million IDR.[13]

Most of the CSR programmes are concentrated in Java with the small exception of the fishing programme which is mainly conducted in Sulawesi. Several major projects are described below:

■ Sustainable Clean Brantas River Project

This project started in August 2001 and continued until 2006. The location was in Surabaya. The programme was designed and those areas were chosen because of their geographical closeness to Unilever Indonesia's factory. This project was designed to improve the quality of the Brantas River through promoting a healthy lifestyle and an environmentally oriented social economic development. It also aimed to improve the quality of life of the local population by reducing river pollution and improving hygienic living conditions (including fishing and recreation), and encouraging other industries along the river. The project also involved government bodies.

■ Sustainable Small and Medium Enterprise Development

This programme gives ordinary Indonesians encouragement, skills, access to finance and connection to the marketplace through forming partnerships in the area of new market channels, commodity supply and finished goods. The benefits to the SME partners are substantial, such as job creation, skill development, upgraded equipment, better quality, consistently produced goods and greater efficiency.

■ Sustainable Fishing

As one of the largest buyers of frozen fish, Unilever Indonesia formed a unique partnership with the World Wide Fund for Nature (WWF) to establish the Marine Stewardship Council (MSC). This relationship aims to ensure the long-term future of fish stocks and the health of the marine environment and the safeguarding of the marine ecosystem.

■ Sustainable Public Health Education

Unilever Indonesia works together with the Indonesia National Family Planning Agency (BKKBN) to teach the importance of hygiene education from an early age with a family approach (healthy lifestyle). This includes free dental check-up programmes and an oral care education programme, promoting the hand-washing campaign and setting up Integrated Family Planning and Community Health Posts (*posyandu*).

■ Sustainable Waste Management Programme

In 2001, Unilever Indonesia also initiated a community-based environmental programme in the Jambangan sub-district of Surabaya, focusing on waste management recycling. ULI started by identifying informal leaders within the community, who were then trained as members of the programme. These community leaders then started to introduce the concept of garbage separation into organic and non-organic garbage. Organic garbage is processed by simple local technologies. Starting with 44 leaders, the programme succeeded in encouraging the community to improve the environment by supporting the establishment of sanitation facilities. By September 2006, the programme had been replicated in 14 districts in Surabaya.

In this programme, ULI established a network with local government, academicians, local NGOs and local communities and their activities gained the attention of the international community. In 2005, ULI ranked first in the International Energy Globe Awards 2005 for the water category. ULI is the first company from Indonesia to receive this kind of award.

QUESTIONS

1. How do the CSR programmes of ULI contribute to sustainable development?
2. How do the CSR programmes of ULI contribute to society in a time of crisis?
3. What is the significance of ULI's CSR programmes for the country?
4. What should be developed in their future CRS programmes?

Sources: Clay, J.W. (2005). *Exploring the Links between International Business and Poverty Reduction: A Case Study of Unilever in Indonesia.* Oxfam-Unilever; and several publications of ULI Perduli Foundation.

INTERESTING WEB LINKS

For a case study of Unilever's CSR practice in Indonesia: http://publications.oxfam.org.uk/oxfam/display.asp?isbn=0855985666.
For corporate governance and CSR issues: www.asria.org.
National Commission on Corporate Governance: http://www.governance-indonesia.com/index.php.
For doing business in Indonesia: http://www.doingbusiness.org/ExploreEconomies/?economyid=90

Notes

1 IMF (2007). World Economic Outlook Database.
2 *The World Factbook 2007.*
3 Most of them were extraordinarily close to the Soeharto government and his family.
4 Calculation based upon the population census in 2000 conducted by the Indonesian Central Bureau of Statistics *(Badan Pusat Statistik).*
5 OPEC is the Organization of Petroleum Exporting Countries.
6 Indonesia's independence from Dutch colonization was on 17 August, 1945.
7 The eight high-performing East Asian economies (HPAEs) are Hong Kong, Indonesia, Japan, Malaysia, Republic of Korea, Singapore, Taiwan (China), and Thailand.
8 See World Bank (1993). *The East Asian Miracle: Economic Growth and Public Policy.* New York: Oxford University Press.
9 The government basically relaxed the requirement for listing in the Indonesian capital market and therefore the number of listed companies rose from just 24 companies in 1988 to 306 in 1997.
10 The total number of private national banks prior to *Pacto 88* was only 64 with a total of 512 offices. At the end of 1996, the number increased to 240 banks with around 5,919 operational offices.
11 IBRA annual report, 2002.
12 Internal data from Unilever Indonesia.
13 Internal data from Unilever Indonesia. US$1 = 8,400 IDR.

REFERENCES

Adnan, M. and Goodfellow, R. (eds) (1997). *Indonesian Business Culture: An Insiders Guide*. London: Reed Academic Publishing.

Claessens, S., Djankov, S. and Lang, L.H.P. (2000). The separation of ownership and control in East Asian corporations. *Journal of Financial Economics*. **58**(2): 82–112.

Clay, J. (2005). *Exploring the Links between International Business and Poverty Reduction: A Case Study of Unilever in Indonesia*. Oxfam GB, Novib Oxfam Netherlands and Unilever.

Habir, A. and Larasati, A.B. (1999). Human resource management as competitive advantage in the new millennium: An Indonesian perspective. *International Journal of Manpower*. **20**(8): 548–63.

Hamada, M. (2003). Transformation of the financial sector in Indonesia. *IDE Research Paper*, 6, Tokyo: Institute for Developing Economies.

Hofman, B., Rodrick-Jones, E. and Thee, K.W. (2004). Indonesia: Rapid growth, weak institutions. In *Reducing Poverty, Sustaining Growth: What Works, What Doesn't, and Why*. Washington, DC: The World Bank.

Hofstede, G. (1983). The cultural relativity of organizational practices and theories. *Journal of International Business Studies*. **14**(2): 75–89.

Husnan, S. (1999). Indonesian corporate governance: Its impact on corporate performance and finance. *Asian Development Bank draft of RETA 5802 project*. Tokyo: Asian Development Bank.

Kemp, M. (2001). Corporate social responsibility in Indonesia: Quixotic dream or confident expectation. *Technology, Business and Society Programme Paper No.6*, United Nations Research Institute for Social Development.

Mackie, J.B.C. (1990). The Indonesian conglomerates in regional perspective. In Hill, H. and Hull, T. (eds) *Indonesia Assessment 1990*. Research School of Pacific and Asian Studies, Australian National University.

Putranto, B. (1999). A long hard drive for Astra. *Indonesian Business*, August, pp. 12–17.

Sadli, M. (2003). Recollections of my career. *Bulletin of Indonesian Economic Studies*. **29**(1): 35–51.

Sato, Y. (1993). The Salim Group in Indonesia: The development and behavior of the largest conglomerate in Southeast Asia. *The Developing Economies*. **31**(4): 408–41.

Sato, Y. (1996). The Astra Group: A pioneer of management modernization in Indonesia. *The Developing Economies*. **34**(3): 247–80.

Sato, Y. (2004). Corporate Ownership and Management in Indonesia: Does it change? In *Business in Indonesia New Challenges, Old Problems*, M. Chatib Basri and Pierre van der Eng, Singapore: Institute of Southeast Asian Studies.

Simandjuntak, D.S. (2000). Transition to good governance in post-crisis Indonesia. Paper presented at the Columbia University CSIS Workshop on Economic Institution Building in a Global Economy. Jakarta, 24–25 May.

Wibisono, C. (1991). *Proceedings of an International Seminar on Issues of Development*, Institute Teknologi Bandung and Goethe Institute

World Bank (1993). *The East Asian Miracle: Economic Growth and Public Policy*. New York: Oxford University Press.

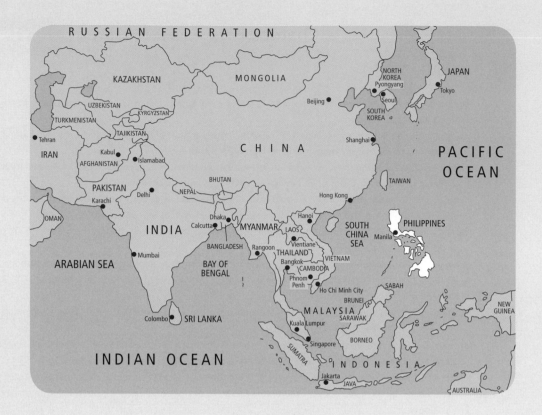

Chapter outline

- Overview of the Philippine economy: Competitiveness and the inequality trap
- Culture, history and state
- Institutions and structures for coordinating business
- The new Philippine puzzle: Growth without competitiveness
- The Philippine management system
- Corporate social responsibility (CSR)
- Living in the Philippines and hopes for the future

Chapter objectives

After reading this chapter, you should be able to:

1. Understand the Philippine puzzle: How the prolonged high level of inequality has weakened the competitiveness of Philippine business
2. Understand the new Philippine puzzle: How globalization relates to its growth without competitiveness
3. Contemplate how CSR can be designed to narrow a gap, including its potentials, limits and pitfalls

Chapter 17

Management in the Philippines

Mari Kondo

OVERVIEW OF THE PHILIPPINE ECONOMY: COMPETITIVENESS AND THE INEQUALITY TRAP

The Philippine Puzzle

The Republic of the Philippines lies close to the world's most dynamic and best performing economies such as China, Korea and Singapore. However, unlike its neighbours, the Philippines' economy is not competitive, ranking 40th among 55 countries in the World Competitiveness Report, and 12th among the 13 Asian Pacific countries (IMD, 2008). The Failed States Index even classified it as a 'borderline' country together with Bosnia, Cambodia, Georgia and Iran (Fund for Peace and the Carnegie Endowment for International Peace, 2008).

The performance of the Philippine economy has been a great puzzle. After it gained independence from the US in 1946 and through the 1950s, the Philippines was Asia's second richest country, and was considered the most promising, having all the elements for success – an educated English-speaking people, natural resources, links to the big US American market, and US-type institutions for democracy and capitalism. Half a century later, it is one of the poorest. Why?

The Philippine Economy

Internationally, the Filipinos are known to be pleasant, capable and well-educated English-speaking workers. The Philippines' population of 90.4 million,[1] majority of Malay-stock, registered as Asia's most highly increased. Their religious affiliations are Roman Catholic (81 per cent), followed by Protestant and other Christian denominations (11 per cent), Islam (5 per cent) and others (2 per cent).[2] Their official languages are 'Filipino' and English, but 78 languages and 500 other dialects have been identified. The literacy rate is 92 per cent.[3]

In 2006, gross domestic product (GDP) was US$117 billion; gross national income (GNI) per capita was US$1,420. The economy consisted of a large and growing service sector (53 per cent of GDP), which absorbed 48 per cent of employment including semi-informal sector jobs for the urban poor. The relatively smaller and stagnating industry sector (33 per cent) accounted for 15 per cent of jobs; and an even smaller, low-productivity agriculture sector (14 per cent) absorbed 37 per cent, probably the rural poor.[4]

Self-rated poverty is around 50 per cent.[5] The Philippine manufacturing sector, supposedly the engine of growth, remains small and internationally uncompetitive. Low production and low technology characterize domestic manufacturing, which has a higher share of low value-added industries such as food, beverages, tobacco and textiles (ADB, 2007b). Since the 1960s, it could absorb only around 10 per cent of the workforce. Consequently, the Philippines has high unemployment (7.8 per cent) and underemployment (22.0 per cent) rates.[6] To survive, some 8.5 million or almost as many as a quarter of the domestic labour force works abroad. Their remittances home constituted more than one-tenth of GDP in 2006, while their families' consumption kept the economy afloat (World Bank, 2007).

Blessed by globalization, the Philippines, in addition to labour, exports hi-tech products and offers business process outsourcing (BPO) services, mainly through multinationals. Recently, the economy has been experiencing record growth, but without competitiveness, so presenting a new puzzle (World Bank, 2008).

The Ten Catalysts and the Inequality Trap

Many factors explain why the Philippine economy has not achieved its full potential. For example, the Philippines has particularly inefficient public administration, endemic corruption, and very low levels of trust beyond the specific clan circles. Redding and Young (2008) summarized ten catalysts for economic success, particularly the evolution of strong, growing enterprises in society. These are presented in Table 17.1. The Philippines shows weaknesses in almost all aspects, systemic ones to a certain extent. Does a root cause exist?

At the risk of being accused of oversimplification, one might advance inequality as a possible answer, because with the Gini coefficient hovering at 40–42,[7] inequality in the Philippines stands out for its historical length and level among Asian countries (although many African and Latin American countries show higher ratios) (ADB, 2007a).[8] IBON Foundation in Manila reported that the net worth of the country's 10 richest families is equivalent to the combined income of its poorest 49 million, or around 55 per cent of the population in 2006.[9]

Beyond the Philippines, there is growing evidence that a long-lasting, very high level of inequality (in opportunities) adversely affects various aspects of competitiveness and the long-term prosperity of society. Society can be caught in a so-called inequality trap.[10] Inequalities reproduce themselves through the interaction of political, economic and sociocultural inequalities, because the initial existence of unequal power tends to shape institutions that regenerate initial conditions, or exacerbate the status quo. If a high level of inequality persists, it makes reduction of poverty difficult even as the economy grows. Also it can hurt the economic growth itself, and bring political instability and undesirable social consequences (Cornia and Cort, 2001; World Bank, 2005). Latin American countries, which generally face higher levels of inequality and lower growth than Asian (miracle) countries, attest to this phenomenon (Perry et al., 2006; for the inequality trap in Mexico, a country that historically influenced the Philippines, see Guerrero et al., 2006).

Table 17.1 The ten catalysts and some Philippine phenomena

Ten catalysts	Philippine phenomena (some examples)
Scientific and technical innovation	Lack of incentive Management difficulties (communication, engagement, coordination) Government's limited capability to orchestrate Human resource/talent constraints => lack of innovation, low R&D expenditure, minimum technological linkage to FDIs
Professional public administration; clean disinterested	Weak state, regulatory capture, inefficiencies in collecting taxes from wealthy and so on Having many political positions occupied 'for the family' until next elections (graft and corruption opportunities) => lack of public goods and services to build competitiveness (infrastructure, education and so on), unpredictable regulations
Legitimate organizational authority	Business is for family. Excessive family-centredness diminishes workers' desire to cooperate and contribute to the owning families' success
Rationalism	Psychological deprivation fosters fatalism, dependency Extreme sensitivity to reciprocity ('we') – against rationalism
Information codification and diffusion	English, many dialects, Catholicism as common ethic Lack of knowledge workers – brain drain, education crisis, 'easy to borrow, quick fix' mentality
Law, available, acceptable and reliable	Weak confidence in legislature due to imperfect democracy (self-serving law by the wealthy for the wealthy) Weak confidence in judiciary (for example some judges can be bought) => weak system trust, weak protection of property rights
Allocative and productive efficiency	Oligopolies => price leadership, restricted outputs Small, concentrated financial sector => restricted role in mobilization of savings, financing business Land reform yet to be effective, regressive tax
Equality and pluralism	A high level of inequality => helplessness, fatalism, dependency on authority, mistrustful of society beyond family
Human talent and skill	Brain drain, deteriorating public education, difficulty in skills formation and innovation
Property rights	Weak protection (social unrest, high crime, unreliable judiciary, inefficient public administration and so on) => fewer investments and transactions, moral hazard problems in organization, motivation problem and so on

Source: Redding and Young, 2008.

The Philippines is often called the 'Latin America of Asia' because of its unique history of Spanish (around 1565–1899) and US American (1899–1941, 1945–46) colonization. Before then, the Philippines consisted of fragmented chiefdoms, without much wealth to concentrate. While nearly 400 years of colonization brought Catholicism, basic education in English and other numerous influences, it also effected a concentration of wealth among the landed, business and/or highly educated elite families, with *political, economic* and *sociocultural institutions* to support it. Having inherited those initial conditions and institutions, the post-independence Philippine economy has suffered inequality and stagnant growth; while its Asian neighbours,

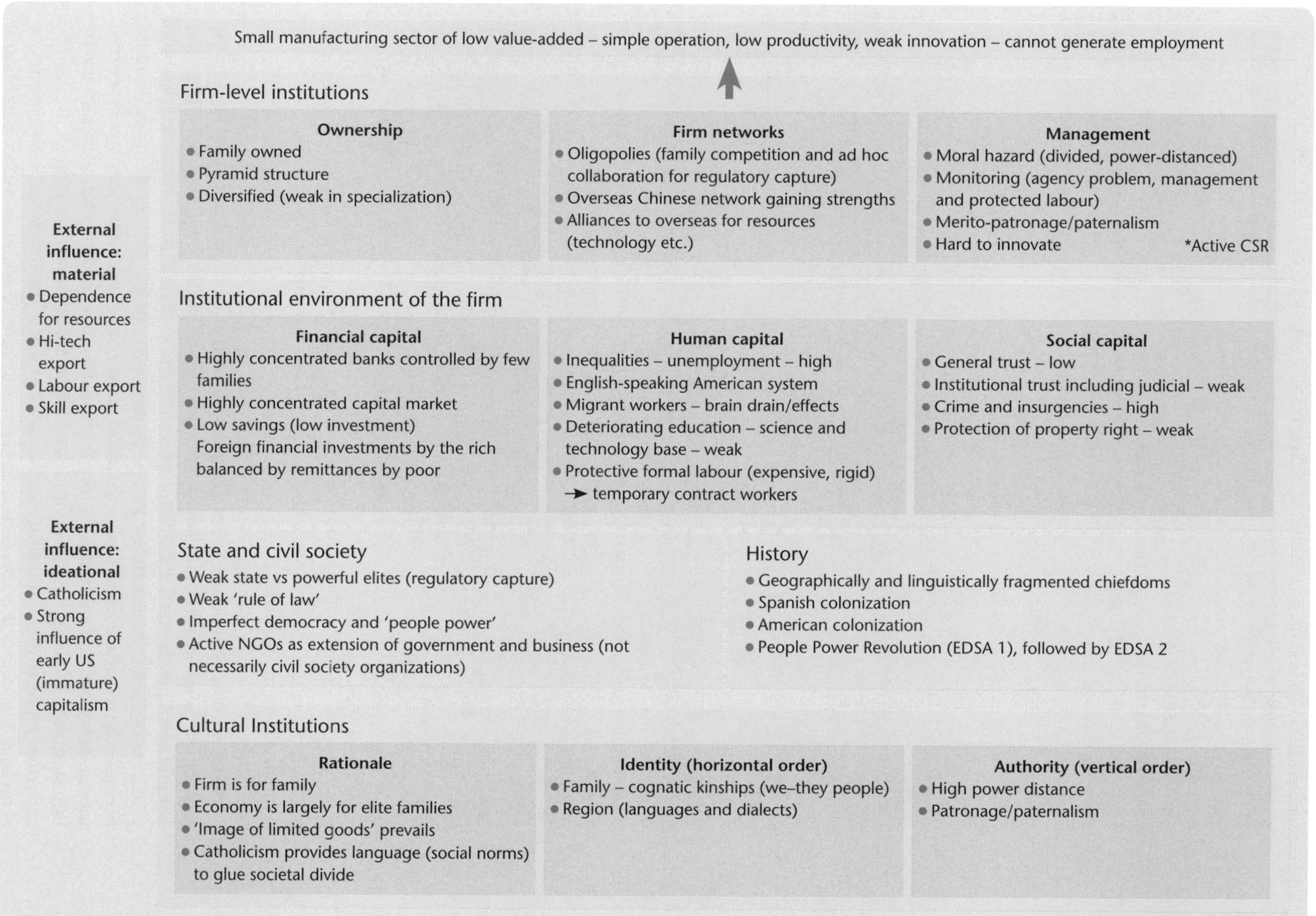

Small manufacturing sector of low value-added – simple operation, low productivity, weak innovation – cannot generate employment

Firm-level institutions

External influence: material
- Dependence for resources
- Hi-tech export
- Labour export
- Skill export

Ownership
- Family owned
- Pyramid structure
- Diversified (weak in specialization)

Firm networks
- Oligopolies (family competition and ad hoc collaboration for regulatory capture)
- Overseas Chinese network gaining strengths
- Alliances to overseas for resources (technology etc.)

Management
- Moral hazard (divided, power-distanced)
- Monitoring (agency problem, management and protected labour)
- Merito-patronage/paternalism
- Hard to innovate   *Active CSR

Institutional environment of the firm

External influence: ideational
- Catholicism
- Strong influence of early US (immature) capitalism

Financial capital
- Highly concentrated banks controlled by few families
- Highly concentrated capital market
- Low savings (low investment)
Foreign financial investments by the rich balanced by remittances by poor

Human capital
- Inequalities – unemployment – high
- English-speaking American system
- Migrant workers – brain drain/effects
- Deteriorating education – science and technology base – weak
- Protective formal labour (expensive, rigid)
  → temporary contract workers

Social capital
- General trust – low
- Institutional trust including judicial – weak
- Crime and insurgencies – high
- Protection of property right – weak

State and civil society
- Weak state vs powerful elites (regulatory capture)
- Weak 'rule of law'
- Imperfect democracy and 'people power'
- Active NGOs as extension of government and business (not necessarily civil society organizations)

History
- Geographically and linguistically fragmented chiefdoms
- Spanish colonization
- American colonization
- People Power Revolution (EDSA 1), followed by EDSA 2

Cultural Institutions

Rationale
- Firm is for family
- Economy is largely for elite families
- 'Image of limited goods' prevails
- Catholicism provides language (social norms) to glue societal divide

Identity (horizontal order)
- Family – cognatic kinships (we–they people)
- Region (languages and dialects)

Authority (vertical order)
- High power distance
- Patronage/paternalism

Figure 17.1 Major characteristics of the Philippine business and management system

Source: Based on Redding (2005) model.

particularly those which gained equality through land reform have been enjoying rapid economic growth.

In describing Philippine business and management systems, the following sections use the framework that Redding (2005) developed. The major characteristics are italicized in the rest of the chapter and presented in Figure 17.1. On the premise that their inequality dynamically relates to its competitiveness in the Philippine case, the phenomena observed in relation to the ten catalysts are presented in Table 17.1. Big firms are the key players of the economy – although they constitute only 3 per cent of enterprises, they accounted for more than 80 per cent of revenues and assets in 2005 (ADB, 2007b). Thus, the characteristics described in Figure 17.1 are more relevant to them.

CULTURE, HISTORY AND STATE

Cultural Institutions

Rationale

Without exaggerating, one learns that the main rule of Philippine society is *'for the family'*. Thus, businesses and firms are family owned. Consequently, the Philippine economy has been arranged largely for elite families, who possess both economic and political power (for example see McCoy, 1993).

Psychological deprivation affects an individual's motivation, reduces initiative and creativity, limits cooperation and encourages fatalism. Various studies around the world have found that long-term deprivation tends to result in a certain common mindset, for example, Foster (1965) found mutual exploitation and fatalism (helplessness and dependency). Ortigas (1994) observed the same among the Filipinos and termed it *'psychology of poverty'*, a vicious cycle whereby deprivation leads to helplessness and dependency, which, in turn, causes further deprivation.

Identity (horizontal order)

Like many in Southeast Asia, Filipinos are bound by *cognatic kinship*, whereby families trace their roots along both their father's and mother's lines, and both boys and girls have equal inheritance rights. Because it is broad and constantly spreading, the family works for an individual as though it were a mutual insurance/help system; hence, the more members there are, the stronger the family.

Because of its expanding nature, the group boundary becomes unclear, and Filipino groups tend to be flexible and inclusive. Filipinos extensively observe the Catholic practice of getting several godfathers and godmothers for baptisms and other sacraments to expand their 'families'. They sometimes end up having hundreds of 'families', including workplace colleagues and superiors, to extend social ties. (In a similar manner, one's hometown and home region are seen as extensions of one's big family; Filipinos strongly identify themselves with their town/region, language, or people with whom they have shared experiences.)

Because of this extensiveness, families and clans, and sometimes alliances of them, become the foundations of competition for power and resources. Family competition can be observed, for example, in national elections, local labour union leaderships, office politics and business competition by elite families.

To make the family system work as mutual insurance/help for the members, social norms such as *utang na loob* (debt of gratitude to be paid back) and *awa* (compassion for people in need) are instilled from an early age to give reciprocal order within the extended family. (These norms also function to create social mechanisms for vertical order, that is, paternalism and the patronage system.)

With those norms, Filipinos are brought up to identify themselves strongly with their extended family as 'we'. Although it is a debated concept, Enriquez, known for the 'Indigenization of Psychology' movement, thinks the core of Filipino interpersonal behaviour is this 'we' feeling, that is, the 'recognition of shared identity with others' (Church and Katigbak, 2002). Once recognized as a part of the 'family', Filipinos seem to feel the other's pain like their own, and exhibit amazing degrees of compassion for those who suffer. This tendency sometimes translates into a tolerance for morally hazardous behaviours in society or in corporate management.

The gender-equal, distributive inheritance system implies easy acceptance of female professionals and leaders. It may imply, however, weakness in capital accumulation over generations, and relatively shorter time perspectives, compared to the patrilineal system of overseas Chinese, for example.

In terms of leadership, a leader, in general, cannot gain legitimacy through his/her inheritance role in cognatic kinship. Therefore, the leader needs to constantly provide (spiritually and) materially, in order to be recognized as a Man of Prowess (Wolters, 1999).

As discussed, the Filipinos' family centredness is deeply rooted in their survival mechanism to cope with a long-term deprivation. However, the extreme sensitivity to reciprocity in relations obfuscates rationality and professionalism, which can cause inefficiencies in public and corporate management.

Authority (vertical order)

There is a state of dependency on authority, which relates to the psychological deprivation discussed above.

Paternalism and patronage: Reflecting centuries-long inequality, the Philippines is one of the largest power-distanced and status-conscious societies when compared internationally (Hofstede, 1980). Since the time of Spanish colonization, peasants could survive only by forging patron–client relations with the land owners. So today, paternalism and patronage still prevail in almost all aspects of vertical relations in the Philippines.

Catholicism: Catholicism provided Filipinos with a way of understanding the universe. Widely and diligently practised across all levels of the population, it is often understood as reflecting their 'worldview', which includes animism and family-centredness (Abinales and Amoroso, 2005). Catholicism provides symbols and analogies for familial and authoritarian norms that are often used to cement society or organizations.

History

Post-independence Philippine history can be divided into three periods. During the first period, Philippine democracy was strongly influenced by the elite families, established during the Spanish and US American periods. Philippine industries were protected by an import-substitution policy, overvalued local currencies and high import tariffs (1950s and 1960s). The overvalued currency made foreign machinery cheaper and labour relatively more expensive, thereby making the companies capital intensive. These created a concentrated industry structure, dominance by large companies, and an orientation towards domestic markets. Oligopolistic behaviours, that is, price leadership, output restrictions and the rise of industry lobby groups, were observed (Saldaña, 2001).

During the second period, under the 20-year rule of the dictator, President Marcos, tariff protections for government-preferred industries remained. Some businesses of elite families were sequestered for the benefit of the Marcos family and their cronies (1970s and early 1980s). His rule ended in 1986 following the first *people power movement* called the People Power Revolution or EDSA I. It was a peaceful popular movement organized by NGO coalitions and alliances of the business elite, the middle classes, the military, labour and the Catholic Church.

During the third period, electoral democracy was restored, again under a strong elite influence, but this time with some NGO influence. Gradual liberalization started in the late 1980s, and later accelerated in the 1990s. President Estrada was charged for corruption and ousted by the second people power movement (EDSA II) in 2001. Some scholars are concerned about this tendency to use 'people power' to remove incumbent presidents using quasi-constitutional means when the status quo is threatened, as doing so hampers the healthy development of a representative democracy (Abinales and Amoroso, 2005).

State and Civil Society

Weak state (vis-à-vis strong business)

Weak bureaucracy: The basic structure of the Philippine government is similar to that of the US. However, among Asian countries (many were British colonies), the Philippines uniquely inherited a poorly developed bureaucratic structure, with the historically rooted concept of 'public service' creating opportunities for graft since the Spanish time. For example, it has twice as many politically appointed positions as the US in order to accommodate families and friends of those in power (World Bank, 2000). Transparency International rated its corruption as one of the highest in Asia (CPI 2.5, 2007).[11]

Regulatory captures: Philippine regulators are often 'captured' by the business they are supposed to regulate, and therefore allow high entry barriers and lucrative rent-seeking practices, which lead to the high cost, low quantity and quality supply of goods and services (Hutchcroft, 1998; World Bank, 2008). Regulatory captures frequently occur in sectors which supply key inputs, for example, electricity. The Manila power tariffs for businesses were reported to be about 20 per cent to 80 per cent higher than those of comparable Southeast Asian cities in 2003, while frequent power disruptions have caused SMEs up to 8 per cent in production losses (ADB, 2007b).

Resource constraints: The Philippine state suffers resource constraints because it cannot collect adequate taxes from the wealthy, and pays large debt services. The Philippine government cannot therefore provide basic services to the population, or the infrastructure for business competitiveness. Of 55 countries considered in the *World Competitiveness Yearbook*, Philippine public finance ranked 48th while its basic infrastructure ranked 54th. Both health and education expenditures ranked 54th (IMD, 2008).

Unreliable judicial system (rule of law): A well-functioning, independent judicial system is essential for rule of law, and thus the protection of property rights, to ensure sound investments and exchange decisions. The Philippine judicial system has been perceived to be notably weak, with judges seen to be serving mostly the interests of the wealthy (World Bank, 2000).

Imperfect democracy: Although the Philippines is one of the most democratic countries in Southeast Asia,[12] unequal power allows the wealthy to influence the decisions of the masses, many of whom are poor, through vote buying, violence and patronage. As a result, historically, the landed and/or business elite have controlled the Philippine legislature. The narrow representation makes it hard to adopt policies to promote the efficient distribution of resources, for example, land (ADB, 2007b).

'Civil society' of ambiguous nature

The Philippines has a vibrant *NGO and PO* (people's organization, such as membership associations of farmers) sector, the third largest in the developing world (Quimpo, 2005). Although some NGOs function as check and balance institutions for state and business, some scholars view the Philippine NGOs and POs as not necessarily 'civil society' organizations, because some function as extensions of the state (Abinales and Amoroso, 2005). Similarly, some NGOs are extensions of business. Nevertheless, NGOs and POs are the essential players in 'people power'.

SUMMARY POINTS

- Business is for the family; thus, the economy is arranged largely for the elite business families.

- Powerful businesses tend to dominate state and 'civil society'.

REFLECTIVE QUESTIONS

- What is your cognatic orientation towards wealth? Why is it important?

INSTITUTIONS AND STRUCTURES FOR COORDINATING BUSINESS

Institutions

Social capital

Societies with a very high level of inequality possess certain commonalities – erosion of social cohesion, social conflicts and uncertain property rights (Cornia and Court, 2001). Philippine society suffers similarly. The general level of trust among Filipinos is much lower than international standards (European Values Study Group and World Values Survey Association, 2006),[13] as is their level of trust towards social institutions.[14]

As described in the above section, reflecting the weakness of the public sphere versus the wealthy or the family, credentials such as licences are sometimes forged and accounting audits may be weak (World Bank, 2006a). The crime rate is high and access to guns is easy. Both communist and Muslim insurgencies occur frequently. Again, property rights are not well protected. Social capital exhibits low trust among the people and society.

Financial capital

Banks dominate the small Philippine financial sector. All large domestic Philippine commercial banks are controlled by a few powerful elite families. A long history of regulatory capture and widespread cartel practices have been reported (Hutchcroft, 1998). Most of the people are too poor to save, and the interest rates for savings are low. The Philippines has the lowest saving mobilization rate among ASEAN countries (though it is higher than in Mexico) (Krinks, 2002).

On the lending side, the World Bank (2008) reported, 'Most banks, given their corporate ownership, lend within their conglomerate, limiting access to outsiders or unconnected companies, which face a declining availability of credit.' Instead of lending to business, Philippine banks make easy money from (perceived) risk-free, high-yielding government bills, because the resource constrained government has to keep borrowing (Krinks, 2002; World Bank, 2008).

Likewise, the Philippine Stock Market is thin, volatile and highly concentrated. Only 237 companies were listed, and the top 10 shared 80 per cent of capitalization in 2006 (World Bank, 2007). As public stock offerings dilute family control, families have been hesitant to go public; or if they do, the owning family effectively controls the business through a multilayered pyramid structure. This structure can easily create minor shareholder rights issues, making the market unattractive to investors (Saldaña, 2001).

Philippine corporations use retained earnings for their operations and project investments, with only a few relying on equity (5 per cent) and bank financing (15 per cent) (World Bank, 2006b). Meanwhile, SMEs suffer from difficulty in obtaining access to financing and from the high cost of financing (ADB, 2007b). The small and highly concentrated financial sector has made a limited contribution to saving mobilization and financing business.

Human capital

Unemployment, inequality, deteriorating education, the brain drain and highly protected formal labour characterize human capital. The Philippines loses human talent crucial to its economic success.

Deteriorating public education: In a society with a high level of inequalities, the education of the wider public tends to be neglected because this requires the transfer of resources from the wealthy, who can afford high quality private education (Birdsall, 2007). In the case of the Philippines, the aforementioned, coupled with the increasing population, has caused the quality of public education to deteriorate seriously. The government has been unable to provide enough classrooms, textbooks and teachers for basic education. However, many students drop out due to poverty. Filipino students' proficiency in maths and science now ranks among the lowest internationally. Further, the Filipinos' English competency has dropped. For tertiary education, the state needs to rely on private institutions, many of which have become mere diploma mills (Abrenica and Tecson, 2003).

Protected formal labour: In order to avoid social and/or labour unrest, the government and business try to buy 'peace' from formal labour. Doing so is easy because formal labour is relatively small in number, and tends to be in the traditionally protected sectors, which enjoy high rents, and thus a proportion of rents is transferred to the union.

The Labor Code issued in the 1970s, when the militant unions linked up with the insurgents, ensures workers, particularly the rank and file, both job and income security regardless of their performance. The labour unions remain well protected, though they are not as active as before. In addition, wages, including minimum wages, have been set high compared with the neighbouring countries (World Bank, 2008). Institutions which buy 'national labour peace' make formal labour in the country more expensive, render labour-intensive industries uncompetitive, generate more informal sector workers, and push more to find work overseas.

Brain drain: The Philippine state facilitates the migration of workers systematically, many of them top quality knowledge workers. Society has consequently lost many of its most educated and talented resources in their most productive years, despite having shouldered the cost of their education. Moreover, reflecting of the lack of opportunities at home, many highly skilled workers, who have acquired knowledge and skills overseas, do not return to the Philippines (Alburo and Abella, 2002).

Firm-level Institutions (Structures for Coordinating Business)

Ownership

Family-owned: Almost all the domestic enterprises in the Philippines are family businesses. By and large, the Philippine economy serves powerful elite families, who constitute a very loosely organized, wealth-based social group, comprising around 60 families (Krinks, 2002). Ethnically, the elite families are mostly composed of the Chinese-Filipinos, descendants of Spanish colonial elites and the wealthy indigenous groups.

Highly diversified: The major elite families tend to own highly diversified conglomerates, which reflect their responses to rent-seeking opportunities. Hardly any specialization can be seen (Hutchcroft, 1998).

Firm networks

Oligopoly: The sectors where high rent can be generated are similar, so that conglomerates show a high concentration within each sector; and different families compete over the pie. However, when faced with challenges to the status quo, they forge ad hoc alliances to influence the sectors' regulatory agencies (Hutchcroft, 1998).

Chinese-Filipino business network: Though the elite unite to maintain the status quo, subtle tensions sometimes arise along ethnic lines. For a long time, the Philippine state adopted an exclusion policy towards the ethnic Chinese. However, with their collective power to fund elections through what they called their 'war chest', ethnic Chinese businesses gradually emerged as political allies, and, especially in the 1990s, were fully recognized in society (Abinales and Amoroso, 2005).

Overseas networks: Overseas networks are important to creating access to resources, including technologies. Sometimes they can be also used for political reasons (see the Ayala case at the end of this chapter).

SUMMARY POINTS

A prolonged high level of inequality, together with other causes, might have induced:

- Low trust among people and the social system, inclusive of property rights and the rule of law. The fragile social capital hinders transactions and investments.

- A small and highly concentrated financial sector. Its contribution to the allocative and productive efficiency needed for economic success, is limited.

- Deteriorating education and the brain drain. The Philippines loses human talent crucial for economic success.

- A necessity to buy labour peace, which, in turn, makes Philippine labour internationally uncompetitive.

THE NEW PHILIPPINE PUZZLE: GROWTH WITHOUT COMPETITIVENESS

In the current globalization, while other countries seriously invest in science and technology as key to competitiveness, Philippine businesses lack any orientation towards innovation, particularly in science and technologies. The Philippines invested only 0.11 per cent of GDP on R&D in 2005, much lower than Thailand (0.26 per cent), Malaysia (0.69 per cent) and most countries in the world. It is dependent on borrowed technologies, usually embodied in new machinery from abroad (ADB, 2007b).

There are various reasons for this. One is that big business can reap enough profits from the domestic market without innovation. Second are the difficulties arising from their people management style and human resources (discussed in the next section). Thirdly, the state is not equipped to play an important role in technology accumulation via its policies and interventions (Abrenica and Tecson, 2003). Meanwhile, without science and technology innovation, the Philippines benefits from globalization by connecting its people directly to outside systems. It exports hi-tech products (using only labour in export processing zones), skills (service outsourcing) and people (including 'knowledge workers').

Export processing zones: The Philippines is the number one hi-tech export country in the world (IMD, 2008) with electronics comprising 61.6 per cent of total exports (NSO, 2008). However, these are assembled by multinationals in export processing zones, that is, semi-outside the Philippine system, using imported parts and Philippine labour. Because the products fall under only two categories with high technological sophistication, such as hard disks and semiconductors, linkages to the domestic industry are virtually non-existent and technology spillover is minimal. If the multinationals relocate, the Philippines will be left without any other major products to export; prompting it to join the race to the bottom and provide one of the most generous FDI conditions in the region (Abrenica and Tecson, 2003).

Outsourcing: Business process outsourcing (BPO) is currently the fastest growing sector in the country, inclusive of call centres, back office services, software development and so on. Around three-quarters of BPO businesses are call centre operations, a low-end BPO sub-sector. BPO does not have much linkage to domestic industry and, unlike manufacturing, its scope of job generation is limited. The ability of the sector to move up the knowledge ladder to sustain the current growth is uncertain (Magtibay-Ramos et al., 2007).

Migrant workers: The state-coordinated system of migrant workers, which started in the 1970s, has evolved into a well-organized national system for maintaining the status quo. Domestic businesses enjoy higher consumption rates from remittances received by the overseas Filipino workers' families, while the state has been saved from social unrest arising from high unemployment. Thus, motivating and exporting workers has become a very serious state business, with the president herself praising them as 'modern-day heroes', somehow hinting at an image of a saviour, in a national ceremony at the presidential palace. As discussed earlier, however, this brain drain damages Philippine competitiveness.

Current economic growth is largely fuelled by remittances from overseas and BPO growth, and to a certain extent by the hi-tech exports. They are quick and easy fixes, which help maintain the status quo of domestic business, almost without any effort to innovate. As it is not based on the competitiveness of Philippine businesses, the World Bank (2008) warns 'Growth is not inclusive – the recent growth is jobless – and poverty reduction is slower.' This is a typical description of an inequality trapped economy.

THE PHILIPPINE MANAGEMENT SYSTEM

With the hope that market liberalization and increased competition would instantly make Philippine manufacturing competitive, in the 1990s, the Philippines rushed into almost unilateral liberalization without any preparation. Businesses could not adjust quickly, thereby resulting in massive unemployment (Abinales and Amoroso, 2005). (If the Philippine manufacturing sector provided more jobs, the Philippines would not have to contend with poverty and inequality issues.) Why has the Philippine manufacturing sector failed to adjust? Why does it still focus on low value-added industries which require only simple coordination and technologies? Why can't it innovate? Significant challenges exist in people management.

Challenges

Coordination, innovation and knowledge creation

Generally, employing those with talent, together with the free exchange of ideas and information within the organization, triggers innovation and knowledge creation. Without these, Philippine business organizations find it difficult to move up to the higher value-added industries which require sophisticated coordination, innovation and knowledge creation.

Vertical communication: A high level of inequality creates broad differences among workers in terms of their education, proficiency in English, lifestyles and cognitive orientations. In addition, people feel a high power-distance, which inhibits upward communication. The vertical flow of information within the organization is constrained.

Horizontal communication: Trust level among people is low, except among family members. Although many pleasantries are exchanged to ease interpersonal tensions, individuals tend to keep critical information to themselves, knowledge being the source of power.

Engagement: Businesses and firms are for the owning family. As employees are not family members, they tend to feel exploited and are thus less engaged.

Human talent: The deteriorating quality of education and the brain drain constrain available talent, especially among knowledge workers. Many seek local jobs to gain the experience needed to get overseas jobs. Some firms have stopped recruiting top graduates, in anticipation of their quickly leaving for overseas.

Skill formation among workers

In addition to the aforementioned, below are two factors that make skill formation a challenge:

Rigid and protected regularized workers: Though rank and file workers cannot be promoted, their wages and jobs are secure regardless of their performance. It is hard to motivate them to acquire skills.

Casual labour: Because employment of regularized workers is expensive and rigid, management extensively resorts to casual workers, who often receive lower than minimum wages. By law, they can work only up to six months to protect regularized workers. The possibility of skill development is constrained.

Moral hazards and monitoring

Many Filipino firms suffer from moral hazard behaviour[15] because of weak property rights protection, excessive family centredness, mistrust and a feeling of being exploited, a protective labour law, difficulties in communication and information sharing, and other odds. Much of the management effort is directed to monitoring workers. Below are two examples:

Divide and rule: In some companies, in order to control and monitor labour, managements, as the Spanish colonizers did, tend to 'divide and rule' workers so they do not collude against management. For this, managements use divisions in society, such as status, home regions and languages/dialects.

Agency problem: Given the ambiguous rule of law and property rights protection, family business owners directly involve themselves in management and make the decisions. Some also rely on inner-circle professional executives. They are highly paid so that they do not loot company assets.

Patronage and Paternalism

However, once Filipino workers feel they are part of the 'family' at the workplace, they show tremendous dedication to the work. Confronted by the challenges described above, many managements resort to patronage and paternalism to bring 'family' into the organization. However, both practices may harm organizational efficiency.

Patronage: Just as in Philippine politics, hierarchies of patron–client networks are observed from the top (the owner), to the bottom (casual employees) of the organization, and quietly but strongly affect every aspect of people management (Selmer and de Leon, 2001). Protégés of executives function as the 'eyes and ears' of the patron in monitoring other workers. Expected to work hard and stay in the organization, they are subjected to training to avert the possibility of a brain drain in the company. Many Philippine corporations try to weave a patronage into meritocracy, in order to minimize its negativity (Kondo, 2008).

Paternalism: Through paternalism, the use of Catholicism and other cultural symbols to enhance norms of familial and hierarchical reciprocities, business organizations try to convey a godfather image to their employees. Thus, they give a 50-kg sack of rice to each employee every month and initiate the holding of Holy Mass and festive meals on special occasions, like a good Filipino family would do.

To promote familial feelings, Philippine management also shows considerable tolerance for workers' moral hazard behaviours. For example, many bosses allow subordinates to sell goods to their fellow workers at the workplace during office hours so that the subordinates can augment their incomes for their families.

SUMMARY POINTS

- Philippine (domestic manufacturing) organizations experience difficulties in coordination, innovation and skill formation. Much of the management effort is used to monitor workers.

- Patronage and paternalism are used to bring 'family' into the organization. In the process, Philippine management tends to show considerable tolerance for workers' moral hazard behaviours.

REFLECTIVE QUESTIONS

■ How does the management system in your home country relate to divisions within your society? How does it relate to competitiveness?

CORPORATE SOCIAL RESPONSIBILITY

Philippine CSR, largely conducted by the elite businesses, including well-established multinationals, and traditionally understood as philanthropy, has been very active and even highly praised internationally. Reflecting a weak state vis-à-vis strong business, Philippine CSR is becoming a national institution such that the state set a 'CSR Week' when the annual 'CSR Expo' was conducted. At the event, the president herself appealed to rich corporations to shoulder more responsibility along the lines of what, traditionally, the state should provide.

Philippine CSR has a long history, having originated from the donations made to churches and hospitals. After government allowed donations for social development to be tax deductible in 1958, many big firms created their own corporate foundations (Magno, 2004). In 1970, hoping to counter the rise of social unrest and insurgency, elite businesses jointly formed an umbrella CSR NGO, which eventually promoted community relations (*comrel*) techniques among member companies (Philippine Business for Social Progress, 2000). In essence, *comrel* is a firm's way of depicting itself as the socially just 'godfather' of the community, getting the right to operate. Widely practised, it has helped contain insurgency at the community level.

With the emergence of 'people power', a popular movement with a new concept of 'democracy', the capability to organize the masses through a coalition of NGOs and POs became critical for businesses to maintain their influence over state power – including ousting two presidents in the past. Philippine CSR further evolved as the 'people power' movement in the late 1980s to the 1990s, with the formation of nationwide CSR NGO networks for issues beyond *comrel*'s purview. For instance, after the 1991 Baguio earthquake, an elite business association organized the Corporate Network for Disaster Response (CNDR), which has helped many Filipinos (Roman, 2007). Meanwhile CSR NGO executives, who became political appointees to cabinet positions, have started to address the concerns of the poor.

In the 2000s, global enthusiasm represented by the UN Global Compact to achieve its Millennium Development Goals enhanced the legitimization of Philippine CSR institutions. A social consensus appeared to be developing whereby big business should consolidate CSR efforts to shoulder national development agendas such as education (Roman, 2007). Criticisms were directed at CSR efforts for being a mere drop in the ocean, however, but given the constrained resources of the state, the Philippines has been left with no choice but to depend on CSR.

Meanwhile, a recent survey found that donations to communities and other charities may discourage the elite from paying higher taxes (Clarke and Sison, 2003), a propensity that may raise concerns regarding CSR's unintended result of weakening state power. The state which cannot collect enough tax from the wealthy cannot provide the much needed basic services to the wider public.

Spotlight on CSR: Textbook Corruption and the Red Trucks of Coca-Cola

In the 1990s, the Department of Education (DepEd) was acknowledged as one of the five most corrupt Philippine government agencies. After textbook production for the country's 17 million students was privatized, costs increased, quality deteriorated and deliveries were delayed or sometimes not made as department officials colluded with suppliers. The result – as many as eight students having to share one textbook in nearly all of the nation's 42,000 public elementary and secondary schools.

From 2003 to 2005, in order to arrest this problem, DepEd, under a newly appointed secretary, carried out the 'Textbook Count' programme which reengineered the bidding process and the manner by which textbooks would be delivered. For example, the DepEd publicly announced the exact date and the number of textbooks to be delivered by producers to each school, and arranged to have local boy and girl scouts physically count the textbooks delivered. As an initial result of Textbook Count, both textbook prices and production times were halved, and the correct number of deliveries was made on time.

Yet, problems remained for remote district offices, which were responsible for the final delivery of textbooks to far-flung schools. As a solution, an agreement was reached with Coca-Cola Philippines, which delivers Coke products even to the country's hard-to-reach areas, to pick up textbooks from the district offices and have them delivered to schools at no additional cost to DepEd. From then on, it appeared as though the governance problem was solved by the state's orchestrating CSR and people and the programme was hailed as an institutional best practice by the World Bank and OECD.

However, immediately after a change in the leadership of DepEd in 2005, the programme was discontinued. The monitoring efforts of the textbook deliveries have been continued, though with greater difficulty because less information has been reported.

Sources: Luz, J.M. (2004). Reflections on institutional reform at the Department of Education. *The SGV Review*, 2(1). Luz, J.M. and Carpintero, A. (2006). National Textbook Delivery Program, a paper presented at the Joint Venture on Procurement Meeting, Manila; Personal interview with J.M. Luz, former undersecretary, DepEd and C. Alcantara, Coca-Cola Foundation.

Peace is essential to development. Looking back, one can conclude that it is an honourable achievement that Philippine CSR has helped the country in terms of its peaceful development through *comrel;* and, to a certain extent, through peaceful transitions of presidential power. Philippine CSR has also helped provide channels for the voice of the marginalized to somehow reach the state's agenda, through CSR NGOs.

On the other hand, Philippine CSR can also be viewed as a historically evolved mechanism to 'buy peace' and 'buy political influence' so that the elite's power can be maintained. In order to facilitate the peaceful and gradual advancement of Philippine society, therefore, the following three points may need to be carefully considered in designing CSR:

- Implications on the power and role of the state: CSR should not induce possible distortions, especially in tax and basic service delivery systems, which further weaken the people's confidence in the state.
- Implications on the healthy development of constitutional (electoral) democracy
- Effectiveness of the globally standardized CSR, as a universal 'civil regulation' in the Philippines weak state vis-à-vis strong business context. For example, Vogel (2005) argues, 'Not only is CSR not a substitute for effective government, but the effectiveness of much civil regulation depends on a strong and well-functioning public sphere.'

LIVING IN THE PHILIPPINES AND HOPES FOR THE FUTURE

The Philippines is a pleasant country to work in because of its being largely English-speaking and the existence of US American business systems. Given their gender-equal cognatic kinship with blurred boundaries, Filipinos accept either gender with amazing ease.

The Philippines is a paradise for an expatriate because most of the country's systems are made for the wealthy, and prices are the lowest in the world (IMD, 2008). Many expatriates can thus afford to live in huge houses resembling resort villas in gated residential communities, complete with swimming pools, beautiful tropical gardens, and special quarters for domestic helpers, who can prepare international cuisine thanks to their overseas experience.

Nonetheless, living in the Philippines means living in a dichotomy. A high incidence of crime means that gated residential areas have to be protected by armed security guards, as does one's office. Once troubled, many expatriates simply flee the country for security reasons.

Hopes for the Future

Living in a dichotomy requires considerable energy. But it is a rather invigorating experience to witness the various efforts that concerned Filipinos have initiated to narrow the gap. For example, at the level of culture, through education and media, Filipinos are trying to raise awareness for empowerment. In fact, 'empowerment' is probably one of Philippine society's most frequently used words. Another example is the efforts to strengthen the state. In 2006, government increased the VAT rate and substantially improved its fiscal position. It is hoped that the state regains the people's confidence in its ability to utilize taxes for equity-based growth.

There have also been substantial efforts to reform the institutional environment of firms. In the financial sectors, comprehensive banking and market reforms have been in progress. As for human capital, with the increase in tax revenue, the state was able to allocate more to education in 2007, and businesses in the Philippines, including those of multinationals, are also actively contributing.

Changes can be also witnessed at the firm level. Newly emerging business leaders hope to reform the state and business by addressing corruption and corporate governance issues. To this end, they have created alliances with reputable watchdog NGOs. The way people are managed is also changing. In order to instil trust within the organizations, many Philippine firms conduct 'value-formation seminars', which espouse Christian-based familial values, for the workers, including the lowest ranked.

Filipino society accepts expatriates easily. Because there is so much that even an expatriate can do to assist the efforts of Filipinos to advance their society, living and working in the Philippines can be an especially exciting and rewarding experience for those who would like to take a proactive role.

SUMMARY POINTS

- Getting out of the inequality trap is difficult, but at all levels, Filipinos are tackling the problems; some expatriates are joining their efforts.

CROSS-CHAPTER REFLECTIVE QUESTION

- One important message we get from this chapter is that the Filipino government does not seem to take much initiative in enhancing technology or innovation development. That is why the current puzzle is, as mentioned by the author, 'growth without competitiveness'. The situation is very different in India (Chapter 10) where the Ministry of Information Technology takes the lead in supporting R&D activities. Can you reconcile what one country is doing but the other is not, and why?

CHAPTER SUMMARY

- The Philippine economy has not achieved its potential due to its uncompetitive, low value-added manufacturing sector.
- Its economic, political and sociocultural institutions are shaped largely to allow powerful elite families to maintain their power.
- Filipino family centredness is deeply rooted on how the family functions for an individual to survive deprivation, and tends to come before public concerns.
- The weak state cannot provide goods and services needed for development. It suffers from endemic corruption.
- Oligopolistic behaviours of key sectors have constrained Philippine competitiveness.
- The small and highly concentrated financial sector has made limited contributions to saving mobilization and financing business.
- Unemployment, inequality, deteriorating education, the brain drain and highly protected formal labour characterize human capital.
- Social capital exhibits low trust among people and the system in society.
- The Philippines enjoys those aspects of globalization that connect its people directly to outside systems. The economy has grown but not business competitiveness. Investments by Philippine businesses in R&D remain scant.
- Philippine management faces challenges in coordination, innovation and skill formation, the essentials to moving up to higher value-added industries.
- Patronage and paternalism constrain organizational efficiencies.
- Philippine CSR has helped the country's peaceful development. For further effectiveness, however, the Philippines may need to strengthen its public sphere.
- At all levels, Filipinos are trying to regain the country's competitiveness by closing the gap.

KEY CONCEPTS

Inequality traps: Inequalities (in opportunities) reproduce themselves through the interaction of political, economic and sociocultural inequalities. (Prolonged severe inequality can damage economic growth, and bring political instability and undesirable social consequences.)

Cognatic kinship: Filipinos subscribe to cognatic kinship which recognizes equal descent through males and females. Because of their extensiveness, families and clans become the foundation of competition for power and resources.

Migrant workers: The Philippine state coordinates 'people exports' to earn foreign exchange and ease social unrest, thereby maintaining the status quo.

Philippine CSR: Philippine CSR, which started as a business response to social unrest, has evolved to become an important subsystem in the country through extensive NGO networks.

REVIEW QUESTIONS

1. What are the specific features of the Philippine economy?
2. Why could the Philippine economy not achieve its potential?
3. How has globalization affected the Philippines?
4. What are the challenges that Philippine management faces?
5. What roles has Philippine CSR played in society?

LEARNING ACTIVITIES AND DISCUSSIONS

1. Search the internet for countries which have had high levels of inequality over a long period. Discuss with your classmates, the impacts of inequality on their business and management systems.
2. Search the internet for the migrant policy of your country. Considering the cost to sending and receiving countries, what are the options for making migration beneficial to both sides? As a manager, what points should you be careful about in management and negotiations?
3. Discuss kinship with your classmates. What are the main differences between Chinese, Indian, Japanese and cognatic kinships? How can businesses reflect those options in their management?
4. With your classmates, discuss how CSR can influence a developing country: what possibilities exist, and what are the potential pitfalls?

MINI CASE

AYALA GROUP The Philippines' most reputable conglomerate

The Ayala Group of Companies, one of the most reputable conglomerates in the Philippines, represented 25 per cent of market capitalization in 2002. Pyramidically arranged, the Ayala family's Mermac, a private corporation, holds a majority of the shares of the public Ayala Corporation (AC). AC effectively controls several public operational companies and their subsidiaries, through direct or cross shareholdings.

Founded in 1834, Ayala has grown with the history of the Philippines. For example, its Bank of the Philippine Islands issued the country's first currency notes. After World War II, the Ayalas successfully converted their Hacienda Makati into the country's biggest business centre. Then, during the Marcos era, Ayala avoided sequestration by incorporating AC to allow wider shareholdings, inviting Mitsubishi of Japan, from which country Marcos obtained large funds in development aid; and strictly upholding the family policy of not being 'clearly' involved in politics.

In the 1990s, Ayala entered the liberalized sectors through alliances with multinationals, thereby creating the nation's second largest telecommunications company and a water utility. Both have been recognized as successful businesses and social projects providing services to the poor. Ayala also developed an export-oriented industrial park which has helped to attract many hi-tech FDIs. In the 2000s, Ayala invested in IT and the BPO industries.

The excellence of the Ayala management vis-à-vis other Filipino family conglomerates has been proven by its water concession business. In 1997, Ayala took on the eastern half of water concession in Metro Manila, effectively raising the 24-hour availability of water from 26 per cent to 89 per cent in seven years. Meanwhile, a different family conglomerate which took on the western half went bankrupt. The success of Ayala's operations can be attributed to good corporate governance which does not allow connected companies to loot; good financial management; and innovations by management to let the poor have access to water, while allowing them to pay through a group responsible scheme. Ayala is also known for the Ayala Foundation which organizes the annual CSR Expo and seeks to contribute 'to the eradication of poverty in all its forms'.

Several internal factors have contributed to Ayala's success:

- one side of the Ayala family holding a majority of Mermac, while the other managed AC
- Ayala purposely restricting the number of family members involved in top management to three, with a mandatory retirement age of 60 for all
- paternalistic policies, though which Ayala has instilled 'stewardship' even among its non-family management teams.

QUESTIONS

1. What internal and external factors have helped Ayala grow?
2. In which aspects has the management of Ayala been typical or atypical of Philippine business?
3. What role can Ayala play to advance Philippine society?

Sources: Ayala Corporation homepage www.ayala.com.ph; Ayala Foundation homepage www.ayalafoundation.org; Batalla, E. (1999). Zaibatsu development in the Philippines. *Southeast Asian Studies*, **37**(1): 18–49; Gibson, K. (2002). A case for the family-owned conglomerate. *McKinsey Quarterly*, (4): 126–37; Wright, C. (2006). All about Ayala. *Asia Money*, May, 26–8; Wu, X. and Malaluan, N. (2008). A tale of two concessionaires. *Urban Studies*, **45**(1): 207–29.

INTERESTING WEB LINKS

Socioeconomic data and research papers: http://www.pids.gov.ph/
On culture: http://www.bansa.org/
On society: http://www.sws.org.ph/

Notes

1   2008 estimate. http://www.census.gov.ph/
2   https://www.cia.gov/library/publications/the-world-factbook/
3   http://www.census.gov.ph/
4   http://www.census.gov.ph/data/quickstat/index.html http://www.census.gov.ph/data/sectordata/2006/lf060405.htm
5   http://www.sws.org.ph/
6   http://www.census.gov.ph/
7   It continues to increase mainly due to the lack of access to education (ADB, 2007a)
8   Income inequality in the Philippines declined between 1960 and 1990. (Cornia and Court, 2001).
9   http://info.ibon.org/index.php?option=com_content&task=view&id=140&Itemid=50
10 The mechanism of the trap was explained as follows: 'The interaction of political, economic, and sociocultural inequalities shapes the institutions and rules in all societies. The way these institutions function affects people's opportunities and their ability to invest and prosper. Unequal economic opportunities lead to unequal outcomes and reinforce unequal political power. Unequal power shapes institutions and policies that tend to foster the persistence of the initial conditions' (World Bank, 2005).
11 http://www.transparency.org/news_room/in_focus/2007/cpi2007/cpi_2007_table
12 http://www.freedomhouse.org/template.cfm?page=363&year=2007
13 Abad's (2005) detailed study on social capital shows that the kin network provides a strong base for human relations in the Philippines, and that social capital is more developed among the ranks of the privileged than among the lower classes.
14 www.sws.org.ph/pr070629.htm
15 http://www.aim.edu.ph/media/Corrupt%20Practices%20II%20Exec.%20Summary%20final.pdf

REFERENCES

Abad, R.G. (2005). Social capital in the Philippines: Results from a national survey. *Philippine Sociological Review* 53: 7–63.

Abinales, P. and Amoroso, D. (2005). *State and Society in the Philippines.* Lanhan: Rowman & Littlefield Publishers, Inc.

Abrenica, J.V. and Tecson, G.R. (2003). Can the Philippines ever catch up? In Lall, S. and Urata, S. (eds) *Competitiveness, FDI and Technological Activity in East Asia.* Cheltenham: Edward Elgar.

ADB (2007a). *Key Indicators 2007: Inequality in Asia.* Manila: Asian Development Bank.

ADB (2007b). *Philippines: Critical Development Constraints.* Manila: Asian Development Bank.

Alburo, F.A. and Abella, D.I. (2002). Skilled labour migration from developing countries: Study on the Philippines. International Migration Papers, 51. Geneva: ILO.

Batalla, E. (1999). Zaibatsu development in the Philippines. *Southeast Asian Studies,* **37**(1): 18–49.

Birdsall, N. (2007). Inequality matters: Why globalization doesn't lift all boats. *Boston Review*, March/April 2007. Available at: http://bostonreview.net/BR32.2/birdsall.php.

Church, T.A. and Katigbak, M.S. (2002). Indigenization of psychology in the Philippines. *International Journal of Psychology*, **37**(3): 129–48.

Clarke, G. and Sison, M. (2003). Voices from the top of the pile: Elite perceptions of poverty and the poor in the Philippines. *Development and Change*, **34**(2): 215–42.

Cornia, G.A. and Court, J. (2001). Inequality, growth and poverty in the era of liberalization and globalization. Policy Brief No. 4. Helsinki: UNU/WIDER.

European Values Study Group and World Values Survey Association (2006). European and World Values Surveys Four-wave Integrated Data File, 1981–2004, V. 20060423.

Foster, G.M. (1965). Peasant society and the image of limited good. *American Anthropologist*, **67**(2): 293–315.

Fund for Peace and the Carnegie Endowment for International Peace (2008). The Failed State Index 2008. Available at: http://www.foreignpolicy.com/story/cms.php?story_id=4350.

Gibson, K. (2002). A case for the family-owned conglomerate. *McKinsey Quarterly*, (4): 126–37.

Guerrero, I., López-Calva, L.F. and Walton, M. (2006). The inequality trap and its links to low growth in Mexico. Available at: http://iepecdg.com/DISK%201/Arquivos/Leiturassugeridas/walton-ingles-24-11-17122006.pdf.

Hofstede, G. (1980). Motivation, leadership and organization: Do American theories apply abroad? *Organizational Dynamics*, **9**(1): 42–63.

Hutchcroft, P.D. (1998). *Booty Capitalism: The Politics of Banking in the Philippines*. Quezon City: Ateneo de Manila University Press.

IMD (2008). *IMD World Competitiveness Yearbook 2008*. Available at: http://www.worldcompetitiveness.com/OnLine/.

Kondo, M. (2008). Twilling bata bata into meritocracy: Merito patronage management system in a modern Filipino Corporation. *Philippine Studies*. **56**(3): 251–84.

Krinks, P. (2002). *The Economy of the Philippines: Elites, Inequalities and Economic Restructuring*. London: Routledge.

Luz, J.M. (2004). Reflections on institutional reform at the Department of Education. *The SGV Review*. **2**(1).

Luz, J.M. and Carpintero, A. (2006). National Textbook Delivery Program. A paper presented at the Joint Venture on Procurement Meeting, Manila.

McCoy, A.W. (ed.) (1993). *An Anarchy of Families: State and Family in the Philippines*. Madison, WI: Center for Southeast Asian Studies, University of Wisconsin-Madison.

Magno, F.A. (2004). Investing in corporate social responsibility: Corporate-community engagement in Cebu City, Philippines. In Contreras, M.E. (ed.) *Corporate Social Responsibility in the Promotion of Social Development*. Washington, DC: Inter-American Development Bank.

Magtibay-Ramos, N., Estrada, G. and Felipe, J. (2007). An analysis of the Philippine business process outsourcing industry. ERD Working Paper (93). Manila: Asian Development Bank.

NSO (National Statistics Office) (2008). Foreign trade statistics of the Philippines: 2007. Available at http://www.census.gov.ph/data/sectordata/sr08337tx.html.

Ortigas, C.D. (1994). The psychology of poverty and the dynamics of empowerment. In Ortigas, C.D. (ed.) *Human Resource Development: The Philippine Experience: Readings for the Practitioner*. Manila: Ateneo de Manila University Press.

Perry, G.E., Arias, O., López, J.H., Maloney, W.F. and Servén, L. (2006). *Poverty Reduction and Growth: Virtuous and Vicious Circles*. Washington, DC: World Bank.

Philippine Business for Social Progress (2000). *Our Legacy*. Manila: Philippine Business for Social Progress.

Quimpo, N.G. (2005). Oligarchic patrimonialism, bossism, electoral clientelism, and contested democracy in the Philippines. *Comparative Politics*, **37**(2): 229–50.

Redding, G. (2005). The thick description and comparison of societal systems of capitalism. *Journal of International Business Studies.* **36**(2): 123–55.

Redding, G. and Young, L. (2008). The ten catalysts. Working paper, INSEAD Euro-Asia Center.

Roman, F.L. (2007). Philippine CSR over five decades: Networks, drivers, and emerging views. In *Doing Good in Business Matters: CSR in the Philippines.* Manila: Asian Institute of Management and De La Salle Professional Schools.

Saldaña, C.G. (2001). Philippines. In Capulong, M., Edwards, D., Webb, D. and Zhuang, J. (eds) *Corporate Governance and Finance in East Asia.* Manila: Asian Development Bank.

Selmer, J.C. and de Leon, C. (2001). Pinoy-style HRM: Human resource management in the Philippines. *Asia Pacific Business Review*, **8**(1): 127–44.

Vogel, D. (2005). *The Market for Virtue.* Washington, DC: Brookings Institution Press.

Wolters, O.W. (1999). *History, Culture, and Region in Southeast Asian Perspectives.* (revised edition). Ithaca, NY: SEAP Publications.

World Bank (2000). *Combating Corruption in the Philippines.* Washington, DC: World Bank.

World Bank (2005). *World Development Report 2006: Equity and Development.* Washington, DC: World Bank.

World Bank (2006a). *Philippines – Report on the Observance of Standards and Codes (ROSC): Accounting and Auditing Update.* Washington, DC: World Bank.

World Bank (2006b). *Philippines – Report on the Observance of Standards and Codes (ROSC): Corporate Governance Country Assessment.* Washington, DC: World Bank.

World Bank (2007). *Philippines – Invigorating Growth, Enhancing its Impact.* Washington, DC: World Bank.

World Bank (2008). *Rising Growth, Declining Investment: The Puzzle of the Philippines Breaking the 'Low-Capital-Stock' Equilibrium.* Washington, DC: World Bank.

Wright, C. (2006). All about Ayala. *Asia Money*, 26–28 May.

Wu, X. and Malaluan, N. (2008). A tale of two concessionaires. *Urban Studies*, **45**(1): 207–29.

Epilogue

As our study tour around Asian business comes to a close, it is time to review what we have learned and consider future implications.

Asia has bounced back from the financial crisis of 1997 to become a production base for the world, with Japan, China and India at the heart of this phenomenon. Yet, as we have seen, Asia has been encountering difficulties with the shadow side of its enormous export-led economic growth – the need for sustainable development and environmental care. Our investigation has involved seven themes common to business management, and the assessment of them in ten specific Asian countries; and we see that Asian business management is like a carpet, composed of many diverse strands, but run through with a single common thread – the twin issues of sustainability and democracy. At this point in time, that thread calls for Asia, more than anywhere else in the world, to become a beacon of sustainability and democracy in business, if economic development is to become real development.

We have used systems theory to gain a perspective on Asian business management, eschewing the customary profit-led perspective more commonly employed in international business to date. Our approach turns the focus on to systemic entities, by looking at the linkages and relationships built up between the whole and individual components, examining the openness and circularity of their relationships in an 'introspective development' paradigm. 'Looking from inside', as it were, in this way can be highly effective in seeking strategies for sustainable development in Asia's economy, society and environment, as the focus is on the integral dynamics of the overall system. We can now review our seven themes from the viewpoint of our common thread.

From the perspective of business systems, business management can be studied in its social, economic and cultural context through interconnected concepts of coordination, order and meaning. Therefore, geography, history, religion, values, people, capital, governance rules, institutions, regulations and social relations become important system components and exert processes that influence economy and society, shaping Asia's diversity and uniqueness. Connections, patterns, network, interaction and process are key concepts for understanding business management, and systems theory is a way to understand the dynamic nature of company management in relation to its context.

The notions of CSR and sustainable development make us rethink the meaning of company activities. These factors are essential for any continuing economic and social development and reflect enduring human values; the energy to pursue them will emerge from the people's perception of democracy. Deepening this perception in popular consciousness will help raise social awareness among management executives and generate a democratic countervailing force in society at large. Among the initiatives that may redefine company behaviour in relation to civil society can be counted voluntary action, legislative reform and democratic activism, including labour unions and non-governmental organizations. Through such activities, a proactive stance on CSR and sustainable development will become a requirement for companies seeking to strengthen their competitiveness in Asia.

History shows us how the present is but a tiny ripple in the tides of time, and the history of technology reaffirms this. Fragmentary discoveries in physics and chemistry developed into systematic sciences, which produced the substantial technologies we know today. The East was once the world's technological powerhouse, before the tides shifted westwards; today, with globalization as an agent of transfer, there is a shrinking gap in technological capability between regions. Current concerns about the environment and sustainable development are contemporary manifestations of the social relationships that spin off at all times during the historical process. When technologies are transferred by capitalist entities, differential development will inevitably appear. To ensure that technologies will enter the preserve of civil society, recognition of the values of social responsibility and sustainable development is needed.

The concept of 'network' also relates to technology. Linkages between the individual components (companies and people) that constitute networks have great significance, carrying important political and economic implications. It is vital to ask why a network has arisen and how it is constructed. East Asia's production network shows how Western technologies are being transferred to Japan and that Japanese technologies are being transferred to Asia, while economic development in China and India raises the possibility that it may be Asia pushing at the frontiers of science, technology and knowledge in the 21st century. If Asia can create a regional production system that transcends narrow profit-oriented functionality and does not degrade human dignity or ecological sustainability, it will achieve high distinction around the world.

Human history and experience is reflected in culture, built upon foundations of religious thought and normative values, influencing the way people think and behave, and at the same time being constantly refreshed by behavioural adaptations to changing conditions. Culture dwells in human consciousness rather than existing objectively and becomes visible as a way of thinking or acting. Understanding different cultures is essential to run an organization efficiently and achieve its objectives, so cultural diversity has become an important issue for international business management; culture, of course, can also be used as a governance tool to influence behaviour. Culture obviously impinges in a number of ways on the themes discussed in this book, and in the current climate of global awareness there is scope for developing wider regional or even common cultural values applying to ethical issues that transcend traditional culture zones.

Leadership, moreover, is greatly influenced by the culture of the country in which it is located. Leadership styles in Asia are different from those in the West, and even among Asian countries, leadership styles vary. As Asian companies globalize further and their management attracts more attention, leadership issues will become more prominent. Much work is still required on causal relationships subsisting between leadership and management outcome, and also on the relationship between leaders and other people. While leadership can improve an organization's efficiency, we also know that the behaviour and political will of business leaders can mould the direction of history, which underlines the importance of further research into leadership issues.

Working conditions and standards of living are crucial constituents of a social system, and are obviously causally affected by company policy and activity. It is an irony that while companies provide people with the means for living, when human beings are drawn into the logic of a company, labour and living tend to become the dominant means for corporate objectives, that is to say, company executives may see labour merely as a means towards management objectives, or as a cost factor. In studying business management, interactive relationships must be identified and understood. For instance, if human rights are suppressed or poverty exists, then company governance and wealth distribution must be examined. Increasing GDP will not eliminate poverty or enhance civil society in any direct way – for economic development to contribute positively to social improvement, social liberalism must be operative within society. Wherever problems with sustainable development or the environment arise, one is likely to find also degraded working and living conditions, and this implies a causal connection with the local business system.

The thread that runs through our overviews of Asian business management studies is an acute warning that narrow management-oriented business and uncaring capitalistic development are themselves detrimental to social and natural conditions. In 21st-century Asia, more stress must be put on concepts and models that broaden the understanding of social responsibility in business activity. A mature democracy at company level and diversified democracy, or social liberalism, in civil society are also needed. A value system which is democratic, transcends national and ethnic boundaries and has an inclusive ethical perspective is required for the maintenance of a mature business environment. This presupposes mature democracy as a common culture across Asia, and thereby issues of leadership come into play; how leadership is performed will affect and reflect ownership relations, governance style, and even the state of democracy in that society.

Part 2 switched the focus from general themes to their application in specific countries. Japan, China and India in particular, despite their own distinctive histories, possess what we can identify as Asian business systems, because they influence other regions and act as a driving force for development in Asia.

Japan is the most economically developed nation in Asia, and consequently in company management has created unique organizations and systems, including *keiretsu* and the Toyota Production System. Large Japanese companies are supported by a huge number of small and medium-sized companies, and the concept of Japanese-style management and production systems has spread across the world. Japan's current situation is a summation of its experience from the introduction of knowledge and technologies from the West after 1868 to their modern adaptation and development. Japan has also developed interrelationships between market, state and companies which have become a development model for Asia, especially Korea, Taiwan and China. Questions that are to be asked of Japan's future include whether the Japanese model will decline in the 21st century or be integrated further into regional models, and how does the Japanese model influence sustainable development, civil democracy and national welfare?

China will continue to offer rich pickings for social science research. After its command economy (1949–78) was displaced by economic and management reforms in 1978, leading to the adoption of 'market socialism' in 1992 and membership of the World Trade Organization (WTO) in 2001, China's market economy is flourishing. China is also experiencing rapid and extensive globalization, exposing severe contradictions. Divides are opening between urban and rural communities and between the rich and the poor in cities, and serious environmental problems have emerged as the shadow side of a market economy introduced too hastily. However, China's development process is typical, and shows how economic growth, company activities, environment and human lifestyles are closely and systemically related to each other. A short-term focus on tackling negative outcomes is to be expected but, in the long term, the key to solving such problems probably lies in the development of democracy in Chinese civil society. A new theoretical framework is required to make sustainable development a reality in a state as huge as China.

Business management in India contrasts well with that of China. Historically under influences from Britain and the Soviet Union, economic reform (liberalization) since the 1990s and the development of an IT industry have had enormous impact on the Indian economy and business system. A shift from traditional small-scale management to new capitalist management in a manner unique to India is apparent. However, India's development is in scale and speed similar to China's, generating similar contradictions. Critical wealth disparities, environmental problems and human rights infringements, including child labour, are a challenge for the future development of its business systems.

Korea, Singapore and Vietnam, with Japan, share a Confucian culture and have certain cultural overlaps. Recovering from the trauma of the Korean War, Korea, as a medium-sized capitalist nation, has created since the 1960s a unique development model, characterized by foreign investment and *chaebols*. Its emphasis has been on the export potential of its manufacturing industries (including Samsung, LG, Hyundai, Kia and SK), and the dual industrial structure between large companies and small and medium-sized companies is a characteristic of its system. Influences from Japan and the US have made the Korean business management system gain strength through hybridity. In any capitalist system, opposition between labour and management is inevitable, but unlike Japan's relatively calm labour–management relations, the Korean experience has been more conflictual. Labour's countervailing force in Korea has brought about high labour costs, a factor which has accelerated globalization among big Korean companies. Corruption ingrained within the business system is not just a negative aspect of the system, but is also related to Korean companies' social responsibility. Countervailing forces of democracy and growing demand for CSR are expected to significantly influence future business development in Korea.

Singapore has a unique geopolitical position as island city state. Having developed its key trading position during the long British colonial period, Singapore has continued to function as an economic hub. But since independence, Singapore has also moved towards a knowledge-intensive industrial economy through three stages of development led by the People's Action Party (PAP). Foreign multinationals and government-related companies play an important role in Singapore's business system. However, its Confucian-style 'cramming' education system is incongruous with the flexible thinking and creativity required for contemporary business, so attention is being drawn to resolving this discrepancy between Confucian values useful in preserving order, and individualistic values that will enhance Singapore's business prospects. Although CSR until recently has been of low priority, Singaporean companies will be increasingly required to demonstrate that their corporate ethical stance meets world standards.

Vietnam, following its period of socialist controlled economy, introduced a market economy in 1986. After the collapse of the Soviet Union in 1990–1, Vietnam achieved 7–8 per cent economic growth in the 1990s, transforming itself from an agricultural to an industrial country. Vietnam, too, has a Confucian foundation, but Western values, including individualism and materialism, have entered with foreign corporations under globalization since the 1990s. Vietnam's globalization has accelerated further since it joined international organizations – ASEAN in 1995, the Asia-Pacific Economic Cooperation (APEC) in 1998 and the WTO in 2007. However, balancing globalization and the development of the domestic economy and society has become an important issue. In respect of business management, Vietnamese companies are required to deliver international-standard performance in quality, cost, delivery and environmental measures, while laws have been established relating to labour codes, environmental protection, corruption and intellectual property. Nonetheless, Vietnam still has many problems related to the CSR umbrella, and other contradictions generated along with the country's rapid development.

Thailand, Indonesia and Malaysia have created a business system different from the Confucian-style models of their neighbours, and enjoyed high economic growth of over 7 per cent during the 1980s and 1990s through export orientation. Thailand, though at root an agricultural country, has been pursuing capitalist development through a unique philosophy, Sufficiency Economy, aimed at combining traditional values with the logic of globalization. This philosophy is very attractive in the respect that it prioritizes internal development. More than rhetoric, this philosophical concept is expected to be enacted through official policies and strategies. How traditional Thai culture, based on Buddhism, will accept globalization driven by the West and Japan, and how Thailand will deal with CSR and environment issues and develop democracy are questions to be resolved in the near future.

The archipelago state of Indonesia is rich in natural resources, and has the world's fourth largest population. Indonesia was under the influences of the Netherlands, the US and Britain during the post-war period, but has been developing in its own way since 1966. Its business culture shows influences from the Dutch colonial period, Indonesian Islam and overseas Chinese culture. Its capitalist system is undergoing rapid development, but its progress has been supported by a strong traditional culture distinct from that of Korea or China and further development in the area of CSR and so on can be anticipated.

Malaysia boasts the greatest cultural diversity of all ASEAN countries, and in integrating its various cultures, it has changed from an agricultural to an export-driven industrial country. Building on stable development policies, state-owned companies, foreign corporations, joint ventures with foreign capital and local businesses have created diverse business management styles displaying influences from Britain, Korea, Japan, the Chinese diaspora, Islam and India. Therefore, no business management style can be identified as a Malaysian format. On the whole, traditional values are strong, so prevailing attitudes are collectivistic, paternalistic and respectful of authority and hierarchy, and human relationships are highly regarded. Sustainability and social responsibility nonetheless still have room for improvement.

The Philippines pursued a distinctive economic development until the late 1960s, but suffered economic stagnation under dictatorship in the 1980s. In the 1990s, an open economic policy was adopted, but has not worked well. The Philippines was long colonized by Spain (1565–1899) and the US (1899–1941 and 1945–1946), and due to Catholic influence, Filipino culture differs markedly from other Asian countries. The country has many problems, including inequality, corruption in government and local officials, difficulty in economic development, weak social capital due to low trust, and a vicious circle of poverty. How can this country deal with the influence of globalization and utilize it for economic development, and how can it improve democracy and sustainable development? The Philippines faces familiar Asian issues, but more severely than elsewhere.

In sum, then, Asia has great potential for further development in the 21st century. But for that to happen, it has to confront and resolve the issues that threaten the very basis of the civilization it is developing towards – issues of environment, sustainable development and democracy. We hope the ideas discussed in this textbook will take root and help business leaders now and in the future to create policies and strategies that benefit not just Asia's further development, but the world's.

HARUKIYO HASEGAWA
CARLOS NORONHA

Index

palgrave
macmillan

www.palgrave-journals.com/abm/

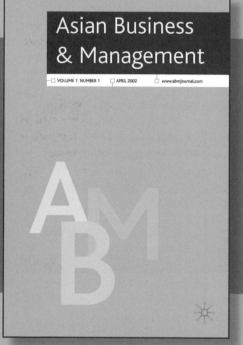

Asian Business & Management (ABM) is a key source of research for academics, researchers, policy-makers and those with an interest in this significant area. International and peer-reviewed, ABM provides a unique perspective on business and management issues, both within Asia and between Asia and the wider world.

In association with the Euro-Asia Management Studies Association (EAMSA), the Japan Academy of Labor and Management (JALM), the Japan Society of Business Administration (JSBA) and the Association of Japanese Business Studies (AJBS)

Editor:
Harukiyo Hasegawa,
Doshisha University, Japan/ University of Sheffield, UK

2009 Volume 8
Four issues per volume
ISSN: 1472-4782
ESSN: 1476-9328

Subscribe to ABM now!

Institutional Print Subscription:
N. America only: US$831
Rest of World: £447
Online access is available through a site license. For information on how to purchase a site license please contact your local NPG sales representative or visit
www.nature.com/libraries/contact_npg/